THE EMERGENCE OF INTERNATIONAL BUSINESS 1200–1800

THE RISE OF INTERNATIONAL BUSINESS

Other titles forthcoming in this series:

THE EVOLUTION OF INTERNATIONAL BUSINESS 1800–1945
Selected and with a new introduction by Mark Casson

British Investments in Latin America 1822–1949
J F Rippy

British Investments and the American Mining Frontier 1860–1901
C C Spence

The Enterprising Scot
W T Jackson

France and the Economic Development of Europe
R E Cameron

Private Investment in India 1900–1939
A K Bagchi

American Industry in Europe
F A Southard Jr

Migration of Industry to South America
D M Phelps

Foreign Investment and the Economic Development of China
C Howe

THE HEGEMONY OF INTERNATIONAL BUSINESS 1945–1970

Selected and with a new introduction by Mark Casson

Volume II

MONEY, BANKING AND CREDIT IN MEDIEVAL BRUGES

Italian Merchant-Bankers Lombards and Money-Changers

A Study in the Origins of Banking

Raymond de Roover

Routledge
Taylor & Francis Group
LONDON AND NEW YORK

First published by The Medieval Academy of America in 1948

This edition published by Routledge 1999
2 Park Square, Milton Park, Abingdon, Oxfordshire OX14 4RN
711 Third Avenue, New York, NY 10017

First issued in paperback 2014

Routledge is an imprint of the Taylor and Francis Group, an informa business

The Emergence of International Business 1200–1800
7 Volumes: ISBN 978-0-415-63054-2 (set)
ISBN 978-0-415-19074-9 (volume)

ISBN 978-1-138-86551-8 (pbk)
ISBN 978-0-415-19074-9 (hbk)

British Library Cataloguing in Publication Data
A CIP record of this set is available from the British Library

Library of Congress Cataloging in Publication Data
A catalog record for this book has been requested

Publisher's note
The publisher has gone to great lengths to ensure the quality of this reprint, but points out that some imperfections in the original book may be apparent.

THE MEDIAEVAL ACADEMY OF AMERICA
PUBLICATION NO. 51

MONEY, BANKING AND CREDIT IN MEDIAEVAL BRUGES

MONEY, BANKING AND CREDIT IN MEDIAEVAL BRUGES

Italian Merchant-Bankers Lombards and Money-Changers

A Study in the Origins of Banking

by

RAYMOND DE ROOVER, Ph. D.

Associate Professor of Economics
Wells College

THE MEDIAEVAL ACADEMY OF AMERICA
CAMBRIDGE, MASSACHUSETTS
1948

The publication of this book was made possible by grants of funds to the Academy from the Carnegie Corporation of New York and the Business History Foundation, Inc.

Printed in U. S. A.

A

MONSIEUR REMI A. PARMENTIER

CONSERVATEUR DES ARCHIVES COMMUNALES

DE BRUGES

qui, pendant près de vingt ans,

n'a cessé de suivre et d'encourager

ce travail sur l'histoire de la

banque à Bruges

Preface

THIS book is the outcome of my finding a casual reference to the existence of several account books of mediaeval merchants in the Bruges Municipal Archives. For some time I had been interested in the history of accounting and I had delved in the archives of Antwerp, my native city. Antwerp is rich in business records of the sixteenth and later centuries but I had seen no earlier account books. Upon learning of their existence in Bruges I immediately wrote a letter of inquiry to the Curator of the Bruges Archives. The reply was courteous but not encouraging. Yes, there were some mediaeval account books in the Bruges Archives, but the script was nearly illegible and the interpretation of those documents, I was tactfully given to understand, would require the combined talents of a palaeographer, a bookkeeper, and a financier. At that time I knew some bookkeeping and I had worked in a bank, but I could qualify neither as a financier nor as a palaeographer. Nevertheless, undaunted by the difficulties, I made arrangements with the Archivist, Monsieur Remi A. Parmentier, to visit the Bruges Archives and to examine those mysterious and alluring account books.

The first visit took place in May 1929. It was followed by many others because Monsieur Parmentier had not exaggerated the difficulties. Several of my short vacations—I was then working in a business office—were spent bending over the huge ledgers of Collard de Marke and Guillaume Ruyelle in the *salle du public,* where only the carillon interrupted from time to time the archival silence. As the years passed my acquaintance with Monsieur Parmentier grew into a warm and enduring friendship. Not only did he grant me unusual privileges and facilities for research but he introduced me to Professor Egide Strubbe and thus enabled me to publish the preliminary results of my investigation in the *Annales de la Société d'Emulation de Bruges.* My last visit to the Bruges Archives was in 1938. By that time I had completed my research and had conceived the general scheme of this book. Its completion was prevented for a long time by other duties and when it was finally completed publication was delayed by the War. During all these years Monsieur Parmentier never lost hope. It is only fitting that this book for which he has waited so long be dedicated to him.

Before leaving Bruges, I must also thank Monsieur Albert Schouteet, the Assistant Archivist. He has helped me in many ways by answering repeated queries and by sending me transcripts of various documents. He was also generous enough to communicate to me the text of a hitherto unknown document, which he had discovered, and which established beyond doubt that Guillaume Ruyelle, one of the two money-changers whose account books are preserved in Bruges, actually failed in 1370. This bit of evidence, which confirmed my suspicions, was particularly welcome to me, and due credit should, therefore, be given to the finder.

This work would have been impossible without the financial aid of the Belgian Fonds National de la Recherche Scientifique which enabled me to spend a summer in Italy and to photograph a great many mediaeval business papers in the Datini Archives, Prato (Tuscany). This material has yielded a crop of extremely valuable information on the money market in Bruges toward the close of the fourteenth century. Chapters Four and Five are based to a large extent upon the records found in the Datini Archives. In this connection I am particularly indebted to Professor François L. Ganshof and the late Henri Laurent who both sponsored my application for a grant-in-aid.

I owe a great deal to the teaching of Professors N. S. B. Gras and Abbott Payson Usher, of Harvard University, and of Professor John U. Nef, of The University of Chicago. Each of them has influenced me in a different way. The emphasis on managerial problems, on business policy, and on administration is traceable to the teaching and the writings of N. S. B. Gras. Professor Usher's valuable studies on negotiable instruments and on early deposit banking have provided the starting point from which I have gone on to develop the theory of interest in exchange and to find the solution to other puzzling problems concerning the mechanism of the mediaeval money market. Professor Nef has awakened my interest in the social and intellectual aspects of economic history and its relation to other fields of knowledge and of human endeavor. If economic history is not to be merely descriptive, only theory can provide the means for an analysis and an interpretation of the data. I am, therefore, especially grateful for the excellent training I received at The University of Chicago from such prominent economists as Jacob Viner, Frank H. Knight, and Lloyd W. Mints.

My friend Benjamin N. Nelson read this study in typescript and made several suggestions for improvement. From my conversations with him I have also gained better insight into the usury doctrine of the mediaeval Church. I wish to thank Hans van Werveke, Jean A. van Houtte, James Lea Cate, Elizabeth Chapin Furber, Frederic C. Lane, Robert S. Lopez, Mary Lucille Shay, and Mary Catherine Welborn, who supplied me with transcripts or responded graciously to my requests for information. The chart was prepared under my supervision by Mary Alice Mactaggart, my student at Wells College. It would be ungrateful on my part not to mention the kindness of Edith Weld Peck who placed at my disposal her summer cottage in Ogunquit, Maine. Several chapters were written in the peaceful surroundings of Miss Peck's cottage by the sea.

I have a special debt of gratitude to my wife, better known in the academic world under her maiden name of Florence Edler. I have greatly benefited from her experience in historical research, her knowledge of bibliography, and her ability to read the Italian letters photographed in the Datini Archives. She has helped me throughout, not only with advice and criticism but with typing, checking, copying, and other unavoidable drudgery. All this required so much of her time that she had to postpone the completion of her own projects.

The publication of this volume has been made possible by a generous subsidy from the Business History Foundation, Inc., in cooperation with the Mediaeval Academy of America. I value greatly the assistance of Dr Van Courtlandt Elliott of the Mediaeval Academy, who is seeing the volume through the press.

Much time and effort have gone into this volume. But I shall not have labored in vain if it arouses more interest in the history of my native land which, despite new loyalties, I can neither forget nor forsake.

RAYMOND DE ROOVER

Wells College
Aurora-on-Cayuga, N. Y.
June 15, 1948

Table of Contents

List of Illustrations

List of Tables

Charts

List of Appendices

MONEY, BANKING AND CREDIT IN MEDIAEVAL BRUGES

Chapter 1

INTRODUCTION

IN the Middle Ages, banking was far more developed than most people, especially in English-speaking countries, realize. It is true that the modern banking system based on the circulation of notes and the discounting of commercial paper was evolved in England during the seventeenth century. This development originated in the exchange, deposit, and lending activities of the London goldsmiths under Elizabeth and James I and culminated in the foundation of the Bank of England in 1694, during the reign of William and Mary. But the London goldsmiths of the Tudor and Stuart periods were far from being the 'pioneers of banking.' In Italy, the most developed country of mediaeval Europe, the origins of banking can be traced back to the twelfth century with a reasonable degree of certainty.

The mediaeval banking system differed from the later system in two important respects: it was characterized by the absence of negotiable credit instruments and by the transferability of deposits instead of the free circulation of notes. Professor Abbott Payson Usher of Harvard University has recently published a volume on the origins of banking in Spain and is preparing another on Italy. Outside of this region, Bruges, Paris, London, and Avignon (at the time of the Babylonian Captivity) were the only commercial centers of importance. Germany can be left out of the picture because of the backwardness of its economic development and the primitiveness of its business methods as compared with those in Italy, Spain, and the Low Countries. London was behind Paris and Bruges. International finance was entirely in the hands of the Italians, and the Englishmen—according to R. D. Richards—do not appear 'to have carried out any major operations in the "business of exchange" prior to the age of the Tudors.' Furthermore, it is doubtful whether there were in mediaeval London banks of deposit which were used on an extensive scale to make local payments. As for Paris, any investigation is greatly hampered by the lack of adequate source material, especially business records and other documents which would throw light on the internal organization of the banks. Avignon can be considered as an Italian colony, since the papal bankers were all Italians, so that there remains only Bruges.

Fortunately, original sources, both published and unpublished, are extant in sufficient quantity to make possible a detailed study of banking in Bruges. The most valuable series of documents is a collection of account books pertaining to two native money-changers, called Collard de Marke and Guillaume Ruyelle or Ruweel. Additional information is supplied by charters of various kinds, court decisions, bankruptcy records, the municipal accounts, and the monetary ordinances of the counts of Flanders and their successors, the dukes of Burgundy of the House of Valois.

The local archives are not rich in documents concerning the activity of the Italian merchant-bankers in Bruges, but Italian source publications and unpublished records have yielded an abundant crop of information. Most useful were the statutes of the Lucchese colony in Flanders published by Dr Eugenio Lazzareschi, the correspondence of the Medici branch in Bruges, edited by Dr Armand Grunzweig, and the account books of the Peruzzi Company, whose text has been made accessible through the painstaking and careful editorship of Professor Armando Sapori. Much valuable material, hitherto unused, was found in the well-known merchant manuals attributed to Francesco Balducci Pegolotti, Giovanni di Antonio da Uzzano, and Giorgio di Lorenzo Chiarini. Among the unpublished sources, I have used chiefly the fragment of a ledger once belonging to the Medici branch in Bruges and numerous business letters written by Italians residing in Flanders and addressed to the branch office which the Tuscan merchant, Francesco Datini of Prato (d. 1410), had established in Barcelona. This correspondence gave especially valuable information concerning the operation of the money market.

The plan of this study is very simple. It is divided into three parts. Part One deals with the Italian merchant-bankers; Part Two, with the lombards, or Italian pawnbrokers; and Part Three, with the money-changers. As will appear later, there are very good reasons for making a clear-cut distinction between these three groups of money-dealers. This plan has the great advantage of avoiding any possible confusion. The first chapter in each section deals with the legal status of the class of money-dealers under consideration. The other chapters are devoted to the economic activities of each group. However, in Part Two, dealing with the lombards, special chapters have been devoted to the social problems arising from consumers' credit and to the struggle for the suppression of casual credit and secret usury. The purpose of this study is to supplement Professor Usher's work on the Mediterranean region as far as Bruges and—to a minor extent—the Low Countries are concerned. As banking in Bruges appeared much later than in Italy, I have felt the need of making many comparisons in order to point out the influence of Italian practices on the development of banking in the North. In some cases, I have not hesitated to fill in gaps by using material not relating to Bruges but to other parts of the Low Countries. Although such a procedure is admittedly dangerous, it is safe to assume that financial institutions varied little within the narrow boundaries of the Low Countries, regardless of whether the different provinces owed allegiance to the Crown of France or to the Empire.

This study has in its title the words 'money, banking, and credit' because these three topics are so closely interwoven that they cannot be separated, as banking necessarily involves the trade in money and the extension of credit. Banking, moreover, leads to the creation of credit, that is, of money substitutes or of additional purchasing power.

The author accepts the quantity theory of money as formulated in Irving Fisher's equation of exchange and as modified and further elaborated by the leading economists of today. His interpretations are based on the assumption that this theory holds true.

PART I

THE ITALIAN MERCHANT-BANKERS

Chapter 2

THE ITALIAN COLONIES IN FLANDERS

THEIR ESTABLISHMENT, THEIR LEGAL STATUS, AND THEIR SOCIAL LIFE

ANY investigation into the early development of credit and banking should center around the rise of a class of professional money-dealers. Such a class did not appear in Flanders before the end of the thirteenth century. Its appearance was accompanied by the wholesale introduction of already well-developed financial institutions either by aliens who established themselves in Flanders or by natives who, through commercial contacts, became acquainted with methods used abroad. There is, therefore, no problem of origins as far as the Low Countries are concerned.

It is true that casual credit was not unknown and that the records abound in examples of credit transactions as far back as the eleventh century. Abbeys and monasteries that possessed hoards of coined money and a treasury of gold and silver ornaments often made loans to neighboring lords who needed money to carry on war, to alleviate famine conditions, or to go on a crusade.[1] In the thirteenth century such loans frequently took the form of *mort-gage,* a kind of loan in which the fruits of the pledged property were collected by the creditor and were not deductible from the principal.[2] By thus lending money on *mort-gage,* the abbeys were often able to enlarge their domains because they did not hesitate to foreclose if the debtor failed to repay the principal. But these transactions, however frequent, never took a professional character; money-lending never became a full-time occupation of the monks. In the early Middle Ages, the abbeys and monasteries of Flanders and Lotharingia were certainly casual lenders, but it would be an untenable theory to consider them as credit institutions.

The chronicles and the lives of the saints, which are our main sources of information for this early period, refer indignantly to the existence of *foeneratores* who took advantage of the want of their neighbors. As early as 1082, some *mercatores leodienses,* by scraping their resources together, were able to lend two hundred marks which the abbot of Saint-Hubert needed to buy the important domain of Chevigny from Countess Richilde of Hainaut. In 1044 thieves who took away church ornaments from the treasury of the abbey of Lobbes were able to pawn the stolen goods with a *trapezita* (pawnbroker?) in Mons. During the famine of 1096, these *usurarii* and *foeneratores* became a scourge: they lent money to distressed landowners and mercilessly doubled the debt if it were not repaid at maturity.[3] As loans in this early period were overwhelmingly made for consumption purposes, it is in connection with the extortions of these *foeneratores* that the Church first formulated the usury doctrine which later proved so ill-adapted to the requirements of nascent capitalism.

Although the available information is very scant and unreliable, nothing proves the existence of a professional class of money-lenders in the early Middle Ages. What little trade survived the impact of the barbarian and Arab invasions was carried on by traveling merchants who were always on the lookout for a bargain and who welcomed famines as unexpected opportunities for profits. There was little or no specialization. Money-lending was often a by-employment intertwined with trade and concealed under the form of credit sales and of other transactions.

Even the important *financiers d'Arras,* at the end of the thirteenth century, were not professional money-dealers. These financiers of Arras had accumulated huge fortunes in the cloth trade with Genoa and at the fairs of Champagne. Members of the Crespin family, one of the richest of Arras, are mentioned as cloth merchants in the Genoese notarial records as far back as 1184.[4] By the end of the thirteenth century, most of the financiers of Arras had apparently retired from business and were seeking to invest their funds in the purchase of urban property and in the acquisition of *seigneuries* and other landed estates. Some of the funds, however, went into loans to princes and to municipal governments, especially to the count of Flanders and to the cities of Ghent and Bruges.[5] The importance of these loans should not be underrated. According to a statement made in 1290, Gui de Dampierre, Count of Flanders, owed as much as £65,166 *parisis* to the financiers of Arras, or many times more than to any other group of creditors.[6] If the statement is reliable, his debts to the lombards, or Italian pawnbrokers, residing in Flanders did not exceed £7,100 *parisis,* and a total of £18,400 *parisis* was owed to ultra-montane merchants at the fairs of Champagne, in particular to the 'Gran Tavola dei Buonsignori,' the famous banking house of Siena.[7]

The importance of these government loans did not promote the financiers of Arras to the rank of professional money-lenders. They never formed any partnerships and they never accepted deposits. They lent only their own funds and not money belonging to other people. The financiers of Arras always stipulated in their contracts that their loans were repayable in Arras, their place of residence. As far as is known, the financiers of Arras did not have any agents or correspondents abroad and were not even in active business relations with the Italian bankers who used the fairs of Champagne as their base of operation.[8]

In short, the financiers of Arras were very rich *rentiers* who had money to invest and were attracted toward government loans by the prospect of a handsome return. Most of the loans were placed at 14 per cent.[9] Alas! these expectations were delusive. As early as 1295 the City of Bruges wrote to the pope accusing the financiers of Arras of extortion and usury which caused the city to be in desperate straits.[10] Thereupon, the pope issued a bull, dated January 21, 1296, by which he ordered the clergy of Arras to warn Robert and Baudouin Crespin, the two principal creditors of the City of Bruges, that they had to moderate their claims or to face the penalties provided by the canon law and the councils of the Church. This admonition probably did not make any impression, because the pope had to issue another bull on June 12, 1297, this time addressed to the dean of Douai who was enjoined to take drastic steps against the Crespin family.[11] It is likely that this second bull had no effect, either, and did not prevent the financiers of Arras from putting pressure on the City of Bruges in order to obtain payment of their claims, principal as well as interest, which were considerably in arrears. An arrangement was finally reached, in 1299, by which the City of Bruges pledged herself to repay a total sum of 110,000 pounds *parisis* spread over a period of eleven years.[12] Nothing came of this agreement because of the war with France which broke out shortly thereafter and which was waged intermittently until 1320.

About 1330, members of the Crespin family made another attempt to collect their outstanding claims. The Italian Thomas Guidi worked out a compromise by which the total due from the City of Bruges was reduced from £110,000 *parisis* to £30,000 *parisis,* but the agreement was not carried out.[13] Fifty years later, in 1386, Rolant Crespin, knight, who still held the original titles, waived all claims in exchange for a token payment of a few pennies in the pound.[14]

Professional money-dealers did not appear in Flanders until the end of the thirteenth century, when the Italian merchant and banking houses began to establish permanent branches in Bruges and to desert the fairs of Champagne. This migration of the Italian merchants to Flanders is an important development, because it meant the end of the traveling or caravan trade, which centered around the fairs of Champagne, and its replacement by a more efficient form of organization. Henceforth, merchants ceased to visit the fairs and began to conduct all their business from the counting-house, using partners, factors, or correspondents to represent them in foreign parts.[15] This evolution involved such a drastic change in the methods of doing business that the transition from one system to the other could be called, without exaggeration, 'the commercial revolution of the end of the thirteenth century.'[16] The most permanent result of the commercial revolution was to pave the way for the advent of mercantile capitalism which, in most European countries, was not displaced by industrial capitalism before the middle of the nineteenth century.

The decline of the fairs of Champagne has often been ascribed to certain ill-advised fiscal measures of the French kings, to the establishment of direct sea connections between Flanders and Italy, and to the wars between Flanders and France which prevented, so the argument runs, the Flemish merchants from going to the fairs.[17] But, after critical analysis, none of these three causes appears to be of decisive importance.[18] The determining factor seems to have been the introduction of new methods in international trade, especially the growing tendency to do business by correspondence and the establishment of the Italians in Flanders near the centers of cloth production.[19] This change was in the offing from the time that the Italian merchant-bankers gained a foothold in England as papal collectors of revenue or maintained quasi-permanent branches and agencies at the fairs of Champagne or in nearby Paris.[20]

The existence of companies having a number of branches or correspondents abroad was made possible only because of considerable progress in business administration and because of the gradual development of new techniques in control and management. First of all, instead of forming partnerships for the duration of a single venture, a new type of agreement was evolved: the terminal partnership which was intended to last for several years unless prematurely dissolved by the death of one of the partners. These terminal partnerships were perhaps first developed in connection with the overland trade with the fairs of Champagne by the merchants of the inland cities of Siena and Florence rather than by those of the coastal cities of Genoa and Venice.[21] The traveling merchants knew the letter obligatory and the exchange contract in notarial form, but these instruments proved inadequate when the sedentary merchants began to work with agents and correspondents abroad, and when import and export tended to become separate transactions. A new instrument, the 'letter of payment' or bill of exchange was created to meet the needs of the new type of sedentary merchants.[22] The bill of exchange made it possible to transfer purchasing power from place to place without the shipping of actual coins. The greater security along the roads was another factor which contributed to the decay of the traveling trade.[23] It became unnecessary for the merchants to convey their goods themselves and to travel in armed caravans. Goods could safely be entrusted to specialized common carriers on land as well as on sea.[24] The development of maritime insurance made it possible to shift the sea risk to the underwriters instead of dividing that risk by chartering space on several different ships.

A more important development was the progress made in the keeping of accounts. The bookkeeping of the traveling merchant had been crude, though adequate for his purpose. Business records were simply memorandum entries of credit transactions; no record was kept of cash or barter transactions. This system ceased to meet the requirements of business when the merchants began to work with agents and correspondents. In the late thirteenth, and the beginning of the fourteenth, century, perhaps more than at any other period of history, accounting advanced with great strides in order to adapt itself to the changes in business organization. One innovation of major importance was the current account kept in bilateral form, that is, the personal account divided vertically into two columns, one for debit and one for credit. Later double-entry bookkeeping was introduced by adding impersonal accounts for tangible assets and for operating results to the existing personal accounts. [25]

The Italians were the first to master the new business technique with the result that foreign trade in Western Europe became virtually an Italian monopoly. They were able to maintain their supremacy until well into the sixteenth century, long after the trade of Italy itself had declined in consequence of the geographical discoveries and the shift in trade routes.[26]

The Flemish traveling merchants, who used to visit the fairs of Champagne, were driven out of business or retired of their own accord, like the financiers of Arras. The Flemings succeeded in maintaining themselves only in the wine and salt trade with Brittany, Gascony, and the Loire region.[27] Otherwise the carrying trade was almost completely taken out of their hands. The Flemings, consequently, had to confine themselves to a purely passive role and relied on foreigners, chiefly the Italians and the Hanseatic merchants, to find markets abroad for the products of the Flemish cloth industry.[28] The native upper-class in Bruges, during the fourteenth and fifteenth centuries, was not made up of merchants, save for a few exceptions, but of brokers, inn-keepers, *drapiers,* and commission agents.

The exclusion of the Flemings from the carrying trade has been attributed to a variety of causes, but appears to be chiefly a consequence of the 'commercial revolution' of the thirteenth century. It is true that during this same period the staple policy of the English kings, the erection of new tolls in the Rhineland, and the hard-handed methods of the Hanseatic League, tended to undermine the position which the Flemings occupied in those markets.[29] But, except in the trade relations with Germany, the unquestionable superiority of Italian business organization was the decisive factor which made it impossible for the Flemings to compete on anything like equal terms.[30]

As soon as the Italians established themselves permanently in Flanders, they began to organize 'nations' or colonies which were composed of all the merchants from the same city. The Italians were thus divided into Genoese, Venetian, Lucchese, Florentine, and Milanese nations, but they occasionally presented a united front, when common interests were at stake.[31] One of the first tasks of the newly formed nations was to secure official recognition of their incorporation and to obtain commercial privileges from the local authorities. The purpose of obtaining such privileges was threefold: first, to secure protection against arbitrary action of the local authorities, especially against retaliatory arrest and seizure of property; secondly, to fix the tariff of tolls and port dues, so that no extra dues could be exacted by irresponsible officials; thirdly, to temper the full rigor of the feudal law, especially with regard to the *droit d'aubaine* and the 'right to wreck.' There was little difference between the privileges granted to the different Italian groups by the Flemish authorities. These privileges were confirmed from time to time and extended to cover unforeseen cases, as the necessity arose.

According to a charter of December 31, 1395, which replaced an earlier grant, the Genoese could not be arrested, nor their property confiscated in retaliation for damages caused by war (art. 1). If the count of Flanders wished to expel the Genoese from his dominions, he would have to notify them eight months in advance, so that they would have time to dispose of their belongings before leaving the country (art. 2). Articles three and four are of little interest to us, because they concern the rights and privileges of the mariners on the Genoese galleys anchored in the port of Sluys.

Article five, on the contrary, is more interesting. The Genoese were not to pay any other duties except those specified in an agreement which had been concluded in October 1395. The importation of English cloth was severely restricted in Flanders, but the Genoese were allowed to keep such cloth aboard their galleys, if it were not to be unloaded.[32]

The grant of 1395 was followed by a treaty concluded on October 1, 1414.[33] Only article five of this new treaty directly concerns the Genoese merchants: it provided that no merchant might be arrested for debt if he offered to give bond. All the other provisions, or nineteen out of twenty, deal in minute detail with regulations concerning shipping. Article two, for example, preserved the right of the masters of the galleys to punish their own crew, except in cases affecting life and limb, or to put down any mutiny which might break out on board. When the galleys were ready to sail, they were not to be delayed for flimsy reasons by the *bailli de l'eau* ('water-bailiff') or other authorities. Articles twelve to fourteen practically abolished the count's right to wreck, even in case of derelict and jettison. The Genoese merchants had the right to recover any goods which were cast ashore and which could be identified by their trademarks. The mariners of the Genoese galleys were allowed to fish for their lost anchors and to beach their ships for repairs. If ballast was taken in, only the customary dues had to be paid.

The treaty of 1414 was revised in 1422, in 1434, and in 1459.[34] A few changes were made in the second of these revisions: the claims of the Genoese to salvaged goods were further defined and port dues were fixed at two pounds groat for each Genoese vessel entering the harbor of Sluys.[35]

In 1468, a new charter was added to the existing privileges.[36] Articles one and three again dealt with the apparently important subject of wrecks, and article two decided that runaway slaves had to be returned to their Genoese

PLACE DE LA BOURSE IN BRUGES
MEETING PLACE OF THE ITALIAN EXCHANGE-DEALERS

From left to right: the consular houses of the Genoese (with crenelations and large windows), of the Venetians (also without gable) and of the Florentines (with the graceful turrets). The consular house of the Venetians was the former inn owned by the van der Beurse family. From Sanderus, *Flandria illustrata.*

owners. Article five presents more interest from our point of view. The local court had the right to initiate criminal proceedings against a Genoese merchant only after informing the consul, so that he might defend his countryman. According to other provisions, the Genoese were promised prompt justice in any suit at law in which they were either plaintiffs or defendants. No dilatory expedients were to be tolerated in order to prevent execution of a judgment against a defaulting debtor. If a debt were witnessed by a letter obligatory, either given under seal or simply signed by the debtor, such a debtor would no longer be admitted to deny his obligation under oath, provided that the creditor was able to prove that the seal or the handwriting was genuine. This was an important step forward toward the recognition of informal credit instruments as conclusive evidence in court. Hitherto, only deeds (*actes échevinaux*) enjoyed such recognition. Protection was also given to the Genoese merchants against frivolous litigation, and fines unjustly imposed had to be refunded. A special provision dealt with the sale of water-soaked goods. The Genoese had the right to sell such damaged goods 'as is' in the Halle des Epices to either burghers or non-burghers, but the burgher was to be given preference at the same price.

In the fifteenth century all the Italian nations enjoyed about the same rights, and the Flemish authorities had apparently come to the conclusion that to make no discrimination was the best policy.[37] The charter of March 13, 1468, by which Charles the Bold confirmed and renewed the trade privileges of the Venetians, shows that they enjoyed the same immunities as the Genoese.[38] In the early fourteenth century, however, the Venetians had been able to obtain exceptional advantages for a short while. In 1319 a Venetian embassy reached Flanders with instructions to demand: (1) the right to set up a consulate with jurisdiction over the Venetians, (2) immunity from arrest for debt without writ from the municipal court, (3) the right to sell goods both at wholesale and at retail, (4) the reduction of the brokerage charges, (5) a better regulation of weights and measures, and (6) freedom to come and go without being molested (an indication, by the way, that the traveling trade had not yet completely died out).[39] All these demands were granted by the count of Flanders on May 22, 1322. On the following eighth of June the municipal authorities of Bruges gave their approval, too, but they allowed only forty days during which imported goods could be freely sold. Despite this restriction the trade privileges granted to the Venetians aroused the suspicions of the gilds. The treaty of 1322 was not carried out, probably because of this opposition and because of the uprising in 1323 among the peasants of the lowlands along the coast.

On March 23, 1332, a new trade agreement was concluded, but it was less favorable than the earlier one.[40] The Venetians obtained full safeguards for their persons and their property, the right to appoint a weigher enjoying their confidence, and immunity from arrest without a writ from the local court. In case a Venetian died, the consul became automatically the custodian of the property left by the deceased. However, the complete freedom to trade was not restored and the Venetians were placed on the same footing as other aliens.

In Bruges, as elsewhere, foreign merchants were excluded from the retail trade which was completely in the hands of the mercers, the grocers, and the local gilds (Fr. *métiers,* Fl. *ambachten*).[41] They watched jealously over their monopolies and any infringement was likely to provoke immediate and vigorous reaction. Even the wholesale trade was not entirely open to foreigners. They were not permitted to deal directly with native buyers or sellers, but all such dealings had to pass through the hands of a broker.[42] Alien merchants also were not allowed to buy local products for resale in Bruges.[43] Because of these regulations, the activity of foreign merchants was practically restricted to the sale of imported goods and the purchase of local products for export. Only commercial transactions between aliens remained free from any sort of interference.

The charters granted to the Italian merchants residing in Bruges were not unilateral concessions, but real trade agreements or commercial treaties. Their terms were usually the result of lengthy negotiations in which official envoys of the Italian republics often played a conspicuous part. Both sides bargained hard for advantages, and concessions could be secured only by compromise. For example, in 1395 the Genoese agreed to keep their staple in Bruges, that is, they agreed that their galleys would call in Flanders before going to England, and that the goods aboard were first to be offered for sale in Bruges.[44] In exchange for the staple, the duke of Burgundy, for his part, granted liberal privileges and the city of Bruges promised in addition to pay as much as 9,500 gold francs.[45] This agreement was ratified by the doge of Genoa, Antoniotto Adorno, who added a decree punishing with banishment any Genoese who dared to violate the staple.[46]

The importance of trade privileges from the point of view of economic and business history should not be overestimated. They were mainly diplomatic documents which settled a number of legal points, but which shed as little light on actual trade relations as a modern treaty of commerce. The privileges granted to the Italian colonies in Bruges are more informative about the customs of the sea than about any other topic. At least one point is established beyond question: the members of the Italian colonies were mostly and primarily merchants, hence their interest in speedy justice, in the respect of property rights, in the reduction of tolls, and in shipping. Not a single word about financial transactions: the reason is undoubtedly that such transactions, unlike shipping and trade, did not give rise to legal conflicts or to local jealousies. The Flemings knew that they were unable to compete with the Italians in international finance. Neither did the Flemish authorities, unlike the English kings, attempt to control the money market or to regulate exchange dealings. Consequently, there was no need to mention banking in the trade privileges.

One should not conclude from this silence that the trade privileges did not determine the legal status of the Italian merchant-bankers, a mistake made by the Belgian historian, Georges Bigwood. He gives the impression that the legal status of the Italian merchant-bankers was determined not by the trade privileges but by the licences which the count of Flanders and the city of Bruges granted to the lombards or Italian pawnbrokers. Bigwood overlooks the fact that the lombards needed a special licence because they publicly lent money at interest, or usury. Such an activity was illegal, and a licence was required to engage in it. But the Italian merchant-bankers did not lend openly at interest: they dealt in bills of exchange. Since such dealings were perfectly legal, there was no need for special concessions. Why should the trade privileges have dealt with a type of activity whose legality was beyond question and which did not infringe upon sovereign rights or conflict with the privileges of other groups?

On the other hand, the Italian merchant-bankers were not exclusively financiers but merchants as well. It is therefore quite natural that their privileges contain minute regulations with regard to shipping, tolls, staple rights, and other matters pertaining to the trade in commodities.

In Bruges, the consular houses of the Genoese, the Venetians, and the Florentines were located on the Place de la Bourse in the heart of the business district and in the vicinity of the Grand' Place and the famous crane.[47] Only the Lucchese had their *loggia* or consular house in Bruges off the Place de la Bourse at the corner of the rue des Aiguilles and the rue des Tonneliers.[48] The Place de la Bourse took its name from the inn kept by the Bruges family van der Beurse or de la Bourse ('of the purse'), who were broker-innkeepers from father to son all through the fourteenth and the first half of the fifteenth centuries.[49] Above the door of the inn were the van der Beurse family's canting arms: Or, on a bend gules, three purses argent.[50] Because of the presence of the three consular houses, the Place de la Bourse soon became the favorite meeting place of the Italian merchants.[51] This circumstance explains why the name *bourse* was later given to the galleries which the city of Antwerp erected around an open square, early in the sixteenth century, so that the merchants could meet without being disturbed by traffic and could find shelter in case of rain.

The internal organization of the Italian 'nations,' 'universities,' or 'communities' in Bruges is known in some detail because of the survival of a Lucchese statute dated July 18, 1478, and of a Florentine statute dated February 8, 1427 (n.s.), with several later amendments. The date of the extant Lucchese statute is rather late, but it does not differ in essential details from an earlier one which was drawn up in Bruges on March 28, 1369, and approved by the General Council (*Consiglio degli Anziani*) of Lucca on September 27 of the same year.[52]

According to the statute of 1478, the Lucchese 'nation' was at the same time a trade association, a social club, and a religious brotherhood formed to promote the devotion to the *Volto Santo,* the national cult of Lucca.[53] As always in the Middle Ages, the religious and mystical element was closely interwoven with political, social, and other activities.

The Lucchese nation in Bruges was headed by a committee composed of a consul, three councillors (only two after 1478), two *operari* ('secretaries'), and two *pacieri* ('ushers') whose duties were of minor importance.[54] These officers were appointed each year at a general meeting of all the Lucchese residents, held for a time on the first Sunday in September, but this date was too close to the national holiday, the Exaltation of the Holy Cross (September 14), and was changed in 1378 to August 15 or Assumption.[55] The consuls were elected by a written ballot. All male members of the Lucchese colony above fourteen years of age had the right to cast their votes.[56] Consuls could not be reelected for a second term, but the outgoing consul became automatically one of the three councillors for the following year, the other two being appointed by a committee composed of the incoming and outgoing consuls and the former councillors. As soon as the new officers were installed, they promised under oath to uphold the statutes and to defend the honor and the welfare of the nation. All proposals approved by a majority of three-fourths of the members present at a meeting were binding for all and had to be enforced by the consul. If a consul or a councillor was out of town for more than eight days, he had to appoint a substitute with power to act in his absence.[57]

The office of consul was important. The consul acted as a diplomatic agent unless the importance of the matter under discussion justified the sending of a special envoy. If an Italian had any trouble with the local authorities, the consul was often requested to iron out the difficulties. For the Italians, the consul was the official representative of the home government and his orders had to be obeyed. According to the Lucchese statute of 1478, the consul had jurisdiction in all disputes over money or merchandise which one Lucchese had with another. The consul's decisions, however, were not final and could be appealed to the local court or some other jurisdiction.[58] The consul also had disciplinary power over the Lucchese, but only in so far as his measures did not violate the sovereign rights of the count of Flanders nor conflict with the decisions of the *Loya di Bruggia,* that is, the municipal government. On the other hand, the Lucchese were entitled to aid and assistance from the consul and, if necessary, to the support of the entire nation.[59]

Membership in the 'university' was not optional, but compulsory for every Lucchese resident in Bruges. Those who refused to join were ostracized and exposed themselves to commercial boycott. The same fate was held in store for those who disobeyed the orders of the consul and were expelled from the 'university.'

The Lucchese had a pew and a chapel dedicated to the *Volto Santo* in the church of the canons regular of the Augustinian Order in Bruges, where the Genoese and the Hanseatic merchants also worshipped.[60] Every member of the Lucchese colony was expected to participate in the religious and social activities on the feast of the Exaltation of the Holy Cross, September 14. He was also expected to attend High Mass in the nation's chapel on the first Sunday of each month and to be present at the meeting which usually followed. Failure to attend was punished with a fine.

Expenses were covered by the proceeds from fines and from compulsory offerings of one groat at each mass celebrated by the nation in the church of the Augustinians. In addition, a tax of one-half groat per pound (or 1/480), called *il diritto di Santa Croce*, was levied on all sales and purchases made by Lucchese in the Low Countries. The tax was also assessable on any Lucchese goods consigned to merchants of another nationality who could be constrained by the consul, if they refused to pay.[61] The Florentine and Genoese colonies raised a similar turnover tax, but the former called it *consolaggio* and the latter, *il denaro della Masseria o della Nazione*.[62]

Wealthy people of the Middle Ages lived in pomp but in discomfort. The receipts of the Lucchese colony must have been quite high. Probably a considerable sum of money went into display or was spent on social activities, such as the torchlight procession on the feast of the Holy Cross or the parades in which each member wore the livery of the nation. This livery, by the way, was changed every year and two officers were appointed to choose the kind and the color of the cloth.[63] According to the available information, the Genoese spent most of their society funds in the same way: the upkeep of the consular house and the chapel, religious ceremonies and other festivities on the feast of St George (April 23), local charities, aid to mariners, and social activities of all kinds.[64]

The organization of the other Italian nations in Bruges varied little from that of the Lucchese, save for some details concerning the appointment of officers and the days of festivals. In the case of the Florentine nation, it seems that it did not enjoy as much autonomy as the Lucchese one, but that the control of the home government was much stronger.[65] Until the end of the fifteenth century, the consul was not elected by the Florentine residents in Bruges, but was appointed by the Captains of the Guelph Party and the Consuls of the Sea in Florence.[66] The Florentine consul in Bruges had full authority to settle without appeal any disputes in civil matters involving a Florentine as defendant. The Florentines worshipped at the chapel of the Friars Minor. All the heads of the Florentine agencies or business houses and their factors were supposed to attend High Mass which was celebrated there on the first Sunday of each month.[67]

It is clear from the Lucchese and the Florentine statutes that all merchants from the same city were strongly held together, and that they did not sever their ties with their mother country. Even from a purely business point of view, it was to the advantage of the Italian merchant to keep in touch with his relatives and friends in the homeland. This point is stated nowhere in the statutes but is very important. The main purpose of the consular organization was not to provide entertainment, but to bring social pressure to bear upon the members of the group and, as there were no newspapers nor trade journals, to facilitate the exchange of information on business failures, wars, market conditions, exchange rates, and similar topics of interest to practical merchants and financiers.[68] If a member of the Lucchese colony in Bruges misbehaved and neglected his business, for example, it is likely that his principals or his partners in Lucca would soon be informed either directly or indirectly and would thus be able to remedy the situation, before it was too late. On the other hand, the Lucchese in Bruges, because of their frequent contacts with their mother city, would surely find out if their interests in Italy or elsewhere were neglected.

Incidentally, the Florentine and Lucchese statutes strengthen the impression that the Italian colonies of Bruges were made up of merchants who earned a good living and were primarily interested in everything connected with foreign trade. Some of them, as we know from other sources, were also deeply involved in financial transactions, but trade was always the backbone of their business. Among the Lucchese, Forteguerra di Forteguerra and Dino Rapondi in the fourteenth century, and Giovanni Arnolfini in the fifteenth century, were prominent both as merchants and as financiers. Even the famous Florentine 'banking' houses, like the Bardi and the Peruzzi in the fourteenth century, and the Medici in the fifteenth, were great trading companies as well as credit institutions.

Those merchants who combined foreign trade and international finance were often the most influential members of their nations and frequently held the office of consul. Forteguerra, for instance, was consul of the Lucchese colony in 1384, as is known with certainty from an entry written by himself in the consular records.[69] Dino Rapondi, in all probability, held the same office more than once in his long career, as the inscription engraved on his tombstone seems to imply.[70] In the fifteenth century, Tommaso Portinari, the manager of the local branch of the Medici, was elected several times to the dignity of consul of the Florentine nation.[71]

In 1378 and 1379, the Lucchese nation, which was one of the most important Italian colonies in Bruges, counted thirty-five residents.[72] In 1393, thirty-eight Lucchese, including the consul, ratified an agreement between the city of Bruges and the Italian colonies with respect to the limitation of credit sales.[73] Only twelve Lucchese merchants, in 1478, signed the petition to renew the statutes.[74] This drop was probably due to the decay of the Lucchese silk industry rather than to the beginning of the decline of Bruges as a trading center. According to the description of Olivier de la Marche, the chronicler of the Burgundian court, twenty Florentines—ten merchants and ten factors, with Tommaso Portinari at their head—marched in the parade which was organized to celebrate the wedding of Charles the Bold and Margaret of York, in 1468. The Genoese were represented in the same procession by one hundred eight merchants. The number of Venetians is unfortunately not given, but there were thirty-four Spaniards and one hundred eight Germans. These figures are plausible enough as approximations, but one may doubt whether they are absolutely correct and whether the chronicler had an opportunity to count heads while he was watching the parade.[75]

It is perhaps needless to say that the foreign merchants, because they were aliens, were not eligible to any function in the municipal government of Bruges. But their status of aliens did not prevent them from entering the service of the count of Flanders and later of the duke of Burgundy. During the fourteenth and fifteenth centuries, offices which required administrative ability and knowledge of finance were often filled by Italians. As early as 1306, Thomas Fini, a factor of the Gallerani company, became '*receiver of Flanders,*' a function similar to that of finance minister today.[76] During the fourteenth century mintmasters were, as a rule, of Italian origin.[77] The Lucchese merchant Dino Rapondi was a close adviser to the Duke of Burgundy, Philip the Bold, and later to his son and successor, John the Fearless.[78] As late as 1468, Tommaso Portinari marched in the parade for the wedding of Charles the Bold 'vestu comme les conseillers de Monseigneur le Duc, car il est de son conseil,' explains Olivier de la Marche.[79]

The Italian business enterprises abroad were managed in the same way as those in the home cities. The surviving records of the Bruges branch of the Medici bank and a number of other documents show that the administrative standards in Bruges were as high as in Italy. The branches kept their books with the utmost care. Double entry was probably in general use after 1400. Italian was the language used for internal administration and for all correspondence with headquarters in Italy, as well as with business firms in other trading centers.[80] French, rather than Flemish, was used in public relations and in business dealings with the natives. The clerical staff of each *fondaco* or agency in Bruges was composed exclusively of Italians and frequently included apprentices sent abroad in order to acquire business experience. Only porters and other minor employees were presumably chosen from local residents. Kinship, in business as well as in social life, played an important role and many firms were family concerns to which outsiders were only reluctantly admitted. Business information was a closely guarded secret, probably more so in the Middle Ages than it is today.

Italian business organization during the fourteenth and fifteenth centuries was vastly superior to that of any other nation. By keeping the foreigners out, the Italians succeeded for a long time in maintaining their control over foreign trade, but they could not entirely prevent outsiders from learning and copying their methods. The uniformity of Italian business procedure at home and abroad was a potent factor in the slow elaboration of a law merchant which was nearly the same all over Europe. In Bruges, for example, the local court often consulted the Italian merchants about the prevailing customs or practices, and decided lawsuits accordingly.

Politically the Italian colonies enjoyed extraterritorial rights, so to speak, and were not part of the local community. Socially, too, the Italians stayed aloof from the rest of the population. Marriages with Flemish women, even of high rank, were not encouraged. Moreover, the Italians did not fit into the social pattern of the Low Countries. Most of them were nobles, but the local nobility considered trade as degrading. Economically, the Italian colonies were one of the cornerstones on which rested the prosperity of Flanders. Only the trade and the credit of the Italian merchants kept the looms humming in this country dependent upon the exportation of cloth and other fabrics.

A word should perhaps be added about the contributions of the Italian colonies in Bruges to cultural advance. The Italian merchants played an important role in promoting the exchange of works of art between Flanders and Italy. Flemish tapestry makers were set to work with designs prepared by Italian artists.[81] As a result, the decorative qualities of the Flemish tapestries were improved. The branch of the Medici imported from Italy a tomb made to order by Andrea della Robbia for a bishop of Tournai.[82] The Lucchese merchant Giovanni Arnolfini had his portrait painted twice by Jan van Eyck, once with his wife, Jeanne Cenami, and once alone.[83] The latter picture, in particular, shows a face which radiates the shrewdness of the crafty banker and business man. The local representatives of the Medici banking house, following the example of their principals, distinguished themselves as patrons of the arts. Tommaso Portinari, the Medici agent, had his portrait and that of his wife, Maria Baroncelli, painted by Memling.[84] Portinari also patronized Hugo van der Goes to whom he gave a commission for an altarpiece which was presented to the Hospital of Santa Maria Nuova in Florence.[85] This famous painting, 'The Adoration of the Shepherds,' is now in the Uffizi Gallery. It is through the tapestries and the paintings sent to Italy by the Medici agents that the Italian artists became acquainted with the works of the Flemish primitives, with their acute observation of detail, and their predilection for vivid colors.[86]

In 1473, a galley flying the flag of Burgundy was captured on its way to England by a Danzig privateer.[87] On board was a rich cargo of velvets, brocades, spices, tapestries, and Memling's 'Last Judgment,' now in St Mary's in Danzig. On the back of the side panels are painted the portraits of the donors, Agnolo Tani and his wife Catarina Tanagli.[88] Agnolo Tani was a former manager of the Bruges branch of the Medici and was still a partner at the time Memling painted the 'Last Judgment' for him.[89] Catarina Tanagli was presumably the daughter of Jacopo Tanagli who managed the silk-manufacturing 'shop' of the

Medici in Florence.[90] Art critics are of the opinion that the nude figures of the Blessed, on the left and central panels, are portraits of Florentine merchants in Bruges, while, on the right, tonsured monks appear among the Damned who are being cast by devils into the eternal flames.[91]

The Italian merchants did not escape the influence of their environment. They shared in the Flemish people's love for pageantry and display which is distinctive of the Burgundo-French culture of the expiring Middle Ages.[92] At the festival celebrating the marriage of Charles the Bold and Margaret of York, all the foreign nations participated in the parade. The Venetians came first, all the merchants and their servants on horseback. They were preceded by fifty torch-bearers; the masters wore magnificent costumes of crimson velvet and the servants, of red cloth. After them came the Florentines dressed in black satin hose with crimson doublets. The Genoese were preceded by a man on horseback representing St George and by a maiden, also on horseback, representing the princess whom St George saved from the dragon. The merchants were all dressed alike in a livery of violet cloth.[93] While the Italian merchants proudly filed past the princely couple, the voice of the bells, high up in the belfry, proclaimed the glory of Burgundy.

NOTES TO CHAPTER 2

[1]Hans van Werveke, 'Monnaie, lingots ou marchandises? Les instruments d'échange aux XIe et XIIe siècles,' *Annales d'histoire économique et sociale* [hereafter referred to as AHES], IV (1932), 459-60.

[2]van Werveke, 'Le mort-gage et son rôle économique en Flandre et en Lotharingie,' *Revue belge de philologie et d'histoire* [hereafter referred to as *RBPH*], VIII (1929), 54-55,

[3]van Werveke, 'Monnaies, lingots ou marchandises?' *op. cit.*, pp. 458-59.

[4]Robert L. Reynolds, 'Merchants of Arras and the Overland Trade with Genoa, Twelfth Century,' *RBPH*, IX (1930), 526.

[5]Georges Bigwood, 'Les financiers d'Arras: contribution à l'étude des origines du capitalisme moderne,' *RBPH*, III (1924), 465-508, 769-819; IV (1925), 109-19, 379-421.

[6]Bigwood, *Le régime juridique et économique du commerce de l'argent dans la Belgique du moyen âge* ('Mémoires de l'Académie royale de Belgique, Classe des lettres et des sciences morales et politiques, Collection in 8°,' 2d series, Vol. XIV, 2 parts; Brussels, 1921-22), Part II, pp. 293-94.

[7]*Ibid.*, pp. 295-96. The Buonsignori are referred to as 'chiaus de le Grant Table.' The total sum due to the lombards includes the following items:

	£	*s*	*d parisis*
A Jakemon de Calot et ses compagnons	500	0	0
Item as freres Jakemon de Calot	200	0	0
As lombars de Biervliet	300	0	0
As lombars de Hulst	200	0	0
Encore doit-on as lombars ki deurent demorer en Flandres	4,672	11	4
A Biche et à ses compagnons demorans à Gant	1,200	0	0
Total	£7,072	11	4 *parisis*

[8]Henri Pirenne, *Economic and Social History of Medieval Europe* (New York, 1937), p. 130.

[9]Bigwood, *Régime*, I, 103.

[10]Louis Gilliodts-van Severen, *Inventaire des archives de la Ville de Bruges* (Bruges, 1871-85), I, 45-46, No. 87; Gilliodts-van Severen, *Coutume de la Ville de Bruges* ('Coutumes des Pays et Comté de Flandre, Quartier de Bruges'; Brussels, 1874-75), I, 515-16.

[11]Bigwood, 'Les financiers d'Arras,' *op. cit.*, III, 475.

[12]Bigwood, *Régime*, I, 105.

[13]Gilliodts, *Inventaire*, I, 461-63, Nos. 399, 400.

[14]Bigwood, 'Financiers d'Arras' *op. cit.*, III, 477.

[15]N.S.B. Gras, *Business and Capitalism: An Introduction to Business History* (New York, 1939), pp. 67-74, especially p. 71.

[16]See Raymond de Roover, 'Discussion of N.S.B. Gras' paper "Capitalism—Concepts and History",' *Bulletin of the Business Historical Society*, XVI (1942), 34-39.

[17]There is general agreement among historians that the fairs of Champagne began to decline rapidly after 1275 (see Henri Laurent, *Un grand commerce d'exportation au moyen âge: la draperie des Pays-Bas en France et dans les pays méditerranéens, XIIe-XVe siècle* [Paris, 1935], p. 308). On the causes of the decline, see Gino Luzzatto, *Storia del commercio*, Vol. I, *Dall'antichità al Rinascimento* (Florence, 1914), p. 346, Laurent, *op. cit.*, pp. 94, 114-26, 141-50; Hans van Werveke, 'Der flandrische Eigenhandel im Mittelalter,' *Hansische Geschichtsblätter*, LXI (1936), 19.

[18]The author intends to devote a separate study to the subject.

[19]Pirenne, *Economic and Social History*, p. 103: 'The essential cause was undoubtedly the substitution for peripatetic commerce of more sedentary practices at the same time as the development of direct shipping from the Italian ports to those of Flanders and England.'

[20]The presence of the Italians in England is mentioned by Matthew Paris early in the thirteenth century. The Sienese companies, especially, had such temporary agencies at the fairs of Champagne or had a permanent representative in Paris. See André-E. Sayous, 'Dans l'Italie à l'intérieur des terres: Sienne de 1221 à 1229,' *AHES,* III (1931), 199; Mario Chiaudano, 'I Rothschild del Duecento, la Gran Tavola di Orlando Bonsignori,' reprint from *Bullettino senese di storia patria,* N.S., Vol. VI (1935), fasc. 2, p. 16.

[21]Sayous, 'Dans l'Italie, à l'intérieur des terres,' *op. cit.,* p. 205.

[22]On the early origins of the bill of exchange, see André-E. Sayous, 'L'origine de la lettre de change: les procédés de crédit et de paiement dans les pays chrétiens de la Méditerranée occidentale entre le milieu du XIIe siècle et celui du XIIIe,' *Revue historique de droit français et étranger,* 4th series, XII (1933), 66-112, and the bibliography cited therein.

[23]Henri Sée, *Histoire économique de la France* (Paris, 1939), I, 59.

[24]Freight contracts between merchants and common carriers in overland trade between Marseilles and the fairs of Champagne appear as early as 1248 (cf. L. Goldschmidt, *Universalgeschichte des Handelsrechts* [Stuttgart, 1891], p. 332, n. 114). Adolf Schaube devotes a long discussion to these contracts in his masterly work, *Storia del commercio dei popoli latini del Mediterraneo sino alla fine delle Crociate,* trans. Pietro Bonfante (Turin, 1915), pp. 457-60, esp. p. 459: 'Il transporto affidato ai vetturali non era sempre accompagnato dal mercante o da un socio o impiegato . . .' On the early bills of lading, see Enrico Bensa, *The Early History of Bills of Lading* (Genoa, 1925), 13pp.

[25]Raymond de Roover, 'Aux origines d'une technique intellectuelle: la formation et l'expansion de la comptabilité à partie double, *AHES,* IX (1937), 176-82.

[26]For evidence on this point, see Jean Denucé, *Italiaansche koopmansgeslachten te Antwerpen in de XVIe-XVIIIe eeuwen* (Malines, 1934). Even in the seventeenth century, the leading merchants in Antwerp were Italians (cf. Chiaudano, *op. cit.,* pp. 16-17).

[27]van Werveke, 'Flandrische Eigenhandel,' *op. cit.,* pp. 19-20. In 1366-69, the Bruges money-changer Collard de Marke had money invested in this trade.

[28]There is general agreement on this point among Belgian historians. See, for example, Laurent, *Un grand commerce d'exportation,* p. 150 'Le commerce actif des Flamands est de plus en plus remplacé par celui des Italiens, qui vont jusqu'aux centres de production en Flandre, et par celui des Brabançons et des Hanséates.' Still today, the Belgians sell mainly f.o.b. and let the foreigner market their products abroad (cf. *ibid.,* p. 313).

[29]van Werveke, 'Flandrische Eigenhandel,' *op. cit.,* pp. 14-20.

[30]The Italians were even active in the trade between England and Flanders. See, for example, the great number of Italian names in a document concerning this trade, dated 1371 (Bruges, Municipal Archives, Chartes politiques, lre série, No. 616 [Gilliodts, *Inventaire,* II, 188]).

[31]For an example, see Telesforo Bini, 'Su i Lucchesi a Venezia, memorie dei secoli XIII e XIV,' *Atti della I. e R. Accademia lucchese di scienze, lettere ed arte,* XV (1854), 153 ff. According to the document, dated August 1, 1393, and published by Bini, the following Italian colonies existed then in Bruges: the Venetians, the Genoese, the Florentines, the Lucchese, the Milanese, the Sienese, the Bolognese, and the merchants from Piacenza.

[32]The text of the grant of December 1395 was published by L. Gilliodts-van Severen (*Cartulaire de l'ancienne Estaple de Bruges* [Bruges, 1903-06], I, 391, No. 469) and by Cornelio Desimoni and L. T. Belgrano ('Documenti ed estratti inediti o poco noti, riguardanti la storia del commercio e della marina ligure: Brabante, Fiandra e Borgogna,' *Atti della società ligure di storia patria,* Vol. V [1867], fasc. 3, pp. 387-88, doc. No. 3). Cf. Jules Finot, *Etude historique sur les relations commerciales entre la Flandre et la République de Gênes au moyen âge* (Paris, 1906), p. 49.

[33]Gilliodts, *Cartulaire de l'Estaple,* I, 503-10, No. 610; Desimoni and Belgrano, *op. cit.,* pp. 399-406, doc. No. 32. Cf. Finot, *op. cit.,* pp. 80-84.

[34]The exact dates are March 31, 1422, June 23, 1434 (Gilliodts, *Cart. de l'Estaple*, I, 510) and December 18, 1459 (*ibid.*, II, 97-98, No. 1023).

[35]Finot, *op. cit.*, pp. 103-106.

[36]The text is found in Gilliodts, *Cart. de l'Estaple*, II, 167-70, No. 1110, and in Desimoni and Belgrano, *op. cit.*, pp. 440-46, doc. No. 128. Cf. Finot, *op. cit.*, pp. 188-89.

[37]Alfred Doren, *Italienische Wirtschaftsgeschichte* (Jena, 1934), I, 370.

[38]The text of this charter is found in Gilliodts, *Inventaire*, V, 559-64 (cf. *Cart. de l'Estaple*, II, 174-75).

[39]Carlo Antonio Marin, *Storia civile e politica del commercio dei Veneziani*, V. (Venice, 1800), 304; Roberto Cessi, 'Le relazioni commerciali tra Venezia e le Fiandre nel sec. XIV,' *Nuovo Archivio Veneto*, N. S., XXVII (1914), 27-28; Adolf Schaube, 'Die Anfänge der venezianischen Galeerenfahrt nach der Nordsee,' *Historische Zeitschrift*, CI (1908), 64.

[40]Cessi, 'Relazioni commerciali,' *op. cit.*, pp. 47-48.

[41]Richard Ehrenberg, 'Makler, Hosteliers und Börse in Brügge vom 13. bis zum 16. Jahrhundert,' *Zeitschrift für das gesamte Handelsrecht*, XXX (1885), 407; van Werveke, 'Flandrische Eigenhandel,' *op. cit.*, p. 21.

[42]Ehrenberg, *op. cit.*, p. 411. On the importance of brokers in the Middle Ages, see J. A. van Houtte, 'Les courtiers au moyen âge,' *Revue historique de droit français et étranger*, 4th series, XV (1936), 105-41, and Roberto Lopez, 'Sensali nel medio evo,' *Nuova rivista storica*, XXII (1938), 108-12.

[43]Ehrenberg, *op cit.*, p. 417; van Werveke, 'Flandrische Eigenhandel,' *op. cit.*, p. 21; Francesco Balducci Pegolotti, *La pratica della mercatura*, ed. Allan Evans (Cambridge, Mass.: 1936), p. 241. Pegolotti informs us that aliens who resold in Bruges what they had purchased there were liable to a fine of five pounds groat for the first and second, and to banishment for the third, offense.

[44]Gilliodts, *Cart. de l'Estaple*, I, 342, No. 405; Finot, *op. cit.*, p. 52.

[45]*Ibid.*, p. 55.

[46]Gilliodts, *Cart. de l'Estaple*, I, 392-93, No. 469.

[47]Only the building which was once the consular house of the Genoese (and later the *Saeihalle*) has been preserved more or less in its original state.

[48]Malcolm Letts, *Bruges and its Past* (2d ed.; Bruges, 1926), pp. 118-19.

[49]Ehrenberg, *op. cit.*, pp. 445-56; Hans van Werveke, 'Les origines des bourses commerciales.' *RBPH*, XV (1936), 133-41. The inn of the van der Beurse family became, after 1450, the consular house of the Venetians. The building was well suited for such a purpose, because it contained many rooms, large and small, and cellars for the storage of merchandise.

[50]Gilliodts, *Coutume*, I, 458, and *Inventaire*, I, 391, No. 323, item 26.

[51]Each nation met in front of its own consular house. There was not in Bruges a general meeting place for all the merchants (see Ehrenberg, *op. cit.*, p. 451).

[52]The statute of 1478 has been published by Eugenio Lazzareschi, 'Gli statuti dei Lucchesi a Bruges e ad Anversa,' *Ad Alessandro Luzio gli Archivi di Stato italiani: miscellanea di studi storici* (Florence, 1933), pp. 75-88.

[53]Florence Edler, 'The Silk Trade of Lucca during the Thirteenth and Fourteenth Centuries' (Unpublished Ph.D. dissertation, Dept. of History, University of Chicago, 1930), p. 146.

[54]*Ibid.*, pp. 147-48.

[55]Bini, *op. cit.*, pp. 144-45.

[56]Lazzareschi, *op. cit.*, p. 84. The Genoese consuls were elected by an assembly or *masseria* composed only of the heads of business firms or agencies (*majores domus*), whether nobles or not, over eighteen years of age. Apparently Genoese serving in a subordinate capacity did not have the right to vote (Gilliodts, *Cart. de l'Estaple*, I, 394, No. 469).

[57]Lazzareschi, *op. cit.*, pp. 85f. Bini (*op. cit.*, p. 145) quotes as an example the case of

the consul Jacopo Fava, who went to Aix-la-Chapelle on a pilgrimage and appointed Ciucchino Tignosini to transact all business during his absence.

[58]Lazzareschi, *op. cit.*, p. 85: '. . . ma pure quando ad alcuna delle parti paresse doversi ritrarre ad altra loya li sia licito poterlo fare; . . .' The word *loya* in this text is derived from the French *loi* and is very uncommon, the Italian word being *legge*.

[59]*Ibid.*, p. 86: '. . . debbino dicti consolo e consiglieri fare ogni assistentia possibile in ogni loro affare quando da alcuno ne fusseno richiesti, e che ne avessero bisogno, prestando loro tutto il favore della natione quando che il caso lo richiedesse.'

[60]Edler, *op. cit.*, p. 144; Letts, *op. cit.*, p. 109.

[61]Lazzareschi, *op. cit.*, pp. 85-87.

[62]Concerning the Genoese, see Gilliodts, *Cart. de l'Estaple,* I, 395. The Florentines raised *consolaggio* on all transactions in foreign exchange as well as on all purchases and sales. In 1441, the rate was 1/3 groat per pound on merchandise and two mites or 1/12 groat per pound on exchange (Florence, State Archives, Mediceo avanti il Principato, filza No. 134, item No. 2: Ledger of the Medici Branch in Bruges, 1441 [fragment], fols. 231, 246). Apparently this rate was not high enough to cover the expenses, because it was increased in 1461 to three mites or 1/8 groat on bills of exchange and to twelve mites or one-half groat on all sales and purchases (see Armand Grunzweig, 'Le fonds du Consulat de la Mer aux Archives de l'Etat à Florence,' *Bulletin de l'Institut historique belge de Rome,* X [1930], 111, art. 24; 112, arts. 26 and 27). These taxes were further increased in 1498 to one-fourth groat per pound on bills and to one groat per pound on purchases and sales (*ibid.*, p. 120, art. 2).

[63]Bini, *op. cit.*, p. 142: ' . . . a dì 17 aprile 1379 fue eletto per la nostra comunità in della nostra loggia Jacopo Maullini e Luiso Anguilla a dovere levare lo panno per la nostra livrea di tutta la comunità, la quale si de' vestire per la Santa Croce . . . che dè venire.'

[64]Gilliodts, *Cart. de l'Estaple,* I, 395.

[65]A French translation of the statutes of the Florentine nation of February 8, 1427 (n.s.), with several later amendments is found in Grunzweig, 'Le fonds du Consulat de la Mer,' *op. cit.*, pp. 103-21. The Italian text of this statute is now available in print, *Statuti delle colonie fiorentine all'estero,* Gino Masi ed. (Milan, 1941), 1-33.

[66]*Ibid.*, p. 104. See also the letter by which Bernardo Portinari was appointed consul for a term of two years on May 13, 1443 (Armand Grunzweig [ed.], *Correspondance de la filiale de Bruges des Medici* [Brussels: Commission Royale d'Histoire, 1931], I, 5). Later on the consul was apparently elected each year by the Florentine merchants resident in Bruges (Grunzweig, 'Consulat de la Mer,' *op. cit.*, p. 117, art. 50 and p. 120, art. 3).

[67]*Ibid.*, p. 115.

[68]The 'nation' apparently also organized the mail service. Lazzareschi, *op. cit.*, p. 79.

[69]Bini, *op. cit.*, p. 140. These consular records were still extant in 1854, when they were consulted by Bini, but have disappeared since then.

[70]Léon Mirot, 'La société des Raponde, Dine Raponde,' *Bibliothèque de l'Ecole des Chartes,* LXXXIX (1928), 382. The inscription on the tombstone reads as follows: Hic jacet Dynus de Rapondus, mercatorum *prepositus* Luca oriundus in Italia, consiliarius Philippi et Joannis ducum Burgundie, etc. [italics mine].

[71]Grunzweig, *Correspondance de la filiale de Bruges des Medici,* I, xxxix.

[72]Bini, *op. cit.*, p. 144.

[73]*Ibid.*, p. 157.

[74]Lazzareschi, *op. cit.*, p. 87.

[75]Olivier de la Marche, *Mémoires (1435-1488),* eds. H. Beaune and J. d'Arbaumont, III. (Paris, 1885), 112-13,

[76]Bigwood, *Régime,* I, 202-13.

[77]From 1343 to 1362, the master of the mint was an Italian named Percheval dou Porche, except for a short interruption from 1356 to 1357 when his functions were taken over by

another Italian named Bardet Malpilys, who absconded leaving a great many debts. Another master of the mint during the same period was Aldrigo Interminelli, a Lucchese (see *ibid.*, pp. 227-35).

[78]Mirot, 'Raponde,' *op. cit.*, p. 319: ' . . . car le duc de Bourgogne parloit souvent a luy pour avoir conseil et advis.'

[79]de la Marche, *op. cit.*, III, 113.

[80]In the Datini Archives in Prato (Tuscany), the author handled and photographed hundreds of letters in Italian sent by Italian firms in Bruges to a correspondent in Barcelona. On the education of the Italian merchant in the Middle Ages, one should consult the important article of Armando Sapori, 'La cultura del mercante medievale italiano,' *Rivista di storia economica,* II (1937), 89-125; republished in his *Studi di storia economica medievale* (2d ed., Florence, 1947), pp. 285-325.

[81]Grunzweig, *Correspondance,* I, 28, 40, 82.

[82]*Ibid.*, xxiv, n. 1.

[83]J. Huizinga, *The Waning of the Middle Ages* (London, 1924), p. 237 and illustration opp. p. 252; A. Warburg, 'Flandrische Kunst und florentinische Frührenaissance,' *Gesammelte Schriften,* I (Leipzig, 1932), 185-206, 370-80 (notes). Warburg thought that Jeanne Cenami was Flemish. Her father, Guglielmo Cenami, was a Lucchese merchant in Paris and her mother was French. See Leon Mirot, 'Etudes lucquoises: les Cename,' *Bibliothèque de l'Ecole des Chartes,* XCI (1930), 107.

[84]These two portraits are now in the Metropolitan Museum of New York City.

[85]Grunzweig, *Correspondance,* I, xxxi, n.2; Warburg, *op. cit.*, I, 190. Cf. Doren, *op. cit.*, I, 352.

[86]Warburg, *op. cit.*, I, 205-206.

[87]*Ibid.*, p. 192; Otto Meltzing, 'Tommaso Portinari und sein Konflikt mit der Hanse,' *Hansische Geschichtsblätter,* XII (1906), 101-24; Florence Edler de Roover, 'A Prize of War: A Painting of Fifteenth Century Merchants,' *Bulletin of the Business Historical Society,* XIX (1945), 3-12.

[88]Warburg, *op. cit.*, I, 193.

[89] Memling's 'Last Judgment' was probably begun in 1469 when Tani and his wife were in Flanders and in England, where he had gone to liquidate the London agency which had suffered heavy losses (*ibid.*, p. 375).

[90]*Ibid.*, p. 193. Cf. Heinrich Sieveking, *Die Handlungsbücher der Medici* ('Sitzungsberichte der Kais. Akademie der Wissenschaften in Wien, Philosophisch-historische Klasse,' CLI, No. 5; Vienna, 1905), 9.

[91]The art critics have even been able to identify among the Blessed Tommaso Portinari, the Bruges representative of the Medici, and Pierantonio Baroncelli, the Bruges representative of the Pazzi (Warburg, *op. cit.*, I, 197, 203).

[92]Huizinga, *op cit.*, pp. 227, 231.

[93]de la Marche, *op. cit.*, III, 113.

Chapter 3

THE ORGANIZATION OF THE ITALIAN MERCANTILE AND BANKING HOUSES WITH BRANCHES IN BRUGES

AS already explained, the Italian merchant-bankers combined trade and banking. They had a network of connections which extended from London to the Levant. Bruges was one of the most important focal points in this network because it was the meeting place of the Italian and Hanseatic merchants and the point of contact between Mediterranean and Baltic commerce.

In order to understand conditions in Bruges, one must keep in mind that the Italians residing there were usually not independent merchants but factors, or branch-managers of mercantile and banking companies with headquarters in Italy. It is, therefore, impossible to deal with Bruges without considering the relations of the branches with their headquarters and the structure of the Italian banking houses as a whole.

The study of the institutional framework will show that it would be wrong to have contempt for mediaeval business methods or organization, at least those of the Italians who were the leaders in this field. It is not true, as Sombart claims, that economic rationalism was non-existent in the Middle Ages, because there was no planning (*Planmässigkeit*), no intelligent direction (*Zweckmässigkeit*), and no adequate accounting control (*Rechnungsmässigkeit*).[1] On the contrary, the behavior of the Italian sedentary merchants was essentially rational, and they strove to make the best of the available means in organizing either banking and foreign trade or industrial production. The Italians constantly tried to innovate and to improve the existing methods. Contrary to what Sombart believes, it was impossible to conduct mediaeval business in a haphazard fashion: competition was strong and profit margins were so small that merchants were forced to weigh their decisions.[2]

In view of the slowness of mediaeval communications, to conduct foreign trade from behind a desk presented a stupendous problem of organization, planning, supervision, and management.[3] The only solution was for the merchant to secure permanent representation abroad either through partners, factors, agents, or correspondents. Goods were sent to them on consignment as most commodities were sold neither according to sample nor according to description, but after inspection by the prospective buyer.[4] The turnover of stocks was exceedingly slow, with the result that foreign trade required large investments of capital. If the merchant dealt extensively in bills of exchange as well as in commodities, his chances of gain were greatly increased, because he would be in a position to switch his capital from one form of investment to the other. But in order to be able to operate successfully on the money market, he needed to have, in all important commercial centers, agents and correspondents who would collect and honor his bills. These representatives were expected to report on the demand and the prices of commodities, on the rates of exchange, on the state of the money market, and on any other events, political as well as economic, which were likely to influence business decisions. For example, in 1464, the Medici branch in Bruges wrote to headquarters in Florence that the Flemish market was gutted with alum from the papal mines in Tolfa, in which the Rome branch was financially interested, and that the production should be regulated so as to keep the price up.[5] According to Italian business practice it was customary to give the exchange rates at the end of all business letters.[6] Mediaeval business men never failed to report to their correspondents when there was unusual stringency or abundance of money in a given trading center. Political events were not ignored because of their possible repercussion on business. A coronation, for example, was likely to boost the sale of silk, whereas a court mourning was bound to increase the demand for black cloth. In the latter case foreign correspondents were advised to stop sending silk, as it would not sell.

In the late Middle Ages, independent merchants and big companies with several branches existed side by side. In general—but there are exceptions—the large firms placed less emphasis on trade and more emphasis on finance, that is, on dealings in foreign exchange or the dangerous loans to princes, ecclesiastics, and great secular lords. Independent merchants, because they had only limited means and no widely-scattered connections, were at a certain disadvantage, if they wanted to deal in bills of exchange. But this disadvantage should not be overestimated. A merchant who had a good credit standing usually had no trouble in establishing new contacts, if he wished to extend his business. The leading, and even the less prominent, Italian merchants in Bruges were well known in other places, and vice versa.

Even the large companies did not have branches in all business centers. Where such companies had no branch office of their own, they were represented by a trustworthy correspondent. The Barcelona branch of Francesco Datini (d. 1410), an important merchant-banker with headquarters in Avignon and later in Tuscany, represented in Catalonia a number of Italian houses established in Bruges. Among them there were three independents, Guglielmo Barberi, Matteo Doni, and Zanobi Taddeo, a Venetian, and the following companies, which had branches elsewhere, but not in Barcelona: Deo Ambrogio e Giovanni Franceschi & Co., Alberto e Bernardo degli Alberti & Co., Diamante e Altobianco degli Alberti & Co., Giovanni Orlandini e Piero Benizi & Co., Luigi e Salvestro Mannini & Co., and Antonio Quarti & Co.

THE LAST JUDGMENT

by Hans Memling

Tommaso Portinari, according to the art-critics, is the man kneeling in one of the scales held by St Michael. Maria Bandini-Baroncelli, Portinari's wife is the woman sitting in the foreground. Farther back, near the angel brandishing a staff, is Pierantonio Bandini-Baroncelli, the Bruges manager of the Pazzi bank. Triptych until recently in the *Marienkirche, Danzig.*

The large Italian mercantile and banking houses with a number of branches abroad were all unlimited companies, that is to say, the partners were fully liable for all the debts of the company. From a structural and legal point of view, however, it is possible to distinguish two different types of companies: the centralized and the decentralized companies. The first type, which was apparently more common in the fourteenth century, is represented by the Bardi, the Peruzzi, and the Acciaiuoli companies. It is possible that the failure of these three companies around 1345 led to the abandonment of the centralized form of organization until it was revived much later by the Fuggers and the Welsers.

A good example of the second type, or of decentralization, are the combinations of interdependent partnerships set up by Francesco Datini late in the fourteenth century. Other examples are found among similar combinations formed by the Borromei of Milan, the historic Medici of Florence, and a less-known branch of the same family.[7]

The principal difference between the two types of organization was that, in one case, there was only one company with branches managed by factors and that, in the other case, there was a separate partnership for the main office and each of the branches. These branches were managed by junior partners who received a share in the profits, and not by salaried factors for whom increases in salary, promotion, and occasional bonuses were the only incentives to increase earnings.

The centralized form of organization typified by the Peruzzi and the Bardi companies was probably evolved during the thirteenth century. It is also found in the organization of the Francesi (failed in 1304), the Macci (failed in 1312), the Frescobaldi (failed in 1315), and the Cerchi Bianchi (failed in 1320).[8] In all these companies the capital was divided into shares which were held chiefly by the members of the family from which the company took its name and by a minority of outsiders. For example, the Francesi Company, in 1297, was composed of ten partners including the three brothers, Niccolò, Musciatto, and Albizzo Francesi, and a number of outsiders, who did not exercise control.[9] In 1331, the capital of the Bardi Company was made up of fifty-eight shares divided among eleven partners: six members of the Bardi family held 36¾ shares and five outsiders, the remaining 21¼ shares.[10] In 1312, the capital of the Peruzzi Company was £118,000 *a fiorino,* of which £68,000 *a fior.* were allotted to eight members of the Peruzzi family; £48,000 *a fior.,* to nine outsiders; and £2,000 *a fior.,* to the poor or *la compagnia per elimosine.*[11] In 1331, when the Peruzzi Company was already on the decline, the participation of the outsiders was increased and the family lost control over the majority of the capital.[12] Profits and losses were divided among the partners proportionately to their share in the capital.[13] The surviving records do not reveal whether the partners who took an active part in the management were entitled to any extra compensation or not. Probably they did not receive anything extra as long as they stayed in Florence, the seat of the central administration.[14]

The Peruzzi Company did not have an uninterrupted existence from 1275, or thereabouts, to 1343, when it went bankrupt. In reality, there were several successive partnerships due to the fact that new articles of association were drawn up in 1300, 1308, 1310, 1312, 1324, 1331, and 1335. Each time a new partnership was begun the old one was terminated. For this purpose the books were closed and a general financial statement or *saldamento generale* was prepared.[15] The partners then proceeded to a division of the profits. Usually the division was not final and was subject to later adjustments, because the financial statement was apt to include a great many contingent claims and other items which had to remain in abeyance.[16] The final liquidation normally took several years, as is evident from the surviving fragments of the account books. Between two *saldamenti generali,* or renewals of the partnership agreement, no new partners were admitted and no partner could withdraw, but each renewal gave rise to a rearrangement in the distribution of the capital.[17]

The distinctive feature of partnerships such as the Peruzzi Company was the absence of autonomous subsidiaries. It is true that the extant fragments of a general ledger (*libro dell'asse*) covering a period from 1335 to 1343 contain several references to a *compagnia della tavola,* a *compagnia della draperia,* and a *compagnia della mercatantia.*[18] Mediaeval terminology was sometimes inadequate. The likelihood is that there were no separate companies, but separate departments for the trade in cloth and in general merchandise as distinct from banking. Very probably the size of the business made some division of labor necessary. Apparently each department kept a separate set of subsidiary books.

The Peruzzi Company had at least fifteen branches abroad, namely in Bruges, in Paris, in Avignon, and in all important trading centers around the Mediterranean. In each branch the company was represented by factors: a manager and one or more assistants.[19] Today the word 'factor' applies to several kinds of business agents, but it had a precise meaning in the Middle Ages. It is evident from the Peruzzi account books that a factor (It. *fattore*) was a clerk serving abroad in one of the branches of a trading company or a banking house.[20] He received a salary 'for the donation of his time' (*per dono del tempo*), but no share in the profits.[21] Factors who were also branch managers were provided with a general power of attorney which allowed them to act in the name of the company. If a contract, because of its importance, had to be surrounded with full legal safeguards, a special power of attorney was sometimes supplied by headquarters in Italy.[22]

The factors were evidently recruited among enterprising young men of good family who had acquired business experience at home or abroad by serving a number of years as apprentices or *giovani.* Factors were in general well paid.

Francesco Balducci Pegolotti, the compiler of a famous handbook for merchants, was a factor of the Bardi in Flanders and Brabant.[23] In 1315, being in Antwerp, he secured trade privileges from the duke of Brabant in favor of the Florentine merchants.[24] In April 1317, Pegolotti left for England where he was in charge of the London office of the Bardi from 1318 to 1321.[25] He continued to serve the Bardi in various capacities for a number of years. His maximum salary was £290 *a fiorino* a year. After the bankruptcy of the Bardi in 1346, Pegolotti was one of the syndics or receivers appointed to settle the affairs of his former employers.[26] All factors were not equally well paid. Andrea Portinari, who was in Flanders for the Bardi from 1321 to 1332, did not receive more than £175 *a fior.* a year, but the company, when he left, decided to give him £80 *a fior.* extra, because 'he had been badly provided for.'[27] Riccardo del Maestro Fagno, who was the Bruges representative of the Peruzzi Company for at least six or seven years, earned 150 florins or £217 10*s. a fior.* per year, a sum which in those days represented a good deal in terms of purchasing power.[28] Assistants were not as well paid. For example, Simone di Gherardo Baroncelli who served the company in Bruges from November 20, 1335, to April 29, 1339, received annually a stipend of only £40 *a fior.* for the first two years. Thereafter it was raised to £60 *a fior.* When he returned to Florence in 1339, he was granted a bonus of thirteen *lire a fiorino* in final settlement.[29]

Sometimes a partner of the Peruzzi Company went abroad as a factor. A conspicuous example is the famous Florentine chronicler Giovanni Villani who represented the Peruzzi first in Naples (1305) and then in Bruges (1306).[30] He is mentioned as having contributed £2,000 *a fior.* to the capital of the *ragione* of 1300.[31] In 1308, or at the next renewal of the articles of association, Giovanni Villani withdrew as a partner, but his place was taken by his brother Filippo, who was still one of the partners at the time of the bankruptcy in 1343.[32] When a partner thus went abroad as a factor he was paid a regular salary in addition to his eventual share in the profits. Pacino di Tommaso di Arnoldo de' Peruzzi, who was at the helm of the company when it failed, had been a factor in Bruges from August 9, 1334, to July 1, 1335.[33] For his services abroad he received a salary of £221 5*s.* 10*d. a fior.,* irrespective of his share in the profits as a partner.

The factors, naturally, were supposed to devote all their time and all their energy to the service of the company. They were reprimanded and denied promotion or a raise in salary, if they neglected their duty or if the returns of the branch fell short of the expectations of their employers. In extreme cases, salaries were even cut, and careless and incompetent factors were recalled.[34] Immediate dismissal was the rule in case of flagrant dishonesty. In 1330, the Peruzzi Company sued in the *Uffizio della Mercanzia* or commercial court of Florence a certain Silimanno Botteri, who had been the company's factor in Bruges and in London and who was accused of defrauding his employers. The accused pleaded guilty. While he was in London, he had deceived the company by charging more than the price actually paid for English wool. He also had garbled gold coins and sold them in Paris as bullion. The dishonest factor had pocketed the profits made in this way.[35]

The organization of the Medici banking house was entirely different from that of the Peruzzi or the Bardi. Instead of one company with several branches managed by salaried employees, the Medici concern was a loose combination of quasi-independent partnerships. In each of them the members of the Medici family, that is, Cosimo and his brother Lorenzo and later their descendants, were the senior partners and controlled the major part of the capital, even when the name of Medici did not appear in the style of the partnership. In 1458, according to a statement prepared in connection with the levy of the property tax (*il catasto*), Cosimo de' Medici was a partner in eleven different enterprises: (1) the 'bank' in Florence managed by Francesco Inghirami; (2) one *bottega d'arte di lana* or a cloth manufacturing firm managed by Antonio di Taddeo; (3) second *bottega d'arte di lana* managed by Andrea Giuntini; (4) a silk manufacturing company managed by Berlinghieri Berlinghieri and Jacopo Tanagli; (5) the branch in Venice managed by Alessandro Martelli; (6) the branch in Bruges managed by Gierozzo de' Pigli and Agnolo Tani; (7) the branch in London managed by Simone Nori; (8) the branch in Avignon, styled 'Francesco Sassetti e Giovanni Zampini,' and managed by Giovanni Zampini and Francesco Baldovini; (9) the branch in Milan managed by Pigello Portinari; (10) the branch in Geneva, styled 'Amerigo Benci e Francesco Sassetti,' managed by Amerigo Benci; (11) a partnership between Cosimo and Simone di Nerone, which was in the process of liquidation.[36] It is to be noted that Cosimo de' Medici, the senior partner, very wisely did not manage any of these enterprises, but confined himself to distant control and to the making of important decisions.[37] In each case, including the 'bank' in Florence, the management of everyday affairs was left to a junior partner who, as we shall see for Bruges, had little or no money invested in the partnership, but received a share in the profits instead of a fixed salary.[38]

Each partnership was a separate legal entity.[39] In dealing with each other the branches behaved like independent enterprises and charged each other commission and interest.[40] The only common link was that the Medici family controlled the conduct of the business of each subsidiary. In all important matters of policy, the head of the Medici family had the final say. The branch managers who were also junior partners were expected to report regularly in private letters (*lettere private*) to the head of the firm. The tone of these letters was that of someone writing to his superior and not to his equal. The senior partner was addressed with the words *Honorando e maggiore mio* ('my honorable senior').[41] This obsequious formula was not used in ordinary business letters (*lettere di compagnia*) even in those exchanged between the branches and the main office in Florence.

The contents of these *lettere di compagnia* are also quite different. The style is dry and matter of fact. They deal with bills of exchange drawn or accepted, consignments sent or received, memoranda for the bookkeeper, and so forth.[42] The exchange rates are always quoted. The *lettere private*, on the contrary, have a personal touch and contain chiefly confidential information regarding the conduct of the business, the personnel, the current political events, and even family affairs.

The branches were expected, of course, to promote each other's business. The Bruges branch, for example, sold the silk manufactured by the 'shop' of the Medici in Florence.[43] The different subsidiary companies referred to each other as 'ours'—*i nostri* of Florence, Bruges, Venice, or *i nostri della seta* ('ours of the silk'), as the case might be.

The nature of the relations between the different branches is perhaps best illustrated by a case which was tried in 1455 before the municipal court in Bruges.[44] In this case a Milanese named Damiano Ruffini brought suit against Tommaso Portinari, acting manager of the Bruges branch in the absence of Agnolo Tani, for damages resulting from defective packing of nine bales of English wool. The defendant argued that the bales in question never belonged to the Bruges branch, but had been sold for account of the London branch managed by Simone Nori. The plaintiff replied to this argument that 'the Medici branch in Bruges and the one in London were all one company and had the same master.'[45] But Tommaso Portinari was allowed to affirm under oath that 'the said bales had been sold for, and in the name of, Simone Nori and that the company of Bruges had nothing to do with the whole business.'[46] Thereupon the Bruges branch was relieved from all responsibility, but the court decided to uphold the claims which the plaintiff might have against Simone Nori and the London branch. Perhaps Portinari did not play fair, but he did not commit perjury, as the Bruges and the London branches were legally separate partnerships.

The same question came up in an entirely different connection. By 1467, the London branch had suffered heavy losses due to the mistakes of Gherardo Canigiani, the local manager. Its liquidation was decided upon in 1471. When in 1475, Lorenzo the Magnificent, probably on the advice of Francesco Sassetti, who acted at that time as 'general manager,' wanted the Bruges branch to take over the liabilities of the London branch for a given sum of money, this proposal was strenuously opposed by Agnolo Tani, the former manager of the Bruges branch who still had a share in its capital. He wrote a report in which he repeated over and over again that the London branch was a separate unit from a legal, as well as from an accounting, point of view (*perchè la ragione di Londra era ragione da parte*).[47]

TABLE 1

Bruges Branch of the Medici Banking House

Division of the Capital and Distribution of the Profits

Names of the Partners	Shares in the Capital in Pounds Groat	Per Cent of Total	Distribution of Profits in Shillings per £	Percentage of Total
Contract of July 25, 1455				
Piero & Giovanni di Cosimo and Pierfrancesco di Lorenzo de' Medici, senior partners	£1900	63⅓	12*s.*	60
Gierozzo de' Pigli, investing partner	600	20	4*s.*	20
Agnolo Tani, managing partner	500	16⅔	4*s.*	20
Total	£3000	100	20*s.*	100
Contract of August 6, 1465				
Piero de' Medici, senior partner	£2000	66⅔	12½*s.*	62½
Agnolo Tani, investing partner	600	20	2½*s.*	12½
Tommaso Portinari, managing partner	400	13⅓	5*s.*	25
Total	£3000	100	20*s.*	100
Contract of October 14, 1469				
Lorenzo and Giuliano di Piero de' Medici, senior partners	£2000	66⅔	10*s.*	50
Agnolo Tani, investing partner	400	13⅓	2½*s.*	12½
Tommaso Portinari, managing partner	400	13⅓	5½*s.*	27½
Antonio de' Medici, assistant manager	200	6⅔	2*s.*	10
Total	£3000	100	20*s.*	100
Contract of May 12, 1471				
Lorenzo and Giuliano de' Medici, senior partners	£2075	69⅙	10*s.*	50
Agnolo Tani, investing partner	375	12½	2½*s.*	12½
Tommaso Portinari, managing partner	400	13⅓	5½*s.*	27½
Tommaso Guidetti, assistant manager	150	5	2*s.*	10
Total	£3000	100	20*s.*	100

Sieveking, *Die Handlungsbücher der Medici*, pp. 48–52.

Only one of several extant partnership agreements pertaining to the Bruges branch is available in print.[48] The text confirms what has just been said about the organization of the Medici house and sheds additional light on the fundamental relations between the partners. These articles of association were drawn up on July 25, 1455, and were signed by the partners on the second of August. According to Article One, the partnership was to last for four years, from March 25, 1456, to March 24, 1460, and was to be styled 'Piero di Cosimo de' Medici e Gierozo de' Pigli e Compagni.' The partnership was allowed to use the mark of the Medici, but it was to remain their property at the end of the contract. The capital (*corpo*) was three thousand pounds groat, of which the senior partners, namely Piero di Cosimo de' Medici, his brother Giovanni, and Pierfrancesco, a first cousin of the other two, supplied the major part or £1,900 groat. Gierozzo de' Pigli, a former manager of the London branch, subscribed another £600 groat; the balance of £500 groat was furnished by Agnolo Tani, the managing partner. Profits were not to be divided among the partners in proportion to their share in the capital; but twelve shillings out of every pound were to go to the senior partners; four shillings, to Gierozzo de' Pigli; and four shillings, to Agnolo Tani. The managing partner who owned only one-sixth of the capital thus received one-fifth of the profits. A similar arrangement is found in later agreements concerning Bruges and in a London contract of 1446 (see Table I).[49] The reason for allocating a larger share of the profits to the managing partner than his share in the capital would justify was evidently to reward him for his services, since he had to devote all his time to the management of the partnership's affairs.

The articles of association of the year 1455 explicitly entrusted the management of the Bruges agency to Agnolo Tani, the junior partner ('il quale debbe essere al ghoverno di detta compagnia'). Except for the provisions concerning the ownership of the capital and the distribution of the profits, the main purpose of the contract was evidently to define the duties and to limit the powers of the managing partner. He was to stay in Flanders for the duration of the agreement and was not allowed to leave except on business trips to the fairs of Antwerp and Bergen-op-Zoom or to Calais, Middleburg, and London, if necessary (art. 12). He was not free to engage, either directly or indirectly, in any other mercantile venture or exchange business under the penalty of £50 groat for each offense (art. 6). It should be noted that the freedom of action of the other partners was not limited by a similar restriction. The managing partner was not permitted to play at cards or at dice, or to entertain women in his quarters, under the penalty of one hundred pounds groat (art. 7). He was not empowered to hire any apprentices or factors (*alchuno giovane o fattore*) except with the permission of the other partners (art. 10). In practice, as we have seen, apprentices and factors were sent from Italy, and the branch manager had no voice in the matter.

Once a year, on March 24, or more often if requested, the manager was expected to close the books and to send a copy of the balance to headquarters in Italy. He could even be summoned to Florence to render accounts (art. 8). Purchases of cloth and wool, together, were not to exceed the sum of six hundred pounds groat in any one year (art. 13). The branch manager was expressly forbidden to underwrite insurance policies (art. 15). If he shipped any goods by sea, they were to be fully insured. Only on goods shipped by the Florentine or Venetian galleys, could he take a chance and be his own insurer up to a maximum of £60 groat on each shipment. If goods were sent to Italy overland, the question of insuring them or not was left for the manager to decide. In any case, he was not to send goods exceeding the value of three hundred pounds groat at one time (art. 14).

After termination of the partnership, the manager was to remain in Bruges and to be helpful in winding up the business (art. 19). The buildings in which the branch office was housed remained the property of the Medici. After liquidation, they were also to receive in custody the books and the archives of the partnership (art. 9).

When a branch manager left Florence to take up his duties abroad, he was often given specific instructions concerning the policy which he was expected to follow with his subordinates, with local customers, and with merchants in other places.[50] Wherever there were branches of the Medici house, the branch managers were urged to deal with them rather than with strangers. According to the instructions given to Gierozzo de' Pigli, when he went to London in 1446, he was cautioned against granting credit facilities and was advised to deal only with houses in good standing which were specifically listed.

Cosimo de' Medici and his son Piero made it their policy to keep their branch managers well in hand; they insisted upon receiving regular reports and yearly balance sheets and saw to it that their instructions were obeyed to the letter.[51] When Cosimo de' Medici learned, in 1457, that his agents in England and in Flanders had dealt with people of ill-repute like the Italian pawnbrokers in Bruges, he was so incensed that he threatened to close both branches and to terminate the existing partnerships before they had expired.[52] Lorenzo the Magnificent did not follow in the footsteps of his father and grandfather and neglected to apply the brake to Tommaso Portinari, the manager of the Bruges branch, a brilliant and gifted personality, but incautious in his business dealings and blinded by ambition and by an unbounded admiration for Charles the Bold, Duke of Burgundy.[53]

With regard to management, there was of necessity a great deal of decentralization regardless of legal structure. It did not make much difference whether or not the branches were separate legal entities, or whether the branch managers were junior partners or simply factors who received a fixed salary instead of a share in the profits. Because of the slowness of mediaeval communications, the branch managers had to be given a free hand within the limits of the policy which was outlined in their instructions. Policy was formulated by headquarters in Italy. In the case of the Peruzzi, it seems that major decisions had to be submitted to some kind of 'board of directors' composed of the partners residing in Florence. The head of the Medici firm was not bound to consult the junior partners and assumed solely the responsibility for all important decisions. In fact, however, he often took the advice of the manager of the 'bank' or main office in Florence: Francesco Ingherami at the time of Cosimo de' Medici and Francesco Sassetti after his death.

Even in the case of the Medici, it is untrue to state that 'the head office in Florence managed everything.'[54] All that the senior partners in Florence did, or could do, was to determine the general policy and to require that the junior partners manage the branches accordingly. Another safeguard was great care in the selection of branch managers.[55] In this respect, Cosimo de' Medici usually made a better choice than his grandson Lorenzo the Magnificent.

The form of organization adopted by the Medici house, far from being exceptional, was rather typical, although details probably varied from one firm to another. In 1438, the Bruges branch of Filippo Borromei e Compagni, a Milanese firm combining banking and trade, was also headed by a manager who was not a salaried factor, but a junior partner with the title of *governatore*.[56] The branch was an autonomous organization, but the head of the Borromei family owned most of the capital.[57] In turn, the Bruges branch supplied the entire capital of the London branch or £1,431 17*s.* 1*d.* sterling, equivalent to £1600 groat.[58] A curious setup is found in the Cenami company of Lucca. In 1381, the personnel of the parent company was composed of three partners, three factors, and five apprentices.[59] A subsidiary company or *ragione* headed by Betto Schiatta apparently specialized in *cambio* transactions or the trade in bills of exchange.[60] This subsidiary had its own trademark. Betto Schiatta employed two factors in Bruges and one factor and three *giovani* or apprentices in Lucca.[61] The main seat of the subsidiary was probably in Bruges, as Betto Schiatta was consul of the Lucchese there in 1394.[62]

It would be a mistake to visualize the mediaeval trading companies as enterprises of gigantic size with hundreds of employees. Nothing of the sort existed in the Middle Ages. At the beginning of the fourteenth century, the Acciaiuoli company, the third largest company of Florence (only the Bardi and the Peruzzi being larger), had fifteen branches and employed forty-one factors, the home office not included.[63] The Bruges and London branches each had two factors; the Paris branch, only one. In 1372, the personnel of the Guinigi company, the largest commercial firm in Lucca, numbered nineteen persons including the seven partners.[64] The company was represented in Bruges by four factors, in Venice and Naples, by three. Nine years later, in 1381, the staff totaled only sixteen persons including the seven partners.[65] The Genoa and Venice branches had been closed and the Naples branch had been transferred to Rome, but a new branch had been opened in London. The staff of the Bruges branch had been reduced from four to three factors. One of the smaller Lucchese companies had only two partners, Giannino and Filippo Spada, one stationed in Bruges and the other in Lucca.[66] In 1371, eighty-nine companies and independent merchants were registered with the *Corte dei Mercanti*. Two companies only, the Guinigi and the

Panichi, employed more than ten factors. Only five had over eight factors.[67] Among those five is the Balbani company which is known to have combined trade and banking.

In 1466, there were six factors and one *giovane* or apprentice on the pay-roll of the Bruges branch of the Medici, not including the branch manager and junior partner, Tommaso Portinari.[68] The assistant manager was Antonio de' Medici who, although only a distant relative of the heads of the firm, felt that he was protected by his name and made himself unpleasant to all the other members of the staff. Cristofano Spini was in charge of the purchases of wool and cloth, a department which required the keeping of special subsidiary books. Carlo Cavalcanti, because of his perfect knowledge of French and probably because of his handsome figure and glib tongue, took care of the sale of silks at the court of the duke of Burgundy. It requires little imagination to visualize Carlo Cavalcanti, dressed like a *damoiseau,* courting the ladies in order to sell his silks. Adoardo Canigiani's job was to keep the books, especially the ledger. No information is available concerning the functions of Tommaso Guidetti and Folco Portinari, a nephew of the manager.[69] The *giovane,* Antonio Tornabuoni, a nephew of Piero di Cosimo de' Medici, had just arrived from Florence: he still needed training and his job was probably to copy all outgoing correspondence in the letter book.

In 1469, according to the notes of the Florentine merchant Benedetto Dei, the staff of the Bruges branch included eight persons: Tommaso Portinari (the manager, Antonio de' Medici (the assistant manager), Cristofano Spini, Tommaso Guidetti, Lorenzo Fanini, Folco Portinari, Antonio Corsi, and Antonio di Filippo Tornabuoni (factors).[70] Carlo Cavalcanti was still in Bruges, but apparently was no longer in the service of the Medici.[71] The same source discloses that there were eight persons on the staff of the branch in Lyons and five on the staff of the one in Avignon.[72] However incomplete these figures are, they suggest that the Medici at their zenith did not have in their employ more than forty or fifty factors, not including the ten or eleven branch managers, who were not employees, but partners. This figure of forty or fifty may not seem very impressive, but it is a large number according to mediaeval standards.

The extent of the operations of the merchant-bankers, both in foreign trade and in international finance, required considerable funds. How were their enterprises financed? In general, the capital invested by the partners was only a fraction of the total financial resources of the large Italian trading companies. The remainder consisted of money invested *fuori del corpo* or *sopracorpo* ('above and beyond the capital') at a fixed rate of interest.[73] The *sopracorpo* was made up of three elements: (a) of funds supplied by the partners themselves in addition to their share in the capital, (b) of reinvested earnings, (c) of money placed on deposit by outsiders, mainly wealthy Italians, for a fixed return per year. The legal position of these outsiders was not unlike that of modern bondholders. *Sopracorpo* deposits, it should be emphasized, were not readily transferable and, as a rule, were not repayable upon request or on short notice.

It is not difficult to find examples of the three kinds of *sopracorpo* just mentioned. According to the entries in the *libro segreto* of Giotto di Arnoldo de' Peruzzi, the partners were allowed a return of 8 per cent on money which they might invest *sopracorpo* or in addition to their share in the capital or *corpo*.[74] In another entry it is stated that net profits were obtained after deducting from gross profits all expenses, all salaries, all bad debts, and the interest on all money invested *fuori del corpo* whether it belonged to partners or to outsiders.[75] That profits were frequently plowed back into the business by being added to the *sopracorpo* is shown by the records of Rossi degli Strozzi, a partner of the Strozzi bank. According to the entries in his *libro segreto,* all the profits which he earned from 1318 to 1340, the date of his death, were credited to his *sopracorpo* account and thus became productive of interest at the rate of 8 per cent. As Rosso degli Strozzi did not withdraw all that he earned, the credit balance of his *sopracorpo* account increased sevenfold during the period from 1318 to 1340.[76] In 1438, the bookkeeper of the Bruges branch of the Borromei banking firm charged to 'profit and loss' two items relating to interest due on money which was placed 'on deposit' by the senior partner, Vitaliano Borromei, and by the heirs of Giovanni del Barza of Milan, apparently outsiders.[77] The total amount invested in the Bruges branch of the Medici house certainly exceeded by far the *corpo* or capital of three thousand pounds groat.[78] It is doubtful whether any local investors placed money at interest with the Italian companies. The published correspondence of the Medici gives very definitely the impression that most financing was done in Italy.[79] The following episode is significant in this respect. The financial results of the fiscal year beginning March 25, 1463, and ending March 24, 1464, had not been very good. When Tommaso Portinari sent a copy of the balance sheet to Florence on the following fourteenth of May, he wrote that 'the profits had been few and the expenses great, and that he had omitted to add the interest to several deposit accounts,' evidently in order to conceal the full extent of the deficit.[80]

A typical Italian investor is, for instance, the wealthy Florentine Francesco Sassetti. He was closely connected with the Medici, as we have seen, and part of his fortune was invested in either the *corpo* or the *sopracorpo* of their companies. With the Milan branch, for example, he had a deposit of fl.6,000 *di suggello* or fl.5,000 *larghi* on which he was paid interest or *discrezione* at the rate of 10 per cent.[81] In Italian sources there are numberless instances of members of the aristocracy and even of the clergy—who were not connected with business—having part of their fortune invested at interest in trading and banking companies.[82]

The importance of these investments in the *sopracorpo* cannot be overstressed.

In the Middle Ages, Italy was perhaps the only country of Europe which had any foreign investments. These investments were mainly in the form of time deposits with the trading companies or of shares in their capital. As the investors were usually wealthy, profits and interest received were not withdrawn but reinvested in the business. Foreign investments thus tended to increase rapidly, and there arose the problem of finding productive uses for surplus funds. In other words, there existed in all likelihood a tendency for savings to outstrip investments. Under such conditions, loans to princes appeared as an attractive outlet for idle capital. But such loans were destructive of savings, in the end, as the bankruptcies of the Bardi and the Peruzzi illustrate.

Many persons have fantastic notions about the productivity of capital in the Middle Ages. It was certainly higher than within the last century, but not as high as is often asserted. According to the *libro segreto* of Giotto di Arnoldo de' Peruzzi, the profits of the Peruzzi Company amounted to 20 per cent a year from 1308 to 1310, to about 14.5 per cent annually from 1310 to 1312, to 14.3% from 1312 to 1319, and to 18% from 1319 to 1324.[83] But one should not overlook the fact that the return on the total investment was much below those figures. All expenses deducted, the Peruzzi made perhaps 10 or 12 per cent on *all* the money invested in their business and not more. The explanation is that profits were swollen by whatever was earned in excess of the 7 or 8 per cent which was paid on the *sopracorpo*. The same happens today: the stockholders of a corporation can increase their dividends by trading on the equity, for example, if money borrowed at 5 per cent from the bondholders yields as much as 6 per cent to the company. Under those conditions the larger the bonded debt, the greater are the dividends. Profits, consequently, are not a reliable index of the productivity of capital. If, however, the return on the total investment, *corpo* and *sopracorpo* combined, dropped below the rate of interest paid on the *sopracorpo*, the *corpo* was likely to melt away. A state of bankruptcy was bound to ensue, should the contributors to the *sopracorpo* withdraw their deposits. This is what happened in the case of the Peruzzi: although the company did not fail until 1343, the *corpo* or capital was entirely lost as early as 1335. The crash came when bad rumors reached the ears of the depositors and they began to ask for their deposits.[84]

From this discussion on finance, it clearly appears that the Italian merchant-bankers in Bruges operated with funds provided by partners or investors residing in Italy. Little, or no, capital was raised in the Low Countries. As the source of capital was in Italy, it is not surprising that the source of power was located there, too. Some Italian merchants in Bruges were independent, but the majority of them were the representatives of firms with headquarters in Italy. Those headquarters formulated policies and exercised ultimate control over the 'governors' or 'factors' who managed the local branches in Bruges or elsewhere.

[1]Frank H. Knight, 'Historical and Theoretical Issues in the Problem of Modern Capitalism,' *Journal of Economic and Business History,* I (1928), 119-36. See also the long preface of André-E. Sayous to the French translation of Sombart's *Hochkapitalismus* (Werner Sombart, *L'Apogée du Capitalisme* [Paris, 1932]), and N.S.B. Gras, 'Economic Rationalism in the Late Middle Ages,' *Speculum,* VIII (1933), 304-312.

[2]Profit margins were perhaps very high during the eleventh and twelfth centuries, but the same conditions did not obtain during the fourteenth and fifteen centuries. For example, the Peruzzi never distributed dividends exceeding 20 per cent on the *corpo,* or capital stock, and the rate of profit on all invested capital, *corpo* and *sopracorpo* combined, must have been much lower. Despite this evidence, historians, especially Marxian writers, continue to assert that profits were fantastically high and easily made. Those writers forget that high profits usually corresponded to high risks. Moreover, mediaeval business firms had a high mortality rate and most of them ended sooner or later in bankruptcy.

[3]Clemens Bauer, *Unternehmung und Unternehmungsformen im Spätmittelalter und in der beginnenden Neuzeit* (Jena, 1936), pp. 17-23.

[4]There were exceptions: for example, tapestries were made to order according to specifications sent from abroad.

[5]Grunzweig, *Correspondance des Medici,* I, 104, 107.

[6]*Ibid.,* p. xlv. There are also countless examples in the Datini letters.

[7]The expression 'historic Medici' refers to the descendants of Giovanni di Averardo or Bicci de' Medici (d. 1429), the father of Cosimo and the great-grandfather of Lorenzo the Magnificent. This branch, which eventually ruled over Tuscany, is now extinct. The other, less-famous branch descends from Giuliano di Giovenco, a second cousin of the aforesaid Giovanni, and is represented today by the marquises of Castellina and the princes of Ottaiano. Most of the business records of this branch—which is apparently elder than the historic line—including partnership agreements and a considerable number of account books are in the Selfridge Collection, now on deposit at the Harvard Graduate School of Business Administration.

[8]Otto Meltzing, *Das Bankhaus der Medici und seine Vorläufer* (Jena, 1906), pp. 16-55.

[9]Robert Davidsohn, *Geschichte von Florenz,* IV^2 (Berlin, 1925), 192. Musciatto and Albizzo Francesi are the famous Mouche and Biche frequently mentioned in French sources of the period. See also *ibid.,* pp. 188-93, for figures on other companies.

[10]Armando Sapori, *La crisi delle compagnie mercantili dei Bardi e dei Peruzzi* (Florence, 1926), p. 249.

[11]See Armando Sapori, 'Storia interna della compagnia mercantile dei Peruzzi,' *Archivio storico italiano* 7th series, Vol. XXII (1934), pp. 20-23; republished in his *Studi di storia economica medievale* (2d ed., Florence, 1947), pp. 243-84.

[12]*Ibid.,* p. 23. The members of the Peruzzi family, in 1331, owned only £37,500 *a fior.* out of a total capital of £90,000 *a fior.*

[13]*I libri di commercio dei Peruzzi,* ed. Armando Sapori (Milan, 1934), pp. 434-41. According to the entries of Giotto di Arnoldo de' Peruzzi in his *libro segreto* or private account book, profits were to be divided among the partners on the basis of so much per thousand florins of capital. For example, p. 434: 'E ordinato si è, quando faranno ragione de la detta conpagnia, ciascun abia sua parte si come ne tocherà per miliaio.'

[14]Sapori, 'Storia interna,' *op. cit.,* p. 13, n. 3.

[15]*Ibid.,* p. 12.

[16]*Ibid.,* p. 15, and the entries in the account book of Giotto di Arnoldo de' Peruzzi (*Libri dei Peruzzi,* pp. 434-41). For example, in 1308 the accounts of the Paris branch could not be closed, because of the considerable sums of money due from the king of France and the barons of his court (*ibid.,* p. 435). In September, 1335, the previous partnership, which had terminated July 1, 1335, was charged with £19 15*s.* 6*d.* groat or

£593 5*s.* *a fior.* because the Bruges branch did not collect as much in receivables as was expected at the time of the *saldamento generale* (*ibid.*, p. 7).

[17]Sapori, 'Storia interna,' *op. cit.*, p. 13.

[18]*Libri dei Peruzzi*, p. 555 (index).

[19]A list of branches is given in Sapori, 'Storia interna,' *op. cit.*, p. 53.

[20]On this topic, see the study of Armando Sapori, 'Il personale delle compagnie mercantili del medioevo,' *Archivio storico italiano,* 7th series, Vol. XXXII (1939), pp. 121-51. That factors were employees is further confirmed by an interesting document dated August 16, 1300. This document is the will of a young Sienese, son of Bonifazio Ricci. The maker of the will, apparently feeling that he was mortally ill, declared that he came to Paris as a factor and agent (*nuntius et factor*) of the Gallerani Company at at annual salary and did not have any property of his own. As he had spent more than his salary and owed money to the company, he begged one of the partners, probably his superior, to give him nevertheless a decent funeral, 'for the love of God and the honor of the company' (*ut amore Dei et honore societatis et sociorum suorum*); see Bigwood, *Régime,* II, 309.

[21]*Libri dei Peruzzi,* pp. 304, 378, and passim.

[22]Gilliodts, *Inventaire,* I, 422, No. 347. Cf. Pegolotti, *op. cit.*, p. xviii. According to the statutes of the *Calimala* gild of Florence, any partner or factor who was sent abroad by a company had to be provided with a general and special power of attorney. See Paolo Emiliani-Giudici, *Storia politica dei municipi italiani* (Florence, 1851), II (*Appendixes*), p. 78, No. 66: *di fare procuratore che fie mandato fuori di Firenze per le compagnie.* Cf. Max Weber, *Zur Geschichte der Handelsgesellschaften im Mittelalter* (Stuttgart, 1889), p. 137.

[23]Pegolotti, *op. cit.*, p. 251.

[24]*Ibid.*

[25]Sapori, *Crisi,* p. 263. The successor of Pegolotti in Flanders was apparently a certain Francesco di Lapo Baldovini who was manager of the Bruges branch from 1319 to 1323 (*ibid.*, p. 264).

[26]Pegolotti, *op. cit.*, p. xxv.

[27]Sapori, *Crisi,* p. 255.

[28]*Libri dei Peruzzi,* p. 304. Cf. Sapori, 'Storia interna,' *op. cit.*, p. 64. The total paid to Riccardo del Maestro Fagno amounted to £1250 10*s.* *a fior.* or his salary for five years, £1087 10*s.* *a fior.*, plus a bonus of £163 *a fior.* At the time of the bankruptcy in 1343, Riccardo del Maestro Fagno fled from Florence, as did the partners and many of the other factors. Fagno was allowed to return with other fugitives under a safe conduct (Sapori, *Crisi,* p. 161). The explanation is that factors were liable for the debts of a company as well as the partners. This rule was not changed until 1393 (Max Weber, *op. cit.*, p. 133).

[29]*Libri dei Peruzzi,* p. 313: According to the records, a total of £179 10*s.* *a fior.* was written to the credit of Simone di Gherardo Baroncelli. This sum was made up as follows:

Salary from November 20, 1335, to November 20, 1337, or two years at £40 *a fior.* a year	£80	*a fior.*
One year's salary from November 20, 1337, to November 20, 1338	£60	
Five months and 9 days up to April 29, 1339, at £60	£26 10*s.*	
Bonus	£13	
Total	£179 10*s.*	

[30]Robert Davidsohn, *Forschungen zur Geschichte von Florenz* (Berlin, 1896-1908), III, 93, No. 477, and 96, No. 502; V. Fris, 'L'historien Jean Villani en Flandre,' *Compte rendu des séances de la Commission Royale d'Histoire,* LXIX (1900), 1-7.

[31]Sapori, 'Storia interna,' *op. cit.*, p. 20.

[32]*Ibid.*, pp. 22-25, and Sapori, *Crisi,* pp. 160-61.

[33]*Libri dei Peruzzi,* p. 378. Paccino de' Peruzzi succeeded his brother Bonifazio who died in London on October 3, 1340, where he had gone to make a settlement with the English crown.

[34]Sapori, 'Il personale delle compagnie mercantili,' *op. cit.*, p. 134.

[35]Davidsohn, *Geschichte* IV², 200, and Forschungen, III, 193 f., No. 975. According to Sapori, the name of this factor was Silimanno di Lottieri (*Studi di storia economica*, p. 469).

[36]Sieveking, *Handlungsbücher der Medici*, pp. 9-10. The table given by Sieveking contains a few obvious mistakes which have been corrected here. In the Avignon branch, styled 'Francesco Sassetti e Giovanni Zampini,' the Medici owned one half of the capital, Francesco Sassetti and Giovanni Zampini each having one fourth. A similar arrangement existed for the Geneva branch. This information is based on the *libro segreto* ('private account book') of Francesco Sassetti: Florence, State Archives, Carte Strozziane, Series II, No. 20; Libro segreto di Francesco Sassetti, 1462-1472.

[37]Curt S. Gutkind, *Cosimo de' Medici, Pater Patriae, 1389-1464* (Oxford, 1938), p. 203. The author makes here and there some penetrating remarks, especially in his chapter on Cosimo's business interests (pp. 172-205) and in Appendix VI (pp. 265-69), but he also makes a number of misstatements, because he is clearly not familiar with business terminology or with the operation of a business. For example, it is not true that 'double-entry bookkeeping had not yet been introduced' (p. 174), that Tommaso Portinari was a son of Bernardo (p. 174, n. 1), that partnership agreements are documents of unusual 'cultural' interest (p. 182), that Cavalcanti was 'an expert on French connexions' (p. 183), that 'all the books were occasionally sent to Florence' (p. 186), that 'de Wale' as used on p. 192 was a Flemish or Walloon family name (it is Low German for Welsch, which means Italian or French, i.e., from a Latin country), that Cosimo was 'the real manager of the combined business' (p. 200), and that the Bruges establishment bought wool, spun, and wove it (p. 202).

[38]This statement is based on numerous partnership agreements of the Medici, published in full or analysed in historical publications: Grunzweig, *Correspondance*, I, 53-63, No. 22; Gertrude R. B. Richards, *Florentine Merchants in the Age of the Medici* (Cambridge, Mass., 1932), pp. 227-51; Florence Edler, *Glossary of Mediaeval Terms of Business, Italian Series*, 1200-1600 (Cambridge, Mass., 1934), Appendix I: 'Medici Partnerships,' pp. 335-47; Lewis Einstein, *The Italian Renaissance in England* (New York, 1902), pp. 242-45; Raymond de Roover, 'A Florentine Firm of Cloth Manufacturers: Management and Organization of a Sixteenth-Century Business,' *Speculum*, XVI (1941), 5-9.

[39]I agree with Gutkind on this point (*op. cit.*, p. 173).

[40]Bauer, *op. cit.*, p. 143, n. 27. The same applies to the Datini partnerships (*ibid.*, n. 26). Bauer's statement that 'Die Filialgesellschaften nähern sich manchmal einem Scheingesellschaftsverhältnis, in dem eben der Leiter der Filiale als Gesellschafter erscheint,' is not quite correct. The branch manager in the Medici set-up was *always* a partner. See also Sieveking, *Handlungsbücher der Medici*, p. 37.

[41]Grunzweig, *Correspondance*, I, 6, No. 5, Cf. *ibid.*, p. xlvi. Under Lorenzo the Magnificent, the formula became even more obsequious and all *lettere private* began with *Magnifico Maior mio*.

[42]*Ibid.*, pp. xlv-xlvi.

[43]*Ibid.*, pp. xxii-xxiii.

[44]Gilliodts, *Cartulaire de l'Estaple*, II, 36-37, No. 958, dated July 30, 1455. Portinari acted as manager, because Agnolo Tani, the manager, was away. He had gone to Florence to renew the partnership contract. Cf. Grunzweig, *Correspondance*, I, 53.

[45]Gilliodts, *Cart. de l'Estaple*, II, 36: 'Le dit Damian ad ce répondant . . . et disans et maintenans que la dite compaignie et la compaignie du dit Simon en Angleterre estoit une mesme compaignie et avoient un mesme maistre.'

[46]*Loc. cit.*: ' . . . mais fu la dite vente faicte pour et au nom de Simon Nory de Londres, et la dite compaignie de Bruges n'y avoit que faire.'

[47]Warburg, 'Flandrische Kunst und Frührenaissance,' *op. cit.*, I, 375.

[48]Grunzweig, *Correspondance*, I, 53-63, No. 22, and Gutkind, *op. cit.*, pp. 308-12. The later partnership agreements were scheduled to appear in Volume II of Grunzweig's *Correspondance* but this volume has not yet been published. These later contracts are all extant

in the State Archives of Florence, Mediceo avanti il Principato, Filza 84, Nos. 27, 29, 32, and 84.

[49]An excellent digest of the London contract is given in Einstein, *op. cit.*, pp. 242-45.

[50]Einstein (*ibid.*, pp. 245-49) gives an excellent analysis of the instructions with which Gierozo de' Pigli was supplied, when he left for London in 1446.

[51]Gutkind, *op. cit.*, p. 203.

[52]Armand Grunzweig, 'La correspondance de la filiale brugeoise des Medici,' *RBPH*, VI (1927), 729.

[53]In 1464 Portinari wrote to his brothers that he preferred honor to money and that he would rather be poor than become rich under Agnolo Tani, whose assistant he was and whom he wanted to replace as head of the Bruges branch. This is not the language of a business man (Grunzweig, *Correspondance*, I, 122, 123-24).

[54]Gutkind, *op. cit.*, p. 172.

[55]Bauer, *op. cit.*, p. 34: 'Der Faktor handelt nach den Direktiven der Zentrale, freilich bei der grossen Entfernung vom Hauptsitz und bei der Unvollkommenheit des Verkehrs- und Nachrichtenmittel mit weitgehender Freiheit und Eigenverantwortlichkeit. Deshalb ist das Korrelat der Faktoreiverfassung als Organisationsform der Fernhandelsunternehmung eine sorgsame "Personalpolitik" d. h. eine Begabten- und Erprobtenauslese für die Besetzung und Leitung der Faktoreien.'

[56]Gerolamo Biscaro, 'Il banco Filippo Borromei e compagni di Londra (1436-1439),' *Archivio storico lombardo*, 4th series, Vol. XIX [total series Vol. XL] (1913), p. 41.

[57]*Ibid.*, p. 40.

[58]*Ibid.*, p. 45.

[59]Lucca, State Archives, Corte dei Mercanti, No. 84: Libro dei Mercanti, 1381.

[60]This is the implication in a letter written by Giovanni Lazzari, the Venice representative of the firm, to Giusfredo Cenami, one of the partners, on February 23, 1375. This letter was published by Bini, *op. cit.*, XVI, 130-35. The relevant passages are on pp. 132 and 133.

[61]Lucca, State Archives, Corte dei Mercanti, No. 84: Libro dei Mercanti, 1381.

[62]Luigi Fumi, (ed.), *Registri del Archivio di Stato di Lucca*, Vol. II: *Carteggio degli Anziani, 1333-1400* (Lucca, 1903), Part II, p. 306, No. 1511.

[63]André-E. Sayous, 'Les transformations des méthodes commerciales dans l'Italie médiévale,' *AHES*, I (1929), 170. The Acciaiuoli Company had:

	Total
6 factors in Genoa	6
5 factors in Naples	5
4 factors in Barletta	4
3 factors in Avignon, Rhodes, Famagusta, Sicily	12
2 factors in Pisa, Bruges, London, Rome, Chiarenza (Greece), Tunis	12
1 factor in Paris and Bologna	2
	41

[64]Lucca, State Archives, Corte dei Mercanti, No. 83: Libro dei Mercanti, 1372.

[65]*Ibid.*, No. 84: Libro dei Mercanti, 1381.

[66]*Ibid.*, No. 83: Libro dei Mercanti, 1372.

[67]These figures are based on data compiled by Florence Edler de Roover from the Libro dei Mercanti of 1371 in the State Archives of Lucca, Corte dei Mercanti, No. 82.

[68]Grunzweig, *Correspondance*, I, xxvi. The names of the factors were: (1) Antonio de' Medici, (2) Cristofano Spini, (3) Carlo Cavalcanti, (4) Adoardo Canigiani (5) Tommaso Guidetti, (6) Folco Portinari. The *giovane* was Antonio Tornabuoni.

[69]Folco Portinari replaced a young man of the Corbinelli family who was so stupid that he could not be used and had to be sent back to Italy.

[70]Gian-Francesco Pagnini, *Della Decima* (Lisbon and Lucca, 1765-66), II, 136. Cf. Grunzweig, *Correspondance*, I, xxvi, n. 4.

[71]Pagnini, *op. cit.*, II, 305. [72]*Ibid.*, p. 304.

[73]For the meaning of *fuori del* (or *di*) *corpo* and *sopracorpo*, see Edler, *Glossary*, pp. 130, 274. The discussion which Max Weber (*op. cit.*, p. 143) devotes to the *sopracorpo* in his work on mediaeval partnerships is far from exhaustive.

[74]*Libri dei Peruzzi*, p. 437, date November 1, 1308: 'E ancora si è ordinato che quali conpagni tengono de' loro danari fuori da corpo di conpagnia e dovranoli ricievere da la conpagnia che la conpagnia ne doni a que' cotali conpagni a ragione d'otto per cientinaio.'

[75]*Ibid.*, p. 438, date November 1, 1312: 'E trovòsi guadagniati ne' detti due anni, netti di spese e salario di fattori e di ma' debiti e di danari dati per guadagnio a que' c'ànno tenuti i denari fuori dal corpo de la conpagnia sia conpagni come ad altri di fuori la conpagnia . . . '

[76]An analysis of Rosso degli Strozzi's account is given by Florence Edler, 'Eclaircissements à propos des considérations de R. Davidsohn sur la productivité de l'argent au moyen âge,' *Vierteljahrschrift für Sozial- und Wirtschaftsgeschichte* [hereafter VSWG], XXX (1937), 375-80. This article also shows that the figures given by Davidsohn (*Geschichte*, IV^2, 201-204, and *Forschungen*, III, 200-201) concerning the productivity of capital in the Middle Ages are unreliable (cf. Sapori, *Crisi*, pp. 227-41).

[77]Biscaro, *op. cit.*, p. 43, n. 3: 'Disavanzi di merchantia e cambi deono dare . . . a dì 31 de detto [dicembre 1438] £40 facemo buoni a Vitaliano Borromei per discrezione de £752 tegniamo da lui in deposito, i quali sono per l'anno presente a loro in credito in questo a fol. 219 .... £40

A dì ditto £45 faremo buoni alli eredi de Giovanni del Barza di Milano per discrezione de £915 abiamo da loro in deposito per l'anno 1438 a loro in credito a fol. 151 £45. '

[78]According to the partnership of May 12, 1471, the credit which the Bruges branch could extend to the duke of Burgundy was limited to £6,000 groat (Sieveking, *Handlungsbücher der Medici*, p. 52). As the capital of the branch did not exceed £3000 groat, one must conclude that funds were supplied from other sources.

[79]Robert J. Lemoine, 'Les étrangers et la formation du capitalisme en Belgique,' *RHES*, XX (1932), 263: 'Comme dans les provinces belges, la plupart des banquiers italiens étaient les agents des grandes maisons de la péninsule, il paraît donc très logique de considérer qu'en dehors des dépôts indigènes qu'ils recevaient, la masse de leurs capitaux provenait de la maison-mère ultramontaine. C'est d'ailleurs ce que prouvent indirectement les études publiées sur les maisons-mères et l'importance des opérations de change. Pour les Médicis, la correspondance publiée par M. Grunzweig paraît probante.'

[80]Grunzweig, *Correspondance*, I, 131: 'I nostri avanzi, come vedrete, sono quest'anno molto scharsi e la spesa è stata grande, a più dipositi ci troviamo nonn ò messo la discrezione.'

[81]Florence, State Archives, Carte Strozziane, Series II, No. 20: Libro segreto di Francesco Sassetti, 1462-1472, 71 fols., especially fol. 11, debit of the account 'Piero et Johanni de' Medici e Compagnia di Milano.' See Florence Edler de Roover, 'Francesco Sassetti and the Downfall of the Medici Banking House,' *Bulletin of the Business Historical Society*, XVII (1943), 65-80. The full text of this account has recently been published with comments in Raymond de Roover, *The Medici Bank* (New York, 1948), pp. 70-72.

[82]Davidsohn, *Geschichte*, IV^2, 204-208.

[83]*Libri dei Peruzzi*, pp. 421, 422, 439, 440. Cf. Sapori, 'Storia interna,' *op. cit.*, pp. 29-31.

[84]Sapori, *Crisi*, pp. 105 f., 141 f.

Chapter 4

THE BUSINESS OF EXCHANGE AND THE MECHANISM OF THE MONEY MARKET

ONCE we know how the Italian mercantile and banking houses were organized, managed, and financed, the next question which comes to mind is what did they do with the funds that were placed at their disposal? An answer to this question is provided by the articles of association of the year 1455 relating to the branch which the Medici banking house maintained in Bruges. These articles state unambiguously that the purpose of the contract was to form 'a company for the trade in merchandise and in foreign exchange in the city of Bruges in Flanders' ('compagnia per traficare nella villa di Bruggia in Fiandra di mercatantia e cambi').[1] By the word *cambi* we should understand the trade in bills of exchange and not manual or petty exchange which was the special province of the money-changers. In other words, the agreement provided that the funds available for investment were to be used in trade either directly by dealing in commodities or indirectly by extending loans to other merchants who could profitably employ additional funds.

The partnership agreement makes this purpose clear by stipulating in Article Two that Angelo Tani, the junior partner and branch manager, was to limit his activity to legitimate business practices, *bona-fide* commercial transactions, and licit exchange contracts. This stipulation—at least in principle—excluded *ipso facto* all contracts tainted with usury. More specifically, Tani was permitted to lend money only to merchants or master-artificers either by giving them credit in the books or by purchasing their bills of exchange (*dare a cambio*).[2] Credit was to be granted only with caution and with due regard to the financial standing and business reputation of the customers. Sales of foreign exchange on credit (*cambi a credenza*) to lords temporal and spiritual—prelates, priests, clerics, or officials—were explicitly forbidden except by special written consent of the senior partners. These provisions, it is clear, excluded all consumption loans, for credit was restricted to merchants, to master tapestry-makers, and to industrial entrepreneurs, such as *drapiers*.

In so far as the merchant-bankers extended credit to customers who bought merchandise from them, they did only what every merchant did, and still does, and cannot for that reason be considered as bankers. The merchant-bankers deserve this qualification, however, because they financed foreign trade by purchasing bills of exchange from merchants who were not their customers and because they concerned themselves with arbitrage between different places. The purchase of bills necessarily involved the extension of credit. Although mediaeval bills were not discounted and did not circulate by way of endorsement, they should be considered as money substitutes, since they reduced to a minimum the shipments of specie which were necessary in order to make international payments. As for arbitrage, this practice achieved the same result and, in addition, provided a self-regulating mechanism for the international distribution of specie. As Bernardo Davanzati pointed out already in the sixteenth century, the merchant-bankers, even though they sought only their private gain, promoted the general welfare and performed a useful function by adjusting any inequalities which might occur in the balance of payments between the different places of Europe.[3]

One of the oldest extant exchange contracts in which Bruges is mentioned is dated May 15, 1306. The two parties involved in this contract were both prominent: on the one hand, Giovanni Villani, the famous Florentine chronicler, representing the Peruzzi Company, and on the other hand, Tommaso Fini, *receveur de Flandre,* representing the Gallerani Company of Siena.[4] In this document Tommaso Fini acknowledges having received an unspecified sum in reals—an imaginary coin reckoned at twenty-four groats—*pro justo pretio et cambio* from Giovanni Villani and promises to return the equivalent, or £2,500 *tournois,* at the forthcoming May Fair of Provins either to Giovanni Villani himself, or to Uguccione Bonaccorsi Bentacorde, or to Filippo Villani, or to any other partner or certain attorney of the Peruzzi Company.[5]

This document, it should be noted, is not yet a bill of exchange and it is, therefore, safer to call it a *cambium,* or exchange, contract. For one thing, the document is a notarial deed, not an informal letter missive. Furthermore, no mention is made of a third party, the drawee. In all probability, Tommaso Fini himself or his agent intended to go to the Fair of Provins to sell Flemish cloth and to repay there the Peruzzi from the proceeds of the sale. The German legal writers, especially Levin Goldschmidt, give to such a contract the name of *Eigenwechsel* because the drawer and the drawee are the same person or members of the same firm.[6] The contract concluded between Giovanni Villani for the Peruzzi Company and Tommaso Fini for the Gallerani Company unquestionably involved the extension of credit, since the former advanced money to the latter and received in exchange an instrument promising repayment at a later date, in a different place, and in a different kind of currency. All the essential elements of an exchange transaction were present, but the instrument for implementing the agreement between the contracting parties was not yet the bill of exchange.

Apparently the *cambium* contract in notarial form was fairly common during the thirteenth, and the first decades of the fourteenth, century. There are a great many examples among the Genoese notarial records recently published by Dr Renée Doehaerd.[7] In most cases money borrowed in Genoa was made repayable at the fairs of Champagne. One of the later documents, however, refers to Bruges. According to its contents, two brothers, Daniel and Uguetus Lomellini, confessed on April 23, 1313, to have received an unspecified amount (*tot denarios*) of Genoese currency from their kinsman, Manfredo Lomellini, acting in the name of Bonvilano Lomellini, and promised to repay in Bruges, on the following first of June, the sum of five hundred gold reals at twenty-four groats per real. However, if the debtors failed to pay in Bruges at the set date, then they promised to repay the creditor in Genoa at the rate of forty-five sous *Genovini* per real after another period of two months, or on August 1, 1313.[8]

The contract is said to be made *nomine vendicionis et cambii,* but I doubt very much whether it rests on a real and genuine exchange transaction. In my opinion, the contracting parties never intended to effect a settlement in Bruges. In all probability this is a spurious, or fictitious, exchange contract which was used to conceal a straight loan with interest, or usury, as it was still called in the Middle Ages. In reality the borrowers received an unspecified sum in Genoese currency on the strength of a solemn promise to repay on August 1, 1313, an amount of £1,125, or five hundred times 45*s*., in the same currency.[9]

There were in this period two kinds of exchange contracts: the ordinary *cambium* and the *cambium nauticum*. Perhaps the latter should be considered as an outgrowth of the sea loan (*foenus nauticum*) rather than as a different form of exchange contract. In any case, the ordinary *cambium* contract usually contained the clause that payment was due *salvus in terra* or unconditionally. In the case of the *cambium nauticum* or *cambium maritimum,* however, the borrower's promise to pay was not given unconditionally but was contingent upon the safe arrival of a certain vessel or a certain cargo.

From 1278 onward, if not earlier, the Genoese began to send galleys through the Straits of Gibraltar to England and Flanders. After 1298 these voyages became regular, and Sluys, the seaport of Bruges, became the terminal of the galley fleets to the West.[10] Genoese merchants who had goods aboard the galleys often raised the funds necessary to finance their ventures by means of a *cambium nauticum*. For example, on April 4, 1312, Dagnanus Ventus acknowledged having received from Nigro de Coturno an unspecified sum in Genoese currency and promised to pay to the lender 518 reals and eight old groats one month and a half after a certain galley had safely reached the port of Sluys (*applicuerit ad portum Cluse*). This galley, according to the deed, belonged to the said Ventus and a Manuel de Bonaver and was ready to sail from Genoa to the parts of Bruges (*ad partes Bruges*). The contract explicitly stipulated that the debt, or *cambium,* was subject to the act of God, the fortunes of the sea, and the risks of men-of-war (*ad rixicum et fortunam Dei, maris et gentium*). In other words, fulfillment of the promise to pay depended upon the safe arrival of the galley at destination. As security, the borrowers pledged ten bags of ginger and fifty bales of alum which were loaded aboard the galley and were registered under the lender's name in the ship's chartulary.[11]

Apparently the *cambium* contract in notarial form was still popular in 1327. On August 6 of that year the Bruges representative of the Acciaiuoli Company entered into such a contract with a merchant of Piacenza. The former declared in the deed that he had received from the latter an unstated amount in gold reals to the equivalent of 240 florins. This sum of 240 florins was to be repaid in Piacenza on the following first of November to the said merchant or his accredited agent.[12]

The *cambium* contract in notarial form was particularly well suited to the needs of the traveling trade because of the legal safeguards which surrounded a formal deed requiring the intervention of a notary. The emphasis was still on the promise to pay.[13] Usually the borrower promised that he himself or his agent would repay the lender, the latter's agent, or, less frequently, the bringer of the instrument at the fairs or in another place.[14] The insertion of such clauses meant only that the debtor could validly pay to a partner, a factor, a proxy, or an accredited agent of the creditor, and did not transform such instruments into negotiable paper in the modern sense.[15] It is true that the creditor by virtue of his title had the right of recourse against the original borrower if his agent failed to carry out the promise to pay.

The notarial instruments lost much of their popularity after the Italian merchants began to conduct their business by correspondence from the counting house and to keep balances with permanent agents or correspondents abroad. In Western Europe this development occurred at the same time as the decline of the fairs of Champagne and, as already explained, there is a close connection between the two phenomena. From then on, legal safeguards became less important than expediency, and the notarial contract was replaced by an informal letter missive which eliminated all superfluous legal verbiage. Thus emerged a new instrument: the bill of exchange, called at first *lettera di pagamento* and later *lettera di cambio*.[16] From a solemn and verbose promise to pay the instrument was reduced to a brief command to pay given by the maker to his correspondent abroad. The old formulas, however, survived in the Northern trade, and *cambium* instruments emphasizing the acknowledgment of a debt were still used among Hanseatic and Flemish merchants in the sixteenth century.[17]

The *cambium nauticum* shared the fate of the *cambium* contract and became less and less common during the fourteenth century. Most probably this decline was due to the development of marine insurance which made possible a more satisfactory division of risks.

It seems likely that the bill of exchange developed out of the letter of advice which usually accompanied the more solemn notarial instrument. There is at least one Bruges document which sheds some light on this transition from the formal *cambium* contract to the informal bill of exchange. The document in question is an acceptance given in notarial form and dated March 30, 1330. According to this instrument, Nado Spiliato, the representative of the Acciaiuoli Company in Bruges, accepts a bill drawn on him for an amount of six hundred reals of twenty-four groats, equivalent to £1,342 10*s*. *Genovini* at the rate of 44*s*. 9*d*. *Genovini* per real. This sum had apparently been advanced in Genoa by Antonorio Grimaldi to Niccolò Guicciardini, the Genoese representative of the Acciaiuoli Company on the preceding fifteenth of February. The Italian text of the bill is quoted in full in the Latin text of the acceptance. As soon as the bill is paid, the payee in Bruges promises to notify Antonorio Grimaldi so that he will cancel the solemn acknowledgment of debt given before a notary by Guicciardini, the maker of the bill.[18]

If I interpret the evidence correctly, it discloses the existence of two documents: a principal instrument which is still the solemn promise given before a notary and a complementary instrument which is the Italian letter missive containing the order to pay.' Jurists and historians have quibbled a great deal over the existence of two documents during the transition period from the notarial *cambium* contract to the informal bill of exchange without reaching an agreement.[19] Those who favor the existence of two instruments are presumably right on the basis of the available evidence. In any case, the final result is the same: by the end of the fourteenth century, if not before, the bill of exchange had emerged as the sole document. However, bills of exchange continued to be made out in duplicate or triplicate as a safeguard against the loss of one copy in the mail.

According to the document of 1330, the acceptance, also, was considered sufficiently important to require the intervention of a notary. This formality was soon discarded, and acceptance was given simply by writing the word *accettata* across the face of the bill as is still the custom today.[20] The intervention of a notary continued to be required only for the drafting of protests in case the drawee of a bill either refused to accept or to pay.[21] Today still protests are made by a notary, a *huissier,* or some other public official.

The essential difference between the mediaeval bill of exchange and the modern draft is that, in the Middle Ages, a bill always originated in an exchange contract. Such a contract may be defined as an agreement by which a deliverer, usually a merchant-banker, gave a certain sum of money in local currency to another merchant and received from him a letter missive which was payable at a future date (credit transaction), in another place, and in another currency (exchange transaction). By definition such a contract involved *both* a credit and an exchange transaction.[22] Because of the slowness of communication, even a sight draft was in effect a time bill, since it had to travel from the place where it was issued to the place where it was payable.[23] The difference of place (*distantia* or *differentia loci*) and the conversion of domestic into foreign currency (*permutatio pecuniae absentis cum praesenti*) were two essential features of the exchange contract. To this rule there was one exception, namely, when the same money was current in the place of issue and in the place of payment.[24]

Such a case is illustrated by one of the earliest bills which happens to be known. On October 5, 1339, Barna da Lucha and Co., a firm established in Avignon, drew a bill of 312 3/4 florins on Bartalo and Co. in Pisa. In exchange for the bill the drawers had received an advance of three hundred florins from Tancredi Bonagiunta.[25] There was consequently an 'advantage,' or agio, of 4 1/4 per cent in favor of the lender.[26] As the bill was payable on November 20, 1339, or forty-six days from date, the lender's gross profit corresponded to thirty-four per cent a year.[27]

A typical exchange contract involved four parties and two payments: an advance of funds in the place where the bill was issued and a repayment in the place where the bill was due. The four parties who participated either in the conclusion or the execution of the contract were: (1) the deliverer (It. *datore,* Fr. *donneur*, and Fl. *gever*) who furnished the value of the bill; (2) the taker (It. *prenditore,* Fr. *preneur,* and Fl. *nemer*) who took up the money supplied by the deliverer and made out the bill to the person or the firm designated by the latter; (3) the payor or drawee on whom the bill was drawn and who was expected to accept it and to pay it at maturity; and (4) the payee in whose favor the bill was made out. In most cases the payor was a correspondent of the taker and the payee, a correspondent of the deliverer. Sometimes two of the parties to the contract were merged in the same individual or the same firm. Such an anomaly did not alter the substance of the contract in the least.

The terms *datore* and *prenditore* are likely to create confusion, especially *prenditore* or *preneur,* as this word has changed its meaning in both French and Italian. Since the middle of the seventeenth century, the terms *preneur, nemer,* or *prenditore,* refer to the person to whose order a bill is payable and not to the drawer or maker.[28] In mediaeval sources, however, *prenditore* and *datore* have always the meaning given above.[29] Further evidence is given by the writings of the English mercantilists prior to Mun: they consistently used the terms 'deliverer' and 'taker' as they are defined here.[30]

As already explained, the mediaeval bill of exchange in contrast to the modern draft, or *traite,* was based on a real or fictitious exchange transaction. The two instruments differ in two other important respects. The mediaeval bill unlike the modern so-called bill of exchange was neither discountable nor negotiable.

To discount a bill would have been illegal in the Middle Ages, since the

Church was strongly opposed to the taking of interest. It was usury to exact anything beyond the principal on a *mutuum,* or straight loan.[31] By definition a *mutuum* was always a gratuitous contract. If it ceased to be gratuitous, it became *ipso facto* a usurious contract.[32] In other words, it was usury to take 'a certain gain' on a *mutuum.* The emphasis is on the word 'certain.'[33] Instead of being discounted, mediaeval bills were bought and sold at a price which was determined by the rate of exchange. The result was that the profit of the banker, instead of being certain as it is today, became uncertain since it depended upon the fickle and unpredictable behavior of the exchange rates. It is this speculative element which justified exchange dealings in the eyes of the Churchmen.[34] To be sure, interest was concealed in the exchange rates, that is to say, in the price at which bills were bought and sold. But it made no difference. The logic of the Churchmen was impeccable: they argued that a *cambium* contract was not a straight loan since it involved an exchange transaction.[35] Moreover, exchange dealings were justified *pro utilitatem reipublicae* or for the benefit of the common weal. Only fictitious exchange was condemned as a contract *in fraudem usurarum* because it was merely a cloak for a straight loan.

This theory was not a rationalization invented by the merchant-bankers to appease a troubled conscience but the accepted doctrine of the Church as it was built up by several generations of canonists and theologians. The outcome was that exchange dealings, provided they were genuine and not fraudulent, were perfectly lawful and were not branded as usurious.

Mediaeval bills were not negotiable credit instruments.[36] The earliest known examples of endorsed bills date back to the years 1610 and 1611.[37] Prior to the beginning of the seventeenth century, bills of exchange, as a rule, were not payable to order, to the bearer, or to a certain person or his assigns.[38] I have not found a single example of such formulas among the numerous Italian bills which are available in print or which I had the opportunity to examine in the Datini Archives.[39] Further evidence that negotiability was lacking is found in the books of the Italian merchant-bankers, especially of the Medici and of Francesco Datini, with which I am familiar. The entries in the ledgers indicate clearly that bills were actually paid to the person or the firm named in them as the payee. These entries usually give a detailed description of each transaction and include the names of all the parties to the contract. The lack of negotiability, of course, was not as great an obstacle to the assignability of debts as it might seem because of the extensive use of book transfers both in foreign and in local trade. Thus specie payments were eliminated as much as possible not only in the clearance of local debts but also in the settlement of international balances. Negotiability should not be confused with assignability. These two terms are by no means synonymous, although they are often used carelessly as if there were no shade of difference in the meaning.

Italian business practices in the Middle Ages were more advanced than those of other nations but, perhaps, were also more rigid and stereotyped. The extensive use which the Italians made of bills of exchange rested on the existence of organized money markets in which the price of bills was regulated by the forces of supply and demand. Those who chose to utilize the mechanism of the money market were expected to play the game according to the rules. Organized money markets existed in only the most important centers of Western Europe, including Bruges and London. In those places exchange rates were actually market prices at which bills were bought and sold.[40] In all centers, not excepting Bruges, the great Italian banking houses were the principal lenders and practically dominated the money market.

Bruges was, of course, the most important money market in northwestern Europe during the fourteenth and fifteenth centuries. At that time London was only a satellite of Bruges. Contrary to what some historians have written, Bruges was *una piazza di cambio,* or a place where the exchange was located and where there existed a well-organized bill market.[41] The evidence is conclusive in this regard. The Italian merchant-bankers were in the habit of giving the exchange quotations at the end of all their business letters.[42] Frequently the latter also contained reports on the conditions prevailing in the money market. Such information was extremely valuable to the bankers in other places who kept balances in Bruges and who needed to know whether they should draw or remit.

Bills of exchange were apparently bought and sold through brokers who brought the deliverers in contact with the takers. According to Pegolotti's handbook for merchants (*ca.* 1340), the brokerage charges were two groats per hundred reals on bills for all parts with the exception of England.[43] Since the real was worth twenty-four groats, these charges corresponded to 1/1200.[44] On English bills the rate was one-half denier per pound from each party, or 1/480. According to the ledger of the Medici bank in Bruges, the tariff of brokerage charges was presumably one per thousand from each party in 1441.[45]

It is fortunately possible to study in detail the mechanism of the Bruges money market toward the year 1400 because of the invaluable material which is extant in the Datini Archives, Prato, Tuscany. These archives possess not only hundreds of bills of exchange but also the related account books and business correspondence.

Francesco Datini (also called Francesco di Marco da Prato, that is, 'Francesco, son of Marco, from Prato') was born around 1335. He started his career as an office boy in Avignon and later entered into a partnership with a dealer in arms and armor. As Francesco had unusual ability, the business prospered and soon became an important firm with branches and correspondents in foreign parts. In 1382, Francesco Datini left Avignon and returned to Prato where he established the headquarters of his firm. It had branches in Florence, Pisa,

Avignon, Barcelona, Valencia, and Palma de Mallorca. As was customary in the Middle Ages, this firm combined trade in all sorts of commodities with dealings in bills of exchange. Datini also controlled a local bank and a cloth-manufacturing establishment in Prato. When he died in 1410, he was one of the richest merchants of his time. Like the Medici later, he received the permission to augment his armorial bearings with the fleur-de-lis of France.[46]

Francesco Datini had no branch in Bruges but was represented in this place by several correspondents, among whom the firms Giovanni Orlandini and Piero Benizi & Co. and Alberto and Bernardo degli Alberti & Co. were probably the most important. There are in the Datini Archives many bills issued by these Bruges correspondents and paid by the Datini firm or its branches in Italy and Spain. The account books also give information about bills which the Datini firm drew on Bruges and on other places. The originals of outgoing bills, of course, have not been preserved with the exception of a few bills which were returned after being protested.

The following bill is a typical sample. Let us examine in how far it fits the description given above.

> Al nome di Dio, amen. dì 12 di dicenbre 1399
> Paghate per questa prima al usanza a Domenicho Sancio schudi seicento a s.10 d.5 per ▽ i quali ▽600 a s.10 d.5 per ▽ sono per la valuta da Jachopo Ghoscho, e ponete a nostro chonto chostì. Idio vi guardi.
> Giovanni Orlandini e Piero Benizi
> e chonpagni in Bruggia
> [In a different handwriting:]
> Acettata a dì 11 di gennaio 1399 [1400]
> [On the back:] Francescho da Prato e chonpagni
> in Barzalona
> Prima[47]

Like most mediaeval bills this one involves four parties (two in Bruges and two in Barcelona) and two payments (an advance of funds in Bruges and its repayment in Barcelona). In this case the four parties to the contract are: (1) the drawer or taker, the firm Giovanni Orlandini and Piero Benizi & Co. in Bruges, who made out the bill; (2) the payor or drawee, the Barcelona branch of the Datini firm, to whom the bill was addressed; (3) the payee or presentor, Domenico Sancio, probably a Spaniard or a Catalan, in whose favor the bill was made out; and (4) the deliverer or remittor, Jacopo Gosco, who gave consideration for the bill. According to the text, the drawer received an advance of six hundred écus (▽) at twenty-two groats, or £55 groat in Flemish currency, and requested the drawee to repay this amount to Domenico Sancio at the exchange rate of 10*s.* 5*d.* Barcelonese per écu of twenty-two groats. In the Middle Ages it was customary to state the exchange rate in the text of a bill. The date given in the bill is December 12, 1399. It was accepted on January 11, 1400. According to the records of the Datini firm an amount of £312 10*s*. Barcelonese, or the equivalent of ∇600 at 10*s*. 5*d*. per écu, was charged to the drawer and credited to the payee upon acceptance of the bill.[48] This entry shows plainly that after acceptance the payor considered himself as primarily liable for the bill or, in other words, as the principal debtor. It appears from numberless letters in the Datini Archives that the drawee was notified of the issuance of a bill not by a special letter of advice but by an ordinary business letter which usually dealt also with other topics.[49]

The above bill was payable at usance. Between Bruges and Barcelona, the usance was thirty days after sight, according to Uzzano's handbook for merchants (1442).[50] The exactness of this information is corroborated by the Datini records.[51] About 1450 there was probably a change in commercial practice because the *Libro di mercatantie et usanze de' paesi,* compiled between 1460 and 1481, and other manuscript sources state that the usance was twenty days after sight instead of thirty days.[52] The usance between Bruges and Florence was seventy days from date according to Pegolotti and sixty days from date according to later sources.[53] The usance was always sixty days from date between Bruges and places in Italy (Genoa, Pisa, and Venice) but only thirty days between Bruges and London and between Bruges and Paris or Avignon, regardless of the direction in which the bill was traveling.[54] Usance bills to and from Montpellier did not fall due until forty days from date.[55] In the Middle Ages bills were usually payable at usance. Exchange quotations, unless otherwise specified, applied to usance bills.

It would be a mistake to believe that bills were usually paid in specie. The records of the Datini branch in Barcelona disclose that such was not the case and that bills of exchange were often paid by assignment in bank or by book transfer of one kind or another. For example, a bill drawn by the Orlandini of Bruges on the Datini branch in Barcelona was accepted by the drawee on August 30, 1398, and paid by assignment in bank, that is, by transfer in the books of a money-changer on October 1, 1398, or thirty-two days later.[56] In another instance, the same Orlandini sent a remittance of ∇200 at 10*s*. 6*d*. Barcelonese per ∇, or £105 Barcelonese, for collection to the Datini firm of Barcelona. The bill matured on January 20, 1400, but was not honored until January 24. On this date, the payor, one Giovanni Bibero, a Barcelonese draper, ordered his banker, Pere Brunet, to credit the Datini firm with £105, Barcelonese currency. The entries in Datini's ledger enable us to follow this transaction step by step.[57] No specie comes into the picture at any time. Conditions in Bruges were the same. There, too, it was the custom to pay bills of exchange by transfer in bank rather than in specie.[58]

As already explained, a typical exchange transaction involved four parties.

There were hardly any exceptions to this rule, but it was possible for two parties to be represented by the same individual or the same firm. Frequently either the payee and the payor or the deliverer and the taker were one and the same person or firm. In the first case the bill usually contained the formula *pagate a voi medesimi* ('pay to yourselves') as in the following example:

> Al nome di Dio dì 25 febraio 1400 [n. s.]
> Pagharete per questa seconda lettera se per la prima non avessi paghato al usanza a voi medesimo lb.420 barzalonesi, le quali lb.420 sono per la valuta sono qui contento da Giovanni Orlandini e Piero Benizi e compagni. Fatene buon paghamento e ponete a mio conto. Che Idio vi ghuardi.
> Ghuiglielmo Barberi salute di Brugia
> [On the back:] Franciescho di Marcho e compagni
> in Barzalona
> Seconda[59]

This bill not only contains the formula *paghate a voi medesimi,* but the reader will notice that the exchange rate is not given, contrary to the prevailing custom. The explanation for this omission is probably that the drawer, whose business affairs were in bad shape, did not want to disclose that he was not able to sell his bills at the current rate. As a matter of fact, the drawee refused to carry out the order given in the above bill and returned the first copy to the Orlandini because he learned that Guglielmo Barberi was on the verge of bankruptcy.[60] As the bill was payable to the drawee himself, probably no protest was necessary.[61]

How could a drawee pay himself and be at the same time payee and payor? The jurists have been baffled by this problem and have not succeeded in offering a satisfactory explanation.[62] Fortunately, the Datini records give the clue to the mystery. Bills payable *a voi medesimi* were not paid in cash but by transfer in the books of the payor who was also the payee. For example, on December 26, 1399, the same Barberi drew a bill on the Datini firm in Barcelona similar to the one quoted above. In accordance with the contents of the bill, the payor who was also payee simply transferred a sum of £520 16*s.* 8*d.*, Barcelonese currency, from the debit of Barberi, the drawer, to the credit of the Orlandini who had furnished the value of the bill in Bruges. The matter was adjusted by such a transfer because both Barberi and the Orlandini happened to have the same correspondent in Barcelona. The result of the transfer was that the Datini firm in Barcelona now owed £520 less to Barberi and £520 more to the Orlandini. In short, bills payable *a voi medesimi* were orders to transfer rather than to pay.[63]

Mediaeval bills of exchange sometimes contained the formula *per la valuta ricevuta da noi medesimi* ('for the value received from ourselves').[64] This type of bill was normally issued by a person who had money both to collect and to pay in a foreign place. In order to satisfy his creditor, such a person naturally found it convenient to draw on his debtor in the same city. The drawer of such a bill was at the same time deliverer and taker. In his books the amount of the bill would simply be written to the debit of the creditor and to the credit of the debtor. Thus mediaeval bills could either originate in a transfer or be settled by transfer. It even happened that adjustment was made by transfer at both ends. The extensive use of transfers gave flexibility to the mediaeval bill despite the lack of negotiability, as has been pointed out.

It is impossible to understand exchange dealings in the Middle Ages without some knowledge of the manner in which exchange rates were quoted. At first, exchange quotations in Bruges were based on the real of twenty-four groats, of the coinage of Saint Louis, as appears from the Genoese notarial records published by Dr Doehaerd. In 1313, for example, the real was rated at about forty-five sous, Genoese currency.[65] The real went out of existence early in the fourteenth century. For a time, exchange quotations continued to be based on an imaginary real. This impractical system was soon abandoned, for Pegolotti's handbook which was written around 1340, contains a table of equivalence which gives the value of the real in sous and deniers *a fiorino* corresponding to different rates of the florin in Flemish groats.[66] Thus, according to Pegolotti's table, the real was worth 58*s*. *a fiorino* if the florin was rated in Bruges at twelve groats, and only 43*s*. 6*d*. *a fiorino* if the florin was rated at sixteen groats.[67] Apparently two methods of quoting the exchange were in use: one based on the real and the other on the Florentine florin. It is probable that at the time of Pegolotti the new system was coming in and the old system was falling into disuse.

After 1350, in any case, the exchange in Bruges on all Italian places was quoted in a variable amount of groats per florin (Genoa and Florence) or per ducat (Venice).[68] The exchange on Paris was also quoted in an uncertain number of groats per franc, a gold coin at that time, but Bruges gave the certain to London and Barcelona. In the case of London, exchange quotations were expressed in so many sterlings, that is, English pennies, per écu of twenty-four groats, Flemish currency. In the case of Barcelona, however, the exchange was based on an imaginary écu of twenty-two groats—and not twenty-four—and quoted in sous and deniers, Barcelonese currency.[69] This system with very few changes, if any, continued in use throughout the fifteenth century. Toward the middle of that century the fairs of Geneva and later those of Lyons acquired great importance as international clearing centers. Exchange rates for bills payable at those fairs were quoted in groats per écu of sixty-six to the gold mark.[70]

According to the merchant handbooks, Bruges quoted regularly the course

TABLE 2
EXCHANGE QUOTATIONS IN BRUGES DURING THE FIFTEENTH CENTURY FOR BILLS PAYABLE ABROAD

Place of payment	Exchange quoted	High*	Low*	Usance
Avignon	In so many groats, Flemish currency, per florin (*fiorino di pitetto*)	30 gr.	24 gr.	30 days from date
Barcelona	In so many sous and deniers, Barcelonese currency, per écu of 22 groats, Flemish currency	9 *s.*	7 *s.*	20 days after sight
Florence	In so many groats, Flemish currency, per florin (*fiorino di suggello*)	54 gr.	45 gr.	60 days from date
Geneva	In so many groats, Flemish currency, per écu of 66 to the gold mark	50 gr.	46 gr.	Payable at the end of each fair
Genoa	In so many groats, Flemish currency, per florin of 25*s.*, Genoese currency	29 gr.	25 gr.	60 days from date
London	In so many sterlings, English currency, per écu of 24 groats, Flemish currency	24 st.	20 st.	30 days from date
Valencia	In so many sous and deniers, currency of Valencia, per écu of 22 groats, Flemish currency	10 *s.*	8 *s.*	60 days from date
Venice	In so many groats, Flemish currency, per Venetian ducat of 24 *grossi d'oro in oro*	54 gr.	47 gr.	60 days from date

*The figures in these two columns are valid for the third quarter of the fifteenth century only, since they are based on a source compiled around 1460. Changes in monetary standards at home or abroad were apt, of course, either to raise or to lower the limits between which the exchange rates fluctuated. The reader will notice that the range of fluctuation was greater than it would be today under an automatic gold standard.

Source: *El libro di mercatantie et usanze de'paesi*, ed. Franco Borlandi, Turin, 1936.

of the exchange on London, Paris, Barcelona, Genoa, Venice, Florence, and later Geneva and Lyons. Any reference to German places is conspicuous by its absence. This omission can be explained only by the fact that there were no organized exchange markets in Germany, not even in Lübeck, the leading Hanseatic city. The business methods of the German merchants were much more primitive than those of the Italians. It is not until the sixteenth century that Frankfort-on-the-Main and Hamburg became banking centers. The lack of banking facilities in Germany greatly hampered the *camera apostolica* or papal treasury throughout the fourteenth and fifteenth centuries. For example, it took a full year to transmit funds from Cracow to Avignon. Usually such funds were conveyed to Bruges by traveling merchants and thence relayed to Avignon by the papal bankers who had permanent branches in Flanders.[71] The first lap of the journey was slow and hazardous: usually the papal bankers did not receive any funds until the traveling merchant had reached Bruges and sold the goods which he had brought from Poland. Once the funds were in the hands of the bankers, the transfer was made with speed and efficiency.

They notified their representatives in Avignon who promptly credited the papal treasury. This last transaction required only a letter of advice and two bookkeeping entries: one in the books of the papal bankers in Bruges and one in those of their representatives in Avignon. The contrast between the two methods of transferring funds is illuminating and does not require further comment.

In the Middle Ages, when two places dealt with each other, it was customary for the exchange to be based on the currency of one of them. Thus the exchange between Flanders and England was based on the écu both in Bruges and in London. In the same way the exchange was based on the Florentine florin and quoted in Flemish groats in both Florence and Bruges. Similarly the exchange ran upon the ducat in both Venice and Bruges and upon the écu in both Bruges and Barcelona. The only exception to this general rule was that of two places which used the same currency, such as Paris and Montpellier.

Today, a banker who discounts commercial paper knows his profit in advance, since the discount is deducted at once from the face value of the draft or the promissory note. In the Middle Ages, however, a merchant-banker who bought a bill of exchange acquired after a while a credit balance in foreign currency and in a foreign place. His profit, far from being certain, remained indeterminate, until he made his returns by reconverting this balance into local currency. The result was that an exchange transaction, in order to be complete, involved two bills instead of one: one for the exchange and the other for the re-exchange (*cambium et recambium*). It is true that the banker could make his returns in specie, in merchandise, or by exchange. The first of these three alternatives need not be considered, since specie shipments were profitable only under exceptional circumstances. The second possibility may be excluded, too, since it involved a speculation in commodities and not in exchange.

In order to explain how a banker determined his profits, it is inadvisable to use a real case taken from documents. Real cases usually involve technical complications.[72] It is, therefore, preferable to proceed by analysis and to deal with a hypothetical case. Let us suppose that a merchant-banker established in Bruges bought a bill of 600 ducats, payable in Venice, at the rate of 50 groats, Flemish currency, per Venetian ducat. The cost of such a bill was £125 groat in Flemish currency. Since the usance of bills on Italy was two months, this banker's correspondent in Venice collected the sum of six hundred ducats at the end of this period. Up to this point, the merchant-banker in Bruges was unable to figure out whether he had gained or lost on this transaction. All he knew was that there were now six hundred ducats standing to his credit in Venice. This money could not remain idle. In order to keep it running upon the exchange, the merchant-banker had the choice between two alternatives: either he could resell the six hundred ducats in Bruges by drawing a bill on Venice or he could instruct his correspondent in Venice to buy a bill on Bruges and to remit.

Usually a remittance was more profitable than a draft.[73] Let us, therefore, suppose that the banker's correspondent in Venice had received instructions to remit and that he bought a bill on Bruges, let us say, at 52 groats per ducat with the proceeds of the first bill. This second bill matured in Bruges after two months. At the end of this period the merchant-banker in Bruges collected £130 groat, or the equivalent of six hundred ducats at 52 groats per ducat. He had consequently made a profit of £5 groat in the space of four months, since he had paid £125 for the first bill and received £130 for the second.[74] This profit arose from the difference of two groats between the rate of the ducat in Venice and in Bruges.

Let us now examine this case with greater scrutiny. If the correspondent in Venice had bought the second bill at 53 groats, the banker's profit would have been increased to three groats per ducat. At the rate of 51 groats in Venice, he would have gained only one groat per ducat. At the rate of 50 groats, he neither gained nor lost, since he paid and recovered the same number of groats for each ducat. At any rate below 50 groats, the Bruges banker suffered a loss instead of making a profit.[75]

This analysis leads to the conclusion that the banker's profits or loss depended entirely upon the price of the second bill or, in other words, upon the margin between the rate of the ducat in Venice and in Bruges.[76] As long as the ducat was rated higher in Venice than in Bruges, the banker made a profit. He just broke even if the two rates were equal. But he lost as soon as the rate in Venice sank below the rate in Bruges. The same analysis may be applied to exchange between any two places where there existed an organized exchange. The equilibrium of the money market required that the rate of exchange be always higher in that one of the two places which gave its currency to the other. Under conditions of equilibrium, the écus of twenty-four and of twenty-two groats were always rated higher in Bruges than in London and in Barcelona, respectively. In the same way the rate of the franc in Paris was always above the rate of the franc in Bruges. This rule is of general validity, and there are no exceptions.[77]

It may be well to keep in mind that exchange dealings in the Middle Ages were limited to time bills. The purchase of a bill necessarily involved an extension of credit. Since interest could not be charged openly, it was concealed in the rate of exchange. It is the presence of the time factor which explains the discrepancy between the rate of the ducat in Venice and in Bruges, for example. Any rise of the interest rate tended to raise the exchange rate in Venice and to

BILLS OF EXCHANGE (RECTO)

The first bill was issued by the firm Alberto e Bernardo degli Alberti of Bruges; the second, by Guglielmo Barberi, an Italian merchant residing in Bruges; the third, by Bernardo degli Alberti of Venice. The text of the third bill is given on p. 74 n 82. *From the Datini Archives, Prato (Tuscany).*

lower the exchange rate in Bruges or, in other words, to increase the gap between the two rates. Conversely, any fall of the rate of interest tended to close the gap between the two exchange rates. This gap also tended to increase or to decrease with the remoteness of the maturity date. Thus bills payable at double usance were rated higher than usance bills in Venice and lower than usance bills in Bruges.

If the rate of interest had been the only factor which influenced the exchange rates, a buyer of bills would always have made a profit on transactions involving exchange and re-exchange. Unfortunately the exchange rates fluctuated in response to factors which were much more powerful than the rather weak influence of the rate of interest. These forces were often strong enough to upset temporarily the equilibrium of the money market. As a result of this instability the profits of a banker were never certain but were speculative, since they were determined by the undependable oscillations of the exchange rates and the uncontrollable forces which operated in the money market.

The forces other than the rate of interest which regulated the course of the exchange were three: (1) changes in the monetary standard either at home or abroad, (2) disturbances in the balance of payments between any two places, and (3) speculation based on the expectations of the exchange-dealers or on the criminal attempts of manipulators who sometimes tried to corner the money market. To this list one should perhaps add the disturbing effects of regulations enacted by the public authorities who, especially in England and to a lesser extent in Flanders, made from time to time clumsy attempts to interfere with the freedom of the money market or of the exchanges. Those forces influenced the course of the exchange as they still do today and caused violent upward or downward movements of the rates. For example, a debasement of the currency in Flanders was bound to cause an immediate and sudden rise of the ducat, the florin, and the franc both in Bruges and abroad. At the same time the écu was likely to drop drastically not only in Bruges but also in London and in Barcelona. Disturbances in the balance of payments had a similar effect upon the exchange rates. If there was, for example, a shortage of ducats in Bruges for making payments in Venice, the ducat was bound to rise in Bruges until the demand equaled the supply. A shortage of ducats in Bruges frequently corresponded to an oversupply of Flemish currency in Venice. As bills on Bruges would be offered for sale in excessive quantities, their price was likely to fall and to cause a rise of the ducat in Venice, too.[78] Moreover, the rise of the ducat would probably affect all the other exchange rates because of arbitrage transactions and the interdependence of all markets.[79]

Speculation caused the exchange rates to deviate from their normal level, but such deviations did not outlast the first change in the temper of the money market. As for government regulations, they were usually designed to protect the national currency, to prevent an outflow of bullion, or to attract specie from abroad. Needless to say, the results were often the opposite of those that were intended.

All these forces tended to pull the exchange rates up or down and increased the risks which were run by takers and deliverers alike. Violent exchange fluctuations, however, did not occur every day, and the money market was in equilibrium most of the time. As already explained, the lender was bound to gain in a stable market. The result was that the bankers, who were mostly lenders, made a profit in the majority of cases. However, it could and did happen that they lost because adverse exchange fluctuations sometimes overruled the stabilizing influence of the rate of interest.

The correctness of this analysis is fully confirmed by the business records of the merchant-bankers and the actual behavior of the exchange rates. The account books of the Datini branch in Barcelona, those of the Medici bank in Bruges, and those of the Borromei bank in London show clearly that profits originated in exchange speculation, and not in fixed interest charges, and that not all exchange transactions were profitable. However, the profits outbalanced the losses.[80] There are almost no statistical data available on mediaeval exchange rates, but I have been able to make use of the only more or less continuous series that exists. The data are plotted on Chart I. As this chart reveals, the écu of twenty-four groats was rated higher in Bruges than in London. According to

CHART 1

Rate of Ecu of 24 Groats, Flemish Currency, in Bruges and London

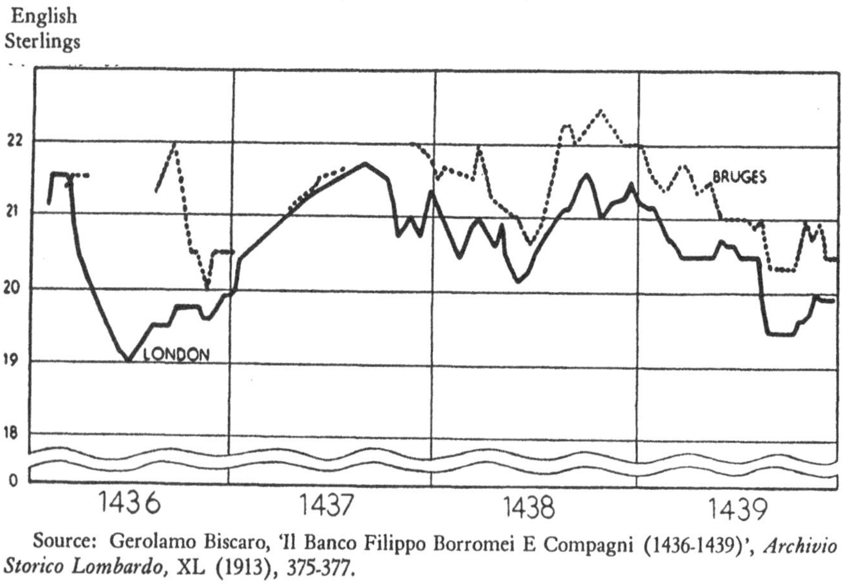

Source: Gerolamo Biscaro, 'Il Banco Filippo Borromei E Compagni (1436-1439)', *Archivio Storico Lombardo,* XL (1913), 375-377.

the few surviving records of the Medici bank, the exchange rate of the ducat in Bruges usually remained below the same rate in Venice.[81] As already explained, the ducat was quoted in Flemish groats both in Bruges and in Venice. The actual behavior of mediaeval exchange rates thus confirms the correctness of the foregoing analysis.

The merchant-bankers always operated on two places at least and sometimes on three. There are many examples of three-cornered exchange transactions in the only surviving fragment of a ledger of the Medici bank in Bruges (1441). Earlier examples are found in the Datini records. Datini's correspondents in Bruges frequently used their credit balances in Barcelona to make remittances to Italy. In other cases, the same merchant-bankers allowed their correspondents in Italy to draw on Barcelona. For example, on February 21, 1400, the firm Bernardo degli Alberti of Venice drew a bill of four hundred ducats at 16*s.* 8*d.* Barcelonese per ducat on the Datini firm in Barcelona with the request to charge the amount of this bill, £333 6*s.* 8*d.* Barcelonese, to the Alberti of Bruges.[82] The Orlandini of Bruges followed the same policy as the Alberti. On March 26, 1400, the Orlandini of Florence drew a bill of three hundred florins on Datini's *fondaco* in Barcelona with instructions to debit their Bruges office.[83] On another occasion, the Datini firm remitted three hundred florins to Florence and charged £228 2*s.* 6*d.* Barcelonese against the Orlandini of Bruges for this remittance.[84] In a letter of January 9, 1400, the same Orlandini instructed the Datini in Barcelona to remit one thousand florins to Genoa, one thousand ducats to Venice, and one thousand florins to Florence, and to cover these transactions by drawing on Bruges.[85] Apparently it was less profitable to remit directly to Italy than indirectly by way of Barcelona. In another letter dated February 26, 1400, the Orlandini strongly expressed their dissatisfaction with their Barcelona correspondents because they kept balances idle and failed to remit either to Bruges or to Italy (*nostro paese*) under the pretext of not finding any suitable takers.[86]

If these facts are typical, they seem to suggest that the balance of payments between Flanders and Catalonia was favorable to the former so that bankers' balances tended to accumulate in Barcelona. On the other hand, the balance of payments between Flanders and Italy was probably favorable to the latter. The records of the Medici branch in Bruges indicate that conditions were still the same forty years later. In any case, the Medici of Bruges were constantly drawing on Barcelona to replenish their balance in ducats with the Medici of Venice.

Contrary to the common belief, it is untrue that mediaeval bills were usually drawn by an exporter on his customer abroad in settlement of a *bona fide* commercial transaction.[87] Such a view, to put it bluntly, is in contradiction with the facts and disregards the great difference between mediaeval and modern business practices. Mediaeval merchants were commonly 'adventurers' who sent goods to correspondents abroad in the hope that the latter would be able to sell the consignments at a profitable price. For example, Guglielmo Barberi, who exported Flemish cloth to Spain, consigned his shipments to the Datini firm which was his agent in Barcelona. Barberi took up money in Bruges by selling bills on his agent in Barcelona and expected him to pay the bills with the proceeds of the cloth. Sometimes Barberi drew before all the goods were actually sold, and the Datini firm was forced to give him credit. In any case, mediaeval bills were as a rule drawn by a principal on his agent or by an agent on his principal.

Not all mediaeval bills of exchange were commercial bills. A large proportion of bills were what might be called finance bills. They were issued by bankers to adjust international balances or to make a profit on arbitrage. This was the rule with exchange dealings involving three places instead of two. Another fact is sometimes overlooked: merchants who did not want to sell their wares at prevailing prices often raised the funds necessary to carry inventories by selling foreign drafts. In other instances merchants financed their trade with one country by drawing bills on another. A striking example is the case of Andrea Barbarigo, a Venetian merchant, who financed his trade with the Levant by drawing bills on London, Bruges, and Geneva.[88] It is not surprising that the volume of exchange transactions was much larger than the volume of trade. I have always been impressed by the fact that the account books of mediaeval merchant-bankers with which I am acquainted contain many more items relating to bills than to dealings in commodities.

As Bernardo Davanzati has pointed out, the business of exchange was an art which was practiced by the merchant-bankers who delivered money on the exchange not because they needed funds elsewhere but because they were thus able to lend at a profit without violating the ban of the Church against usury.[89] An important consequence was that the extension of commercial credit was tied to the exchange, and that exchange rates were very sensitive to any change in the conditions of the money market. The existence of recurring movements of contraction and expansion is attested by the mediaeval handbooks on commerce. They use the expressions *strettezza* when referring to a tight money market and *larghezza* when referring to an easy money market. The same terms occur again and again in the correspondence of the merchant-bankers. Stringency was usually caused by a shortage of loanable funds relative to the demand for short-term credit. Such market conditions tended, of course, to depress the price of bills because deliverers were willing to lend only on their own terms. On the other hand, *larghezza* meant that money was cheap, that bills were sold at a high price, and that deliverers were seeking reliable takers.

A low price of bills corresponded either to a low or to a high exchange depending upon the way in which the exchange rates were quoted. When the rate was based on a foreign coin, a low price of bills also corresponded to a low exchange. When the rate was based on a domestic coin, a low price of bills corresponded to a high exchange. The same rules, in reverse, apply to a high price of bills. In Bruges, a tight money market and a rising rate of interest was likely to cause a fall of the ducat, the florin, and the French franc and a rise of the two imaginary écus. *Ceteris paribus,* an easy money market had the opposite effect, that is, of raising the rate of the ducat, the florin, and the franc in Flemish currency and of lowering the rate of the two écus in English and Barcelonese currency.

The merchant-bankers were skilled in their art and watched carefully the course of the exchange and the trend of the market both at home and abroad. According to Uzzano, an exchange-dealer ought to be well informed about trade practices, mint regulations, and market conditions so that he might decide whether, under given conditions, it was more profitable to remit by bill of exchange or to ship specie.[90] There is no doubt that the merchant-bankers followed Uzzano's advice. As much as possible, they tried to be deliverers, or lenders, where money was scarce and to be takers, or borrowers, where it was abundant and where bills sold for a good price.[91] In most places the money market tended to contract at certain times of the year and to expand at other times. The pattern of these seasonal variations was well known to the bankers and is described in detail in the mediaeval handbooks. In Bruges money was usually dear in March before the fair and in June and December before the sailing of the galleys. The tension usually eased during the intervening months, especially during August and September when many merchants from other towns in the Low Countries and from Germany came to Bruges to buy supplies and brought in a flow of specie.[92]

Chart I shows that the exchange rate actually followed the seasonal pattern described by the handbooks for merchants. Both in 1438 and in 1439 the money market was presumably stringent late in the autumn, since the rate of the écu rose in Bruges and dropped in London, thus increasing the distance between the two curves. The same happened in both years during Lent. In March, 1438, the écu did not rise much in Bruges but there was a sharp drop in London. The following year, the écu actually rose in Bruges while it continued to fall in London. According to the chart, the distance between the rate of the écu in Bruges and the rate of the écu in London was less in mid-summer and in January than at any other season in both 1438 and 1439. It is regrettable that the available statistical data are so scanty. It is probable, however, that more complete data, if they were available, would not invalidate the preceding analysis or contradict the observations of contemporaries who had practical knowledge of the mechanism of the money market.

[1]Grunzweig, *Correspondance*, I, 55 f.

[2]*Ibid.*, p. 57: Article Four of the partnership agreement.

[3]Bernardo Davanzati, 'Notizia de' cambi a M. Giulio del Caccia, dottor di Legge,' *Scrittori classici italiani di economia politica, Parte Antica*, II (Milan, 1804), 55.

[4]The text of this document has been published in full by Fris, 'L'historien Jean Villani en Flandre,' *op. cit.*, pp. 4-6 (cf. Davidsohn, *Forschungen*, III, 96, No. 502). On Tommaso Fini, see V. Fris, 'Note sur Thomas Fin, receveur de Flandre,' *Compte rendu des séances de la Commission Royale d'Histoire*, LXIX (1900), 8-14; Bigwood, *Régime*, I, 202-15, and *passim*.

[5]These men were all partners in the Peruzzi Company. See Sapori, 'Storia interna,' *op. cit.*, p. 20, No. 1.

[6]Goldschmidt, *op. cit.*, pp. 417-30.

[7]Renée Doehaerd, *Les relations commerciales entre Gênes, la Belgique et l'Outremont d'après les archives notariales génoises aux XIIIe et XIVe siècles* (3 vols., Brussels, 1941). A list of such contracts is given in the index (*ibid.*, III, 1284-85).

[8]*Ibid.*, III, 1085, No. 1788. Cf. III, 1061, No. 1757.

[9]Dr Doehaerd (*op. cit.*, I, 129) comes to the same conclusion. She correctly points out that such a contract involves *cambium et recambium*, or exchange and rechange. I would add that the contract eliminated all element of risk due to exchange fluctuations by stipulating in advance the rate at which returns from Bruges to Genoa would be made. There is nothing to distinguish such a contract from a *mutuum* or straight loan.

[10]Renée Doehaerd, 'Les galères génoises dans la Manche et la Mer du Nord à la fin du XIIIe et au début du XIVe siècle,' *Bulletin de l'Institut historique belge de Rome*, XIX (1938), 1-76.

[11]Doehaerd, *Relations commerciales*, III, 1057, No. 1754. Similar contracts are listed in the index under the heading 'Change maritime,' III, 1284.

[12]Davidsohn, *Forschungen*, III, 180, No. 899.

[13]Doehaerd states correctly that the instrument was still in the form of a *reconnaissance de dette* or an acknowledgment of debt (*Relations commerciales*, I, 128).

[14]A common formula was the following: 'Tibi vel tuo certo misso per me vel meum missum dare et solvere promitto' ('I promise to give and to pay either myself or through my agent to you or to your accredited agent').—Doehaerd, *Relations commerciales*, II, 305 f., No. 577, and *passim*. Sometimes the contract stipulated that the debt was payable to the creditor or to his agent, bringer of the instrument ('promitto tibi vel tuo misso danto mihi hanc cartam') as in the document of 1207 (?) first published incorrectly by Canale.—Goldschmidt, *Universalgeschichte*, pp. 423 f. According to Goldschmidt, the *cambium* contract contained frequently 'a passive and an active order clause' (*aktiver und passiver Orderklausel*).—*Ibid.*, p. 433. In my opinion this terminology is simply misleading.

[15]Sayous, 'L'origine de la lettre de change,' *op. cit.*, p. 95. For example, a contract of 1244 stipulates that it is payable to the original lender, or to his certain attorney, or to any one of his partners (Doehaerd, *Relations commerciales*, II, 266, No. 507). In this connection one may also consult the section on notarial contracts in Abbott P. Usher, *The Early History of Deposit Banking in Mediterranean Europe* (Cambridge, Mass., 1943), I, 61-70. I do not wish to discuss further this controversial matter which is outside the scope of this study.

[16]Edler, 'Lettera di cambio' and 'Lettera di pagamento,' *Glossary*, pp. 154 f.

[17]The text of these instruments is found in notarial protests published by Jakob Strieder *Aus Antwerpener Notariatsarchiven; Quellen zur deutschen Wirtschaftsgeschichte des 16. Jahrhunderts* (Stuttgart, 1930), Nos. 132, 174, 192, 216, 237, and *passim*. In nearly all cases the contracting parties are Flemish, Hanseatic, or High-German merchants and the language used in the instruments is invariably either Flemish or a form of German. These documents should be compared with the Italian bill also published by Strieder (*ibid.*, p. 53, No. 47).

In my opinion these German and Flemish credit instruments have been unjustly neglected. Despite their unconventional wording, they should be considered as genuine bills of exchange.

[18]*Davidsohn, Geschichte,* IV², 220, and *Forschungen,* III, 191, No. 962.

[19]The thesis that there were two documents, a principal *instrumentum* and a complementary letter, was first propounded by the German jurists, notably by Goldschmidt (*Universalgeschichte,* pp. 433-36). This thesis was later challenged by Sayous ('L'origine de la lettre de change,' *op. cit.,* p. 103) and by Enrico Bensa, but it was supported by Alessandro Lattes in his article 'Genova nella storia del diritto cambiario italiano,' (*Rivista del diritto commerciale,* XIII¹ [1915], p. 188), in his review of Bensa's *Francesco di Marco* (*ibid.,* XXVII¹ [1929], 101 f.) and in his 'Note per la storia del diritto commerciale,' (*ibid.,* XXXI¹ [1933], 535-40). Further evidence is given by Doehaerd, *Relations commerciales,* I, 131, and III, 617-18, Nos. 1126, 1127.

[20]Numerous examples will be found among the bills published by Enrico Bensa, *Francesco di Marco da Prato: notizie e documenti sulla mercatura italiana del secolo XIV* (Milan, 1928). pp. 321-51.

[21]Goldschmidt, *Universalgeschichte,* p. 457.

[22]A polemic has raged over this point among the jurists (Goldschmidt, Schaube, Lattes) in which the French historian Sayous joined. I do not see why they wasted so much time and ink in discussing the obvious, but I do see that the lawyers have done their best to blur and to confuse the issues.

[23]As was pointed out by Sir Thomas Gresham in the sixteenth century! The text is quoted by Tawney in his introduction to Thomas Wilson, *A Discourse upon Usury* (New York, 1925), p. 72.

[24]This was often the case between two places within the same realm. In the fifteen century, for instance, Montpellier and Paris, and Avignon and Paris, exchanged one franc for one franc and a certain percentage more or less according to the conditions of the money market. See *El libro di mercatantie et usanze de' paesi,* ed. Franco Borlandi ('Documenti e studi per la storia del commercio e del diritto commerciale italiano,' No. VII; Turin, 1936), p. 120: 'Chostumi di Vingnione: per Parigi vi si chanbia franchi contra a franchi.'

[25]The text of this bill is given by Goldschmidt, *op. cit.,* p. 441. It was first published by Francesco Bonaini (*Statuti inediti della città di Pisa dal XII al XIV secolo* [Florence, 1857], III, 201 ff.) and later by Heinrich Brunner ('Beiträge zur Geschichte und Dogmatik der Werthpapiere: I. Brügger Schöffensprüche zur Geschichte des Wechselrechts im fünfzehnten Jahrhundert,' *Zeitschrift für das gesamte Handelsrecht,* XXII [1877], 8 ff.); by C. Freundt (*Das Wechselrecht der Postglossatoren* [Leipzig, 1899-1909], I, 24); and by André-E. Sayous ('Note sur l'origine de la lettre de change et les débuts de son emploi à Barcelone [XIVe siècle], *Revue historique de droit français et étranger,* 4th series, Vol. XIII [1934], p. 319).

[26]The Italian term is *vantaggio,* from which the term 'agio' is obviously derived. Edler, *Glossary,* p. 310.

[27]One must be careful not to call this profit interest. Probably Pisan money was at a premium in Avignon. The 4¼ per cent agio included both premium and interest.

[28]This change in meaning has been so misleading that Edler (*Glossary,* pp. 99 and 222) gives wrong definitions for *datore* and *prenditore. Prenditore* should be defined as drawer or seller of a bill instead of purchaser and *datore* should be defined as remitter, deliverer, or buyer of a bill instead of drawer. The confusion in terminology has been increased by the German jurists, especially Goldschmidt, who coined the terms *Wechselnehmer* and *Wechselgeber.* These terms were unknown to the Middle Ages and should be avoided. In mediaeval sources, the *prenditore* is always the person who takes up the money given, or lent, by the *datore* and makes out the bill. On the other hand, the *datore* is always the party who gives, or lends, the money and receives the bill. *Prenditore,* consequently, corresponds to what the Germans understand by *Wechselgeber* and *datore,* to what they mean by *Wechselnehmer.*

[29]Here are some of the most common terms used in Italian records of the fourteenth and fifteenth centuries relating to the bill of exchange:

dare a cambio: to buy a bill, to invest money on the exchange or in the purchase of bills.
mandare debito: to draw, to be drawn on.
mandare a pagare: to draw (supplanted by *trarre* in the fifteenth century).
mandare a riccvere: to remit, to send a bill for collection to a correspondent.
prendere (or *pigliare*) *a* (or *per*) *cambio:* to take up money, or to borrow, by selling bills.
dare compimento: to pay or to honor a bill.
carestia or *strettezza:* scarcity of money, tight money market.
dovizia or *larghezza:* abundance of money, easy money market. A few of these definitions do not agree with those given by Florence Edler in her *Glossary* but she has come to the conclusion, after a careful study of the Datini letters and account books, that the new definitions given here, including those of *datore* and *prenditore,* are the correct ones.

[30]Raymond de Roover, 'What is Dry Exchange? A Contribution to the Study of English Mercantilism,' *The Journal of Political Economy* [hereafter referred to as *JPE*], LII (1944), p. 252.

[31]'Quicquid sorti accidit usura est,' Decretum Gratiani, pars II, causa XIV, quest. III, c. iii. E. Friedberg (ed.), *Corpus Juris Canonici,* I (Leipzig, 1879), 735.

[32]T. P. McLaughlin, 'The Teachings of the Canonists on Usury (XII, XIII and XIV centuries),' *Mediaeval Studies,* I (1939), 101. The other gratuitous contract was the *commodatum.* If a *commodatum* was not gratuitous, it became a *locatio* which, however, was not a usurious type of contract.

[33]Tawney, Intro., Wilson, *Discourse,* p. 109. The gain was 'certain' in the sense (1) that the lender assumed no risk and that the loan yielded a profit to him whether the borrower gained or lost in investing the proceeds of the loan and (2) that usury usually was computed on the basis of a given percentage a year, that is to say, it varied proportionately to the duration of the loan *(ratione temporis).*

[34]This was the opinion of Thomas de Vio, Cardinal Cajetan, among others. Wilhelm Endemann, *Studien in der romanisch-kanonistischen Wirtschafts- und Rechtslehre* (Berlin, 1874-83), I, 150.

[35]This was the prevailing opinion with a few exceptions including the orthodox Henricus de Segusia (Hostiensis) and, much later, the heretical Dr Thomas Wilson.

[36]Usher (*Early History of Deposit Banking,* p. 26) states that 'discounting could not develop until the doctrine of negotiability was established.' This statement is true, but it should be added that the opposition of the Church to the taking of interest was another factor which prevented this development. The merchants could not and did not openly defy the canons of the Church but were resourceful in finding new forms of contract which were not objectionable. Cf. Gennaro Mondaini, *Moneta credito banche attraverso i tempi* (2d ed.; Rome, 1942), p. 127.

[37]One of the earliest of these bills has been published by Usher (*Early History,* p. 104) and republished with his kind permission in my article, 'Le contrat de change depuis la fin du treizième siècle jusqu'au début du dix-septième,' *RBPH,* XXV (1946-47), 112-13. These bills were found by me in 1938 after considerable search among hundreds of other bills preserved in the Antwerp Municipal Archives. Apparently endorsed bills were still scarce in 1610 but the practice of endorsing bills spread rapidly within the next twenty or thirty years. I found one example after another of endorsement among the bills dating from 1640 onward, while I was selecting the samples which I photographed for Professor Usher (*Early History,* p. xii).

[38]There is no rule without exception. One of the sixteenth-century bills published by Strieder (*op. cit.,* p. 165, No. 237) is payable 'to Johan van Kasteren or the bringer of the bill' ('Johan van Kasteren oft tom brynger der billen'). It is significant that the Lucchese merchants protested in 1565 or thereabouts to the Antwerp municipal authorities against the use of the payable-to-the-bearer clause in bills of exchange and other credit instruments. Jan A. Goris, *Les colonies marchandes méridionales à Anvers de 1488 à 1567* (Louvain, 1925), pp. 338-39. I do not wish to go further into the legal aspects of this controversial subject of negotiability, since it is outside the scope of this study. However, I would like to make two re-

marks in this connection. One, I am not ignorant of the fact that the bearer clause occurs frequently in the great variety of credit instruments—bills of debt, chirographs, letters obligatory, recognisances, bonds, and other obligations—which were used in the Northern and Baltic trade. I might refer to the chirographs of Ypres and Nivelles published by Des Marez and by Bigwood (*Régime juridique,* I, 507-15). The Italian merchant-bankers adapted themselves to the business practices followed in the Northern trade and made advances secured by such instruments. The Borromei in London, for example, lent money to Robert Utingham, mayor of the Staple, on instruments payable 'to the said Utingham or to the bearer' ('a Robert Utingham vel al portator').—Biscaro, *op. cit.,* pp. 364-65 and *passim.* Two, even in the Low Countries the status of the bearer was uncertain at law. At best the insertion of the payable-to-the-bearer clause enabled the bearer to sue a recalcitrant debtor in his own name without power of attorney from the original creditor. But all courts did not allow such a procedure and some required a power of attorney despite the presence of the bearer clause. The bearer, in any case, was not a holder in due course. In other words, defenses opposable to the original creditor were also opposable to the subsequent assignee or to the bearer of the instrument.

[39]This statement is in agreement with that of Alessandro Lattes, *Il diritto commerciale nella legislazione statutaria delle città italiane* (Milan, 1884), p. 181: 'Di quelle formule più o meno perfette al portatore, che sono così frequente in altre carte del Medio Evo . . . manca quasi ogni esempio per le cambiali.' There are apparently two or three exceptions among the bills of exchange published by Bensa, but upon closer inspection it appears that the bills in question are actually letters of credit issued to travellers rather than real bills of exchange. One of the so-called bills is payable to a cardinal or to his proxy. Bensa, *Francesco di Marco,* p. 323, Nos. 16, 17; p. 326, No. 20.

[40]The Churchmen even argued that in matters of exchange the just price was the market price, or the current rate of exchange. It was lawful to buy bills at the current price or above but not below. Those who bought bills below the current price were taking advantage of the borrower's need and were suspect of usury.

[41]Bigwood, *Régime,* I, 653: 'Il n'y eut pas, à proprement parler, de commerce de change, et Bruges ne devint pas une place de paiements.' This statement is simply false and is contradicted by the evidence which the author himself gives in a footnote. The fact that papal revenues collected in Germany and Poland were transmitted to Avignon by way of Bruges proves by itself that this city was an important financial center.

[42]There are plenty of examples in the business letters of the Medici branch in London and in those of Datini's correspondents in Bruges. The Medici letters only are available in print. —Grunzweig, *Correspondance,* pp. 19, 24, 26, 98. Exchange rates are quoted in the following way (*ibid.,* p. 26): 'Per costì 36⅔, Vinegia 40⅔, Bruggia 19⅔ in ¾, Genova [and not Ginevra] 22¾.' This sentence means: Florence, 36⅔ sterlings per florin, Venice 40⅔ sterlings per ducat, Bruges from 19⅔ st. to 19¾ st. per écu of 24 groats, Genoa 22¾ st. per Genoese florin.

[43]Pegolotti, *op. cit.,* p. 243.

[44]*Ibid.,* pp. 239, 247.

[45]Florence, State Archives, Mediceo avanti il Principato, filza 134, No. 2; Fragment of a ledger belonging to the Bruges branch of the Medici bank, fol. 231.

[46]The Datini Archives in Prato, Italy, are the most valuable collection for mediaeval business and economic history. The wealth of material contained in this collection is almost unbelievable. There are more than five hundred account books, over three hundred bundles of business letters—each package containing several hundred letters—and countless other commercial documents ranging from insurance policies to small slips of paper on which were jotted down the quotations of exchange rates and the prices of commodities. Historians who have tried to work in the Datini Archives have been overwhelmed by the mass of material. Only a small part has been explored as yet. The best work on Datini is Bensa, *Francesco di Marco da Prato.* The only publication in English is Robert Brun's article, 'A Fourteenth-Century Merchant of Italy: Francesco Datini of Prato,' *Journal of Economic and Business History,* II (1930), 451-66. The Datini Archives suffered no damage during World War II.

[47]Prato (Tuscany), Datini Archives, No. 1146, Cambiali:

In the name of God, amen.

December 12, 1399

Pay at usance by this first of exchange to Domenico Sancio six hundred écus at 10*s*. 5*d*. [barcelonese] per ▽, which ▽600 at 10*s*. 5*d*. per écu are for the value received [here] from Jacopo Gosco, and charge them to our account. God be with you.

Giovanni Orlandini and Piero Benizi & Co.
in Bruges

Accepted January 11, 1400
[Verso:] Francesco da Prato & Co. in Barcelona
First [of exchange]

[48]The entry by which the amount of £312 10*s*. Barcelonese was charged to the firm Orlandini and Benizi, of Bruges, reads as follows: 'E deon dare a dì 11 di genaio ▽600 a sol. 10 den. 5 per ▽ trasonci per uso in Domenicho Sancio in questo a c. 293 debino avere, per altre n'ebono da Giachopo Ghoscho........£312.10.0' Datini Archives, No. 802, Libro nero D, fol. 283v.

[49]The usual formula was: 'Avisamovi di ▽ [amount] vi traemo in [name of payee] a s.— d.— per ▽ i quali al termine paghate e ponete a conto per noi.' Another formula was: 'V'abiamo tratto ▽ [amount] a sol.— den.— per scudo per uso in [name of payee] per la valuta a dì [date of bill] da [name of remitter]. Ponete a conto per noi.'

[50]Giovanni di Antonio da Uzzano, *La pratica della mercatura* (Vol. IV of Gian-Francesco Pagnini, *Della Decima;* Lisbon-Lucca, 1766), pp. 102 f.

[51]Bensa, *Francesco di Marco,* p. 350.

[52]*El libro di mercatantie,* p. 15. The same figure of twenty days after sight is given in a manuscript handbook: Florence, Biblioteca Nazionale, Codice Magliabechiano, XI, 97, Abaco Benedetto [after 1474], fol. 60v.

[53]Pegolotti, *Pratica,* p. 195; *El libro di mercatantie,* p. 10.

[54]Uzzano, *op. cit.,* pp. 100-103. There may be an exception in the case of Genoa. According to the *Libro di mercatantie* (p. 13), usance bills drawn from Bruges on Genoa were payable two months from date, but those drawn from Genoa on Bruges matured ten days after sight. Pegolotti, however, states that the usance was two months in both directions (*op. cit.,* p. 195).

[55]Uzzano, *op. cit.,* p. 101. According to the *Libro di mercatantie,* exchange transactions between Bruges and Montpellier were very rare *(radissimi).*

[56]The bill was issued in favor of Giovanni Gharone. His account was credited upon acceptance of the bill:

> Giovanni Gharone dè avere a dì 30 d'agosto [1398] ▽ cinqueciento a soldi 9 denari 10 [per] ▽, promettemo loro per lettera da Brugia di Giovanni Orlandini e compagnia, in questo carta 199 debino [dare]. Sono per altri ▽500 da Antonio Salella....£245 s.16 d.8

The entry relating to the payment of the bill reads as follows:

> Giovanni Gharone dè dare a dì primo d'ottobre [1398] £ dugientoquarantacinque s. 16 d.8 disonli per noi Giame di Pue di Lucho e Giovaneto Savasso [money-changers] in questo carta 223 dèbi avere........£245 s.16 d.8

As this entry shows, Gharone was paid by credit to his bank account. Datini Archives, No. 801, Barcelona Branch, Libro Verde C, fol. 213.

[57]When the bill reached Barcelona, the Datini firm at once charged the account of Bibero, the payor, and credited the Orlandini. On January 24, the Datini firm was notified that it had received credit at the bank of Pere Brunet, a Barcelonese money-changer (called Piero Brunetto by the Italians). Consequently, his account was charged and Bibero's account was discharged. Datini Archives, No. 802, Barcelona Branch, Libro nero D, fols. 284, 297. The entries are quoted in the footnotes to my article 'Early Accounting Problems of Foreign Exchange,' *The Accounting Review,* XIX (1944) 405, nn. 27, 30.

[58]This practice was also followed in Genoa. An early example (1315) is given by Doehaerd, *Relations commerciales,* III, 1136, No. 1853.

[59]Datini Archives, No. 1146: Cambiali:

In the name of God February 25, 1400

Pay by this second of exchange, if you have not paid by the first, at usance to yourselves £420 Barcelonese which 420 pounds are for the value received here from Giovanni Orlandini, Piero Benizi, and Partners. Make good payment and charge to my account. May God protect you.

Guglielmo Barberi
Greetings from Bruges

[Verso:] Francesco di Marco and Partners
in Barcelona

Second

[60]According to a letter of the Orlandini dated March 17, 1400.

[61]Although protests were sometimes made even when the payor and payee were the same, as appears from an entry in the ledger of the Medici bank in Bruges. They caused a bill drawn by Nicolo di Bartolomeo of Venice and payable to themselves to be protested by a Bruges notary. The protest charges were debited to the Medici branch of Venice which apparently had furnished the value. Florence, State Archives, Mediceo avanti il Principato, Filza 134, No. 2. See de Roover, *Medici Bank,* p. 80.

[62]Goldschmidt (*op. cit.,* p. 443, n. 131) states correctly that bills containing this formula were credited by the payor to the remitter, but such a statement does not explain anything. Bensa (*Francesco di Marco,* p. 158) also deals with the problem and states that such bills were paid by compensation, which is true but does not clear up the matter.

[63]The text of the entries in the ledger is given in my article 'Early Accounting Problems,' *op. cit.,* p. 405, n. 34.

[64]An example is given by Bensa, *Francesco di Marco,* p. 329, No. 27.

[65]Doehaerd, *Relations commerciales,* III, 1085, No. 1788.

[66]Pegolotti, *op. cit.,* p. 247.

[67]The figures given by Pegolotti are correct and can be easily checked by using the Chain Rule:

1 real = 24 groats
12 groats = 1 florin
1 florin = 29*s. a fiorino*

These equations give the result that one real was worth 58*s. a fiorino.* Different results are obtained for different values of the florin.

[68]My sources on exchange quotations in the fifteenth century are the handbook of Uzzano and *El libro di mercatantie,* sometimes attributed to Giorgio Chiarini, especially p. 132.

[69]Uzzano, *op. cit.,* pp. 141, 149, 149-50; *El libro di mercatantie,* pp. 5, 15-16; and Florence, Biblioteca Nazionale, Ms. Palatino, No. 573, Abaco Benedetto, fol. 54: 'A Bruggia si fanni e' paghamenti a lire, soldi, e denari . . . Ed è vi 2 ragioni di schudi immaginati che l'uno vale grossi 24 e l'altro grossi 22.'

[70]*El libro di mercatantie,* p. 17. Uzzano does not mention the fairs of Geneva.

[71]Yves Renouard, *Les relations des Papes d'Avignon et des compagnies commerciales et bancaires de 1316 à 1378* (Paris, 1941), p. 211.

[72]In actual practice merchant-bankers determined their profits by using a bookkeeping device and by opening to each of their correspondents abroad two accounts, one *Nostro* and one *Vostro* account. This question is so technical that full development would require several pages and interest very few readers who are not accountants. Those who are not discouraged by a technical discussion will find that the matter is fully explained in my article, 'Early Accounting Problems of Foreign Exchange,' *The Accounting Review,* XIX (1944), 381-407.

[73]A draft was profitable only in the case of a rising exchange in Bruges and unprofitable

in the case of a falling exchange. Moreover, in the case of a draft, the lender had no speculative advantage over the borrower.

[74]Proceeds of the second bill in Bruges,

600 ducats at 52 groats per ducat	£130 gr.
Deduct: cost of the first bill, 600 ducats at 50 groats per ducat	£125 gr.
Gross profit, 2 groats per ducat	£ 5 gr.

[75]The same analysis is presented in my article, 'Le contrat de change depuis la fin du treizième siècle jusqu'au début du dix-septième,' *RBPH,* XXV (1946-47) 111-128.

[76]It is the existence of this margin which gave to the lender a speculative advantage over the borrower.

[77]A complete analysis of 'the theory of interest in exchange' will be found in my article, 'What is Dry Exchange? A Contribution to the Study of English Mercantilism,' *JPE,* LII (1944), 250-66. This article deals with the exchange between London and Antwerp in the sixteenth century but the same analysis may be applied to mediaeval cases by simply changing the factual data.

[78]A fall in the price of bills corresponded to a falling exchange in Bruges and to a rising exchange in Venice.

[79]This analysis, of course, is incomplete, but I deal here with well-known phenomena that are explained in almost any book on economic theory.

[80]The question is so technical that it is impossible to go into more detail here but a full description of the accounting procedure is given in my article, 'Accounting Problems of Foreign Exchange,' *op. cit.,* 381-407. In my opinion the evidence presented in this article is decisive.

[81]Raymond de Roover, *The Medici Bank,* p. 36.

[82]Datini Archives, No. 1146:

Al nome di Dio a dì 21 di febraio 1399 [1400]

Pagate per questa prima a usanza a Andrea de' Pazzi e compagnia £ treciento trentatre s.6 d.8 barzalonesi, cioè £333 s.6 d.8, per £ quaranta grosso da Manette Davanzati e compagnia e ponete a chonto de' nostri di Bruggia e R. [rimandate?]. Cristo vi guardi.

Bernardo Alberti e compagnia
in Vinegia

Acettata dì 30 marzo 1400
[On the back:] Franciescho di Marcho e conpangni
in Barzalona

Prima

The exchange rate is not explicitly stated but appears to be 16*s.* 8*d.* Barcelonese per ducat. The *lira grosso* (i.e., *lira di grossi*) mentioned in the bill was equal to ten ducats.

[83]Datini Archives, No. 1146. The bill in question was for 300 florins at 15*s.* 8⅜*d.* Barcelonese per florin, or £235 15*s.* Barcelonese. The bill was in favor of Antonio d'Allesandro & Co. in Barcelona, and the value had been received in Florence from Filippo di Piero Rinieri. The bill contains the sentence: 'Ponete a conto de' nostri di Bruggia.'

[84]Datini Archives, No. 802, Libro Nero D, fol. 284:

Giovanni Orlandini e Piero Benizi e conpagni di Brugia..........................

E deon dare a dì 7 di genaio [1400] F. 300 rimettemo loro a Firenze a loro per uso in Diamante e Altobiancho degli Alberti e conpagni per valuta a soldi 15 d.2½ per fiorino qui a Nicholaio degli Alberti e Filipozo Soldani in questo carta 288...............£228.2.6

According to this entry the bill was drawn by Nicolaio degli Alberti and Filipozo Soldano in Barcelona on Diamante and Altobianco degli Alberti of Florence and payable to the Orlandini in the same city. The Datini firm bought the bill for account of the Orlandini firm in Bruges at the rate of 15*s.* 2½*d.* Barcelonese per florin.

[85]Datini Archives, No. 853: Fondaco di Barcellona, Carteggio di Bruggia, II. The instructions are repeated in later letters dated February 9 and March 13, 1400.

[86]*Ibid.* Orlandini letter of March 4, 1400. Similar complaints were expressed in a later letter dated January 9, 1401 (*ibid.*, No. 854: Carteggio da Bruggia, III). Of course, idle balances did not yield any profits.

[87]It is untrue, as Bigwood states (*Régime juridique,* I, 653), that 'il n'y eut guère à Bruges que des opérations de change consécutives ou connexes à des opérations commerciales.'

[88]Frederic C. Lane, *Andrea Barbarigo, Merchant of Venice, 1418-1449* ('Johns Hopkins University Studies in Historical and Political Science,' Series LXII, No. 1; Baltimore, 1944), pp. 25-26, 188-92. As Barbarigo borrowed by selling bills, it is no wonder that he usually lost on his exchange dealings. At one time, he lost £14 *di grossi* or 140 ducats on exchange and re-exchange with London. As he himself explains in his ledger, he incurred this loss because he drew on London at 45 and 44 sterlings per ducat but his correspondents redrew on Venice at about 40 sterlings per ducat. There was, consequently, a loss of about 4 sterlings per ducat in six months or two usances. This loss corresponds to an interest rate of about 18% a year, which is plausible. The text of the entry is given by Vittorio Alfieri, *La partita doppia applicata alle scritture delle antiche aziende mercantili veneziane* (Turin, 1891), p. 79. At another time Barbarigo lost £2 6*s. di grossi* or 23 ducats on exchange with Bruges. Although he bought cloth in England and Flanders, the funds raised by the sale of bills were apparently not used for this purpose but for financing his purchases of cotton in the Levant.

[89]Davanzati, 'Notizia de' cambi' *op. cit.*, pp. 54-55.

[90]Uzzano, *op. cit.*, p. 152.

[91] Fra Luca Paciolo, 'De cambiis seu cambitionibus,' distinctio 9, tractatus 4, *Summa de arithmetica, geometria, proportioni et proportionalita* (Venice, 1494), fol. 167. Cf. Uzzano, *op, cit.*, p. 152: 'La buona regola del cambiare vuole essere questa: guardarsi di non si trovare debito nella terra ne' tempi che di ragione i denari vi debbono essere buoni.'

[92]*El libro di mercatantie,* p. 168.

Chapter 5

THE VICISSITUDES OF THE MONEY MARKET AND THE PERILS OF INVESTMENT IN PUBLIC LOANS

THE letters written by Datini's correspondents in Bruges give decidedly the impression that economic fluctuations are nothing new and that there were already in the Middle Ages alternating periods of prosperity and depression, of good and bad trade. Whether those fluctuations were cyclical in character cannot be ascertained as yet from the available evidence, but further study on mediaeval business conditions will undoubtedly throw more light on this important subject. In any case, business letters disclose that both great scarcity and great abundance of money were harmful to business activity. Credit contraction, or an acute scarcity of money, as it was called in the technical parlance of the Middle Ages, was often the prelude to a depression and was accompanied by a drastic fall in prices, forced sales, and business failures. Usually, *larghezza,* or an easy money market followed upon the heels of *strettezza,* or a period of tension and liquidation. An easy money market, however, was by no means an unmistakable sign of prosperity. Often money was plentiful because it failed to circulate, because trade was dull, and because prices were generally depressed. The merchants were loath to take any risks, and stocks were lying dead on the hands of the *drapiers* or cloth manufacturers. Under such circumstances the interest rate —as reflected in the course of the foreign exchange—was generally low for the good reason that there were many *datori* or lenders but few *prenditori* or borrowers.

The disturbing effects of both abundance and scarcity of money are graphically described in the letters of the Italian merchant-bankers in Bruges to Francesco Datini's branch offices in Genoa and Barcelona. On May 3, 1399, the Orlandini of Bruges reported that money was easy rather than tight but that spices were low in price.[1] As the Venetian galleys were due to arrive, prices were expected to drop still further, since there was no demand. Two months later, on July 31, 1399, the Orlandini wrote to Barcelona that the exchange rates were at a normal level (*intorno al usato*), but they did not know whether the money market would contract or expand after the arrival of the Venetian galleys, which were expected at Sluys at any time.[2] On August 2, 1399, after the galleys had arrived in port, the money market was rather tight (*più tosto ristrietto*), but the Orlandini were not able to forecast any important change in the near future.[3] At the end of September, money was 'rather good,' meaning dear, and was expected to remain so until the galleys had left.[4]

At this juncture the public authorities appeared on the stage to upset the equilibrium of the money market and to precipitate a crisis by a series of ill-advised monetary ordinances. On November 26, 1399, in the midst of the crisis, the Orlandini wrote to Genoa that money in Bruges was dear but that prices were low. Trade was apparently at a standstill. The commodity market, in particular, remained 'cold' to spices which were little in demand. 'Those,' the letter continues, 'who are able to buy for cash are sure to find bargains.'[5] In March, 1400, the crisis was over. Money was cheap but trade bad. The Orlandini, in a letter to Datini's Barcelona branch, expressed the hope that business would improve during the approaching May Fair of Bruges which was held three weeks after Easter.[6] Diamante and Altobianco degli Alberti, another firm of Italian merchant-bankers established in Bruges, writing to Genoa on March 31, 1400, also stated that money was plentiful but that 'very little business was being done' (*qui si fa pochissimo al presente*) and that the price of spices was low because of lack of demand.[7] This description suggests that Bruges was at that time in the grip of a business depression which was attributable to the fact that the merchants expected a further decline in prices and that money did not get into circulation. Everyone was waiting and unwilling to make any commitments. Eventually trade returned to normal because the public authorities were finally persuaded to repeal the obnoxious ordinances.

In February, 1401, money was again plentiful in Bruges, as it usually was in that season, but business prospects were rather good: the exchange-dealers were in an optimistic mood and expected the money market to tighten and the demand for credit accommodation to increase. On February 26, 1401, the Orlandini made the following significant statement in a letter to Barcelona: 'Money is now plentiful . . . but it would be well to remit here at favorable rates because scarcity always follows an easy money market.'[8]

It is significant that Uzzano, in his handbook for merchants, gives the same advice and cautions merchants against remitting to those places where money is dear and against drawing on those places where it is cheap.[9] Such a statement may seem paradoxical, but Uzzano argues that conditions in the money market are likely to change before the remittances or the drafts reach their destination. What a clever exchange-dealer should do is to watch the trends of the market and to make correct forecasts. As far as possible he should anticipate the course of events so that he will not find himself without funds when the stringency occurs or with excess funds when there is no demand for credit accommodation. According to Uzzano, places where the market is tight attract specie from everywhere with the result that the tension is bound to lessen and even to cause a swing of the pendulum in the other direction.

Those matters must have been common knowledge among the merchant-bankers.[10] They were probably better informed about foreign exchange and monetary phenomena than some economists who consider anything prior to Adam Smith as 'prehistoric' are willing to admit.[11]

The crisis of 1399, which caused so much disturbance in the Bruges money market, was brought about by an ill-fated attempt to force gold into circulation. In 1399 the Flemish currency had apparently been mismanaged for some time because the monetary ordinances underrated the gold coins in terms of silver currency. As usual in such a case, gold had disappeared entirely or circulated under cover at rates higher than those set by the monetary ordinances. The circulation was made up mostly of white money (silver) and of subsidiary black money (an alloy containing little silver). Mediaeval authorities often had a blind faith in their omnipotence and in the virtues of governmental interference. In the autumn of 1399 the authorities decided to restore the circulation of gold, not by adjusting the official rates to the market rates, but by decreeing that all bills of exchange were to be paid at first partly in silver and partly in gold, and later entirely in gold.

TABLE 3
EXCHANGE RATES IN BRUGES

Date	BARCELONA	GENOA	VENICE	LONDON	PARIS
	Per écu of 22 groats	In groats per florin	In groats per ducat	Per écu of 24 groats	In groats per French franc
July 31, 1399	9*s.* 10*d.*	gr. 32 5/6	gr. 35 2/3	st. 25 1/4	gr. 33 2/3
September 20, 1399	9*s.* 11*d.*	gr. 32 1/3	gr. 35 1/12	st. 25 5/12	gr. 33 2/3
October 7, 1399	10*s.*	gr. 32 1/12	gr. 35	st. 25 1/12	gr. 33 11/12
November 13, 1399	10*s.* 4*d.*	gr. 30 3/4	gr. 34	st. 26 7/8	gr. 33 1/2
November 26, 1399	10*s.* 6*d.*	gr. 30 5/12	gr. 33 7/8	st. 27	gr. 32 11/12
December 19, 1399	10*s.* 5*d.*	gr. 31 3/4	gr. 34 5/6	st. 26 1/3	gr. 33 1/3
January 3, 1400	10*s.* 5 1/2*d.*	gr. 32 1/4	gr. 34 1/3	st. 26 1/8	gr. 33 1/3

Source: Datini Archives, Prato, Tuscany, No. 853: Fondaco di Barcellona, Carteggio da Bruggia, II.

The first step in this direction was an ordinance issued on October 2, 1399, according to the letters of Datini's correspondents in Bruges. This ordinance became effective immediately and prescribed that all bills of exchange were to be paid henceforth in specie and not by assignment in bank, as was customary among merchants.[12] The new measure took the bankers completely by surprise. The money market immediately tightened, and the foreign exchanges reacted vigorously. The écu of twenty-two groats went up from 9*s.* 11*d.* Barcelonese on September 20, 1399, to 10*s.* 6*d.* Barcelonese on November 26. The exchange on London followed suit and jumped from 25 5/12 sterlings per écu on September 20 to twenty-seven sterlings on November 26. At the same time, both the Genoese florin and the Venetian ducat dropped several points. The French franc also suffered a setback. As these rates were quoted in local currency, they

BILLS OF EXCHANGE (VERSO)

All three bills are addressed to the firm Francesco di Marco Datini & Co. in Barcelona. *From the Datini Archives, Prato (Tuscany).*

moved up and down contrary to the London and Barcelona rates which were quoted in foreign currency.[13]

The stringency of the money market is easy to explain, since the ordinance created a need for more coin in place of money substitutes. This additional specie had to be attracted from abroad by a rise in the rate of interest which affected the exchange rates and caused the écu to rise and the ducat, the florin, and the franc to fall. But, in the meanwhile, there was an acute shortage of money, prices were forced down, and the merchants complained of hard times.[14]

By January, 1400, the tension in the money market had decreased somewhat, but prices were still low and business was in a slump (*fassi molto pocho*).[15] On February 18, 1400, the authorities considered the moment favorable to strike another blow. A proclamation was issued according to which all foreign exchanges were to be paid one-third in gold and two-thirds in silver after May 1. 1400; two-thirds in gold and one-third in silver after September 1, 1400; and entirely in gold after January 1, 1401.[16] The ordinance created great excitement among the merchants. Prices and the volume of business were adversely affected, but the money market did not contract immediately. The Orlandini wrote to Genoa that it would be difficult to comply with the ordinance, especially when payments were to be made two-thirds in gold and one-third in silver, because there was so little gold in circulation.[17] In another letter, addressed to Barcelona, they remarked pointedly that the rate of gold coins had been set ten years previous—a reference to the monetary reform of 1389-1390—and had ceased to correspond to existing conditions.[18] The situation resulted in a deadlock: on the one hand, it did not pay to import gold coins, as they were undervalued; on the other hand, the authorities stubbornly refused to change the official valuation and punished with banishment anyone who dared to accept gold coins at a higher price.[19]

After the ordinance went into effect on May 1, 1400, there was for some time little activity in the exchange business, as everyone was waiting for further developments.[20] No one was willing either to give or to take up money, that is, there were neither deliverers nor takers. In general, stringency prevailed in the money market throughout May and June. The tightness was expected to become worse after the arrival of the galleys.[21] The Orlandini advised their correspondent in Barcelona to remit and not to draw. On July 3, 1400, the Genoese, the Venetians, and the Catalans went in a body to the *Loya,* or the city council of Bruges, asking for the repeal of the ordinance, but they were not supported by the Milanese, the Lucchese, and the Florentines.[22] As a result of the split in the ranks of the foreign colonies, the ordinance was allowed to stand. But the Genoese and their supporters did not give up the struggle.

At the end of July, the authorities finally decided to grant more delay and to amend the ordinance: up to December 1, 1400, exchanges were to be paid one-

TABLE 4
COURSE OF THE EXCHANGE IN BRUGES ON MAY 11, 1401

Place of Payment	Exchange Quotation	Value Payable
Genoa	32⅛ groats per florin	Half in gold and half in silver
	33 groats per florin	All in silver
Venice	34½ groats per ducat	Half in gold and half in silver
London	25 5/12 sterlings per écu	Half in gold and half in silver
	24⅚ sterlings per écu	All in silver

Source: Datini Archives, No. 753: Fondaco di Genova, Carteggio da Bruggia. Letter dated May 11, 1401.

fourth in gold and three-fourths in silver; from December 1, 1400, half in gold and half in silver; from April 1, 1401, three-fourths in gold and one-fourth in silver; and from July 1, 1401, all was to be paid in gold.[23] The immediate effect of this revision was relief of the strain on the money market. The exchange rate on Barcelona dropped from 10*s.* 8½*d.* Barcelonese to 10*s.* 4½*d.* per écu of twenty-two groats, but the change in the other rates was not as great. In the autumn, the forecast was that the money market would contract after December 1, when exchanges would become payable half in gold and half in silver.[24] Actually the money market improved a little in January 1401[25] Several Genoese merchants refused to carry out the ordinance and did not pay their bills half in gold and half in silver.[26] Apparently, no effort was made to constrain the offenders. In order to avoid litigation, the Orlandini advised their correspondents to specify in bills of exchange that they were payable 'according to the municipal ordinances' (*chome per la villa è ordinato*).[27] Despite the confusion resulting from the stand taken by the Genoese, the money market eased considerably. On March 5, 1401, the exchange rate on Barcelona stood at 10*s.* per écu of twenty-two groats. In May, money was easy but business was depressed.[28]

In the end the forces of the market proved to be stronger than the municipal ordinances. The merchants resorted to the simple device of quoting two different exchange rates: one for bills of which the value was payable half in gold and half in silver and the other for bills of which the value was payable entirely in silver. The first of the two rates included the premium on gold, as is evident from the figures given in Table 4. Thus a taker who wanted gold received only 32⅛ groats for each florin payable in Genoa. If he was satisfied with silver he received 33 groats instead of 32⅛ groats per florin. On the other hand, a borrower who wanted gold had to give 25 5/12 sterlings in London for each écu received in Bruges. He promised only 24⅚ sterlings if he was content with receiving payment in silver.

By means of this clever device the circulation of gold coins remained circumscribed within a small group of merchants and international bankers. The ordinance thus failed to achieve its purpose of increasing the circulation of gold among the public at large. The authorities finally gave up the struggle and repealed the ordinance in September 1401 to be effective October 1. If a payor offered payment in white money, that is, in silver, the payee had no right to refuse unless the bill of exchange specified that it was payable wholly or partly in gold.[29]

Governments have short memories and do not seem to learn by experience. About 1410, or less than ten years after the events related in the preceding paragraphs, another attempt was made to increase the circulation of gold by passing an ordinance that bills of exchange were to be paid half in gold and half in silver. The ordinance was to go into effect immediately but the Italians protested strongly to the Loya and pleaded for delay so that they might inform their correspondents abroad.[30] This request was granted, but it is doubtful whether this second ordinance was more successful than the first. A third attempt of the same kind was made in the sixteenth century, when Charles V, on December 10, 1541, issued a decree ordering that all bills were to be paid in specie, two-thirds in gold and one-third in silver.[31] At first this decree caused a serious stagnation in business activity. Although it soon became evident that the decree could not be enforced, it remained on the statute books for several years and it was not repealed until 1551.

Loans at interest could easily be concealed under the color of exchange with or without the connivance of correspondents abroad. Such spurious exchange transactions were known under the names of dry exchange and fictitious exchange. They generally involved exchange and re-exchange, or *cambium et recambium*. The common characteristic of all contracts of this sort was that the contracting parties, or the taker and the deliverer, agreed in advance to make no real payments abroad. In the case of dry exchange, a bill was actually sent to a correspondent abroad, but he redrew at the prevailing rate as soon as the bill in question fell due. The banker's profit (or loss) was still uncertain, since it depended upon the price of the redraft. Fictitious exchange was based either upon fictitious bills or upon fictitious rates, that is, rates other than market prices.[32] In the first instance, the contracting parties did not even bother to send bills abroad but made them out *pro forma* to be used only in case of litigation. In the second instance, all speculative risks were eliminated by stipulating in advance the rate at which returns would be made, that is, the price of the *recambium* or redraft. By so doing the profit of the lender became certain, since it ceased to depend upon the unpredictable swing of the exchange rates.

Although the Medici professed to deal only in licit and honorable exchange, the surviving fragment of the ledger of their Bruges branch records several clear cases of dry exchange. In the first of three such cases, the Medici of Venice bought a bill on Bruges from one Antonio di Niccolò del Conte at 51½ groats. The bill in question was payable to and by the Medici of Bruges.[33]

As soon as it matured, the latter redrew on Antonio del Conte at the prevailing rate of exchange which, in this case, happened to be 51½ groats. The Medici of Venice neither gained nor lost on this transaction, since the *cambium* and the *recambium* were made at the same rate. In other words, they broke even because they paid and received the same number of groats for each ducat. The second case involved the same parties and was similar to the first with this difference: the Medici of Venice made a profit of three groats because they obtained 54½ groats per ducat for the first bill, from Venice on Bruges, but paid only 51½ groats per ducat for the second bill, from Bruges on Venice. In the third case they made a profit of 2¼ groats which also arose from the difference in price between the first and the second bill (53¼ groats as against 51 groats per ducat).[34]

These three cases illustrate what has been explained in the preceding chapter. A banker, whether he resided in Bruges or in Venice, made a profit as long as the ducat was rated higher in the second of these two places; he just broke even when the two rates were the same; and he lost if the ducat was rated lower in Venice than in Bruges. It should be added that the profit became certain if the price of the redraft was determined in advance by the contracting parties instead of being determined by the uncontrollable fluctuations of market rates.

Let us suppose, for example, that a banker residing in Bruges bought a bill on Venice at fifty groats per ducat and agreed *in advance* with the taker that the banker's correspondent in Venice would redraw at 52 groats instead of at the current rate. Such a banker was then certain of his profit. He earned two groats per ducat in two usances or four months whether the exchange in Venice went up or down. A transaction of this sort might be either to the advantage of the borrower, if the ducat in Venice went above 52 groats, or to his disadvantage, if the ducat fell below 52 groats. But that is not the point which the Churchmen considered. They argued, quite logically from their point of view, that the speculative element was absent and that there was in fact no difference between such a contract and a straight loan at interest. As such, fictitious exchange was condemned by all theologians for being what it actually was: a contract *in fraudem usurarum*.

Dry exchange, although the profit was uncertain, was also censored by most theologians and jurists because it was not a genuine exchange contract but a loan with lucre. They pointed out that no real payment was made abroad but that contracting parties agreed from the outset to effect a final settlement in the same place and in the same currency.

One more interesting fact should be brought out in connection with fictitious exchange. It was considered as foul play even by the merchants themselves. This attitude may seem strange but it is easily explainable. Fictitious exchange violated the rules of the game which required that exchanges be contracted at current, or market, rates. In the opinion of the merchants any violation of this rule interfered with the free play of supply and demand. The delicate mechanism of the money market could hardly be expected to function properly if private parties were allowed to tamper with the rules. It is not surprising, therefore, that the merchants considered fictitious exchange as an infringement of business ethics, just as gamblers consider it bad form to stack the cards or to load the dice.

In emergencies the city of Bruges sometimes raised money by means of bills of exchange, but the records give little information beyond the amount which was paid for agio by the municipal treasury.[35] The Lucchese merchant, Dino Rapondi, was instrumental in finding a market for the bills among his business connections. Most probably Dino Rapondi took up money by exchange on his own credit, since it is unlikely that the city of Bruges was named in any of the bills. It has been asserted that those bills were actually 'discounted,' but the sources do not support such an assertion and the word 'discount' is not found in any of the texts.[36] The municipal accounts refer only to the 'loss' (*verliese*) which the city incurred on the exchange. It is true that discounts under the form of allowances for prompt payment were not unknown in the Middle Ages, but it does not follow that bills were actually discounted in the modern sense of the term.[37]

As a complement to the exchange business the international bankers sold letters of credit to travelers, pilgrims, and students in mediaeval universities.[38] These transactions were relatively unimportant and deserve only passing mention. In 1441, for example, Anselmo Fabri, dean of the collegiate church of Our Lady in Antwerp, who resided at the Curia and neglected the duties of his deanship, paid the sum of £106 5*s.* groat to a factor of the Medici for two letters of credit, one of one hundred ducats and the other of four hundred ducats, payable in Rome.[39] The smaller sum was collected by the dean's servant in Rome before February 28, 1442. The remainder was still standing to Dean Fabri's credit when the ledger was closed on March 24, 1442, the end of the year according to Florentine style.[40]

The business of exchange was speculative, it is true, but it did not expose the bankers to heavy risks because the structure of the money market was such that it favored the lender to the detriment of the borrower. By being cautious a banker could hardly fail to make a profit on most transactions and to reduce to a minimum the losses due to bad debts. Moreover, risks could easily be divided; and the merchant-bankers did not fail to do so: (1) by scattering their working balances among many places, (2) by picking out reliable takers and by refusing to buy bills from merchants of doubtful standing, and (3) by restricting the amount of credit which was granted to any one borrower.[41] On the average, however, profits were limited by what merchants could earn if they invested more money in foreign trade or, in other words, by the expected return on alternative opportunities for investment. As compared with exchange dealings, loans to princes and municipal governments were often more attractive but also more dangerous, because such loans involved a prolonged immobilization of funds and always tied the lender to the political fortunes of the borrower. The rise and fall of the financiers of Arras was only the prelude to a tragedy which was to be reenacted many times in the course of history.

The municipal loans were somewhat better than the loans to rulers because municipal governments could sometimes be coërced to live up to their obligations by reprisals or by court action. Municipal governments in the Middle Ages were corporations—as they still are in the United States and in Great Britain—and all burghers were jointly liable for the debts of the community. Just as it was considered advisable to have the heir apparent ratify any promise made by a ruler, so it was deemed a safeguard to have all leading citizens put their seals to any document in which a municipal government assumed financial obligations. A splendid example of this practice is furnished by a charter dated December 14, 1328, in which the municipal authorities of Bruges acknowledged that they owed £20,000 *parisis* to Donato di Pacino de' Peruzzi, a partner of the Peruzzi Company, and promised to repay this sum in monthly installments of £333 6*s*. 8*d*. *parisis* covering a period of five years. To this document are appended the seals of no less than 316 persons: the *échevins* or aldermen, the *doyens* or deans of the forty-seven gilds, and a number of leading burghers.[42] It is true that the contract did not relate to an ordinary loan but to a penalty which had been imposed upon the city of Bruges for participation in the uprising of the *Flandre maritime*. The creditor, Donato de' Peruzzi, was at that time *receveur de Flandre*.[43] He had probably lent money to the count of Flanders to equip an army with which to quell the rebellion. When the rebels surrendered, after the crushing defeat of Cassel (August 23, 1328), the count assigned to his *receveur* the penalty of £20,000 *parisis* which was levied on the city of Bruges in accordance with the terms of the peace treaties of Arques and St André-lez-Bruges.[44]

The charter of December 14, 1328, presents some interesting features. It is stated that the loan does not involve any illicit covenants (*sans nulle vilaine convenanche faire*), but there is no doubt that interest was concealed in some way or other. The charter does not mention anywhere the sum that was actually advanced to the count of Flanders by his *receveur*. The installments were payable to the said Donato de' Peruzzi himself, or to his proxy, or to his agent who would be the bearer of the original obligation or of any transcript made under the seal of the *Châtelet de Paris* or any other authoritative seal.[45] Despite this provision the city of Bruges was asked to make out a new obligation when Donato de' Peruzzi transferred his claim, in 1331, to the Peruzzi Company of which he was a partner.[46] The loan had still two years to run and the new charter was made out for the balance of £8,000 *parisis* which remained to be paid.[47] Again, a number of citizens, 192 persons to be specific, including the two burgomasters, the twelve aldermen (*échevins*), and the twelve city councillors, were asked to append their seals to the contract.

After the battle of Cassel, peace was not disturbed for a few years, and the city of Bruges was able to meet the monthly installments. The receipts extant in the municipal archives and the Peruzzi account books show that the loan was fully repaid.

The second contract gave rise to a clerical error in the books of the Peruzzi Company. The factor in Bruges mistakingly wrote in his books that the transfer did not become effective until February 1333, instead of 1332. This matter was not adjusted until 1345, two years after the bankruptcy of the Peruzzi, when 933⅓ florins representing the equivalent of £560 *parisis* at the rate of 12*s. parisis* per florin, were written to the credit of Donato de' Peruzzi for one year's interest on £8,000 *parisis* at seven per cent.[48] It seems, therefore, probable that Donato de' Peruzzi borrowed money from his company and then lent it to the count of Flanders in his own name.

Not all creditors of the city of Bruges fared equally well. In 1379, the Lucchese merchant-bankers, Lazzaro Guinigi and Forteguerra di Forteguerra, lent three hundred pounds groat to the city of Bruges.[49] The increasing bitterness of the civil war which had just broken out soon interfered with the repayment of the loan. For many years the creditors tried to collect their claim, but their efforts were of no avail. After the restoration of peace in 1385, Forteguerra di Forteguerra and Lazzaro Guinigi finally came to terms with the municipal authorities. The debt was reduced to 1,864 francs, which were to be repaid within four years by installments of 116½ francs falling due four times a year, on the fifteenth of August, November, February, and May.[50] If the payment of any of these installments was delayed until the next became due, the contract gave the creditors the right to sue the city and the municipal officials personally for the entire balance which was still unpaid.

At certain times the city of Bruges was in such dire need of cash that the municipal authorities had to resort to all kinds of subterfuges. In the beginning of the fifteenth century, the city, on several occasions, bought pepper, silk, ginger, dyestuffs, woad, and other commodities on credit from Italian and Flemish merchants and resold these commodities for cash at a loss.[51] Although the city of Bruges was often hard pressed for money and was slow in repaying loans, her finances were managed much better during the fourteenth and fifteenth centuries than at the end of the thirteenth century. Ordinary expenses were usually met out of current income, but the extraordinary expenses caused by war, revolt, and penalties brought about deficits which made it necessary to contract loans.

At the end of the fourteenth, and the beginning of the fifteenth century, the Lucchese merchant-banker Dino Rapondi wielded considerable influence at the court of Philip the Bold and his son John the Fearless.[52] They often consulted him on monetary and financial matters. Dino Rapondi was apparently a man of great administrative ability who could keep the threads of his multifarious business activities well in hand. His financial career reached a climax when he brought to a successful conclusion the negotiations connected with the ransom of John the Fearless, Count of Nevers, who later became Duke of Burgundy. He was taken prisoner by the Turks at the disastrous battle of Nicopolis in 1396. The sultan demanded 200,000 florins. The payment of such a huge sum created a serious transfer problem. Dino Rapondi traveled for this purpose to Venice and arranged for the transfer of the ransom to the Turkish potentate by way of bills of exchange on Italian merchants in the Levant. These drafts were apparently covered by other bills drawn on Paris and Bruges. The merchants were eventually paid from the proceeds of a special tax levied on all the subjects of the duke of Burgundy. It is useless to try to describe these transactions in detail without more information than is at present available.

Dino Rapondi did not share the fate of a great many others who went bankrupt because of their loans to princes. One reason is probably that Rapondi lent only on good security and was careful not to become too deeply engaged. Another reason is that Philip the Bold and John the Fearless never became involved in a major war which would have forced them to default on the payment of both principal and interest.

One will recall that the partnership contract of 1455 did not allow the Medici branch in Bruges to extend credit to lords temporal or spiritual, including evidently the duke of Burgundy. The first breach in this policy was made in 1457, when both Tani and Portinari, the manager and the assistant manager of the Bruges branch, wrote to Florence for permission to sell silk on credit to the Court of Burgundy.[53] They insisted that the risk was about the same as on any other transaction ('perchè al pericholo si è circa tutto uno'), that they were now foregoing handsome profits, and that the purchases of the Court were substantial and would give plenty of work to 'those of the silk' (*chotesti della seta*), that is, the silk 'shop' of the Medici in Florence.

It is difficult to say where credit sales end and loans begin. The Court was such a good customer that the temptation was great to be lenient on terms. However, as long as Cosimo and Piero de' Medici lived, they tried to steer away from the dangerous course toward which Portinari was drifting. Piero de' Medici warned that loans 'to rulers involved more risk than profit,' and he stated that 'his policy was to keep what he had rather than to enrich himself still more by hazardous undertakings.'[54] Even before Piero's death in 1469, the affairs of the London branch had become hopelessly entangled because of excessive loans to Edward IV as well as to the supporters of the House of Lancaster.[55]

Lorenzo the Magnificent did not follow the cautious policy of his father and his grandfather. When the partnership contract of the Bruges branch was renewed in 1471, he took the fatal step of allowing Portinari to extend credit to Charles the Bold, but only up to £6,000 groat or twice the capital of the partnership, 'lest we be ruined as happened to Gherardo Canigiani [the manager of the London branch] and to many merchants of our nation in the past.' If Lorenzo was conscious of this peril, why did he allow Portinari to go ahead? Lorenzo felt that he had to acquiesce to Portinari's policy 'because of the qualities and virtues of this illustrious prince [Charles the Bold] and because of the favor which the said Portinari enjoyed at the Court and which placed him on a footing of familiarity with His Highness.'[56] If this was the real reason, it was a poor one. Lorenzo should not have fostered Portinari's ambition to play an important part in international diplomacy. One should consider, however, that the real reason for lending money to Charles the Bold may not have been explicitly stated.

In 1471, the Medici had become the leading members of a cartel which controlled all the most important deposits of alum in Western Europe and was trying to establish a monopoly by excluding from the market all rival products. In exchange for loans, the Medici expected Charles the Bold to promote the interests of the cartel and to help them eliminate competition by prohibiting the importation of Turkish alum into his dominions and by other measures. In these hopes the Medici were disappointed because the Duke was forced to consider the opposition of his subjects to the cartel's monopoly. The plans of the Medici miscarried in another respect: after they had made the loans, they were unable to enjoy their monopoly for more than a few years because they lost the farm of the papal alum mines at Tolfa as a result of the Pazzi conspiracy (1478) which brought Lorenzo into conflict with the pope.

At the next renewal of the articles of association, in 1473, the question of a maximum limit to government loans was dropped, and Portinari was given a free hand. When Charles the Bold died in battle in 1476, he owed to the Bruges branch of the Medici the considerable sum of £57,000 Artois of forty groats each, or £9,500 groat.[57] This sum was more than thrice the capital invested by the partners in the Bruges branch of the Medici bank. Portinari had been financing the ambitious schemes of Charles the Bold on a grand scale! In the next years an additional sum of £20,000 Artois was lent to Mary of Burgundy and her impecunious husband Maximilian of Austria in order to save the Burgundian state from utter destruction by Louis XI and to prevent a financial catastrophe.

The loans to the government certainly cut into the financial resources which were available for other purposes. The loss of working capital was further aggravated by the failure of the court to meet its interest payments and by the withdrawal of deposits. In 1478, the financial condition of the Bruges branch of the Medici bank was so serious that Lorenzo took alarm. He sent an emissary to Bruges and forced Portinari to liquidate the share of the Medici and to take over the branch in his own name.[58] For a time Portinari tried to carry on but he soon had to give up, because he found himself assailed by creditors, without working capital and with uncollectible claims on the Burgundian court as his only assets.[59] Maximilian finally assigned to him gratuitously the toll of Gravelines which was a very important source of revenue because of its location at the gates of Calais—the staple for English wool. But the income from the toll extinguished the frozen credits very slowly. In 1488, Tommaso Portinari was forced to sell his rights to his nephews Benedetto and Folco Portinari in order to obtain ready cash.[60] He also transferred to them his claim on the Hansa for the captured galley carrying Memling's 'Last Judgment,' an affair which had been pending before the courts since 1473 and was not to be settled until 1499.[61] Tommaso Portinari died in 1501 in the Hospital of Santa Maria Nuova in Florence to which he had given the famous triptych by Hugo van der Goes.

The catastrophic liquidation of the Bruges branch of the Medici bank has been blamed on Lorenzo the Magnificent. It has been pointed out that he was a man of letters, a patron of the arts, a great statesman, but a poor business man. 'Fu,' wrote Machiavelli, 'quanto alla mercanzia infelicissimo' ('in business he had no luck').[62] It seems that this view is only partly correct. The blame should certainly be shared by Francesco Sassetti who, as the general manager of the Medici bank, was the close adviser of Piero and Lorenzo de' Medici in all business matters.[63] Sassetti, it is certain, failed to control the policy of the branch managers and followed their lead instead of giving them guidance.

The mistake made by the Medici was not due to the fact that they were confronted with a novel situation. Among merchants it was generally known that loans to princes were perilous. In 1399 the Mannini, a firm of Italian merchant-bankers with offices in London and Bruges, were forced to liquidate after the fall of Richard II to whom they had lent money. In a letter to Datini's *fondaco* or branch in Barcelona, the Orlandini of Bruges commented as follows: 'No one ever becomes embroiled with great lords without losing his feathers in the end.'[64] In a Florentine document of 1424, a merchant complained that his agents had sold silk to the brother of the king of Aragon but could not obtain payment. He added philosophically: 'Well, you know how these lords are.'[65] Another to whom the Emperor was indebted stated bluntly that 'there is no worse payer than the Emperor.'[66]

Any study of the Italian merchant-bankers in Bruges is greatly hampered by the absence of business records. Of the account books of the Medici branch, only a few pages from one ledger have survived. The Borromei bank maintained a branch in Bruges during the greater part of the fifteenth century. Several ledgers and other material of great interest were until recently in the possession of the family. In August 1943, during one of the air raids on Milan, the old Borromei palace was hit by an incendiary bomb and burned to the ground. All the collections, including the family archives, were destroyed.[67] The loss of the Borromei papers is a grievous one because the records were nearly complete for the fifteenth century. The Italian historian Gerolamo Biscaro, who had access to them, published some excerpts from the London ledgers but left the Bruges material untouched. Even so, Biscaro's article is extremely interesting. It has unfortunately not received the notice that it deserves. The State Archives in Ghent contain several account books of the Gallerani Company of Siena from the early fourteenth century. This material was almost ready for publication when the editor, the Belgian historian Georges Bigwood, suddenly died. His widow turned the manuscript over to a Belgian archivist who, for some unexplained reason, has made no headway with the publication of the text.[68] In the absence of fairly complete records of a typical firm, a detailed picture of the activity of the merchant-bankers can be obtained only by piecing together little bits of information found in scattered sources. The final result is not very satisfactory, but it is impossible to do better for the present.

As this study is primarily devoted to banking, little or no attention has been paid to the commercial dealings of the merchant-bankers. It is important to bear in mind that banking was only one aspect of their many-sided business. Trade came first, banking was next, commission and agency were often scarcely less important, and shipping and underwriting were usually a poor fourth. In the Middle Ages, there was as yet little or no specialization. A merchant-banker could easily switch his capital from banking to trade, and from trade to banking. The diversity of interests of the mediaeval merchants has been emphasized by Professor N. S. B. Gras in his recent description of the activities of the 'sedentary merchant.'[69] The available information on the Italian merchant-bankers in Bruges plainly confirms the truth of his description.

The financial undertakings of Dino Rapondi have already been mentioned in connection with the ransom of John the Fearless, but the variety of his other interests is astonishing, even in an age when diversity was the dominant characteristic of the merchant. Rapondi had several offices: one in Bruges, another in Paris, and a third in Avignon.[70] He supplied the courts of France and of Burgundy with all kinds of luxury articles, including illuminated manuscripts. To the duke of Burgundy he sold a copy of the *Légende dorée* for five hundred gold écus, another volume for four hundred écus, and a French Bible for six hundred écus.[71] Dino Rapondi was evidently in touch with the best illuminators of his time. The city of Bruges bought from him gold cloth which was presented to the duchess of Burgundy. He also supplied the city with two silver pitchers and twelve cups made to order in Paris for the same purpose.[72] To Yolande of Flanders, Lady of Cassel and Countess of Bar, a member of the ruling family, Rapondi sold oranges, sugar, ginger, cinnamon, cloves, and other spices in small quantities of ten pounds or less.[73] She also entrusted him with more delicate and confidential matters such as the settlement of her accounts with the lombards or Italian pawnbrokers of Bruges. Rapondi even proved to be a contractor and a military engineer: he supervised the building of a stronghold which the duke of Burgundy decided to erect at Sluys, the seaport of Bruges.[74]

The Medici were not any more specialized than the Rapondi or other firms of merchant-bankers. The surviving fragment of the ledger of the Medici in Bruges shows that they were interested in an amazing variety of business ventures and were careful to divide their risks whenever they enjoyed no monopolistic advantages over their competitors. The fragment contains one entry after another relating to the purchase, the sale, the collection, or the payment of bills—which proves the importance of exchange dealings. Some of the accounts represent balances held in Bruges for correspondents abroad; others represent balances held abroad by foreign correspondents. Besides these interbank accounts, the fragment contains several accounts concerning lots of pepper, almonds, turnsole, sugar, and Florentine cloth. Only a few of these lots had been bought by the Medici of Bruges for their own account and were their exclusive property. A number of lots had been acquired jointly by two branches of the Medici bank or by a branch in association with outsiders. One of these joint ventures had as many as four partners. The Medici had no interest at all in several consignments and were selling them on a commission basis. For example, there were three or four different lots of pepper: one had been bought by the Medici of Bruges for their own account, another belonged jointly to the Medici branches in Bruges and in Venice, a third was sold on commission for the latter, and a fourth had been consigned to the Bruges branch by an outsider and was being sold for his account at the best price obtainable. The same was true of almonds and other commodities. Diversification was the dominant consideration in business policy.

Although the Medici were the greatest foreign bankers of their time, the emphasis in their business was on trade rather than on banking. As late as 1464, Portinari made this significant statement in a letter to Cosimo de' Medici:

> The foundation of our business is in merchandise which absorbs most of our capital so that there is little left for dealings in exchange. It seems to me that trade today is no more hazardous than exchanges, especially if we do not run any risk by sea; nor is trade less profitable. And dealing in commodities is certainly more honorable than dealing in bills of exchange.[75]

Perhaps Portinari had a somewhat guilty conscience about certain deals involving dry exchange and other doubtful practices!

Although the Medici emphasized trade rather than finance, they called themselves bankers and are described as such in contemporary sources. The main office of the Medici in Florence is always referred to as a 'bank.'[76] According to the chronicler Benedetto Dei, there were in Florence in 1472, thirty-three *banchi grossi* ('large banks') which dealt in bills of exchange and in commodities (*e chanbiano e fanno merchantia*).[77] This combination is highly significant. In the Middle Ages a merchant-banker was always a person who was at the same time a dealer in exchange and a dealer in commodities.

NOTES TO CHAPTER 5

[1]Prato, Datini Archives, No. 753: Fondaco di Genova, Carteggio da Bruggia, Letter of Giovanni Orlandini and Piero Benizi & Co. to Datini & Co. in Genoa, May 3, 1399.

[2]*Ibid.*, No. 853: Fondaco di Barcellona, Carteggio da Bruggia, II, Orlandini to Datini & Co., in Barcelona, July 31, 1399. The expression *intorno al usato* is often used in the Orlandini letters. The Venetian galleys had actually arrived in Sluys the day before, on July 30, 1399.

[3]*Ibid.*, No. 753: Orlandini to Datini in Genoa, August 2, 1399.

[4]*Ibid.*, Letter of September 27, 1399.

[5]*Ibid.*, Letter of November 26, 1399: 'Le spezie si stanno qui molto frede e pocho richieste; e per la charestia che c'è di danari, chi a chontanti volese chonperare n'arebbe buono merchato.'

[6]*Ibid.*, No. 854: Fondaco di Barcellona, Carteggio da Bruggia, III, Orlandini to Datini in Barcelona, March 29, 1400.

[7]*Ibid.*, No. 753: Diamante e Altobianco degli Alberti in Bruges to Datini in Genoa, March 31, 1400: 'Qui si fa pochissimo al presente e le spezie sono in bassi pregi; è perchè nulla si domanda, a' danari c'è dovizia.'

[8]*Ibid.*, No. 854: 'Qui è larghezza di danari ma più non li debbe potere alarghare ma faranno il chontrario . . . e troverete innanzi che sia maggio i danari faranno vertù di qua e lodiamo la rimessa a buoni pregi, perchè dopo la larghezza viene la strettezza.'

[9]Uzzano, *op. cit.*, pp. 152 ff.: 'Regole da tenersi nel rimettere e trar danari,' Cf. Florence, Biblioteca Nazionale, Codice Panciatichiano, No. 71 [1418], fol. 20^r.

[10]The exchange rates, of course, oscillated around the par, and the exchange-dealers certainly were not ignorant of this rule. In 1441, the Medici of Bruges paid a special courier who was sent from Venice to Bruges to bring the news of a debasement of the currency, presumably in Venice. Florence, State Archives, Mediceo avanti il Principato, filza 134, No. 2, fol. 241. The principle of the specie points was also understood, and the merchant-bankers knew that, beyond a certain point, it became profitable either to import or to export specie. Cf. Uzzano, *op. cit.*, p. 152.

[11]The author of a recent book on the history of economic doctrines actually uses the expression 'the prehistory of economics' in the title of his chapter dealing with economic thought before Adam Smith. Less than one paragraph is devoted to the doctrines of Thomas Aquinas and his followers. Out of charity I shall refrain from giving my reference. There is no excuse for such a contemptuous attitude toward the Middle Ages. It only betrays the ignorance of the author on mediaeval developments.

[12]Datini Archives, No. 853: Orlandini to Datini in Barcelona, October 1, 1399. Alberto degli Alberti to the same, October 2, 1399: 'Facianvi solo questa per avisarvi chome qui si chomincia a paghare di danari contanti dove prima si paghava di scritta ma se si pagherà d'oro o di biancha moneta non si sa. . . .' Orlandini to the same, October 4, 1399: 'A dì 2 di questo fu chomandato per la loia di qui [the municipal authorities of Bruges] a tutti merchanti che di lettere di chanbio e de' chanbi che si facino caschuno paghi di chontanti, e non più di scritta ne di poliza, e non si pagha però che di biancha moneta. . . .' *Pagare di scritta* means 'to pay by transfer in bank,' Such transfer orders were commonly given by word of mouth. *Polizza* evidently refers to a written order similar to the modern check. The ordinance applied both to payments in settlement of bills issued abroad and to payments connected with the creation of bills payable abroad, as the Orlandini letter explicitly states.

[13]*Ibid.*, No. 753: Orlandini to Datini in Genoa, October 16, November 20, November 26, and December 17, 1399.

[14]*Ibid.*, Orlandini to Datini in Genoa, November 26, 1399.

[15]*Ibid.*, Orlandini to Datini in Genoa, January 14, 1400 (n.s.).

[16]The date of the ordinance is given in a letter written by the Orlandini to Datini's Barcelona branch (Datini Archives, No. 853), February 20 (?), 1400 (n.s.). 'All foreign ex-

changes' refers to the purchase of a bill made out in Bruges as well as to the payment at maturity of a bill drawn on Bruges from abroad. The expression used is *tutti i chanbi.*

[17]*Ibid.*, No. 753: Orlandini to Datini in Genoa, February 21, 1400.

[18]*Ibid.*, No. 853: Orlandini to Datini in Barcelona, February 26, 1400.

[19]For example, the official rate of the English noble was set at seventy-two groats as late as July 30, 1400. In England the noble circulated at 6*s*. 8*d*. sterling, or 80 sterlings. According to the official rate in Flanders, 72 groats were thus equal to 80 sterlings. This equation gives a value of $26\frac{2}{3}$ sterlings to the écu of 24 groats. Actually the exchange rate was only $25\frac{5}{12}$ sterlings per écu on September 20, 1399, which shows that the noble was underrated in Flanders. According to the prevailing rate of exchange, the English noble was actually worth 75.5 groats. It is not surprising that no nobles were circulating in Flanders. In November, 1399, the exchange rate rose to 27 sterlings which probably made the importation of nobles profitable, but the premium on gold was included in the rate of exchange. According to the letters of Datini's correspondents in Bruges, some nobles and other gold coins were actually imported from London and Paris.

The official rate of the noble is taken from Louis Deschamps de Pas, *Essai sur l'histoire monétaire des comtes de Flandre de la maison de Bourgogne* (Paris, 1863), p. xx, No. 100. This volume is a reprint of a series of articles published in the *Revue Numismatique,* but the book contains a calendar of documents which was not published in the journal. As far as I know the only copy of the book available in this country is in the New York Public Library.

[20]The merchants expected the ordinance to be repealed eventually. Datini Archives, No. 854: Guglielmo Barberi to Datini in Barcelona, May 5, 1400: 'Non ciè persona che donni ne pigli.' Cf. Orlandini to the same, May 18, 1400.

[21]*Ibid.*, Letters of June 2, 7, and 15, 1400.

[22]*Ibid.*, Orlandini to Datini in Barcelona, July 1, 1400, with a postscript dated July 3.

[23]*Ibid.*, Letter of July 30, 1400.

[24]*Ibid.*, Orlandini to Datini in Barcelona, October 11, 1400.

[25]*Ibid.*, No. 753: Orlandini to Datini in Genoa, January 6, 1401 (n.s.).

[26]*Ibid.*, No. 854: Orlandini to Datini in Barcelona, February 26, 1401.

[27]*Ibid.*, No. 753: Orlandini to Datini in Genoa, March 5 and April 9, 1401.

[28]*Ibid.* Domenico Caccini and Piero Cambini, the Orlandini representatives in London, who happened to be in Bruges, made these comments in a letter addressed to Datini's branch in Genoa and dated May 11, 1401.

[29]*Ibid.*, Diamante e Altobianco degli Alberti in Bruges to Datini in Genoa, September 4, 1401.

[30]Gilliodts-van Severen, *Cart. de l'Estaple,* I, 478-79, No. 583, and *Coutume de Bruges,* I, 455-57, No. LVIII.

[31]Gottfried Pusch, *Staatliche Münz- und Geldpolitik in den Niederlanden unter den Burgundischen und Habsburgischen Herrschern besonders unter Kaiser Karl V* (doctoral dissertation, Munich, 1932), p. 70; Florence Edler, 'The Effects of the Financial Measures of Charles V on the Commerce of Antwerp, 1539-1542.' *RBPH,* XVI (1937), 671; *idem,* 'The van der Molen, Commission-Merchants of Antwerp: Trade with Italy, 1538-44,' *Medieval and Historiographical Essays in Honor of James Westfall Thompson,* eds. James L. Cate and Eugene N. Anderson (Chicago, 1938), p. 123.

[32]Fictitious exchange was a form of dry exchange and it is difficult to distinguish between the two. See Endemann, *Studien,* I, 144.

[33]In cases of dry exchange, the first bill usually contained the clause *pagate a voi medesimi.* The redraft or second bill usually mentioned that it had been issued *per la valuta ricevuta da noi medesimi.* All bills containing one of these two clauses, however, did not necessarily originate in dry exchange.

[34]A full description of these three cases with an illustrative diagram will be found in my article, 'What is Dry Exchange,' *op. cit.,* pp. 262-64. The entries in the ledger show plainly that the profit of the Medici in Venice arose from the difference between the rate of the ducat

in Venice and in Bruges and did not originate in interest charges. This point is absolutely beyond dispute. The account of Antonio del Conte is published in my book on the Medici Bank, Appendix VI, pp. 82-85.

[35]Gilliodts, *Inventaire,* III, 248, 287, 289, 396, 397, 527; IV, 45, 49, 63 f.; Bigwood, *Régime,* I, 124-31; Mirot, 'La société des Raponde,' *op. cit.,* p. 372.

[36]Louis Gilliodts-van Severen in his article, 'La lettre de change, son emploi à Bruges au moyen âge et dans les siècles suivants,' (*La Flandre,* XI [1880], p. 331) quotes a court decision of 1441 in order to prove that bills were not only discounted but also endorsed. The text of this court decision, which was published by Heinrich Brunner ('Brügger Schöffensprüche zur Geschichte des Wechselrechts im fünfzehnten Jahrhundert,' *op. cit.,* pp. 22-24) does not mention endorsement and concerns a legal claim in connection with a bill which was paid twice: once by the payor and the second time by the drawer to whom a copy had been returned after protest. Gilliodts also asserts that protested bills were productive of interest, but the French word *intérêts* as used in the expression *dommages et intérêts* means compensation for damages and not interest or usury (Gilliodts, 'La lettre de change,' *op. cit.,* p. 333). This article of Gilliodts is entirely unreliable.

[37]Several examples of cash discounts for early payment are given by Sapori, 'La cultura del mercante medievale italiano,' *op. cit.,* pp. 99-100, esp. n. 43.

[38]Examples of such letters of credit are given by Bensa, *Francesco di Marco,* p. 323, No. XVI (to a cardinal), No. XVII (to a student); p. 325, No. XIX (to a traveler), No. XX (to the cardinal of Ravenna); p. 327, No. XXII (to a doctor of law), No. XXIII (to a student in canon law).

[39]According to these figures the dean paid 51 groats per ducat.

[40]Florence, States Archives, Mediceo avanti il Principato, No. 134 (2), fol. 245. On Dean Fabri, see Floris Prims, 'Heer Anselmus Fabri, onze tiende deken (1415-1449),' *Antwerpiensia, losse bijdragen tot de Antwerpsche geschiedenis,* XI (1937), 19-26.

[41]For example, the Mannini, important merchant-bankers in Bruges and in England, wrote to Genoa that they did not want to commit themselves beyond a certain sum in granting credit to the same taker: 'Perchè noi siamo datori di qua ogni dì, espezialmente per costì e non vogliamo che a nesuna compagnia di genovesi che qui sieno, diate danari a cambio per noi nè per nostra compagnia, perchè non vogliamo essere se non a una certa somma, e dando voi costì et noi qui e a Londra verano a essere tropo grossi.' Datini Archives, No. 753: Letter dated October 7, 1397.

[42]Gilliodts, *Inventaire,* I, 389-99, charter No. 323.

[43]*Ibid.,* p. 389, No. 322. In this charter Louis de Nevers, Count of Flanders, refers to 'Donat de la Peruche, son receveur en Flandre.' Cf. *ibid.,* p. 401, No. 327; pp. 413-14, No. 338.

[44]*Ibid.,* p. 428, n. 1; cf. Henri Pirenne, *Histoire de Belgique,* II (3d ed., Brussels, 1922), 94-100.

[45]Gilliodts, *Inventaire,* I, 390, No. 323.

[46]He is listed among the partners of the *ragione* of 1324 and of the subsequent *ragioni* of 1331 and 1335. See Sapori, 'Storia interna,' *op. cit.,* pp. 22-24.

[47]Gilliodts, *Inventaire,* I, 428-34, charter No. 357.

[48]*Libri de' Peruzzi,* ed. Sapori, pp. 164, 274-75.

[49]Gilliodts, *Inventaire,* II, 347. For a biography of Forteguerra, see Léon Mirot, 'Etudes lucquoises: V. Forteguerra Forteguerra et sa succession,' *Bibliothèque de l'Ecole des Chartes,* XCVI (1935), 301-37. This study contains very little that is of value to economic historians.

[50]Bruges, Municipal Archives, Chartes politiques, 1e série, No. 1307, Obligation No. 26.

[51]Gilliodts, *Inventaire,* IV, 49-51, 62-63, 423-25. Cf. Bigwood, *Régime,* I, 132-44. The same practice was followed by other cities, for example, Genoa.

[52]The facts about Rapondi's career are given in considerable detail by Mirot, 'La société des Raponde,' *op. cit.,* pp. 299-389.

[53]Angelo Tani and Tommaso Portinari to Cosimo de' Medici, February 19, 1458. Grunzweig, *Correspondance,* I, 73.

[54]Sieveking, *Handlungsbücher der Medici*, p. 50: '. . . vuol essere molto maggiore pericolo che l'utile. . . . Nostra intenzione è trafficharé per conservare quanto abiamo di substanzie, credito e honore più tosto che volere pericolosamente cerchare d'arichire più.'

[55]Grunzweig, *Correspondance*, I, xxviii-xxix.

[56]Sieveking, *Handlungsbücher der Medici*, p. 52: '. . . attesa la virtù e bontà di quello illustrissimo principe e la grazia e familiarità del sopradetto Thommaso Portinari con la sua Illustrissima Signoria e sua chorte ed eziando i beneficii ricevuti.'

[57]Bigwood, *Régime*, I, 89, 470, 663.

[58]Grunzweig, *Correspondance*, I, xxxii-xxxiv; Sieveking, *Handlungsbücher der Medici*, pp. 53-54.

[59]The documents seem to indicate that this description is entirely accurate. See, for instance, Portinari's lawsuit with the heirs of Tommaso Soderini who had 4,204 1/2 ducats invested in the former Bruges branch of the Medici bank. The heirs of Soderini claimed that the 4,204 1/2 ducats were a deposit, repayable after four months' notice, but Portinari maintained that the said sum represented a share in the capital and profits of his company. —Gilliodts, *Cart. de l'Estaple*, II, 260, No. 1240: *Heirs of Tommaso Soderini* v. *Tommaso Portinari*, September 11, 1487.

Concerning the loss of working capital, the following text is especially significant: '. . . avecq le grand et insupportable dommage qu'il a eu d'avoir délaissé et abandonné entièrement son négoce, lequel estoit par lui autant exercé et fréquenté que par quelque autre marchand de toutes les nations d'Italie ou d'autres.' The date of this text is January 6, 1488.—L. Gilliodts-van Severen (ed.), *Cartulaire de l'ancien grand tonlieu de Bruges*, I (Bruges, 1908), 343-45.

[60]Grunzweig, *Correspondance*, I, xxxvii-xxxix.

[61]Meltzing, 'Tommaso Portinari und sein Konflikt mit der Hanse,' *op. cit.*, pp. 101-24; Florence Edler de Roover, 'A Prize of War,' *op. cit.*, pp. 3-11.

[62]Niccolò Machiavelli, *Istorie fiorentine*, ed. Plinio Carli (Florence, 1927), II, 218.

[63]Florence Edler de Roover, 'Francesco Sassetti and the Downfall of the Medici Banking House,' *op. cit.*, 65-80; A. Warburg, 'Francesco Sassettis letzwillige Verfügung,' *Gesammelte Schriften* (Leipzig, 1932), I, 130.

[64]Datini Archives, No. 853: Orlandini to Datini in Barcelona, October 4, 1399: '. . . ma niuno s'impaccio mai chon singniori che poi alla fine non vi rimetta le penne.'

[65]Heinrich Sieveking, *Aus Genueser Rechnungs- und Steuerbüchern: ein Beitrag zur mittelalterlichen Handels- und Vermögensstatistik* ('Sitzungsberichte der Kais. Akademie der Wissenschaften in Wien, Philosophisch-Historische Klasse,' Vol. CLXII, No. 2; Vienna, 1909), pp. 94-95: 'Dichono vendevano al fratello del re una parte, e non si possono avere. Sapete chome fanno questi signori!'

[66]*Ibid.*, p. 95: '. . . perchè chome sapete, lui [l'imperatore] è chativissimo paghatore.'

[67]According to a letter which I have received from Professor Tommaso Zerbi of Milan, who was working in the Borromei archives when the disaster occurred. Some of his notes were burned, too, but he had others at home. He hopes that he will be able to publish the result of his research tragically interrupted by the fire. I am sorry to state that the Borromei family did not like to be reminded of its mercantile origins and discouraged research in the family archives.

[68]Ghent, State Archives, Varia III, 239, 239*bis*, and Varia D, 3109, 3116, 3117.

[69]Gras, *Business and Capitalism*, pp. 67-119.

[70]Mirot, 'La société des Raponde,' *op. cit.*, p. 318.

[71]*Ibid.*, p. 342.

[72]Gilliodts, *Inventaire*, III, 118, 121, 262, 263, 264, 298.

[73]Mirot, 'La société des Raponde,' *op. cit.*, p. 320, n.3.

[74]*Ibid.*, pp. 349-353.

[75]Grunzweig, *Correspondance*, I, 131.

[76]In 1458 the Medici declared that they had 5,600 florins invested 'in the bank of Florence'

(*nel bancho di Firenze*) as their share in the *corpo* or capital (Sieveking, *Handlungsbücher der Medici,* p. 9). A Flemish document of 1473 mentions Portinari as the representative of the Medici 'bank' in Bruges ('Portner van Florente van der banck van Medicis bynnen Brugge residerende'). Max Neumann, *Geschichte des Wuchers in Deutschland bis zur Begründung der heutigen Zinsengesetze, 1654* (Halle, 1865), p. 370.

[77]Pagnini, *Della Decima,* II, 275.

PART II

THE LOMBARDS OR 'CAHORSINS'

Chapter 6

THE LEGAL STATUS OF LICENCED USURY

DURING the Middle Ages the merchant-bankers were not the only Italians established in Flanders who were concerned with finance and money-lending. For the sake of completeness, we should include the Italians who had loan offices, pawnshops, or *tables de prêt,* in a number of cities and towns. These were commonly called 'lombards' or 'cahorsins.'

In the Bruges records these two words are treated as synonyms and are sometimes used jointly as equivalent expressions.[1] Whereas there is no doubt about the etymology of the term 'lombard,' that of 'cahorsin' or 'caursin,' is one of those puzzles on which historians have wasted a great deal of ink without reaching any certainty.[2] Some believe that the word 'cahorsin,' in the meaning of usurer, lombard, or money-lender, owes its origin to the fact that merchants of Cahors, a small town in southwestern France, played quite a prominent role as traders—and to some extent as financiers— in the early Middle Ages.[3] But this fact does not explain why the name 'cahorsin' became identified with 'usurer.' Other surmises with regard to the etymology of 'cahorsin' are even more hypothetical. Although this problem is interesting, it is not important for our purpose. It is sufficient to know that 'lombard' and 'cahorsin' convey one and the same meaning and can be used interchangeably.

The lombards made their appearance in Flanders during the last quarter of the thirteenth century, that is to say, at about the same time that the big Italian houses began to establish branches in Bruges. As we have seen, the arrival of these newcomers corresponded to the disappearance of the system based on the traveling merchant and its replacement by an entirely different organization of international trade.[4] The penetration of the lombards into Flanders was only one of many aspects of this 'commercial revolution.'

In order to avoid any misunderstanding, let us state at once that money-lending and especially pawnbroking was the main business of the lombards. As the mediaeval church was violent in its condemnation of usury, the pursuit of such a profession was considered evil and was subject to severe repression according to both the canon and the secular law. This situation had important legal consequences.[5]

Like the other Italians established in Flanders, the lombards or cahorsins were foreigners—but foreigners who were tolerated rather than privileged. They were not allowed to follow their calling peacefully without a license or special permit to do so. Even thus provided, their position remained precarious and was in many ways comparable to that of the Jews. The lombards in Flanders as elsewhere lived in constant fear of a sudden reversion to repressive methods and under the permanent threat of expulsion and of spoliation.[6] They succeeded most of the time, it is true, in warding off those threats by placing themselves, as was customary in feudal times, under the direct protection of the ruling prince: king, duke, or count, as the case might be. It is almost needless to add that such protection could not be obtained without giving something in exchange, either a loan or, more often, the payment of an annual fee.

In Flanders the lombards were granted their first charters in 1281 by the count, Gui de Dampierre, who was hard pressed by the needs of an empty treasury. They were consequently allowed to settle in the three *chefs-villes* or principal cities of Bruges, Ghent, and Ypres and in half a score of smaller towns, such as Alost, Dixmude, Ardenbourg, Furnes, and so forth.[7] In Douai, lombards had gained a foothold as early as 1247 but they had vanished before the end of the century and they did not reappear until 1373.[8] In contrast with the merchant-bankers and their representatives who could only be found in Bruges and in a few important manufacturing centers, the lombards swooped down like vultures upon even small communities. In the absence of other evidence, this fact alone would indicate that not the honorable practice of international trade but the sordid pursuit of usury is the explanation for their presence.

The charters granted by the Count of Flanders, Gui de Dampierre, in 1281 were among the first of a long series of similar documents which he and his heirs, the rulers of the other provinces, and, later, the sovereigns of the united Low Countries were in the habit of granting to the lombards until they were irrevocably expelled at the beginning of the seventeenth century, when their place was taken by the newly organized *monts de piété*. These charters of the Belgian rulers vary, of course, somewhat in detail but exhibit at the same time a striking degree of uniformity on all essential points. As time goes on, their provisions gain in clarity, precision, and completeness; the differences tend to fade away and they disappear completely after the unification of the Low Countries under the House of Burgundy. This growing comprehensiveness and uniformity is probably attributable to the fact that the charters were drafted in accordance with the requests presented by the lombards themselves and it was evidently to their advantage to provide against every possible contingency, as experience revealed loopholes and gaps. The result, at any rate, was the steady elaboration of a uniform body of law with regard to the lombards and the licenced practice of usury.[9]

A considerable number of the charters granted to the lombards by the counts of Flanders, the kings of France, and other princes are still extant and quite a few have been published.[10] With the exception of some minor gaps, this statement applies also to the grants concerning Bruges. From these extant grants and from other sources the names of the principal grantees are well known.[11] The first lombards of Bruges were Jakemon de Calochs (Jacomo di Caloccio) and Centurin de Montfaucon (Centurino di Montefalcone) who received a licence on February 28, 1281.[12] In 1307-1308 the municipal accounts mention a certain Bernière de Calots or de Calochs, probably a relative of the earlier lombard of that name.[13] A few years later, in 1311-1316, Jacques Puyele and his partners are referred to as the owners of the pawnshop.[14] In 1333 ownership passed for twelve years into the hands of an association which included representatives of the families Garet or Garetti, Royer or Roerio, and Deal. These three families remain in control until at least 1380.[15] After an interruption during which there was no licenced pawnshop in Bruges, the Royers alone reappeared as proprietors around 1400. In 1405 their charter was extended for fifteen years.[16] In 1420 the Royers were succeeded by a partnership of which the members were Pol Machet, Jean Machet (Macetti), George du Solier (Solari), and a certain Frederic Casul. Their grant was renewed in 1432, but with some changes in membership. This time the partnership was composed of Jean du Solier, his son George, and four brothers: Paul, Jean, Nicolas, and Dimanche (Domenico) Machet.[17] They retained ownership of the pawnshop until 1457 when the Machet went bankrupt.[18]

The last licencees were Oudenin de Ville and Gabriel du Solier who had been granted a charter for twenty years in 1480, but left Bruges in 1492, probably because of the city's decline.[19] From then onward, there was no licenced pawnshop in Bruges. Its disappearance must have cleared the way for a resurgence of surreptitious usury. The resulting evils probably prompted the authorities to establish a *mont-de-piété* as early as 1572, or forty years before such institutions became general in the Low Countries.[20]

It should be noted that none of the great Italian merchant families are listed among the grantees of the *table de prêt* or pawnshop of Bruges. On the contrary, these grantees, without a single exception, belong to clans of professional usurers who were scattered all over Western Europe and whose home towns were Asti and Chieri in Piedmont.[21]

In Bruges the lombards were careful to have the count's charter confirmed by the municipal council, that is, by the burgomasters and *échevins* or aldermen of the city. This was an exceptional procedure because, in the Low Countries, the granting of licences to lombards was deemed a princely prerogative which did not require the approval of local authorities.[22] Between these municipal licences and those of the count, there is sometimes a slight discrepancy as to dates, but this fact does not seem to have any practical importance. A more important result of having dual grants was that this system entailed payment of a double annual fee, one to the count and another to the city.[23]

The first grants, those of 1281, had been made by the Count Gui de

Dampierre in exchange for loans, amounting to 1,400 *livres,* money of Flanders, for the Bruges grant and to lesser sums for the other towns.[24] The grants were to be valid for a minimum of six years, and thereafter until complete repayment of the loans.[25] This method was discontinued after a few years, when it was deemed preferable to impose upon the lombards the payment of an annual fee. Along with the domain, the tolls, and the courts of justice, the lombards thus became a permanent source of revenue to the Count. The yearly fee which they paid to the city also appears regularly among the receipts in the municipal accounts, of which there is an almost complete set for the fourteenth and fifteenth centuries.

The amount of the fee was determined in each licence and remained unchanged for the duration of the grant. In case of renewal, of course, the amount could be adjusted upward or downward. It is very likely that this gave rise each time to a great deal of higgling and haggling. The presence or absence of competitors, past profit records of the pawnshop, expectations of good or bad trade, and bargaining ability and shrewdness on the part of the lombards were probably the factors which ultimately determined the amount of the fee.

According to the municipal accounts, Bernière de Calochs and his partner paid in 1308 £133 6*s*. 8*d*. *parisis* to the city of Bruges, not including, of course, the claim of the Count of Flanders.[26] In 1310 the fee apparently soared to £400 par. but fell back in 1315 to £144 par.[27] After 1360, it was increased to £216 par. and stayed at this level for many years.[28] In 1391, probably as a result of the return to the *monnaie forte,* the fee was lowered to £172 16*s*. par.[29] but in 1396 it was raised again and set at £288 par. or £24 groat.[30] This figure remained unchanged for almost half a century.[31] Not until 1454 was it moved up to £30 gr. or £360 par.[32] Another increase occurred in 1479; this time the fee was advanced to £400 par. or £33 6*s*. 8*d*. groat.[33]

As for the annual payment to the count of Flanders, there is little information available on the subject. In 1404, when the lombards paid £24 gr. to the city, the count received £30 gr.[34]

If consideration is given to the purchasing power of money, these fees which the lombards were under obligation to pay both to the count and to the city represented quite substantial amounts. It is only fair to assume that the lombards received in return equally substantial advantages and privileges. It will, therefore, be worthwhile to examine in more detail what those privileges were.

First of all, the count and the municipal authorities allowed the lombards to settle in Bruges and to maintain whatever establishments were necessary for their business.[35] In other words, they were given a permit of residence. As the lombards' business of money-lending was an illegal occupation, this authorization, in and by itself, was a big favor. However, one should not forget that the authorities were inclined to consider the establishment of licenced money-lenders as a lesser evil and as a means of keeping in check the more dangerous activities of clandestine usurers.[36] In many respects, the situation was not unlike that which prevails in certain countries where licenced houses are tolerated as a means of protection against uncontrolled prostitution.

In the second place, the count of Flanders and the municipal authorities declared that they took the lombards under their 'safeguard, secure protection, and loyal defense.'[37] Moreover, this protection extended not only to the person of the grantees but also to their partners, the members of their households, and all their property.[38] This protection should not be understood to mean only the sort of protection given by the courts or by the police and to which all the inhabitants of a given country or city were entitled. In the case under discussion, the protection is of a more active sort and akin to some kind of guardianship. As a matter of fact, in the duchy of Brabant, the lombards, together with the religious orders and the Jews, were considered as the wards of the duke who had promised to protect them even against papal bulls and imperial edicts.[39]

As early as 1281, Gui de Dampierre, Count of Flanders, declared in a charter granted to the lombards of Ghent that he extended over them his wardship and protection (*à nostre warde et en nostre protection*).[40] There is thus nothing exceptional in the legal status of the lombards of Bruges. As elsewhere, they were placed under the guardianship of the prince. Of course, this safeguard was not worth much in case the prince himself broke his pledged word. But in all other circumstances, it was a shield against arbitrary action and interference on the part of other authorities and, in particular, of the Church.

The grants not only placed the lombards under the high protection of the count, but went further and bestowed upon them some rights of citizenship. In the municipal licences of 1404 and 1432, the magistracy declared that they recognized the lombards as, and held them for, burghers.[41] Does this mean that they enjoyed full citizenship? Probably not. All that the authorities meant and intended was that they would treat the lombards like any other burghers. The authorities never intended to give full political rights to persons who were foreigners and public usurers. One result, however, was that the lombards were to be judged by the aldermen's court (*tribunal des échevins*) according to the law and custom of Bruges. This principle is already written in the charters which the lombards received from Count Louis de Male on June 14, 1349, and April 9, 1359 (n.s.). It seems that the lombards were given full civil rights but no political rights. The charters, moreover, read as if even these limited rights of citizenship were only conceded for the duration of the grant.[42] In short, the lombards, from a legal point of view, were in a special class: they were neither complete aliens, nor full-fledged burghers, but denizens with precarious and revocable rights.

Such was at least their legal status at the close of the fourteenth, and during the fifteenth, century. Prior to that time instances are found of lombards admitted to citizenship by going through the usual procedure. For instance, Jaquemon, the son of the lombard Jacques de Calots, became a burgher of Bruges in 1282 and, at the same time, a member of the Flemish Hansa of London.[43] A year later his father was made a citizen.[44] A few years thereafter, in 1306, the municipal accounts mention that the lombard Denise Rogiere van Harle—probably Denis Rogier of Arles—had been admitted as a full burgher (*volmaect portre*) with the same rights as a born citizen. The municipal accounts of the same year list among the receipts an item of £300 par. which Denise Rogiere had paid for permission to lend at interest.[45]

Later, the practice of admitting lombards to full citizenship was discontinued. That there was still some doubt, however, about their real legal status is shown by the following occurrence. In 1401 the *écoutète* or public attorney caught the cahorsins of Bruges with forbidden coins in their possession. They were heavily fined, but the coins were not confiscated because—it is explained in the *écoutète's* account—'the said cahorsins are free burghers of Bruges and hence their property cannot be seized.'[46] This document, however, has a marginal note which shows that the *écoutète's* explanation was questioned, and the matter was brought up before the duke's council for reconsideration.

In the first charters which were granted to the lombards, those of 1281, for instance, it is explicitly stipulated that usury is not permitted under the penalty of heavy fines, which, in the case of Bruges, amounted to one hundred pounds Flemish. Similar provisions also appear in later licences, namely in those of 1333, 1349, and 1359, in favor of the lombards of Bruges. For example, it is stated therein that they are perfectly free to trade as they see fit but are not supposed to enter into any unethical covenants of manifest usury under the penalty of twenty pounds par.[47] But this fine, it is added immediately, will be due only once a year, regardless of the number of transgressions. It is clear that the provision regarding usury should not be taken seriously. The real purpose of the grant was to permit rather than to prohibit usury.

That this is the correct interpretation is established beyond the slightest doubt by the municipal accounts. As early as 1306, it is stated bluntly in them that the lombards are licenced to lend at the weekly rate of 2*d.* a pound and not higher.[48] Later, it is recognized with equal frankness that the lombards lend 'money for money' (*ghelt omme meer ghelts*), as it is expressed in Flemish.[49]

From the fifteenth century onward, less ambiguous language also finds its way into the official charters and grants, and all pretense to conceal the real nature of the lombards' business is discarded. In the municipal licences of 1404 and 1432, it is said without subterfuge 'that, within the city of Bruges, the lombards are free to lend to all kinds of people gold and silver monies at a profit of 2*d.* a pound per week, but not more, without incurring a fine payable to the city.'[50] And even if it could be proven that this maximum rate was exceeded, still the lombards would be liable to the fine called *jetter au sacq* only twice in seven years.[51] This, of course, was practically equivalent to saying that they were perfectly free to charge whatever interest they pleased. The sole purpose of providing a penalty at all was evidently to maintain the principle that lending at excessive rates remained unlawful.

These texts reveal clearly a change in the official treatment of usury during the fourteenth and fifteenth centuries. Whereas, at first, the taking of any interest was regarded as wicked, later on only the lending of money at exorbitant rates was considered reprehensible.[52] This evolution is noticeable not only in Bruges, but elsewhere in the Low Countries, Northern France, and Western Germany. In Douai, around 1250, the cahorsins were not supposed to lend money at usury, nor to take any usury under some concealed form, nor even to ask any gratuity beyond the principal of their loans.[53] According to a charter granted to the lombards of Ghent in 1281, they were allowed 'to make profit out of their pennies but without evil device or usury.'[54] The text unfortunately fails to explain how this could be done.

The fifteenth century licences all over Northwestern Europe no longer pretend to ban usury completely but openly allow the lombards to lend money 'for profit.'[55] In general, a maximum rate of interest, almost always *2d.* a pound per week or 43⅓ per cent a year, is stipulated.[56] Occasionally, no rate is specified, as in Cologne where the cahorsins were authorized to charge interest 'according to the custom of the lombards' (*secundum consuetudinem lombardorum*).[57]

It is difficult to say why the attitude toward money-lending became more tolerant in the fifteenth century than it had been before. The Church certainly had not changed its stand. The greater leniency which prevailed after 1400 may have been due to candid recognition of existing practices and social necessities, to the widening loopholes in the canonist doctrine of usury, or to the growing laxity in morals which is so well depicted in Huizinga's *The Waning of the Middle Ages.*

Besides money-lending, the lombards of Bruges were given leave to trade in all kinds of commodities just like other burghers who paid excise.[58] The purpose of this provision was apparently to free the lombards from the obligation, imposed upon other aliens, of resorting to a broker in their business dealings with natives.[59]

It would have been contrary to the dominant tendencies of mediaeval society if the lombards of Bruges had not been granted monopoly privileges. In all the licences—in those of the fourteenth century as well as those of the fifteenth—the authorities emphatically declare that they will not tolerate within the city of Bruges any other 'Lombards or Tuscans' engaged in the same line of business—read 'money-lending'—as the grantees.[60] This privilege, however, did not protect the lombards from the competition of other usurers—either Italians or nationals—who had their pawnshops on the territory of the provost and chapter of the canons of St Donatian. This territory formed little islands—here a street, there a few houses— which, although they were located within the city walls, were not under the jurisdiction of the municipal government but under that of the local ecclesiastical authorities. Thus, legally, these islands were outside the city boundaries, and there was nothing the magistracy could do if the provost, head of the local clergy, allowed usury to flourish under his benevolent protection.

In the fifteenth century the same association of lombards controlled, for a time, both the pawnshop of Bruges and another one called 'The Peacock' located on the provost's territory. The problem of monopoly was thus satisfactorily solved in a very modern way by the merger of the two competing institutions.[61]

There were other limitations to the monopoly enjoyed by the lombards. None of the grants for Bruges mention money-changing among the authorized activities. This omission is significant because money-changing is authorized in the early licences concerning smaller Flemish towns.[62] As a matter of fact, money-changing in Bruges was the monopoly of the money-changers, and the lombards were thus *ipso facto* excluded. Philip the Bold's ordinance of December 20, 1389, also explicitly excluded them from the trade in bullion.[63] In case of infringement of the tacit prohibition to exchange money, the lombards of Bruges could be fined, as appears from the municipal accounts for the year 1290.[64] Similar conditions existed in other important centers, for instance, in Cologne where money-changing was also strictly forbidden to the lombards.[65]

The records show that attempts were made to enforce and uphold the monopoly of the lombards. Unlicenced usurers, if they could be caught, were heavily fined. Article Two of the privileges granted to the Hanseatic Merchants in 1307 gives them the greatest freedom to trade and to do business but explicitly excludes money-changing and pawnbroking.[66]

To sum up, special protection, denization, freedom to lend money at interest, and monopoly rights were the main advantages which the lombards derived from their charters. These dealt, besides, with a few other points of minor importance.

In all the grants the lombards were promised fair and speedy justice. This implied, in particular, that the courts could not refuse redress of any claims which were supported by writing or other satisfactory evidence.[67] In other words, claims arising from money lent were recoverable at law, both for principal and interest.[68] Moreover, loans had to be repaid in the currency agreed upon or its equivalent in legal tender at the time the payment was made.[69] The lombards were thus adequately protected against losses due to debasement of the coinage.

According to the licences, the lombards of Bruges were exempt from military service outside the city (*ost et chevauchées*), from watch duty on the walls (*guet*), and from any *taille,* extraordinary levies (*zettingen*) or forced loans (*pointingen*).[70] Yet the sources indicate that, in spite of this provision, the lombards were not infrequently called upon to contribute their share in an emergency.

If any lombard committed a crime or was found guilty of misdemeanor, only the culprit was liable to trial and punishment, and his relatives or partners could not be held responsible[71] This was an important exception to the rule of reprisals, so common in mediaeval times, according to which the group was answerable for the individual.

The Bruges grants are silent about the lombards' ability to bequeath their property.[72] This is surprising because other licences, for instance, those for Hainaut, often mention this matter and free the lombards from any disability which might result from *aubaine* or *mainmorte.*[73] The reason for the omission of such a provision from the Bruges grants was probably that it would have been redundant. As denizens, the lombards, like the burghers of Bruges, could not be subject to *aubaine* or *mainmorte.* Of course, if a lombard died intestate and without heirs, his property would escheat to the prince. This happened in 1363, when the estate of a lombard named Jacques Mancegas who owned a share in the pawnshop of Bruges reverted to the count, because no heirs heritable filed a claim before the lapse of one year and one day.[74]

The Bruges grants contain one odd provision. It is stated that if the lombards wished to change their names, the magistracy was bound to comply without offering any objections.[75] This clause is the more surprising because names were commonly translated. Thus the Italian name *Solari* became *du Solier* in French and *van den Zoldere* in Flemish.[76] Who would ever suspect this thoroughly Flemish-sounding name of concealing a lombard?

After a licence had expired, the lombards were given a delay of six months to collect their receivables, to liquidate their business and to take their property out of the country.[77] Though this provision does not appear in the later licences, it probably remained in force on the basis of precedent.

In Bruges the lombards enjoyed about the same rights and privileges and assumed the same obligation of paying an annual fee as elsewhere in the Low Countries, Northern France, and Western Germany. From a legal standpoint conditions in Bruges were not very different from what they were in Brussels, or Liége, or Valenciennes, or Nivelles, or even Cologne. They can thus be considered as fairly typical of those prevailing in the northwestern section of Continental Europe.

There is, however, one important difference. In the smaller centers, the lombards often were the only resident Italians. In Bruges, on the contrary, there were many fellow-countrymen from every Italian city and from every station in life—merchant-bankers as well as humble mariners. The presence of all these different groups brings out the contrast that much the better. The striking fact is that the other Italians did not mingle with the lombards. The charters which the latter enjoyed allowed them to engage in a type of economic activity which was barred to the others. But legal distinctions do not explain everything. As professional money-lenders, the lombards were surrounded with so much social odium that the other Italians did not care to associate with them. It is surprising that this fact has not been noted sooner, because it is of the greatest importance for a clear understanding of mediaeval financial organization.

NOTES TO CHAPTER 6

[1]For example, in a document of April 12, 1373, the Italian pawnbrokers are called *lombars de Bruges caourcins* and *lombars caversins de Bruges* (Bigwood, *Régime,* II, 363-66, doc. No. 77). See also Gilliodts, *Inventaire,* II, 140; Bruges, Municipal Archives, Comptes Communaux, 1368-69 (n.s.), fol. 32, No. 3. In Douai, the word *cahorsins* seems to have fallen into disuse by the end of the XIIIth century. Georges Espinas, *La vie urbaine de Douai au moyen âge* (Paris, 1913), II, 159.

[2]Franz Arens, 'Grundsätzliches zur Problematik der "Kauwerschen",' *VSWG,* XXV (1932), 251-60. See also Georg Liebe, 'Die Anfänge der lombardischen Wechsler im Deutschen Mittelalter,' *Zeitschrift für Kulturgeschichte,* 4th series, I (1894), 273-74.

[3]William Servat of Cahors, merchant of London, was primarily a trader but he also became involved in some financial ventures, as many merchants did. He is never referred to as a pawnbroker. See Franz Arens, 'Wilhelm Servat von Cahors als Kaufmann zu London (1273-1320),' *VSWG,* XI (1913), 477-514.

[4]Pirenne, *Economic and Social History of Medieval Europe,* p. 103; Gras, *Business and Capitalism,* p. 67.

[5]The title of an article by Adolf Schaube, 'Rechtsgeschäfte und Rechtsstellung der "Lombarden" in der älteren Zeit ihres Auftretens in Frankreich,' (*Zeitschrift für das gesamte Handels- und Konkursrecht,* LXI [1908], 289-322), is misleading as it does not contain a single word about the lombards as pawnbrokers. This study deals with Italian merchants visiting the fairs of Champagne in a period prior to the one discussed here.

[6]For instance, in 1302 the prince-bishop of Liége, Adolf of Waldeck, disregarding the protests of the municipal authorities, led a mob to the house of the lombards and—dressed in full regalia with miter and staff—directed the plundering of their pawnshop. Then he expelled them from the city (Ferdinand Hénaux, 'Les banquiers liégeois au XIVe siècle,' *Bulletin de l'Institut d'Archéologie liégeois,* III [1857], 316). Later, in 1473, Charles the Bold, Duke of Burgundy, ruler of the Low Countries, etc., suddenly suppressed all the pawnshops and repealed all the licences of the lombards. It is true that he was forced to recall and to reinstate them after a few months (Bigwood, *Régime,* I, 386).

[7]*Ibid.,* p. 319 and II, Appendix II, 44 ff.

[8]Espinas, *La vie urbaine de Douai,* II, 159.

[9]Sylvain Koch, *Italienische Pfandleiher im nördlichen und ostlichen Frankreich* (doctoral dissertation, Breslau, 1904), p. 18. Cf. Aloys Schulte, *Geschichte des mittelalterlichen Handels und Verkehrs zwischen Westdeutschland und Italien* (Leipzig, 1900), I, 323.

[10]Bigwood, *Régime,* II, docs. Nos. 10, 11, and 29; Paul Morel, *Les Lombards dans la Flandre française et le Hainaut* (Lille, 1908), docs. Nos. 13, 16, 19, 22, 23, 24, 37, 38, 39; Koch, *op. cit.,* p. 18 (charter granted on October 7, 1313, to the lombards of Quesnoy and Forest). With regard to Bruges, the earliest grant, dated October 28, 1281, has never been published *in extenso,* but a summary is found in Octave Delepierre, *Précis analytique des documents que renferme le dépôt des archives de la Flandre Occidentale,* I (Bruges, 1840), lxxxvii f. The text probably differs little from a charter granted the preceding day, i.e., on October 27, 1281, to the lombards of Furnes, and published by Bigwood, (*Régime,* II, 288). Count Thierry de Limburg-Stirum has published four grants, dated respectively, June 14, 1349, April 7, 1350, July 23, 1357, and April 9, 1359 (n.s.), in his *Cartulaire des chartes de Louis de Male, comte de Flandre* (Bruges, 1898-1901), I, docs. Nos. 114, 352, 578, 663. Gilliodts gives extensive excerpts from a grant, emanating from the magistracy of Bruges and dated March 1, 1404, in his *Cartulaire de l'ancienne Estaple de Bruges,* I, 433, No. 518. Another charter dated February 14, 1432 (n.s.), is published in full by the same editor in his *Coutume de la Ville de Bruges,* I, 510, No. 70.

[11]They are listed in Bigwood, *Régime,* II, 55-58.

[12]Delepierre, *op. cit.,* I, lxxxviii, Gilliodts, *Inventaire,* Intro., p. 353.

[13]Gilliodts, *Coutume*, I, 515 and 520.

[14]Gilliodts, *Cartulaire de l'Estaple*, I, 137, No. 192; *idem, Coutume*, I, 520.

[15]Limburg-Stirum, *op. cit.*, Nos. 114 and 663; Bigwood, *Régime*, II, 56.

[16]Gilliodts, *Inventaire*, V, 3, No. 981; *idem, Cart. de l'Estaple*, I, 433, No. 518; *idem, Coutume*, I, 513. Gilliodts is probably mistaken when he writes that the grant of the Royers was extended in 1420 for another 12 years. This statement is in contradiction with the text of the charter granted in 1432 to the Macetti and the Solari. In this text it is stated explicitly that the grant is the continuation of another one, dated 1418, in favor of Pol Machet, Jean Machet, George du Solier, and Frederic Casul, at that time all members of the same financial group *(lors leurs compagnons)*. See *Coutume*, I, 511.

[17]*Ibid.*, pp. 511 and 525; *idem, Inventaire*, V, 3, No. 981.

[18]Bigwood, *Régime*, I, 380 ff.

[19]*Ibid.*, 379.

[20]Pierre de Decker, *Etudes historiques et critiques sur les monts-de-piété en Belgique* (Brussels, 1844), p. 34.

[21]The families Garetti, Roerio or Royer, Deal, Solari or du Solier were from Asti (Koch, *op. cit.*, pp. 11 ff.). The Machet came from Chieri (Bigwood, *Régime*, II, 424, No. 93). Cf. Schulte, *op. cit.*, I, 311.

[22]Only in Malines did the grants emanate from the municipality without interference from higher up. This lasted until 1457, when the city of Malines was accused of encroaching upon the sovereign authority of the dukes and was threatened with forfeiture of all her privileges. The city had to yield and was lucky to get out of the dispute with the payment of a heavy fine. J. Laenen, 'Les Lombards à Malines, 1295-1457,' *Bulletin du Cercle archéologique, littéraire, et artistique de Malines*, XV (1905), 38-39.

[23]Bigwood, *Régime*, I, 332-33 and esp. 333, footnote 2.

[24]Delepierre, *op. cit.*, I, lxxxviii.

[25]These loans are listed among the debts of Gui de Dampierre, Count of Flanders, that remained unpaid on September 15, 1290. Bigwood, *Régime*, II, 296, No. 15.

[26]*Ibid.*, I, 336; Gilliodts, *Coutume*, I, 520.

[27]*Ibid.*, 520-21. It is to be presumed that the fee stayed at the figure of £144 for several years. It was still there in 1333 (Bruges, Municipal Archives, Comptes Communaux, 1333, fol. 19^{v}, No. 6: 'Ontfangen van den Cauwersinen up 't wyc: van Williams dou Galoos ende sinen ghesellе, 144 lb. *par.*').

[28]For instance, in 1371 (Bruges, Municipal Archives, Comptes Communaux, 1371-72, fol. 11: 'Item, ontfanghen van den Caworsinen, van dat zie wonachtich zyn up 't Wyc ende lenen ghelt omme meer ghelds: somma 216 lb. *par.*'; cf. Comptes Communaux, 1372-73, fol. 12 and 1375-76, fol. 9).

[29]Gilliodts, *Coutume*, I, 521.

[30]*Loc. cit.*

[31]See, for instance, the grant of February 1432 (*ibid.*, p. 512): 'Et pour grâces et franchises dessus dictes devront donner et payer le diz Jehan du Solier, George du Solier, Pol, Jean, Nicolet et Dimanche Machet, frères, à la dicte ville de Bruges chacun an 24 livres de gros, monnoye courran en icelle ville durant le terme dessus dit, assavoir: douze livres de groz au jour de Noël et douze livres de groz au jour de Saint Jean Baptiste, dont le premier terme d'icelles seize années escherra au jour de Noël l'an de l'Incarnation Nostre Seigneur Jehu Christ 1436.'

[32]*Ibid.*, p. 526.

[33]*Loc. cit.;* Bigwood, *Régime*, I, 336. Cf. Bruges Municipal Archives, Nieuwen Groenenboeck, p. 314, February 24, 1480: 'Wouckeraers bij de wet gheconsenteirt huerlieder wouckere binder stede te houdene, midts ghevende eene somme van penninghen eens comptant ende vier hondert ponden parisis tsiaers.'

[34]Bigwood, *Régime*, II, 57.

[35]The text of the grants dated 1349 and 1359 runs as follows: ' . . . leur avons donneit et

donnons congiet de demourer et de manoir en nostre ville de Bruges et de tenir tels hosteulx que leur plaira.' Limburg-Stirum, *op. cit.*, I, Nos. 114, 663.

[36]This was also the opinion of no less a person than St. Thomas Aquinas. George O'Brien, *An Essay on Mediaeval Economic Teaching* (London, 1920), pp. 197 f.

[37]Grants of 1349 and 1359. Limburg-Stirum, *op. cit.*, I, Nos. 114, 663.

[38]*Loc. cit.*; cf. Morel, *op. cit.*, p. 15.

[39]J. Laenen, 'Usuriers et Lombards dans le Brabant au XVe siècle,' *Bulletin de l'Académie royale d'archéologie de Belgique*, 1904, p. 131; Bigwood, *Régime*, I, 259, n.2. Cf. Schulte, *op. cit.*, I, 323.

[40]Bigwood, *Régime*, II, 287, No. 10.

[41]Gilliodts, *Cart. de l'Estaple*, I, 433, No. 518 and *Coutume*, I, 511, No. 70.

[42]This seems to have been the case in Cologne. Bruno Kuske, 'Die Handelsbeziehungen zwischen Köln und Italien im späteren Mittelalter,' *Westdeutsche Zeitschrift für Geschichte und Kunst*, XXVII (1908), 408.

[43]Rudolf Häpke, *Brügges Entwicklung zum mittelalterlichen Weltmarkt* (Berlin, 1908), p. 245; Gilliodts, *Coutume*, I, 514.

[44]Bruges, Municipal Archives, Comptes Communaux, 1283, fol. 8.

[45]Gilliodts, *Inventaire*, IV, 406. *Van Harle* probably refers to Arles in Provence. If this is true, Denise Rogiere was a Provençal and not a Lombard or a Piedmontese. His real name was probably Denis Rogier.

[46]Gilliodts, *Cart. de l'Estaple*, I, 414, No. 494.

[47]Delepierre, *op. cit.*, I, lxxxviii; Bigwood, *Régime*, I, 451; Limburg-Stirum, *op. cit.*, I 117 f., No. 114; 632 f., No. 663.

[48]Comptes Communaux, 1306B, fol. 2v, No. 15. Cf. Gilliodts, *Inventaire*, IV, 416. Numerous other examples are found in later years, for instance: Gilliodts, *Coutume*, I, 520; *Cart. de l'Estaple*, I, 128, No. 176 and 137, No. 192. The rate of 2*d*. a pound per week corresponds to 43⅓% a year.

[49]Comptes Communaux, 1371-72 (n.s.), fol. 71; 1372-73, fol. 12; 1375-76, fol. 9v; 1378-79, for. 11; 1389, fol. 14. Cf. Gilliodts, *Inventaire*, II, 347.

[50]The 1432 grant reads as follows: '. . . eulx, leurs hoirs, compaignons et facteurs puissent prester en la dicte ville de Bruges à toutes manières de gens, monnoyes d'or et d'argent pour deux deniers la livre la sepmaine de prouffit, tant seulement, sans cheoir pour ce en amende envers la dicte ville.' Gilliodts, *Coutume*, I, 511; cf. *idem*, *Cart. de l'Estaple*, I, 433, No. 518.

[51]*Loc. cit.*

[52]Pirenne, *Economic and Social History of Europe*, p. 135.

[53]Espinas, *La vie urbaine de Douai*, III, 159, No. 234.

[54]Bigwood, *Régime*, II, 287, No. 10: '. . . faire leur prouffit de leur deniers einsi k'il lor semblera ke boen soit, bien et loiaument sanz mal engien et sans usure . . .'

[55]The expression *prester à prouffit* is found in a charter granted in 1462 by Louis XI, King of France to the lombards of Tournai. Morel, *op. cit.*, p. 223, No. 39.

[56]There were a number of exceptions to this rule. In Antwerp the lombards could charge only 2*d*. to burghers, but up to 3*d*. to aliens. Bigwood, *Régime*, I, 452.

[57]Kuske, *op. cit.*, p. 409.

[58]Grants of 1404 and 1432. Gilliodts, *Coutume*, I, 512 and *Cart. de l'Estaple*, I, 433.

[59]Ehrenberg, 'Makler, Hosteliers und Börse in Brügge,' *op. cit.*, p. 411.

[60]Grants of 1349, 1359, 1404, and 1432. Cf. Morel, *op. cit.*, p. 7.

[61]Bigwood, *Régime*, II, 424, No. 93.

[62]*Ibid.*, I, 391 f.

[63]Gilliodts, *Inventaire*, III, 134: 'Item, que aucuns *taflettiers* n'achatront billon sur paine d'estre dix ans banniz, s'ilz sont bourgois ou soubzmanans; et s'ilz sont estraigniers, ilz seront banniz comme dessus dix ans, et le billon fourfait à nous.' *Tafletier* means any owner of a *table de prêt* or loan agency. It applies consequently to the lombards as well as to any other pawnbrokers.

[64]Gilliodts, *Cart. de l'Estaple,* I, 75, No. 100.

[65]Kuske, *op. cit.,* p. 409.

[66]Gilliodts, *Inventaire,* I, 267, No. 222.

[67]Grants of 1349 and 1359. Limburg-Stirum, *op. cit.,* I, Nos. 114, 663.

[68]This was a departure from the general rule according to which all usurious covenants (i.e., any agreements involving the payment of interest) were illegal and claims arising from such contracts were irrecoverable at law. See J. Lameere, "Un chapitre de l'histoire du prêt à intérêt dans l'ancien droit belgique,' *Bulletin de l'Académie royale de Belgique, Classe des lettres* (1920), p. 93.

[69]Gilliodts, *Coutume,* I, 512.

[70]Grants of 1404 and 1432 (see above, n. 58). The same provision is found in a charter of 1336 in favor of the lombards of Montbéliard in Franche-Comté. Léon Gauthier, *Les Lombards dans les Deux-Bourgognes* (Paris, 1907), p. 56.

[71]Grants of 1349 and 1359.

[72]Except in the grant dated September 9, 1445 (see Bigwood, *Régime,* I, 296, n. 8).

[73]*Ibid.,* p. 291 ff.

[74]*Ibid.,* II, 352, No. 48. This Jacques Maucegas is probably the same as Jakemars Manciah or Jakemon Manciah mentioned in the 1349 and 1359 licences.

[75]Gilliodts, *Coutume,* I, 512.

[76]*Ibid.,* p. 525.

[77]Grants of 1349 and 1359 (see above, n. 67).

Chapter 7

THE PAWNBROKING BUSINESS

WITH regard to the exact nature of the lombards' business only private business records, especially account books, could supply precise, reliable, and conclusive information. Unfortunately, no such records are known to be extant,[1] with the exception of a few sheets relating to a pawnshop in Pistoia, Italy.[2] While the absence of business papers is to be regretted, the available data are abundant enough to leave little doubt that pawnbroking, or the lending of money on the pledge of personal property, was the lombards' favorite and principal field of activity.[3] Other lines of business might be entered into, but only occasionally and on the side.

The pawnshop of Bruges was located on the Quai Long or Lange Reye in the parish of St Gilles, a rather outlying and quiet district (called in Flemish *'t Wyc*) far from the movement of the Grand' Place and the bustle of the Place des Orientaux or the Place de la Bourse where the Easterlings, the Florentines, the Genoese, and the Venetians had their headquarters and transacted their business.[4] The location of the lombards in a remote part of the town is rather significant. If they had been connected with trade and international finance, they would certainly have chosen a more conveniently situated residence. But, for pawnbroking, it was an advantage rather than a disadvantage to be far away from busy and crowded thoroughfares. After dark, the *quartier Saint-Gilles* must have been deserted, and through the empty streets customers could find their way to the pawnshop, without being seen or recognized.

The lombards' place of business is described in the documents by the term *hostel* which suggests a rather large establishment.[5] Its exact location along the Quai Long or Lange Reye was beyond the Pont de la Tour (Torenbrugghe) and between the Nieuwstraete (now rue de la Main d'Or) and the 't Coorstraete (now rue longue de la Rame), a side street running towards the church of St Gilles. After 1425, if not earlier, there were two adjoining buildings belonging to the lombards: a smaller house standing on the corner of the rue longue de la Rame and a much larger one next to it. Because of their difference in size, the documents talk about *de cleene* and *de groote Cauwersinen* ('the small and the big houses of the cahorsins'),[6] and the pawnbrokers themselves are frequently referred to as the *Grands Cahorsins du quartier Saint-Gilles*.[7] The sources seem to indicate that the pawnshop itself was located in the larger of the two houses and that the smaller was used only as living quarters.

The residence of the lombards is clearly discernible on Marc Gheeraerts' detailed map of Bruges (1562).[8] It is a cluster of buildings—two fronting on the quay and others surrounding a courtyard. Between the *cleene* and *groote Cauwersinen,* there is a gate or passageway leading from the street into the courtyard which extends as far as the choir of the church of St Gilles.[9] In the yard there is a tower, but not as graceful as the neighboring towers adorning the *maison de la Tour,* on the corner of the rue de la Main d'Or, and the *hôtel de Saint-Pol,* a little farther down the quay toward the Porte Saint-Léonard or Porte de Damme.

After the lombards left Bruges, shortly before 1492,[10] their residence stood empty until it was rented in 1503 by the municipal authorities in order to house a workshop for clothmaking. At that time the city was engaged in a project to introduce into Bruges the light drapery of Leyden.[11] Two Dutchmen, Govaert Philipszone and Jacob *filius* Joris, had been hired to manage the shop and to teach the weavers of Bruges how to make the new kind of cloth.[12] This was one of the many attempts to stem the city's decline and to revive the dying Flemish cloth industry. The project, of course, involved organizing a weaving school, setting up a score of looms, and providing decent quarters for the two managers and their families. Only a very large house would be spacious enough for all these purposes.

In 1571, for the levy of the tenth and twentieth penny, the former house of the lombards' was assessed on the basis of a yearly income of £20 gr. a year, which is rather high.[13] By 1581 it had reverted to its old use and was sheltering the public pawnshop or *mont-de-piété* of Bruges, established in 1572.[14]

There are two reasons why the lombards needed a rather large establishment. For one thing, the pawnshop was owned by several partners, and it is very likely that their residence had to be roomy enough to accommodate more than one family, not to mention any servants. The main reason, however, was that the pawnbroking business by its very nature required a lot of storage space.[15] As security for their loans, the lombards accepted all kinds of pledges ranging from jewelry and plate to more bulky articles such as clothing, kitchenware, kettles, tubs, bedding, and furniture. All these things had to be stored away until the pledges were either redeemed or otherwise disposed of. Warehousing was thus an essential feature of pawnbroking.

There is no doubt that the interior of the lombards' residence in Bruges resembled that of a storehouse. This appears clearly from an inventory which was taken in 1457 in pursuance of bankruptcy proceedings.[16] This document mentions a series of rooms in which pawned articles were kept. Those of the same nature were probably stored in the same room because the inventory speaks of a *chambre des manteaulx* and a *chambre des cauderons,* which means apparently that clothing was packed away in one room and kitchenware and brass kettles, in another. The inventory also mentions a *chambre des sacs.* It is reasonable to suppose that pawns of small size were neatly wrapped in bags and placed on shelves along the walls. Unredeemed pledges were kept separate, because the inventory mentions a *chambre haulte* and a *chambre basse des gaiges passez.*

The inventory of 1457 gives us a fairly good idea of the lombards' place of business. In all probability, it included an office facing the street and a number of storerooms located behind and above the office. The latter contained a counter (*table*)[17] and behind it, shelves for books, papers, and pledges which had just come in and awaited removal to one of the storerooms.

The house of the lombards in Bruges was certainly a brick building and not a timber structure. In Ghent it was probably built of stone, as the sources talk about a *Lombaardensteen,* which, incidentally, must have been quite large and was located on the Couter (Place d'Armes), where the Club des Nobles stands today.[18] The use of brick or stone in preference to timber is quite understandable, if one considers the hazards of fire. Buildings used for the safekeeping of valuables have naturally to be immune from this danger, as far as possible.

All this shows that the residence of the lombards in Bruges was especially arranged to fit the particular needs of their business. Evidence shows that the same was true in other cities, as, for instance, Ghent and Antwerp.[19] Often the pawnshop gave its name to the street where it was located, as the famous 'Lombard Street' in London and the less famous 'Rempart du Lombard' in Antwerp both exemplify.

None of the grants for Bruges or for any other town were ever made out in favor of a single individual. As a rule there were several grantees who were frequently related to each other by family ties. As far as can be ascertained from the existing sources, they never dealt singly, but always collectively, either with the public authorities or with other people.[20] Often only one of the lombards is mentioned by name and the others are referred to as *et ses compaignons* in French and as *ende sine ghesellen* or *ende zinen gheselscepe* in Flemish.[21] The chronicler Georges Chastellain intimates the same thing when he writes that the lombards 'faissoient tous d'une commune bourse.'[22]

Unfortunately, no partnership agreements have survived, except one concerning the pawnshop of Dijon in the duchy of Burgundy. The text of this document, dated April 14, 1382, is rather disappointing as it does not give much information beyond the fact that the partners promised each other 'to form a loyal company, without fraud or deception.'[23] In the absence of more comprehensive partnership agreements, a few clues can be gathered from occasional references in other documents, but still there is very little we know about the internal organization and the management of the pawnshops.

Most probably the capital was made up of shares, and profits were divided accordingly. When the father of Simon de Mirabello died in prison around 1330, his son claimed his inheritance which had been seized by the duke of Brabant. The estate included, among other things, 'several pawnshops in which he [the father] had shares with other lombards.'[24] That lombards frequently had money invested in several pawnshops, as this text indicates, is corroborated by other evidence. For instance, in 1473, a Gabriel du Solier (Solari) owned the pawnshop of Sluys and had a share in the ones of Bruges and Antwerp. Oudenin de Ville, his partner in both of these places, also had 'a finger in the pie' at Ghent, Courtrai, Audenarde, Herenthals, and Lierre.[25] Shares in the ownership of a pawnshop were evidently an object of trade. In 1417 one Mikiel Sackier bought from a Jehan de Cordes his half in the pawnshop of Nivelles. This purchase involved one half of the outstanding claims and one half in the property of a house which was used as a place of business. About five years later the same Jehan de Cordes, acting in behalf of his brother Wallefroy, bought back Mikiel Sackier's share in the house and in the business. The latter included all licences, privileges, claims, account books, letters obligatory, and other public instruments, in short, one half in all the assets and liabilities of the pawnshop.[26]

As the lombards did not enjoy the gift of ubiquity, the management of the pawnshops had to be entrusted to a resident partner or, exceptionally, to a factor, who was merely a salaried employee. A distinction, therefore, has to be made between investing and managing partners. For their time and services, the latter probably received, not a fixed salary, but a larger share in the profits than they would otherwise have been entitled to. It is also very likely that some fixed percentage rather than a share in the profits was paid on all money invested *fuori del corpo,* or above and beyond the partners' share in the capital.

The advantages derived from entering into partnerships with others were very great, but family ties and tradition also had an important role to play. The Royer family, for instance, remained in control of the pawnshop of Bruges for almost a century, more precisely from 1333 to 1420. At one time or another members of this same family were established as pawnbrokers in Alost, Bergues St Winoc, Forest and Quesnoy, Termonde, Tournai, Ypres, Cologne, Bar-sur-Aube, and other places.[27] This is not an isolated instance. There were other dynasties of usurers, for example, the Garetti, the Macetti (Machet), and the de Villa or de Ville.

The strength of family relations was due to powerful economic and social forces. In general, kinship played a far greater role in mediaeval than in modern society. Furthermore the lombards, being virtually outcasts, reacted like the Jews; they became group conscious and clung together as a means of defense against a hostile environment. Among the economic causes, there was the necessity of dividing risk by scattering investments and of forestalling competition from outsiders. Moreover, pawnbroking, as we shall see, required as much ability as any other profession, and it can safely be assumed that business secrets and experience were passed on from one generation to the next, and that intruders without such a family background were seriously handicapped from the start.

In spite of the strong solidarity within the group, the lombards never formed a 'nation' until the end of the fifteenth century.[28] The reason was that they were not concentrated chiefly in Bruges like the Florentines, the Genoese, the Venetians, and the Lucchese, but were sprinkled all over Flanders, Brabant, and the other provinces. The nation of the Piedmontese or 'lombards' did not, therefore, come into existence until after the unification of the Low Countries. The new institution, moreover, was chiefly an agency created in order that the sovereign might deal collectively with the lombards. It was, consequently, something very different from the other 'nations' whose functions were not confined to public relations but affected the whole life of the Italian communities in Flanders.

One of the main reasons why the lombards formed partnerships and pooled their resources was, apparently, that their business absorbed quite substantial amounts of capital. After the failure of the Grands Cahorsins in 1457, a group of lombards represented by Pierre de Ville offered as much as £13,000 groat—to be paid in several installments distributed over a period of eight years—for the assets of the bankrupt business. It is not known whether the creditors accepted this offer or not.[29]

Unlike deposit bankers, the lombards did not work mainly with the money of someone else; they depended largely on their own financial resources. This situation, incidentally, proves once more that the lombards were not bankers, but merely pawnbrokers. It also explains why they had to charge such a high interest rate and why pawnbroking was (and still is) an expensive form of credit. The reason is obvious. The money lent by the lombards had not only to earn interest, but a trader's profit besides. In other words, they made a living out of money-lending and were, consequently, entitled to a compensation for their time and services in addition to a fair return on their investment.[30]

While the lombards did their own financing, as much as possible, they sometimes accepted deposits in order to increase their working capital.[31] This practice was very old. As early as 1247 it was found in Douai where the lombards paid the *taille* and the other municipal taxes on the basis 'of all the money which they handled, their own as well as that of others.'[32] In a small town like Douai, the capital placed on deposit with the lombards probably did not amount to much. It must have been considerable in important centers like Bruges where there was both a great demand for consumers' credit and an ample supply of capital seeking safe investment. Although a well-managed pawnshop was not a risky enterprise, it did not attract capital easily nor on favorable terms. Strong social and religious prejudices, unfortunately, stood in the way of the free flow of capital. According to the canonist doctrine, to make deposits with a money lender was clearly partaking in usury and hence sinful.[33] As a result, the lombards, if they wished to borrow, had to allay the scruples of prospective investors by the alluring offer of a return which was well above that on other investments of comparable security. No precise information is available concerning rates of return, but in 1369, Jewish pawnbrokers resident in Brussels paid as much as ten per cent a year to Christian depositors.[34] As the lombards could not borrow cheaply, they were not in a position to relend the borrowed money at low rates. The practical effect of the canonist doctrine was thus to increase the cost of lending to the borrower—a result which the canonists certainly did not intend and never understood.

When the pawnshop of Bruges went bankrupt in 1457, it was discovered that widows, maidens, orphans, and a number of rich people had placed money 'for profit' with the lombards.[35] 'Which they should not have done' (*Ce que point ne devoient*), adds the chronicler Chastellain in relating these facts.[36] The duke Philip the Good was quite irate, too, when he learned that rich burghers from Bruges and elsewhere were not ashamed to seek gain from usury. He ordered them to surrender their claims in bankruptcy to the treasury,[37] and Chastellain reports that they were heavily fined besides.[38] Only the widows, maidens, orphans, and *aultres misérables personnes* were treated with more clemency and allowed to come in for their pro-rata share of the assets.[39]

There is no evidence that deposits with pawnbrokers were either transferable or payable on demand. On the contrary, the fact that they yielded a handsome return is sufficient indication that the lombards were not bound to repay their depositors on short notice. Such deposits, consequently, should be regarded as time deposits. They constituted more or less permanent investments. They did not by any means give rise to a system of payments which could replace and displace coin.

We have seen that the lombards specialized in pawnbroking and that they financed their business largely out of their own capital and to a minor extent out of money entrusted to them for investment. But this is not quite enough to give a thorough idea of their business. In particular, we should like to know more precisely what they did with their money. Who were the people to whom they lent? What was the real character of their loans—large or small, long or short term?

The people who borrowed from the lombards really belonged to all classes—from the prince down to the poor artisan or journeyman.[40] In emergencies, the count of Flanders himself and the feudal nobility would pawn their jewels, plate, tapestries, rich hangings and splendid court attire. In 1334 the lombards of Bruges released the crown jewels which they had held for some time as security for a loan to the count of Flanders.[41] A few years later, in 1370, the Duke of

Burgundy, Philip the Bold, borrowed from the same pawnbrokers and gave them his jewels as collateral.[42]

A member of the reigning family, Yolande of Flanders, Countess of Bar and Lady of Cassel, was constantly in debt to lombards.[43] In order to obtain a loan at an interest rate of fifty per cent she had to pawn her beautiful golden coronet adorned with twelve jeweled ornaments and nine fleurons.[44] On May 11, 1364, she contracted a loan of 1,010 *moutons* with the Grands Cahorsins of Bruges and gave them as pledges her coronet, two golden tiaras (*chapeaux*), and twelve silver cups. Countess Yolande must have been in serious financial trouble because she had raised in Bruges another loan of 6,000 francs by putting up as collateral golden and silver figurines (*ymages*) and other jewelry.[45] The first loan seems to have been repaid promptly on November 3, 1364, but the second one dragged on for several months, and a small balance was still due in April, 1365. Though the cahorsins of Bruges had received several installments, they refused to release any of the pledges until the entire debt had been discharged. In the meantime, the Countess wrote the most pathetic letters to her stewards, begging them to keep her out of the lombards' clutches and to press the repayment of the loan, so that interest would not accumulate.[46] The worries of the poor lady are quite understandable as she was paying interest at excessive rates.

In spite of this disheartening experience, she again ran into debt. On April 20, 1370, she had to pledge her jewels once more to the lombards of Bruges as security for the considerable amount of 5,000 French francs, 3,000 Hungarian florins, and 3,000 common florins.[47] The repayment of this loan was quite slow and part of it was still outstanding after three years. The lombards for some unknown reason caused trouble when it came to returning the pledges.[48] Their ill will did not discourage Countess Yolande, for she kept on borrowing. Her career as an inveterate borrower reached a climax, when, in 1395, at the age of 69, she was arrested and jailed for debt in Tournai—outside her domains—at the request of a money-changer named Thierry Prévot, who had lent her sundry amounts 'on and without security' (*à gaige et sans gaige*) and who could not obtain satisfaction.[49]

Advances to the prince and the feudal lords were in general for considerable amounts and were secured by collateral of great value.[50] As large loans are not more expensive to handle than small ones, it would appear on the surface that such advances were a very desirable investment. Alas! princes and feudal lords, while they enjoyed large incomes, had also heavy expenses, and their finances were often in bad shape. As a result, this class of borrowers was slow in making payments, and any money lent to them was likely to be tied up for a considerable period of time. As the lombards had to pay their running expenses (servants, fees, rents, interest charges, etc.) during the meanwhile, delay could lead to great inconvenience and even endanger their solvency. Furthermore, borrowers of high social rank had to be handled with kid gloves and it was difficult to proceed against them in case of default. If the reigning prince himself was the borrower, such a course was entirely out of question, and, worse, the lombards were more or less at his mercy because of the power he wielded to repeal or to renew their licences and even to seize their property.[51]

Though the pledges given as security represented a great value, one should not overlook the fact that such things as crown jewels or even Countess Yolande's coronet were not readily salable. They could, of course, be broken up and the gold, pearls, diamonds, and precious stones sold separately, but only at a considerable loss, because the value of jewels is partly determined by the artistic quality of the setting.

For all these reasons, it would have been unwise for pawnbrokers to favor loans to princes and other feudal lords. As the lombards were shrewd business men, they avoided such loans as much as possible. However, they were not always able to do so, if pressure was brought to bear upon them.

The available documents indicate clearly enough that the bulk of the lombards' business came from less prominent borrowers. Because of the absence of account books and of loan contracts, there is little information concerning this clientele of the lombards of Bruges beyond a mention that weavers—probably working under some form of the putting-out system—whose wages were not paid within three days had the right to borrow on the cloth belonging to their employers, up to the amount of the unpaid wages.[52] Such loans were evidently made by small people and for petty amounts.

Fortunately, a survey made for Nivelles, a small town south of Brussels, fills the gap left by lack of information concerning Bruges. This survey covers 1,464 loan contracts drawn up before the *scabini* or aldermen and dating from 1330 to 1428.[53] It shows that the clientele of the lombards of Nivelles was made up of people in all walks of life: the lower clergy, neighboring barons, knights, and squires, well-to-do burghers, minor officials, craftsmen, village-mayors, and tenants. Merchants are conspicuous by their absence. Only a few craftsmen are listed, but it is unlikely that, for very small loans, the lombards went to the trouble of drawing up a deed in the presence of the aldermen. It is also noteworthy that most of the contracts stipulate repayment in stable gold coins (francs, *moutons, couronnes* or *écus*), evidently as a protection against the depreciation of the silver coinage. In Hainaut, the story is much the same, and public records reveal that the people who owed money to the lombards were not wealthy as a rule and that, on the average, the loans were for small amounts.[54]

A telling document is the fragment of an account book, dated 1417, which belonged to a pawnbroker in Pistoia (Tuscany).[55] Though Pistoia is far from Bruges, there is no reason to believe that the lombards operated in Italy itself on

TABLE 5

FREQUENCY DISTRIBUTION OF EIGHTY LOANS MADE BY A PAWNSHOP IN PISTOIA (1417)

Amount of Loan (In *Lire piccioli*)	Number of Loans	Per Cent of Total	Cumulative Per Cent
Less than 10*s*. *piccioli*	7	8.8	8.8
10*s*. and under £1 *piccioli*	17	21.2	30.0
£1 and under £1 10*s*.	12	15.0	45.0
£1 10*s*. and under £2	12	15.0	60.0
£2 and under £2 10*s*.	8	10.0	70.0
£2 10*s*. and under £3	4	5.0	75.0
£3 and under £3 10*s*.	2	2.5	77.5
£3 10*s*. and under £4	..	.....	77.5
£4 and under £4 10*s*.	7	8.8	86.3
£4 10*s*. and under £5	2	2.5	88.8
£5 *piccioli* and above	9	11.2	100.0
Total	80	100.0	.....

Source: Lodovico Zdekauer, 'L'interno d'un banco di pegno nel 1417,' *Archivio storico italiano*, 5th Series, XVII (1896), 63–105.

TABLE 6

DISTRIBUTION ACCORDING TO ARTICLES PLEDGED IN SECURITY

Kind of Article	Number of Loans	Per Cent of Total
Articles of clothing and apparel	46	57.5
Tools and agricultural implements	9	11.2
Jewelry (pearls, silver, buckles, etc.)	9	11.2
Arms and armor (sword, dagger, cross bow, etc.)	7	8.8
Bedding (mattress, pillows, sheets, coverings, etc.)	6	7.5
Kitchenware and household utensils	2	2.5
Calf skins	1	1.3
Total	80	100.0

Source: Zdekauer, *op. cit.*

different principles than in Flanders. The fragment is, unfortunately, very incomplete and contains only the business transactions for five days, April 14 and 15 and May 7, 8, and 9, 1417. In all, eighty loans are recorded. With the exception of a broker and a goldsmith, the pawners were all craftsmen or peasants, many of them poor weavers, spinners, and shoemakers (*calzolai*).[56] In general, they borrowed only trifling amounts. Out of eighty loans, seven did not attain 10 *soldi piccioli*, twenty-four were below one *lira piccioli* and only eighteen were over one florin or 4 *lire piccioli*.[57] More than half did not exceed the figure of two *lire piccioli*. The pawns are described in the account book as being of poor quality and little value. Articles of clothing, most of the time well worn and torn, were given as security in forty-six instances; the remainder of the pawns was made up of tools, arms, jewelry, kitchenware, bedding, and one lot of calf skins pawned by a currier. The presence of tools is significant: one carpenter pledged his saw; peasants, their ploughshares, their hoes, and their axes. This practice was bound to work much hardship on the poor borrowers if they needed the pledged tools but were unable to redeem them. The items in the account book, quite unwittingly, give us a glimpse into the social problems created by distress borrowing.

What little evidence there is suggests that, in the Low Countries, too, the lombards received as pledges an amazing variety of things, but that the bulk of them was made up of household articles and clothing. In 1361, the pawnbrokers of Nivelles held as security for a loan to one of their customers: five *lis stoffés* or the equipment for five beds, twelve cushions, table covers, several garments, eleven ells of cloth, silverware, pewter, an array of kitchenware and other utensils including kettles, pots, pans, shovels, one tripod, and one waffle iron![58] In Bruges itself the poor artisans were often reduced to the necessity of pawning their clothing. In 1371 a number of weavers were called up for military duty but were not able to answer the call, because their clothes and equipment were pawned with the lombards. So the weavers' gild had to step in and to assume the expense of taking the needed equipment out of pawn.[59]

With regard to the repayment of the loans, the Pistoia manuscript supplies valuable information. The pledges, in ten cases out of eighty, were never redeemed and consequently sold by the pawnee, but only after having been kept for one year or longer. For instance, a blouse (*camiciotto*) pawned on May 8, 1417, was not sold until August 22, 1418. Because of the bad condition of the manuscript, the dates of repayment written in the margin are not always legible. As a result they are only known in thirty-nine instances out of a total of seventy. Twenty loans were liquidated within thirty days. One loan, only, was repaid after one year and nineteen days. Table 7 shows how this information compares with similar statistical data compiled by a Belgian author, Georges Bigwood, for the pawnshop of Tournai in the late thirteenth century and for that of Nivelles in the fourteenth and early fifteenth centuries.

There is one important difference between data available for Pistoia and that for Nivelles and Tournai. The table for Pistoia, based on business records, gives the distribution of forty loans according to actual dates of repayment. The two other tables, on the contrary, have been prepared from legal contracts whose provisions with regard to maturity might or might not have been complied with. Another difference is that the data for Tournai and Nivelles do not include any small loans. As has been pointed out before, the lombards probably did not bother to draft regular contracts when petty sums were involved. It was far more convenient for them to mention the amount due on the pawnticket, a businesslike procedure which did not entail any loss of time or expense.[60]

Another difficulty of interpretation arises from the fact that twenty-four per

TABLE 7

Repayment of Loans Made by Mediaeval Pawnshops

Duration of Loan or Terms of Repayment	Pistoia			Nivelles			Tournai		
	Number of Loans	Per Cent of Total	Cumulative Per Cent	Number of Loans	Per Cent of Total	Cumulative Per Cent	Number of Loans	Per Cent of Total	Cumulative Per Cent
From 1 to 9 days	12	30.0	30.0	52	3.7	3.7	4	3.3	3.3
From 10 to 30 days	8	20.0	50.0	310	21.6	25.3	12	10.0	13.3
From 31 to 60 days	2	5.0	55.0	378	26.4	51.7	32	26.0	39.3
From 61 to 90 days	3	7.5	62.5	120	8.2	59.9	24	20.0	59.3
From 3 to 6 months	5	12.5	75.0	96	6.7	66.6	28	23.0	82.3
From 6 to 12 months	8	20.0	95.0	45	3.1	69.7	18	14.5	96.8
More than one year	1	2.5	97.5	28	2.0	71.7	1	0.8	97.6
Installments	...	...	...	38	2.6	74.3	1	0.8	98.4
Upon request (*a volonté*)	...	...	...	344	24.0	98.3	...	...	...
Unredeemed or unknown	1	2.5	100.0	25	1.7	100.0	2	1.6	100.0
Total	40	100.0		1436	100.0		122	100.0	

Sources: Zdekauer, 'L'interno d'un banco di pegno nel 1417,' *op. cit.*, pp. 63–105; Georges Bigwood, *Le régime juridique et économique du commerce de l'argent dans la Belgique du moyen âge*, (Brussels, 1922), Vol. II, Appendices 3 and 4, pp. 103–262.

cent of the Nivelles loans are mentioned as 'payable at will' (*payable à volonté*).[61] The purpose of this provision was to make interest appear as a measure of damages for failure to pay a loan at the first request of the lender. In other words, it was one of the numerous devices which were resorted to in order to conceal that interest was charged. As the lombards were not under any obligation to keep pledges longer than one year, loans payable at will were presumably payable within a year's limit.[62]

Despite all these differences of period, place, and source material, the table shows a really remarkable uniformity in results. In all three cases, about 60 per cent of the loans were repaid or repayable within three months, and 67 to 82 per cent within six months. Very few loans were outstanding after one year.

This table, combined with the precious evidence contained in the few extant sheets of the Pistoia account book, shows conclusively that the lombards granted mainly short term credit, that their loans were in the great majority for small amounts, and that their customers borrowed almost exclusively for consumption purposes. It is the type of business which is still carried on today by official and private pawnshops and small loan companies. It is fittingly described by the French expression of *prêt à la petite semaine,* because interest was generally computed by the week or month.[63] In Flemish, the word for usurers is *woekeraers* which comes from *woeke* meaning 'week.'[64] Usurers are thus people who reckon interest per week. In the Rhineland the verb *lombardieren* is synonymous with 'pawning.'[65] At Liége, the populace still calls any pawnshop *un lombard* and the *mont-de-piété* is referred to as the *Grand Lombard.*[66] The same is true in Holland where *lombert* or *lommert,* obviously derived from 'lombard,' are the colloquial names for the municipal loan offices.[67]

The lombards performed the important function of supplying the demand for consumers' credit. This demand was relatively of greater importance in mediaeval society than it is today, because there was little accumulated wealth, and there existed few investment opportunities for productive purposes. Also in a society visited by plague, famine, and war, life was surrounded with uncertainties and the poorer classes lived in the shadow of death and dire misery. Should an emergency arise, they had no reserves to fall back upon, and their meager belongings took the road to the pawnshop.[68] These were the social and economic conditions which the canonist doctrine tried to meet. It has not always been clearly recognized that the position of the canonists was fundamentally correct, even in the light of the most orthodox economic theory. There is no doubt that money devoted to consumption is barren and cannot be used without being spent.[69] The result of a loan to a consumer is merely a transfer of purchasing power from the lender to the borrower. This is the theory which is at the bottom of the canonist doctrine, but confusedly expressed and only dimly perceived. Unfortunately, the canonists did not push their analysis a little farther. They did not see that the transfer of purchasing power from the lender to the borrower allowed the latter to anticipate his future income. For society as a whole, anticipation of income is impossible, because commodities cannot be consumed unless they are first produced. With individual members, the story is different. It is quite possible for someone to spend more than he earns, if he can borrow from someone else who does the saving, in other words, who spends less than he earns and stores up purchasing power. This process involves, however, a sacrifice on the part of the lender in order to be of service to the borrower. If money lending is a profession, such a service can only be produced at a cost and purchased at a price, which usually takes the form of a rate of interest on the money lent.

As we have seen before, the lombards were permitted by their licences to charge as much as *2d.* a pound per week, a rate which corresponds to 43⅓ per cent a year. There is little doubt that this legal rate was also the actual rate for most of the small loans, though it is difficult to find specific instances. There is at least one clear case. In 1414, the famous St John's Hospital in Bruges borrowed from the Grands Cahorsins the sum of £10 groat for a period of eight weeks. As interest, the Hospital paid *20d.* gr., equivalent to £1 *parisis* a week or £8 par. for the eight weeks.[70] This rate corresponds exactly to the above-mentioned *2d.* a pound per week.

Princes, feudal lords, or municipal authorities, who borrowed large amounts, frequently paid different rates which varied widely, probably depending upon the nature of the security offered, the duration of the loan, the state of the money market, the political outlook, and the measure of confidence which the borrower enjoyed.

The lombards of Lessines lent to Countess Yolande on January 12, 1364, an amount of 1,200 *moutons* for a consideration (*courtoisie*) of 300 *moutons* at the end of one year or at the rate of 25 per cent.[71] As was to be expected from her record, she was not able to repay the loan when the year was up. As a result, the consideration of 300 *moutons* was added to the principal, and interest at the rate of 25 per cent had to be paid henceforth on 1,500 *moutons.* On August 3, 1365, Countess Yolande was finally in a position to make a first payment of 1127 *moutons.* By that time, the loan totalled up, principal and interest, to exactly 1,700 *moutons.* The lombards probably began to lose patience with the dilatory habits of Countess Yolande, for the rate of interest on the balance of 573 *moutons* was raised from 25 per cent to the legal maximum, 43⅓ per cent. The Countess was fortunately able to pay off her debt after fifteen days or on August 17, 1365, by offering 580 *moutons* in final settlement.[72] The loan was thus liquidated in about one year and seven months. Incidentally, it is perhaps noteworthy that interest was compounded after one year.[73]

Besides the debt to the lombards of Lessines, Countess Yolande also owed money to the Grands Cahorsins of Bruges. The interest on a loan of 6,000 francs amounted to 1,200 francs for one year or 20 per cent.[74] These were very favorable terms. In 1368, Countess Yolande had to pay to the lombards of Bruges two francs a month per hundred francs or 24 per cent a year on a loan of 2,000 francs.[75] Later on, the rate was still further increased. In 1370, when she borrowed 5,000 French francs, 3,000 Hungarian florins, and 3,000 other florins, interest was computed on the basis of 25 per thousand a month or 30 per cent a year.[76]

Sometimes Countess Yolande could not avoid paying the maximum or legal rate of 2*d*. a pound per week, as, for instance, on an accommodation of £135.16.8 *gr*. secured on June 1, 1368, from the Grands Cahorsins of Bruges.[77] When the loan was repaid on July 17, 1369, or after one year and seven weeks, interest charges amounted to £66.15.8 gr. or almost 50 per cent. At the same time, on other loans, Countess Yolande was charged only 24 per cent.[78] The sources give no clue to explain the discrepancy. Very likely the difference in rate was due to the fact that one loan was backed by better security than another.

Cities and towns occasionally did borrow from the lombards, but only in great emergencies. Their credit standing was much better than that of the nobility and they could easily raise money from other sources and by other means, as, for example, by the sale of life annuities or of *rentes perpétuelles*.[79] These methods of financing were also much cheaper than any loan which could be obtained from the lombards. It is significant that small towns had to resort to them more frequently than important cities.[80] As towns or cities had no jewelry to pledge, they borrowed either on the basis of their credit standing or on the personal surety of municipal officers. Sometimes creditors were granted a lien on specific sources of revenue.

In the municipal accounts of Bruges, there are only a few references to dealings with the lombards and they involve rather unimportant amounts. In 1339-1340 a sum of £120 gr. or £1,440 par. is listed among the income of that year as borrowed from the Grands Cahorsins of St Gilles' parish.[81]

In 1426 the Machet, who were at that time licenced pawnbrokers, in response to urgent pleas of the burgomasters and *scabini,* advanced to the city £200 gr., with the understanding that the lenders could recover this amount from their annual fees and their excise taxes.[82] Unfortunately, in both of these cases, nothing is said about the interest rate. It is even likely that no interest at all was chargeable on the later loan.[83].

At first, during the thirteenth century, the taking of interest was carefully concealed in all documents or contracts concerning loans. In order to dispel suspicion, it is even frequently stated that the money is lent 'without cost, without usuries, or without any evil covenants.' In some documents it is even stated that the loan is made 'out of pure friendship,' though probably interest was charged under some form or other.[84] In the fourteenth and fifteenth centuries, those phrases are dropped, but interest still is never mentioned openly in any public instrument. This ceased to be true of records other than contracts, such as municipal and private accounts, and even court sentences. A common euphemism for interest was *courtoisie*[85] or *bonté* in French and *hovescede*[86] ('consideration') in Flemish. The words most frequently used, however, were in French, *montes*[87] and *accrois,*[88] which stress the idea of increase, and in Flemish, *wasdom,*[89] which conveys the same idea, or *verloop,*[90] which means compensation for the lapse of time. To summarize briefly, the lombards charged interest at the legal rate of 43⅓ per cent on the small loans which formed the backbone of their business. Borrowers of large sums occasionally paid a lower rate, which varied greatly according to the circumstances of each loan, but which rarely fell below 20 per cent. There is no reason to believe that the yield on capital invested in mediaeval business enterprises ever attained those percentages. The rates at which the lombards computed interest were thus far above any normal return which might be expected from productive investments[91] An economist would say that those rates were above both the average and marginal productivity of capital. This observation leads once more to the unescapable conclusion that the lombards specialized in consumers' credit.

It is as true now as it was in the Middle Ages that consumers' loans are ruinous to the borrower unless he does not commit himself beyond his capacity to pay. This capacity to pay is not impaired, if the amount of the loan is small in relation to income and if the borrower's budget is only temporarily unbalanced. Under all other circumstances, consumers' loans at high interest rates bring only momentary relief at the price of increased financial difficulties in the near future.[92] 'Money borrowed is soon sorrowed' is an old saying of perennial truth.

The high interest rates charged by the lombards have aroused the pious indignation of modern historians as well as of mediaeval friars. Both have been equally vehement in denouncing the excessive interest rates and the high cost of credit to the poor borrower, but nobody, as far as I know, has whispered one word about the cost to the lender. Impartiality requires the historian to look at all sides of the problem.

It is quite clear that the lombards were not in the pawnbroking business for the love of humanity but for the sake of earning a living. First of all, in order to be profitable, a pawnshop needed a certain volume of business. In the late thirteenth and early fourteenth centuries, lombards settled in small towns like Ardenbourg, Audenarde, Biervliet, Bouvines, Furnes, Calais, and Gavre, but they soon discovered that these localities were not large enough to support a pawnshop.[93] The lombards, therefore, moved elsewhere and disappeared after a short while.

In the second place, the rates of interest charged by the lombards had, first, to cover all their incidental expenses; next, to yield a fair return on their investment; and, finally, to compensate them for their time and services. Like any other business man, the Italian pawnbrokers operated on a gross and a net margin of profit. The high interest rates which they charged suggest that their gross profit was very high, but this fact does not mean much, as it is net profit that determines whether a business pays or not. Very likely the lombards' net income was not large and there was little left after all opportunity costs had been deducted from gross earnings.

The lombards carried a very heavy burden of overhead charges. The most important items were licence fees, rent of a suitable house, wages of servants and employees, commission to canvassers, interest on till money and sometimes—when business was bad—on idle cash, selling expenses on forfeited pledges, legal fees, office supplies (account books, stationery, etc.), charities, storage charges, and losses through theft, insolvency, and decline in value of unredeemed pledges.[94]

The licence fees, as we have seen, were far from being negligible and certainly contributed to raising the rate at which the lombards could profitably lend. Rent certainly was another important item, because they needed a well built house with plenty of storage space. It is also quite evident that they had to keep on hand, at all times, a certain amount of cash in order to accommodate applicants for loans. Interest on this idle money had, of course, to come out of the earnings on the money actively employed. Selling expenses were probably in many cases high enough to make a great number of transactions unprofitable. When business was slack, the lombards frequently employed canvassers, who called on people and tried to persuade them to borrow. As not many calls produced the expected results, this was an expensive way of securing more business. Although the lombards were careful not to lend up to the full value of the pledges, still it frequently happened that sales did not produce enough to cover the principal and accrued interest on unpaid loans. Such losses might be due to a decline in price, to deterioration, to lack of proper care, or to an initial mistake in appraising the value of the pledge. Whatever the cause, these losses had to be made good by higher profits on other transactions.

One case of outright deception is even known. About 1452 the lombards of Bruges discovered too late that they had made a loan on a chain of false gold. The case was taken to court and the sureties of the borrower were ordered to repay the lombards.[95]

Another cost-raising factor was the premium which the lombards, in order to relieve their lack of working capital, had to offer to prospective investors or time depositors.

After taking into account all these various expenses, the remaining net profit had to be high enough to reward the lombards for their time and exertion. It is very likely that several persons were permanently busy in a pawnshop like that of Bruges. During office hours, at least one person had to be behind the counter waiting on customers. Probably someone else acted as cashier or book-keeper. Still another person took care of the storeroom: carrying pledges to and from the office, wrapping and tagging them, keeping track of those which had to be sold.

The selling of unredeemed articles was probably another full-time and important job, because pledges ranged from crown jewels to rusty ploughshares. The person in charge had to know, of course, how these many things could be most advantageously disposed of. Obviously jewels, plate, or illuminated books did not have the same outlet as ploughshares, broken spinningwheels, or ragged garments.

Above all these persons, employees or junior partners attending to the routine of the business, there were probably one or two senior partners vested with the necessary authority to supervise and coordinate the different departments and to make all decisions of general policy.[96] Running a pawnshop was not a simple proposition. Not only did it entail heavy expenses, but it also required a great deal of managerial ability. Despite the high interest rates charged to customers, such an enterprise without careful management, could easily be steered on the rocks. This is another aspect which the clerical mind of the churchmen was unwilling or unable to see.

As no account books are extant, there is little definite proof of all these facts except in a rather late document (1624) concerning the lombards of Tournai.[97] These lombards were being prosecuted by the *procureur général de Flandre* for persisting in the practice of usury after having received absolution. In reply to the charges made against them, they pointed out that they were regularly licenced, that the Bishop of Tournai had granted them general dispensation, and that their business was burdened with so many expenses that it barely afforded a livelihood. The lombards emphasized further that they earned less and with more toil than other merchants engaged in legitimate business, and that 'all things well considered, they only received a just reward for their labors.' They concluded their plea by asserting that they did not commit any sin of usury so long as their interest rates represented only *usuram compensatorium aut interesse que licitum est.*

At least one attempt was made to reduce by decree the rate of interest which the lombards were allowed to charge. Because the rate was so high, the pawnbroker was, of course, very unpopular among numerous classes of borrowers. For the common people of the Middle Ages, the pawnshop was at the same time a terror and a necessity.[98] They naïvely believed—and the friars confirmed them in this belief—that the greed of the lombards was the source of all evils and that the legal rate of 2*d.* a pound per week could be reduced by a legislative fiat. Failure to do so was a permanent source of grievance, and it is not surprising that the populace clamored for redress when the death of Charles the Bold in 1477 almost led to the collapse of the Burgundian state. Poor Mary of Burgundy, threatened by internal revolt and foreign invasion, was not in a position to refuse even the most impossible demands, and by article nine of the Great Charter of April 21, 1477, the legal rate was brought down from 2*d.* to 1*d.* a pound per week.[99] It is needless to say that the measure proved to be unenforceable, and that legislative action could not prevail over the economic forces which made consumers' credit expensive.

Another illustration of an attempt to reduce the interest rate is furnished by the history of the *monts-de-piété* which superseded the lombards in the beginning of the seventeenth century during the reign of the Archduke Albert and the Archduchess Isabella, sovereigns of the Belgians (*Belgarum Domini*).[100] It was hoped that these institutions, copied from Italy, would solve the problem of consumers' credit.[101] As a matter of fact, they were only partially successful. Though the *monts-de-piété* were not run for profit, it proved impossible to reduce the interest rate to borrowers below 15 per cent, because incidental expenses amounted to at least $8\frac{3}{4}$ per cent, and $6\frac{1}{4}$ per cent had to be paid on the invested capital.[102] A few years of operation also revealed that, in general, small loans were more expensive than big loans and very small loans were entirely unprofitable, except at rates well above 15 per cent. As a result, the regulations made in 1752 adopted a graduated scale. The outcome was that the poor man, who borrowed only petty sums and needed help the most, paid the highest rate.

The capital of the *monts-de-piété* was soon depleted by mismanagement, forced government loans, and outright dishonesty.[103] The founder, Wenceslas Cobergher, an architect and civil engineer,[104] was a poor administrator, and, at his death, the affairs of the *monts-de-piété* were in a terrible state. He, himself, had borrowed several thousand florins from them, in order to finance one of his projects, the draining of the *moeren* or marshes of West Flanders.[105] This turned out to be a disastrous investment with the result that the entire estate of the deceased did not suffice to make up for the loss. Several *monts-de-piété* were badly managed; salaries were too high and managers, inexperienced and incompetent.[106]

During the disastrous campaign against the Dutch, the Governess Isabella had borrowed a huge sum of money giving her jewels and parts of the public domain as security.[107] This also turned out to be a calamitous transaction, as the loan was never repaid and her jewels were sold, several years later, for less than was anticipated.

The *monts-de-piété* in the Low Countries really never recovered from these blows. They lingered on, were patched up from time to time, but never were thoroughly reorganized. In 1750 four-fifths of the initial capital had been lost and interest payments were in arrears for thirty-five years.[108] If the lombards, instead of being expelled, had been allowed to run the *monts-de-piété,* their experience would, perhaps, have put these institutions on a sound and firm basis from the very start.

Today conditions with regard to consumers' credit resemble very much those which prevailed in the Middle Ages. Careful inquiries conducted under the auspices of the Russell Sage Foundation have yielded conclusive evidence that pawnshops and small loan offices cannot operate profitably except at interest rates of 2½ per cent to 3 per cent a month or of 30 per cent to 36 per cent a year.[109] Many states of the union have adopted small loan and pawnbroking acts making it legal for licenced money-lenders to lend at those rates, but only up to $300. Even so, very small loans frequently do not pay the cost of handling them, because any loan, regardless of the amount, involves examining and appraising the collateral, making the required entries in the books, issuing a pawn ticket, wrapping and storing the pledges with due precaution against loss and damage.[110]

The routine of the lombards' business was also much like that of modern pawnbrokers. Unless the transaction was important enough to justify the drawing up of a formal contract, the lombards issued for each loan a document which was the equivalent of what we call today a pawnticket.[111] Such a document was called *woekerbriefje* or *lombardbriefje* in Flemish[112] and *reconnaissance* in French. It was designed to serve as proof of the transaction to the borrower. The lender did not need any evidence beyond the entries in his own books, as he held a pledge, the value of which supposedly exceeded the amount of the loan.

As it generally happens that business and private records are destroyed after having fulfilled their purpose, it is not surprising that no mediaeval pawntickets have survived. We are, however, fortunate enough to know the contents of one of them, owing to the happy accident that the text is quoted in full in a court decision. Though it has been published thrice, the full significance of this text has never been properly emphasized.[113] To the pawnbroker, the pawnticket is as basic an instrument as the check to the banker, the bill of exchange to the merchant, the insurance policy to the insurer, or the bill of lading to the common carrier.

The court decision in question relates to a lawsuit which involved the Grands Cahorsins of Bruges and a Scottish clergyman named Patrick Home, Apostolic prothonotary and archdeacon of Tyndale in Scotland.[114] Passing through Bruges on his way to, or from, Rome, he was probably short of cash for he left part of his wardrobe with the lombards in order to raise twenty gold crowns. The pawnticket relating to this transaction reads as follows:

Ego, Johannes de Cellario, fateor me habere de bonis magistri Patricii Home, apostolice sedis prothonotarii, archidiaconi Teindalie, etc., tres togas foderatas, unam rubeam, aliam brunam, terciam nigram, et unum caputium nigrum, unam foderaturam de bevere, unam tunicam de worset, unam bursam de panno deaurato et unum coopertorium blavii coloris; et super ista bona prestavi eidem magistro Patricio viginti coronas monete Francie, ad usum banchi nostri.

Aldus gheteekent: Ego Johannis antedictus hanc cedulam signavi manu mea propria, die xij julii anno 1465.

The document is very concise and gives only essential information: the names of both the lender and the borrower, an enumeration and brief description of the pawned articles, the amount due, the signature of the lender, and the date. All the rest is summarized in the words *Ad usum banchi nostri.* This innocent-looking phrase is, however, the most important part of the contract. It says little, but it implies a great deal, as Archdeacon Patrick Home was to discover to his dismay.

Now what does the phrase *ad usum banchi nostri* exactly mean or imply? It evidently means the same thing as the *consuetudine lombardorum* to which some mediaeval documents refer. It is the law of the lombards as determined by their licences and established by custom.[115]

Ad usum banchi nostri consequently implied that interest was to be computed at the legal rate of 43⅓ per cent or 2*d*. a pound per week. The formula conveniently relieved the lender from the necessity of revealing to the borrower the leonine character of the contract. After all, money-lenders today resort to the same trick when they advertise that loans are made at the *legal* rate of interest. They know that only well-informed persons are aware of the fact that the legal rate on small loans is 30 per cent or 36 per cent in most states.

Ad usum banchi nostri was also a cloak covering important provisions and regulations regarding the redemption and disposal of the pledges. The lombards of Bruges, according to their licences, were under no obligation to keep unredeemed pledges longer than one year and one day.[116] After that the pledges were forfeited and the lombards could dispose of them as they chose. They were under no obligation to refund any surplus, if the proceeds of the sale exceeded the amount of the loan—principal and interest. It was because of these rules that Archdeacon Patrick Home became involved in difficulties.

Returning to Bruges after two years, he offered to redeem his pawned wardrobe and was told that it had been sold.[117] Thereupon, he brought suit against the lombards, who pleaded that the loan was made subject to the customary restrictions, that they were not bound by their licences to keep pledges over one year, but that, in fact, they had kept the plaintiff's wardrobe much longer before selling it. To make their argument even stronger, the defendants further claimed that the proceeds of the sale had barely covered the principal and accrued interest of the loan, so that they would owe nothing to Archdeacon

Home under any circumstances. The court had to admit that the lombards were within their rights and turned down the Archdeacon's plea.

The story of this lawsuit illustrates clearly that unredeemed pawns were simply forfeited, and that the pawner did not have any right to the surplus.[118] But what happened if the sale of a pawned article did not cover the claims of the lombards? In such a case, it seems that they had no recourse against the borrower. The question, though, is merely of academic interest: since most borrowers who did not redeem their pledges were insolvent, there was no use in suing them anyhow. Moreover, the lombards were shrewd enough to understand that they were unpopular, even with the judges. Although we have no direct evidence, it is probable that the lombards followed the policy of lending only on good security and of avoiding subsequent litigation as much as possible. If, by any chance, a mistake was made in appraising the sale value of a pledge, they undoubtedly preferred to take the loss rather than to go to court and to have trouble.

The licences of 1404 and 1432 provided that the oath of the lombards would be decisive in any dispute with regard to the fulfillment of the one year requirement. The *usus banchi nostri* was thus all in favor of the lender. The rule that pledges had to be sold by auction, that the sale had to be announced in advance by public crier, and that the pawner had an unquestionable right to the surplus, if any, did not become universal in the Low Countries until the reign of Charles V.[119] Isolated examples, however, are to be found in the fifteenth century, and the lombards of Grammont had been enjoined to follow such a rule as early as 1401.[120]

An interesting document shows that the lombards of Sluys, the seaport of Bruges, lent up to 60 per cent of the estimated market value of a pledge of silverware.[121] Whether this ratio is typical or not, cannot be decided on the basis of a single instance. Sixty per cent is, perhaps, too high a ratio on articles whose value was more uncertain than that of silverware. However, let us accept the figure of 60 per cent. On this basis, principal plus interest at the rate of $43\frac{1}{3}$ per cent would surpass the value of the pledge in one year and a half. As the lombards had to keep the pledges for at least one year and would have lost money, if they had kept them longer than one year and a half, it was to their advantage to sell them during the intervening six months. And this doubtless was the lombards' policy, as the lawsuit with Archdeacon Patrick Home clearly illustrates.

The licences for Bruges contain a provision that the lombards could not be compelled to surrender pledges unless they were fully paid—both the principal and the interest.[122] The practical effect of this provision was to protect the Italian pawnbrokers against claims made by owners of stolen goods.[123] According to a city ordinance of March 11, 1409, a money-lender who knowingly or unknowingly accepted stolen goods as pledges was not entitled to any compensation, if they were claimed by their rightful owners. This rule, it is stated explicitly in the ordinance, did not apply to the Grands Cahorsins of St Gilles.[124]

While the lombards certainly did not deliberately acquire all kinds of loot, it was very difficult for them to prevent this altogether.[125] As a matter of fact, the pawnbroking business today is confronted with the same problem. It is not the business of a pawnbroker to inquire into the morals or character of each applicant for a loan or the ownership of everything that is offered as security.[126] Practically all a pawnbroker can do is not to deal with people whom he strongly suspects of dishonesty. In the Middle Ages, the problem was much the same or even more difficult. Most people loathed the pawnshop because of social prejudice or for reasons of face-saving. In the sixteenth century a lombard stated that most pledges were not brought in by their owners, but by servants and other persons, so that, as a result, lending on stolen goods could not be entirely avoided.[127]

The lombards were forbidden to lend on church ornaments and liturgical vestments. The lombards of Bruges were forced to return a dalmatic, belonging to the church of St Walburge, which had been pawned by someone who had no authority to do so.[128] In Louvain pawnbrokers were forbidden to lend money on school texts to students of the university.[129] Similar prohibitions existed elsewhere. In Troyes, for instance, loans on agricultural implements were illegal.[130] According to a fourteenth-century statute of Valenciennes, the cahorsins and other money-lenders were not permitted to make advances secured by wool, yarn, unfinished or finished cloth, unless these materials were the property of the applicant for a loan. Violation of this rule not only entailed the loss of the money lent, but was also punishable with a heavy fine.[131] The purpose of the statute of Valenciennes was evidently to prevent cabbaging by home-workers to the detriment of their employers, the rich and influential *drapiers*.

While pawnbroking was certainly the lombards' *raison d'être* and their main line of business, it does not follow that our Italian pawnbrokers never engaged in any other type of economic activity.[132] Quite the contrary. Trade was an essential part of their business because of the necessity of getting rid of forfeited pledges. The Bruges aldermen, sitting as a court, decided in a test case that such trading did not encroach upon any of the monopoly privileges of the craft gilds. This principle had been challenged by the gild of fustian-makers, which complained that the sale of fustians (probably secondhand) by the lombards was an infringement of the gild's monopoly.[133]

Did the lombards go further and engage in any trade other than the local sale of unredeemed pledges? It is significant that their licences are silent on trade matters. Quite the opposite is true of the charters of the other Italian nations, in particular those of the Genoese and the Venetians, which deal almost exclusively with trade relations and shipping and are, in fact, commercial treaties. There is, furthermore, no indication in the records of any active trade between Bruges and the towns of Asti and Chieri in Piedmont whence the lombards came. Nor do the latter seem to have had branches, agents, or correspondents abroad. The conclusion should therefore be that the lombards, as a rule, did not take any active part in foreign trade. Of course, it is not difficult to find examples to the contrary, and there is little doubt that the lombards occasionally participated in a commercial venture, when they had idle money to invest and saw an opportunity to strike a bargain.

In 1464 a lawsuit resulted from a contract between Ulric Cheringher, a German merchant from Nuremberg, and Claude de Ville, one of the lombards connected with the Antwerp pawnshop. The contract was partly a barter agreement according to which Claude de Ville and his partners undertook to deliver eighty-nine pieces of English cloth in exchange for eleven sables and a sum of money. As the importation of English cloth into the Low Countries was severely prohibited at the time, delivery had to be made abroad.[134] It would be rash to conclude from this single instance that the lombards of Antwerp were cloth-dealers.[135]

A more disturbing case is one involving the Grands Cahorsins of Bruges, because, on the surface, it seems to undermine the thesis that the lombards were mainly pawnbrokers. In reality, the case, far from disproving this theory, confirms that the lombards were not well placed to engage in foreign trade and that hazardous operations in commodities were likely to endanger their solvency and to cripple their entire business.

When the pawnshops of the Peacock and of the Grands Cahorsins failed in 1457, there occurred in Bruges, according to the chronicler Chastellain, a panic without precedent.[136] The papers of the lombards were seized and an audit of their books revealed that they had not only accepted money on deposit, but they had also been speculating in commodities, probably in wool.[137] This proved to be their undoing. The speculations did not turn out as the lombards had anticipated, and, according to Chastellain, one of their partners, a certain Berthélémieu, manager of the pawnshop of Louvain, pulled them all down by drawing accommodation bills in the vain hope of gaining time and making good the losses.[138] This story of Chastellain's is at least partly, if not wholly, true, because public documents also state that the downfall of the lombards was caused by the fact that excessive amounts of money were due on purchases from several merchants of Bruges.[139] Although the available evidence is confusing and incomplete, the likelihood is that the bankruptcy originated in an unsuccessful attempt to corner wool. The plan seemingly miscarried because the lombards were not financially strong enough to dominate the market and because they did not have the proper connections either among the producers in England or among the buyers in the Low Countries. As a result, the lombards had to buy rather dear from importers in Bruges. The fact that several creditors were merchants established in Bruges lends credence to this theory. *Qui trop embrasse, mal étreint.* There is little doubt that the lombards, instead of confining their operations to pawnbroking, nearly wrecked their business by overexpansion and pure gambling.[140]

While the lombards were not organized to engage successfully in foreign trade, they were also practically excluded from local trade, except, of course, for those transactions connected with the sale of forfeited pledges. In the Middle Ages, there was no, or little, independent wholesale trade. It was as a rule combined with retailing, and the lombards were shut out of the retail trade by gild regulations or staple rights. The contracts regarding purchases of grain on future delivery which were entered into by the lombards of Nivelles are without doubt disguised loans.[141] It is well known that short-term agricultural credits frequently took the form of dealings in futures. Sometimes such contracts were prohibited because of the harm done to poor and guileless country folk whom the authorities thought it their duty to protect.[142]

Whether the lombards engaged in manufacturing as well as in money-lending has given rise to some debate. Georges Bigwood, the most authoritative writer on the subject, contends that they were not interested in manufacturing, but his position has been challenged by Etienne Sabbe, another Belgian scholar, who was able to show that the Italian pawnbroker of Courtrai, in the first half of the fifteenth century, also managed a dyeing establishment.[143]

The factual evidence presented by Dr Sabbe is unassailable. The lombard in question, a certain Roland à Nya, was not only the proprietor of the pawnshop of Courtrai, but he also bought in 1433 a share in the one of Bruges, after the death of one of the partners named Antoine de Mourion.[144] Roland à Nya must have been a rich man: he owned a dozen houses in Courtrai, and his dyeing establishment was seemingly quite important. As it is described under the Flemish name of *blauw verwerij,* the probabilities are that à Nya specialized in the dyeing of cloth in all shades of blue and green, using woad as the principal dyestuff. According to the available information, à Nya installed in 1433 a suction pump in order to provide his establishment with water. A special sewer was also built to drain off the waste.

These are the facts. Do they elicit the conclusion, as Dr Sabbe seems to imply, that the lombards in general were manufacturers as well as money-lenders? In other words, are the conditions prevailing in Courtrai representative or not?

In most Flemish cities the lombards were either explicitly or implicitly excluded from industrial occupations, especially in the cloth industry which was almost everywhere controlled by monopolistic gilds. As a rule the gilds required full citizenship of their members. As the lombards were denizens, but not full citizens, they were *ipso facto* excluded from gild-controlled industries. Moreover, the particularistic municipal authorities watched anxiously over the cloth industry, and any intrusion of foreigners was likely to arouse fears and suspicion. It is, therefore, not surprising that the licences granted to the lombards of Malines explicitly stipulated that they were not allowed to engage in the manufacturing of cloth either directly or indirectly by having others work for them.[145] In Douai not the licences but a municipal statute excluded all money lenders from the woolen industry. The same applies to Ghent where it was enacted, in 1338, that no lombards nor any other foreigners were permitted to process wool or to have it processed for them. A heavy fine threatened any *drapier* or master-dyer who might be helpful in circumventing this rule.[146]

Courtrai was a small town and the gild organization was probably not very strong. This circumstance seems to explain why à Nya was able to combine pawnbroking with the management of a dyeing establishment. Such a combination, therefore, was not representative of conditions existing elsewhere. The evidence presented by Dr Sabbe proves only that there are always exceptions to the rule.

As the lombards were not much interested either in trade or in industry, there remained the possibility of other types of money-lending besides pawnbroking. The lombards occasionally lent on security other than personal property, but these operations never outbalanced pawnbroking in importance. Loans secured by real estate did not tempt the lombards for three decisive reasons: such loans did not yield a return high enough to be profitable to pawnbrokers, they were perpetual in character, and they involved time-consuming legal formalities.[147] Real estate owners could obtain credit more cheaply from institutions and private investors, interested in a steady flow of income, than from professional lenders. Conditions were thus similar to those prevailing today with regard to mortgages.

Loans to public authorities secured by a lien on specific sources of revenue occasionally found favor with the lombards. Around 1368 those of Bruges had made a loan to Louis de Male, Count of Flanders. As guaranty against default, they were assigned for repayment the £3,000 par. or £250 gr. which the city of Bruges yearly paid to the count for the right of levying excise duties on wine, beer, mead, and other commodities.[148] Though similar instances are not rare, the records convey the impression that the lombards did not specialize in this kind of transaction.[149]

Sometimes the lombards were willing to accept surety instead of the pledge of personal property, but instances are extremely rare.[150] More often, surety was required in addition to other pledges. A good example is afforded by the loan the lombards of Bruges granted, in 1370, to Countess Yolande of Bar. The loan, which has been previously mentioned, amounted to 5,000 French francs, 3,000 Hungarian florins, and 3,000 other florins or the equivalent of £1562½ groat.[151] The conditions imposed upon the debtor were particularly harsh and burdensome, though this might have been due to the character of Countess Yolande, whose reputation for promptness in repaying her debts was none too good. At any rate, the safety of the loan was bolstered not only by the pledge of jewelry but also by the surety of two knights, three squires, and the towns of Dunkirk and Gravelines.[152] The contract, moreover, provided for hostages, if the loan was not repaid on maturity. Should this happen, then the debtor was to send to Bruges five knights, each with three horses, four squires, each with two horses, and four municipal officials, each with two horses, both from Dunkirk and Gravelines, or, in all, seventeen people and thirty-nine horses.[153] This party was to remain in Bruges at the expense of the debtor until complete repayment of the loan.

In the archives of the Low Countries, there are records of other similar cases, but not many. Surety and hostage were, of course, of limited applicability. They were best adapted to important contracts in which princes or nobles were concerned, but were not as well fitted to the small transactions which, after all, were the sinews of the lombards' business.

Although most of the licences stipulated that the lombards could not be asked anything beyond the payment of their annual fees, this provision was sometimes disregarded in times of war or social unrest. This happened when, in the fall of 1379, the weavers in Bruges, Ghent, and Ypres revolted against the existing social order, overthrew the city governments, and nearly got control of the whole of Flanders.[154] As civil war was threatening, they could not think of any better way to raise money than to decree a forced loan.[155] Since the weavers established a reign of terror, nobody dared to resist. The loan was highly successful and produced the considerable amount of £26,207 15*s*. *parisis*. Whoever had any money was compelled to contribute: the well-to-do burghers, the money-changers, the foreign merchants resident in Bruges, the abbeys of the Dunes and of St Andrew and the *smale steden,* or small towns, which the bigger cities of Bruges, Ghent, and Ypres held under their heel. Naturally, the lombards were not passed over, but, on the contrary, more heavily assessed than any others. Their contribution amounted to a total of £350 groat.[156] It is significant that in the municipal accounts where all the contributors are listed, a distinction is made between the cahorsins of St Gilles' parish and the other Italian colonies, including the Milanese. This little fact shows clearly that contemporaries, too, set the lombards apart from the other national groups. It is extremely doubtful whether the lombards or, for that matter, any of the other contributors to the forced loan of 1379 ever saw their money again. Forced loans almost always turned out to be extraordinary war contributions. They can therefore not even be regarded as a bad investment, but are to be considered as an *exactio* with which the lombards had to cope and against which there was no protection.

On the whole, there were practically no other possibilities open to the lombards outside of pawnbroking and the activities closely connected with it. Other investment opportunities were rare and not profitable enough for people who derived their living from money-lending. All things considered, pawnbroking was a profession which, like any other, required special training and ability. The organization had also to be adapted to the nature of the business and, consequently, was not very flexible. The result was strict specialization. Pawnbroking could not very well be combined with other forms of economic activity.

The justification for the services supplied by the lombards is to be found in the local demand for consumers' credit, chiefly for small loans by people who were not wealthy and who were confronted with some emergency.[157] Half the time their solvency was already impaired, when they applied for a loan, and usually they needed financial help so badly that they were not in a position to bargain about the price. This situation suited the lombards very well. Their high operating costs made it impossible for them to lend money at a rate below the normal return on productive investments. As a result, the lombards were thrown back on consumers' loans for which they could charge a rate high enough to meet their expenses.[158] Risk was largely eliminated by lending only on good security and by selling all pledges which were not redeemed within the appointed time.

Professional money-lending rested on a delicate equilibrium of economic forces in which necessity on the one side, cost and the balance sheet on the other, played a more important part than cupidity and merciless exploitation of other people's needs. It is undeniable, however, that equilibrium resulting from the blind operation of economic forces is not always conducive to social well-being as well. The rate of interest was so high that borrowers were often crushed under the weight of their commitments. Inability to redeem pledged tools, clothing, or household articles caused undoubtedly a great deal of suffering which was the source of deep-seated bitterness against the lombards.

The amazing volume of literature on the subject of usury and the numerous pronouncements of the Church show clearly that consumers' credit constituted a social problem of major importance, and that it was foremost in the public mind.

[1]Bigwood, *Régime,* I, 343: 'Malheureusement, il semble bien que les archives de nos contrées ne contiennent aucun document, contrat, livre de comptabilité ou autre, qui fasse connaître l'organisation intérieure de ces associations.'

[2]Lodovico Zdekauer, 'L'interno d'un banco di pegno nel 1417,' *Archivio storico italiano,* 5th series, XVII (1896), 63-105.

[3]Most historians agree on this point but some do not. For instance, Hénaux (*op. cit.,* p. 316, n. 2) writes: 'Au moyen âge, le mot Lombard était synonyme de prêteur d'argent sur gages.' Morel (*op. cit.,* p. 38) also considers the lombards as *prêteurs sur gages* but thinks mistakingly that they combined this function with that of banker and money-changer. Kuske (*op. cit.,* pp. 407 f.) is of another opinion and writes: 'Lombarde ist sonach jeder italienische Kaufmann, der sich völlig oder teilweise dem Geldhandel widmet. . . . In dieser Zeit liehen übrigens die Lombarden durchaus nicht immer gegen Pfand. In Köln lässt sich sogar kein Fall nachweisen, dass es geschah. Sie liehen dort vielmehr auf Risiko und nahmen dafür einen hohen Zins von etwa 54%.' It is needless to say that I do not agree with Kuske's point of view. Kuske's information is based exclusively on local sources which are incomplete and misleading. Schulte (*op. cit.,* I, 325), on the contrary, writes: 'Im wesentlichen war ihre [der Lombarden] Thätigkeit auf das Gewähren von zinsbaren Darlehen beschränkt, welche durch Pfänder oder Bürgen gesichert waren.' In my opinion Schulte is right and Kuske wrong. The municipal accounts of Bruges are most emphatic on this point; for example, in the accounts for the financial year 1429-30, it is stated as plainly as possible that the lombards are licenced by the city to lend money on *pledges*: '. . . over 't consent dat zy hebben van der stede *omme te leenene up pandde*' (Gilliodts, *Inventaire,* IV, 521).

[4]Gilliodts, *Coutume,* I, 521.

[5]This is true already of the first charter granted to the lombards in 1281 by Gui de Dampierre (Delepierre, *op cit.,* I, lxxxviii). This document speaks about three *hosteulx.* The grants of Louis de Male of 1349 and 1359 also mention *hostels.* In 1457 a document refers to the residence of the lombards as *l'ostel des Caoursins en Bruges* (Gilliodts, *Cart. de l'Estaple,* II, 73, No. 992).

[6]Gilliodts, *Coutume,* I, 521; Emile Van den Bussche, 'De Groote Cauwersine,' *La Flandre,* IV (1872), 79-82.

[7]Gilliodts, *Coutume,* I, 519.

[8]Panoramic map of Bruges: Marc Gheeraerts, 'Brugae, Flandrorum Urbs et Emporium Mercatu Celebre (1562).' Reprints published by Charles Beyaert (ed.), Bruges (n.d., [but after 1900]). See extracts from the map in Letts, *Bruges and its Past,* pp. 20-24. A biography of Marc Gheeraerts with a description of his work has recently been published by Albert Schouteet, *De zestiende-eeuwsche schilder en graveur, Marcus Gerards* (Bruges: Gidsenbond, 1941), 56 pp.

[9]This courtyard was walled in. It is clearly visible on the map and is also explicitly mentioned in other descriptions of the premises. Cf. Louis Gilliodts-van-Severen, 'Les registres des "Zestendeelen" ou le cadastre de la Ville de Bruges de l'année 1580.' *Annales de la Société d'Emulation pour l'étude de l'histoire et des antiquités de la Flandre Occidentale,* XLIII (1894), 294-95; *idem,* 'La levée du dixième et du vingtième denier à Bruges, 1571-1583,' *Annales de la Société d'Emulation de Bruges,* LX (1910), 316; *idem, Coutume,* I, 521.

[10]Bruges, Municipal Archives, Comptes Communaux, 1499, fol. 32, No. 1; 1502, fol. 34^{v}, No. 2; cf. Gilliodts, *Coutume,* I, 526.

[11]Comptes Communaux, 1503, fol. 96, No. 1: 'Betaelt ter cause van der huere van den huuse ter Cauwerchine, 't welke dese stede in hueren ghenomen hadde omme daer inne te doene de neeringhe ende draperye van den Leyschen lakenen, te drien ponden grooten tsiacrs.'

[12]Gilliodts, *Coutume,* I, 526.

[13]Gilliodts, 'La levée du dixième . . . denier,' *op. cit.,* p. 316.

[14]Gilliodts, *Coutume,* I, 521. The *mont-de-piété* started operations on January 15, 1572. Above the door there was a figure of Charity with the inscription:

Hier hout men den berch der oprechte charitate
Om te leenen sonder crois ofte baete

('Here is the mount of genuine charity for lending without accrument or profit.' See de Decker, *op. cit.,* p. 34).

[15]Morel, *op. cit.,* p. 38: 'Les Lombards, à la fois banquiers, changeurs, prêteurs sur gages, ont besoin de vastes établissements où peuvent se mouvoir à l'aise ces différents services.' The statement regarding the size of the establishments of the lombards is perfectly correct, but the reason given is erroneous. Except in small towns the lombards never were at one and the same time bankers, money-changers, and pawnbrokers.

[16]Gilliodts, *Cart. de l'Estaple,* II, 73-74, No. 992, December 17-18, 1457.

[17]Whence the name of *tables de prêt* which was given to the pawnshops of the lombards. The Flemish equivalent is *bank van leening,* which is still the official name of the *mont-de-piété* all over the Flemish-speaking part of Belgium and the Netherlands.

[18]Bigwood, *Régime,* I, 324.

[19]Bigwood, *Régime,* I, 324-27.

[20]*Ibid.,* p. 343.

[21]Gilliodts, *Coutume,* I, 520 f; cf. Espinas, *La vie urbaine de Douai,* II, 160.

[22]Georges Chastellain, *Chronique, 1419-1470,* ed. by Baron Kervyn de Lettenhove, III (Brussels, 1864), 315.

[23]Gauthier, *op. cit.,* pp. 267-68, No. 133.

[24]Bigwood, *Régime,* II, 332, No. 36.

[25]Morel, *op. cit.,* p. 237, No. 42.

[26]Bigwood, *Régime,* I, 344-45, 353-54; II, 417-18, No. 88, 418-19, No. 89.

[27]*Ibid.,* II, 44 ff.

[28]Morel, *op. cit.,* p. 237, No. 42. This document, dated November 29, 1473, mentions Oudenin de Ville, Anthoine Fallet, Thomas de Laval, Jehan de Rubis as 'consulz de la nacion des Piedmontois résidens ès pays de mon trés-redoubté seigneur, monseigneur le Duc de Bourgoigne.' Oudenin de Ville was a partner in several pawnshops. Anthoine Fallet owned, wholly or partly, those of Lille and Namur; Jehan de Rubis, those of Saint-Omer, Nieuport, Bergues-Saint-Winoc; and Thomas de Laval was the lombard of Bois-le-Duc.

[29]For more details, see Bigwood, *Régime,* I, 382-85; II, 424-44, No. 93.

[30]Dorothy Johnson Orchard and Geoffrey May, *Money Lending in Great Britain* (New York: Russell Sage Foundation, 1933), p. 30.

[31]Bigwood, *Régime,* I, 346. In 1399, councilors of the duke of Burgundy learned that many of the duke's subjects 'demorans par decha ont grandes finances prestées aux usuriers de Bruges pour laquelle chose il ne pourroient estre en loy ne en office.' The councilors wrote to friends in Bruges in order to inquire whether or not all this was true.

[32]Espinas, *La vie urbaine de Douai,* II, 158.

[33]Thomas Aquinas, *Summa Theologica,* Part II, ii, quest. 78, art. 4, translated in Arthur Eli Monroe (ed.), *Early Economic Thought: Selections from Economic Literature prior to Adam Smith* (Cambridge, Mass.: Harvard University Press, 3d printing, 1930), pp. 76 f.

[34]Placide Lefèvre, 'A propos du trafic de l'argent exercé par les juifs de Bruxelles au XIVe siècle,' *RBPH,* IX (1930), 908. The Christian depositors in question were two priests named Jean and Guillaume de Halle, most probably of lombard descent and related to the usurer Simon de Mirabello. Usury was thus a family trait. Their dealings with the Jews brought our two priests before the ecclesiastical court on a charge of usury. They sought vainly to put all the blame on their maid, but apparently were convicted on her testimony. What action was taken by the court is not disclosed by the extant documents. According to the decretals of the Church, members of the clergy who were found guilty of usury were to be deprived of their office.

[35]Bigwood, *Régime,* II, 428.

[36]Chastellain, *op. cit.*, III, chap. lxi, 315.

[37]Bigwood, *Régime*, II, 428; I, 380 ff.

[38]Chastellain, *op. cit.*, III, chap. lxi, 315.

[39]Bigwood, *Régime*, II, 428.

[40]Morel, *op. cit.*, p. 59: 'Les Lombards avaient deux catégories de clients, les seigneurs et le peuple.' For a comparison with conditions today, consult R. Cornelius Raby, *The Regulation of Pawnbroking* (New York: Russell Sage Foundation, 1924), p. 51: 'Pawnbrokers today will lend money on an article of jewelry worth thousands of dollars as well as on a household utensil or piece of wearing apparel worth only one dollar.'

[41]Bigwood, *Régime*, I, 500.

[42]*Ibid.*, p. 504.

[43]Jules Baudot, *Les princesses Yolande et les ducs de Bar de la famille des Valois* (Paris, 1900), pp. 2-35. Yolande, daughter of Robert, Lord of Cassel and granddaughter of Robert de Béthune, Count of Flanders, was born in 1326. Married to Count Henry of Bar in 1340, she was left a widow at the age of eighteen with two small children. She courageously protected the County of Bar for her son from various nobles who tried to seize it. In 1352 she remarried, but five years later she and her second husband, Philip of Navarre, Count of Longueville and Valois, were separated. He died in 1363. It was after her second husband's death—he left her nothing—that Yolande borrowed money so frequently. Her son was ruling in Bar and had married the daughter of Charles V of France, but he apparently was not in a position to give her much financial assistance. Her chief source of revenue was her dower lands, the *seigneurie* (or *terres et châtellenies*) of Cassel. Yolande died December 12, 1395.

[44]Morel, *op. cit.*, p. 59: 'C'est encore aux Lombards qu'un siècle plus tard Yolande, dame de Cassel, donne en garantie "sa belle couronne d'or et de pierreries à douze grands ornements et à neuf fleurons" pour obtenir un prêt à 50% d'intérêt.'

[45]Bigwood, *Régime*, I, 502 and II, 20 f.

[46]*Ibid.*, I, 502; II, 355, No. 51. The letter is dated from Clermont, March 22, 1365. The following sentence is significant: 'Si faites tant l'un parmi l'autre que briefment tous noz joiaux soient rachetez afin que la *finance ne monte mie sur nous*' (italics mine).

[47]*Ibid.*, II, 362 ff., No. 57.

[48]*Ibid.*, I, 503.

[49]*Ibid.*, p. 504.

[50]Morel, *op. cit.*, p. 59.

[51]Note that Yolande was arrested outside her domains. Otherwise it would not have been possible to deal so firmly with her.

[52]Häpke, *op. cit.*, p. 244; Georges Espinas and Henri Pirenne, *Recueil de documents relatifs à l'histoire de l'industrie drapière en Flandre* (Brussels, 1906-24) I, 367, No. 138, § 29. The editors date the document before 1282.

[53]Bigwood, *Régime*, I, 370 ff. In the Low Countries deeds were drawn up in the presence of *échevins* ('aldermen') instead of by notaries. See below, note 60.

[54]*Ibid.*, 370.

[55]Zdekauer, *op. cit.*, pp. 63-103. Only two folios are extant and part of the text is illegible.

[56]*Ibid.*, p. 71. Zdekauer writes that merchants (*mercanti*) were among the customers. In an appendix, he publishes the full text of the fragment, but no mention of a merchant is found.

[57]The largest loan amounted to seven florins, or £28 *piccioli*, and was secured by a man's robe which is described as old and damaged by moths (*ibid.*, p. 96, No. 3). The next to largest loan amounted to £13 4*s.* *piccioli* and was secured by a green belt with silver ornaments and a house robe of white cloth which is described as old and full of moth holes (*ibid.*, p. 97, No. 10). It seems that the pawnbroker was an expert who discovered traces of moths in nearly every garment that was pledged!

[58]Bigwood, *Régime*, II, 349, No. 45.

[59]P. de Stoop, 'Particularités sur les corporations et métiers de Bruges,' *Annales de la*

Société d'Emulation pour l'étude de l'histoire et des antiquités de la Flandre Occidentale, 2d series, I (1843), 158.

[60]In the Low Countries notaries were not so important as in mediaeval Italy. Deeds and other legal contracts were drawn up in the presence of two or more aldermen, called *échevins* in French and *schepenen* in Flemish, who were also criminal judges and town-councillors. The drafting of a deed was, of course, a time-consuming procedure, as it involved going to the town hall in order to appear before the aldermen. This was not done unless the importance of the contract or legal requirements made going to such trouble unavoidable.

[61]Bigwood, *Régime,* I, 520 f. Cf. O'Brien, *op. cit.,* p. 185. According to the canonist doctrine, the lender was supposed to suffer damage and was entitled to compensation if the borrower failed to pay at maturity. This compensation was called *poena conventionalis.*

[62]Bigwood, *Régime,* I, 521.

[63]P. Boissonnade, *Le travail dans l'Europe chrétienne au moyen âge: Ve-XVe siècles* (Paris, 1921), p. 358. Cf. Morel *op. cit.,* p. 56.

[64]The modern Flemish is *week* (spelled as in English), but in the dialect of Bruges and West Flanders, the old form *woeke* has been preserved.

[65]Kuske, *op. cit.,* p. 408.

[66]Hénaux, *op. cit.,* p. 316, n. 2. The same is true of Lille. C. Piton, *Les Lombards en France et à Paris,* I (Paris, 1892), 245; A. Benôit, 'Le "Beauregard" de Lille,' *Revue du Nord,* XXV (1939), 16-17.

[67]'Lombard,' *Oosthoek's Geillustreerde Encyclopaedie,* VIII (1936), 612.

[68]Morel, *op. cit.,* p. 60: 'Leurs opérations furent si considérables qu'on put les accuser de ruiner tout un pays et d'apporter la misère où ils séjournaient et les débiteurs après avoir mis "le peu de meubles qu'ilz ont aux Lombards ou souventes fois se consument et ainsi desnouez de tous moiens se mettent à la besace et brimberie à la surcharge des povres de la ville." '

[69]Cf. Wilhelm Endemann, 'Die nationalökonomischen Grundsätze der canonistischen Lehre,' *Hildebrand's Jahrbücher für Nationalökonomie,* I (1863), 346. If money is used for productive purposes, the problem is entirely different.

[70]Gilliodts, *Coutume,* I, 519: 'Item van dat wy staende hadden ten grooten cauwersinen in den wouker 8 wouken lanc gheduerende 10 tb. gr.; over elke wouke 20*s.*; somma 8 tb. par.

[71]Bigwood, *Régime,* I, 448.

[72]The figures and other information are taken from an account of one of Countess Yolande's stewards. This account is entitled: 'Ce sont les parties que madame la contesse de Bar et dame de Cassel doit as Caoursins à Lessines.' The text is published in full by Bigwood, *Régime,* II, 356-8, No. 52. The transactions relating to the loan can be summarized as follows:

Principal borrowed on January 12, 1364	1,200	*moutons*
One year interest at 25% on 1,200 *moutons*	300	
Balance due on January 12, 1365	1,500	
Interest from Jan. 12 to July 12, 1365, or six months at 25% on 1,500 *moutons*	187½	
Interest from July 12 to August 3, 1365, three weeks, as per agreement	12½	
Balance due on August 3, 1365	1,700	
Deduct repayment	−1,127	
Balance carried over	573	*moutons*
Interest from August 3 to Aug. 17, 1365, two weeks at 43⅓%, 9½ *moutons,* rebated 2½ *moutons,* remains	7	
Final Balance on August 17, 1365	580	*moutons*

[73]This practice was sometimes prohibited; for example, instructions dispatched by the duke's council to the lombards of Grammont explicitly forbade them to compound interest

at the end of the year ('. . . et ne pourront lesdiz lombars mettre usure au bout de la dicte année'). Bigwood, *Régime,* II, 394, doc. No. 77, dated November 6, 1401.

[74]Bigwood, *Régime,* II, 20-21, Appendix I, item No. 98.

[75]*Ibid.,* pp. 22-23, Appendix I, item No. 103.

[76]*Ibid.,* item No. 106 and p. 364, doc. No. 57: 'Item doit avoir pour la monte des 5000 frans pour ung an 1500 frans, dont il ont le moix pour cascun millier 25 frans.' The information given in the document published by Bigwood is too incomplete and too confusing to permit us from the available data to prepare a summarized account, as was done for the loan from the lombards of Lessines.

[77]Bigwood, *Régime,* I, 448; II, 22-23, Appendix I, item No. 101.

[78]*Ibid.,* item No. 103.

[79]*Ibid.,* I, 120: 'La création de rentes a été le mode normal pour les villes du moyen âge de se créer des ressources extraordinaires.'

[80]*Ibid.,* pp. 116-17.

[81]Gilliodts, *Cart de l'Estaple,* I, 189, No. 257.

[82]*Idem, Inventaire,* IV, 521.

[83]Bigwood, *Régime,* II, 38-39, Appendix I, item No. 199.

[84]Espinas, *op. cit.,* II, 153.

[85]Bigwood, *Régime,* II, 356, No. 52: 'Et il doivent avoir 300 vies moutons du Roy en *courtoisie* pour le premier an . . .' *(italics are mine).*

[86]Hans van Werveke, *De Gentsche stadsfinanciën in de middeleeuwen* ('Memoires de l'Académie royale de Belgique, Classe des lettres, etc.,' Collection in 8°, 2d series, Vol. XXXIV; Brussels, 1934), p. 277.

[87]Bigwood, *Régime,* II, 364: 'Ensi demeure qu'il devoit avoir pour les *montes* des frans dessus ditz pour un an entier fenissant le 21e jour d'avrilg l'an 1371 tant en *montez* comme du principael rabatu ce que on en a payet' *(italics mine); ibid.,* 357: ' . . . dont la livre de gros monte 2 gros de Flandre le simaine.'

[88]Gilliodts, *Cart. de l'Estaple,* I, 433, No. 518. The word 'interest' is not used except in its original meaning of compensation, as in the legal expression *dommages et intérêts.* Non-payment on maturity of a bill of exchange gave rise to a claim for *despens, dommages et interetz* (Gilliodts, *Coutume,* I, 461). This text is from 1470.

[89]*Ibid.,* p. 531. Sometimes the word *bate,* meaning 'profit' in English, is used in Flemish texts. (Bruges, Municipal Archives, Chartes politiques, No. 445, fol. 3 [*ca.* 1340]).

[90]*Ibid.,* p. 450. Text is dated March 11, 1409.

[91]It is very difficult to give any figures, as profits varied from year to year and from one enterprise to another. A prominent economic historian, Professor Armando Sapori, estimates that profits in the Florentine wool trade oscillated between 7% and 15%. See his article 'Il commercio internazionale nel medioevo,' reprint from *Archivio di studi corporativi* (1938, fasc. 3), pp. 32-33. (The same article with some changes was republished in the *Rivista storica italiana* [1938]). See also Sapori's book, *Una compagnia di Calimala ai primi del Trecento* (Florence, 1932), pp. 136-37. Money invested at interest with banks or commercial firms yielded from 6 to 10% a year (see Armando Sapori, 'L'interesse del danaro a Firenze nel Trecento: dal testamento di un usuraio.' *Archivio storico italiano,* 7th series, X [1928], 179; Edler, 'Eclaircissements à propos des considérations de R. Davidsohn sur la productivité de l'argent au moyen âge,' *op. cit.,* pp. 375-80). In the Florentine woolen industry, 10% on invested capital was a fair return (de Roover, 'A Florentine Firm of Cloth Manufacturers,' *op. cit.,* p. 25, n. 4). For further evidence, see also Gino Luzzatto, 'Sull'attendibilità di alcune statistiche economiche medievali,' *Giornale degli economisti e rivista di statistica,* 4th series, LXIX (1929), p. 132, Melvin M. Knight, *Economic History of Europe to the End of the Middle Ages* (New York, 1926), p. 116; Frank H. Knight, 'Interest,' *Encyclopaedia of the Social Sciences,* VIII, 139; *Josef Kulischer, 'Zur Entwickelungsgeschichte des Kapitalzinses,' Jahrbücher für Nationalökonomie und Statistik,* LXXIII (1899) 305-71. The title of this article is very misleading, as it hardly touches upon the question of the productivity of capital

(Kapitalzins). Most of the discussion is devoted to trade with primitive tribes and to monopoly profits.

[92]This was recognized long ago as is evident from the following Flemish verses:

In den wouker draegt syn panden
En daer vooren creyght wat ghelt.
Maar wanneer hy lost de cleeren
Compt den armen man te leeren
Dat den wouker is een dief,
En gherief vol ongherief.

('Carrying one's pledges to the pawnshop—Will bring in some cash—But, when it comes to redeeming them—Then the poor borrower finds out—That the pawnshop is a thief—And does not bring relief.') Quoted from L. L. De Bo, *Westvlaamsch Idioticon* (Bruges, 1873), p. 1406. Cf. Louis N. Robinson and Rolf Nugent, *Regulation of the Small Loan Business* (New York: Russell Sage Foundation, 1935), p. 209.

[93]Bigwood, *Régime*, I, 320.

[94]Morel, *op. cit.*, pp. 51-52.

[95]Gilliodts, *Coutume*, I, 453: a court sentence of January 22, 1452.

[96]Bigwood, *Régime*, II, 424, No. 93: 'Comme nagaires Anthoine et Cathelan Macet, frères, filz de feu Pol Macet, en son vivant natiif de la ville de Ker en Piemont, eussent eu tant en leurs propres et privez noms comme ès noms des aultres Macets et de leurs compaignonx la *principale* charge, gouvernement et administracion des bancs, maisons et tables nommez en la ville de Bruges les Grands Caoursins et le Paon . . .' (italics mine).

[97]Morel, *op. cit.*, pp. 300-15, doc. No. 63.

[98]Tawney, Intro., Wilson, *Discourse upon Usury*, pp. 29 f.

[99]Gilliodts, *Inventaire*, VI, 147, charter No. 1155.

[100]J. H. Darings, 'Over de Lombaerden en Bergen van Barmhartigheid in België,' *Belgisch Museum voor de Nederduitsche Tael- en Letterkunde*, VI (1842), 357.

[101]The first two *montes pietatis* were founded in Perugia and Orvieto (Umbria) around 1465 by the Franciscan Order. The new institution spread rapidly to other Italian cities, and from there to the Low Countries and Spain. In France the *monts-de-piété* were not introduced until the XVIIIth century; there was one in Marseilles before 1696, but the one in Paris was not founded until 1777. The creation of *montes pietatis* or *monts-de-piété* was essentially a Catholic movement which was not paralleled in Protestant countries (de Decker, *op. cit.*, pp. 27 ff.).

[102]*Ibid.*, p. 206.

[103]*Ibid.*, p. 141.

[104]Darings, *op. cit.*, p. 355.

[105]de Decker, *op. cit.*, p. 129.

[106]*Ibid.*, p. 141.

[107]*Ibid.*, pp. 117 f., 139. The story repeated itself in 1705, when the Elector-Governor General pawned part of his jewelry with the *mont-de-piété* of Brussels (*ibid.*, p. 181).

[108]*Ibid.*, p. 182.

[109]Consult the various publications of the Russell Sage Foundation, chiefly Raby, *op. cit.*,; Robinson and Nugent, *op. cit.*, Orchard and May, *op. cit.*

[110]Raby, *op. cit.*, p. 6.

[111]In the Low Countries such a formal contract often took the form of a letter obligatory which was called *chirographe* in technical language. A *chirographe* was usually drawn up in the presence of the municipal officers, *échevins* or *jurés*, as the case might be, and differed from the English bond in that the *chirographe* was not a letter close given under seal, but a letter patent. The lombards of Bruges occasionally accepted *chirographes* as evidence for their loans. Two examples are mentioned by Gilliodts (*Inventaire*, I, 499, No. 455; 501, No. 460). The dates of these two documents are respectively August 1, 1346, and June 29, 1347. Gilliodts unfortunately does not publish the full text, but gives only a very unsatisfactory sum-

mary of the contents. In both cases the creditor is the lombard Otto Garet. Bigwood (*Régime,* II, 285, 292, 341, 343, 350) publishes several *chirographes* involving the lombards of Nivelles as creditors. The dates range from 1275 to 1362. Bigwood's statement (*ibid.,* I, 457) that the letter obligatory rather than some kind of pawnticket was the typical document used by the lombards is not correct in my opinion. The use of the letter obligatory involved burdensome and time-consuming formalities and was limited to a few important loans.

[112]L. Gilliodts-van-Severen, *Inventaire des archives de la Ville de Bruges: Table des noms de familles, Table des noms de lieux et Glossaire flamand,* prepared by Edward Gaillard (Bruges, 1879), p. 832, 'Caoursin;' E. Feys et D. Van de Casteele, *Histoire d'Oudenbourg* (Bruges, 1873), II, 454.

[113]Gilliodts, *Coutume,* I, 527; *idem, Cart de l'Estaple,* II, 161, No. 1102; Bigwood, *Régime,* I, 494.

[114]Gilliodts, *Coutume,* 1, 526 ff; *idem, Cart. de l'Estaple,* II, 160 ff., No. 1102.

[115]Pirenne, *Economic and Social History,* p. 135.

[116]Gilliodts, *Cart de l'Estaple,* I, 433, No. 518; *idem, Coutume,* I, 512.

[117]Gilliodts, *Cart. de l'Estaple,* II, 160-62, No. 1102; *idem, Coutume,* I, 526-28.

[118]The same was true in many towns of Western Germany (see Schulte, *op. cit.,* I, 324).

[119]Laenen, 'Usuriers et Lombards dans le Brabant au XVe siècle,' *op. cit.,* p. 132.

[120]Bigwood, *Régime,* II, 394, No. 77.

[121]*Ibid.,* p. 395, No. 78. Document dated September 18, 1404. The lombard lent £3 12*s.* gr. on a pledge appraised at £5 18*s.* 4*d.* gr.

[122]Gilliodts, *Cart. de l'Estaple,* I, 433, No. 518; *idem, Coutume,* I, 512.

[123]Apparently the rightful owner could recover damages only from the pawner of stolen goods (see Gilliodts, *Coutume,* I, 531).

[124]*Ibid.,* p. 450.

[125]Morel, *op. cit.,* p. 61.

[126]Raby, *op. cit.,* p. 5.

[127]de Decker, *op. cit.,* p. xxxv.

[128]Gilliodts, *Coutume,* I, 529-31.

[129]de Decker, *op. cit.,* p. xxiii.

[130]Koch, *op. cit.,* p. 29.

[131]Georges Espinas, *Documents relatifs à la draperie de Valenciennes au moyen âge* (Paris, 1931), p. 108, No. 135, arts. 1, 2.

[132]Morel, *op. cit.,* pp. 9 f.

[133]Gilliodts, *Coutume,* I, 529.

[134]'Het "Register van den Dachvaerden",' *Bulletin des Archives d'Anvers* (*Antwerpsch Archievenblad*) XIX (n.d.), 337.

[135]Bigwood, *Régime,* I, 303: 'Les de Ville, lombards établis à Anvers, font le commerce de draps.'

[136]Chastellain, *Chronique,* III, chap. lxi, 314 f.: 'En ce mesme temps, en Bruges, sur la fin du mois de may [1457], advint un cas estrange, car les trois tabliers qui tenoient les bancs des usures piémontois, s'enfuirent par nuyt, et chargeans en bouges multitude d'avoir, s'en allèrent en divers lieux en franchise, les uns tout loings, autres en Valencines et ailleurs, et *emportèrent merveilleuse chevance* des marchans et bourgeois de la dite ville, *dont la criée devint si grande que nulle onques telle*' (italics mine).

[137]Bigwood, *Régime,* I, 380-85, gives a detailed narrative of the facts concerning the bankruptcy of the lombards of Bruges (cf., *ibid.,* II, 424-44, No. 93). Chastellain says that one of their partners became involved in financial difficulties 'par avoir trop embrassié de marchandises en Angleterre.' This certainly means wool, the English commodity *par excellence.*

[138]Chastellain, *op. cit.,* III, 315.

[139]Bigwood, *Régime,* II, 424: '[Les dits caoursins] qui se sont absentez desdits lieux ou maisons pour grandes et excessives sommes de deniers par eulx deuz à cause de pluiseurs marchandises achatez de certains marchans demourans et habitans en icelle ville de Bruges . . .'

The list of these merchants included Angelo Tani (the local representative of the Medici), the Welsers, the Spinolas of Genoa, the Justiniani of Venice, and others.

[140]I say *nearly,* because the lombards were apparently able to reorganize their business, though the information concerning the settlement of the bankruptcy is incomplete. According to Bigwood, the same company of lombards was still in control of the pawnshop of Bruges in 1465 (*Régime,* II, 58) and was probably slowly paying off past liabilities. In any case, Anthoine Macet, the senior partner, was kept in prison for several years until the creditors had obtained full satisfaction either by payment or by assignment on his property (Chastellain, *op. cit.,* III, 316; cf. Bigwood, *Régime,* I, 385). Chastellain's text seems to suggest that the pawnshop in Bruges and several others remained closed, until the creditors and the lombards had reached some kind of an agreement. Though the bankruptcy occurred in May, 1457, negotiations were still going on in January, 1459 (*ibid.,* II, 424) and no agreement had been achieved as yet. Cf. Grunzweig, 'La correspondance de la filiale brugeoise des Medici,' *op. cit.,* pp. 725-32. Grunzweig believes that the proposal of Pierre de Ville, who offered to take over the pawnshop of the Machet, was actually accepted. There is a third possibility: Pierre de Ville might have been a strawman. In any case, the problem raised by Grunzweig cannot be solved without more information than is now available.

[141]Bigwood (*Régime,* I, 361-66) is of a different opinion and considers that these dealings in grain have an exclusively commercial character. This statement has been disproved by subsequent research undertaken by another Belgian scholar. See J. Bolsée, 'Une enquête sur les usuriers dans l'Ammanie de Bruxelles en 1393,' *Bulletin de la Commission Royale d'Histoire,* CII (1937), 141-210.

[142]Koch, *op. cit.,* p. 27: Licence of 1413 concerning the lombards of Forest (cf. Bigwood, *Régime,* I, 366).

[143]Bigwood, *Régime,* I, 303. Cf. Etienne Sabbe, 'De Lombarden te Kortrijk in de XIIIe, XIVe en XVe eeuwen,' *Annales de la Société d'Emulation de Bruges,* LXVII (1924), 173-80.

[144]Bigwood, *Régime,* I, 294.

[145]Laenen, 'Les Lombards à Malines,' *op. cit.,* p. 31.

[146]Bigwood, *Régime,* I, 303 f.

[147]The use of the word 'mortgage' has been purposely avoided here. In the Low Countries, as in many other places on the European continent, there existed three different types of loans secured by real estate: *le mort-gage, le vif-gage,* and *la rente foncière.* In the case of *mort-gage,* the income produced by the property given as security, went to the lender, and it was not deductible from the principal of the loan. In the case of *vif-gage,* the lender still collected the income, but it was applied against the principal due to him. The loan thus automatically became extinct after a period of time. See Hans van Werveke, 'Le mort-gage et son rôle économique en Flandre et en Lotharingie,' *op. cit.,* pp. 54 f. The *rentes foncières* or rent-charges (in Flemish *erflyke renten*) are in many ways similar to present-day mortgages and should not be confused with *loyers* ('rents') or *cens* ('feudal dues'). The *rente foncière* involved the yearly payment by the borrower to the lender of a given sum, called *rente.* The *rente foncière* was repayable at the option of the debtor at a rate of capitalization determined by contract. Thus a *rente au denier vingt* meant that the loan could be redeemed by paying a lump sum equal to twenty times the annual *rente.* This is equivalent to an interest rate of 5%. A *rente au denier seize* corresponds to 6¼% and *au denier vingt-cinq,* to 4%. From the point of view of the lender, *rentes foncières* were perpetual in character. He could sell his rights to a third party, but he could not exact payment of the principal from an unwilling debtor. If the latter defaulted on the yearly income payments, however, the property given as security could be seized by the creditor. By the fourteenth and fifteenth centuries, the *rentes foncières* had become far more common than either the *mort-gage* or the *vif-gage.*

[148]Gilliodts, *Inventaire,* II, 140 and 182.

[149]For another example for Bruges, see Delepierre, *op. cit.,* I, clvi (September 5, 1359); cf. Bigwood, *Régime,* I, 526-39.

[150]Bigwood (*Régime,* I, 472-76) gives, however, a few examples involving the lombards of

Tournai, Nivelles, and Mons. One reason why examples are not more numerous is apparently that most borrowers wanted to keep their troubles secret. They would have been revealed, if friend or relative had been asked to give surety.

	£ s d
[151]5,000 francs at 36 groats	750. 0. 0
3,000 florins of Hungary at 33 groats	412.10. 0
3,000 florins at 32 groats	400. 0. 0
Total	1,562.10. 0

These rates are given in an incomplete statement of account (Bigwood, *Régime, II,* 362, No. 57).

[152]*Ibid.,* pp. 22-23, Appendix I, item No. 106.

[153]*Ibid.,* I, 551.

[154]Pirenne, *Histoire de Belgique,* II, 207.

[155]The Flemish name is *pointinghen.* See Gilliodts, *Inventaire, Glossaire flamand,* II, 504 f. The assessment was in theory based on the capacity to pay, but in practice it was probably very arbitrary.

[156]Gilliodts, *Inventaire,* II, 349-53.

[157]Schulte (*op. cit.,* I, 315) writes: 'Die Schuldner waren meist kleine Leute.' He states further (p. 316): 'Es fehlt ja nicht an Zeugnissen auch über wirkliche "Anleihen" von geistlichen oder weltlichen Fürsten und Herren, aber wie die erhaltenen Akten solcher Casanen uns lehren, ist das Darlehen auf oder ohne Pfand, das kleinen Leuten gewährt wurde, der Mittelpunkt des Geschäftslebens.'

[158]Schulte thinks erroneously that the lombards' credit helped people to start in business or to expand existing enterprises (*op. cit.,* I, 325). It would have been foolish for anyone to borrow at 43⅓% in order to earn only from 7% to 15%. The lombards specialized decidedly in consumers' credit.

Chapter 8

THE SOCIAL PROBLEM OF CONSUMERS' CREDIT

THE lombards were often accused of bringing ruin and distress wherever they settled down, and of squeezing the poor until they were reduced to beggary and became public charges.[1] Some went even farther and denounced the lombards as extortioners, money-mongers, and suppliers to the gallows because they supposedly drove their despairing victims to delinquency and crime. These commonplaces, resting on sheer prejudice and superficial analysis have been accepted and endorsed by modern historians. More careful investigation of the facts, however, would have revealed immediately that any such statements confused cause and effect.

Borrowing in itself, even for consumption purposes, cannot lead to insolvency, unless the borrower foolishly makes commitments inconsistent with his income. This might be, and often is, the result of ignorance on the one hand and of deceit on the other. The borrower could wait before making some purchases, but he is persuaded to take advantage of the 'attractive' offer of some clever money-lender. If trouble develops later, it clearly results from inconsiderate borrowing.[2] But the borrower has only himself to blame.

In most cases, however, borrowing is not at the root of the trouble, but the real cause of financial difficulties is to be sought in some individual misfortune or social maladjustment. It may be death, illness, unemployment, bad crops, or drinking, shiftlessness, improvidence, and sheer prodigality. As a result, the borrower's budget is either temporarily or permanently out of balance. Borrowing will only postpone difficulties and lead to ultimate insolvency unless some way is found to eliminate the disturbing factor which caused the borrower to spend beyond his income.

While loans for consumption purposes are rarely the primary cause of financial troubles, one should not be blind to the fact that such troubles are certainly aggravated by the high interest rates wrested from the borrower. The result is to make the repayment much more difficult and painful. In many cases it requires threats of court action or other forms of pressure to make the debtor fulfill his commitments. Pitilessness is an integral part of a money lender's business, and resentment and wrath are the most common feelings among the borrowers.

Those are the conditions today; those were the conditions in the Middle Ages. No wonder that the lombards were needed, feared, and hated, all at the same time.

In Flanders and elsewhere, several attempts were made to dispense with the lombards. Such attempts were invariably shattered on the rocks of economic and social realities. Failure of such attempts was bound to ensue as long as conditions prevailed which often made borrowing for consumption purposes an imperative necessity.

As soon as the lombards were driven out, their place was taken by a throng of secret money-lenders who would grind their victims under the crushing weight of usurious interest rates, much higher than those charged by the lombards. Popular complaints would soon compel the authorities to recall the lombards as the lesser of two evils.

By the end of the fourteenth century, the pawnshop of the Grands Cahorsins in Bruges had been vacant for some time. When a group of lombards applied for a licence, the authorities were glad to grant the request and candidly admitted that they did so 'in order to eschew greater harm and loss to the public.'[3] While the licenced pawnshop was closed, people from Valenciennes, Tournai, and elsewhere had been prompt to take advantage of this situation. They had engaged in money-lending and were exacting much higher rates than the lombards had been accustomed to charge.[4]

The story was reenacted three-quarters of a century later, when Charles the Bold, in June, 1473, suddenly suspended the licences which were in operation throughout the Low Countries. After a few months, or more exactly in November of the same year, he saw himself compelled to reestablish all the pawnshops at the urgent request of deputations from the boroughs. The lombards, it was pointed out to the Duke, were indispensible 'to keep trade and business going.'[5] The same note is struck in a document which is a little late—it dates from 1601—but what it says was true earlier. In this significant document, it is stated squarely that it is a matter of record that the common people are constantly in need of small advances of money, and that great distress would consequently result, if they were cut off from means of pawning in order to obtain cash.[6] For these reasons, the document adds, it has been necessary to tolerate the lombards who are licenced by the sovereign to lend money for profit to the needy.

In view of this avowed social need for consumers' credit, the attitude of the Church and the canonist doctrine on usury were woefully inadequate, because they were based exclusively on a few theological concepts, legal principles, maxims drawn from classical pagan authors, either directly or via patristic authors, and obscure biblical quotations, but overlooked almost entirely the economic and social conditions which allowed usury to exist. The fundamental truth is that people in need of financial help had to depend upon the money-lender either because they had not been able to find a Christian soul willing to lend them without interest, or because they preferred to keep their troubles concealed from relatives and friends.[7]

The creation of the *monts-de-piété* under the auspices of the Church or in alliance with the government was certainly a step in the right direction. Despite the reduction of the interest rate from 43⅓ per cent to 15 per cent, achievements fell short of the expected results, partly because of mismanagement and partly because of unbusinesslike procedure. Sometimes credit accommodation was made subject to inquisitive and irksome investigation about the borrower's needs.[8] In other instances, the borrower was made to feel that granting him a loan was a favor almost equivalent to charity.[9] Another major grievance against government controlled pawnshops was, and still is, the extremely low valuation put upon pledges. As appraisers are personally responsible for any losses arising from the sale of unredeemed pawns, this evil is difficult to eradicate.[10] It has unfortunately led to a greater evil, since the buying up of pawntickets has developed into a real swindle.[11]

In view of these conditions, it is not surprising that people would shun the *monts-de-piété* and prefer to deal with the secret usurers who maintained themselves alongside the official loan agencies. The creation of the *monts-de-piété* was, of course, the death-knell of public or licenced usury.

According to the doctrine of the mediaeval Church, usurers were excluded from the communion of the Faithful: they were not supposed to attend Divine service; they were not admitted to the sacraments; and they were denied burial in hallowed ground.[12] This was the theory, at least. In practice things were a little different. Because of God's infinite mercy, usurers always could obtain absolution *in articulo mortis* provided that they repented their sins and offered to make restitution. As this involved some practical difficulties, the Church never objected to accepting bequests as a substitute.[13] The ban could also be lifted by obtaining dispensation.[14] As we have seen, an attitude of leniency prevailed in the Low Countries during the fourteenth and fifteenth centuries, and it became customary to grant dispensation to usurers licenced by the secular authorities. We know with certainty that this practice was followed in the bishopric of Cambrai. The situation was doubtless the same in the neighboring diocese of Tournai whose jurisdiction extended over Bruges. In the sixteenth century, however, a reaction set in, apparently in an attempt to counteract the spread of the Reformation. The Church reaffirmed its traditional doctrine on the matter of usury and reverted to the uncompromising attitude which had prevailed prior to the fifteenth century. The secular authorities, however reluctantly, continued to issue licences, but the Church henceforth refused to grant dispensation to the lombards. They were, and remained, excommunicated. According to Charles V's ordinance of January 30, 1546 (n.s.), licenced usurers were forbidden to attend mass or to enter any church under the penalty of forfeiting their licences. The same prohibition applied to anyone who was in partnership with them, who owned a share in their *tables de prêt,* or who participated in their management.[15]

Very often members of the lower clergy and of the preaching orders would not conform to the line of conduct adopted by the higher ecclesiastical authorities and would deplore the 'corruption' which had crept into the Church. Dispensation or no dispensation, the lombards were branded from the pulpits as 'manifest usurers, public sinners, and servants of Lucifer.'[16] It is, perhaps, needless to add that the views of the priesthood were fully shared by the flock.

In a profoundly religious society like that of the Middle Ages, the ban of the Church meant social isolation. Although the lombards, being nominally Christians, were not exactly outcasts like the Jews, they were not socially acceptable, either, and did not play an active part in the life of the community. Decent people—in case of need—would deal, but not associate, with them.[17] In mediaeval Bruges the *Joyeuses Entrées* of the princes were important social events. On such occasions the foreign 'nations' or colonies would march in procession through the streets of the city, and the different groups—the Venetians, the Genoese, the Florentines, the Spaniards, the Easterlings—would vie with each other in mustering the greatest number of participants and in displaying the richest costumes.[18] It is significant that the lombards were never represented in any of such processions. Notorious usurers, of course, could not conspicuously parade through the city.

Though the lombards were socially isolated, they were not homeless like the Jews. They called themselves proudly *cives astenses.*[19] Many of them were of gentle birth and belonged to the most prominent families of Asti and Chieri, their home-cities.[20] This was the case of the families Garetti, Royer or Roerio, Solari, and Macetti, which, at one time or another, were represented in Bruges. In view of the prevailing social conditions, it is probable that the lombards intermarried a great deal, although there is no positive evidence on the subject. Marriages into the local upper classes must have been exceptional.[21]

In 1388, however, the son of a lombard of Nivelles took as bride the daughter of a neighboring nobleman, the lord of Bois-Seigneur-Isaac. It should be added that the bridegroom, far from engaging in money-lending, was himself in debt to the lombards who had taken over his father's business.[22] There is, unfortunately, no information available at present with regard to the matrimonial alliances of the lombards of Bruges.

Whether or not the lombards succeeded in accumulating much wealth depended on the earning possibilities of a given pawnshop and the importance of their share in the profits. It is, moreover, clear that those possibilities were limited by the volume of business and that, consequently, pawnshops in small towns were less profitable than those located in important cities like Bruges. It is therefore not surprising to read in the records that the lombard of Bois-le-Duc, an unimportant town in Brabant, was so poor that he could not pay the fines which he had incurred as a result of frivolous litigation.[23]

According to popular belief, money-lenders could not be anything but rich.[24] As we have just seen, some of them were poor, others were persons of means or even very wealthy. The estate of Jacques Mancegas, a lombard of Bruges, who died around 1363 without leaving any heirs, amounted to £419 10*s*. groat which escheated to the count of Flanders. This is not a very large amount, but Jacques Mancegas was probably not one of the principal partners.[25] Another lombard, Benoit Royer of Ghent, in the hope of saving his soul, bequeathed all his property to Pope John XXII.[26] The estate included two houses, one in Brussels and one in Courtrai, and several claims, totalling £256 groat, though this total is probably incomplete.[27] A more important estate is that of Simon de Mirabello's father, who died in prison on October 10, 1333, and whose property had been confiscated by the duke of Brabant.[28] The son claimed that the seizure of his inheritance had been illegal and demanded restitution of the following property: a house in Brussels, the seigneurie of Perwez, land in Huisdine, Heyst-op-den-Berg, and Lierre, woodland bought from the duke at the price of £1,500 groat, a flock of sheep valued at £4,000 *tournois,* plate and jewelry worth £600 groat, claims against the count of Cleves for £13,000 *tournois,* letters of indebtedness under the duke's great seal for an amount of £1,725 groat, and shares in several pawnshops of Brabant.[29] All this wealth, though, did not originate in the pawnbroking business, as the deceased had been for some time the Duke's *receveur* or treasurer, a circumstance which explains why he died in prison under a charge of misappropriation of funds.[30]

The son, Simon de Mirabello, had an even more eventful and extraordinary career. His start, like that of his father's, was in the pawnbroking business. On March 20, 1307, Simon de Mirabello, his brother John, and three members of the Royer family were granted for ten years the exclusive rights of money lending in Ghent.[31] This licence was probably renewed several times in favor of the same group. In 1345 Simon de Mirabello still had an interest in the pawnshop of Ghent.[32] It is possible that, in the beginning, Simon might have taken an active part in the management, but there is no doubt that, as time went on, he withdrew more and more into the background and left the administrative duties to his partners. Most likely, he kept a hand in the business, but interfered only when important decisions were involved.

As Simon de Mirabello gained in wealth and social prestige, he probably became more eager to have people forget that he was a lombard.[33] He preferred to be called Simon de Halen or de Mirabel, sire de Perwez, *chevalier*.[34] His investments also changed in character, and his surplus income was increasingly devoted to the acquisition of *seigneuries* and other landed property.[35] Simon de Mirabello, however, never lost all interest in money-lending. As late as 1342 or only four years before his death, he obtained a licence by which he was authorized to open a pawnshop in Malines.[36]

Besides pawnbroking, successful loans to the count of Flanders[37] and the city of Ghent[38] contributed a great deal to the enrichment and rise of Simon de Mirabello. As such transactions involved the risk of default, he was presumably very careful in his dealings with public authorities. His tactics were probably to play safe, to avoid tying up borrowed funds, and to lend only on good security, i.e., on assignment of specific sources of revenue.[39] By following this policy, Simon de Mirabello escaped having his credits frozen and even succeeded in maintaining friendly relations with his borrowers. In 1327, when he, his father, and his brother were arrested in Brabant, the city of Ghent obtained the release of the two brothers on the ground that they were burghers of that city.[40] Later, the count of Flanders used his influence with the duke of Brabant to have the estate of Simon de Mirabello's father restored to the son.[41] After the death of his first wife, the shrewd financier married a natural sister of the count of Flanders.[42] Simon was knighted and, in 1329, became for a short time 'receiver general' or treasurer of Flanders. Why he did not retain this office is not known, but certainly it was not because of lack of competence.

Despite his family ties with the ruling house, Simon de Mirabello was opposed to the count's policy of loyalty to the French crown. He espoused the cause of the democratic party led by Jacques van Artevelde who favored the alliance with England.[43]. This allegiance brought new honors to Sir Simon, who was proclaimed *Ruwaert* or Regent of Flanders after the count's flight.[44] A lombard, regent of Flanders! However, Simon de Mirabello never assumed actual leadership, but was the puppet behind which Jacques van Artevelde pulled the strings.[45] Apparently, our lombard was better at making money than at playing the political game. In his capacity of *Ruwaert,* Simon de Mirabello entertained lavishly Edward III of England, who, in 1340, resided in Ghent for several weeks.[46]

He also lent money to the King on the strength of an assignment on 1,030 sacks of wool to be shipped from England. Besides this guarantee, several princes of the Low Countries, including Reginald, Duke of Gelderland, a brother-in-law of Edward III, were sureties for the latter.[47]

It is not difficult to guess why Simon de Mirabello favored the cause of the *communes* rather than that of his relative and debtor, the Count of Flanders. Mirabello, there is not the slightest doubt, had a big stake in the wool trade and in the woolen industry. Consequently, the alliance with France, which would have cut off the supply of the English wool necessary to the Flemish cloth industry, was against his economic interest and he threw in his lot with the *communes* rather than with the Count and his feudal following. It is difficult to tell whether this decision was impelled by other more personal motives, such as ambition and craving for social recognition. It is likely that the profit motives dominated all other impulses.

After the murder of Jacques van Artevelde in July, 1345, his faction began to lose ground and Simon de Mirabello became apprehensive for his life. On January 15, 1346, he made his will which included generous legacies to the Church and to charities. This precaution proved to be wise, because Simon de Mirabello was killed by political opponents on May 9, 1346.[48] He was buried with great pomp in the collegiate church of St Pharaïlde in Ghent, which he had richly endowed.

The career of Simon de Mirabello is interesting because it is exceptional rather than typical.[49] It is extremely unlikely that many lombards followed his example and took root in the Low Countries. Probably only very few accumulated wealth. Some of them, as we have seen, failed, but most of them apparently saved enough money to return to their homeland and to spend the rest of their days in comfortable retirement as respectable citizens. How their fortunes had been made, probably nobody asked or cared much about.

Simon de Mirabello's success was certainly due to a strong personality, which overcame all economic handicaps and was not hampered by any religious scruples. Even a Mirabello could not have risen to social prominence if he had stayed in the pawnbroking business. It is noteworthy that as his career progressed, pawnbroking became more and more a sideline carried on indirectly through partners and factors. Surplus profits were increasingly invested in landed property, the form of wealth which par excellence conferred social prestige.

NOTES TO CHAPTER 8

[1]The medieval Flemish poet, Jan Boendaele (d. 1365), accuses the lombards of bringing about the decay of towns and cities, in his poem 'Boec van der Wraken,' III, vss. 528-31:

Van woekeneren of persemieren
Hoedt u in alder manieren
Want dese twee, sonder waen,
Doen een stat te nieute gaen.

('Usurers and money-lenders—Beware of them by all means—Because these two, without boasting—Bring towns and cities to naught.') Quoted by Laenen ('Usuriers et Lombards dans le Brabant,' *op. cit.*, p. 128), from Ferdinand Augustijn Snellaert, *Nederlandsche Gedichten uit de veertiende eeuw van Jan Boendale, Hein van Aken en anderen, naer het Oxfordsch handschrift* (Brussels: Académie Royale de Belgique, 1869), p. 421. Cf. Morel, *op. cit.*, p. 60; G. G. Coulton, *Medieval Panorama: the English Scene from Conquest to Reformation* (Cambridge: University Press, 1939), p. 357.

[2]A typical case is that of a young beginner who borrowed at the rate of more than 100% per annum in order to start a business. He soon found out that his business was not that profitable and, as a result, was unable to live up to his obligations. The creditor was threatening to lay his hand on three tenements owned by the borrower, when the latter petitioned a London court to rescind the contract for being usurious. The young beginner, in my opinion, was a gullible fool and hardly deserves the sympathy which a kind-hearted and socially-minded historian so generously bestows upon him. See Tawney, Intro., Wilson, *Discourse Upon Usury*, p. 28.

[3]Bruges, Municipal Archives, Ouden Witten Bouck, fol. 65. In this document, dated March 1, 1404, the municipal authorities declare that they have decided to grant a licence to the lombards 'pour eschiever le plus grant perte et dommaige du peuple d'icelle ville.' An ordinance of Charles V (1524) concerning Tournai proclaims that the lombards are necessary 'au support et commodité du pauvre peuple.' (Morel, *op. cit.*, p. 89, and doc. No. 45, p. 248). Cf. de Decker, *op. cit.*, p. xxx. In 1382, the municipal council of the town of Gemona in Italy commissioned two of its members to look around for a pawnbroker, either a Jew or a Christian, who would be willing to set up his business in the town (Zdekauer, *op. cit.*, pp. 79 f.). In 1404, the citizens of Siena in Tuscany petitioned the *Signoria* to abolish the system of licences and to make money lending free except for some general restrictions with regard to a maximum rate of interest (*ibid.*, p. 80 and doc. No. 4, pp. 104 f.).

[4]Gilliodts, *Cart. de l'Estaple*, I, 433, No. 518; *idem, Coutume*, I, 515.

[5]The representatives of the boroughs pointed out that 'iceulx marchans [the lombards] leur estoient duysables et nécessaires pour l'entretenement de la marchandise' (Bigwood, *Régime*, I, 386). Cf. Morel, *op. cit.*, p. 231, No. 41; Darings, *op. cit.*, p. 348. Another attempt to do away with the lombards was made in 1511. According to the decree of April 9 of that year, all the licences were cancelled on the ground that usury was contrary to the divine, the canon, and the civil, law and that they had been obtained by trickery, entreaty, and other dubious means. The toleration of usury, the decree added, had caused great scandal in the Church, had led astray many souls, had done great harm to the common weal, and had allowed many persons to squander their substance. Despite all those evils, the decree of 1511 was never put into effect and the lombards continued to be tolerated for another century. For the text of the decree, see *Recueil des ordonnances des Pays-Bas sous le règne de Charles-Quint (1506-1555)*, eds. Ch. Laurent, J. Lameere et H. Simont ('Recueil des anciennes ordonnances de la Belgique,' 2d series), I (Brussels, 1893), 164.

[6]Morel, *op. cit.*, p. 286, No. 58: '. . . toutefois l'expérience quotidienne et la nécessité publicq at démonstré et démonstre que, pour éviter plus grandz maulx et ruyne des bonnes gens, signament du commun peuple ayant à touttes heures besoing d'estre secouruz de quelque argent comptant, il convient tolérer aucunes personnes à faire quelque gaing du prest de leur argent . . .'

[7]A document of 1601 refers pointedly to the fact that men were not very charitable: '. . . pour la petite charité quy est entre les hommes. . . .' Morel, *op. cit.*, p. 286, No. 58.

[8]Zdekauer, *op. cit.*, p. 86.

[9]*Ibid.*, p. 89.

[10]Solomon Kuznets, 'Pawnbroking,' *Encyclopaedia of the Social Sciences*, XII, 38. The rule of making the appraisers personally responsible for mistakes in valuation was evolved by the Antwerp *mont-de-piété* and is known as the 'Antwerp Scheme.'

[11]Gustav Schmoller, 'Die öffentlichen Leihhäuser sowie das Pfandleih- und Rückkaufsgeschäft,' *Jahrbuch für Gesetzgebung, Verwaltung und Volkswirtschaft*, IV (1880), 120.

[12]This rule was universal in the Roman Church. It was embodied in the canon law and based on decisions of the third Lateran Council (1179), and the Councils of Lyons (1274) and Vienne (1312). See R. H. Tawney, *Religion and the Rise of Capitalism* (Pelican Books ed.; Harmondsworth, Eng.: Penguin Books Ltd., 1938), chap. i, sec. ii, p. 57. For the Low Countries, see de Decker, *op. cit.*, p. xxi; Laenen, 'Usuriers et Lombards dans le Brabant,' *op. cit.*, pp. 135 ff.

[13]Tawney cites the interesting case of a bishop of Paris who urged a usurer to dedicate his ill-gotten wealth to the building of Notre Dame rather than to make restitution (*Religion*, p. 43 and n. 30 for chap. i). For a longer account of the story, see Achille Luchaire, *Social France at the time of Philip Augustus*, trans. E. B. Krehbiel (New York, 1912), p. 166. Another striking example is given by Armando Sapori. It relates to the manner in which the will made on August 23, 1389, by a notorious usurer of Florence, Bartolomeo dei Cocchi-Compagni, was executed. The will called for complete and unconditional restitution to all persons who could prove that they had been wronged by the testator. Despite this provision, all the bequests in favor of the Church were paid in full prior to any restitution. What remained of the estate did not suffice to satisfy all the claimants. Moreover, the archbishop of Florence was awarded by the executors a grant of 100 florins 'pro incertis omnibus et singulis que petere et habere posset' ('L'interesse del danaro a Firenze nel Trecento.' *op. cit.*, pp. 174-77). Bartolomeo dei Cocchi-Compagni was buried in state under the steps of the high altar of Santa Maria Novella (*ibid.*, p. 164, n. 1), and expenses for the funeral amounted to the fantastic sum of 800 fl. (*ibid.*, p. 162, n. 2). In many Florentine wills of the period, lip service was paid to the principle of restitution by setting aside *pro incertis* a small amount for this purpose, or by leaving this matter to the discretion of the executors (*ibid.*, p. 163). On this important matter of restitution, one will profit by consulting the recent and excellent study of Benjamin N. Nelson, 'The Usurer and the Merchant Prince: Italian Businessmen and the Ecclesiastical Law of Restitution, 1100-1550,' *The Tasks of Economic History*, supplement to the *Journal of Economic History*, VII (1947), 104-122.

[14]Laenen, 'Usuriers et Lombards,' *op. cit.*, p. 135.

[15]*Recueil des ordonnances des Pays-Bas sous le règne de Charles-Quint*, V (Brussels, 1913), 215, art. 5. In Italy, the ecclesiastical authorities stiffened their policy toward usury earlier than in the Low Countries. In Florence, during the twelfth, thirteenth, and fourteenth centuries pawnbrokers had always been Christians, but in 1437 the *Signoria* granted a monopoly to Jewish money-lenders to whom, because of their religion, the prohibition of usury did not apply. See Marino Ciardini, *I banchieri ebrei in Firenze nel secolo XV e il monte di pietà fondato da Girolamo Savonarola* (Borgo S. Lorenzo, 1907), pp. 24, 28-30.

[16]Laenen, 'Usuriers et Lombards,' *op. cit.*, pp. 135 ff.

[17]The ordinance of 1546 actually proclaims that it is a scandal to see the lombards behaving like, and mixing with, decent people.

[18]Pirenne, *Histoire de Belgique*, II, 431; Olivier de la Marche, *Mémoires (1435-1488)*, III, 113; Chastellain, *op. cit.*, III, 304.

[19]Schulte, *op. cit.*, I, 314.

[20]Koch, *op. cit.*, pp. 11-17, 55.

[21]Bigwood (*Régime*, I, 306) contends that 'le mariage avec une femme belge ne fut pas rare,' and gives an impressive list of half-a-dozen lombards who married natives of the Low

Countries. He apparently overlooks the fact that no word is to be found in the Belgian archives of the more frequent marriages contracted in Italy. As a rule, the lombards did not break the ties with their homeland. There are, of course, exceptions. A hint is given in a proclamation, issued in 1473 by Charles the Bold, which contains an article referring to the marriages contracted by the lombards in Italy. This article states clearly that any marriage contracts concluded by the lombards beyond the Alps will be held valid in the Low Countries, even if the provisions of the contract are contrary to local custom (*ibid.*, p. 295).

[22]*Ibid.*, I, 306; 316, n. 2; 345.

[23]*Ibid.*, p. 380.

[24]Jean Gessler (ed.), *Le livre des mestiers de Bruges et ses dérivés: quatre anciens manuels de conversation* (New York, 1931) contains four versions of conversation manuals. In version C (*Dialogues in French and English* published by William Caxton *ca.* 1483) appears the following lines (p. 42): 'Johan, the usurer, hath lente so moche that he knoweth not the nombre of the good, that he hath alle evyll gadred togedyr; he leneth the pounde for four pens.' (Cf. Version M, p. 35, and Version D, p. 50.)

[25]Bigwood, *Régime*, I, 316; II, 352, No. 48. The estate was made up as follows:

	£	s	d groat
On deposit with the money-changer, Jacques Reubs	332	0	0
In mature and unmatured claims	65	0	0
In chattel and Jacques Mancegas' share in the house of the lombards	22	10	0
Total	419	10	0

[26]The Pope collected all the outstanding claims and there was no question of restitution.

[27]Bigwood, *Régime*, I, 307, 315-16.

[28]*Ibid.*, p. 236.

[29]*Ibid.*, II, 331-32, No. 36.

[30]*Ibid.*, I, 220.

[31]*Ibid.*, II, 316-17, No. 29.

[32]*Ibid.*, p. 66.

[33]He did not always succeed, and in the *Chronique de Saint-Trond* he is called *usurarius maximus* (Pirenne, *Histoire de Belgique*, II, 121, n. 2).

[34]Simon de Mirabello's seal bore the following inscription: *Signum Symonis de Mirabello, militis, domini de Peireweys.* While de Mirabello was *receveur de Flandre,* the words *Receptoris Flandriae* were substituted for *domini de Peireweys.* Later, when he became regent or *Ruwaert* of Flanders, the following legend appeared on the seal: *Signum Flandriae Reuwardi, per communem patriam ordinati.* See Napoléon de Pauw, 'Les Mirabello,' *Biographie Nationale,* XIV (Brussels, 1897), 873. The family also called itself 'de Halen' from the name of a village in Brabant (Bigwood, *Régime*, I, 236). Cf. Gilliodts, *Inventaire*, I, 478.

[35]Bigwood, *Régime*, I, 238.

[36]Laenen, 'Les Lombards à Malines,' *op. cit.*, p. 24.

[37]Bigwood, *Régime*, II, 14, Appendix I, item 70; Gilliodts, *Inventaire*, I, 334, 339, 345.

[38]van Werveke, *De Gentsche Stadsfinanciën in de Middeleeuwen*, pp. 277-281.

[39]Gilliodts, *Inventaire*, I, 334, 339, 345. Some of his loans to the city of Ghent were secured by the excise taxes on wine (van Werveke, *De Gentsche Stadsfinanciën*, p. 279).

[40]Bigwood, *Régime*, I, 236.

[41]*Ibid.*, p. 238.

[42]*Ibid.*, p. 237.

[43]It should be added that a sister of de Mirabello had married Guillaume van Artevelde, *watergrave* of Flanders, a brother of Jacques van Artevelde, the famous Flemish leader (de Pauw, 'Les Mirabello,' *op. cit.*, p. 872).

[44]Bigwood, *Régime*, I, 239; Pirenne, *Histoire de Belgique*, II, 121.

[45]Pirenne, *Hist. de Belgique*, II, 123.

[46]A brother of Simon, François de Mirabello, was in this king's service and became famous for his valor. When Edward III founded the Order of the Garter, this François de Mirabello was among the first Knights of the Order (de Pauw, 'Les Mirabello,' *op. cit.*, p. 878). By the way, John of Gaunt, Duke of Lancaster, was born during the stay of Edward III in Ghent.

[47]Henry Stephen Lucas, *The Low Countries and the Hundred Years Wars, 1326-1347* (Ann Arbor, 1929), pp. 429, 435.

[48]Bigwood, *Régime*, I, 239.

[49]The only lombard who had a somewhat similar career, seems to have been Barthélémy Trabukier. In 1457 he obtained a licence to open a pawnshop in Malines. Twenty years later, in 1478, he had become *seigneur de Bautersem* and *receveur du duc de Bourgogne*. Laenen, 'Usuriers et lombards dans le Brabant,' *op. cit.*, p. 141.

Chapter 9

THE STRUGGLE AGAINST SECRET USURY AND THE SURVIVAL OF CASUAL CREDIT

THE mediaeval church advanced the claim that jurisdiction over usury cases belonged to the courts Christian, but the Bruges sources indicate that laymen who violated the usury prohibition were punishable by the civil authorities.[1] The municipal accounts contain numerous items relating to fines exacted from secret usurers. The reasons for fining them were several: one offense was to lend at a rate higher than two *deniers* per pound, another was to practice money-lending without being licenced, and a third was to lend money on 'charters.'[2] In some cases no specific reason is given beyond the mere statement that the offender was guilty of usury.[3]

Fines exacted from usurers were a regular, if unimportant, source of income and almost every year a number of usury cases are listed in the municipal accounts. In 1304 twenty-one persons, including two women, were fined for lending money at interest. The next year the number of infringers was twenty-four. In 1310, the list of usurers who were fined included nineteen names.[4] In 1367, there were seven transgressors, but there were only six the following year.[5] The fine was fifty pounds *parisis* of which one-third went to the city and two-thirds to the count of Flanders.[6] Often the offender did not pay the full amount but succeeded in having the fine reduced, probably by pleading extenuating circumstances.

The municipal authorities apparently were not drastic enough in suppressing the activity of surreptitious usurers, because the duke of Burgundy decided, in 1397, to step in, thereby breaking all precedent. Several residents of Bruges, burghers as well as non-burghers, were brought before the *Chambre des Comtes* of Lille and accused of lending 'money for money or usury without special licence or permission.'[7] The fines this time exceeded by far the usual amount and ranged from ten to one hundred and fifty nobles or from three to forty-five pounds groat, at the rate of 72 groats for a noble. This sudden outburst of activity did not last: the exceptional procedure which was followed aroused so much opposition among the existing bodies that further attempts were given up.

Professional money-dealers are rarely listed among the transgressors of the usury laws. The only example is the money-changer Jan Moreel who was fined fifty pounds *parisis* in 1368 for charging more than two *deniers* a pound per week on loans secured by pledges of personal property.[8] Another name on the same list is that of Belen Sceerrers, a woman who was nicknamed *Mankebele* or 'Limping Isabelle.' She was fined twice in the same year, once for usury and the second time for having kept a house of ill fame.[9] Limping Isabelle was probably a professional procuress, but it would be difficult to consider her as a professional money-lender. In all probability she belonged to the world of François Villon, where gambling, usury, ribaldry, and crime held undisputed sway.

The lombards, being more or less protected by their licences, were able to avoid trouble most of the time. In 1403, Philip the Bold, Duke of Burgundy, caused the lombards of Bruges and Sluys to be fined the considerable sum of 600 nobles at 72 groats per noble. The reason for imposing this heavy penalty was presumably that the lombards had been charging a higher rate of interest than the one allowed by their licences.[10] This action of Philip the Bold's was probably an exceptional step. As long as the lombards did not misuse their licences, they were entitled to the help of the authorities in recovering outstanding claims. The *écoutète* of Bruges, who was some kind of criminal officer and state attorney combined, even received the *quinq denier* or one-fifth of any claims which he was able to collect by putting pressure on recalcitrant debtors of the lombards.[11] In 1392, they paid five *pieters* to the *écoutète* for executing a judgment against a debtor who owed them twenty *pieters* by letter obligatory. Entries of this kind are frequently found in the accounts of judicial officers like *baillis* and *écoutètes* throughout the Low Countries.

One kind of usury punishable according to the custom of Bruges was to lend money 'on charters' (Fr. *prêter sur chartes,* Fl. *leenen up tsaerters*).[12] Historians have been puzzled by the meaning of the word 'charters,' but it evidently refers to the letter obligatory or the *chirographe,* the Flemish equivalent of the English bond. The letter obligatory, misnamed *lettre de foire* by Des Marez, was called *chirographe, conissance, charte partie,* or briefly *charte,* even in the text of the documents themselves.[13]

There is no doubt that the letter obligatory lent itself to fraud, because it was often made out for a sum which was higher than the one actually received by the debtor. Under the influence of the canonist doctrine, the courts in the Low Countries recognized the validity of the *exceptione non numeratae pecuniae* which placed upon the creditor the burden of the proof that the debtor had really received the full amount for which he was obligated.[14] In view of this practice, it is unlikely that the prohibition of 'lending money on charters' was intended to forbid the use of the letter obligatory as a credit instrument. Another explanation must therefore be found.

An important text, dated 1409, relating to the lombards of Nivelles gives the clue to the whole problem. This text mentions two kinds of *chirographes* or letters obligatory, which were in possession of the lombards of Nivelles: first, those made out directly in their favor as obligees, and, secondly, those pledged to them in security for loans.[15] The letter obligatory, consequently, was being used as collateral by creditors in order to borrow money from the lombards or from third parties. This practice was possible because the letter obligatory often contained the 'payable to bearer' clause. The presence of this clause did not transform the letter obligatory into a truly negotiable instrument but it facilitated transfers to a certain extent, because the debtor could validly pay to the bearer and because the latter could sue an unwilling debtor in the capacity of proxy or agent of the obligee.[16] What the Bruges authorities evidently tried to prevent was the misuse of the letter obligatory as collateral security because usury was fostered by such a practice.

Despite the great number of usury cases recorded in the municipal accounts, the impression is strong that the authorities were slipshod in enforcing the canon law. They often resorted to informers who were rewarded with part of the fine.[17] The efficacy of such a method of detection is open to question. Occasional raids, when the complaints about usury grew too loud, were not effective, either, so that the authorities were fighting a losing battle in their attempts to eradicate usury. Perhaps the evil would have been greater still, if it had not been for the preachings of the Franciscan and Dominican friars and for the quiet enforcement of the canon law in the confessional.

As often occurred in the Middle Ages, there was in Bruges, with regard to usury, an abyss of difference between the teachings of the Church and the actions of the clergy. The same divines who preached against the sin of usury from their pulpits covered usurers with their protection by sheltering them on the territory of the Church.

In Bruges throughout the fourteenth and fifteenth centuries, pawnshops were established on property belonging to the provost and the chapter of canons of the collegiate church of St Donatian. The territory on which these pawnshops were located was called in Flemish *Oost-Proossche* and *Zuid-Proossche* and formed little islands which were not under the jurisdiction of the municipal government but under that of the provost and the local ecclesiastical authorities.[18] The owners of these pawnshops operated under licences granted to them by the provost. It is easy to see how this situation was likely to create conflicts, as the municipal authorities had no control whatsoever over the pawnbrokers of the *prévôté*.[19]

In 1380, there were seven pawnshops in one section, and the same number in the other section, of the *prévôté*. Judging by the names, the pawnbrokers were mostly Flemings and Walloons. There were at that time no Jews nor Lombards.[20] The most important pawnshop in the territory of the *prévôté* was called 'The Peacock.' In the fifteenth century, this establishment was operated for a time by the same lombards who managed the pawnshop of the *quartier Saint-Gilles* in municipal territory.[21]

The usurers of the *prévôté* charged higher rates than the lombards. In 1397, Philip the Bold pretended to put a stop to the extortion of the usurers established on the territory of the *prévôté*.[22] Several of them were fined, and their books and papers were seized. This action aroused vigorous protests on the part of the provost who claimed that from 'time immemorial' he had enjoyed the right to 'regulate' the practice of usury. After much discussion, the provost and the delegates of the duke reached a provisional agreement. Henceforth, a proclamation, renewable every year, was to forbid usury on the territory of the *prévôté*. Transgressors were made liable to a fine of eighty pounds par. It is significant that the officers of the provost were not allowed to reduce this fine without permission of the *bailli* or duke's representative. Fines were actually collected in 1402.[23] After that the agreement presumably became a dead letter. In any case, the fine was in the nature of a yearly licence fee. By paying it, the usurers acquired the right to practice their trade in perfect freedom. Another aspect which should not be overlooked is that the intervention of the duke was part of a program of centralization. The suppression of usury was only a pretext. The real purpose was to increase the power of the central government to the detriment of the local authorities.

The provost, by allowing usurers to settle on his territory, clearly defied and openly violated the decretals and the canons of the Church, especially the decisions of the councils of Lyons (1274) and of Vienne (1312).[24] The Council of Lyons, in particular, forbade any individual or society to let houses to usurers under pain of excommunication or interdict. The Council of Vienne, no less emphatically, declared that any authorities who granted licences to public usurers committed an offense against God. The additional income which the provost received under form of higher rents, fines, and licence fees were apparently too attractive to forego, with the result that the territory of the Church was transformed into a paradise for usurers. This extraordinary situation, far from being shortlived, was allowed to continue for more than a century, at a time when the Church and the predicant orders were most vehement in their denunciation of usury and everything connected with it.

As we have seen, the lombards in the Low Countries were found only in the cities and in a number of the smaller towns. Most of their customers were recruited among the urban population. But there was also a need for credit among the peasants, exposed as they were to the common risks of illness and death, of uncertain seasons, bad harvests, and perishable livestock. How was this need for short-term credit among the peasantry met? The only document which throws any light on this problem is an inquiry conducted in 1393 in the villages around Brussels.[25] This document, consequently, does not relate to Flanders but to the neighboring principality of Brabant. It can safely be assumed, however, that conditions were much the same on both sides of the boundary.

The inquiry of 1393 in the *ammanie* or district around Brussels reveals first of all that the countryfolk, in general, did not go to the lombards, but usually borrowed from casual money-lenders. The inquiry does not give much information about these lenders, but the majority of them were living in the same village as the borrowers. This situation may serve as an indication that the lenders were mostly wealthier or more provident villagers. Among the lenders who did not reside in the same locality as the borrowers, the inquiry mentions the abbot of the Premonstratensian Abbey of Affligem, several burghers of Brussels and Louvain, the servants of noblemen, and minor judicial officers, among whom one Pierre de Roeke, a former *sous-mayeur* of the district, was singled out by the inquiry.[26]

Those who lodged complaints with the inquirers, as they toured the district and stopped in one village after another, were almost all people of small means, chiefly peasants and tenants who did not possess any land of their own. In a number of credit transactions, interest was concealed in several ways—not infrequently under the form of services. In one case, the borrower had to take care of the lender's cow for a whole winter or until the loan was repaid.[27] There were a few cases in which money was openly lent for more money (*gelt voor gelt*). The rate of interest varied greatly from one loan to another. On the average, however, the rate did not exceed twenty per cent, except on some short-term loans where interest was computed on a weekly or a daily basis.[28]

The most common form of loan was the so-called *voircoep,* a type of contract in which the lender advanced money against the future delivery of grain. If, as often happened, the borrower was not able to live up to his commitments, the contract was extended, but with the provision that the borrower was to deliver wheat instead of rye, rye instead of barley, or barley instead of oats.[29] The interest rate was thus regulated by the price differences between the different kinds of cereals. Most of the peasants who appeared before the commission of inquiry complained about the hardships which resulted from these transmutations. The debt increased rapidly and, if the borrower had some land, he was in grave danger of forfeiting it to the lender.

The lombards were not entirely averse to the *voircoep* or future delivery contract. Those of Nivelles, a small town in the center of a rich agricultural district, often made advances repayable in kind.[30] Deliveries to be made by the borrower sometimes extended over a period of years. In one contract, concluded on June 8, 1358, the borrower undertook to deliver 109 measures (*muids*) of grain on six different dates extending from Christmas 1358 to St John's Day (June 24), 1361.[31] A licence granted in 1413 to the lombards of

Quesnoy and Forest in Hainaut expressly forbade their entering into any future delivery contracts with countryfolk, 'because of the losses, damages, and hardships which were likely to result.'[32]

The inquiry of 1393 gives the impression that conditions in the rural districts were very different from those prevailing in the towns. In the country there was no credit organization and no specialized class of money-lenders.[33] Only occasionally did peasants resort to the lombards of the nearest town. Under the primitive conditions which survived in the country, the usury problem reduced itself to a simple question of mutual assistance and of neighborly or unneighborly conduct. The usury doctrine still retained its validity as far as it applied to the petty transactions of a rural society barely touched by the rising power of commercial capitalism. In spite of the elaborations which the canonist doctrine received at the hands of the glossators and post-glossators, it was inadequate wherever casual credit had given way to professional money-lending, be it for consumption or production purposes.

[1]Clerics who violated the usury prohibition were, of course, subject to the ecclesiastical courts rather than the civil ones.

[2]Gilliodts, *Coutume,* I, 521. Cf. Bruges, Municipal Archives, Municipal Accounts, 1368-1369 (n. s.), fol. 18v:'Ontfanghen van den ghenen die 't pond parisis dierre gheleent hebben danne 2*d.* par. up pande;' *ibid.,* 1355 (n. s.) fol. 28: 'Ontfanghen van den ghenen die bevonden waren dat si leenden up tsaerters. Cf. Gilliodts, *Cart. de l'Estaple,* I, 457, No. 549: 'Item de ceulx qui prestent plus hault que 2*d.* de la livre ou argent sur chartes 50 ℔.'

[3]Bruges, Municipal Archives, Municipal Accounts, 1367-1368, fol. 15: 'Ontfanghen van den ghuenen die wouker gheleend hebben van boeten.'

[4]Gilliodts, *Coutume,* I, 519.

[5]Bruges, Municipal Archives, Municipal Accounts, 1367-1368, fol. 15; 1368-1369, fol. 18.

[6]Gilliodts, *Coutume,* I, 519.

[7]Bigwood, *Régime,* II, 391-93, Nos. 75, 76, especially p. 391: '. . . d'avoir presté en son pays de Flandre et par especial en la ville de Bruges, argent pour argent que l'on appelle usure, senz son congié ou licence espéciale.'

[8]Bruges, Municipal Archives, Municipal Accounts, 1368-1369, fol. 18.

[9]*Ibid.,* fol. 19: 'Ontfanghen van den ghuenen die huze te bordeellen verhuert hebben: van Belen Scerrers 20*s.*'

[10]Bigwood, *Régime,* I, 602.

[11]Gilliodts, *Inventaire,* IV, 185.

[12]Gilliodts, *Cart. de l'Estaple,* I, 457, No. 549 (1408); *Coutume,* I, 521.

[13]Des Marez, *La lettre de foire,* pp. 10, 13, 26, 34, 60, 109, and *passim.*

[14]Lameere, 'Un chapitre de l'histoire du prêt à intérêt,' *op. cit.,* p. 97.

[15]Bigwood, *Régime,* I, 457, n. 2: '. . . chirographes obligatoires faitez à l'usage del tauble ensi bien comme les chirographes de cognissance qui estoient enwagiez en la dicte tauble.'

[16]Henri Brunner, 'Les titres au porteur français du moyen âge,' *Nouvelle revue historique de droit française et étranger,* X (1886), 148-49, 152.

[17]Gilliodts, *Coutume,* I, 518-19.

[18]Gilliodts, *Inventaire,* II, 348.

[19]Gilliodts, *Coutume,* I, 515.

[20]These are the names of the fourteen usurers listed in the municipal accounts: (1) Jan de Wulf, (2) Jan Walepijn, (3) Jan van Valenchine, (4) Willem Faghoot or Fagot, (5) Lotaerd Desplechijn, (6) Pietre Commere, (7) Jan van Bochout, (8) Allard Bataille, (9) Jan de Brifuil, (10) Jan Campioene, (11) Woutre de Smed, (12) Jacop Mues, (13) Jan Bandette, (14) Willem Moluun (Gilliodts, *Inventaire,* II, 348). Cf. Bigwood, *Régime,* II, 392. Some of the userers were still in business in 1397, for example, Gautier le Fevre (Woutre de Smed) and Jehan de Valenciennes (Jan van Valenchine).

[21]Bigwood, *Régime,* II, 58, 424.

[22]*Ibid.,* I, 593-96; II, 391-92, Nos. 75, 76.

[23]*Ibid.,* I, 595, n. 1.

[24]McLaughlin, 'The Teachings of the Canonists on Usury,' *op. cit.,* I, 84; II, 9. Cf. Tawney, *Religion and the Rise of Capitalism,* p. 57; Sir William J. Ashley, *An Introduction to Economic History and Theory* (London, 1931), Vol. I, Part I: The Middle Ages, p. 150.

[25]Bolsée, 'Une enquête sur les usuriers dans l'Ammanie de Bruxelles en 1393,' *op. cit.,* pp. 141-210.

[26]*Ibid.,* p. 147.

[27]*Ibid.,* p. 145.

[28]*Ibid.,* pp. 145-46.

[29]*Ibid.,* pp. 144-45.

[30]Bigwood, *Régime,* I, 356-67. Bigwood, it seems to me, is not justified in calling these

purchases of grain 'commercial transactions,' (*ibid.*, p. 360). In reality, these so-called commercial transactions were disguised and speculative loans.

[31]*Ibid.*, p. 362.

[32]Koch, *op. cit.*, p. 27: '. . . sauf tant que nous ne volons mie que as censeurs, laboureurs et autres gens de nostre dit pays puissent accater bleds ou autres grains à argent secq pour recevoir as termes lointains, car telle marchandise avons nouvellement deffendu à faire par tout nostre pays de Haynau pour les très grans pertes, damages et inconveniens qui au peuple d'icelui nostre pays en avendroit souvent. . . .' Cf. Bigwood, *Régime*, I, 366-67.

[33]For a comparison with conditions in rural England, see Tawney, Intro., Wilson, *Discourse upon Usury*, pp. 19-21.

PART III

THE MONEY-CHANGERS

Chapter 10

THE LEGAL AND SOCIAL BACKGROUND

UNLIKE the Italian merchant-bankers and the lombards, the money-changers were neither aliens nor denizens. Several lists of money-changers practicing in Bruges during the fourteenth century are extant in the municipal accounts. A checking of those lists reveals at once the fact that Flemish names predominate.[1] A priori this fact does not prove much, since foreign names were frequently translated. Did not a lombard named Giovanni Solari become Jan van den Zoldere in Flemish and Jehan du Solier in French? Flemish or French-sounding names, consequently, are sometimes merely a mask. It is significant, however, that many of the names appearing on the lists of money-changers are those of well-known families of Bruges. The name Metteneye, belonging to one of the most prominent native families, occurs twice in each of several lists of money-changers for the period, 1305-1310. A little less prominent are the families Danwilde, van Wulfsberghe, van Hertsberghe, and van Zomerghem, which are also mentioned.

About half a century later another list is given in the municipal accounts. It contains the name of Evrard Goederic, who became an alderman of the city, after he retired from business.[2] Other names listed are those of van Oudenaerde, Vlaminghe, Reubs, Cortscove, Moens, and de Vos, all belonging to families of local standing.[3]

While most of the money-changers were Flemings, it does not follow, however, that no foreigners crept into their ranks. In 1435 one of the money-changers was a woman called Donorye uten Zacke, wife of Lauwereins or Laurence Paelvoysin.[4] She might have been, and very likely was, a Fleming for her maiden name 'uten Zacke' appears in the records more than a century earlier. Her husband's surname, however, is obviously a corruption of the Genoese name Pallavicini. This example is, perhaps, not well chosen, because native women who married outsiders not only retained their citizenship, but conferred it upon their husbands.[5]

A much better case is that of Tideman Bloumeroot, a German from Cologne.[6] He is known to have been a money-changer for he is designated as such in the municipal accounts of the fiscal year 1359-1360 (n.s.).[7] Tideman Bloumeroot had apparently started his business career as a merchant and had been a member of the Hanseatic League for a number of years. He did not get along very well with the elders who managed the affairs of the League in Bruges and he sued them in the local court or *tribunal des échevins.* This action was a serious offense, because the League claimed exclusive jurisdiction over all disputes arising among its members. As a consequence, Tideman Bloumeroot was expelled from the League and deprived of all the privileges which went with membership.[8] Henceforth, no Hanseatic merchant was permitted to enter into a partnership with him nor to ship goods in the same vessel.[9] This boycott does not seem to have harmed Bloumeroot a great deal in his economic interests. His expulsion from the League occurred in 1350. When he died about ten years later, he left a considerable fortune.[10] Together with the widow of Simon de Mirabello, he was one of the two principal creditors of the city of Ghent, according to the accounts for the fiscal year, 1352-1353.[11]

There is more than one legal angle to Tideman Bloumeroot's story. First, he could never have become a money-changer had he remained a member of the League. The reason is that the privileges granted by the count of Flanders and the city of Bruges allowed the Hanseatic merchants the greatest freedom in trade, but specifically excluded money-changing and usurious practices, which presumably meant pawnbroking. This prohibition was embodied in the charter of privileges which the Hanseatic League received in 1307 from Robert de Béthune, Count of Flanders.[12] Article Two of the charter provided that the merchants of the Holy Roman Empire could trade by land and by sea, in whatever way they wished, *excepto cambio pecunie et omni conventione usuraria.*[13] The same clause is repeated verbatim in the charter by which Louis de Male, Count of Flanders, in 1360 solemnly renewed the privileges of the Hansa.[14] The first draft of the charter which the city of Bruges—in order to end a boycott—was forced to grant to the Hanseatic League in 1359, also contains the provision forbidding money-changing and usury,[15] but such a provision is not found in the final text.[16] It is not clear why this was dropped in the course of the negotiations carried on in Lübeck between the diplomatic representatives of Bruges and those of the League. In any case, the Hanseatics never engaged in either money-changing or usury. Usury, as already explained, was the monopoly of the lombards. As for money-changing—and this brings us to the second point—citizenship was a necessary requirement and one could not be a burgher of Bruges and a member of the Hansa at one and the same time.[17]

It is, therefore, probable that Tideman Bloumeroot, after his expulsion from the League, applied for, and was admitted to, citizenship. Once a burgher of Bruges, there was no legal impediment to his becoming a money-changer. As the example of Bloumeroot shows, the fact that money-changers had to be burghers of Bruges does not mean that all money-changers were of native stock. Occasionally, one of them could be of foreign birth, provided he had acquired citizenship (Fr. *bourgeoisie,* Fl. *poorterschip*).[18] It should further be pointed out that the epithet 'foreign' applied to all persons born outside of Bruges, whether within or without the county of Flanders.[19] 'Citizenship,' as used here, has nothing in common with the modern concept of nationality, but should be understood in its narrow and original meaning.

The fact that only burghers by birth or adoption could be money-changers had one important legal consequence. The money-changers, unlike the Italian merchants or the lombards, did not enjoy any special privileges, but were subject to the 'common' law (*droit commun*) except in matters pertaining to their profession. In practice, this exception involved compliance with the regulations of the municipal authorities and the monetary ordinances emanating from the prince. As time went on, the power to regulate passed more and more from the former to the latter. After the accession of the dukes of Burgundy, the monetary ordinances gained in comprehensiveness, and definite rules were laid down for matters which formerly had been left to the discretion of the local government.

Charles the Bold, in his monetary ordinance of October 13, 1467, even ordered all new money-changers to relinquish their *bourgeoisie* or citizenship, but only so far as the observance of the ordinance was concerned.[20] This provision did not apply to the duchies of Brabant and Limburg,[21] but was to be effective in Flanders and the other provinces of the Low Countries which were under the dominion of the duke of Burgundy.[22] The purpose of the provision is not clear. Most probably, it was intended to make money-changers, who might violate the ordinance, liable to heavier penalties than local custom would allow.

Money-changers, in their capacity of burghers, were eligible to public office. In Bruges, several of them became *échevins, scabini,* or aldermen. About 1330 the city kept money on deposit and had other business dealings with the money-changer, Jan Cortscoef,[23] who happened to be also an alderman.[24] This connection very likely explains why the city favored him with her patronage. In 1369 one of the aldermen was Evrard Goederic, a retired money-changer.[25]

The same conditions prevailed in other cities of the Low Countries. In Douai, for instance, the money-changers were among the richest and most prominent citizens.[26] The records mention at least two of them who were aldermen at the end of the thirteenth century. In Brussels, an Everminus Campsor, evidently a money-changer, held public office from 1275 to 1297.[27] There is no doubt that many more cases would be brought to light if the question were more carefully investigated.

In mediaeval Bruges, the profession of money-changer was open to women, who did not suffer from any legal disability in this respect. The records show that quite a few of them did engage in money-changing; it seems that widows frequently carried on their husbands' business. That they were not always successful is proven by the failure of the widow of the money-changer Diederic Urbaens sometime between 1340 and 1350.[28] In 1304, two women, Joncvrauwe Marie Danwilde and Kateline van Ghent, appear on a list of eighteen money-changers who were fined for doing business during Holy Week.[29] More than a century later, in 1435, women were owners of two of the four exchange banks which were held in fief from the count of Flanders.[30]

In the Middle Ages money-changing was apparently one of the few professions where there was no discrimination against women. In this respect the conditions found in Bruges are duplicated in Ghent,[31] and elsewhere in Western Europe. No less than six women appear on a list of eleven money-changers who were doing business in the year 1368 at Frankfort-on-the-Main, already famous for its fairs.[32]

In Bruges the number of money-changers was strictly limited. In accordance with a tendency common in feudal times, four of the exchanges were hereditary fiefs held from the count of Flanders and placed under the jurisdiction of the old feudal court which had its seat in the Burg.[33] They were called in French *les quatre francs fieffés changeurs* and in Flemish *de vier vrije wisselen.* The holders of the fiefs practically enjoyed monopoly rights which were transmittable from father to son, but were occasionally bought and sold. Such an arrangement cannot be deemed felicitous in view of the fact that business ability is not hereditary. It is therefore not surprising that the fiefs did not remain long in the same family. Failures of money-changers were not infrequent. In the absence of records of bankruptcy proceedings, it is not known, however, whether the fiefs were dealt with in the same way as other assets, that is, whether they were sold for the benefit of the creditors.

No one knows exactly when the four fiefs were created, but they certainly date back at least to the beginning of the thirteenth century.[34] By 1300 the growing volume of trade had necessitated an increase in the number of money-changers.[35] The owners of these additional exchanges presumably were allowed to practice their trade under a licence or commission from the original four who held their offices in fief. In order to avoid any confusion, the latter will be called the 'four free money-changers' and the former, the 'licenced money-changers' (the French is *changeurs non libres;* the Flemish, *onvrije wisselaars*). The licenced money-changers had to pay a yearly fee or royalty of 20*s. parisis* to each one of the free money-changers, apparently for the privilege of sharing in their monopoly.[36] According to the municipal accounts, the city of Bruges collected on November 16, 1306, a tax or *taille* from seventeen money-changers.[37] The following year the number of taxpayers was the same, but the contribution was nearly doubled and made payable in two installments, one due on St John's Day and the other, on St Martin's Day.[38] Two years later, in 1308, twenty money-changers paid the tax on St John's Day, but only

THE BUSINESS DISTRICT OF MEDIAEVAL BRUGES
ACCORDING TO THE MAP OF MARC GHEERAERTS

The location of the pawnshop (15) is in the left corner of the picture, between St Gilles Church (14) and the river. Other landmarks, going from left to right and more or less following the river, are: the house of the Easterlings with tall and slender tower (79), the monastery of the Augustinians (33), the Poorterslogie also with a tower (83), the house of

the Biscay merchants (67,80), the consular house of the Florentines (81), the Place de la Bourse (63), the consular house of the Genoese (82), the Pont Saint-Pierre where the money-changers had their offices (A,A), the Waterhalle 72 or B,B), and the Old Cloth Hall (71 or C) with the high belfry. In the right corner of the map, at some distance from the river, are: the Hôtel Bladelin, seat of the Medici Bank (85), the Mint (77), and the Palace or Prinsenhof (76). The Burgh (70) is the square surrounded by the Town Hall and other public buildings.

nineteen on St Martin's.[39] A check of the lists reveals that, between 1307 and 1308, two names were dropped, but five new names were added, which accounts for the jump from seventeen to twenty. The discrepancy of one between the two lists extant for the year 1308 is easily explained by the fact that two of the taxpayers were seemingly partners; both are mentioned in the first list, but only one, in the second. In the course of 1309 the tax was collected twice as before, but only once in 1310. Thereafter, the municipal accounts cease to mention contributions from money-changers among the regular sources of revenue. It is probable that collection of the tax was discontinued from then on.

In 1309 and 1310 the list of taxpayers includes only fourteen names against nineteen in 1308.[40] Among those missing is a Boidine Weghebedde. This money-changer is known to have failed sometime before 1315, a fact which undoubtedly explains why his name does not recur.[41]

The money-changers do not reappear in the municipal accounts until 1359, when the city of Bruges, being in financial straits, asked them for help. The trouble originated in unforeseen expenditures brought about by unrest and threatening revolt among the weavers.[42] Fifteen money-changers responded to the appeal of the city and lent £2,400 8*s*. par.[43] In 1362 another loan was made by sixteen money-changers and the lombards of St Gilles' parish.[44]

All the stalls in which the money-changers had their place of business belonged to the city of Bruges. In 1346 the city paid for repairs to fifteen stalls which were rented to the money-changers.[45] This confirms our other information and leaves no doubt that there were approximately fifteen money-changers in Bruges about the middle of the fourteenth century. Strangely enough, there were not so many a few years later. In 1379, eight of the stalls were rented to persons other than money-changers.[46] Records for the year 1389 mention four stalls, located in the New Cloth Hall (*de Nieuwe Halle*), which 'formerly had been used as exchanges.'[47]

By the middle of the fifteenth century, either the four free money-changers alone had survived, or very few of the licenced money-changers were still doing business. The available evidence is so vague and confusing that it is impossible to tell what the situation actually was. One thing is certain: by 1450 the species of the licenced money-changer was slowly dying out if it was not already extinct. The monetary ordinances from the late fourteenth century are silent about the existence of any other money-changers besides those who held fiefs. The ordinance of December 20, 1389, which paved the way for important monetary reforms, mentions only the free money-changers (*changeurs fiefvez*), but does not specify their number.[48] Carelessness or lack of accuracy may be responsible for the absence of any reference to the licenced money-changers. The same applies to later monetary ordinances, to wit, those of October 12, 1433,[49] and of October 13, 1467.[50]

For the historian, it is difficult to interpret legislative statutes, because one never knows how far they reflect existing conditions and to what extent they were, or could be, enforced. In this case the monetary ordinances are fortunately supplemented by a few other bits of evidence which, though they may not be very important, are not entirely devoid of significance.

In 1456 the four free money-changers, designated by name, were reminded by the local court that they were bound by oath to observe the monetary ordinances and that it was against the law to send bullion out of the country.[51] If no writ was served on any other money-changers, the reason apparently is that they had passed out of existence. They are last referred to in 1435 when it is stated in the records that the free money-changers, because of their fiefs, are entitled to a yearly fee from each of the licenced money-changers.[52]

By the end of the fifteenth century, interlopers must have engaged in exchange dealings, for the free money-changers complained about this unfair competition and this encroachment upon their monopoly. In 1498, they petitioned Philip the Handsome, Archduke of Austria, and asked him for confirmation of their monopoly privileges. Among other points, the petitioners claimed that 'from time immemorial, there had been in Bruges no money-changers other than those who held their office in fief from the count of Flanders.' This claim, of course, may have been made in good faith, but it was certainly contrary to the truth. The petitioners further argued 'that the interlopers availed themselves of so-called commissions and perpetrated all kinds of frauds which were detrimental to the common weal and the rights of the prince.' As proof, the petition pointed to the notorious fact that one of the interlopers had recently been executed for felony. Philip the Handsome granted the request and proclaimed on November 12, 1498, that, in Bruges 'no bankers, nor dealers in bullion, nor anyone else was allowed to buy or exchange coins except the four free money-changers'.[53]

This text is difficult to interpret. It has no meaning, unless one admits that the prohibition was aimed at intruders from outside, because licenced money-changers no longer existed.

The legal character of the relations which existed for a time between the four free, and the licenced, money-changers can best be understood by making a comparison. These relations were similar to those prevailing today between a patentee and the persons to whom he has sold licences to use his patent. The patentee has the exclusive right to his invention and can make use of this right in different ways. One way is to grant licences in exchange for a royalty. The result of such a contract is that the licencee by paying a royalty obtains the right to participate in the patentee's monopoly. The licencee is not an infringer of the patent so long as his licence is not revoked and he continues to pay the royalties which have been agreed upon. This was exactly the relationship which existed in Bruges between the two classes of money-changers from the end of the thirteenth to the early part of the fifteenth century. The free money-changers were monopolists who, for an annual fee, allowed a number of persons to share in their monopoly.

Later on, the four free money-changers, whose feudal title put them in a strong legal position, began to revoke the existing grants or refused to renew them as they lapsed. Whatever the method employed, the result was a more rigid monopoly and drastic action against infringers. As happens frequently when a trade is bad or declining, people seek refuge in protection or the elimination of competition as a cure for their ills.

The proclamation of Philip the Handsome restored conditions which had not existed since the middle of the thirteenth century. It was distinctly a regressive measure.

Historians have expressed the opinion that the decline of Bruges was responsible for the shrinking of the money-changers' business.[54] A thorough examination of the facts shows, however, that this explanation does not hold water. In the first place, people have overlooked the fact that the money-changers' trade had begun to slip long before the city itself lost its preponderance as a commercial center. In the second place, the trade of the money-changers did not contract in Bruges alone, but the same downward trend can be observed in other cities. In Lille, for instance, there had been originally ten money-changers, who had their offices in a building called 'le Beauregard,' which stood on the marketplace and was part of the domain of the count of Flanders. Only five offices remained in 1391, each of them occupying twice the space of the original stalls. Already in 1397, one of the remaining offices had its destination changed after the death of the tenant, a money-changer named Jehan de Villers, and became the public weighing office. In 1412 another vacancy occurred; this time the empty exchange office was transformed into a courtroom. By 1422, when the 'Beauregard' was rebuilt and embellished by the addition of a lofty belvedere, only two offices of the original ten were still occupied by money-changers.[55]

It is doubtful whether, either in Bruges or in Lille, the reduction in number was compensated by a greater concentration of capital or an increase in the volume of business. On the contrary, there seems to have been contraction all along the line. A full explanation cannot be attempted at this point, but will be given in connection with a discussion of the 'hard money' policy of the dukes of Burgundy. In the meantime it will be well to remember the important fact that money-changing was on the wane from the end of the fourteenth century onward.

As the number of money-changers was strictly limited, there was, of course, no free entrance into the profession. It was completely closed to newcomers unless there happened to be a vacancy. The probabilities are that people paid quite a sum of money in order to buy out a money-changer, just as today they are willing to pay a big price for a seat on the stock exchange.

As appears from the foregoing explanation, money-changing was the monopoly of a small group. This does not mean that there was absence of competition. Each money-changer probably tried to attract customers by offering better service, or by making the most of his personality, professional ability, financial backing, and strategic connections. It is not humanly possible that all the money-changers of Bruges possessed these advantages to an equal degree. It is further impossible that the money-changers always acted as a unit, and that they all followed the same business policy. Consequently, the monopoly of the money-changers was far from being perfect, and competition survived among them to a considerable extent.

The money-changers' monopoly was protected in several ways, by a fence of legal enactments and regulations. As has been stated before, neither the Hanseatic merchants, nor the lombards, nor any other aliens were allowed to deal in exchange. The word 'exchange,' as used here, should be interpreted literally, and means manual exchange from one currency into another. In other words, the prohibition applied only to the trade in bullion and specie, but not to dealings in bills of exchange.

The municipal authorities kept a jealous watch in order to prevent money-changers from establishing themselves in any of the smaller towns within the orbit of Bruges. These efforts were at least partially successful. About 1297, however, an exchange office, which was to be held in fief, was established in the town of Ardenbourg by Gui de Dampierre, Count of Flanders, in order to spite the Bruges patricians who sided with the king of France against the Count.[56] This office probably existed for some time, but must have disappeared after the town's short-lived prosperity had come to an end. At any rate, the monetary ordinances of the fifteenth century are silent about a money-changer in Ardenbourg. The presumption is that the trade of the little town had dwindled away to the point where no money-changer could make a living.

Whereas Ardenbourg caused little concern to the municipal authorities, the establishment of an exchange office in Sluys (or l'Ecluse), the seaport of Bruges, was not viewed with the same equanimity. For more than a century, the city of Bruges persistently and successfully opposed such a move. In 1323 Bruges resorted to open revolt in order to maintain her hegemony over the small neighboring towns. Louis de Crécy, Count of Flanders, was forced to yield and to issue a charter which placed a number of restrictions upon the further development of Sluys.[57] One of them was that 'in Sluys there would be no exchange nor melting of silver.'[58] The people of this town were, however, unwilling to abide by the count's decision and this question along with others remained a bone of contention between Bruges and Sluys. In 1367 Count Louis de Male was called upon to settle the points at issue. His decision was again favorable to Bruges as far as money-changing was concerned.[59] Still this decision was not final, because the question came up again in 1441, when Duke Philip the Good was asked to arbitrate twenty-four points about which Bruges and Sluys could not come to an agreement. The Brugeois contended, among other things, that there was to be in Sluys no exchange nor melting of silver. Their opponents, of course, contested this point and boldly asserted that there was no evidence to support such a claim.[60] Whether the Brugeois failed to dig up the charters of Louis de Crécy and Louis de Male or whether the duke, for whatever reason, preferred to brush this evidence aside, one thing is certain: his decision settled most of the disputed points, but remained quiet about money-changers. The chances are that the people of Sluys took advantage of this omission and had their way, because the monetary ordinance of 1467 mentions the existence of a money-changer in Sluys, whereas such a mention is lacking in previous ordinances, for example, in that of 1433.[61]

There is no doubt that the attitude of the Bruges authorities was not inspired by the desire to protect the monopoly of the city's money-changers, but was part of a general policy designed to prevent Sluys from developing into a rival commercial and industrial center. This is brought out sufficiently by the fact that the matter of money-changers was not the only issue at stake, but was linked with other disputes over staple rights and industrial privileges.[62] It is also beyond doubt that the exchange office in Sluys, once it was established, took little business away from the money-changers of Bruges. The reason is not far to seek: the two did not compete for the same business. This statement requires, perhaps, some explanation.

Sluys was only a satellite of Bruges; the town had neither trade nor industry of its own, but was merely a harbor where all the incoming and outgoing goods had to be transshipped from seagoing vessels to rivercraft or vice versa.[63] Most of the time a number of ships were anchored in the roadstead, either loading, unloading, or waiting for cargo. Under those circumstances, there was a real need for a place where the crews, when they went ashore, could exchange their foreign money for local currency at a fair rate.[64] It is easy to see why the people of Sluys were so insistent and why the policy of Bruges was so shortsighted and so unfair. The money-changer of Sluys, in all probability, specialized in a type of business in which his colleagues of Bruges were but little interested. As long as there was no exchange in Sluys, they doubtless secured some of this business, but what they got was only a negligible fraction of their total volume.[65]

The statutes not only shielded the money-changers against any competition from outside the community, but also against any encroachment upon their monopoly on the part of their fellow-citizens. The protective measures taken in this respect were formulated in a city ordinance of the year 1309.[66] This ordinance is important, because it was presumably the first codification of previous decisions, and because it determined legal precedent.[67] The main provisions of the municipal statute of 1309 were later reenacted in the monetary ordinances and thus served as a basis for all subsequent legislation.

According to these provisions, anyone, except a money-changer, was liable to a fine of fifty pounds *parisis,* if he was caught dealing in exchange or even occasionally changing money.[68] Of course, it was perfectly lawful at any time for anyone to give change for a gold or silver piece presented in discharge of a commercial transaction.[69] What the statutes really intended to forbid was the exchange for a fee of foreign currency for local currency, or of gold for silver, or in general of one currency for another. The city ordinance of 1309 further forbade anyone to act as a broker between a money-changer and the public under the penalty of a fine of ten pounds.[70] Philip the Bold's monetary ordinance of December 20, 1389, further extended these restrictions to include the trade in bullion and changed the penalty from a fine to ten years' banishment.[71] Only the goldsmiths were allowed to buy gold or silver up to five troy marks at one time.[72] Later on, the trade in bullion became apparently free, at least in theory. The monetary ordinance of 1433, for instance, provided that no one (money-changer or otherwise) was allowed to buy up bullion except in order to deliver it to the mint.[73] The implication evidently was that everyone might buy bullion with the purpose of having it minted. But as only the money-changers were regularly doing business with the mint, the trade in bullion practically remained restricted to them. The same provision as in the ordinance of 1433 is found in other monetary ordinances of the fifteenth century, for example, in the one of 1467.[74]

As this instance about the trade in bullion shows, it is always advisable to ascertain what the practical results of regulations really are, irrespective of their legal implications. A cursory perusal of the municipal accounts seems to indicate that fines were rarely collected for infringement of the money-changers' monopoly.[75] As explanation, there are three possibilities: either nobody ever tried to challenge it openly, or the authorities did not press the enforcement of the statutes, or they were frequently violated in secret, but such transgressions were difficult to detect. In any case, we do not hear about encroachment of the monopoly until the very end of the fifteenth century, when the four free money-changers petitioned Archduke Philip and asked him to confirm their age-old privileges. Whether this petition yielded any practical effect is unfortunately not known. On the whole, the documents give the impression that the monopoly of the money-changers was perhaps better protected by their professional knowledge, their business experience, and the need for their services than by way of statutes and regulations.

The legal position of the money-changers, unlike that of the lombards, which was more or less uniform throughout the Low Countries, varied widely from one principality to another and from town to town. The question, unfortunately, has never been thoroughly studied and much material that would throw light on the subject lies buried in local archives. As a result, the evidence available at present is incomplete and confusing.[76] Concerning the money-changers of Ghent, for instance, we know very little except that they paid a tax to the city and that they were twelve in 1366, but their number subsequently dropped to two.[77] The fact that they paid a special tax to the city seems to suggest that the count of Flanders had nothing to do with their appointment. The question whether, in Ghent, the profession of money-changer was free or closed has not been elucidated as yet. We are a little better informed with regard to Lille. In August, 1294, Gui de Dampierre, Count of Flanders, granted to six burghers of this city a ten years' monopoly of all exchange dealings and banking operations.[78] The Bruges public records are silent about this latter aspect of the money-changers' activity. It must, therefore, be assumed that, in Bruges, the monopoly of the money-changers legally applied only to exchange dealings, but did not extend to banking, although in practice the two functions were frequently combined.

In the smaller towns of Flanders the exchange offices were often farmed out by the count's representatives and the income derived therefrom became a regular source of public revenue.[79] In the fifteenth century, however, it proved increasingly difficult to find bidders, and several offices in the smaller towns remained vacant—another symptom that money-changing was on the decline at the end of the Middle Ages. In Courtrai, for example, there was no money-changer from 1398 to July 1465, except temporarily during the fairs. As this condition was detrimental to the town's prosperity, the municipal authorities repeatedly tried to find someone willing to establish himself as money-changer in Courtrai.[80] According to the monetary ordinance of 1433, each of the following cities in Flanders (not including Bruges) had the right to have two money-changers: Ghent, Ypres, Lille, and Douai. Only one was allowed in half a score of smaller towns, namely in Alost, Audenarde, Bergues, Courtrai, Dixmude, Furnes, Grammont, Hulst, Nieuport, Termonde, and Wervicq.[81] Sluys, as we have seen, was added to this list later.[82]

In Brabant there was even less uniformity than in Flanders. In Antwerp every burgher had the right to open a public exchange office as long as money-changing was not forbidden altogether, but foreigners were rigidly excluded even during the fairs.[83] According to a municipal ordinance dated August 22, 1387, it was furthermore declared illegal for a burgher to lend his name to someone who was not a citizen and thus help him evade the above rule. But it was apparently lawful for a burgher to be actively in partnership with a non-burgher.[84]

In Brussels, too, the profession of money-changer was free, the only restriction being the payment of a fee of ten *tours d'or* to the duke, and of eight *vieux écus* to the city.[85] In Louvain conditions were entirely different. There the duke had the right to appoint money-changers without consulting the local authorities, but the latter needed the duke's consent to make appointments. The proceeds of a tax on money-changers were shared equally by the duke and the city.[86] In several towns of Brabant one of the exchange offices was called the *stadwissel* or municipal exchange and the owner was exempt from the tax levied on money-changers. In compensation for this advantage he probably had to handle the municipal business free of charge. The institution of the *stadwissel* in Brabant never developed into city-owned offices as in Strasbourg and Frankfort-on-the-Main.[87]

In Liége the money-changers were organized into a brotherhood or *confrérie*. All money-changers were expected to join the brotherhood. On the other hand, their number was not limited. Any burgher of good character and family background could enter the profession by complying with the requirement concerning membership in the brotherhood.[88] Such conditions were found nowhere else in the Low Countries. They resembled more those prevailing in Florence, where all money-changers and bankers were affiliated with the *Arte del Cambio* or the Money-Changers' Gild.

If, on the one hand, the money-changers in Bruges enjoyed a monopoly, this privilege, on the other hand, entailed some compensatory obligations. The authorities felt that it was their duty to protect the public against exploitation with the result that the money-changers' fees were strictly regulated by statute. In Bruges a money-changer who charged more than the tariff was liable to a fine which, according to the monetary ordinances of 1433 and 1467, amounted to three pounds *parisis* per coin exchanged.[89] No money-changer had the right to refuse to serve the public at the official rate. This principle was already laid down in the city ordinance of 1309, and each transgression was made punishable by a fine of ten pounds.[90] The same principle is restated in the monetary ordinances of the fifteenth century which specify that a money-changer must exchange gold and silver coins whenever his services are requested.[91]

The mediaeval public authorities had to rely on the money-changers for the enforcement of the monetary ordinances. It is, therefore, only natural that the money-changers were required to take an oath in order to ensure the observance of the law. In Flanders this oath was administered by the local authorities in the presence of the count's representative, *bailli* or *écoutète* as the case might be, and was frequently renewed.[92] The statute of December 20, 1389, prescribed that the oath was to be repeated each year.[93] This rule probably did not remain in force. During the fifteenth century, the custom prevailed of requiring the oath as a matter of routine each time that a new monetary ordinance appeared or that the personnel of the local government was changed.[94] Besides the officials had the right to require a new oath whenever it suited them. According to Philip the Bold's statute of 1389 the money-changer had to swear not only that he himself would comply with the monetary ordinances, but also that he would not allow them to be violated by his wife, his clerks. his servants, or any members of his household.[95] The purpose of this requirement was evidently to prevent any collusion. The legal result of the oath was, of course, to make a transgressing money-changer guilty of perjury, which was considered a serious offense entailing severe penalties.[96]

During the Middle Ages, the money-changers were often accused of cunning and fraudulent practices which caused the deterioration of the currency. One of these malpractices was called 'picking and culling' or, sometimes, 'garbling the money.'[97] It consisted in picking or sorting out the heavier coins either in order to carry them abroad or to melt them down and to sell the metal as bullion. This practice was encouraged by the imperfect technique of mediaeval coinage. While it is certain that picking and culling was not an uncommon practice, it is nonetheless questionable whether it was as widespread as people have been inclined to believe, because it could only be profitable under certain conditions; for instance, if there was debasement of the currency[98] or an outflow of specie to pay for imports.[99] Picking and culling was less likely to be remunerative when economic and monetary conditions were rather stable.[100] Because of the high seigniorage, the intrinsic or metallic value of mediaeval coins was generally much below their current or face value. The deviation from standard weight had, therefore, to be considerable before it compensated for the difference between the intrinsic and the current value. This was not likely to happen in the case of silver coins, but was far less improbable in the case of gold coins which paid a relatively low seigniorage and served as international means of payment.

The result of garbling was to leave only the lighter coins in circulation, a condition eminently favorable to further debasement of the currency.[101] It is, therefore, not surprising that the practice of picking and culling was considered unlawful.[102] Already the city ordinance of 1309 forbade the buying of coins of full weight and sufficient alloy in order to send them outside the *portus* or to convert them into bullion, under the penalty of a fine of fifty pounds and forfeiture of the picked money.[103] The ordinances of the dukes of Burgundy in the fifteenth century contain a similar provision and stipulate that anyone who, for profit, picks or culls any new gold or silver coins is to be banished for ten years.[104]

Picking and culling was a far less harmful and deceitful practice than clipping or diminishing the coin by scraping off some of the substance. This fraud could be perpetrated in several ways. One method consisted in paring the edge of the coins, another in filing off the surface, and a third in washing them with aqua regia or some other corrosive acid. In Flanders no distinction was made between clipping and counterfeiting; they were both crimes punishable on the gallows.[105] Money-changers were too much in evidence to practice clipping with any chance of escaping detection. They were also too rich and too solicitous of their social and professional prestige to venture foolhardily their lives, their wealth, and their reputation in a criminal enterprise. For these reasons it is safe to conclude that clippers came from the same criminal class as counterfeiters and were not recruited among the professional money-dealers.[106]

Judging by the numerous complaints about the poor state of the currency, clipping must have been quite prevalent in the Middle Ages, despite the risks which were involved. This is due chiefly to technical conditions. Clipping, unlike counterfeiting, did not require great dexterity and was not easy to detect until the introduction of a machine for milling coin in the middle of the sixteenth century.[107] Until that time it was well-nigh impossible for the average person to tell whether irregularities in the shape, weight, or appearance of a coin were due to clipping, to abrasion, or to defective minting or stamping. This situation greatly enhanced the opportunities for fraud.

The authorities not only took drastic action against clippers and counterfeiters, if they could be caught, but tried also to prevent, as far as possible, the circulation of adulterated or spurious coin. In Bruges the city ordinance of 1309 threatened with a fine of ten pounds Flemish any money-changer who would reissue clipped or defaced money.[108] According to the monetary ordinances of the fifteenth century, no one, whatever his station in life or social condition, was permitted to receive or to utter any underweight gold pieces under the penalty of a fine of three pounds par. per gold piece and of forfeiture of the coins.[109] This penalty was raised to ten year's banishment in the case of money-changers.[110] However, they could buy diminished or mutilated gold and silver coins, paying a fair price, if the coins were cut in two and converted into bullion under the eyes of the seller.[111] It is clear that such legislation penalized the innocent holder of false money rather than the falsifier.

The same legal rules which applied to clipped coin were also applicable to forbidden or non-current coin. In the Middle Ages this expression covered all native coin that had been called in and all foreign coin whose circulation was not explicitly authorized by the monetary ordinances. It was unlawful for anyone to accept, or to pass on, any non-current coin, and the fines were graduated according to the importance of the amount involved in each offence.[112] In addition to the fine, offenders ran the risk of ten years banishment, if they were money-changers, tax-collectors, inn- and tavern-keepers, mercers, brokers, money lenders, or usurers. Persons belonging to these professions were also answerable for any offence committed by their clerks, servants, or relatives.[113] As in the case of clipped coin, money-changers had, however, permission to purchase any non-current coins for what they were worth as bullion.[114] The shears to cut such coins in half had always to be in evidence on the money-changer's table or *bank*.[115] Failure to comply with this requirement gave rise to a heavy fine of sixty pounds *parisis* or five pounds groat.

All the bullion which the money-changers acquired through their exchange-dealings had to be delivered to the count's mint and not elsewhere.[116] This was an old rule which had found its way into the city ordinance of 1309 and became part of all subsequent legislation on currency.[117] Money-changers were not supposed to let bullion accumulate in their strongboxes in excess of ten marks troy in the case of gold and of fifty marks troy in the case of silver.[118] The local officials had the right to enter the offices and houses of the money-changers in order to search for any clipped or forbidden coins and any bullion exceeding the said quantities. Even if the stock on hand did not attain the legal maximum, the officials were empowered to put into sealed bags whatever bullion they found and to have it delivered to the mint.[119] The bullion thus taken away from a money-changer was not forfeited and had to be paid for at the mint's price.

The export of bullion was, as a rule, severely prohibited during both the fourteenth and fifteenth centuries. As early as 1303, Philip de Thiette, who ruled Flanders while his father Gui de Dampierre was a prisoner in Compiègne, issued a statute which denounced the export of bullion, and the washing and picking of coin as illegal practices.[120] In 1349, [121] and again in 1389,[122] it was declared unlawful to carry bullion out of the country. The same policy remained in force during the fifteenth century and exporters of bullion, if caught, ran the risk of having their bullion confiscated and of being fined at the rate of twelve pounds groat or 144 pounds *parisis* per mark gold and of thirteen pounds *parisis* per mark silver.[123]

The money-changers, as we have seen, were obligated by their oath to buy non-current coins for their value in bullion and to exchange current coins at the legal or official rate which was set by proclamation. This rule was so well established that it is not always explicitly stated in the monetary ordinances, but it is clearly implied in the text. The statute of December 20, 1389, however, is an exception in that it contains a specific provision. It provided that henceforth no one would be allowed to accept the noble of Flanders at a higher price than seventy-two groats and that all other current coins would be valued or appraised accordingly. Transgressors were to be banished for ten years, if they were money-changers or belonged to a number of other professions. This penalty was reduced to three years in the case of ordinary burghers and denizens and to a fine in the case of aliens.[124] A similar provision is found in a statute of June 20, 1434, which supplements the ordinances of 1433.[125] It is perhaps significant that both the statute of 1389 and the one of 1433 were connected with an attempt to reverse the trend toward debasement of the currency.

The duties of the money-changers were not limited to conformance with the official valuation. They were also expected to report to the authorities if base or counterfeit money was introduced into the country, or if coins circulated at a price above the legal rate, or if the monetary ordinances were in any way disregarded.[126]

All these measures were not taken, of course, for the sole purpose of regulating the money-changers' business and were not even designed primarily to keep the mints going and to increase the revenue which the count of Flanders derived from his seigniorage. The main concern of the authorities was to establish a sound and stable currency.[127] It is immaterial at the moment whether or not this policy was always successful.[128] The point is that it served to justify the minute regulation of exchange and bullion transactions.

These regulations would have been watertight, indeed, if only they had been enforceable. As always, to enact is one thing but to enforce is another. At this stage we are concerned only with the letter of the law. How it is put into effect depends upon so many circumstances that this problem will have to be considered later.

There is one more legal requirement which the money-changers were supposed to meet. As far back as the fourteenth century they were required to give bond 'for the protection of the merchants who had dealings with them'—in the words of the monetary ordinances.[129] It was the duty of the local authorities to see to it that the sureties offered were satisfactory, so that the merchants would not suffer any losses. This question of sureties, too, is not so simple as it looks and cannot be fully discussed at present, because it is related to other problems which will be discussed later. It is therefore better to wait than to deal piecemeal with the question.

The legal obligations which were incumbent on the money-changers were the same in Flanders as elsewhere in the Low Countries, even before they were united under the rule of the dukes of Burgundy of the House of Valois. In Brabant, for instance, according to an ordinance of June 6, 1381, the money-changers were also bound to take an oath, to bring their bullion to the mint, and to report on the state of the currency. On the other hand, they were restrained by statute from exporting bullion and from uttering clipped or debased coin.[130] The same or similar provisions were in force in Utrecht, Middelburg, and Deventer.[131] These are found even outside the Low Countries, as far as Frankfort-on-the-Main[132] and Italy.[133] According to the statutes of Genoa, the money-changers had to swear that they would make all their payments in good money and that they would cut and withdraw from circulation all false coins coming into their hands.[134]

In the Middle Ages, the regulation of the currency practically rested upon the money-changers; hence they performed a very important and quasi-public function. As such a function involved certain responsibilities, money-changers had to be men of means and of executive ability. Often, as we have seen, they belonged to the best families and not infrequently held public office. The social position of the money-changers was naturally proportionate to their wealth and their standing in the community.

We unfortunately, do not know very much about their milieu, their social relations, their cultural background, and their ideas and prejudices. It is certain that the mediaeval money-changers were educated persons, because the conduct of their business required a fair degree of intelligence and executive ability.[135] They evidently had to be quick at figures and to be familiar with the use of counters and of the abacus.[136] Furthermore, they had to have an understanding of bookkeeping and finance, and to be conversant with the monetary regulations, the law-merchant, and the art of letter writing. It is clear from available evidence that the money-changers of Bruges knew both Flemish, the local tongue, and French, the language of the court, of fashionable society, and of the business world.[137] It is significant that the extant account books of Bruges money-changers are in French, not in Flemish. From the linguistic point of view the situation was thus much the same as in present-day Belgium.[138]

The type of knowledge which a mediaeval money-changer was likely to possess was thus primarily practical and factual. It was chiefly made up of the kind of information which one finds, for instance, in Francesco Balducci Pegolotti's handbook for merchants. In other words, a money-changer had to know quite a bit about commercial geography, coinage, weights and measures, rates of exchange, trade routes, and commodity markets.

Whether the money-changers of Bruges had any other intellectual interests is difficult to determine because no inventories of their libraries have come down to us. One should not forget that, in the late Middle Ages, boys preparing for a business career started their training at an early age, first as messengers, then as bookkeepers, cashiers, factors, or agents. They consequently acquired their knowledge of business by doing things rather than by learning them in books. Working from morning till night, they did not have much time left for outside study or reading. It is therefore safe to assume that the cultural level of mediaeval money-changers was the same as that of businessmen, past and present, who have come up from the ranks and know their trade thoroughly, but not much else. One should also consider that, in the Middle Ages, books were rare and expensive and that a liberal arts education was still largely the monopoly of the higher clergy and of the legists. There are, however, exceptions. Occasionally one finds a money-changer who had a university degree as, for example, that Jan Raepsade who was certainly a Master of Arts, since he is consistently labelled 'Meester' in the municipal accounts.

In business, success depends perhaps more on personality and plain common sense than on culture and learning. As Luca Paciolo, himself a learned cleric, remarks: 'It requires more ability to make a merchant than a doctor of laws.'[139] From the intellectual viewpoint, our Bruges money-changers—at least the most successful of the lot—should be pictured as able and hardworking men, not very much interested in knowledge for knowledge's sake, but only in knowledge as a means of earning a living.

Our money-changers doubtless preferred to spend their free time less in the quiet enjoyment of books than in the company of friends whom they met in winter at the Poorterslogie and in summer at the contests of butt- and popingay-shooting organized by the archery societies of St Sebastian and St George. The Poorterslogie (the lovely Gothic building still standing on the Quai du Miroir) was at that time an exclusive clubhouse and the seat of the jousting society called the 'White Bear.'[140] Membership in this society was restricted to the *poorterie* or upper bourgeoisie;[141] members of the gilds—with the possible exception of the influential brokers and innkeepers—were rigorously excluded.[142] The archery societies were somewhat less exclusive, but still did not admit the rank and file. In 1354 or 1355, Jacob de Visch, who is mentioned later as a close associate of the money-changer Jacob Reubs, was fêted by the municipal government of Bruges because he had won the prize of the *Epinette* jousting society at a tournament in Lille.[143]

One should not assume that the meetings at the Poorterslogie and at the archery societies were purely social affairs which provided entertainment without serving any useful purpose. On the contrary, at those meetings, news and rumors were passed around: people talked, discussed the general political outlook and the economic prospects, or imparted information that might affect business decisions.

The money-changers naturally shared the ideas and prejudices of their social class and of the people with whom they associated. It is therefore not hard to guess that the majority of the Bruges money-changers sided with the *goede lieden* ('decent people') and opposed the democratic program of the weavers and their following among the common people.[144] The economic interests of the money-changers also coincided with those of the ruling bourgeoisie who had a big stake in the cloth industry. Both favored debasement of the currency: the money-changers, because debasement was often the only measure which could save them from impending bankruptcy; and the merchant-class because inflationary reforms of the currency kept trade going, prices high, and wages down.[145]

This description of the social milieu in which the money-changers moved is not a generalization based on sheer probabilities, but is substantiated by a number of details which center around the life of a certain Evrard Goederic, alderman or *échevin* of Bruges in the second half of the fourteenth century. About his business, we know next to nothing beyond the bare fact that he was a money-changer.[146] But we are a little better informed concerning his social position and political activity. Evrard Goederic seems to have belonged to an aldermanic family, because a Walter Goederyck is mentioned as burgomaster of Bruges in 1275 and a Jacob Goederick, in 1326.[147]

In the records, Evrard Goederic is consistently called '*Der* Evrard Goederic.' *Der* is a contraction of *de her,* a Flemish expression which corresponds to the French *sire* and to the English 'sir.'[148] He is even styled '*her* Evehart Godenrik' in the account book of Vicko van Geldersen, a Hamburg merchant.[149] In the Middle Ages, such a title was not lightly bestowed. It was strictly reserved for the members of the gentry or the patrician class. It is, therefore, not surprising that not all money-changers of Bruges were called *Der.* Evrard Goederic is the only one out of fifteen to receive this honor according to a list which appears in the municipal accounts for the fiscal year, 1359-1360 (n.s.).[150] Should we consider this as an indication that Evrard Goederic, being endowed with exceptional business ability and ambition, rose far above his colleagues in wealth, social prestige, and influence?

By way of comparison, another significant detail perhaps deserves attention. In the account books of the money-changer Guillaume Ruyelle, the bookkeeper consistently calls his master's wife *Medmyselle* not *Medame.*[151] In the Middle Ages, the title of 'Madame' was given only to ladies of rank, whereas women of the middle class were called 'Mademoiselle,' whether married or not, and those of the lower classes were addressed by their Christian name or referred to as the wife of so-and-so. Courtesy titles are indicative of social distinctions. Those applied to the Bruges money-changers and their wives confirm that they belonged to the middle and upper bourgeoisie.

As a member of the *poorterie,* Evrard Goederic had a command in the city's militia and fought on horseback like a knight, whereas the craftsmen fought on foot. During the campaign against Brabant in 1356, he served with the cavalry section of St John which was placed under the command of sire George van Aertrike.[152] According to the roll, Evrard Goederic was able to muster four horses, probably with the necessary attendants, squires and grooms. In 1359, when riots broke out among the weavers, he was called to duty in defense of the social order. The city of Bruges paid him twelve pounds *parisis* for watch and ward during as many nights, or at the rate of one pound per night of duty.[153] The unrest among the workers in the Flemish cities kept smoldering for a long time and called for concerted action on the part of the authorities responsible for the preservation of law and order. In the summer and autumn of 1360, Evrard Goederic, presumably in his capacity of alderman, represented Bruges at several parleys:[154] in Ghent on June 15, at Ursel on September 12, and at Deynze on October 14.[155] When the unrest finally flared up into open revolt in 1379, Evrard Goederic was dead, but his widow was still alive and the triumphant weavers made her contribute to their war chest.[156]

In 1369, when there was still no inkling of the oncoming storm, Evrard Goederic was a member of the delegation which represented the city of Bruges at the marriage of Marguerite of Flanders, only legitimate daughter of Louis de Male, with Philip the Bold, 'prince of the fleurs-de-lis,' Duke of Burgundy.[157] The Bruges delegation was composed of the burgomaster sire Jehan Bonin, three aldermen, one of them being Evrard Goederic, three city councilors, and the two pensionaries, each with their pages and servants. The members of this impressive delegation had been fitted out at the city's expense with magnificent costumes of perse and scarlet cloth with hoods and capes of brocade lined with red cloth of the finest quality.[158] A few days after the wedding celebrated in Ghent on June 19, 1369, the young princely couple made their *joyeuse entrée* into their good city of Bruges. On this occasion, too, Goederic was called to military duty and given command over the guard which, at night, watched over the safety of the princes.[159]

Evrard Goederic used a seal on which was represented his coat-of-arms.[160] The use of a coat-of-arms did not necessarily mean that the user belonged to the gentry. In the fourteenth century a coat-of-arms was still the most common design for seals, and seals were used by all persons of substance in lieu of signatures. Moreover, whether or not one belonged to the gentry was not yet a question of letters patent, but was still determined by one's way of life, the performance of certain military duties, and the general opinion of the public. These factors were, of course, all in favor of Evrard Goederic, who was rich enough to live like a gentleman and to go to war arrayed like a knight.

In Bruges money-changers belonged to the ruling class and at least one of them, sire Evrard Goederic, even played a prominent role. Their influence—at least in the fourteenth century—was perhaps greater than in some Italian cities, like Florence for instance, where the *cambiatori* or money-changers were completely overshadowed in wealth and social prestige by the merchant-princes.[161] In Bruges merchant-princes were only represented through agents who, moreover, were aliens and did not play an active part in the life of the community. The *poorterie* or native upper class was composed of *rentiers* (real estate owners), brokers, and cloth-merchants who were only moderately rich; and the money-changers, if they were successful in their business, were admitted without difficulty.[162]

THE USURER AND DEATH
(L'AVARE ET LA MORT)
by an unknown artist
From a painting in the Musée des Beaux Arts, Bruges

NOTES TO CHAPTER 10

[1]Bruges, Municipal Archives, Municipal Accounts (Comptes Communaux): 1305, fol. 6; 1306-07, fol. 13; 1307, fols. 2-3; 1308-09, fol. 7; 1309-10, fol. 19v; 1310-11, fol. 2v. See also Raymond de Roover, 'Le livre de comptes de Guillaume Ruyelle, changeur à Bruges (1369)' [hereafter referred to as 'Ruyelle'], *Annales de la Société d'Emulation de Bruges,* LXXVII (1934), 88-89, documents Nos. 1, 2, and 3.

[2]*Ibid.,* pp. 88 f.

[3]*Loc cit.*

[4]Gilliodts, *Inventaire, Introduction,* p. 410.

[5]Remi A. Parmentier, *Indices op de Brugsche Poorterboeken* (Bruges, 1938), I, viii.

[6]Bigwood, *Régime,* I, 100. Bigwood's statement that Tideman Bloumeroot or Blommeroede was a burgher of Cologne is probably wrong. It should read that he was a native of Cologne, because he had become a citizen of Bruges.

[7]de Roover, 'Ruyelle,' *op. cit.,* pp. 88 f.

[8]*Hansisches Urkundenbuch,* III, ed. K. Höhlbaum (Halle, 1882-86), 77, No. 160.

[9]*Loc. cit.*

[10]He probably died about 1360. He is listed as a money-changer in the municipal accounts for the fiscal year 1359-60 (n.s.). His name, however, does not appear again on a list of money-changers included in the municipal account for the fiscal year 1362-63. The inference is that he either died or retired from business between these two dates. Cf. *Hansisches Urkendenbuch,* III, 345, n. 2, according to which Bloumeroot died in 1360 and was buried in the Church of the Augustinians, the favorite place of worship of the Germans residing in Bruges.

[11]van Werveke, *De Gentsche Stadsfinanciën in de Middeleeuwen,* p. 366.

[12]*Hansisches Urkundenbuch,* II, ed. K. Höhlbaum (Halle, 1879), 52-54, No. 121 (Latin charter dated December 1, 1307).

[13]*Ibid.,* p. 52, art. 2. Gilliodts makes a mistake when he states in a footnote (*Inventaire,* I, 274, n. 1) that the first part of the charter of 1307 is an exact reproduction of a charter dated April 13, 1253, granted by Countess Marguerite to the Hanseatic merchants in Bruges, thus leading to the false conclusion that the prohibition against money-changing, etc., dates back as early as 1253. This earlier charter (published by Gilliodts in *La Flandre,* I [1867-68], 243-46) deals chiefly with legal protection of the property of the Hanseatic merchants against confiscation, reprisals, etc. Articles 7 to 13 of the charter of 1307 do restate the privileges granted in the earlier charter, but the first six articles are new.

[14]*Hansisches Urkundenbuch,* III, 244, No. 495, art. 2 (Latin charter dated June 14, 1360).

[15]*Ibid.,* p. 211, No. 451, art. 2. This draft is in Flemish. The text says that the Hanseatic merchants are allowed to trade in whatever way they wish except in money-changing and in all forms of usury ('huteghesteken wissel van ghelde ende alle vorworden van woukere').

[16]*Ibid.,* p. 215, No. 452. Flemish charter dated June 5, 1359, art. 2.

[17]The Hanseatic League was not originally a league of towns but a league of merchants engaged in foreign trade.

[18]Citizenship could be acquired by marriage or by residence and could also be granted upon request by the municipal authorities. In general, the applicant had to pay a fee before he was admitted to take the required oath of allegiance (Parmentier, *op. cit.,* I, viii).

[19]Formalities were not a bit easier for Flemings than for people born outside the boundaries of the County of Flanders; only the latter paid a double fee. At least this was so in the fifteenth century (*loc. cit.*).

[20]Gilliodts, *Inventaire,* V, 548 f.: 'Item, voulons et ordonnons que quiconques voudra doresenavant faire et exercer fait de change en aucuns de nosdiz pays de Flandres, d'Artois, Haynaut, Hollande, Zellande, Namur, seignouries et ville de Frise et Malines, il sera tenu de soy deffranchir souffisaument de sa bourgeoisie quant au dit fait de change et à l'entretenement de ceste dicte ordonnance tant seulement pardevant ceulx de la loy soubz laquelle il sera demourant.'

[21]The reason is probably that the provision was in conflict with the constitutional charters, the *Charte Wallonne* of 1314, and the *Joyeuse Entrée* of 1356, of the duchies of Brabant and Limburg. See Henri Laurent, *La Loi de Gresham au moyen âge* (Brussels, 1933), p. 26, n. 3.

[22]This provision, consequently, did not extend to the duchy of Burgundy, Franche-Comté, and the *seigneurie* of Salins. It also excluded Gelderland which was still ruled by its local dynasty.

[23]Gilliodts, *Inventaire,* I, 423 f.

[24]Gilliodts, *Cartulaire de l'Estaple,* I, 183, No. 244.

[25]Gilliodts, *Inventaire,* II, 172, 181.

[26]Espinas, *La Vie urbaine de Douai au moyen âge,* II, 156.

[27]Bigwood, *Régime,* I, 403.

[28]Gilliodts, *Inventaire,* I, 491, No. 445; also see below, Appendix No. I. Diederic Urbaens was still alive in 1340 and paid his share of a forced loan necessitated by the expenses of the campaign against France. In June, 1340, the French fleet had been completely destroyed by the English under Edward III. In July the Flemish troops beleaguered St. Omer and Tournai. They captured neither of them and the hostilities ended with a truce in September. Pirenne, *Histoire de Belgique,* II, 125 f.

[29]Gilliodts, *Coutume,* I, 518.

[30]Gilliodts, *Inventaire, Introduction,* p. 410.

[31]van Werveke, *Gentsche Stadsfinanciën,* p. 221.

[32]Georg Ludwig Kriegk, 'Frankfurter Geldgeschäfte und Handelsbanken im Mittelalter,' *Frankfurter Burgerzwiste und Zustände in Mittelalter* (Frankfurt am Main, 1862), p. 334.

[33]Gilliodts, *Inventaire, Introduction,* p. 410 and *Inventaire,* VI, 466.

[34]At least one of the four fiefs seems to have been created by a charter of the year 1224 (see Bigwood, *Régime,* I, 413, n. 1).

[35]*Ibid.,* p. 394.

[36]Gilliodts, *Inventaire, Introduction,* p. 410: 'Margriete, filia Jans van Cuertrike, houdt een leengoed ende es één van den viere vryen wissele eervelyc binnen der stede van Brugghen up sinte Pieters brugghe, met alsulken rechten als daer toe behoren, te wetene van elken onvryen wisselen twyntich schellinghen parisis aerveliker renten siaers.'

[37]Bruges, Municipal Archives, Municipal accounts, 1306-1307, fol. 13. The date given is Wednesday after St Martin's day or November 16, 1306.

[38]*Ibid.,* 1307, fols. 2^v-3^r. The names of the seventeen moneychangers listed are: (1) Wouter Danwilde, (2) Jan van der Naelde, (3) Heer Wouter van Scathille, (4) Claas de Hond, (5) Loye van Cassele, (6) Pieter Urbane, (7) Joris van der Matte de Jonge, (8) Jacop van Leffinghe, (9) Dierman Metteneye, (10) Pieter Metteneye, (11) Jan van der Angle, (12) Jacop uten Zacke, (13) Willem de Scaerslipere, (14) Willem van Wulsberghe, (15) Meester Jan Raepsade, (16) Jan van der Poele, (17) Boidine Weghebedde. Gilliodts (*Coutume,* I, 518) writes erroneously about thirty-four money-changers. Apparently he failed to see that there are two lists and that each of the seventeen names is listed twice. The same error is found in Häpke, *Brügges Entwicklung zum mittelalterlichen Weltmarkt,* pp. 243 f. Häpke probably never saw the original texts so that his mistake originates in Gilliodts' misstatements.

[39]Municipal accounts, 1308-1309, fol. 7. Heer Wouter van Scathille dropped out before the end of 1307 and was replaced by Jan de Repere. Two more money-changers dropped out in 1308: Jacop uten Zacke and Willem van Wulsberghe. The new names appearing on the list are: (1) Willem van Ansame, (2) Willem van der Lanterne, (3) Gillis van der Matte, (4) Andries van Zomerghem, (5) Pieter van den Rame. Gilliodts makes the same mistake again and thus obtains the wrong figure of nineteen plus twenty or thirty-nine money changers.

[40]*Ibid.,* 1309-1310, fol. 19^v. The number of money-changers dropped from twenty to fourteen through the disappearance of: (1) Boidine Weghebedde, (2) Wouter Danwilde, (3) Claas de Hond, (4) Pieter Urbane, (5) Jacop van Leffinghe, and (6) Pieter van den Rame. Gilliodts again obtains a figure of twenty-nine by adding two lists which include the same names.

[41]Bruges, Municipal Archives, Comptes Communaux, 1315, fol. 2.

[42]Pirenne, *Hist. de Belgique,* II, 200 f.

[43]de Roover, 'Ruyelle,' *op. cit.,* pp. 88 f., docs. 1 and 2.

[44]*Ibid.,* p. 89, doc. No. 3.

[45]Gilliodts, *Coutume,* I, 518: 'gewrocht an die 15 wissele.'

[46]*Loc. cit.*

[47]Gilliodts, *Coutume,* I, 518: '[Ontfanghen van stede lande]: van 4 cameren onder de niewe halle daer men wissele in *placht* te houdene' (italics mine).

[48]Gilliodts, *Inventaire,* III, 131, 133. The reform in question is the raise or the return *à la monnaie forte* of January, 1390.

[49]Ghent, Municipal Archives, Chartres et Documents, No. 561, art. 10.

[50]Gilliodts, *Inventaire,* V, 546. The text is almost exactly the same as that of the ordinance of 1433.

[51]*Ibid.,* p. 385. The names of these four free money-changers were: Hellin le Cuer, Jan Roelands, Jan Grysseel, and Maerc Buengetuer.

[52]Gilliodts, *Inventaire, Introduction,* p. 410.

[53]The money-changers' petition and Archduke Philip's reply are given in full in Gilliodts, *Inventaire,* VI, 466 f.

[54]Bigwood, *Régime,* I, 395, 415.

[55]Benoît, 'Le "Beauregard" de Lille,' *op. cit.,* pp. 7-11.

[56]The date of 1282 given by Gilliodts (*Cart. de l'Estaple,* I, 69, No. 90) is certainly wrong because the grant dates from the war between Gui de Dampierre and Philip the Fair which was waged from 1297 to 1300. Cf. Bigwood, *Régime,* I, 397; *Hansisches Urkundenbuch,* II, 63, No. 152, n. 3.

[57]Pirenne, *Hist. de Belgique,* II, 83-85.

[58]Gilliodts, *Inventaire,* III, 360. 'Item que l'on ne tiengne à l'Ecluse nul change, ne fondeure d'argent.' Cf. *idem, Cart. de l'Estaple,* I, 158, No. 223; *Hansisches Urkundenbuch,* II, 171, No. 401, art. 5.

[59]Gilliodts, *Inventaire,* II, 143. The date of the charter is December 7, 1367, and the text concerning money-changing in Sluys runs as follows: 'dat men ter Sluis niet houde wissel noch smeltinghe van selvere.'

[60]Gilliodts, *Inventaire,* V, 233, 240. The text is as follows: '. . . ne seroit point trouvé que l'on ne peut tenir à L'Escluse estaple d'iceulx biens, ne aussi estaple et taille de draps, hostilles, troncs, liches et taintures, pois oultre 60 livres, change et fondure d'argent . . ."

[61]The relevant passage in the ordinance of October 12, 1433, art. 10, is as follows: 'Item à Courtray, Audenarde, Alost, Grandmont, Tenremonde, Hulst, Furnes, Neufport, Berghes, Dicquemue et Wervy en chascune ville ung changeur et non plus' (Ghent, Municipal Archives, Chartres et Documents, No. 561). This text is virtually the same in the ordinance of October 13, 1467, except for the following additions: 'Item, en nostre ville de L'Escluze sur l'une des kueres aura aussy ung changeur et non plus' (Gilliodts, *Inventaire,* V, 546).

[62]Gilliodts, *Inventaire,* V, 233, 240, No. 1023.

[63]This is made very clear in Pegolotti's handbook for merchants (Pegolotti, *La pratica della mercatura*) p. 239: 'Il porto di mare di Bruggia si è alle Schiuse, che è alla marina del mare del porto di Bruggia, ove tutta la mercatantia si carica e discarica nelle nave o cocche, o galee o altri navili . . .'. Cf. A. De Smet, 'L'origine des ports du Zwin: Damme, Mude, Monikrede, Hoeke et Sluis,' *Etudes d'histoire dédiées à la mémoire de Henri Pirenne* (Brussels, 1937), pp. 125-141.

[64]One should not overlook the fact that the distance between Bruges and Sluys is more than ten miles and that there were no taxicabs in the Middle Ages.

[65]This is evidenced by the account books of the Bruges money-changer Collard de Marke. Several of his customers, chiefly Spaniards and Portuguese, are described as shipmasters (*mestres de naves*). In general these accounts are not very important, and are closed after a few transactions.

[66]Gilliodts (*Inventaire*, I, 300 f., No. 237) gives an analysis of the contents of the ordinance of 1309 but he does not give the full text (Chartes politiques, 1° série, No. 237).

[67]This is certain, because fines provided for in the statute of 1309 were already imposed at an earlier date.

[68]Article 1 of the ordinance of 1309. The fines were divided equally between the Count of Flanders, the city of Bruges, and the officials who indicted the transgressors (art. 14).

[69]About this a very clear statement is found in an ordinance, dated June 6, 1381, of Wenceslas and Jeanne, Duke and Duchess of Brabant and Limburg. The text of this ordinance has been published in-extenso by Henri Laurent in his *La Loi de Gresham au moyen âge*, p. 136, appendix No. 6.

[70]Art. 13 of the ordinance of 1309.

[71]Gilliodts, *Inventaire*, III, 134. The ordinance forbids anyone who is not a money-changer to buy gold or silver in specie or otherwise.

[72]*Loc. cit.*

[73]Ghent, Municipal Archives, Chartres et Documents, No. 561, ordinance of October 12, 1433, art. 12: 'Item que aucun ne porra acheter billon au dit pais de Flandres, se ce n'est pour le livrer en la dicte monnoye sur le ban de trois ans excepté . . .' Exception was made for the goldsmiths up to 20 troy marks, the cutlers up to one-half mark, and lombards to one-half mark. The latter were supposed to sell the bullion to the money-changers or to send it to the mint.

[74]Gilliodts, *Inventaire*, V, 546.

[75]In 1291 or 1292, the city of Bruges collected £16 6*s*. 8*d*. or one-third of 50 pounds (see also footnote 68) from the lombards who had been fined for dealing in exchange (*pro actis de cambio*). See Gilliodts, *Cart. de l'Estaple*, I, 75, No. 100 and *idem*, *Coutume*, I, 517. Another somewhat similar case is that of a man named Arnaude de Meestre. According to the municipal account for the fiscal year 1367-1368 (n. s.), he was fined £12 for melting bullion and silver in violation of the city ordinances. Arnaude de Meestre was not one of the Bruges money-changers. Their names for this period are well known. See Bruges, Municipal Archives, Comptes Communaux, 1367-1368 (n.s.), fol. 15^{v}.

[76]The best survey will be found in Bigwood, *Régime*, I, 391-411. The information given here is only for purposes of comparison.

[77]*Ibid.*, pp. 395 f.

[78]The full text of Gui de Dampierre's grant is given by Bigwood, *Régime*, II, 304, No. 20.

[79]*Ibid.*, I, 397.

[80]Sabbe, 'De lombarden te Kortrijk,' *op. cit.*, p. 176.

[81]Ghent, Municipal Archives, Chartres et Documents, No. 561, ordinance of October 12, 1433, art. 10.

[82]Gilliodts, *Inventaire*, V, 546.

[83]Bigwood, *Régime*, I, 401.

[84]'Clementynbouck (1288-1414),' *Bulletin des Archives d'Anvers (Antwerpsch Archievenblad)* XXV (n.d.) 168: Ordonnantie van den wisselaers. Bigwood's explanation (*Régime*, I, 401-2) does not make sense and is a misinterpretation of the original Flemish text.

[85]Georges Cumont, 'Etude sur le cours des monnaies en Brabant pendant le règne de la Duchesse Jeanne, veuve, depuis 1383 jusqu'à 1406,' *Annales de la Société royale d'archéologie* de Bruxelles, XVI (1902), 157.

[86]*Ibid.*

[87]Cf. Bigwood, *Régime*, I, 430, n. 1.

[88]Hénaux, 'Les Banquiers liégeois au XIVe siècle,' *op. cit.*, pp. 320 f.

[89]Ghent, Municipal Archives, Chartres et Documents, No. 561, ordinance of October 12, 1433, art. 6; Gilliodts, *Inventaire*, V, 544.

[90]Ordinance of 1309, art. 9.

[91]The ordinance of 1433, art. 6 (Ghent, Municipal Archives, Chartres et docs., No. 561) for example, provides that 'Item, que tous changeurs seront tenu de changier à chascun qui le

requerra son or et des deniers qui seront réputez pour billon . . .' Cf. Gilliodts, *Inventaire,* V, 544.

[92]See, for example, the ordinance of December 20, 1389, published by Gilliodts, *Inventaire,* III, 133; and the ordinances of 1433 and 1467 (*ibid.,* V, 548).

[93]Gilliodts, *Inventaire,* III, 133: 'Et de ce feront serment les diz changeurs présentement et chascun an une fois ès mains des baillis et lois des villes et eschevins des lieux.'

[94]See above no. 92.

[95]Gilliodts, *Inventaire,* III, 133.

[96]See, for instance, the ordinance of 1467: *ibid.,* V, 548.

[97]W. Stanley Jevons, *Money and the Mechanism of Exchange* (New York, 1897), chap. viii, p. 80. The French expression is *biqueter et trébucher.*

[98]In case of debasement, the new and lighter coins would drive the old and heavier coins out of circulation.

[99]An exporter of gold has an evident interest in selecting only the heavier coins, because he has to make payment by weight instead of by tale.

[100]'Rather stable' means here no change in the monetary standard or no drain on the gold or silver supply from abroad.

[101]Because it would be impossible to maintain in circulation new and heavy coins at par with the old and worn ones.

[102]It was unlawful but not necessarily dishonest.

[103]Ordinance of 1309, art. 12.

[104]The ordinance of 1467 (Gilliodts, *Inventaire,* V, 550) provides namely that 'Et en oultre que nul ne biquette ne tresbuche aucuns de noz deniers d'or ou d'argent nouveaulx, c'est assavoir de eslire ou prendre les pesans hors des légiers par nombre ou pour y gaigner, et ce sur le ban de dix ans.'

[105]The ordinance of 1467 (*ibid.,* p. 550) provides that 'Item que nul, quel qu'il soit, soit bourgois, forain ou estraingier, ne ronge ou coppe, ne par eaue ou autre industrie diminue en aucune manière aucun de nosdiz deniers sur payne de la hart.'

[106]I believe that a careful examination of the criminal records, especially the accounts of the écoutètes, would prove this point. The accounts of the écoutètes are preserved in Brussels in the Archives Générales du Royaume. Of course, there might have been a few exceptions.

[107]Although the method of coining by machinery instead of with the moneyer's hammer was introduced into the Paris mint in 1552 and in London ten years later, the opposition of the conservative French and English mint authorities prevented the adoption of the new method. Milled coins did not permanently replace hammered coins for another century. See Charles Oman, *The Coinage of England* (Oxford, 1931), pp. 279 f.

[108]Ordinance of 1309, art. 2.

[109]For instance, the ordinance of 1467 (Gilliodts, *Inventaire,* V, 541).

[110]*Loc. cit.*

[111]*Loc. cit.*

[112]Ordinance of December 20, 1389 (Gilliodts, *Inventaire,* III, 132); and of October 13, 1467 (*ibid.,* V, 540).

[113]*Ibid.*

[114]Ordinance of December 14, 1361 (Gilliodts, *Cart. de l'Estaple,* I, 241, No. 317, art. 2 and 4); of December 20, 1389 (Gilliodts, *Inventaire,* III, 133); of October 12, 1433 (Ghent Municipal Archives, Chartres et Documents, No. 561, art. 6); of October 13, 1467 (Gilliodts, *Inventaire,* V, 544).

[115]See ordinances of 1433 and 1467 as indicated above. Cf. the ordinance of 1361, art. 4.

[116]For instance, the ordinance of 1467 provides: 'Item, que les diz changeurs seront tenuz de porter ou faire porter en noz monnoye tout le billon qu'ilz trouveront et auront acquis, sitost qu'ilz l'auront . . .' (*ibid.,* V, 544, 546). For a precedent, see the ordinance of Louis de Male dated December 14, 1361, art. 3, which says that no one is allowed to buy bullion

except with the purpose of sending it to the count's mint at Ghent (Gilliodts, *Cart. de l'Estaple,* I, 241, No. 317 or *Hansisches Urkundenbuch,* III, 356).

[117]Ordinance of 1309, arts. 3 and 5.

[118]Ordinance of 1467 (Gilliodts, *Inventaire,* V, 544). In the ordinance of 1433, the figures are four and fifty marks respectively. Cf. Ordinance of 1389 (*ibid.,* III, 133).

[119]Ordinance of December 20, 1389 (Gilliodts, *Inventaire,* III, 133); of October 12, 1433 (Ghent, Municipal Archives, Chartres et Documents, No. 561, art. 7); of October 13, 1467 (Gilliodts, *Inventaire,* V, 544-545). These three texts vary somewhat in detail, but this is of no importance here.

[120]Philip de Thiette's ordinance is dated October 21, 1303 ('le lundi après Saint Luc') and is published in full by Gilliodts (*Coutume,* I, 458 f.). The text (spelling modernized) reads as follows: 'Nous, Philippe, fils au comte de Flandre, . . . avons ordonné et fait statut que nul ne soit si hardi qu'il mette eau sur denier qui son cours ait et qui bon soit et suffisant, ni ne porte hors de Flandre pour billon, et que nul ne fonde ni ne fasse fondre argent fors ès cinq bonnes villes de Flandre ou ès monnaies de Flandre, fors orfèvre, billon tant seulement pour leur ouvrage, sur peine de cinquante livres et banni un an hors du comté de Flandre.'

[121]Ordinance dated June 1, 1349 and published by Limburg-Stirum, *Cartulaire de Louis de Male,* I, 125, No. 123.

[122]Gilliodts, *Inventaire,* III, 133.

[123]Ordinance of 1467 (*ibid.,* V, 542). Incidentally, it is to be noted that the difference in rates for gold and silver corresponded roughly to the ratio between the value of gold and silver.

[124]*Ibid.,* III, 132 f.

[125]*Ibid.,* V, 18, No. 987.

[126]Ordinance of October 13, 1467 (*ibid.,* p. 548).

[127]Pirenne, *Hist. de Belgique,* II, 420 f.

[128]During the fifteenth century the dukes of Burgundy succeeded in maintaining a stable currency for long periods of years (*ibid.,* p. 420).

[129]Gilliodts, *Inventaire,* V, 549: '. . . pour la seurté des marchans qui auront à faire avecq eulx.'

[130]Laurent, *op. cit.,* document No. 6, pp. 135-37. This document is an ordinance of Wenceslas and Jeanne, Duke and Duchess of Brabant, Limburg, and Luxemburg, dated June 6, 1381.

[131]Z. W. Sneller, 'Het wisselaarsbedrijf in Nederland vóór de oprichting der stedelijke wisselbanken,' *Tijdschrift voor Geschiedenis,* XLIX (1934), 490-94.

[132]Otto Speyer, *Die ältesten Credit- und Wechselbanken in Frankfurt am Main, 1402-1403* (Frankfurt am Main, 1883), p. 21.

[133]Alessandro Lattes, in his *Il diritto commerciale nella legislazione statutaria delle città italiane,* p. 203, gives an excellent summary of the duties of the Italian money-changers. They assumed the same quasi-public functions as their colleagues in the Low Countries.

[134]Heinrich Sieveking, *Genueser Finanzwesen mit besonderer Berücksichtigung der Casa di San Giorgio,* Vol. II, *Die Casa di San Giorgio* ('Volkswirtschaftliche Abhandlungen der Badischen Hochschulen,' Vol. III, No. 3 [Freiburg in Breisgau, 1899]), pp. 44 f. The regulations on money and banking were prepared by the *officium mercantie,* the department of commerce of the Genoese Republic.

[135]Cf. Henri Pirenne, 'L'instruction des marchands au moyen âge.' *AHES,* I (1929), 13-28; Sapori, 'La cultura del mercante medievale italiano,' *op. cit.,* pp. 89-125.

[136]*Ibid.,* pp. 99 f.

[137]de Roover, 'Ruyelle,' *op. cit.,* p. 18.

[138]Today, even in the Flemish-speaking part of Belgium only French is used in the offices of most concerns of any size or importance.

[139]Paciolo, *Summa de arithmetica,* distinctio 9, tractatus 11, capitolo xxxv, fol. 209^{v}.

[140]Letts, *op. cit.,* p. 39.

[141]Pirenne (*Hist. de Belgique,* II, 68) defines the *poorterie* as made up of people who do

not belong to any craft ('poorters, lieden die van ghenen ambachte en zijn').

[142]*Ibid.*, pp. 72 f.

[143]Gilliodts, *Inventaire*, II, 443.

[144]Pirenne, *Hist. de Belgique*, II, 201 ff.

[145]*Ibid.*, p. 199; Hans van Werveke, 'De ekonomische en sociale gevolgen van de munt-politiek der graven van Vlaanderen,' *Annales de la Société d'Emulation de Bruges*, LXXIV (1931), 7-10 and *passim*.

[146]de Roover, 'Ruyelle,' *op. cit.*, p. 88, doc. No. 1. Evrard Goederic is listed in the municipal accounts among fifteen money-changers who lent money to the city during the fiscal year 1359-1360 (n.s.).

[147]Antonius Sanderus, *Flandria illustrata sive descriptio comitatus istius* (2d ed., The Hague, 1732-1735), II, 21 f.

[148]E. Verwijs and J. Verdam, 'Der,' *Middelnederlandsch Woordenboek* (The Hague, 1885-1928), II, 125.

[149]*Das Handlungsbuch Vickos von Geldersen*, ed. Hans Nirrnheim (Hamburg, 1895), p. 92, No. 563; p. 104, No. 665; p. 106, No. 684.

[150]de Roover, 'Ruyelle,' *op. cit.*, p. 88.

[151]*Ibid.*, p. 27. On the other hand, the accounts refer to Medame d'Alost, evidently a lady of the nobility.

[152]Pirenne, *Hist. de Belgique*, II, 185; Gilliodts, *Inventaire*, II, 96.

[153]*Ibid.*, p. 98.

[154]Gilliodts erroneously refers to *parlements populaires*. Exactly the opposite is true, because the texts say emphatically that only *goede lieden* ('decent people') went to the parleys. The troublemakers were called *kwade lieden* ('bad people'). See a significant text at the bottom of p. 101 of Gilliodts, *Inventaire*, Vol. II.

[155]*Ibid.*, pp. 101 f.

[156]*Ibid.*, III, 349-53: 'sher Everaerds goederix wedewe' was forced to contribute £5 groat.

[157]*Ibid.*, II, p. 171.

[158]*Loc. cit.*

[159]*Ibid.*, p. 172.

[160]*Ibid.*, II, 181, No. 608.

[161]Saverio La Sorsa, *L'organizzazione dei cambiatori fiorentini nel medio evo* (Cerignola, 1904), p. 21.

[162]Pirenne, *Hist. de Belgique*, II, 68-70, 196; van Werveke, 'Der flandrische Eigenhandel,' *op. cit.*, pp. 7-24.

Chapter 11

A GENERAL PICTURE OF THE MONEY-CHANGERS' BUSINESS

IN Bruges some of the exchanges or offices of the money-changers were located on the St Peter's Bridge adjoining the Waterhalle, and others, under the arcades of this building.[1] The Waterhalle, also called the 'New Cloth Hall,' was a huge Gothic structure, erected during the years 1285 to 1298 and enlarged in the course of the fourteenth century, which stood on the East side of the Grand' Place, where the post office and the pseudo-Gothic palace of the provincial government are today.[2] The Waterhalle was considered one of the wonders of Bruges, because it was built astride the Reye, the river which meanders through the city. The Waterhalle thus formed a covered dock in which the barges or *schuiten* plying between Sluys and Bruges could load or unload their cargoes without danger of having them spoiled by rain.[3] The building was so spacious that it served many other purposes. It was also used as a cloth hall, whence the name of New Cloth Hall, which was often given to the Waterhalle, in order to distinguish it from the Belfry and Old Cloth Hall, which still stands today on the South side of the Grand' Place. The Waterhalle was demolished in 1787, because it had been standing idle for more than two centuries and its value as an historical monument was not sufficiently appreciated.[4]

At least three of the four free money-changers had their offices on or close to St Peter's bridge which, for this reason, was often called le Pont au Change or Wisselbrugge.[5] This bridge crossed the Reye next to the side wall of the Waterhalle, at the northeast corner of the Grand' Place, or where the rue Philip Stock begins today. Thus the Waterhalle formed the south side of the bridge. On the other side also, buildings concealed the river, so that passersby were not aware that they were going over a bridge. According to the cadaster or survey of 1580, one of these exchanges stood on the south side of the bridge next to the Waterhalle,[6] and a second one was on the other side near the corner of the rue de Cordoue or Cordouanierstrate (Cordwainers' Street').[7] The properties in which the exchanges had been located were still known in 1580 by names recalling their former use. One was called *'t Wisselken* and the other, *de Wissele*. The exact location of the third exchange is uncertain, but it stood somewhere near or on the bridge, probably on the south side against the Waterhalle. As for the fourth of the free exchanges, it was not stationary like the other three. It is described in a text of the fifteenth century as some kind of a booth or truck, twelve feet square, which was mounted on four wheels. The owner had the right to move this cumbersome vehicle around the city and to set it up wherever he pleased.[8]

The offices of the free money-changers were probably located on St Peter's Bridge even before the building of the Waterhalle. This assumption is based on the fact that its erection necessitated the pulling-down of some buildings adjoining the bridge. One of them was held in feudal tenure and the beneficiary, a certain *Hannekin* ('Johnny'), was paid a compensation for the loss sustained.[9] As the only fiefs near St Peter's Bridge were those of the money-changers, our Johnny was presumably one of them. He was apparently allowed to rebuild on approximately the same spot. At least one, or possibly two, of the four free exchanges were housed in the small shops which on Marc Gheeraert's map can be seen leaning against the north wall of the Waterhalle. These shops are even clearer on the picture of this building in Sanderus' *Flandria illustrata*.[10]

Under the arcades of the Waterhalle, on the side of the Grand' Place, the city erected a number of stalls which were rented to the licenced money-changers.[11] This is, perhaps, an indication that the emergence of this second class of money-changers dates from the same period as the construction of the Waterhalle. When the number of money-changers began to shrink at the end of the fourteenth century, the vacant stalls were leased by the city for other purposes.

The exchanges in Bruges were thus all concentrated in or around the Waterhalle. This location was exceedingly favorable because it was in the heart of the business center, at only a stone's throw from the Old Cloth Hall just across the square, and within five minutes walking distance from the Place de la Bourse where the Italian merchants had their meeting-place and their headquarters. This question of location was even more important than it would be today, because, as we shall see, the check did not yet exist and its place was taken by an oral order which had to be delivered in person. It was, therefore, very convenient for the merchants and other businessmen that the exchanges were not only close at hand but were all concentrated in one spot.

No wonder that the situation which we find in Bruges repeats itself in other mediaeval trading centers. In Venice the money-changers' offices were all located on the Rialto Bridge. In Genoa most of the private bankers clustered around the Piazza Banchi[12] near the Cathedral of San Lorenzo and the palace of St George, which was the seat of the famous Casa di San Giorgio and of the quasi-public bank of the same name during the short period of its existence, from 1408 to 1444.[13] In Florence, as in Genoa, most of the money-changers had their offices in the downtown business district: in the Mercato Vecchio, the Mercato Nuovo, and close to Or San Michele, all within the radius of a short walk. A few of them, however, resided in Oltrarno, the suburb across the Arno River.[14] In German cities too, the money-changers' offices were as a rule centrally located.[15] The same was true of Lille where no one was allowed to deal in exchange except on the Place du Marché in one of the stalls built for the purpose.[16]

In our documents the word 'exchange' (in French *change* and in Flemish *wissel*) is the term which is most commonly used to designate a money-changer's place of business, just as today the word 'bank' is used for the building as well as for the institution.[17] Occasionally, one finds in the records an expression which is somewhat more descriptive. A charter of 1280 reveals that money-changers from Lille had *loges* or booths in Thorout, a small Flemish town halfway between Bruges and Courtrai, which at that time was famous for its fairs.[18] It is reasonable to suppose that those *loges* or booths were only temporary shelters which were put up at the beginning of the fairs and taken down at the end. In Bruges, evidently, the money-changers did business all year around and needed permanent quarters. In Lille the money-changers' offices, located on the Place du Marché in the building which in the fifteenth century became known as the 'Beauregard,' are described in the documents as *échoppes* ('shops') or even as *échoppettes* ('little shops').[19] In Bruges itself the Flemish word *cameren* is used in connection with the space let to the money-changers under the arcades of the Waterhalle.[20] The word *cameren,* which literally means 'rooms,' can perhaps best be translated by the English word 'stalls.' From Marc Gheeraerts' map it appears clearly that the offices of the free money-changers on St Peter's Bridge were not large enough to spoil the monumental proportions of the Waterhalle and did not protrude more than a few feet onto the bridge. This pictorial evidence finds support in an old charter of 1224, which evidently relates to the creation of one of the fiefs on St Peter's Bridge. According to this charter, the area of the fief was to be twelve by fourteen feet, the Flemish foot differing very little from the English linear measure of the same name.[21]

All this evidence leads to the conclusion that the money-changers of Bruges and elsewhere, though they were often rich enough to own large and comfortable homes, carried on their business in small stalls or shops whose floor space hardly exceeded 150 square feet.[22] There is, consequently, a great contrast between the money-changers and the lombards whose residences or *hostels* were large establishments containing living quarters, offices, and warehouse facilities. A central location was very important for the money-changers, but the lombards preferred to be away from the crowded districts.

The arrangement of the money-changers' offices could not be very elaborate because of limited space. The best idea of their interior can perhaps be obtained from a number of paintings of the Flemish School representing bankers or tax collectors. These pictures, all treating the same subject, were painted in the first half of the sixteenth century and copies are found in various European art galleries and private collections.[23]

The earliest and most famous is a painting dated 1514 by Quinten Matsys. It is called 'The Banker and his Wife.'[24] The original is found in the Louvre.

The subject apparently appealed to the taste of the public and the genre was further developed by a painter named Marinus van Reymerswael, belonging to the school of Matsys. The theme is not always treated in the same manner.[25] Sometimes the picture represents two men instead of a man and his wife and the pose of the characters varies from one painting to another.[26] The imitators, especially Marinus van Reymerswael, do not treat their subject with the same detachment and refinement as Quinten Matsys. In their works, the theme is no longer a scene from life but a crude caricature of avarice and greed.[27] This remark does not apply to a diptych which belongs to the Bruges Museum of Fine Arts and is labeled 'L'Avare et la Mort'.[28] The attribution of this painting is uncertain: some think the author was a pupil of Matsys, others are inclined to credit J. Provoost, a Bruges painter of the sixteenth century, with the authorship.[29] The diptych of Bruges represents a skeleton who counts money on a table and points to the contents of a bill which is being handed over to him by a fat, old, startled man, evidently a money-changer or a usurer. The Bruges painting displays quiet originality and freedom in the treatment of the familiar theme of a miser having an unexpected rendezvous with Death. There is drama and restraint in the picture, but no satire.

There has been some discussion among art-critics about the question whether the pictures under consideration represent money-changers or tax collectors. Such a discussion is quite superfluous as both were often one and the same person.[30]

For us the details are the most interesting part of the pictures. In all of them the money-changer is the central figure and sits behind a table covered with a green cloth. He either examines a coin or writes in an oblong-shaped account book which lies before him on the table. Incidentally, this is the shape of the journals in which the money-changers wrote down their business transactions as they occurred. In at least three of the van Reymerswael pictures the second figure is a man, probably a customer, whose attitude shows that he is dictating something to the money-changer who evidently is writing from dictation in the account book in front of him. As we shall discover later, this small detail is not devoid of significance. In general the table is covered with the appurtenances of the money-changer's profession: a pile of coins, an inkstand, a set of weights or a queer purse with several baglike compartments, and sometimes beads, necklaces, or other pieces of jewelry. Behind the money-changer, on shelves along the walls, there is a display of account books, bundles of documents, boxes overflowing with papers, candlesticks, scales, and other accessories. All the pictures convey the impression that the money-changers' offices were simply furnished and crowded for space.[31]

There is consensus among the art-critics that the paintings described here were all executed in the sixteenth century. And yet most of them portray people garbed in costumes of the fifteenth century and more especially of the reign of Philip the Good. This little detail is additional proof that the paintings are not meant to be portraits, but genre paintings.

No extant document describes the inside of a money-changer's office in Bruges, but there is no reason why it would be different from similar interiors in other mediaeval cities. When the public authorities of Frankfort-on-the-Main decided to establish a municipal exchange in 1402, they purchased for this purpose two walnut tables, four screens (probably to make a partition), two strongboxes, one other chest, and several assay-balances: one for gold, three for silver coin, and some others for weighing bullion, old plate, or jewelry.[32] This list corroborates the exactness of detail found in the pictures of Quinten Matsys, Marinus van Reymerswael, and the unknown painter of the canvas 'L'Avare et la Mort.'

The most conspicuous piece of furniture in a money-changer's office was the table, whence the name of *table de change* in French and of *wisselbank* in Flemish. In Florence the statutes of the *Arte del Cambio*[33] describe repeatedly the members of the gild as 'sitting at a covered table with a book and a purse' (*sedentes ad tabulam cum tasca, libro et tappetto*).[34]

As petty exchange (or the exchange of one currency for another) is a cash transaction which does not involve much bookkeeping, the presence of account books in the offices of the money-changers arouses the suspicion that they did not confine their dealings to money-changing, but had extended their activity beyond this point. In Italy the *campsores, cambiatori,* or money-changers were also bankers and this was also the case in Flanders from an early date. When, exactly, the two functions were merged, we do not know. This development was probably the result of a slow evolution which came to a head during the decisive period which marks the end of the thirteenth century. In this connection a charter granted by Gui de Dampierre in August, 1294, to six burghers of Lille gives extremely valuable information.[35] As the importance of this document has been hitherto overlooked, it will be worthwhile to discuss its tenor at some length.

Unlike the lombards, the money-changers did not usually receive a special grant, and the charter of 1294 is the only one of its kind. According to its provisions, six burghers of Lille were given permission 'to change and'—this is more significant—'to receive money in the said city' (*k'il soient cangeurs et fachent rechoite*). The grant was to be valid for ten years starting with Pentecost, 1294, and during this period the count promised that he would neither tolerate nor allow any other money-changers or 'receivers' in Lille except the grantees and the heirs of their own blood. As the expressions 'to receive money' and 'receivers' do not refer to the collection of any public revenue, they are rather puzzling at first glance, but their meaning is made clear by other provisions of the same charter. In one of these, the count bound himself to protect and shield the grantees against any unfair demands as long as they were 'honest in their exchange dealings and reliable in their receipts and payments.' He added that, if the king of France should decide to suppress all money-changers within his realm, the grantees would still be allowed 'to receive money from persons who might entrust it to them and to make payments in accordance with the commands of these persons, but without dealing in exchange' (*sans maintenir et sans faire cange*). In other words, in case the king of France should decide to abolish all money-changing within his dominions, the grantees would have to comply and to discontinue their exchange business but they would be permitted to go on with their 'receiving'—read 'banking'—business, accepting deposits and making payments as ordered by the depositors.

In the light of these statements, there can be no doubt that the word 'receivers' as used in the charter of 1294 has the meaning of 'bankers' and that 'to receive money' stands for 'to accept money on deposit.' The text of the grant is admittedly obscure and shows that there did not yet exist in French, in Picard, or in Walloon an adequate terminology to describe banking activities. The presumption is therefore that banking was still something new.

If this interpretation is correct, it is scarcely a debatable question that the money-changers of Lille—and presumably those of Bruges—combined money-changing and deposit banking as early as the end of the thirteenth century. Of course, the text does not state explicitly that only part of the deposits was kept in ready cash in order to meet occasional withdrawals and that the rest was invested or used in credit transactions. It can be safely assumed, however, that the deposits with the money-changers of Lille during the last decade of the thirteenth century were irregular and not regular deposits. This amounts to saying that the depositors did not entrust their funds to a money-changer for safe-keeping in a strongbox, but only expected him to be able to refund the deposit at a moment's notice. Consequently, between the depositor and the money-changer, there existed not a trust, but a debtor-creditor, relationship.

To those who are prone to reject any but the most explicit statements, the evidence advanced here may not be enough. They may still prefer to think that the grant of 1294 does not prove sufficiently that the money-changers in Flanders combined banking and money-changing. This attitude is understandable from a strictly legal point of view. However, from 1365 onward, there can be no longer any doubt about the dual character of the money-changers' activities, so that the question is merely to decide when the practice was introduced.

For the years 1366 to 1369 we have a number of account books belonging to two money-changers of Bruges, named Collard de Marke and Guillaume Ruyelle. A careful examination of this material shows convincingly that these two money-changers did an extensive banking business. They currently accepted deposits and, through book-transfers and clearing agreements with other banks, they had developed a system of payments which did not involve the use of specie or hard money. Our two money-changers undoubtedly operated on a fractional reserve principle, that is to say, they operated on the theory that all deposits would not be called at once and their cash reserve was only a fraction of their liabilities to depositors. The funds thus made available were used partly to extend credit in the form of overdrafts and partly to finance business enterprises by outright investment.[36]

The account books of Collard de Marke and Guillaume Ruyelle give the impression that the banking operations of the money-changers by far outweighed their exchange transactions in relative importance. The participation of money-changers in commercial ventures also was only incidental to their banking activity, as such a participation was one way of finding a productive investment for excess reserves.

The money-changers whose activity originally included only the trade in bullion and the exchange of coins, had thus gradually expanded the scope of their business. In Bruges they had become bankers as well as money-changers by the middle of the fourteenth century and probably before. The abovementioned business records show that the system of payments by book-transfer and by clearing between banks was so perfected that it could not have sprung up overnight but must have been the outcome of a gradual development extending over a period of years.

In the fifteenth century the fact that the money-changers were bankers as well is more and more clearly recognized even in official documents. In a court sentence of July 5, 1460, which concerns the failure of a money-changer named Simon de Cokere, his business is described as *banke ende wissele,* a Flemish expression for which the English 'exchange bank' is a literal translation.[37] The same expression is found in a charter of Mary of Burgundy dated April 21, 1477. In this document the money-changers themselves are called *wisselaers ende banchouders,* which literally means money-changers and bankkeepers.[38] The French form seems to have been *bancq et chambge* which occurs in a Bruges document dated March 29, 1514, and refers to a deposit with the money-changer Nicholas de May who had failed in 1482 or more than thirty years before.[39] The best description is perhaps found in an ordinance of December 11, 1489. Here the money-changers are defined as *changeurs-banquiers* that is to say 'those who keep the money of merchants, burghers, and other people and use these funds to make daily payments.'[40] The idea which this last sentence tries to convey is somewhat clumsily expressed. What is really meant is that the money-changers made daily payments on behalf of their depositors.

It is significant that the Flemish (and Dutch) expression *banke ende wissele* was later changed into *wisselbank* by inverting the two words and writing them together. The new term came to designate the municipal public banks which sprang up in the United Provinces during the seventeenth century. The most famous of these banks, the Bank of Amsterdam, was called in Dutch, *De Wisselbank van Amsterdam*. These questions of terminology have sometimes their importance and should not be dismissed lightly. As we shall see, the public banks are the direct descendants of the mediaeval exchange-banks.

The development which has been sketched here was quite general in mediaeval Europe excluding perhaps some backward regions like Scandinavia, the Baltic countries, and even the Hanseatic towns of Northern Germany. Elsewhere money-changing and banking were almost invariably intermingled, with two notable exceptions. In London, money-changing and the trade in bullion was apparently in the hands of the goldsmiths, a profession which after all has some affinities with that of money-changer. It is commonly believed that the London goldsmiths did not enter the banking business until the period of the Civil War and the Commonwealth, but some historians question that assumption and think that this development should be traced back at least to the reign of Elizabeth if not to the Middle Ages.[41] The other exception concerns some Italian cities and Barcelona. In those centers, there existed two classes of money-changers: petty money-changers who continued to confine their activity to the trade in coins and bullion, and public money-changers who added banking to this function. In Venice, both classes were known at first as *campsores;* but later on the public money-changers became known as *bancherii,* whereas only the petty money-changers continued to be called *campsores.*[42] A document of 1374 foreshadows this change in terminology and significantly defines a banker as a money-changer who runs a deposit-bank (*banco di scritta*).[43] In Barcelona and in Venice public money-changers were required to furnish surety, but not petty money-changers.[44] The reason for this discrimination is obvious: as petty money-changers were not supposed to accept deposits, their going bankrupt could not bring about widespread losses among depositors.

As we have seen, the money-changers of Bruges, from a legal standpoint, were divided into two groups: the free and the licenced money-changers. Another *de jure* division between petty, and public, money-changers certainly did not exist and there is only scant evidence that it ever existed *de facto*. A perusal of the ledgers of Collard de Marke and Guillaume Ruyelle gives the impression that some money-changers made little use of the clearing arrangements between the different exchange-banks, but this is only an impression gathered from the fact that some accounts are not very active. Failure to use the clearing facilities at any rate, would indicate that some of the money-changers were not deeply interested in banking. The Bruges records fortunately throw much more light on another problem: they show that there existed among the money-changers great inequalities in the size of their business. Some, apparently, were more successful than others.

TABLE 8

SPECIAL TAX LEVIED ON THE BRUGES MONEY-CHANGERS FROM 1305 TO 1310

AMOUNT ASSESSED	NUMBER OF CONTRIBUTING MONEY-CHANGERS								
	1305	Nov. 1306	June 1307	Nov. 1307	June 1308	Nov. 1308	June 1309	Nov. 1309	1310
£50 *parisis*	1	..	..	..	..	..	..	..	..
£45–49	..	..	..	..	..	..	..	..	..
£40–44	1	2	2	2	2	2	..	..	..
£35–39	1	..	1	1	1	1	2	2	2
£30–34	2	6	8	7	7	6	1	1	1
£25–29	1	5	3	3	4	7	1	2	2
£20–24	2	3	3	3	3	3	5	3	3
£15–19	2	..	..	1	..	..	4	3	3
£10–14	1	1	..	..	3	..	1	3	3
Total	11	17	17	17	20	19	14	14	14

Source: Bruges, Municipal Archives, Municipal Accounts, Fourteenth Century.

As has been said before, a *taille* or special tax was levied on the money-changers in the beginning of the fourteenth century. While we do not know how this tax was assessed, it is natural enough to suppose that the method of assessment bore some relation to the ability of the taxpayers and the importance of their business.[45] Table Eight covering a period from 1305 to 1310, shows the distribution of the tax among the money-changers. It should be noted that the tax was collected twice in 1307, 1308, and 1309, probably to alleviate the pressing needs of the municipal treasury as a result of the war with France. The amounts collected in 1305 really represent not a *taille*, but a forced loan. This makes practically no difference as the loan was presumably never repaid.

As Table Eight shows, one of the money-changers paid as much as £50 *parisis* in 1305 and another as little as £10, but more than half of them paid £25 *parisis* or more. The next year, two money-changers paid £40 *parisis* and one only £10, but again the greater part of the money-changers paid at least £25 *parisis*. This remains true in 1307 and 1308. In 1309 and 1310, business must have been bad, and the proceeds of the tax decline because of a drop in the individual quotas as well as in the number of money-changers. In consequence of this downward shift the median falls from £25 to £20 *parisis*.

In 1359, fifteen money-changers lent a total amount of £2,400 par. to the City (Table 9).[46] In 1362, the city of Bruges contracted another loan of £3,780 par. of which £480 were subscribed by the lombards and the remaining £3,300 by sixteen money-changers (Table 9).[47] Their contributions were not all equal: the subscription of a few money-changers did not exceed the sum of £60 par. Others subscribed as much as £360 par.

These figures find confirmation in other data. The available information

THE BANKER AND HIS WIFE

by Marinus van Reymerswael

This picture shows a money-changer who is in the process of picking and culling coins. He is holding assay scales in one hand and a coin in the other. *From a painting in the Museo Nazionale (Bargello), Florence.*

TABLE 9

SUBSCRIPTIONS OF BRUGES MONEY-CHANGERS TO MUNICIPAL LOANS RAISED IN 1359 AND 1362

NAMES OF SUBSCRIBING MONEY-CHANGERS	Number of subscrip-tions	Amount of individual subscriptions (in pounds *parisis*)	Total
1359			
Janne de Vos	1	£600	£600 par.
Pieter van Oudenaerde	1	360	360
Jakemaerd Vlaminghe	1	240	240
Here Evrard Goederic	1	180	180
Willem Ruwele, Clais Rapezaet, Christiaen Juedemaere, Jan Moens, Janne van Maerc, Tydeman Bloumeroot	6	120	720
Janne Huerle, Jacob Reubs, Zeghere van Scardauwe, Jacop den Hamer, Clais van Donc	5	60	300
Total	15		£2,400 par.
1362			
Janne de Vos, Pieter van Oudenaerde	2	£360	£720 par.
Jacop Reubs	1	300	300
Willem Ruwele, Jakemaerd Vlaminghe, Jakemaerde van Rouc	3	240	720
Janne Moens, Janne van Maerc, Jan Cortscove, Kerstiaen Juedemaere, Jacob den Hamer, Jan Huerle, Joris Bartoene	7	180	1,260
Janne van Donc, Zeghere van Scardau	2	120	240
Clais Raepzade	1	60	60
Total	16		£3,300 par.

Source: Raymond de Roover, 'Le livre de comptes de Guillaume Ruyelle,' *Annales de la Société d'Emulation de Bruges*, LXXVII (1934), 88–89.

suggests that a few money-changers at the top secured most of the business, while some others at the bottom probably just managed to survive and were always on the brink of bankruptcy. The majority of the money-changers very likely were neither conspicuously successful, nor had much trouble in keeping afloat. From time to time a panic or a business depression came along and swept some away, as in 1309 when their number suddenly fell from nineteen to fourteen. One at least is known to have failed and the others who dropped out probably shared the same fate.[48] Incidentally, it is noteworthy that our acquaintance, sire Evrard Goederic, is not heading the list, but that, in 1359, there were three other money-changers more important than he. Of these three only one, Pieter van Oudenaerde, was still in business in the years 1366 to 1369, since the other two, namely Janne de Vos and Jakemaerd Vlaminghe, have no clearing accounts in the ledgers of Collard de Marke and Guillaume Ruyelle, which cover this period. These same records also show that the clearing account of Pieter van Oudenaerde was one of the most important. This may be taken as a sure indication that he had maintained his position in the business world and still ranked as one of the foremost money-changers of Bruges.

A careful check of the two lists brings to light another interesting fact. In 1359 the money-changer Jacob Reubs is close to the bottom of the list, but already in 1362, he has risen to the top and his name is listed third, after those of Janne de Vos and Pieter van Oudenaerde. From 1359 to 1362, consequently, the business of Jacob Reubs must have expanded more rapidly than that of most of his competitors. By 1369 he was perhaps the leading money-changer of Bruges, or at least as important as Pieter van Oudenaerde if the clearing accounts of these two men in the Collard de Marke account books can be taken as a safe criterion. According to these records, the two clearing accounts compare as follows for a period covering about five months, from December 24, 1368, to May 19, 1369:

Jacob Reubs[49]

Dr.	£	*s*	*d* gr.	Cr.	£	*s*	*d* gr.
Debits from Dec. 26, 1368, to May 19, 1369	5955	18	1	Balance on Dec. 24	77	16	4
Credit balance on May 19, to be carried forward	2	17	1	Credits from Dec. 26 to May 19	5880	18	10
	5958	15	2		5958	15	2

Pieter van Oudenaerde[50]

Dr.	£	*s*	*d* gr.	Cr.	£	*s*	*d* gr.
Total debits from December 26, 1368, to May 19, 1369	5066	3	0	Balance on December 24, 1368	82	11	2
Credit balance on May 19 to be carried forward	134	3	9	Total credits from Dec. 26, 1368, to May 19, 1369	5117	15	7
	5200	6	9		5200	6	9

As can be seen, the total of the amounts charged or credited to the account of Jacob Reubs during these five months are somewhat higher than the figures of Pieter van Oudenaerde's account.

Jacob Reubs was still alive in 1379 and was called upon to contribute to the forced loan which was raised in that year.[51] His share amounted to £10 gr. or twice as much as that of the widows of Pieter van Oudenaerde and sire Evrard Goederic.[52] The career of Jacob Reubs was probably successful up to the end. He was doubtless endowed with unusual business ability, because it would be difficult to explain in any other way his spectacular rise above the heads of his competitors. He must have left property to his widow, because the municipal account for the fiscal year September 2, 1386, to September 1, 1387, records the payment to her of the arrears of a *cens foncier* on the English weighing house in Bruges.[53] This *cens* had not been paid for five years, owing to the civil wars which had raged in Flanders.

The lists of 1359 and 1362 both mention Guillaume Ruyelle or William Ruweel, one of the two money-changers of whom some account books are still extant. As appears from the lists, Ruyelle was not one of the most important money-changers, and his business was only of average size. Collard de Marke, the other money-changer whose account books have also been preserved in the Bruges municipal archives, was certainly far more important. This fact is borne out by a comparison of his records with those of Guillaume Ruyelle. Whereas the latter gets along quite well with only one ledger a year, Collard de Marke, on the contrary, needs each year two huge in-folio volumes, generally one for the time from Christmas to Easter or Pentecost and another one for the remainder of the year. As his ledger also contains many more current accounts than Ruyelle's, one must conclude that he had also many more customers than the latter. Finally, Collard de Marke had more dealings with the other money-changers and made greater use of the existing clearing facilities.

Collard de Marke is not listed as a money-changer in connection with the forced loans of 1359 and 1362 and his name does not appear as such in the municipal accounts until 1366.[54] He must, therefore, have established himself in business between these two dates and have expanded it greatly in a relatively short time.

The disparities among the money-changers of Bruges can only be explained by differences in personality. In the Middle Ages, there existed no large corporations, and business relations were still on a personal basis. In banking especially, lasting success depended on two main factors: the art of inspiring confidence so as to attract deposits and the ability of making profitable and safe investments. A money-changer, of course, had to convince people that their money would be safe, if it were entrusted to him, and that they would be able to withdraw it when needed. Such confidence might be justified or not, but it usually rested on a reputation for reliability and competence in the management of funds. The public would, of course, also be inclined to have greater trust in a money-changer whose liabilities were secured by a private fortune than in another one who had nothing to back him up in case of need.

As a money-changer did not work with his own money, but with that of others, his most difficult problem was to find a suitable investment for the funds entrusted to him. This was made extremely hazardous and difficult because mediaeval banking, as we shall see, was seriously hampered by the lack of negotiable paper, the absence of a central bank, and the dangerous practice of making direct investments in business enterprises which precluded an adequate division of risks. Under those circumstances, unusual caution, ability, and perhaps a bit of good luck were required to keep clear of the rocks. As a result of reckless banking methods, failures were common, and it is a wonder that they did not recur with even greater frequency. In Genoa bankruptcies were so prevalent among the small banks—doubtless more vulnerable than large institutions—that this state of affairs gave rise to an amusing pun. The populace derisively called the small bankers *bancherotto,* a diminutive derived from *bancherius*, which sounds very much like *bancarotta,* the Italian word for 'broken bank' or bankruptcy.[55]

In Flanders the frequent failures of private exchange-banks never led to the creation of public or quasi-public banks as in Barcelona (1401), Genoa (1408), or in some German cities, such as Strasbourg and Frankfort-on-the-Main. Like the private money-changers, these municipal banks all combined banking and petty exchange transactions (manual exchange).

The sketch which has been drawn in the preceding pages leaves no doubt about the general character of the money-changers' business, but is not very detailed. It is possible, however, to go into more detail thanks to the preservation of the business records of two Bruges money-changers named Collard de Marke and Guillaume Ruyelle. These documents shed much light on many aspects of a money-changer's business, but they cannot be fully utilized unless we know something about their contents and the methods of bookkeeping which were in use.

There are extant in Bruges one ledger of Guillaume Ruyelle[56] and the following books of Collard de Marke: five ledgers, two journals, and the indexes belonging to two of the ledgers.[57] The indexes were only recently discovered and identified: by chance the ledgers to which they belong are those for which there is also a corresponding journal. There are, consequently, two complete sets, each including a journal, a ledger and the index pertaining thereto.

The ledger of Guillaume Ruyelle covers the whole of 1369 and part of 1370. In the rear, the ledger contains a fragmentary cash record of daily receipts and expenditures covering a period going from March 21, 1370, to June 27 of the same year. Within the folds of the binding there was found a loose sheet of paper on which was written a financial statement concerning the condition of Ruyelle's business as of May 24, 1370.[58]

The ledgers of Collard de Marke extend over a period of several years, or more exactly, from April 6, 1366, to December 24, 1369. The first two ledgers each cover a whole year but from April 10, 1368, onward, the extent of Collard de Marke's business required the use of two ledgers a year. The two complete sets go from April 19, 1367, to April 10, 1368—or from Easter to Easter—and from December 24, 1368, to May 20, 1369—or from Christmas, 1368, to Pentecost, 1369.[59]

According to a custom prevalent in the Middle Ages, the Collard de Marke ledgers all begin with an invocation to the Holy Trinity and to all the saints and angels of Paradise.[60] Guillaume Ruyelle follows the same usage, but his formula is much simpler and states only that the ledger is begun 'in the name of God and of All Saints.'[61] All the account books in question are kept in French and not in Flemish with the exception of the invocation and an occasional phrase in the Ruyelle ledger. According to references found in the account books, a ledger was called *grant papier;* a journal, *petit papier;* and an index, *le tavle dou grant papier.*[62]

As usual in mediaeval business records, Roman numerals are used instead of Arabic figures in both the narrative and the extension columns. The books are kept in Pounds Flemish, or groat, divided into twenty shillings (*escalins*) of twelve groats (*gros*) each.[63] The groat is further subdivided into three sterlings (*esterlins*) or twenty-four mites (*mites*).[64] Occasionally, amounts are expressed in French francs or in other denominations, frequently without indication of their equivalent in pounds Flemish, the money of account.[65] In a few instances, the rate of conversion is given. Each time that I have used the given rate and checked the conversion into Pounds Flemish, I have obtained results which show that the accounts tally. The computations of our Bruges money-changers were consequently correct. Incidentally, this accuracy shows once more that the German economist, Werner Sombart, was entirely wrong when he contended that mediaeval businessmen did not know how to figure.[66]

For their banking business, our money-changers kept four or five books: a ledger, a journal, a cash book, and a *papier de le monnoie.*[67] The *papier de le monnoie* was evidently used to keep track of the transactions with the Master of the Mint. As no copy has come down to us, we do not know precisely what such a book contained. A *petit papier quaret* is also mentioned somewhere by Collard de Marke, but the purpose of having a small, square-shaped book is not indicated.[68] No cash books have survived, either, but we have some idea of their contents through a fragment included by accident in the Ruyelle ledger. Each page of the cash book was divided into two columns: one for the receipts and one for the expenditures. A daily record was kept both of money received and money paid out. From time to time, each column was added up and one total subtracted from the other. The balance thus obtained should, in theory, have corresponded to the cash on hand, but this was never the case. As our money-changers made a profit on the exchange of coins and kept no record of such transactions, there was always a cash surplus![69]

The ledger contained only personal accounts, but no impersonal accounts, either for tangible assets, expenses, or operating results. The accounts were in bilateral form, that is to say, they were divided into two vertical columns, one for the debit and one for the credit. Collard de Marke used the left side for the debit and the right side for the credit, as is customary today, but Ruyelle did exactly the opposite and thus reversed the usual order. Each account is headed by the name of the customer. In the Collard de Marke ledgers debit is indicated by the phrase *me doit* and credit by *doy* standing for *Je dois.* Guillaume Ruyelle substitutes for these expressions the Latin forms *debet* and *debeo.* Closed accounts were balanced and cancelled with a diagonal stroke on both the debit and the credit sides.

The ledgers of Collard de Marke are divided into three sections. Section one, which extends over by far the greatest number of pages, contains the deposit- and overdraft-accounts. The clearing accounts with the other money-changers are grouped together in section two. As for section three, it is reserved for accounts of non-residents. Most of them have Walloon names and lived apparently in the province of Hainaut.[70]

The two extant journals are oblong in shape as are the Italian journals of the same period. In the journal our money-changers recorded their transactions day by day, as they occurred. As can be seen in several of the paintings described above, the money-changer or his clerk was in the habit of always keeping his journal right on the table, ready for use when a customer walked in. Like the cash book, the journal was a book of original entry. From the journal the entries were posted to the ledger. It is quite possible that this work was done every evening after office hours. Posting to the ledger was indicated by a short stroke across each journal entry.

The purpose of the indexes was, of course, to give the number of the page or folio on which a given account could be found in the corresponding ledgers. The two extant indexes are provided with thumb initials like most dictionaries or modern indexes. The customers listed in the Collard de Marke indexes are not classified under the initial of their last name but under that of their first or Christian name. This method of classification was the usual one during the Middle Ages (because the Christian name was *the* name) but it was not very practical, because of the great number of people with a Christian name like John, James, or Peter. Collard de Marke's bookkeeper had the bright idea of keeping the 'Johns' and the 'Jameses' separate, but still there are too many 'Johns' listed to make the index convenient.

Guillaume Ruyelle and Collard de Marke, as we shall see, invested some of the money entrusted to them directly in business enterprises. These investments were recorded in separate books none of which are extant. We know of their existence by references in the extant ledgers.

It is clear from the explanations given that Collard de Marke and Guillaume Ruyelle kept their books not in double-entry, *but in single-entry.* In other words, they did not keep a record of *all* their transactions, only of those which affected the state of their cash or the balances due to, or owed by, customers or other money-changers. The system of bookkeeping adopted by our Bruges money-changers was, consequently, incomplete in that it did not lead up to a real balance and to a comprehensive statement of profit and loss.

When Collard de Marke wanted to start a new ledger, all the accounts in the old one were closed and balanced. These balances were then transferred from the old to the new ledger. This transfer is indicated by an appropriate formula, always the same. For example, the account of Jehan de Concorighe, on folio 30 of Ledger No. 4, which begins on December 24, 1368, starts out with a debit balance left over from the preceding ledger, No. 3. The formula used for the transfer reads as follows: 'Jehan de Concorighe me doit: par le reste de nos contes dou fuelliet 287 de men autre papier' ('Jehan de Concorighe owes me for the rest of our accounts from folio 287 in my other book'). When an account begins with a credit instead of a debit balance, the formula used is exactly the same with the exception that *me doit* is replaced by *doy* ('I owe him'). Ruyelle followed a similar method in transferring accounts from one ledger to another, though the wording of the formula he uses is somewhat different.

When our two Bruges money-changers wanted to have an idea of the state of their business, they proceeded in much the same way, by closing all the ledger accounts and by listing and adding the open balances on a sheet of paper. Debit and credit balances had to be listed and added up separately. It is evidently in this manner that Ruyelle (or his bookkeeper) prepared the financial statement of May 24, 1370, which was discovered by chance in the binding of his ledger. This statement is not dated, but it has not been difficult to determine the exact date by referring to the ledger. No similar financial statements pertaining to Collard de Marke have been found as yet. But they may still turn up some day.

The essential features of the bookkeeping system which we have just described have to be kept in mind, if one wants to understand the business of mediaeval money-changers. Many details in banking practice rest on accounting procedure and it is impossible to separate the two.

Unlike the lombards, the money-changers did not usually enter into partnerships, at least as far as their money-changing and banking business is concerned. The only known exception is the case of two money-changers, Willemme van der Lanternen and Gillis van der Matte, who jointly paid the *taille* levied in the beginning of the fourteenth century.[71] The same remark does not apply to the direct participation of money-changers in commercial ventures, where partnerships were, of necessity, the rule.

Mediaeval money changers did not employ a large clerical staff. One should remember that their offices were small and that there was no room to have many clerks running around. It does not mean that the Bruges money-changers did all the work themselves and were not dependent upon clerical help. On the contrary, the Collard de Marke and Guillaume Ruyelle account books give a number of clues which prove beyond a doubt that our two money-changers had a small number of employees in their service.

For one thing, it is certain that someone other than the master was in charge of keeping the books. The Collard de Marke account books are mostly written in the same hand, but occasionally one finds another handwriting. The most noticeable is a bad and hardly legible scrawl which may be that of Collard de Marke himself. In the journal corresponding to the ledger No. 4, beginning on December 24, 1369, there is an account relating to his household expenses. Most of it is hardly readable because moisture has made the ink fade. Anyway, the bookkeeper refers to Collard de Marke in the third person and mentions his wife (*se femme*) and his son (*mestre Colin, sen fil*). If Collard de Marke had kept these accounts himself, he would doubtless have written 'my wife' and 'my son.' The bookkeeper of Guillaume Ruyelle is more polite and refers to his master's wife as *Medmyselle*. He probably acted also as cashier and one of his duties was to keep the cash book. Judging by the sample in the rear of Ruyelle ledger, receipts were entered on the credit side under the heading *debeo* and expenditures, on the debit side under *debet*. According to accounting practice, it should be the opposite. Ruyelle's cashier apparently worked on the theory that all money received by him was a debt to his employer and that all money paid out was chargeable to the same.[72] In other words, the cash account was treated like an account payable.

Besides a bookkeeper, our money-changers used one or two assistants and a couple of messengers who were most of the time on the streets and not working in the office. These employees were called *varlets*. One of Collard de Marke's varlets was named Pashier Mis and borrowed from his master an amount of four pounds groat.[73] The account books also contain frequent references to payments made to the other money-changers' varlets or messengers who were apparently sent over to Collard de Marke's office to make collections.[74] Ruyelle was assisted in his business by a cousin named Hannekin (or 'Johnny') Ruyelle.[75]

To conclude, the clerical staff of a money-changer's office was small and included an assistant, a bookkeeper, one or two messengers and sometimes a cashier. All routine work was left to employees,[76] so that the master could concentrate on more important tasks, such as interviewing customers, dealing with the master of the mint, keeping in touch with the market, and making all important decisions of policy, especially concerning loans and investments.

A money-changer, apparently, was liable for any obligations arising from deposits which had been received during his absence by any of his employees. According to Jean Boutillier's *Somme Rural,* such responsibility was based on the rules of Roman Law regarding agency.[77] Jean Boutillier's *Somme Rural* is a treatise on law and legal practice written in the fourteenth century. The author (d. 1395 or 1396) was *bailli royal* in Tournai. His work deals with that part of Northern France which was under the jurisdiction of the *Parlement de Paris*.[78] In our period this region included Flanders as well as Picardy, Artois, and Tournaisis.

These remarks on the organization of the work in the office of a money-changer complete the general picture of his business and professional activity. As we have seen, the money-changers performed three important functions: they traded in money and bullion, they accepted deposits payable on demand, and they reinvested and relent most of the money entrusted to them. These three main functions will now be discussed separately in the next three chapters.

[1]Gilliodts, *Coutume*, I, 518; *idem, Inventaire, Introduction*, p. 409, II, 347. Cf. Bigwood, *Régime*, I, 394, 413.

[2]Letts, *Bruges and its Past*, p. 164.

[3]These barges are referred to in many Italian documents which call them by the name of *scutta.* See Pegolotti, *Pratica della Mercatura*, pp. 17, 442.

[4]Letts, *op. cit.*, pp. 26, 164.

[5]Gilliodts, *Inventaire, Introduction*, p. 410: 'Margriete, filia Jans van Cuertrike, houdt een leengoed ende es een van den viere vryen wisselen eervelyc binnen der stede van Brugghen *up sinte Pietersbrugghe*' (italics mine). The date of the text is 1435. Cf. Gilliodts, *Coutume*, I, 518; *idem, Inventaire*, VI, 466. In 1498 the free money-changers speak of themselves as the 'quatre francs fiefvez changeurs de Bruges scituez et tenans ensemble sur le pont Saint Piere.'

[6]Gilliodts, 'Les registres des "Zestendeelen" de l'année 1580,' *op. cit.*, p. 98, No. 95.

[7]*Ibid.*, p. 42, No. 5 and n. 1.

[8]Gilliodts, *Inventaire, Introduction*, p. 410.

[9]This results from an entry in the municipal accounts for the year 1294, fol. 22, No. 1: 'Hanchins pro restitutione partis feodi sui iacentis iuxta pontem Sancti Petri occupati pro constructione Nova Halle, (Gilliodts, *Coutume*, I, 518). This text seems to indicate that Hankin was only part-owner of a fief adjoining St. Peter's Bridge.

[10]Sanderus, *Flandria illustrata*, II, plate opp. p. 37.

[11]Gilliodts, *Coutume*, I, 518.

[12]Sieveking, *Casa di San Giorgio*, p. 44 [328].

[13]*Ibid.*, p. 62 [346]. The Bank of San Giorgio was revived in 1586 (*ibid.*, p. 200 [484]).

[14]Giulio Gandi, *Le corporazioni dell'antica Firenze* (Florence, 1928), pp. 95, 97.

[15]As, for example, in Strasbourg (Julius Cahn, 'Der Strassburger Stadtwechsel: ein Beitrag zur Geschichte der ältesten Banken in Deutschland,' *Zeitschrift für die Geschichte des Oberrheins*, LIII [1899], 54).

[16]Benoît, "Le 'Beauregard' de Lille," *op. cit.*, p. 16.

[17]'Exchange,' *The Oxford English Dictionary* (rev. ed., Oxford, 1933), III, 377. According to this authoritative work, 'exchange' may mean a money-changer's office, though the word has become obsolete in this meaning. As I am dealing with the Middle Ages, I feel justified in using an obsolete word, because there is no other equivalent in English for the Flemish *wissel* or the French *change.*

[18]Bigwood, *Régime*, II, 286 f., No. 9.

[19]*Ibid.*, I, 412; *Morel, Les Lombards dans la Flandre française. et le Hainaut*, p. 39.

[20]Gilliodts, *Coutume*, I, 518.

[21]Bigwood, I, 413: 'Unam tabulam campsoriam habentem ante in latitudine quatuordecim pedes et retro in longitudine duodecim pedes.'

[22]Benoît, *op. cit.*, p. 17. In Venice, too, a bank building was hardly more than a superior sort of booth or shop (from an article in MS entitled 'News on the Rialto' kindly lent by the author, Professor Frederic C. Lane).

[23]Fernand de Mély, 'Les primitifs et leurs signatures: Quinten Matsys et Marinus, *Gazette des beaux-arts*, XL (1908), 215-27; cf. Fernand Donnet, *Coup d'oeil sur l'histoire financière d'Anvers au cours des siècles* (Antwerp, 1927), p. 32.

[24]Mély, *op. cit.*, p. 218.

[25]*Loc. cit.*

[26]A man and his wife, as in the original of Quinten Matsys, are represented on at least three replicas by Marinus van Reymerswael: one in Munich (Alte Pinacotheca, No. 138), one in Madrid (Prado), and one in Antwerp (Musée royal des Beaux Arts, No. 567). This last picture is called 'Un banquier et sa femme' according to the catalogue. Two men, probably a banker and his customer or his partner, are represented on the following replicas: London

(National Gallery, No. 944), Antwerp (Musée royal des Beaux Arts, No. 244). Windsor Castle, 'The Misers' (attributed to Quinten Matsys).

[27]This applies especially to the pictures in London, Windsor Castle, and Antwerp, No. 244.

[28]No. 218. Description in E. Hosten and Eg. I. Strubbe, *Geillustreerde Catalogus, Stedelijk Museum van Schoone Kunsten* (Bruges, n. d.), p. 207.

[29]*Loc. cit.*

[30]Donnet, *op. cit.*, p. 33.

[31]*Loc. cit.*

[32]Kriegk, 'Frankfurter Geldgeschäfte und Handelsbanken,' *op. cit.*, pp. 335 f.; Speyer, *Die ältesten Credit- und Wechselbanken*, p. 23.

[33]The *Arte del Cambio* was the money-changers' gild.

[34]La Sorsa, *op. cit.*, p. 19; Gandi, *op. cit.*, p. 97; Sieveking, *Casa di San Giorgio*, p. 43 [327], n. 8. Cf. Félix Bourquelot, *Etudes sur les foires de Champagne: sur la nature, l'étendue et les règles du commerce qui s'y faisait aux XIIe, XIIIe et XIVe siècles* ('Mémoires de l'Académie des Inscriptions et des Belles Lettres,' 2d series, Vol. V [Paris, 1865]) Part II, p. 130. The cloth covering the money-changers' tables often had a legal significance. In Milan money-changers who had not taken the required oath and who had not given surety were not allowed to have covers on their tables.—Alessandro Lattes, *Il diritto commerciale*, p. 202. In Valencia the table of the municipal exchange-bank was covered with a cloth on which the city's coat-of-arms was embroidered.—A.-E. Sayous, 'Une caisse de dépôts: la "Table des Changes" de Valence (1407 et 1418),' *AHES*, VI (1934), 137. It is also interesting that the furniture of the municipal bank included two chests: a small one for till money and a larger one used as a safe for the cash reserve.

[35]This document is published in full by Bigwood, *Régime*, II, 304 f., No. 20. The date is August 1294. The document is in Picard dialect and is rather difficult to read.

[36]de Roover, 'Ruyelle,' *op. cit.*, pp. 32, 36, 62.

[37]Bruges, Municipal Archives, Sentences civiles, 1453-1461, fol. 332. The English term 'exchange-bank' was actually used in the sixteenth century. It is even found in Coverdale's translation of the Bible (1535), Luke, 19:23: 'Wherefore than hast thou not delyvered my money to the exchaunge banke.' See 'Exchange,' *The Oxford English Dictionary*, III, 377.

[38]Bruges, Municipal Archives, Chartes politiques, 1st series, No. 1155, art. 13.

[39]Gilliodts, *Cart. de l'Estaple*, II, 448, No. 1422.

[40]Sneller, *op. cit.*, p. 495, n. 2. The text speaks about 'changeurs-banquiers, à savoir ceulx qui gardent l'argent des marchans, bourgeois et aultres personnes, dont ilz faisoyent payemens journelement.'

[41]George Unwin, 'London Tradesmen and their creditors,' *Finance and Trade under Edward III* (Manchester, 1918), p. 26. R. H. Tawney, on the contrary, adhers to the accepted tradition according to which the goldsmiths did not develop banking until the Civil War. He points out that no anticipation of such a practice is found even among the goldsmiths at the time of Elizabeth (Introduction, Wilson, *Discourse upon Usury*, pp. 92-94). If Tawney is right, it only proves once more that England, in the later Middle Ages, was in something of a commercial backwater, very much behind the Low Countries, not to mention Italy and the Mediterranean trading centers.

[42]Roberto Cessi, 'Il problema bancario a Venezia nel secolo XIV,' *Atti della R. Accademia delle Scienze di Torino*, LII (1917), 784. Cf. A. Lattes, *Il diritto commerciale nella legislazione statutaria*, p. 199.

[43]Cessi, 'Il problema bancario a Venezia,' *op. cit.*, p. 786, n. 1: '. . . bancherius vel campsor qui teneat banchum de scripta,' or 'bancha cambiorum a scripta.'

[44]Abbott Payson Usher, 'Deposit Banking in Barcelona, 1300-1700,' *Journal of Economic and Business History*, IV (1931), 125; A. Lattes, *Il diritto commerciale*, p. 219, n. 31.

[45]Gilliodts, *Inventaire, Glossaire flamand*, II, pp. 504 f.: 'Pointinghen: C'était du reste un principe admis que "l'assiette de la *pointinghe* et *zettinghe* se liève aussy bien sur les faisans

mestiers et négociations que sur les laboriers de terre," et qu'il fallait l'imposer "selon les facultés, richesses, mestiers, négociations et bedryfz" . . .'

[46]de Roover, 'Ruyelle,' *op. cit.*, p. 88, No. 1.

[47]*Ibid.*, p. 89, No. 3.

[48]The name of the one who failed is Boidin Weghebedde. Bruges, Municipal Archives, Comptes Communaux, 1315, fol. 2 *(Ghemeene ontfanc)*.

[49]Bruges, Municipal Archives, Account Books of Collard de Marke, Ledger No. 4, beginning on December 24, 1368. This is a summary of Jacob Reubs' account on folios 300, 303, 308-09, 312, 316, 318, 320, and 322 of this ledger.

[50]Summary of Pieter van Oudenaerde's account on fols. 301, 305, 309, 311, 313, 314, 315, 317, 320, 323 of the same ledger.

[51]Gilliodts, *Inventaire*, II, 349-53.

[52]*Loc. cit.*

[53]Bruges, Municipal Archives, Municipal Accounts, 1386-1387, fol. 138: 'Item, bi denzelven [Jan de Grave, *pensionnaire* of Bruges] betaelt joncvrauwe Katelinen, Jacob Ruebs [sic] wedewe, van achterstellen van landcheinse, van 5 jaren tachter up 't vorseide Ingelsche weghehuus, alsoot blyct bi lettren van adquite, 18*s.* 4*d.* grooten . . . . .Somma 11 *lb.*'

[54]Bruges, Municipal Archives, Comptes Communaux, 1366-1367 (n.s.), fol. 16.

[55]Sieveking, *Casa di San Giorgio,* 43 [327], n. 2: 'Minores bancherii quos volgus nuncupat bancherotos.'

[56]Bruges, Municipal Archives, Ledger of Guillaume Ruyelle (not catalogued, in-folio). This MS is described and excerpts are given in Raymond de Roover, 'Le livre de comptes de Guillaume Ruyelle, changeur à Bruges (1369),' *op. cit.*, pp. 15-95. This study has been excellently summarized in English by Lewis A. Carman, 'Researches of Raymond de Roover in Flemish Accounting of the Fourteenth Century,' *The Journal of Accountancy,* LX (1935), 111-22. An Italian translation appeared during World War II: *Il libro dei conti di Guglielmo Ruyelle, cambiavalute di Bruges (1369),* trans. Mario Cittadini (Rome: Casa editrice Castellani, 1941).

[57]Bruges, Municipal Archives, Account Books of Collard de Marke (not catalogued):

1)Ledger No. 1, in-fol., April [4], 1366-April 19, 1367, 310 folios. Some folios are damaged and the ink has faded. Section I, fols. 1-244; II, 251-280; III, 287-301.

2) Ledger No. 2, in-fol., April 19, 1367-April 10, 1368 (from Easter, 1367, to Easter, 1368), 400 folios. Section I, fols. 1-299, 370-388; II, 300-343; III, 352-366; Index.

3) Ledger No. 3, in-fol., April 10, 1368-December 24, 1368 (from Easter, 1368, to Christmas, 1368), 381 folios. Section I, fols. 1-291; II, 291-327; III, 332- 361.

4) Ledger No. 4, in-fol., December 24, 1368-May 19, 1369 (from Christmas, 1368, to Pentecost, 1369), 443 folios. Sec. I, fols. 1-212; II, 300-323; III, 400-406; Index.

5) Ledger No. 5, in-fol., May 20, 1369-December 24, 1369 (from Pentecost, 1369, to Christmas, 1369), 470 folios. Sec. I, fols. 1-321; II, 350-387; III, 410-419.

6) Journal No. 1 (corresponds to Ledger No. 2), half-folio, April 19, 1367-April 10, 1368, no pagination.

7) Journal No. 2 (corresponds to Ledger No. 4), half-folio, December 24, 1368-May 19, 1369, 195 folios. The folios from 117 to 190 and 194-195 are blank.

Henry Pirenne, in his *Economic and Social History of Medieval Europe,* p. 125, n. 4, states erroneously that, for Bruges, there remains only the fragments of an account book of Collard de Marke (1366-1369). As appears from the references given above, there are, in fact, five large ledgers, two indexes, and two journals.

[58]The text of the financial statement has been published in de Roover, 'Ruyelle,' *op. cit.* pp. 92-95, doc. No. 7.

[59]The Collard de Marke account books have been described in various places as far as the bookkeeping technique is concerned: Raymond de Roover, 'Quelques considérations sur les livres de comptes de Collard de Marke (1366-1369), précédées d'un aperçu sur les archives commerciales en Belgique,' reprint from *Bulletin d'Etudes et d'Informations de l'Ecole*

Supérieure de Commerce St. Ignace (Antwerp, 1930), 33 pp.; *idem,* 'Aux origines d'une technique intellectuelle: la formation et l'expansion de la comptabilité à partie double,' *op. cit.*, 189-91; *idem,* 'The Account Books of Collard de Marke,' *Bulletin of the Business Historical Society,* XII (1938), 44-47.

[60]The invocation in Ledger No. 3 reads as follows: 'Chest li papiers Collard de Marke qu'il fist l'an 1368, 10 jours en avril, ou non dou Père et dou Fil et dou Saint-Espri, et de tous Sains et de toutes les Saintes, et de tous les Angles et Arcangles de Paradis, Amem [*sic*].'

[61]de Roover, 'Ruyelle,' *op. cit.*, p. 19, n.1: 'Im de name van Gode ende van Alhelychen moet dit begonnen zyn Amen Amen.'

[62]The index corresponding to Ledger No. 4 begins as follows: 'C'est li papier de le tavle dou grant papier dou tierme dou 24 de décembre l'an [13]68.'

[63]The French name is *la livre de gros, monnaie de Flandre;* the Flemish, *Pond Grooten Vlaamsch.* The abbreviation is *£ s. d.* gr. or *lb. s. d.* gr. The latter is used in the Collard de Marke account books.

[64]These are Flemish sterlings and should not be confused with the English money of the same name. The standard abbreviation for sterling is *st.*

[65]The French franc was a gold coin worth about 32 groats in 1368-1369. Collard de Marke uses the abbreviation *frs. frs.* (francs françoys).

[66]Werner Sombart, *Der Moderne Kapitalismus* (Munich-Leipzig, 1919, 3d ed.) I, 36, 298.

[67]Ledger, No. 5, fol. 3v, account of Thomas Sarlande.

[68]Ledger No. 2, fol. 12, account of Jehan Parmentier: 'Jehan Parmentier me doit que j'ay mis en un petit papier quaret, 10 lb. gr.'

[69]de Roover, 'Ruyelle,' *op. cit.*, p. 27.

[70]There are a great number of references in the account books which prove that Collard de Marke traded with this region. The most important account in Section III is that of a man named Thierry Brochons, who was presumably a *drapier* from Valenciennes. See Journal, No. 2, fol. 48: 'doy Tiery Brochon ke il m'envoia par Colart le Brun, bouchier de Valenchiennes, le 12e en février: 1400 francs dou roy.'

[71]Bruges, Municipal Archives, Municipal Accounts, 1309-1910, fol. 19v.

[72]The supporting evidence is found in de Roover, 'Ruyelle,' *op. cit.*, 25-26; 74, table No. 5; 80, table No. 11.

[73]Ledger No. 2, fol. 1, and Ledger No. 3, fol. 1.

[74]For example, Journal No. 2, fol. 109 and Ledger No. 4, fol. 319, account of the money-changer Pietre le Potre. The journal entry is as follows (italics mine):

Pietre de Potre me doit *par sen varlet* contet 20 moutons doubles
de Hollande ky valent .... *4lb.* 3*s.* 4 *d.*

Each *mouton* was worth 50 groats.

[75]de Roover, 'Ruyelle,' *op. cit.*, pp. 17, 47. In this study I assumed that this Hannekin Ruyelle was probably Guillaume Ruyelle's son. He appears, however, to be a cousin according to a text in Collard de Marke's ledger, No. 5, fol. 385:

Willem Ruyelle me doit par Hanekin sen cousin contet 7 en décembre [1369] . . 50 frs. frs.

[76]Alessandro Lattes (*Il diritto commerciale,* p. 201) writes about conditions in Italy: '. . . essi [i banchieri] tenevano pure discepoli e ministri per eseguire le operazioni di minor rilievo, come il cambio manuale delle monete e la registrazione sui libri mercantili.'

[77]Jean Boutillier, *Le grand coustumier général de practique, aultrement appellé Somme Rural* (Paris, 1537), fol. 89v: *'De varlet de change.* Action institoire est bien douée par la loy escripte que pour celuy qui a mis aucun argent au change d'aucun changeur publique par consignation deue, lequel argent fut mis et consigné au varlet, jassoit ce que son maistre n'y fust présent, puisque ce a esté fait ou nom du maistre, il convient que le maistre face bon tout ce que par son varlet a esté fait, ne différer ny peult. L. eodem [codex 51.4], 1. institoria.'

[78]O. de Meulenaere, 'Jehan Boutillier: Esquisse biographique,' *Nouvelle revue historique de droit français et étranger,* XV (1891), 18-35.

Chapter 12

THE FLEMISH CURRENCY SYSTEM, THE TRADE IN BULLION, AND THE MONEY MARKET

THE trade in money and bullion, the first of the three main functions performed by the money-changers, involved much more than the petty exchange of coins. The money-changers formed the link between the public and the mint. The existence of such a link was essential to the smooth operation of the money market. But the mechanism of the money market cannot be fully understood without some knowledge of the monetary system. Therefore, it appears necessary to give a description of the Flemish monetary system during the fourteenth and fifteenth centuries.

In the field of mediaeval history, there is, perhaps, no topic which has given rise to more confusion than money. Although much has been written on the subject, there are very few satisfactory treatises.[1] The reason is obvious: the solution of an economic problem rests on a correct interpretation of the facts; if the facts are misrepresented or if the interpretation of them is based on a false theory, the whole analysis is likely to suffer from this initial mistake. Most of the writings on money in the Middle Ages are deficient in one respect or the other, and are, therefore, misleading, if not entirely worthless. One cause of the lack of reliable studies is that economists and historians have failed to cooperate. Much writing has been done either by historians, who could read documents but were ignorant of economic problems, or by economists, who were admirable in their logic but unfortunately wrong about their facts.[2] However, most of the work on mediaeval money has been done neither by historians nor by economists, but by numismatists. They certainly deserve great credit for the publication of valuable source material, but their commentaries on the sources have usually been valueless from the standpoint of economic history.[3] The reason is that numismatists look at monetary problems from a collector's point of view and are more interested in the identification of particular coins than in money as a standard of value or a medium of exchange.

The chief fallacy which pervades most of the work on money in the Middle Ages is the mistaken notion that 'money of account' was some kind of 'ideal' or 'imaginary' money which was used as a basis for the valuation of the real coins.[4] This valuation, the theory runs, could be changed arbitrarily by the monetary authorities. The 'money of account' was thus some kind of a standard suspended in mid-air like Rodilard, the cat, in one of the fables of La Fontaine.[5] This theory has been widely accepted.[6] On the basis of it, an Italian economist has even discovered that the Middle Ages enjoyed the blessings of a managed currency which was intended to prevent the fluctuations of the price-level![7] Truly, the mediaeval monetary authorities must have been endowed with a surprising understanding of financial problems.

In reality, the facts do not lend support to the theory of 'ideal money' or of an 'independent' standard. As the studies of Professor Hans van Werveke on Flemish currency and of Professor Gino Luzzatto and Dr Allan Evans on Venetian and Florentine currency clearly show, mediaeval monetary systems were pegged either directly or indirectly to gold or silver. They were based either on a real coin, such as the groat in Flanders, or on a coin which had ceased to circulate, but which still represented a definite weight of gold or silver.[8] In Flanders a unit of this latter type was the *denier parisis.* Originally, a silver groat had been equal to twelve deniers *parisis.* When the denier *parisis* disappeared from circulation in the beginning of the fourteenth century,[9] some people continued to reckon in deniers *parisis* representing a weight in silver equivalent to one-twelfth of the groat, a real coin. Thus the municipal accounts of Bruges were kept in pounds, shillings, and deniers *parisis.* As has been explained, the money-changers of Bruges were less conservative and kept their books in pounds, shillings, and deniers groat, the new monetary unit.

According to this system, the pounds and shillings groat were not represented in circulation by any real coin, but were simply 'monies of account' or mere numerical expressions, just as today one guinea is an expression for twenty-one shillings sterling.[10] In other words, pounds and shillings groat were mere multiples of the basic coin, the groat. One pound, of course, corresponded to twenty shillings or 240 deniers groat, and one shilling, to twelve of such deniers. Neither the pound *parisis* nor the denier *parisis* existed under the form of a real coin, but the shilling *parisis* was represented in circulation by the groat, a silver coin, as both the shilling *parisis* and the groat were equal to twelve deniers *parisis.* From this explanation it appears clear that Flanders, in the fourteenth and fifteenth centuries, was on a silver standard based on the groat.

The gold coins, whose circulation was authorized, were rated at so many groats apiece. These rates were generally determined by the monetary authorities, but it was clearly beyond the power of these authorities to set arbitrary rates. The official valuation had to be made with due regard to the gold content of the coin in question, to the silver content of the basic coin (the groat), and to the market ratio between gold and silver.[11] If a change occurred in any of these elements, an adjustment of the rate became necessary. It is true that the existence of seigniorage gave some leeway to the monetary authorities in the fixing of rates. If a coin was undervalued in the official tariff, it would either disappear from circulation or circulate only at a market rate above the official rate.[12] If, on the contrary, a gold coin was overvalued, it would tend to drive the other coins out of circulation[13] and to create a scarcity of silver.[14] This latter phenomenon was less likely to happen, since the seigniorage was rather high on silver coins and acted as a deterrent to their exportation.

During the fourteenth century the groat was not the only silver coin in circulation, since the mint also coined half-groats, sterlings ($\frac{1}{3}$ of a groat), and double sterlings.[15] The *botdragers* or double groats were apparently not issued until 1373.[16] According to Charles the Bold's monetary ordinance of October 13, 1467, the circulation was made up of pieces of four groats, two groats, one groat, one-half a groat, and one-fourth a groat.[17] These coins were commonly known as 'white money.' Their silver content was not exactly proportionate to their relative value because of differences in seigniorage and mint charges, but the price of the mint for a mark troy *argent-le-roi*—an alloy $\frac{23}{24}$ pure—was nearly uniform for all denominations.[18] The individuals who sold bullion to the mint received a slightly better price, if they asked for pieces of two or four groats, rather than for the smaller denominations.

In addition to white money, the circulation included coins called mites ($\frac{1}{24}$ groat) and double mites ($\frac{1}{12}$ groat), which were known as 'black money.' They were made of an alloy which contained very little silver. As mechanical processes of coinage were unknown in the Middle Ages, the mint charges on black money were very high.[19] In 1418, mint charges alone, not including seigniorage, amounted to as much as fifty-two per cent in the case of mites and forty-six per cent in the case of double mites per mark troy *argent-le-roi*. The intrinsic value of black money was thus far below its face or nominal value. As a result, the mites and double mites were somewhat like token coins. They tended to remain in circulation indefinitely and were never exported for their value in bullion. Even the debasement of white money did not affect the circulation of black money, as the margin between intrinsic and face value was ample enough to provide for automatic adjustment.

It is obvious that any study of mediaeval money should be based on a careful analysis of the monetary ordinances of the period. In other words, does the above description of the Flemish monetary system agree with the text of the monetary ordinances? For this purpose it is not necessary to examine all the published ordinances one by one, but rather it is sufficient to make a selection. Let us, therefore, take one ordinance of the fourteenth century and another of the fifteenth century.

According to Louis de Male's ordinance of November 25, 1356, the master of the mint Bardet de Malpilys, a Florentine, was allowed to coin 'un blanc denier qui aura son cours pour douze deniers parisis et à sys deniers et quatre grains d'aloy d'argent le roy, et de chinq sols et noef deniers de taille au marc de Troyes.'[20] In other words, the ordinance allowed the coinage of a groat (equal to twelve

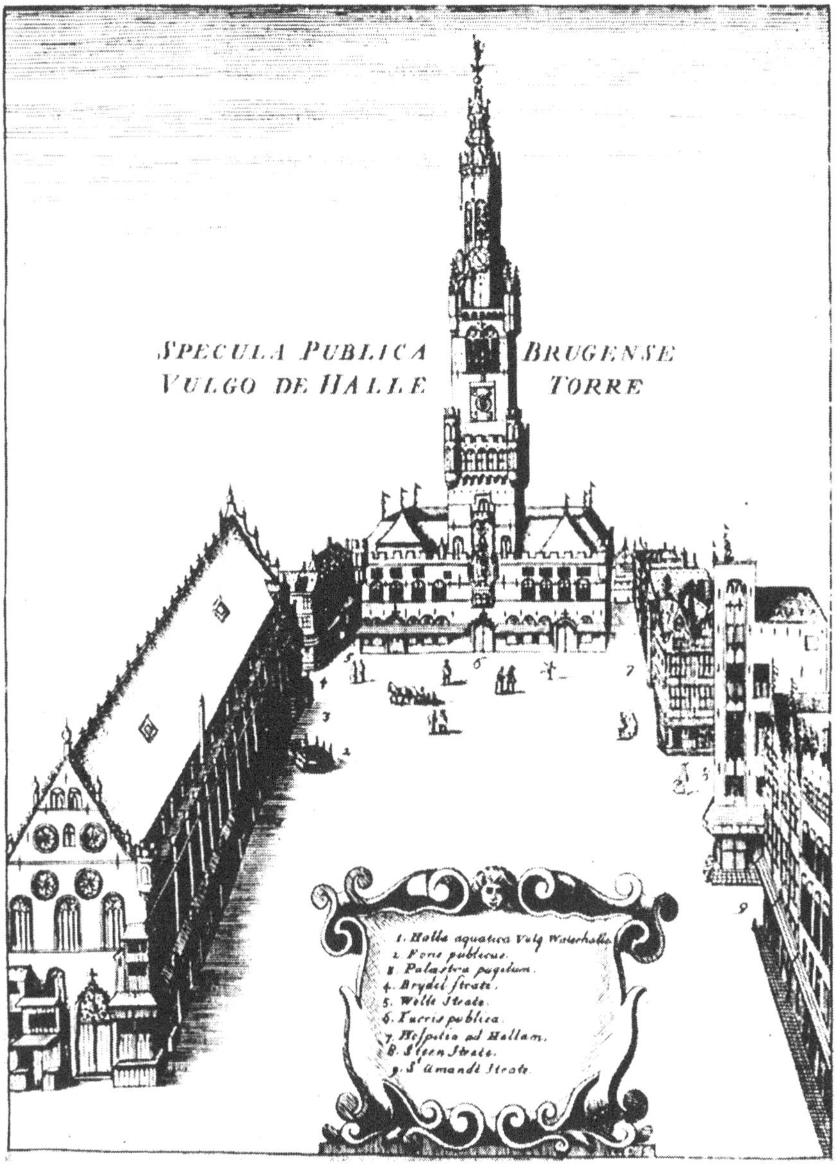

THE GRAND'PLACE OF BRUGES

The Old Cloth Hall with its belfry is in the rear. To the left is the Waterhalle or New Cloth Hall. Some of the stalls once occupied by the money-changers are clearly visible on the picture. From Saderus, *Flandria illustrata.*

deniers *parisis*), weighing $\frac{1}{69}$ of the mark troy and having a fineness of $\frac{37}{72}$ *argent-le-roi.* [21] On this basis the silver groat, in 1356, weighed 3.55 grams and contained 1.82 grams *argent-le-roi* or silver $\frac{23}{24}$ fine.[22] The ordinance added that the merchants who sold silver to the mint were to receive 118 groats or 9*s.* 10*d.* gr. for each mark troy *argent-le-roi.* As 134 groats were struck from each mark *argent-le-roi,* the seigniorage and the mint charges combined amounted to sixteen groats per mark.[23]

The second ordinance which has been chosen as an example is the ordinance of October 13, 1467, promulgated by Charles the Bold shortly after his accession to power as the ruler of the Low Countries, of Burgundy, and of Franche-Comté. This ordinance provided for the coinage of a 'denier d'argent à 4*d.* 12 grains argent le roy et de 130 de taille ou dit marc, qui aura cours pour ung gros de Flandres pieches. . .'[24] According to this text, 130 groats were to be struck out of a mark troy having a fineness of $\frac{9}{24}$ *argent-le-roi.* The groat thus weighed 1.89 grams and contained 0.71 grams *argent-le-roi.*[25] The ordinance further provided that 346⅔ groats or 28*s.* 10*d.* 2*st.* groat were to be coined out of each mark troy *argent-le-roi,* that the merchants were to be paid 26*s.* 11*d.* gr. for each mark *argent-le-roi,* and that the difference of 1*s.* 11*d.* 2*st.* gr. was to cover the seigniorage and the mint charges.

The text of these two ordinances, it seems to me, is susceptible of only one interpretation: the groat was a real coin, and Flanders was on a silver standard all through the fourteenth and fifteenth centuries. There is not the slightest foundation, even by twisting the text, for the theory of an independent standard.

The ordinance of October 13, 1467, provided also for the minting of other denominations besides pieces of one groat. The tabulation of the data given in the ordinance confirms the remarks which have been made in this connection (see Table 10).[26] The reader will notice that the price which the mint paid for one mark troy *argent-le-roi* varied slightly from 26*s.* 11*d.* gr. for the lower denominations to 27*s.* 4*d.* gr. for the highest denomination. The purpose of these small price differences was evidently to encourage the coinage of high standard denominations, as there was always the danger of overstocking the market with inferior white and black money.

According to these data the silver content of the groat had fallen from 1.82 grams in 1356 to 0.71 grams in 1467. This decrease was due to the steady debasement of the currency. In the Middle Ages debasement consisted in reducing the silver or gold content of the monetary unit either by a reduction of the degree of fineness (*mutatio in materia* or *in proportione*) or by a diminution in weight (*mutatio in pondere*). The two methods were even frequently combined. Under the Flemish monetary system, a depreciation of the standard (*pied des monnoies*) involved an upward revision of the official rates at which the gold coins were quoted and an increase in the price which the mint

TABLE 10

REGULATION OF THE SILVER COINAGE ACCORDING TO THE ORDINANCE OF OCTOBER 13, 1467

Denomination	Fineness of Alloy (1)	*Taille** (2)	Weight of Coin (3)	Silver Contents (4)	Number of Coins Struck from One Mark Troy *Argent-le-roi* (5)	Equivalent of Figure in Column (5) in *s* and *d* groat (6)		Seigniorage and Mint Charges (7)		Mint Price of One Mark Troy *Argent-le-roi* (8)	
			Grams	Grams		*s*	*d*	*s*	*d*	*s*	*d*
White Money											
Four Groats	0.9167	77½	3.16	2.90	84½	28	2		10	27	4
Two Groats	.5000	84½	2.90	1.45	169	28	2		14	27	0
One Groat	.3750	130	1.89	0.71	346⅔	28	10⅔		23⅔	26	11
One-Half Groat	.3333	234	1.05	0.35	702	29	3		28	26	11
One-Fourth Groat	.2222	324	0.76	0.17	1458	30	4½		41½	26	11
Black Money											
Double Mite (1/12 Groat)	.0347	204	1.20	0.04	5875	40	9½	13	10½	26	11
Mite (1/24 Groat)	0.0208	264	0.91	0.02	12672	44	0	17	1	26	11

*The *taille* was the number of coins struck from one mark troy of the fineness indicated in column (1).

Source: Gilliodts, *Inventaire*, V, 589–590, and Deschamps de Pas, 'Essai sur l'histoire monétaire,' *Revue Numismatique*, VII (1862). The figures of both authors contain obvious errors which partly correct each other.

paid for one mark troy *argent-le-roi.* Another result of debasement was to bring Gresham's law into play. The new and lighter groats were sure to eliminate the old and heavier groats, if the value of the latter under the form of bullion rose above their value as coins. Only badly clipped and abraded coins were likely to remain in circulation. All other things remaining equal, debasement called for an upward adjustment of the price level.

It sometimes happened that the standard was raised instead of being lowered. Such a 'raise' (*renforcement* or *retour à la forte monnaie*) was most of the time as difficult to carry out as it is today to return to the old parity after an inflation of paper money. A raise involved not only a reduction of the mint price and a scaling down of all the gold coins, but also the demonetization of the existing silver currency. As Gresham's law was likely to operate against the reform of the currency, it was necessary to decry and to call in all the silver coins and to replace them with the new currency.[27] Such a conversion was liable to create at least a temporary shortage of money. But these transitional difficulties were nothing in comparison with the economic problems which were certain to follow in the wake of the currency reform. As a 'raise' was essentially a deflationary measure, it required a downward adjustment of wages and prices. It is here that the policy of the monetary authorities was bound to encounter the greatest resistance. There is no reason to assume that, in the Middle Ages, prices were more flexible than they are today. An artificial reduction of the price level, therefore, was likely to lead to depression, business failures, unemployment, and widespread discontent.

In Flanders, the depreciation of the standard was especially rapid during the fourteenth century. Under Louis de Male the inflation of the currency assumed almost catastrophic proportions. The silver content of the groat sank from 4.22 grams *argent-le-roi* before 1318 to 1.01 grams in 1383.[28] The fifteenth century, on the contrary, was a period of relative monetary stability. Debasement continued, but at a slower pace. Between 1384 and 1480, the silver content of the groat dropped only from 1.225 grams to 0.64 grams *argent-le-roi*.[29] Moreover, the currency remained stable for several years in succession. According to the available information, there was no change in the standard from 1390 to 1407, from 1409 to 1416, from 1418 to 1428, and from 1433 to 1466.[30] The monetary authorities also made an effort to stem the tide of inflation by raising the standard in the face of serious difficulties. Such raises occurred in 1384, in 1390, in 1407, and in 1409.[31] Thus, in 1384, the silver content of the groat was increased by nearly twenty per cent, but the most drastic deflation was carried through by the reform of January 1390. This reform raised the silver content of the groat from 0.81 grams to 1.07 grams *argent-le-roi,* so that the new groats contained one third more silver than the old groats.[32] The reform of 1390 was followed by more moderate raises of the standard in 1407 and 1409.[33] The policy of deflation was pursued steadfastly until 1416, when the monetary authorities relapsed into debasing the currency.

Although Flanders was a fief of the French crown, the Flemish monetary system became independent from the French system after 1337.[34] It is true that the kings of France advanced the claim that they had the right to determine the standard and to set rates throughout their realm.[35] But the counts of Flanders got around this difficulty by minting preferably at Ghent or at Malines.[36] These mints were located on the territory of the Empire and the king of France had no jurisdiction over them. The French silver currency did not circulate in Flanders, but the king's gold coins could not be barred and were always listed among the current coins.[37]

According to a widely current theory, the debasement of mediaeval currencies is explained by the dwindling supply of precious metals in Western Europe due partly to the outflow of gold and silver to the East and partly to the exhaustion of the European mines.[38] While this theory may contain an element of truth, it is far from being satisfactory and neglects many important aspects of the problem. For example, the counteracting effect of the increased use of money substitutes, such as bills of exchange in international trade and bank deposits in the making of local payments, is entirely overlooked. Fundamentally, the theory rests on the assumption that, in order to stop the decline of the price level, it became necessary to strike an increasing number of monetary units out of a diminishing supply of bullion.

But the study of Flemish documents does not reveal the existence of any downward trend of the price level. On the contrary, prices rose sharply during the fourteenth century and more slowly during the latter part of the fifteenth century.[39] They tended neither to rise nor to fall during the intervening period of deflation and relative monetary stability.

As far as the fifteenth century is concerned the main source regarding the movement of the price level is a series of prices published by a Belgian historian Hubert van Houtte. This series is based on average prices of farm produce which were collected by an official body called 'la Chambre des Renenghes' or the 'Tribunal de l'Epier.'[40] This institution existed at least from 1351 and lasted until the end of the *Ancien Régime*. It was the duty of the Tribunal de l'Epier to collect data on prices in order to determine the money value of rents and other dues payable in kind to the public domain. The chart appended to van Houtte's study shows that the price of foodstuffs was subject to violent fluctations, obviously due to famine conditions, bad harvests, and an inelastic demand, but there is no evidence of a downward trend.

For the fourteenth century there are no price series or index numbers available, but other documents give a fairly good idea of what was going on. Apparently, prices and the cost of living rose faster than wages.[41] All through the reign of Louis de Male, there were constant complaints among the workers of the woolen industry about low wages (*cranke loon*) and the high cost of living (*diere tijt*).[42] The workers repeatedly petitioned the authorities for wage increases. That the complaints were justified is evident from the fact that wage rates were usually increased, but not as much as the workers demanded. For example, in 1374 the dyers sent a request to the authorities of Ghent in order to obtain an increase of the rates to which they were entitled for the dyeing of various kinds of cloth. The master dyers submitted figures which showed that their remuneration did not cover their cost of production. Probably the rates were fixed by gild regulations and had not been changed despite the rise in the price of alum and dyestuffs, the main raw materials used by the dyers. They claimed that they were unable to make a living and to support their wives and children. The authorities granted them an increase equal to two-thirds of the difference between the cost figures submitted by the dyers and the prevailing rates.[43] This decision seems to suggest that the dyers were rather generous in figuring out their cost, otherwise they would have continued to lose money.[44] Whatever the truth of the matter, there is no doubt that wages in general did not keep up with the rising price level. The resulting deterioration of the standard of living among the working classes is certainly one of the factors which explain the revolt of 1379. On the other hand, the debasement of the currency must have had a stimulating effect on business. The lower cost of production probably permitted the Flemish cloth industry to hold out much longer against the increased competition of English woolens.[45] The end of currency inflation in 1384 also marked the beginning of the slow decline of the Flemish *draperie.*

The deflation policy, which was adopted after the rise to power of the House of Burgundy, perhaps under the influence of Oresme's ideas, was even more harmful than the currency inflation of the preceding period.[46] Especially the 'raise' of 1389-1390 opened the door to serious trouble. The reform called for a downward adjustment of all prices, but, in fact, prices did not go down, at least not immediately. In all probability, the 'raise' reacted unfavorably upon the balance of payments, created a scarcity of money, and had a paralyzing effect on business, in particular on the all important cloth industry. As the public was accustomed to think in terms of groats rather than in terms of purchasing power, the workers resented the reduction of their wages. In Bruges the city-treasurer, who was responsible for the enforcement of the monetary ordinances, was nearly killed by an angry mob.[47] The only classes to benefit by the reform of the currency were the recipients of house rents and of *cens* or feudal dues—in fact the *rentiers,* the landed gentry, the clergy, and the duke himself in his capacity of landowner and feudal lord. According to the ordinance of December 20, 1389, they were entitled to receive payment in new groats, i.e., on the basis of seventy-two groats to a noble.[48] It is true that the *rentiers* and the fixed-income groups had been the principal victims of the inflation. All other creditors (except the recipients of rents and *cens*) were to be repaid in old groats or on the basis of 102 groats to a noble, the value of the noble before the reform of the silver currency.[49] This was after all a wise measure, otherwise all the banks (all the money-changers) would have been confronted with impending bankruptcy. The protection of the rights of orphans and the regulation of prices were left to the paternal care of the local authorities.[50]

A great many debtors were sorely hit by the ordinance of December 20, 1389. Protests were general. They soon forced the authorities to act in order to 'relieve the people' (*relever le peuple*) from the crushing burden of debts. On December 5, 1390, a new ordinance was passed at the urgent request of the representatives of the three principal cities and of the Franc de Bruges. The municipal authorities and those of the Franc were thereby empowered to scale down the rents due to their own burghers, but not those to the duke, to the Church, or to noblemen who were not burghers of the said cities.[51]

The monetary ordinance of 1389-1390 not only disturbed the relations between debtors and creditors, but also sharpened the conflict between wage-earners and employers. Wages, of course, had to be equated to the new standard. Such an adjustment, it would seem, should be easy, as it is a problem of simple arithmetic. In fact, the wage reductions gave rise to a great deal of bickering as both employers and workers tried to take advantage of the confusion created by the reform of the currency. In Courtrai, for example, the *drapiers* or cloth manufacturers proposed to reduce the wage rate of the fullers from forty-one groats to thirty-two groats for each cloth to be fulled. The *drapiers* argued that wages had to be reduced proportionately to the raise of the standard (*selonc ce que la dicte monnoie estoit plus forte le salaire des diz foulons devoit estre diminué*), but the fullers opposed such a move on the ground that the rate of forty-one groats had been set once and for all by an ordinance of Louis de Male. The case was finally arbitrated by the Council, and an ordinance of August 25, 1390, set the wage rate of the fullers at thirty-six groats, certainly a less than proportionate reduction.[52]

In other cases the employers were the stronger of the contending parties and succeeded in reducing wages more than proportionately. Thus, in Oudenarde, the wage rate of the finishers and shearers was apparently reduced from four groats to eight sterlings or two and two-thirds groats for *raemlakene* and from twelve groats to eight groats for *snijlakene,* another kind of cloth, or a reduction of one third in both instances.[53] It did not take long for the finishers to find out that this reduction was all the more disastrous, because the price level had not fallen. They petitioned the aldermen for a return to the scale of wages which had been in operation before the reform of the currency. These demands were naturally opposed by the *drapiers* who pointed out that business was so bad (*naer de quaede neeringhe die nu es*) that they could not afford to pay higher wages. There was probably something to this argument. Very likely the *drapiers* themselves were hard hit by the business depression which was the result of currency deflation. In any case the perplexed municipal authorities fixed a maximum scale below which wages were to be determined by free competition. On the whole the decision was favorable to the employers since it was a direct blow to the monopoly of the finishers' gild and the practice of collective bargaining.[54]

The evidence concerning the effects of monetary policy on the movement of the price level is admittedly scant. Therefore, it would be dangerous to make any generalizations. It is here that price studies should come in, but their importance should not be overrated. In the Middle Ages, the prices of foodstuffs in particular, were subject to erratic fluctuations due to famine conditions and to the lack of a properly-organized rationing system. As a consequence, the selection of a satisfactory index is extremely difficult. In the absence of price studies, the accessible evidence should not be despised. As far as it goes, it shows clearly that any tampering with the money was likely to have far-reaching and disrupting effects. Perhaps the results of deflation were even less desirable than those of inflation. Prices were not flexible. Wages, especially, were sticky, because they were fixed either by custom or by gild regulations. Today the same is true, and it is notorious that trade union rules have the same effect of freezing wages.

In view of the rigidity of the mediaeval price structure, prices did not respond readily to a contraction of the quantity of money; hence debasement was often the only means by which it was possible to restore economic prosperity and to bring the balance of payments into equilibrium.[55] The continuous debasement of mediaeval currencies, consequently, was not due to any permanent or long-run causes. Very often debasement was only an expedient used reluctantly and in the last resort to meet temporary difficulties.[56]

Today seigniorage has disappeared in most countries, but it was one of the distinctive features of mediaeval currency systems. The effects of seigniorage on the operation of the money market have not always been understood, and many people have only hazy ideas on the subject. The most important result of the existence of a seigniorage charge was to raise the face value of the coins above the value of their metallic content as long as the exchange rates were favorable and bullion was pouring into the mint.[57] If, on the contrary, exchange rates were depressed and if bullion was leaving the country, the market price of gold or silver was likely to rise above the mint price with the result that bullion would cease to flow toward the mint and that the mint would be forced to suspend operation.[58] As mediaeval mints were farmed out, the stoppage of work at the mint was one of the main causes of debasement.[59] The mintmasters, seeing that they were losing money, could be expected to break their contracts if the currency were not debased. It is clear that debasement was likely to entail some recoinage. Debasement also, by lowering the internal price level in terms of foreign currencies, was bound to set forces in motion which would tend to restore the equilibrium of the balance of payments, to stop the drain of bullion from abroad, and to raise the mint price above the market price of bullion.[60] Thus the mint would be enabled to resume operations until the next crisis in the money market. Debasement, in a certain way, fulfilled the same function as does today the raising of the discount rate by the central bank.

The fact that the mints were run for profit was undoubtedly at the root of many debasements.[61] Contrary to common belief, it is doubtful whether mediaeval rulers derived any real benefit from debasing the currency.[62] What the rulers gained from debasement by an increase of their seigniorage, they were apt to lose tenfold in other ways, because the income from other sources of revenue did not increase as fast as the price level.[63] It is not true that debasement increased directly the financial resources of the state as does today the unrestricted issue of fiat or paper money.

Another consequence of the existence of a seigniorage charge was to widen the margin between the import and export specie points.[64] The import specie point was often lowered by granting a refund (*une crue*) to the merchants who delivered bullion to the mint.[65] Such a measure was effective only within certain limits. It did attract bullion to the mint, if the exchange rates were already favorable and if there was only a slight difference between the mint price and the market price of bullion. But under less favorable conditions a refund on the seigniorage was not sufficient to induce people to send bullion to the mint.

As we have seen in a preceding chapter, the existence of seigniorage was to a certain extent a deterrent to the common practice of picking and culling. Seigniorage also conferred a certain elasticity on the mediaeval currency systems by allowing some leeway in the rating of current coins.[66]

The Flemish monetary system which has just been described remained in operation all through the fourteenth and fifteenth centuries. In the beginning of this period, however, it seems that it was still customary between merchants to make payments by weight rather than by tale. For this purpose the city of Bruges maintained an establishment, called *barnecamere* in Flemish or *chambre fondoire* in French, for the refining and assaying of silver.[67] This establishment issued silver bars bearing an assay stamp or hallmark as a guarantee of fineness. According to the municipal statute of 1309 on the trade in bullion, it was unlawful to have silver refined elsewhere than in the municipal *chambre fondoire* or to send any unmarked silver out of the city.[68] The municipal *chambre fondoire* charged six deniers *parisis* for the refining of one mark of high-standard or white silver and three deniers par. per mark of low-standard or black alloy.[69]

The *chambre fondoire* had a monopoly on the weighing of silver used in making payments. The tariff was twenty deniers par. per hundred marks and ten deniers par. from twenty to one hundred marks. Below twenty marks there was a flat rate of three deniers according to weight (*van den ghewichte*), but the exact meaning of this expression is uncertain.[70] Only the money-changers had the right to weigh silver up to the amount of five marks.[71]

The *chambre fondoire* declined rapidly. It is not mentioned any more after the middle of the fourteenth century.[72] The causes of this decline are not far to seek. They were two-fold: (1) the resumption of gold coinage and the preference given to gold coins in the making of large payments, (2) the disappearance of the traveling or caravan merchant, who carried his money in his belt, and the appearance in Bruges of Italian business houses and agencies which used almost exclusively bills of exchange in making payments abroad.[73]

After the resumption of gold coinage, Flanders retained the silver standard, but gold coins were used as a subsidiary or commercial money and circulated at variable rates. As a result of this condition, silver and gold were not freely exchangeable. The money-changers made it their business to supply gold to those who had silver but needed gold, and silver to those who had gold but needed silver. The services of the money-changers entailed the payment of a fee which is called *avantaige* in the Collard de Marke and Guillaume Ruyelle account books. *Vantaggio*, the Italian equivalent of *avantaige*, was soon shortened to *agio* which, in most European languages, has come to designate any difference or premium on exchange.[74]

Curiously enough the agio or commission of the money-changers was not computed on a percentage basis until the end of the fifteenth century. According to the municipal statute of 1309, the money-changers were allowed to charge one mite for every four gold coins that they appraised. In the case of silver the rate was one mite per pound.[75] The pound in question was probably the pound *parisis* so that the rate was $\frac{1}{432}$ per pound.[76] According to Francesco Balducci Pegolotti, whose handbook for merchants was compiled between 1310 and 1340, the tariff for expert advice on the value of coins was apparently one-fourth groat per hundred *royals* from each of the parties or one-half groat per hundred *royals* in all.[77] The *royal* was a gold piece worth twenty-four deniers groat according to Pegolotti.[78] On this basis, the commission of the money-changers was as low as one-fifth per thousand for appraising the value of coins. The agio was higher, if the money-changers actually were a party to the contract and bought or sold gold in exchange for silver. In such a case they were allowed one half-groat or twelve mites per noble of seventy-two groats or $\frac{1}{144}$ according to the ordinances of Philip the Bold dated December 26, 1399.[79] The monetary ordinance of October 12, 1433, provided for a double tariff: the money-changers were authorized to take eight mites or one-third groat on each gold piece which they bought as bullion, but the commission for the exchange of current coins was one-sixth groat or four mites for the smaller, and one-third groat or eight mites for the larger gold pieces.[80] These larger pieces were apparently the English and Flemish nobles which, in 1443, were worth ninety-six and ninety-two groats respectively.[81] The smaller gold coins included presumably the francs, the crowns, the Rhenish florins, the clinkaerts, the pieters, etc., whose value ranged from twenty-eight to fifty groats.[82] The rates of renumeration fixed by the ordinance of October 12, 1433, were still valid in 1467.[83] Maximilian's ordinance of December 14, 1489, however, simplified and improved the existing system considerably by establishing a flat rate of one per cent on all exchange transactions.[84]

The canonist writers did not object to fees being charged on the exchange of coins or 'manual exchange.'[85] For this reason such fees often served the useful purpose of concealing interest. But, even disregarding this possibility, there is no doubt that agio was an important source of profit for mediaeval banks. The ledgers of Collard de Marke and Guillaume Ruyelle do not give any precise information in this connection, because they do not contain any accounts for operating results. The profit derived from exchange transactions simply resulted in a cash surplus.[86]

The ledgers do disclose, however, that the money-changers carefully kept track of any deposits or withdrawals made in gold rather than in silver currency. If an entry relates to a transaction actually settled by a payment in gold coins, one usually finds the word *or* behind the amount written in the extension column of the ledger. A 'p' (for *payement*) behind a ledger entry refers to payments in silver currency. The purpose of these notations was evidently to help the bookkeeper in computing the fees which were ultimately owed by the customer.

Apparently a depositor who made a deposit in silver could withdraw his money gratuitously in the same kind of money, but had to pay agio, if he wanted gold. On the other hand, a depositor could receive credit in £ *s. d.* gr. for the equivalent of a given number of gold coins. In such a case he had the right to be repaid in gold without charge, but it seems that a fee was due, if the repayment took place in another form of currency. A good example is furnished by the account of Jehan de Concorighe in one of the Collard de Marke ledgers. This customer, besides several deposits in silver, made two deposits totalling £151 5*s*. 5*d*. gr. in gold. Later he withdrew from his account £110 16*s*. 9*d*. gr. in gold coins. After a while the balance of his account, £163 0*s*. 3*d*. gr., was transferred to another folio of the ledger. But under the transfer entry there is a notation *si a* 40 *lb. or,* meaning the balance of £163 0*s*. 3*d*. gr. includes forty pounds in gold or the difference between £151 5*s*. 5*d*. gr. and £110 16*s*. 9*d*. gr.[87]

The Collard de Marke ledgers contain numerous entries relating to agio which was charged to customers of the bank. The account of Zegres Onin le Jeune includes such an entry. It is stated explicitly therein that the customer owed the agio on thirty pounds groat, because he had a silver and not a gold account.[88] Probably Zegres Onin le Jeune had taken out gold against credit in silver currency. On May 2, 1369, the account of the Italian merchant-banker Guglielmo Rapondi was charged with £1 5*s*. gr. for all the agio which remained due up to the date of the entry.[89] According to an entry in the account of Roulof Rabonne of Louvain, the fee on £211 15*s*. 1*d*. gr., paid with 510 *grands moutons* at 51 groats apiece, 800 francs at 31 groats apiece and thirteen groats in silver, was £3 9*s*. 2*d*. gr. or a little over 1½ per cent.[90] Agio was even charged between money-changers as appears from an entry in the account of the money-changer Pieter van Oudenaerde. On May 14, 1369, Collard de Marke paid him 29*s*. 6*d*. gr. for agio on £120 gr. received in gold coins.[91]

Sometimes the money-changers also sold bullion to the gold- and silver-smiths, but transactions of this kind were few and unimportant.[92] Besides the exchange of current coins, a much more important source of profit was the purchase of bullion, especially of non-current foreign coins. According to the monetary ordinances, the money-changers were allowed to buy such coins, paying their value in bullion minus the customary fee or agio. The bullion supposedly had to be delivered to the mint. The extant ledgers of Collard de Marke and Guillaume Ruyelle give little information concerning their business dealings with the mint. These dealings were, undoubtedly, very important and were recorded in special books called *papiers de le monnoie,* of which no copy is known to be extant.

From occasional references in the existing records of Collard de Marke, it appears that there was a great deal of cooperation between the money-changers of the same city in their relations with the mint. For instance, on March 26, 1369, Collard de Marke wrote £158 3*s*. 10*d*. gr. to the debit of his colleague Pieter van Oudenaerde 'for a keg of coins which had just come from the mint.'[93] This entry suggests that the money-changers arranged to make joint shipments of bullion to the mintmaster at Ghent.

In Collard de Marke's extant ledgers there is also an account open in the name of Thumas Sarlande, 'à le cause dou mestre de le monnoie'[94] but the connection between him and Jehan Terminel or Interminelli, the master of the mint, is not made clear. The amounts involved are rather high and it is difficult to make out what the entries really mean. Apparently, in April and May 1369, Collard de Marke sent to Ghent, where the mint was located, several shipments of bullion amounting to a total of £501 19*s*. 7*d*. gr. The detail concerning these shipments is not given in the extant ledger, but was recorded in the missing *papier de le monnoie*. The proceeds were partly used to repay an amount of four hundred pounds which had been advanced by Thumas

Sarlande before Christmas 1368. At that time he was paid fifty pounds groat interest (*pour le pourfit de lui*) by Collard de Marke.[95] In settlement of the remaining £101 19*s.* 7*d.* gr., the mint sent new coins amounting to £51 19*s.* 7*d.* gr. about the first of August 1369. The balance of fifty pounds groat was charged to Thumas Sarlande and was still standing on the books in December 1369, when the ledger was closed.[96]

This loan of four hundred pounds groat made to Collard de Marke by Thumas Sarlande is certainly a puzzle. Collard de Marke, it is evident from his records, was in financial trouble at the end of 1368 and his cash position was seriously impaired. Did the mint sometimes come to the rescue of imperiled money-changers by lending them money? It is worthwhile to raise this question, even though it cannot be answered from the available evidence. The problem, at any rate, is of great importance: if such loans were ever made, one has to draw the conclusion that mediaeval mints sometimes performed the functions of a central bank.

In theory, anyone had the right to bring bullion to the mint and was entitled to receive the regular price per mark troy fixed by the monetary ordinances. In practice, however, bullion was purchased from the public by the money-changers and delivered by them to the mint. The general public was never in contact with the officers of the mint. The purveyors of the mint were the money-changers who collected all the bullion which came on the market and usually sold it to the mint.[97]

At the end of the thirteenth century, an attempt was made to do away with the private exchange business. After the conclusion of a monetary union between Flanders and Brabant, Robert de Béthune, regent of Flanders, issued on October 31, 1299, an ordinance which ordered all exchanges 'to be pulled down.'[98] The merchants trading with England could obtain at the mint the foreign money which they needed. There is no evidence that Robert de Béthune's ordinance was ever enforced. If a timid attempt was ever made in that direction, it certainly was given up after a short time because of practical difficulties. The grant of 1294 to the money-changers of Lille and an Antwerp privilege of 1306 contain provisions which indicate that the ruler had, in theory, the right to abolish all private exchanges.[99] In England the authorities actually succeeded in abolishing all private exchanges and in replacing them by the King's Exchanger who had tables at Dover, in the Tower of London, and in other seaports.[100]

The importance of the money-changers as purveyors of the mint is perhaps best emphasized in a document of 1357. This document is a statement of the debts left by an absconding master of the mint, an Italian named Bardet de Malpilys. In July 1357, he suddenly left Ghent for an unknown destination.[101] His liabilities amounted to the formidable sum of 27,598 moutons at 24 groats

TABLE 11
STATEMENT OF THE DEBTS LEFT BY BARDET DE MALPILYS, AN ABSCONDING MASTER OF THE MINT, JULY 1357

NAMES OF THE CREDITORS	Amount of Claims (Moutons d'or)	Per Cent of Total
The Bruges money-changers: Guillaume Ruyelle, Jaquemon Vlaminc, and Jehan Moens	6,091	22.0
The Bruges money-changer, Evrard Goederic	5,867	21.3
The Bruges money-changer, Christiaen Juedemaere	458	1.7
Total claimed by Bruges money-changers	12,416	45.0
Merchants of Ghent (no names given)	4,045	14.6
Money-changers of Ypres	1,579	5.7
Others	509	1.9
Total claimed by private individuals	18,549	67.2
Baudouin de Vos, varlet du Comte	9,049	32.8
Total of all claims	27,598	100.0

Sources: Gaillard, *Recherches sur les monnaies de Flandre*, II, 119–21, doc. LIII; Limburg-Stirum, *op. cit.*, Nos. 925 and 926; Bigwood, *Régime*, I, 230; de Roover, 'Ruyelle,' *op. cit.*, 38–41.

apiece or £2,759 16*s.* groat which the count of Flanders had to make good, because he was responsible for any embezzlement committed by his official, the master of the mint (see Table 11).

The highest single item listed in the statement of Bardet de Malpilys' liabilities is a sum of 9,049 *moutons* due Baudouin de Vos, *varlet du Comte.*[102] This title suggests that Baudouin de Vos was a public official and perhaps a *receveur* or collector of public revenue. If this assumption is correct, the item of 9,049 *moutons* represents minting done for public account. Presumably bullion and abraded coins which, by taxation or in other ways, flowed into the public treasury were turned over to the mint in order to be recoined. As this item does not exceed 32.8 per cent of the total, one must conclude that minting for public account was less important than minting for private account. The statement shows clearly that the money-changers were the chief channel by which bullion found its way to the mint. The debts to the money-changers represent 65.3 per cent of Bardet de Malpilys' total liabilities, if the 'merchants of Ghent' mentioned in the statement, may be considered as money-changers, too. The words 'merchants' and 'money-changers' were often used loosely in the monetary ordinances and other public documents of the period.[103] The money-changers of Bruges, with claims representing 45 per cent of the total, presumably did more business than those of Ghent or Ypres who came in for only 14.6 and 5.7 per cent of the aggregate liabilities. The minting done for private individuals other than money-changers was obviously negligible, if the statement of the debts left by Bardet de Malpilys can be regarded as a reliable guide.

According to law, the money-changers were supposed to deliver all their bullion to the mint. In fact, they did so only if they could not sell their bullion for a better price to some one else. To put it in another way, the money-changers continued their deliveries of gold and silver to the mint as long as bullion did not command a premium over the mint price. Such a phenomenon was likely to happen, if there was a brisk demand of bullion for the industrial arts, if the exchanges were unfavorable and bullion was being sent abroad, or if debased coins from a neighboring country invaded the circulation because the public disobeyed the ordinances and accepted this spurious money.[104] The money-changers were often accused of having a hand in the plot by uttering such adulterated coins.[105] The history of money in the Middle Ages is a continuous struggle between the forces of the market and the unrealistic and obdurate authorities.[106]

Each time that the complaints about the scarcity of money became too loud or that the circulation was swamped with under-weight coin, the authorities awoke from their slumber and clamped down on the money-changers. From time to time one of them ended on the gallows.[107] It happened more often that money-changers were fined and that the unlawful money found in their possession was confiscated. The gold coins may have circulated among the public at the official rate, but the Collard de Marke ledgers, decidedly, give the impression that such coins were bought and sold in the exchange at a market rate which was subject to constant variation. In 1366, nine money-changers, including Collard de Marke and Guillaume Ruyelle, were fined ten shillings groat each for having accepted and uttered nobles at a rate higher than the official price.[108] In 1392 a fine was exacted from the money-changer Henry de Hedes for the same reason.[109]

The authorities were especially anxious to enforce the monetary ordinances after the currency reform of 1390. In 1392 the *écoutète* of Bruges learned that the money-changers bought non-current coins without cutting them in two and thus converting them into bullion. He called two aldermen and searched with them the houses of the money-changers. The above-mentioned Henri de Hedes and the widow of Jehan de Courtrai were found in possession of forbidden coins; the former had £210 14*s.* 6*d.* *parisis* and the latter, £188 10*s.* 4*d.* *parisis*. All the forbidden coins were seized, and the offenders had to pay heavy fines besides.[110] In 1408 several money-changers were fined for sending bullion to foreign mints.[111]

In order to prevent the perpetration of frauds, the money-changers were required to keep their offices wide-open, so that anyone could observe them from the street.[112] One may doubt whether any one of these measures was in the least effective. From time to time a money-changer might be betrayed by an informer or be caught by surprise, but the alarm was soon given whenever the *écoutète* and his sergeants were on the move. However, the real reason why the monetary ordinances could not be enforced lay deeper than in the failure of repressive measures.

Why would a money-changer have converted coins into bullion, if he could find a merchant or a traveler going abroad who needed foreign currency and who was willing to pay a price above that of the mint? The ordinances disregarded completely the conditions which prevailed in the business world and the money market.

The monetary policy of mediaeval public authorities was to favor the import of bullion and to prevent its outflow in order to keep the mint going and to maintain an 'abundant' supply of currency.[113] Such a policy was based on the correct assumption that prices could only be kept stable, if the quantity of money was not diminished, everything else remaining the same. But the mediaeval authorities overlooked entirely the importance of short-run fluctuations, chiefly in a country like Flanders which, already in the Middle Ages, was largely dependent upon foreign trade. No prohibitions could prevent the outflow of bullion if the exchange rates reached the export point, because coins could so easily be concealed and smuggled out. As the interest rate, because of the usury prohibition, played a very subordinate role, debasement was the only method by which mediaeval authorities could relieve the tension which resulted from a loss of bullion to neighboring countries. This analysis leads in a different way to the same conclusion as before: monetary stringency of a recurrent character was the fundamental cause of debasements.

There is another problem to which mediaeval authorities did not give enough consideration, namely, the influence of the money market on the cash position and the reserve ratio of the banks. This phenomenon must have been well known among the merchants, if not among the mintmasters and other financiers, because it is accurately described by Giovanni di Antonio da Uzzano (1442) and by the authors of other handbooks for merchants.

Uzzano observed that there was a seasonal ebb and flow in the money market and that, in the great commercial centers of his time, money tended to be scarce during one season and plentiful during another. In Bruges, according to the Italian merchant manuals, money was usually tight in December and January, when many ships were ready to sail, but expanded in February-March and August-September, when a great number of merchants from outside, especially Germans, came to the town and brought in cash.[114] The reason given by Uzzano and others for the scarcity of money during the winter is only partly true. Actually, the scarcity was caused by the drain of currency due to heavy purchases of cloth in the surrounding manufacturing districts. These purchases were especially heavy in wintertime, because stocks were accumulated for shipment early in the spring, when navigation was resumed.

Uzzano also noted that these seasonal movements of the money market affected the cash reserves of the banks. In Florence, he wrote, money was always dear from September to January because of the payments which had to be made in the country, with the result that cash was withdrawn from the banks in order to meet the demand for hard money.[115] In Florence the cash reserves of the banks were thus depleted in the autumn because of a real 'crop movement.' In Genoa money was generally scarce in July because the galleys sailed at that time for the Levant. They usually carried bullion which had to be taken from the banks and from the offices of the money-changers.[116]

There is no reason to believe that the Bruges banks (the money-changers) were unaffected by the state of the money market. The Collard de Marke ledgers, due in part to the conciseness of the entries, give unfortunately little information in this respect. It is, therefore, necessary to rely a great deal on circumstantial evidence and on theoretical interpretation.

As the Bruges money-changers had no correspondents abroad, they did not import bullion themselves, but it was brought to them by the merchants, who were given either local currency in exchange or, more often, credit on the books.[117] By this process, bank deposits were likely to expand if bullion flowed into Bruges. The cash reserves of the banks would also increase. If this movement kept on, the banks might feel that they could safely expand their loans and their investments. Business, in general, would be promoted, and the banks would be glad to deliver the incoming bullion to the mint in order to get local currency.

On the other hand, the money-changers, as a rule, did not send money abroad. If bullion was needed for export, it was likely to be taken out of the banks by the merchants drawing on their bank accounts.[118] If such withdrawals continued and outbalanced the sales of bullion to the money-changers, their cash reserves would inevitably decline. Eventually this decline would force the banks to curtail their loans and their investments. Such a contraction was liable to have disastrous effects by increasing the pressure on the money market, by bringing down prices, by encouraging the practice of picking and culling (because the heavier coins had more value as bullion abroad), and by stopping the deliveries of bullion to the mint.

As has been explained, a cessation of the work at the mint was the first step toward debasement of the currency. If the money-changers were hard pressed for cash, they could be trusted to favor the same move. As the liabilities of the banks were in groats and multiples of the groat—pounds and shillings—debasement or a devaluation of the groat would improve directly and immediately their financial condition by creating a cash surplus and by stretching out their dwindling cash reserves. In other words, the money-changers could have their cash reserves recoined into a greater number of groats and still owe to their customers the same number of groats as before the debasement. The position of the banks would also be improved indirectly. Debasement was likely to relieve the strain on the money market, to arrest the fall of the price level, to stop the foreign demand for bullion, and thus to check the drain on the coffers of the money-changers. It is not surprising, therefore, that they were in favor of debasement whenever there was an acute scarcity of money and they were threatened with impending ruin by the exhaustion of their cash reserves. An essential difference between the mediaeval and the modern banking systems is that, in the Middle Ages, the commercial banks could not turn for aid to a central bank in times of stress.

[1]The most noteworthy contributions are the following articles: Hans van Werveke, 'Monnaie de compte et monnaie réelle,' *RBPH,* XIII (1934), 123-52; Allan Evans, 'Some Coinage Systems of the Fourteenth Century,' *Journal of Economic and Business History,* III (1931), 481-96; Gino Luzzatto, 'L'oro e l'argento nella politica monetaria veneziana dei secoli XIII e XIV,' *Rivista storica italiana,* 5th series, Vol. II, fasc. 3 (1937), pp. 17-29; Marc Bloch, 'Le problème de l'or au moyen âge,' *AHES,* V (1933), 1-34. On the Flemish monetary system in particular, we are indebted to Professor Hans van Werveke of the University of Ghent for a series of excellent studies: *De Gentsche stadsfinanciën in de middeleeuwen,* chap. vi, pp. 107-61; 'De ekonomische en sociale gevolgen van de muntpolitiek der graven van Vlaanderen,' *op. cit.,* pp. 1-15: 'De Vlaamsche munthervorming van 1389-1390,' *Nederlandsche Historiebladen,* I (1938), 336-47. In connection with these studies of Dr van Werveke, one should also read Henri Laurent, 'Crise monétaire/et difficultés économiques: en Flandre aux XIVe et XVe siècles,' *AHES,* V (1933), 156-60.

[2]Luzzatto, 'L'oro e l'argento,' *op. cit.,* pp. 17 ff.

[3]*Ibid.,* p. 17.

[4]One expounder of this fallacious theory is the French numismatist Adolphe Dieudonné, who writes: 'La livre de compte, c'est la monnaie d'apparence immuable derrière laquelle se dissimulent les espèces; la livre de compte, c'est le billet. Seulement, il intervenait à l'état de promesse verbale et, lorsqu'il s'agissait de regler, au lieu de fournir du papier, on traduisait le compte en monnaie métallique ('L'actualité d'hier: changes et monnaies au moyen âge,' *Revue des Deux Mondes,* 7e période, XXXVII [1927], 931). This statement of Dieudonné's, it seems to me, does not make sense. Dr van Werveke was one of the first to challenge the theory of 'ideal' money in his article, 'Monnaie de compte et monnaie réelle,' *op. cit.,* pp. 123 ff.

[5]Dr van Werveke correctly refers to 'une monnaie fonctionnant dans le vide,' (*ibid.,* p. 127).

[6]Chiefly among the French and Belgian historians. See, for example, Ernest Babelon, *La théorie féodale de la monnaie,* ('Mémoires de l'Académie des Inscriptions et des Belles Lettres,' in-4° series, Vol. XXXVIII; Paris, 1908), Part I, p. 19; Victor Tourneur, 'De la méthode à suivre pour évaluer en monnaies modernes les valeurs anciennes énoncées dans les textes historiques belges du XIe siècle au XVIIIe,' *RBPH,* I (1922), 105; Laurent *La Loi de Gresham au moyen âge,* p. 5. This book of Laurent's is full of contradictions and errors in interpretation. Laurent was an excellent historian, but he made the mistake of accepting the theory of the independent standard. A book on money, unfortunately, stands or falls with the soundness or falseness of the underlying monetary theory. Another characteristic formulation of the theory of the independent standard is given by Joseph Calmette, *La société féodale* (Paris, 1923), p. 64: 'Elles [les altérations] étaient facilitées par la complication du régime monétaire tel qu'il existe au moyen âge, époque où *la monnaie de compte était différente de la monnaie réelle* [italics mine].'

[7]Luigi Einaudi, 'The Medieval Practice of Managed Currency' in *The Lessons of Monetary Experience: Essays in Honor of Irving Fisher* (New York, 1937), pp. 259-69; *idem,* 'Teoria della moneta immaginaria nel tempo da Carlomagno alla Rivoluzione francese,' *Rivista di storia economica,* I (1936), 1-35.

[8]van Werveke, 'Monnaie de compte,' *op. cit.,* pp. 123-34.

[9]*Idem, Gentsche stadsfinanciën,* p. 109.

[10]Cf. A. Luschin von Ebengreuth, *Allgemeine Münzkunde und Geldgeschichte des Mittelalters und der neueren Zeit* (2d ed.; Munich, 1926), p. 195; Pirenne, *Economic and Social History of Medieval Europe,* pp. 109 f.; Walter Täuber, *Geld und Kredit im Mittelalter* (Berlin, 1933), p. 69.

[11]Concerning changes in this ratio, see Tourneur, 'Méthode pour évaluer en monnaies modernes les valeurs anciennes,' *op. cit.,* p. 108; van Werveke, *Gentsche stadsfinanciën,* pp. 115-36.

[12]Money-changers were fined if they received or sold gold coins at a rate exceeding the official valuation.

[13]In 1408, for example, the money market in Flanders was swamped with Rhenish florins. Assays revealed that these florins were worth only 29 groats instead of 33 groats. The municipal authorities of Bruges asked the count of Flanders to ban the Rhenish florins from circulation (Gilliodts, *Inventaire,* V, 28).

[14]Victor Brants, *Esquisse des théories économiques professées par les écrivains des XIIIe et XIVe siècles: l'économie politique au moyen âge* (Louvain, 1895), p. 189: 'Il y a un texte d'un mémoire du XIVe siècle, émané d'un monnayeur inconnu, qui prouve d'ailleurs que cette loi économique était comprise à merveille. Il est curieux de signaler, comme une ancienne formule de la loi attribuée à Gresham, ce texte qui, par des exemples alors récents, démontre le danger de ne pas *ajuster l'or et l'argent,* ce qui fait, selon son énergique expression, que *tantôt l'argent mange l'or, tantôt l'or mange l'argent.*'

[15]Victor Gaillard, *Recherches sur les monnaies des comtes de Flandre depuis les temps les plus reculés jusqu'à l'avènement de la maison de Bourgogne,* II (Ghent, 1857), 159. The Flemish sterling, equal to $\frac{1}{3}$ groat, should not be confused with the English coin of the same name. On the coinage of sterlings, see *ibid.*, p. 74, No. XXVIII.

[16]It is not true, as Dr van Werveke asserts (*Gentsche stadsfinanciën,* p. 142), that the coinage of pieces of one groat was discontinued after the appearance of the double groat. The double groat was simply added to the existing denominations. See the ordinance of July 16, 1384, published by Gilliodts (*Inventaire,* IV, 122). This ordinance mentions the double groat (art. 1) and the single groat (art. 2).

[17]Gilliodts, *Inventaire,* V, 589 f. In 1489, the following denominations were in circulation: *grand double* (4 patards, 8 groats), *double patard* (4 groats), *patard* (2 groats), one groat, half-groat, $\frac{1}{4}$ groat, *denier* ($\frac{1}{6}$ groat, $\frac{1}{12}$ patard), two mites ($\frac{1}{12}$ groat), one mite ($\frac{1}{24}$ groat). See ordinance of December 14, 1489, published in *Groot Placcaet-Boeck inhoudende de Placaten ende Ordonnantien van de Hoogh-Mog. Heeren Staten Generael der Vereenighde Nederlanden,* I (The Hague, 1658), 2580-81.

[18]Seigniorage, strictly speaking, is a tax on the coinage of money paid by the individual who delivered bullion to the mint and received in exchange a smaller quantity of gold or silver under the form of new coins. *Brassage* or mint charges were usually added to seigniorage in order to cover the cost of the coining process.

[19]For instance, according to the ordinance of June 12, 1418, the price of the mint, the seigniorage, and the mint charges per mark troy *argent-le-roi* were as follows:

Groat:				
Mint price of one mark troy *argent-le-roi*	21*s.*	2*d.*	gr.	92%
Seigniorage		4*d.*		1.5%
Brassage or mint charges	1*s.*	6*d.*		6.5%
Total	23*s.*		gr.	100%
Double mites:				
Mint price of one mark troy	21*s.*	2*d.*	gr.	53%
Seigniorage		4*d.*		1%
Brassage or mint charges	18*s.*	6*d.*		46%
Total	40*s.*		gr.	100%
Mites:				
Mint price	21*s.*	2*d.*	gr.	47%
Seigniorage		4*d.*		1%
Brassage or mint charges	23*s.*	6*d.*		52%
Total	45*s.*		gr.	100%

Deschamps de Pas, 'Essai sur l'histoire monétaire des comtes de Flandre,' *op. cit.*, VI, 230-32.

[20]Gaillard, *op. cit.*, p. 102, No. XLV.

[21]Pure silver was 12 deniers fine. The denier was further subdivided into 24 grains.

[22]The mark troy being equal to 245 grams, the figure of 3.55 grams is obtained by dividing 245 gr. by 69. By taking $\frac{37}{72}$ of 3.55, one obtains the figure of 1.82 grams.

[23]The figure of 134 is obtained by dividing 69 by $\frac{37}{72}$. Another good example is the ordinance of July 16, 1384 (Gilliodts, *Inventaire,* IV, 122). This ordinance provided for the coinage of double groats, ½ *argent-le-roi,* at the rate of 50 in a mark troy, standard silver. On this basis 100 double groats or 200 single groats were coined from a mark troy *argent-le-roi.* The equivalent of 200 groats is 16*s.* 8*d.* gr. This figure agrees with the ordinance which fixed the price of the mint for one mark troy *argent-le-roi* at 14*s.* 4*d.*, the seigniorage at 1*s.* gr., and the mint charges at 1*s.* 4*d.* gr.

[24]Gilliodts, *Inventaire,* V, 589.

[25]1.89 grams=245÷130; 0.71 grams= 0.375 x 1.89 grams.

[26]The figures in columns 1, 2, 6, 7, and 8 are based on the data given in the ordinance. The figures in column 3 are obtained by dividing 245 grams by the corresponding figure given in column 2. The figures in column 4 are obtained by multiplying the corresponding figure in column 3 by the fraction in column 1. The figures in column 5 are obtained by dividing 245 grams by the corresponding figure in column 4. The accuracy of the table can be checked by multiplying the figure in column 5 by the value of each denomination. The product of this multiplication should give the equivalent of the values in column 6. Thus 4 groats x 84½ =338 groats=28*s.* 2*d.* gr.

[27]This procedure was not always followed. Thus, after the raise of January 1390, the groats of former issues were allowed to remain in circulation, but at reduced rates. Some of those groats could only be accepted for 20 mites, another kind was rated as low as 2 sterlings or ⅔ of a groat. See Gilliodts, *Inventaire,* IV, 123.

[28]van Werveke, *Stadsfinanciën,* pp. 139-42.

[29]*Ibid.,* p. 145 and *idem,* 'Munthervorming,' *op. cit.,* p. 337.

[30]*Idem,* Stadsfinanciën, p. 145.

[31]*Ibid.,* p. 145 and *idem,* 'Munthervorming,' *op. cit.,* p. 337.

[32]*Loc. cit.*

[33]In 1407, the silver content of the groat was raised from 1.07 grams to 1.17 grams. In 1409, the silver content was further increased to 1.25 grams *argent-le-roi.*

[34]van Werveke, *Stadsfinanciën,* p. 139.

[35]Babelon, *La théorie féodale des monnaies,* p. 45.

[36]Laurent, *La loi de Gresham,* p. 14. The mint of Bruges was not reopened until January 22, 1390, when the claims of the French kings were entirely forgotten as far as Flanders was concerned.

[37]See, for example, the ordinance of Louis de Male, December 14, 1361, art. 2 (*Hansisches Urkundenbuch,* III, 355-56, No. 583 and Gilliodts, *Cart. de l'Estaple,* I, 241, No. 317). This ordinance forbade the giving or accepting in payment of any money other than Flemish currency or the coins of the king of France. The money-changers were, of course, always allowed to buy foreign coins as bullion.

[38]John Maynard Keynes, *Monetary Reform* (New York, 1929), p. 162. Henri Laurent mentions this theory as an unquestionable truth in his article, 'Crise monétaire et difficultés économiques,' *op. cit.,* p. 156.

[39]The rise of the price level after 1450 was probably due not only to debasement, but also the increased production of the German silver mines. As there was certainly no increase, but rather a decline, in the use of money substitutes, increased production of the mines was likely to have a more direct effect on the quantity of money and on the price level. Cf. John U. Nef, 'Silver Production in Central Europe, 1450-1680,' *JPE,* XLIX (1941), 585-86.

[40]Hubert Van Houtte (ed.), *Documents pour servir à l'histoire des prix de 1381 à 1794* (Brussels, 1902), pp. 9-10.

[41]In 1357, the fullers of Hulst, a small town in northern Flanders, were granted an increase of wages, because everything had greatly risen in price (*aensiende dat alle dinghen zere*

verdierst zijn). Espinas and Pirenne, *Recueil de documents relatifs à l'histoire de l'industrie drapière en Flandre,* II, 709, No. 593. Cf. van Werveke, 'Muntpolitiek,' *op. cit.*, pp. 4-5.

[42]Espinas and Pirenne, *Recueil,* III, p. 378, No. 726; p. 384, No. 729. Cf. Pirenne, *Histoire de Belgique,* II, 199 and van Werveke, 'Muntpolitiek,' *op. cit.*, p. 6.

[43]Espinas and Pirenne, *Recueil,* II, 540 f., No. 496.

[44]van Werveke, 'Muntpolitiek,' *op. cit.*, p. 11.

[45]*Ibid.*, p. 15. Cf. Laurent, 'Crise monétaire,' *op. cit.*, p. 158.

[46]Oresme was a staunch advocate of monetary stability and was strongly opposed to any debasement of the currency except in great emergencies. See Nicole Oresme, *Traictié de la première invention des monnoies,* ed. L. Wolowski (Paris, 1864), pp. 26, 60-61.

[47]van Werveke, 'Munthervorming,' *op. cit.*, p. 343 and n. 1.

[48]Gilliodts, *Inventaire,* III, 134.

[49]Except when there was an agreement to the contrary (see *ibid.*, p. 134, and van Werveke, 'Munthervorming,' *op. cit.*, p. 343).

[50]Gilliodts, *Inventaire,* III, 134.

[51]Laurent, *La loi de Gresham,* pp. 169-71, No. 24.

[52]Espinas and Pirenne, *Recueil,* I (1906), 668-69, No. 206.

[53]*Ibid.*, pp. 297-98, No. 122: '. . . hoe hemlieden die loen ghemindert was ende ghevalueert mids den verandrene van den munten.'

[54]The date of the decision is February 12, 1397 (*loc. cit.*).

[55]The subject of price and other rigidities in the Middle Ages has received little attention up to now, save for a short article by N. S. B. Gras, 'The Growth of Rigidity in Business during the Middle Ages,' *American Economic Review,* XXX (1940), suppl., 281-89.

[56]John Maynard Keynes, *The General Theory of Employment, Interest, and Money* (New York, 1936), p. 307.

[57]Jacob Viner, 'Review of Eli F. Heckscher, *Mercantilism,' The Economic History Review,* VI (1935), 101.

[58]In 1381, Duke Wenceslas and Duchess Jeanne of Brabant stated in a report that their mint had been closed for more than three years, because they were not allowed by their subjects to debase the currency (Laurent, *La loi de Gresham,* p. 121, No. 3). At a meeting of the Estates in 1381, Duke Wenceslas left the delegates with the choice of three alternatives: (1) the delegates should allow him to debase the currency, (2) or to close the mint, (3) or they could take over the mint themselves and try to run it (*ibid.*, pp. 33-34). After the reform of 1389-1390, Philip the Bold experienced great difficulty in finding a master of the mint. In 1400, he had to offer two hundred nobles as an inducement to Barthélémy Thomas (Deschamps de Pas, 'Histoire monétaire des comtes de Flandre," *op. cit.*, VI, 129-30). Cf. Laurent, *La loi de Gresham,* p. 68. The table published by Gaillard (*Recherches sur les monnaies des comtes de Flandre,* II, 168-69) which covers with some gaps the period from 1346 to 1383 shows that there were great variations in the output of the Flemish mint. During certain years no silver at all was coined and the mint was frequently operated at a loss (*ibid.*, docs., Nos. 22, 23, 25, and *passim*). See also Laurent, *La loi de Gresham,* pp. 56-57. In 1438, the money-changers were ordered to deliver a given quantity of bullion to the mint 'in proportion to the importance of their exchange dealings.' The purpose of this ordinance was evidently to keep the mint supplied with bullion (Deschamps de Pas, 'Histoire monétaire des comtes de Flandre,' *op cit.*, VII, 118.

[59]Arthur Layton Funk, 'The Movement of Reform and Revolt in Mid-Fourteenth Century France' (Unpublished Ph.D. dissertation, Dept. of History, The University of Chicago, 1940), p. 38.

[60]As early as 1300, Dubois saw that debasement made exports of goods more profitable. Arthur Eli Monroe, *Monetary Theory before Adam Smith* [Cambridge, Mass., 1923], p. 30.

[61]Funk, *op. cit.*, p. 40: 'It seems clear, however, that because of the method of operation in the mints, the currency could not remain stable.'

[62]The mints of the counts of Flanders were frequently operated at a loss. See Gaillard, *Recherches sur les monnaies,* pp. 63, 68, and *passim.*

[63]This was the opinion expressed by Pierre Dubois as far back as the year 1300 in a memoir submitted to Philip the Fair, King of France (Monroe, *Monetary Theory before Adam Smith,* p. 29). Cf. Funk, *op. cit.,* p. 42: 'Actually, debasement seems to have been practiced only under the greatest pressure, when no other solution was available,'; and Bernardo Davanzati, *'Lezioni delle monete' in Scrittori classici italiani di economia politica, Parte Antica,* Vol. II (Milan, 1804), p. 40.

[64]Jacob Viner, *Studies in the Theory of International Trade* (New York, 1937), pp. 206 f, 378.

[65]The technical expression is *accorder une crue aux marchands* and is found in a great number of ordinances of the counts of Flanders and the dukes of Burgundy of the House of Valois. It is not true, as Laurent asserts, that the country with the highest seigniorage charges will change in its favor the distribution of bullion (*La loi de Gresham,* p. 11). Exactly the opposite is true: the higher the charges, the less bullion will be attracted.

[66]Marc Bloch, 'Ecrits sur la monnaie,' *AHES,* X (1938), p. 361.

[67]Such establishments existed not only in Bruges, but in other Flemish cities as well. See Bigwood, *Régime,* I, 423-25.

[68]Gilliodts, *Inventaire,* I, 300 f., No. 237.

[69]*Loc. cit.*

[70]*Loc. cit.*

[71]*Loc. cit.*

[72]Bigwood, *Régime,* I, 422.

[73]It seems that hallmarked silver bars were chiefly used by the conservative and backward Hanseatic merchants. They did not give up the use of silver bars as a means of payment until late in the fourteenth century. See Luschin von Ebengreuth, *op. cit.,* p. 182.

[74]Edler, *Glossary of Business Terms,* 'Vantaggio,' p. 310 and 'Aggio,' p. 25.

[75]Gilliodts, *Inventaire,* I, 301 and ordinance of 1309, art. 8.

[76]In 1316-1317 the mite was worth $\frac{5}{9}$ of a denier *parisis.* See van Werveke, *Gentsche stadsfinanciën,* p. 146.

[77]Pegolotti, *La Pratica della Mercatura,* p. 243: 'Di cambiora manesche a contanti, da ciascuna delle parti ¼ di grosso tornese d'ariento del centinaio di reali.'

[78]*Ibid.,* p. 247.

[79]Bigwood, *Régime,* I, 428 and Simone Poignant, *La foire de Lille: contribution à l'étude des foires flamandes au moyen-âge* ('Bibliothèque de la Société d'Histoire du Droit des Pays flamands, picards et wallons,' VI; Lille, 1932), p. 134.

[80]Ghent, Municipal Archives, Chartres et Documents, No. 561, ordinance of October 12, 1433, arts. 6 and 15.

[81]Gilliodts, *Inventaire,* V, 384. On this basis, the commission of the money-changer was $\frac{1}{288}$ or $\frac{1}{276}$ of the total of each exchange transaction.

[82]*Loc. cit.*

[83]*Ibid.,* pp. 544, 548.

[84]*Groot Placcaet-Boeck,* I, 2594.

[85]Endemann, *Studien,* I, 105.

[86]de Roover, 'Ruyelle,' *op. cit.,* p. 27. According to the cash book of Guillaume Ruyelle, he had in cash on March 30, 1370, £45 14*s.* 7*d.* gr. The next day on April 1, 1370, he reopened his cash book with £47 7*s.* 5*d.* gr. The only explanation for this difference of £1 12*s.* 10*d.* gr. is that it originated in fees on exchange transactions.

[87]Collard de Marke Ledger No. 4, fol. 30, account of Jehan de Concorighe. The amount of £151 5*s.* 5*d.* gr. is made up of two deposits, one of £72 18*s.* 9*d.* gr. and one of £78 6*s.* 8*d.* gr.

[88]Collard de Marke Ledger No. 2, fol. 15: 'Zegres Onin li Jouenes me doit l'avantaige de 30 lb en or en conte blanc argent.'

[89]*Ibid.,* Ledger No. 4, fol. 188. See also the account of Forteguerra (Ledger No. 4, fol. 124) and that of Davin Tedaldin (*ibid.,* fol. 76).

[90]Ledger No. 4, fol . 103. The amount of £215 4*s.* 3*d.* gr. charged to Roulof Rabonne was made up as follows:

	£	*s*	*d* gr.
510 *moutons* at 51 groats	108	7	4
800 francs at 31 groats	103	6	8
in silver currency, 13 groats		1	1
agio or fee	3	9	2
Total	£215	4	3 gr.

[91]*Ibid.,* fol. 320.

[92]See, for example, the account of Jehan de Courtrai, l'orfèvre, Ledger No. 4, fol. 1. When the widow of Diederic Urbaens failed, one of the creditors lodged a claim for five ounces of gold (Bruges, Municipal Archives, Chartes politiques, No. 445).

[93]Ledger No. 4, fol. 315.

[94]*Ibid.,* fol. 3^{v} and Ledger No. 5, fol. 3^{v}.

[95]Ledger No. 4, fol. 3^{v}.

[96]The dealings between Collard de Marke and the mint can be summarized in the following way:

Account of Thumas Sarlande

		£	*s*	*d* gr.
Due to Thumas Sarlande for money lent before Christmas 1368	Cr.	400	–	–
Several shipments of bullion to the mint in March and April 1369 as recorded in the 'papier de le monnoie'	Dr.	501	19	7
Balance outstanding on May 20, 1369	Dr.	101	19	7
Coins delivered by the mint about August 1, 1369	Cr.	51	19	7
Balance due from Thumas Sarlande on December 24, 1369	Dr.	50	–	–

[97]Bigwood, *Régime,* I, 389; Gilliodts, *Inventaire,* V, 19; Z. W. Sneller, *Deventer, die Stadt der Jahrmärkte* ('Pfingstblätter des Hansischen Geschichtsvereins,' XXV; Weimar, 1936), p. 112; *idem,* 'Het wisselaarsbedrijf in Nederland vóór de oprichtung der stedelijke wisselbanken,' *op. cit.,* p. 493.

[98]Gaillard, *Recherches sur les monnaies,* I, 23, No. XIII, October 31, 1299; Gilliodts, *Cart. de l'Estaple,* I, 93, No. 132; Bigwood, *Régime,* I, 426. Art. 3 provided that 'nuls marchands, ne cangieres, ne autres hoirs ne puist achateir argent ne billon, ne cange tenir; c'est à entendre ke toutes les canges soient abatues.'

[99]Bigwood, *Régime,* I, 401; II, 304 f., No. XX.

[100]L. F. Salzman, *English Trade in the Middle Ages* (Oxford, 1931), pp. 20-21. It was illegal in England to charge any fee for the exchange of English coins and to bring non-current foreign coins into circulation. Such coins were to be sold as bullion to the Royal Exchanger. This office already existed in 1223. It was originally created to supply the Mint with bullion and to regulate petty exchange. Later efforts by the Plantagenets and the Tudors to extend the royal monopoly and to bring the trade in bills of exchange under the control of the Royal Exchanger were unsuccessful. Cf. Pegolotti, *op. cit.,* p. 255.

[101]The facts are given in de Roover, 'Ruyelle,' *op. cit.,* pp. 38-41 and Bigwood, *Régime,* I, 229-31.

[102]Baudouin de Vos is called by Louis de Male 'nostre amé vallet' in a public document. See Gaillard, *Recherches,* II, 119, No. LIII, dated August 4, 1357.

[103]The monetary ordinances of the fifteenth century having been drafted with more care

than those of the preceding century, frequently refer to the money-changers and merchants (*marchans et changeurs*) who bring bullion to the mint.

[104]A mintmaster of Philip the Bold, Simon de la Faucille, complains of the fact that the monetary ordinances are disobeyed ('et le peuple n'obeist pas aux ordonnances'). See Laurent, *La loi de Gresham*, pp. 74, 77; Gilliodts, *Inventaire*, III, 131 (ordinance of December 20, 1389) and *ibid.*, V, 537 (ordinance of October 13, 1467).

[105]Laurent, *La loi de Gresham*, p. 74.

[106]Cf. Tawney, Intro., Wilson, *Discourse on Usury*, p. 93.

[107]Such a case is mentioned in a document published by Gilliodts, *Inventaire*, VI, 466.

[108]Bruges, Municipal Archives, Municipal Account, 1366-1367 (n.s.), fol. 16. These are the names of the money-changers who were fined: (1) Colaerde van Maerc, (2) Jakemaerde van Rouc, (3) Stevene van der Meersch, (4) Gillisse Uten-Hove, (5) Pietre de Pottere, (6) Janne van Maerc, (7) Janne van Donc, (8) Janne Huerle, (9) Janne Ruwele.

[109]Gilliodts, *Inventaire*, IV, 184 and *Cart. de l'Estaple*, I, 381, No. 455.

[110]Gilliodts, *Inventaire*, IV, 186 f., and *Cart. de l'Estaple*, I, 381, No. 455.

[111]*Ibid.*, p. 457, No. 549. [112]Gilliodts, *Inventaire*, VI, 466.

[113]Vatican Library, Vat. Lat. MS 4828, fol. 114: 'E fecevisi uno ordine che ciascuno banchiere a cui ne capitasse ne dovesse dare el pregio ch'era messo, poi taglarle, e mettarle in zecca, *acciò vi fusse abondanze delle tre monete dette che v'anno il corso*' (italics mine, date *ca.* 1460).

[114]Uzzano, *La pratica della mercatura*, chap. xlviii, p. 156; Florence, Bibl. Naz., Codice Palatino 601: Aritmetica [*ca.* 1450], fol. 71: 'A Brugia sono buoni que' danari ragionevolmente il magio e giugnio e di dicenbre insino ½ giennaio perchè in questi tenpi vi sono le migliori fiere di tutto l'anno e quando non apare di nuovo senpre in que' tenpi vi sono buoni, ma quando vi vanno navi di Levante che sieno ricche senpre allora vi s'alargha perchè gli Alamanni e paesani vi traghono a chonprare e lascianvi assai danari chontanti e chosì in questo chaso vi si alarghanno e' danari;' *Libro di mercatantie et usanze de' paesi*, p. 168: 'A Bruggia è una fiera di marzo [emend to read "maggio"] che vi gitta gran charo e al giungnio e al dicenbre per ispaccamento di navi.'

[115]Uzzano, *op. cit.*, p. 155: 'Firenze fanno sempre miglioramente di denari, Settembre fino a Gennaio sono buoni, e questo è per molte paghe ànno a fare ai [text has only "i" by mistake] Contadini, che danari entrono in comune ed escono de' banchi.'

[116]*Ibid.*, p. 155: '[I denari] uscissono de' banchi e de' cambiatori.'

[117]The account book of Vicko van Geldersen, a Hamburg merchant of the fourteenth century, contains a great many entries relating to the shipment of coins from Hamburg to Bruges. See *Das Handlungsbuch Vickos von Geldersen*, 101, Nos. 624, 627, 629, 631, 632, 633; p. 102, No. 643; p. 103, Nos. 648, 651, 654; p. 104, No. 659, and *passim*. In Venice, all the deposit banks failed in 1499 except one, the Agostini bank. A few months later, the German merchants complained before the doge that, as a result of these bank failures, they had no market for their silver and *that bullion was not finding its way to the mint.* See Frederic C. Lane, 'Venetian Bankers, 1496-1533: a Study in the Early Stages of Deposit Banking,' *JPE*, XLV (1937), 196. In the fifteenth century English statutes prescribed that the Merchants of the Staple should accept only gold, and no bills of credit, in payment of English wool. This gold was then coined into English nobles at the mint of Calais. The nobles, however, did not stay in England, but were re-exported by English importers of continental goods. The result was that English nobles could easily be bought at the exchange in Bruges and that the mint of Calais was soon left without any supply of bullion. To remedy this situation, Parliament passed another act forbidding the export of bullion!! See Eileen Power, 'The Wool Trade in the Fifteenth Century,' *Studies in English Trade in the Fifteenth Century*, eds. Eileen Power and M. M. Postan (New York, 1933), p. 82.

[118]There is at least one unquestionable example in the Collard de Marke account books. On December 27, 1368, a customer named Raoul Doucemin withdrew £8 1*s.* gr. in cash for export to Brabant (*pour porter en Braibant*). See Ledger No. 4, fol. 26.

Chapter 13

BANK DEPOSITS AS MONEY

As we have seen, it had become customary in Flanders, by the second quarter of the fourteenth century, for merchants and private individuals to deposit with the money-changers any cash which was not immediately needed. The latter did not keep all this money safely locked up in their chests but used the greater part of it for their own purposes. This was not a breach of confidence. The money-changers were indeed expected to meet every demand for repayment at the first request. But the specific coins originally placed on deposit need not be returned, only their equivalent in money. In short, by the fourteenth century, the money-changers had expanded their business to include deposit banking.

The question may now be asked: when and how did this evolution take place? There is, unfortunately, only scant information available for the period prior to 1300. However, there is scarcely any doubt that the growth of banking in Flanders was influenced by the evolution of financial institutions in Italy and went through the same stages of development, but with a considerable lag. In Italy, deposit banking was well developed by 1200, and presumably before.[1] *Bancherii* are mentioned in Genoa as early as the twelfth century, although the word, at that time, may have been used loosely and without precise connotation, like the expression *tafletiers* in the Low Countries.[2] This expression seems to have been a general term for money-dealers and money-lenders of every description, as all of them transacted their business at a table, desk, or bank.[3] It is quite possible that, in the beginning, *bancherius* had the same vague and general meaning. Be that as it may, it is beyond question that money-changing in Italy as well as in Flanders was the starting-point of deposit banking.[4] The money-changers took the first step in this direction when they began to accept money and valuables for safekeeping in their coffers or strongboxes, as did some of the monastic orders, especially the Knights Templars.[5] Such deposits were, of course, regular deposits, and the money-changers who accepted them were simply bailees or depositaries obligated to restore the specific monies or valuables entrusted to their care. As all deposits were not withdrawn at the same time, money-changers soon found out that they would run little risk if they invested for profit some of the money given to them for safe-keeping. The ease with which coins could be interchanged further encouraged such a practice.[6] The Italian notarial records give one the impression that, at first, the depositors neither gave their formal consent nor even knew what was going on.[7] Later—

and this final step completed the evolution—they knew but did not care, so long as they could get their money back at a moment's notice or dispose of it by assignment. Bank deposits thus became *transferable claims to a given sum of money*. The result of this final change was that bank deposits were increasingly used as a means of payment and thus turned out to be a substitute for specie.

The Lille grant of 1294 and the Bruges account books of the middle of the fourteenth century show us deposit banking as an existing institution, but do not explain how it came into being. There is, fortunately, one very important document which throws some light on this problem of origins. This document concerns Liége and not Bruges, but this does not matter very much as business methods presumably varied little within the narrow boundaries of the Low Countries. The Liége document is a statute of the *frairie* or brotherhood of the money-changers and dates from the year 1315 (n. s.).[8] The text was prepared from information supplied by trustworthy persons (*bones gens de foid*) and by the oldest members of the gild (*les anchines cambges*).[9] Consequently, the statute refers to customs and rules which, in 1315, had been in force for a long time. They probably date back to the middle of the thirteenth century and possibly even further. The statute emanated from the municipal authorities. Its purpose was to uphold the good reputation of the money-changers of Liége, to define their duties, and to provide penalties for any offense against professional ethics. Those duties were twofold. First of all, the money-changers were expected to do their best in order to maintain a sound currency. In the second place, they were expected to keep securely and to return faithfully at the first request any money, jewelry, plate or other valuables which were entrusted to them for custody (*en comandiese*).[10]

If the owners of such goods complained to the gild officials (*les maistres delle cambge*) that a money-changer refused to release any property held in custody, he was notified that he had three days in which to comply.[11] If after three days the property had not been restored, the recalcitrant money-changer became liable to a fine equal to the amount of the deposit or the value thereof in currency. The gild authorities had, further, the power to suspend the offender for six weeks (*trois quinzaines*). If at the end of this period he still refused to pay the fine and to surrender what he unlawfully retained, he was deprived of his membership in the brotherhood of the money-changers, and court proceedings were initiated without further delay. Any fines collected as a result of such action were to be shared equally by the brotherhood, the city treasury, and the Mayor of Liége in behalf of the municipal court of justice.

These drastic measures, the authorities declare in the statute, are taken because the exchange of Liége is and ought to remain the strongbox of the good people of the city ('que la cange de la cité de Liége doit estre et est huge de bonnes gens'). In other words, the coffers of the money-changers of Liége were the favorite place of safe-keeping for valuables belonging to the well-to-do people in the community.

It is clear that the statute of Liége does not contain a single word from which one could draw the inference that the money-changers of that city were doing banking. The document deals only with monies and valuables entrusted to them for custody or *en comandiese*. This is the *commenda sive depositum,*[12] the *depositum regulare* of Roman law, the Italian *accomanda.*[13] The conclusion is that, in the thirteenth century, the money-changers of Liége were also depositaries or safe-keepers of monies and valuables, but not yet deposit bankers.

During that same period, the money-changers of Bruges were already taking the final step and it is possible that the statute of Liége was a measure sponsored by the older and more conservative members of the *frairie* in order to counter the same tendency. It is difficult to say whether the money-changers, after becoming deposit bankers, continued to be custodians of valuables. Most probably they did, but the Bruges account books do not give any clue to this problem. This is quite natural. Banks today still perform the same function of safe-keeping, but they do not keep a record in their ledgers of what customers put into their safety-deposit boxes.

Once the money-changers had extended their activity to deposit banking, it ceased to be true that funds were deposited with them primarily for reasons of safe-keeping.[14] Neither did people have money on deposit at the exchange (*en change*) in order to get a small return on idle cash. Today, in some European countries the banks pay a small interest on demand deposits, but the rate is usually very low and varies in accordance with the state of the money market. This does not seem to have been the practice in the Middle Ages. In the Collard de Marke and Guillaume Ruyelle account books, there is nothing which would indicate that interest was paid to depositors. When the widow of the money-changer Diederic Urbaens failed, sometime between 1340 and 1350, the sureties claimed that they were not liable for any debts on which interest was paid.[15] These accounts appeared to be *wesegheld* or money belonging to orphans which was invested by their guardians in the exchange banks. These investments certainly were not subject to sudden withdrawal and we would call them today 'time deposits.' In fact, the statement of the debts of Diederic Urbaens' widow mentions only one such deposit. It had been carried on the books for a long time, and interest payments were in arrears for three years when the crash occurred.

As the public did not have money on deposit with the money-changers either for reasons of safe-keeping or for the sake of a return, we must look for some other motive which explains why people were willing to part with their pennies and to run the risk of losing them in the failure of a bank. This motive is fortunately not hard to find. It is for reasons of convenience that people of today often prefer to have money in the bank rather than in their till, their purse, or their strongbox. In many circumstances it is more convenient to pay by check than to pay with cash. Because of the disorderly state of mediaeval currency, the convenience of having an account at the exchange (with a money-changer) was even greater than is today the convenience of having an account at the bank.[16] In the Middle Ages, of course, there were no checks, but their place was taken by a system of book-transfers which achieved the same purpose.

Mediaeval trade would have been greatly hampered if it had been necessary for all payments to be made in cash. The Venetian Senator Tommaso Contarini goes even so far as to say that trade would have been well-nigh impossible.[17] Because of the great variety of coins in circulation, it was not practical to pay out or to receive large sums without expert advice. If a money-changer were called in for consultation, he would charge a fee for his services. It should also not be forgotten that there existed no banknotes of large denominations in the Middle Ages. As a result, money-telling, when large sums were involved, represented a considerable waste of time.[18] This is not a small matter as one may be inclined to think. The businessmen of yesterday, as well as those of today, were pressed for time and were therefore glad to take advantage of the book-transfer system devised by the money-changers. This system allowed local payments to be made with a stroke of the pen.[19] Moreover, the books of the money-changers were public records and there was no need to give acquittance, to have witnesses, or to draw up legal instruments.[20] This facility was great, indeed, and it is not surprising that it was extensively used—just how extensively it is difficult to determine.

Living in a time when banks in large cities have thousands of customers, we are likely to lose our sense of proportion and to forget that even the largest mediaeval cities were comparatively small. The population of Bruges, in the fourteenth and fifteenth centuries, was somewhere between 35,000 and 45,000 inhabitants. This is not a wild guess. Bruges did not expand beyond her mediaeval walls until the beginning of the twentieth century. At that time the population barely exceeded 56,000 inhabitants; consequently, it could not have been larger in the Middle Ages.[21] According to the cadaster of 1580, there were in Bruges about 8,400 houses. If we assume that each house was occupied by a family of five, we obtain a figure of 42,000 for the total population.[22] In 1580, many houses stood empty because of the city's decay, but this figure of over 40,000 might be valid for the end of the fifteenth century. In 1340, the Bruges militia numbered 6,044 men. On the basis of this figure, a Belgian scholar has arrived at a total of 35,000 inhabitants for the middle of the fourteenth century.[23] This estimate may be a little low. At any rate, with a population of about 40,000 souls, Bruges was a large city according to mediaeval standards. In Northwestern Europe, only near-by Ghent, Paris, and perhaps London, were larger than Bruges.

It is, of course, not possible to produce complete statistical data which would give us an accurate idea of the number of people who had a bank account and of the size of mediaeval banks. For Bruges, we have only a few figures and they are all for the middle of the fourteenth century. At that time, there were fifteen or sixteen money-changers, according to both the municipal accounts and the Collard de Marke ledgers. Let us now accept the above figure of forty thousand for the total population of Bruges. On this basis, if one person out of every hundred had a bank account, each money-changer would have carried on his books an average of twenty-five accounts. If the proportion were one in fifty, the average would have been fifty accounts. If the ratio were raised to one in twenty-five, the average money-changer would have had as many as one hundred accounts. This simple arithmetic shows at once that we should not expect banking on a large scale in fourteenth-century Bruges, and that an exchange-bank was a relatively small business, as were also most mediaeval industrial enterprises. It is possible that as the number of money-changers decreased in the fifteenth century some concentration took place, and that the average bank was somewhat larger than previously. In order to be complete, it should perhaps be pointed out that one thing ties in with another and that—besides the volume of available business—the lack of office space, the smallness of the clerical staff, and imperfect and clumsy methods of accounting were other factors which set definite limits to the size of mediaeval banks.

The transition from average figures to actual figures always presents some difficulties, because deviations from the average may be considerable. This is also true in the present instance. As we have seen, a few money-changers secured a lion's share of the business, while others just managed to survive and had presumably few customers. Figures for one money-changer, consequently, do not mean much unless we know whether he belongs to the top or to the bottom stratum.

When Diederic Urbaens' widow failed, sometime between 1340 and 1350, her records showed that she owed money to twenty-six depositors, but fifteen more creditors presented claims which were not recorded in the books owing either to neglect or to fraudulent intent.[24] In any case, forty-one depositors were affected by the bankruptcy. The liabilities also included balances due to other money-changers, one time deposit, and two debts originating in commercial transactions. Forty-one is not, of course, a very impressive figure, but the widow of Diederic Urbaens might have belonged to the class of money-changers who had a hard struggle for existence and whose business was below the average size.

The financial statement found in the binding of Guillaume Ruyelle's ledger shows that on May 24, 1370, there were in all eighty-two accounts open in the ledger; sixty credit balances originating in deposits and twenty-two debit balances representing overdrafts.[25] The latter figure does not include four drawing or special accounts: one in the name of Guillaume Ruyelle himself, two in the name of *Medmyselle,* his wife, and the last in the name of Hannekin Ruyelle, his cousin and chief assistant. If the information given in the municipal accounts is at all reliable, it appears that Ruyelle was doing a little better than most of his colleagues in so far as securing volume or getting customers was concerned. The above figure of eighty-two probably was slightly above the average.

Collard de Marke, we know from his extant account books, was doubtless one of the three or four most important money-changers of Bruges in the period from 1366 to 1369. His figures, consequently, must be above the average. An analysis of his accounts confirms that he had perhaps more customers than most of his colleagues. The figures are given in Table 12.

A glance at this table will disclose that the business of Collard de Marke was on the upswing during the period from 1366 to 1369. The first ledger starts on April 6, 1366, with approximately 134 balances carried over from a preceding ledger which is not extant. The last of the extant ledgers opens with 305 balances posted from the previous ledger, No. 4. This figure of 305 is certainly above the average number of accounts which other money-changers carried on their books at any one time. Otherwise one person in eight would have had a bank account in fourteenth-century Bruges. It goes without saying that such a ratio is absurdly high. But there is, nonetheless, little doubt that having a bank account was far more common than one would expect at such an early date.

This point can be further illustrated by a different set of figures. Up to now it has been pointed out how many accounts there were open on the books of different money-changers at a given date, but no attempt has yet been made to give an idea of the importance of the movement of funds which were handled by them in the daily course of their business. As may be seen from Table 12, the liabilities of Collard de Marke to his depositors grew in a few years from £2,310 9*s.* 2*d.* to £5,575 6*s.* 1*d.* groat. These figures represent considerable sums in view of the fact that the purchasing power of money was extremely high and that the groat, on which the Flemish pound was based, was still in the middle of the fourteenth century a heavier coin than the English sterling on which the English monetary system rested.

The journal of Collard de Marke gives the best idea of the number of transactions per day. Under the date of December 27, 1368, the journal contains only six entries: five, totalling £115 1*s.* groat and one entry of one hundred *francs dou Roy* or French francs.[26] On December 29, only four transactions are recorded making a total of £109 8*s.* 7*d.* groat, but the next day there are thirty-nine items entered, representing a total of £609 14*s.* 4*d.* groat. No entries are made under the date of December 28, the Feast of the Holy Innocents, of December 31, a Sunday, and of January 1st, 1369, Circumcision. No business was transacted evidently on Sunday and on Circumcision, but December 28 was not a holiday and the absence of any entries for that date can only be explained by the fact that Collard de Marke may have had more than one journal in use. On February 27, 1369, there are thirty-two entries in the journal which total £785 18*s.* 1*d.* groat and one item of 400 francs.[27] As this amount corresponds to £51 13*s.* 4*d.* groat at the rate of 31 groats per franc, the total for the day is £837 11*s.* 5*d.* groat.[28] It is possible that December 30 and February 27, both close to the end of the month were especially busy days. These figures may not impress a modern reader, but they are high, if one considers that the mediaeval exchange-banks were small affairs, run by the proprietor and a couple of clerks.

Thirty-three customers calling in one day: how much time was required to take care of them? Even five minutes per customer would have meant two hours and three-quarters. Surely many customers stayed longer than five minutes, especially when any counting of money was involved. There were probably other callers during the day who simply wanted exchange and did not have bank accounts. The likelihood is that mediaeval money-changers and their clerks were rather busy all day long.

In order to complete the picture, it is possible to give one more figure which is not devoid of significance. Collard de Marke's ledger No. 4, which happens to have been more thoroughly examined than the others and covers a period of about five months from December 24, 1368, to May 20, 1369, contains close to eleven hundred accounts.[29] This is amazingly high, even if it is true that most of these accounts were of a transitory character and were closed and balanced within a few days—after two or three transactions. As we have seen, only three hundred and five accounts were still open when ledger No. 4 was closed and the remaining balances were transferred to a new ledger. One should also consider that a number of individuals might have had accounts at several exchange-banks. Eleven hundred is nevertheless a surprising figure if one keeps in mind that there were in Bruges sixteen money-changers, and that the population did not exceed 45,000 souls.

Professor Frederic C. Lane, who has made a special study of Venetian banking, states that the Lippomani bank, when it failed in 1499, owed money to 1,248 depositors of whom 700 were Venetian nobles.[30] The Venetian *banchi di scritta* were thus considerably larger than the Bruges exchange-banks of the fourteenth century. But it should not be overlooked that, in 1499, there were

TABLE 12

ACCOUNTS OPEN IN THE LEDGERS OF THE BRUGES MONEY-CHANGER COLLARD DE MARKE ON FIVE DIFFERENT DATES

CREDIT BALANCES OR DEPOSITS

Ledger	Date	Number of Balances	Aggregate Deposits			Average Balance		
			£	*s*	*d*	£	*s*	*d*
No. 1	April 6, 1366	85	2,310	9	2	27	3	8
No. 2	April 19, 1367	136	5,566	8	3	40	18	7
No. 3	April 10, 1368	121	5,071	4	4	41	18	3
No. 4	December 24, 1368	171	4,605	16	5	26	18	8
No. 5	May 20, 1369	188	5,575	6	1	29	13	1

DEBIT BALANCES OR OVERDRAFTS

Ledger	Date	Number of Balances	Aggregate Deposits			Average Balance		
			£	*s*	*d*	£	*s*	*d*
No. 1	April 6, 1366	49	660	10	2	13	9	7
No. 2	April 19, 1367	59	1,405	12	10	23	16	6
No. 3	April 10, 1368	91	1,478	10	0	16	4	11
No. 4	December 24, 1368	115	2,611	18	2	22	14	3
No. 5	May 20, 1369	117	2,553	11	9	21	16	6

SUMMARY

Ledger	Date	Total	Deposits	Overdrafts
No. 1	April 6, 1366	134*	85	49
No. 2	April 19, 1367	195	136	59
No. 3	April 10, 1368	212	121	91
No. 4	December 24, 1368	286	171	115
No. 5	May 20, 1369	305	188	117

*The totals for April 6, 1366, are incomplete because of the omission of a few illegible items The above figures also do not include any balances in French francs, *lions d'or*, or units other than £, *s*, and *d* groat, Flemish money. Such items are few in number and can be neglected.

Source: Bruges, Municipal Archives, Collard de Marke Ledgers.

only four, instead of sixteen, deposit banks in Venice: the Garzoni, the Lippomani, the Pisani, and the Agostini. Moreover, Venice was perhaps three times as large a city as Bruges. Professor Lane figures that in Venice one person out of every thirty had a bank account. In Bruges the proportion might be a little lower in the fourteenth century, but not very much: perhaps one out of every thirty-five or forty persons. The Collard de Marke account books corroborate these figures by giving the impression that having a bank account was very common. Certainly, every merchant, every broker, every innkeeper, and every *drapier* had one, and probably also a good many high-class retailers such as mercers, furriers, and goldsmiths, not to mention nobles and other persons who were not in business.[31] Presumably only the poor had no dealings

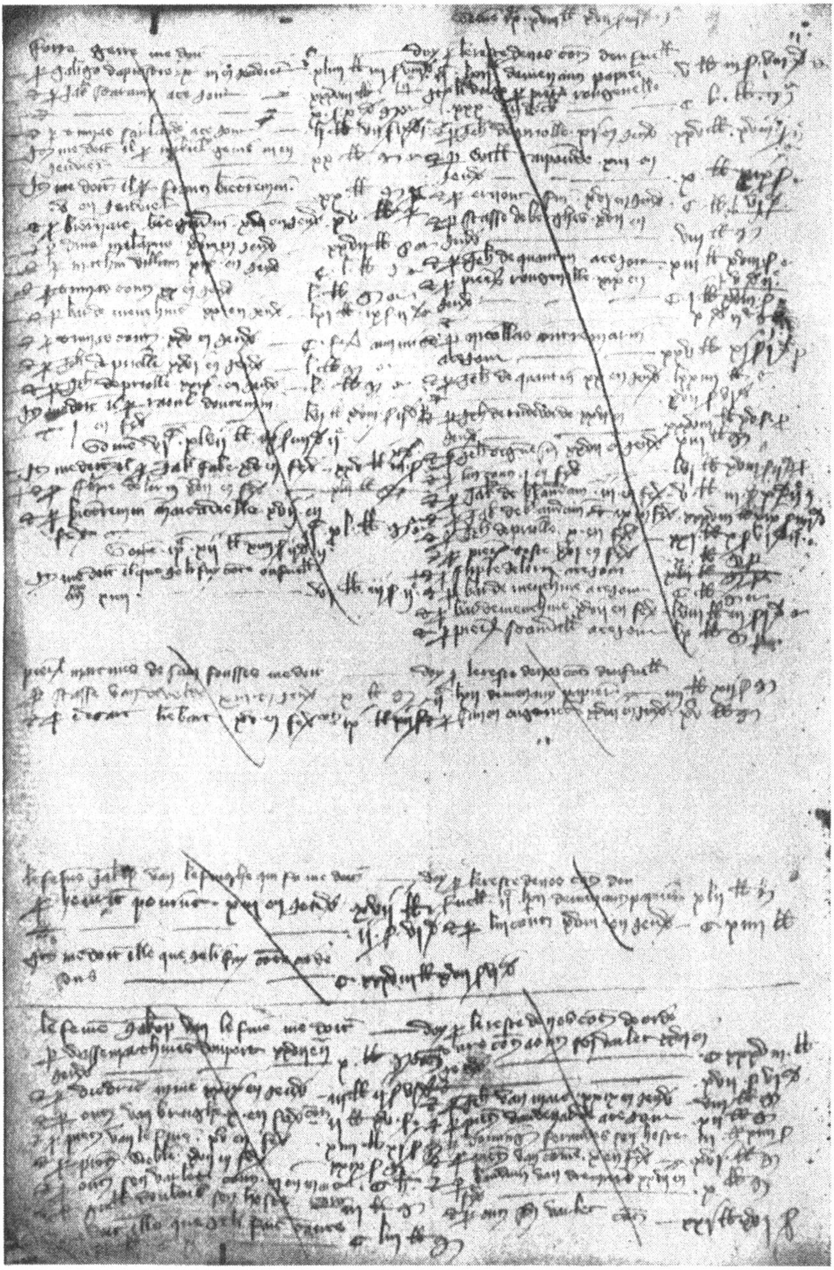

A PAGE FROM THE LEDGER OF COLLARD DE MARKE

This page has the accounts of Forteguerra di Forteguerra (the Lucchese merchant-banker) of the widow of Jakop van Lefinghe, and of the wife of Jakop van le Fine (Bruges inn keeper). *From the original in the Bruges Municipal Archives.*

TABLE 13

CREDIT BALANCES IN THE COLLARD DE MARKE LEDGERS

Frequency Distribution	Ledger No. 1 April 6, 1366			Ledger No. 2 April 19, 1367			Ledger No. 3 April 10, 1368			Ledger No. 4 December 24, 1368			Ledger No. 5 May 20, 1369		
	Number of Balances	Per Cent of Total	Cumulative Per Cent	Number of Balances	Per Cent of Total	Cumulative Per Cent	Number of Balances	Per Cent of Total	Cumulative Per Cent	Number of Balances	Per Cent of Total	Cumulative Per Cent	Number of Balances	Per Cent of Total	Cumulative Per Cent
Below £5 groat	12	14.1	14.1	12	8.8	8.8	18	14.7	14.7	36	21.0	21.0	39	20.8	20.8
£5 and under £10	17	20.0	34.1	19	14.0	22.8	21	17.2	31.9	24	14.0	35.0	23	12.2	33.0
£10 and under £15	11	13.0	47.1	27	19.9	42.7	17	14.0	45.9	27	15.8	50.8	29	15.4	48.4
£15 and under £20	7	8.2	55.3	12	8.8	51.5	8	6.5	52.4	13	7.6	58.4	19	10.1	58.5
£20 and under £25	7	8.3	63.6	12	8.8	60.3	9	7.4	59.8	15	8.8	67.2	14	7.4	65.9
£25 and under £30	5	5.9	69.5	6	4.4	64.7	7	5.8	65.6	10	5.9	73.1	7	3.7	69.6
£30 and under £35	2	2.4	71.9	9	6.7	71.4	4	3.3	68.9	8	4.7	77.8	9	4.8	74.4
£35 and under £40	2	2.4	74.3	1	.7	72.1	2	1.6	70.5	4	2.3	80.1	7	3.7	78.1
£40 and under £45	8	9.4	83.7	5	3.7	75.8	4	3.3	73.8	8	4.7	84.8	...	.....	78.1
£45 and under £50	...	.....	83.7	5	3.7	79.5	1	.8	74.6	4	2.3	87.1	6	3.2	81.3
£50 and under £100	12	14.1	97.8	12	8.8	88.3	17	14.0	88.6	16	9.4	96.5	26	13.9	95.2
£100 and under £200	1	1.1	98.9	10	7.3	95.6	10	8.1	96.7	4	2.3	98.8	7	3.7	98.9
£200 groat and above	1	1.1	100.0	6	4.4	100.0	4	3.3	100.0	2	1.2	100.0	2	1.1	100.0
Total	85	100.0	.....	136	100.0	.....	122	100.0	.....	171	100.0	.....	188	100.0	.....

Source: Bruges, Municipal Archives, Account Books of Collard de Marke

TABLE 14
FREQUENCY DISTRIBUTION OF THE BALANCES DUE TO DEPOSITORS LISTED IN RUYELLE'S STATEMENT OF MAY 24, 1370

Balance due	Number of Balances	Per Cent of Total	Cumulative Per Cent
Below £5 groat	25	41.7	41.7
£5 and under £10 groat	15	25.0	66.7
£10 and under £15 groat	4	6.7	73.4
£15 and under £20 groat	5	8.3	81.7
£20 and under £30 groat	2	3.3	85.0
£30 and under £40 groat	3	5.0	90.0
£40 and under £50 groat	1	1.7	91.7
£50 and under £100 groat	4	6.7	98.4
£100 groat and above	1*	1.6	100.0
Total	60	100.0	

*The balance above £100 was a balance of £167 groat due to Vidua Mathes.
Source: de Roover, 'Ruyelle,' *op. cit.*, pp. 92–95.

with one of the exchange-banks in the course of a year. These remarks are valid only for the middle of the fourteenth century, as we have no data concerning either the preceding or the succeeding period. With regard to the latter it seems that banking in the Low Countries suffered a setback during the fifteenth century.

The Collard de Marke account books and, to a lesser extent, the Guillaume Ruyelle ledger contain thousands of names and it would be an enormous, if not impossible, task to identify them all. It is, furthermore, questionable whether the results would be proportionate to the effort. They are likely to be almost exclusively of local and antiquarian interest, but to contribute woefully little to a better understanding of the development of banking institutions, which is our main concern. The statistical method fortunately supplies additional proof that the clientele of our Bruges money-changers was not restricted to a few big accounts of important merchants and bankers, but was recruited at large among the moderately well-to-do. Nothing shows this better than the prevalence of small accounts. According to the statement of May 24, 1370, Guillaume Ruyelle owed on this date a total of £943 14*s*. 6*d*. groat to sixty depositors, or an average of £15 14*s*. 7*d*. groat per depositor.[32] On the other hand £69 2*s*. 2*d*. groat were receivable from twenty-two individuals who had overdrawn their accounts. The average overdraft amounted thus to £3 2*s*. 10*d*. groat.[33] The figures for Collard de Marke are given above in Table 12.

As this table shows, there are considerable variations in the average from one date to another. On April 10, 1368, the average balance was £41 18*s*. 3*d*. groat. By December 24, 1368, this figure had fallen to £26 18*s*. 8*d*. groat but it went up again and reached £29 13*s*. 1*d*. groat on May 20, 1369. These fluctuations

TABLE 15

BALANCES ABOVE FORTY POUNDS GROAT ACCORDING TO RUYELLE'S STATEMENT OF MAY 24, 1370

Names of Depositors	Amount of Balance			Per Cent of Total
	£	*s*	*d*	
1. Vidua Mathes	167	0	0	17.8
2. Nicolay Amenati	99	0	0	10.5
3. Hatse Tedeledin	79	11	4	8.4
4. Jacob Ranckelos	55	8	8	5.9
5. Michiel Venise	51	0	0	5.4
6. Joris de Matsenare	45	10	11	4.8
Total	497	10	11	52.8
Total of the balances due to depositors	943	16	6	100.0

Source: de Roover, 'Ruyelle,' *op. cit.*, pp. 92–94.

probably reflect changes in the conditions of the money market. There was apparently a contraction of the volume of bank deposits followed by an expansion. It might be objected that averages of about thirty or forty pounds groat are a little too high to justify the statement that small accounts predominated. However, an arithmetic average is unduly influenced by a few large items and is therefore sometimes misleading. Table 13 has been prepared to correct these defects. It is based on the Collard de Marke ledgers and shows the distribution according to size of the balances due to depositors at different dates or, more precisely, each time a ledger was closed and a new one begun.

From Table 13 it appears at the first glance that, at each of the given dates, the majority of the balances are below twenty pounds groat. In all cases, more than 95 per cent of the deposits are below two hundred pounds groat, from 88 to 98 per cent are below one hundred pounds, and from 74 to 87 per cent are below fifty pounds.

In the case of Guillaume Ruyelle a table similar to Table 13 has been prepared on the basis of the data given by a financial statement of May 24, 1370. This table shows that 41.7 per cent of the deposits are not higher than five pounds, 66.7 per cent are below ten pounds, and 81.7 are below twenty pounds groat. There is only one balance exceeding one hundred pounds groat. These figures are in a lower range than those of Collard de Marke. Ruyelle not only had fewer customers than his competitor, but they belonged to a less wealthy class and had less money on deposit at the exchange. This fact confirms what has been said before about the respective importance of our two money-changers.

While the vast majority of deposits were small, it appears, however, that the few big accounts provided most of the funds with which both money-changers operated. In the case of Guillaume Ruyelle, his statement of May 24, 1370, which includes sixty items, reveals that the six largest accounts, or one-

TABLE 16

LIST OF FOURTEEN ACCOUNTS WITH BALANCES ABOVE FIFTY POUNDS GROAT ON APRIL 6, 1366, ACCORDING TO COLLARD DE MARKE'S LEDGERS

	£	s	d groat
1. Jehan van Tinneskin	243	12	0
2. Franchoys Villain	118	4	6
3. Pierre de Leurent	96	12	0
4. Hannebaut Lommelin	92	8	7
5. Jehan Moens (money-changer)	80	18	0
6. Simon Ongeriet	72	12	0
7. Pietre van Erke	60	0	0
8. Olivier van den Berghe	59	6	4
9. Sire Gorres Wandelaire	58	7	11
10. Pierre van Comme	55	17	0
11. Jehan Gonsalles	55	6	1
12. Lambesin d'Alost	51	1	0
13. Cristofle Pelerin	50	0	0
14. Jehan Auls and Jehan van Tinneskin	50	0	0
Total	1,144	5	5 groat

Source: Collard de Marke Ledger No. 1.

tenth of the total, brought in more money than the remaining fifty-four (Table 15).

In Collard de Marke's case, conditions were much the same, and a minority of big accounts were the main source of working capital. On April 6, 1366, fourteen accounts with balances of fifty pounds groat and upward represented 49 per cent of the total liability to depositors, or £1,144 5*s*. 5*d*. groat of a total of £2,310 9*s*. 2*d*. groat (Tables 12 and 16). The next year did not bring much improvement. More than half of the total liability to depositors was made up of sixteen accounts, each having a credit balance of over one hundred pounds groat (Tables 12 and 17). These conditions remained unchanged up to 1369. When on May 20, 1369, a new ledger was started, a total of £5,575 6*s*. 1*d*. groat due to depositors was divided among 188 items not including two items in French francs and one in *escus vies*, or old écus. Out of these 188 items, thirty-five items—each of fifty pounds groat or above—added up to £3,374 3*s*. 11*d*. groat. In other words, less than 20 per cent of the depositors were responsible for over 60 per cent of the aggregate deposits.

It is clear from these figures that the solvency of the Bruges money-changers depended largely upon the continued support of a few customers. The danger came less from a run by small depositors than from the sudden withdrawal of a few important accounts. This condition was a serious weakness. If some of the principal customers suddenly decided to withdraw their funds, the resulting drain would soon exhaust a money-changer's cash reserves. These could not readily be replenished because in the Middle Ages there were no negotiable instruments and no facilities for rediscounting. The smaller the bank, the greater was the reliance on a few big customers and the greater became the danger involved in losing them. Collard de Marke, who in 1369 had

TABLE 17

LIST OF SIXTEEN ACCOUNTS WITH CREDIT BALANCES ABOVE ONE HUNDRED POUNDS GROAT ON APRIL 19, 1367, ACCORDING TO COLLARD DE MARKE'S LEDGERS

	£	*s*	*d* groat
1. Jakoppe van le Fine	290	7	4
2. Sire Pierre Rougenelle	282	13	8
3. Sire Jehan de Castillon	266	10	8
4. Estievene Bieke	259	17	10
5. Sire Jehan van de Nacre (van den Acker)	230	0	0
6. Sire Tiram Enpereal (Imperiali)	228	9	4
7. Pierre Cousin	177	4	5
8. Louis de Robiert	160	11	6
9. Sire Jakes Matenaie (Mettencye)	143	18	9
10. Jakoppe van de Niede	131	11	5
11. Raoul de Coumines	129	0	7
12. Fortegerre (Forteguerra di Forteguerra)	120	0	0
13. Sire Manuyel Prouvende	110	3	2
14. Jehan Ninescat	107	16	4
15. Demiselle Isoie	103	15	8
16. Franche Villain	103	13	3
Total	2,845	13	11 groat*

*The total liability to depositors was £5,566 8*s*. 3*d*. gr.
Source: Collard de Marke Ledger No. 2.

more than thirty important customers, could better afford to lose three than Guillaume Ruyelle, who had only six. As is the case today, small banks had less resilience than big banks. Perhaps the final conclusion should be that there were too many banks in fourteenth-century Bruges.

Besides the size of the balances maintained by depositors at a given date, there exists still another criterion according to which the customers of our money-changers can be divided into different groups. This other classification may even prove to be more useful for further analysis. Even a cursory examination of the Collard de Marke and Guillaume Ruyelle ledgers cannot fail to disclose the fact that some of the customers had dormant accounts, that some others had active accounts, and that still others had accounts which remained open for a short time only. The accounts of those in the first group are mainly overdrafts and will receive attention in the next chapter dealing with loans. The third group is very numerous and is made up of casual customers. Usually things happened in the following way: a new account was opened to a person who was made creditor for a given sum by transfer from an existing account; such a person did not as a rule become a regular customer, but ordinarily disposed of his credit in the course of a few days with the result that his account was closed and balanced after a brief period of existence. Such transitory accounts are those of individuals who either did not usually have a bank account or else had one with a money-changer other than Guillaume Ruyelle or Collard de Marke.

The first type is illustrated by the following case found in the ledger of Guillaume Ruyelle. On May 16, 1369, a new account was created in the name of a certain Jan de Keyser and an amount of six pounds groat was written to his credit by transfer from another account.[34] Already the next day the account was closed, because Jan de Keyser collected all that was standing to his credit. It is likely that he did not have a bank account, otherwise he would not have collected his money in cash, but would have asked to transfer it to his account at the exchange. This method of settlement is exemplified by another case which is interesting because it involved the lombards of St Gilles parish. On March 5, 1369, an account was opened to them in Collard de Marke's ledger No. 4 and they were given credit for an amount of £29 1*s.* 4*d.* groat transferred from the account of a Conrart Boin Adone.[35] This arrangement did not suit the lombards because they had a bank account, not with Collard de Marke, but with the money-changer, Jacob Reubs. Consequently, they gave instructions to adjust the matter. In pursuance of these orders, the account of the lombards was closed on March 7th (two days after having been opened), and the amount of £29 1*s.* 4*d.* groat was written off and transferred to the credit of Jacob Reubs, who probably made in his own books whatever adjustments were necessary. In the Collard de Marke and Guillaume Ruyelle ledgers there are hundreds of cases similar to the two which have just been described. Their frequency explains why the Collard de Marke ledger No. 4, for example, contains as many as 1,100 accounts of which only 305 were still open when a new ledger was started.

There are, however, a few transitory accounts which should be set apart from the rest. These are the accounts of foreigners who did not take up residence in Bruges, but stayed there only for a short while. Collard de Marke had a few of such accounts. Some of them were those of Spanish and Portuguese shipmasters who would open an account for the time they were in port. A good example is the account of a Jehan Diese de Castille, *mestre de naves,* which remained open from February 21 to March 17, 1369.[36] On the latter date, Jehan Diese collected the balance in cash, probably before sailing. Another group of accounts of the same type were those of the Hanseatic merchants. Their commercial methods were backward in comparison with those of the Italians, who maintained permanent branches or correspondents in Bruges. The lack of such an organization among the Germans compelled them not only to operate on a smaller scale but to travel constantly back and forth between Bruges and their home towns.[37] Of course, each trip gave rise to a separate and short-lived bank account.

It is quite clear that the business which the money-changers got from casual customers did not afford a basis broad and secure enough upon which to run a bank. Only the regular customers who had active accounts provided the foundation on which rested the whole system of book-transfers created by the money-changers. Although some of the regular customers were allowed to overdraw their accounts, most of them maintained fair-sized balances which, of course, moved up and down, but in general a decrease in one balance tended to be offset by an increase in another.[38]

In order to avoid any apparent contradiction, it should, perhaps, be pointed out that the group of regular customers included all the big customers whose importance in supplying the money-changers with working capital has been emphasized before. Consequently, the two classifications overlap, but only to a certain extent because all regular customers were not necessarily big customers.

What the social or economic background of the regular customers was is not hard to guess, but difficult to determine by exact historical methods. The reason is that the business or profession of the customers is rarely indicated in our only sources, the Collard de Marke and Guillaume Ruyelle account books. However, as far as can be ascertained, it seems that the group of regular customers consisted of the business men in the community: the native merchants, the broker-innkeepers, the *drapiers,* the resident Italians, not excepting the lombards whose current account was handled by the money-changer Jacob Reubs.[39] The Hanseatic merchants also had bank accounts,[40] but they were not as a rule regular customers for the reasons stated above.

In 1369 Collard de Marke had about seventy to eighty regular customers. Their names recur constantly in the ledger and their accounts, far from being closed and balanced after a few transactions, had frequently to be carried forward, because the allotted space—sometimes a whole page, sometimes half-a-page—had been filled.

The regular customers made extensive use of the existing transfer system. They probably followed the policy of making all local payments by assignment on their bank accounts. As most of the time the assignees did not care to collect their credits in cash, but preferred to have money in the bank, most payments between business men were made by 'writings only' through the banking system.[41] One result was that payments within the group of regular customers simply brought about a shift in balances, but did not affect the total volume of bank deposits. As is the case today, the size of individual deposits varied according to individual choice and decisions, but the aggregate volume of bank deposits obeyed certain economic laws and was determined by the state of the money market. Only today, we would add: 'and also by the policy of the central bank and the monetary authorities.'

These conclusions are fully borne out by the Collard de Marke and Guillaume Ruyelle account books. An examination of these manuscripts reveals the striking fact that book-transfers by far outnumber cash transactions.[42] It is difficult to give any exact ratio, but it would certainly be unbelievably high if it could be computed. The habit of assigning money on deposit to a creditor apparently goes back to the beginnings of banking in the Low Countries. The proof is to be found in a statute of Douai, enacted in 1248, which consequently antedates the Lille grant of 1294 by more than forty-five years.[43] According to this statute, any one who pays a creditor by assignment on a money-changer without having sufficient funds exposes himself to banishment and to a fine of fifty pounds.[44] The same penalties are imposed upon any money-changer who does not return any deposits of money at the first request.[45] One should be on guard against hasty conclusions: there is nothing in the above statute implying that banking existed in thirteenth-century Douai. Nor does the statute contain any reference to book-transfers. It only proves that it was fairly common to pay by assignment and to deposit money with a money-changer, but it is not even clear whether such deposits were regular or irregular deposits. It is certain, however, that such practices were conducive to the settlement of debts by book-transfer, if the debtor and the creditor each had a bank account.

In the Collard de Marke and Guillaume Ruyelle account books we are confronted with a fully developed system of book-transfers. This system made it possible to settle accounts without the employment of specie, not only when both the debtor and the creditor were customers of the same money-changer, but also when they were customers of different money-changers. This arrangement presupposes, of course, some organization of inter-bank relations so as to facilitate such settlements. In substance, such an organization had to perform the same functions as our modern clearing system.

In order to understand the mediaeval banking system, it is necessary to realize that it differed in some essential particulars from any modern system. In the Middle Ages there were no negotiable instruments and no checks. These two essential differences have been properly stressed in the studies which Professor Usher has devoted to mediaeval banking, and especially in his article on the primitive bank deposit, which appeared a few years ago in the English *Economic History Review*.[46] The check was replaced by an oral order which had to be delivered in person and was recorded by the banker in his journal under the dictation of the customer, so to speak. This is undoubtedly the reason why in several of van Reymerswael's paintings the banker is shown writing in an account book while another man, seated beside him, is clearly telling him what to put down. The act of dictating is portrayed by facial expression and gestures of the hands. It is therefore not unlikely that the scene represents a money-changer receiving an oral order of transfer. But perhaps an economic historian does not have the privilege of borrowing his argument from picture galleries.

It would be futile to hunt in the Bruges account books for any specific reference to the use of the oral contract in lieu of checks. The municipal statutes are equally silent on the subject. The lack of explicit mention need not, however, be deplored too much, as there is plenty of circumstantial evidence proving that orders to make transfers on the books of a bank were given by word of mouth. The existence of this practice in Italy and at the fairs of Champagne is established beyond any doubt by a number of texts. A comparison of the account books of Collard de Marke and Guillaume Ruyelle with similar Italian manuscripts shows that these two money-changers kept their books and conducted their business according to methods borrowed from the Italians. There is no reason why the Bruges money-changers should not have taken over the oral contract with all the rest. Their accounting procedure eludes all logical explanation, unless one assumes the existence of either oral contracts or endorsed checks. As the endorsement of commercial paper is not older than the seventeenth century, the other alternative is the only remaining possibility.

The oldest known document which gives some insight into mediaeval banking routine dates from the year 1200 and consists of a series of testimonies collected by a Genoese notary in connection with a lawsuit. From what the witnesses had to say, it appears that ordering a transfer from one's bank account to the account of someone else involved going in person to the bank. If checks had been in use, people could have saved themselves such a trip.[47]

The next document which sheds some light on our problem concerns the Italian money-changers who, in the thirteenth century, had established themselves at the fairs of Champagne.[48] The way in which they dealt with their clientele is described in a manuscript called *Les Coustumes, stylle et usaiges des Foires de Champagne.*[49] The relevant passage begins with the statement that the merchants of Italy and Provence who visited the fairs were accustomed to deposit their monies at the exchange and to make all their payments through the medium of a money-changer (*par le greffe de tel changeur*). If, for instance, one of those merchants bought cloth from a Malines cloth-dealer for the value of one hundred pounds, the buyer would not pay in cash, but would persuade the seller to accept an 'assignment in bank.'[50] Both would then go to the exchange and the buyer would *tell* his money-changer to write the sum of one hundred pounds to the credit of the cloth-dealer from Malines. These instructions would be carried out forthwith in the presence of both parties to the contract (*présent l'un et l'autre*).

From this description it is clear that book-transfers were made on the strength of an oral order, the assignor and the assignee both being present. The text imparts some further information. We learn that the money-changers used wax tablets instead of parchment and kept the accounts of their customers in bilateral form, the debits on one side and the credits on the other. The Bruges money-changers Collard de Marke and Guillaume Ruyelle did not use wax tablets any more, but they had adopted the bilateral form for their ledger accounts so that they knew exactly how they stood with each customer.

The text of the *Us et Coutumes* of the fairs of Champagne has come down to us through a copy made in the seventeenth century by an *avocat* of Provins named Michel Caillot.[51] This copy is believed to be once removed from a lost original which was written about 1368 but described conditions existing at the end of the thirteenth century when the fairs of Champagne were still in full swing.

The Flemish merchants visited the fairs regularly all through the twelfth and thirteenth centuries and of necessity came frequently in touch with the Italian money-changers. Through these contacts, the Flemings undoubtedly became acquainted with the oral order of assignment, the settlement of debts by book-transfer, the current account in bilateral form, and the whole technique of deposit banking. From Champagne these practices probably spread first to French Flanders and thence farther north, to the Flemish-speaking part of the county and to Brabant, in the wake of the expanding cloth industry. It is therefore more probable that deposit banking was introduced into Bruges by native merchants who learned the technique from the Italians at the Champagne fairs than by the Italian merchant-bankers who set up permanent branches in Bruges, but not before the close of the thirteenth century.

All through the Middle Ages the law merchant was partial to the oral contract, and checks or *polizze*—as they were called in Italy—were regarded with suspicion as being tainted by fraud.[52] They did not come into general use until the sixteenth century and only after having overcome considerable opposition.[53] Venice was one of the most conservative business centers. As late as 1526 the Senate promulgated a statute which forbade the bankers on the Rialto to make any transfers in their books, except in the presence of both parties concerned.[54] Still later, in 1584, while the Senate was contemplating the creation of a public bank, a tentative statute was drafted which provided in article 31 that nothing was to be entered in the books of the public bank on the strength of a verbal order given beforehand (*parola data*) or of a written command (*polizza*), but that all entries were to be made in the presence of the client or of his lawful attorney.[55] In other words, all entries were to be made under the eyes of the client or of his proxy and during—not outside—office hours. This provision was incorporated into the statutes of the Banco di Rialto, founded in 1587,[56] and of the Banco del Giro, founded in 1619. The regulation voiding all *polizze* or checks remained in force until the eighteenth century, and only orders given by word of mouth (*a viva voce*) were considered valid according to a contemporary text.[57]

Even in the Low Countries, the oral order of assignment seems to have survived up to the beginning of the seventeenth century. The municipal authorities of Amsterdam, for certain reasons which will be discussed later, were at that time very ill-disposed toward deposit banking or *het kassiersbedrijf*, as it was called. In order to abolish this obnoxious institution, several ordinances were issued which forbade any one to accept deposits or to settle debts by transfer in accordance with orders given by word of mouth or otherwise (*overwijsinge bij monde ofte andersints*).[58]

One result of the oral order of assignment was that the entry in the books of the bank was the only evidence of the contract.[59] It is, therefore, not surprising that bank journals were considered in most Italian cities as public or notarial records and that great pains were taken to ensure their authenticity. As Luca Paciolo, a writer on mathematics and bookkeeping in the last decade of the fifteenth century, expresses it: 'The assignment in bank (*la ditta di banco*) is like the act of a notary, because such an assignment is guaranteed by public authority.'[60] In Genoa the clerk who kept the journal or *manuale notularum bancorum* had to be an imperial notary.[61] In Florence the statutes of the Arte del Cambio required all members to make entries in their books before a customer left the premises.[62]

The journal had to be kept strictly according to chronological order, without blanks and without erasures.[63] The use of Arabic figures was not allowed, because it was thought that they could be easily falsified. All amounts had, therefore, to be written in Roman numerals. The tearing out of leaves from the journal was viewed with great suspicion. If it could be proven that such action was fraudulent in intent, the offender not only laid himself open to heavy fines imposed by the gild authorities, but his case was reported to the *Signoria* or municipal government.[64] The same rules were in force in many other Italian cities and have left their imprint on modern commercial law. The journal kept according to the above principles is still mandatory in Belgium and in other European countries whose codes are derived from the Code Napoleon and the 'Ordonnance du Commerce' of 1673. The law, however, is unworkable under modern conditions and is practically disregarded with the connivance of the courts. Jurists and accountants have been at a loss in trying to understand why so much emphasis was placed on the journal and so little on the ledger which is, after all, the key-book in any well-conceived system of bookkeeping. The problem is nearly solved if one considers the fact that the journal was originally a notarial and chronological record of otherwise oral agreements.

From the legal standpoint conditions in Flanders, where there was little statutory law, were entirely different from those in Italy. The law merchant was still uncertain and in a process of elaboration. It is, therefore, very much open to doubt whether, in Bruges, the journals of the money-changers enjoyed recognition as public records.[65] But whether or not such was the case makes no practical difference. In case of need the money-changer could always be called upon to testify in court with regard to any transaction which he had witnessed and had entered into his books. Furthermore, the *échevins,* who were at the same time the city's administrators and the judges of the local court, were either business men themselves or connected with the business world. They were always willing to be guided by business practice and to sanction it in their court decisions.[66] The law merchant, as Professor Postan has pointed out, is often but another name for the custom of the merchants.[67]

To what extent the account books of the money-changers were to be received as evidence in court was a problem which could not fail to come up some day or other and which actually did come up in connection with the failure of Diederic Urbaen's widow, previously mentioned. A number of creditors including three money-changers, Jan van der Capelle, Jan Moens, and sire Evrard Goederic, lodged claims for which no entries were found in the books of the bankrupt.[68] Her sureties countered these claims by rejecting all liability for the reason that 'no record was found in the papers [books] of the exchange.' That such a contention was made proves at least two things. First, it was up to the money-changers' customers to see that each transaction was duly recorded in their presence. In the second place, it seems that the 'papers' of the exchange were the sole evidence, as no mention is made of vouchers or receipts which the creditors could have used in order to establish their claims. One of the claimants was not even sure of the amount which was due him, but it was somewhere between £3 10*s*. 5*d*. and £5 10*s*. groat. Unfortunately, we do not know whether or not the municipal court accepted the point of view of the bankrupt's sureties. Probably not, since all the means of establishing the truth had not been exhausted. For example, the three money-changers could produce their own books which deserved as much credence as the 'papers' of the bankrupt. Whatever decision was reached, the case brings out the informal character of mediaeval banking procedure and the serious shortcomings of a system based on the spoken word. Apparently Paciolo was aware of these drawbacks when he advised the merchants to play safe and to require a voucher for each deposit regardless of the fact that the public character of bank records made such a formality superfluous.[69]

As an entry recorded in the journal was on a par with an agreement contracted before a notary, several historians have expressed the opinion that the journal entries had to give full particulars or, at least, to state the *causa* or purpose of each transaction.[70] Such a rule, indeed, was embodied in a Genoese statute of the fourteenth century, but probably remained a dead letter as appears from surviving records of the period.[71] The State Archives of Genoa contain a number of journals or *manualia notularum* and cash books or *cartularii capsiae* once belonging to the Lomellini bank; the ledgers are missing. The surviving series of journals and cash books covers with some gaps a period extending from 1386 to 1433.[72] In these Lomellini journals the profession of clients is rarely mentioned and there are only occasional references to the purpose of a given transaction such as *pro vino* (for wine), *pro naulo* (for freight), *pro pensione domus* (for rent), *ex mutuo* (for a loan), or *pro cambio de* Barcelona, Famagusta, etc.[73] Full details are never given. The same remark applies to the journals and ledgers of the famous Bank of St George, which are also preserved at the State Archives of Genoa and extend over the period from 1408 to 1445.

The Lomellini journals are of special interest to us because of their close resemblance to the two extant journals of Collard de Marke. The only difference is that the Lomellini kept their books in Latin, whereas Collard de Marke used French.[74] Otherwise, in shape, appearance, method, and wording they are almost identical.[75] The great number of book-transfers as compared with cash transactions is another common feature. In both the Lomellini and the Collard de Marke journals, the form of the entries is very condensed and is reduced to bare essentials. In the case of a book-transfer, the only information supplied is the name of the assignor, the name of the assignee, and the amount transferred.

Even the journals of the Bank of St. George, which was a quasi-public institution, do not give any more details than those of the private Lomellini bank or of the Bruges money-changer Collard de Marke.[76] Identity in accounting procedure is a sign of identity in methods of doing business. The banking practices in Bruges, therefore, did not differ in any important respect from those in Genoa and elsewhere in Italy and the Mediterranean world.

The predominant use of the oral order instead of checks and the importance assumed by the journal as a public record determined the way in which business was handled by mediaeval banks. Administrative details, as a result, took a form which is rather unfamiliar to us. They can best be grasped by following the accounting procedure step by step. As today, this procedure was different for each type of transaction, but all transactions of the same type were handled in the same way. One or two examples of each will consequently suffice. Bank deposits do not give rise to a great number of different types of transactions. In all there are only four possibilities: 1) the placing of money on deposit; 2) the withdrawal of funds either by the depositor himself or by someone else; 3) the transfer of credit from one account to another, if the assignor and the assignee each has an account with the same money-changer; 4) the transfer of credit, if the assignor and the assignee have bank accounts with different money-changers. This fourth possibility raises, of course, the whole question of inter-bank relations.

Money can be deposited by a client himself or by someone else in his behalf. The first possibility can be illustrated by the following case. On December 29, 1368, one of Collard de Marke's regular customers, Medemiselle de Rudevorde, who apparently was the proprietor of an inn patronized by foreign merchants, made a deposit of 540 francs and twelve *lions d'or,* equal to £72 0*s.* 7*d.* gr. in money of account. As a result the bookkeeper entered in his journal that

£72 0*s*. 7*d*. groat were due demiselle de Rudevorde for 540 francs and twelve lions deposited by her in cash. The exact text of the entry is as follows:

doy le demiselle de Rudevorde par lui contet
pour 540 francs et 12 lion.............................. 72 lb.—.7d. gr.[77]

Par lui contet ('counted by him or her') is a standard formula used in both the Collard de Marke and the Guillaume Ruyelle ledgers to indicate a cash transaction. The kind of coins in which payment was made is specified here, but such a mention is exceptional in the Collard de Marke account books. It will also be noticed that the rate of conversion of the francs and the *lions d'or* into groats, the money of account, is not given.

The above journal entry was subsequently posted to the ledger and the sum of £72 0*s*. 7*d*. gr. was written to the credit of Medemiselle de Rudevorde's account, as appears in the following excerpt. The reader will notice that there is little difference in the wording of the journal and the ledger entries.

Dr. Medemiselle de Rudevorde[78]	Cr.
Medemiselle de Rudevorde me doit par le reste de nos contes dou fuelliet 339 de men autre papier 107 *lb*. 9*s*. 6*d*. gr. etc., etc.	doy par lui contet 29 en décembre pour 540 francs et 12 lion, somme 72 *lb*. 7*d*. gr. etc., etc.

He will also see that Medemiselle de Rudevorde's account is overdrawn and starts with a debit balance of £107 9*s*. 6*d*. gr. carried over from a preceding ledger.

It did not make much difference from the banker's point of view whether money was brought in by the client himself or by someone else acting as his agent. In the Collard de Marke account books the name of such a third party is always recorded, probably for the latter's protection, in case the payment were denied later on. Evidently the customer, to whose credit the amount deposited was placed, did not have to be present. He did not even need to be notified, as the transaction was usually carried out in pursuance of his own instructions. Such was generally the case when employees, factors, or *varlets* made deposits to the account of their employers. For example, on May 11, 1369, Collard de Marke received a deposit of 40 pounds groat made in his master's behalf by Jehan Teste, a factor of the Lucchese merchant Forteguerra di Forteguerra. The journal records this transaction as follows:

doy Fortegere par Jehan Teste contet........................ 40 lb. gr.[79]
('I owe Forteguerra, paid by Jehan Test')

This item is also found, of course, in the ledger on the credit side of Forteguerra's account:

Dr.	Forteguerra di Forteguerra[80]	Cr.
Fortegerre me doit etc., etc.		doy .... Et par Jehan Teste contet 11 en may.......... 40 lb. gr. p. .... etc., etc.

The withdrawal of funds by the depositor himself did not raise any legal problems or practical difficulties. Such withdrawals were naturally charged against the depositor's account. The standard formula used both by Collard de Marke and Guillaume Ruyelle was *par lui contet* ('paid by him'). The withdrawal of funds by someone other than the depositor did, however, involve some difficulties. These were overcome by breaking the rule which required the personal presence of the client and by allowing him to act through an attorney. The Collard de Marke and the Guillaume Ruyelle account books abound in examples of payments made to the wife, the factors, the *varlets* (messengers or employees), or the partners of customers. As Professor Usher has pointed out, such a practice was not inconsistent with the principle of the oral contract, but this principle was further extended by considering as valid any order given orally by a lawful representative of the client.

Mediaeval business men were practical and expediency was more important than red tape. It is certain that a formal power of attorney was not always necessary. Money could be taken out by any one who was known to the money-changer as the regular agent or proxy of a depositor. As a safeguard against any breach of trust the name of such an agent always appears in the account books and the formula *par lui contet* is replaced by phrases like these: *par se femme contet, par sen varlet contet,* or *par sen compaignon* ['partner'] *contet.*[81] For example, the account of Guillaume Ruyelle in the Collard de Marke ledgers includes several items relating to collections made by Hannekin, Ruyelle's cousin and assistant. Here is a typical entry referring to such a transaction: 'Willem Ruyelle me doit: par Hanekin sen cousin contet 7 en décembre [1369] 50 frs. frs.'[82]

Another good example is afforded by the following case. On December 27, 1368, the employee or *varlet* of a certain Raoul Doucemin of Commines withdrew in his master's behalf the amount of £8 1*s*. groat which was paid out to him in currency of Brabant. Then entry in the journal reads as follows: 'Raoul de Coumines me doit par sen varlet contet, en monnoie de Braibant 8 *lb*. 12*d*.'[83] The corresponding entry in the ledger is a little more detailed: 'Rauol Doucemin me doit: par Jehan sen varlet contet 27 jours en décembre, pour porter en Braibant 8 *lb*. 12*d*.'[84] It appears therefrom that Raoul de Commines and Raoul Doucemin were evidently one and the same person, that his *varlet's* name was Jehan, and that foreign currency was needed for a trip to Brabant, possibly for a visit to the Cold Mart at Bergen-op-Zoom. This entry is one of the very few in which the purpose of the transaction is indicated.

Today one may take money out of a bank account by simply cashing a check signed by the depositor. Mediaeval banking practice did not permit this procedure. Withdrawals could be made only by the depositor, and not by a stranger unless the depositor or his agent was actually present and gave his consent. The transaction was thus equivalent either to a withdrawal by the depositor himself—as he had to be present anyhow—or to an ordinary book transfer.

The payee often wanted to make a further assignment or to dispose of his credit partly by a withdrawal of cash and partly by assignment. In such a case, mediaeval money-changers found it expedient to open to the payee a temporary account which recorded all the transactions carried out in accordance with his instructions. This procedure can best be understood by giving an example. On May 2, 1369, a Bruges merchant, Jan van den Vagheviere, who was not a regular customer of the money-changer Guillaume Ruyelle, was assigned an amount of £10 13*s*. 4*d*. groat by a certain Jan Barkin, probably an Englishman. For the sake of convenience, a new account was opened to the assignee, because he wanted to collect only £2 3*s*. 4*d*. groat of his credit in cash and to dispose of the balance of £8 10*s*. groat by assigning it to another Englishman named Jacob Tolbin. These orders were carried out forthwith, so that Jan van den Vagheviere's account with Guillaume Ruyelle was opened, closed, and balanced all in one day. As this account is short, it will be reproduced here. In order to avoid any confusion, the reader is reminded of the fact that Ruyelle does not observe the conventional rules and puts debit to the right and credit to the left instead of the opposite.

Cr. Jan van den Vagheviere[85]	Dr.
Jan van den Vagheeviere debeo 10 lb. 13*s*. 4*d*. par Jan Barkin le 2e de may (1369)	debet Item 8 lb. 10*s*. par Jacop Tolbin le 2e de may Item 2 lb. 3*s*. 4*d*. par li conteit le 2e de may

As this account shows, the whole transaction involved three steps: a transfer of credit from Jan Barkin's to Jan van den Vagheviere's account, a withdrawal of funds by Jan van den Vagheviere himself, and a transfer from his account to that of Jacob Tolbin. The effect was the same as if Jan Barkin had made out two checks payable to Jan van den Vagheviere: one for £2 3*s*. 4*d*. groat which was cashed immediately by the payee, and another for £8 10*s* groat which he did not collect, but passed on by endorsement to Jacob Tolbin.

Thus the peculiarities of mediaeval banking practice explain at least in part why

THE MONEY-CHANGER AND HIS CUSTOMER
by Marinus van Reymerswael
From a painting in the Royal Gallery, Windsor Castle

so many transitory or temporary accounts are to be found in the Collard de Marke and Guillaume Ruyelle ledgers. These accounts introduced greater flexibility into the system, facilitated the circulation of bank deposits, and fulfilled to some extent the same function as the modern endorsement of checks.

As this example already shows, the book transfer was the most efficient and easiest way of using bank deposits as a means of payment. When the assignor and the assignee each had an account with the same money-changer, the procedure was simple and did not involve any problem at all. In the Collard de Marke and Guillaume Ruyelle ledgers the number of transfers from the account of one customer to that of another *runs into the thousands*. All these transfer entries are exactly alike and, as has been stated, are very much condensed. As a result, the Bruges account books contain an array of names, dates, and figures which are invaluable for the history of banking, but cast little light on any other aspect of mediaeval trade.

Because of this uniformity one example picked out at random from among thousands of similar items will be quite sufficient. On March 28, 1369, Collard de Marke's journal records the following entry relating to a transfer of forty pounds groat from the account of Guillaume Rapondi, the Lucchese merchant-banker, to that of another Lucchese, Forteguerra di Forteguerra:

Guillaume Raiponde me doit par Fortegerre..............40 lb. gr. or[86]

As previously explained, such a transfer was entered into the journal under the eyes of both parties or of their agents. The entry was then posted to the debit of the account of Guillaume Rapondi and to the credit of that of Forteguerra:

Dr. Guillaume Rapondi[87] Cr.

Willaume Raiponde me doit .... Et par Fortegerre 28 en march........40 lb. or	

Dr. Forteguerra[88] Cr.

Fortegerre me doit etc., etc.	doy .... Et par Willaume Raiponde 28 en march..........40 lb. gr. or

Sometimes the same amount was transferred several times. A good example of successive transfers is found in Guillaume Ruyelle's ledger. A regular customer named Gyllis Lauwers assigned on July 28, 1369, an amount of four pounds groat to a certain Jan de Vleins who was not one of Ruyelle's clients. Consequently, the above sum was credited to a new account opened in the payee's name. This account did not exist for long, as Jan de Vleins ordered the four pounds groat to be transferred to a certain Goes van Werkene who did not have an account, either. In accordance with these instructions Jan de Vleins' account was closed and the said sum of four pounds groat was written to the credit of another newly created account, this time in the name of Goes van Werkene. This account was short-lived, too, as the latter had the four pounds collected the same day by one Simoen Evelbaren, probably his agent.[89] To sum up, the said four pounds were assigned in one single day by Gillis Lauwers to Jan de Vleins, by Jan de Vleins to Goes van Werkene, and by Goes van Werkene to Simoen Evelbaren who finally collected them in specie.[90] Such a rapid succession of transfers is only possible when assignments can be effected without time-consuming legal formalities; it presupposes either the existence of endorsable instruments or else a system of oral contracts combined with book transfers which, in a devious way, accomplishes the same results.

This transfer system was so perfected that it allowed not only the transfer of credit from one person to another when each had a current account at the same bank, but also when the two had accounts at different banks. This arrangement was made possible by all the money-changers of Bruges having accounts with each other. In the Collard de Marke ledgers the accounts with other money-changers of Bruges are grouped together in a separate section. In ledgers two and four there are fourteen such accounts. This figure tallies with information gathered from other sources concerning the total number of money-changers who were in business at that time.[91]

As was to be expected, some of these accounts were more important than others: the accounts of the most successful money-changers were also the most active, especially those of Jacob Reubs and Pieter van Oudenaerde. It was not uncommon to have several debit and credit items posted to these two accounts in one single day.

Accounts with the smaller money-changers were settled from time to time, but at irregular intervals, by paying off the balance due to them or by collecting whatever was outstanding.[92] This method of settlement was adopted, for example, between Collard de Marke and Guillaume Ruyelle. The relations between the former and his two main competitors Jacob Reubs and Pieter van Oudenaerde were, however, on an entirely different basis. Settlements in specie were rarely resorted to. As a rule accounts remained open year in and year out, the balance being forwarded from one page to another and from one ledger to the next. From time to time two of these money-changers would reckon with each other and bring their balances into agreement if any discrepancies were discovered. Unfortunately, we do not know exactly what procedure was followed. It is quite possible that adjustments were made on the basis of a statement of account which one money-changer sent to the other. One thing is certain, such statements should not be thought of as neatly written copies of the ledger accounts but as rough summaries hastily jotted down on scraps of paper. A couple of these scraps were found in the Collard de Marke ledgers but could not be identified owing to the absence of any guiding reference.

The accounts of Pieter van Oudenaerde (Pierre d'Audenarde) and of Jacques Reubs cover pages and pages in the Collard de Marke ledgers. Whenever the allotted space was filled, the balance was transferred and the account continued on the first blank page. Sometimes such transfers coincide with one of those periodical checkings which have just been discussed. When this is the case, special mention is made that the two parties were in agreement on the balance. For example, on April 30, 1369, Pieter van Oudenaerde's account starts with the following entry: 'doy pour le reste de nos contes dou fuellet [317] contet à sen varlet 30 en avril.'[93] The *contet* here does not stand for a payment in cash, but the text should be read as follows: 'I owe [Pieter van Oudenaerde] for the balance of our accounts, reckoned with his *varlet* on April 30.' The *varlet* or employee probably brought with him some kind of a memorandum which was then compared with Collard de Marke's ledger.

The following summaries of the accounts of Jacques Reubs and Pieter van Oudenaerde cover a period about five months, from Christmas 1368 to May 19 (Pentecost), 1369. These summaries will give the reader some idea of the importance of inter-bank accounts and of the volume of clearing payments. It will be observed that the balance of the account of Pieter van Oudenaerde is always in his favor, whereas Jacques Reubs has sometimes a favorable, and sometimes an adverse, balance. Money-changers could thus draw on each other's resources. This practice gave a little elasticity to the mediaeval banking system.

Luckily for us the only extant ledger of Guillaume Ruyelle covers the same period as one of Collard de Marke's complete sets composed of journal, ledger, and alphabetical index. Therefore we have the account of Collard de Marke in Guillaume Ruyelle's ledger and the corresponding account of Guillaume Ruyelle in Collard de Marke's ledger.[94] It is necessary, of course, to have the accounts of two banks, if one wishes to study the process by which an individual having money standing to his credit in one bank could transfer this money to the credit of another individual in another bank.

Let us take as an example the transfer on March 16, 1369, of an amount of £6 16*s.* groat from the account of France de Busschere, a customer of Guillaume Ruyelle, to the credit of Tideman Geismar, a customer of Collard de Marke. Judging by his name, France de Busschere was probably a native Fleming, but we have no other information concerning him. As for Tideman Geismar, he was an important Hanseatic merchant who owned some real estate in Lübeck and traded chiefly with Sweden, but sometimes also with Flanders. He was not one of Collard de Marke's regular customers, but he had opened a bank account—as

TABLE 18

SUMMARY OF THE ACCOUNT OF THE MONEY-CHANGER PIETER VAN OUDENAERDE IN COLLARD DE MARKE'S LEDGER NO. 4

(December 24, 1368 — May 19, 1369)

DATES	Fol. of Ledger	DEBITS			CREDITS			BALANCES					
								Debit			Credit		
		£	s	d	£	s	d	£	s	d	£	s	d
December 24, 1368					82	11	2				82	11	2
Jan. 24, 1369	301	691	7	1	610	6	0				1	10	1
Jan. 29, 1369	305	79	12	6	89	13	7				11	11	2
Feb. 20, 1369	305	359	3	1	426	8	11				78	17	0
Feb. 15, 1369	309	141	2	0	62	5	0						
March 3, 1369	309	673	10	10	719	17	2				46	6	4
March 6, 1369	311	64	17	4	75	10	8				56	19	8
March 15, 1369	311	506	8	2	643	3	4				193	14	10
March 19, 1369	313	287	6	1	337	19	0				244	7	9
March 24, 1369	314	571	10	3	549	9	1				222	6	7
March 26, 1369	315	186	3	11	33	13	0				69	15	8
April 21, 1369	315	617	17	6	548	16	8					14	10
April 28, 1369	317	343	17	0	380	5	2				37	3	0
May 14, 1369	320	285	7	0	331	3	7				82	19	7
May 19, 1369	323	258	0	3	309	4	5				134	3	9
Balance to be carried forward		134	3	9									
Total		5200	6	9	5200	6	9						

Source: Bruges Municipal Archives, Collard de Marke Ledger No. 4.

TABLE 19

SUMMARY OF THE ACCOUNT OF THE MONEY-CHANGER JACQUES REUBS IN COLLARD DE MARKE'S LEDGER NO. 4

(December 24, 1368 — May 19, 1369)

DATES	Fol. of Ledger	DEBITS			CREDITS			BALANCES					
								Debit			Credit		
		£	s	d	£	s	d	£	s	d	£	s	d
December 24, 1368					77	16	4				77	16	4
December 26, 1368	300	875	16	10	683	8	7	114	11	11			
Jan. 17, 1369	303	165	12	1	271	17	6	8	6	6			
Feb. 5, 1369	303	392	17	11	330	4	8	70	19	9			
Feb. 15, 1369	308	286	15	4	395	4	5				37	9	4
Feb. 17, 1369	308	161	1	2	141	16	4				18	4	6
March 6, 1369	309	950	9	5	919	0	8	13	4	3			
March 28, 1369	312	954	5	3	1191	1	5				223	11	11
April 12, 1369	316	645	4	8	495	7	4				73	14	7
April 20, 1369	318	372	11	5	330	0	3				31	3	5
April 28, 1369	318	343	17	2	231	14	4	80	19	5			
May 12, 1369	320	533	17	8	470	7	8	144	9	5			
May 19, 1369	322	273	9	2	420	15	8				2	17	1
Balance to be carried forward		2	17	1									
Total		5958	15	2	5958	15	2						

Source: Collard de Marke Ledger No. 4.

was customary among the Easterlings—while he was staying in Bruges during the winter and spring of 1369.[95]

It is likely that Tideman Geismar had sold some Baltic products to France de Busschere. Instead of paying in cash, the latter told his banker Guillaume Ruyelle to place the above amount of £6 16*s* gr. at Geismar's disposal. Accordingly the £6 16*s*. gr. were charged to France de Busschere's account and written to the credit of a new account in the name of Tideman Geismar.[96] The latter, however, wanted to have this money in his own bank account at Collard de Marke's. What procedure was followed from then on, we really do not know. It is probable that Tideman Geismar had to call into Ruyelle's office one of the messengers or clerks of his own banker and in the presence of both the messenger and Geismar, the latter's newly opened account was cancelled and the account of Collard de Marke was credited with £6 16*s*. gr.[97] The parties to this last transaction then walked over to the office of Collard de Marke, who wrote down in his journal: "Williame Ruelle me doit par Tildeman Gismar 6 lb. 16s."[98] The result of this entry was the debiting of Ruyelle and the crediting of Geismar with the said sum. It is perhaps well to add that all these transactions took place on the same date, March 16, 1369, as is evident from the records of both money-changers.

This description might convey the impression that the whole process was rather cumbersome and involved a considerable waste of time. One has to consider, however, that the offices of the money-changers were all located in the same vicinity—in the Waterhalle or near it. The exchanges were close together in other mediaeval cities, too, and for the same fundamental reason: the convenience of the customers.

The process which has just been described can be presented in abridged form by giving only the sequence of book transfers. This presentation simplifies matters considerably and will make them clear, if there is still any confusion in the reader's mind.

Bookkeeping of Guillaume Ruyelle

First transfer:

Dr. France de Busschere	£6 16*s*. groat
Cr. Tideman Geismar	£6 16*s*. groat

Second transfer:

Dr. Tideman Geismar	£6 16*s*. groat
Cr. Collard de Marke	£6 16*s*. groat

Bookkeeping of Collard de Marke

Third transfer:

Dr. Guillaume Ruyelle	£6 16*s*. groat
Cr. Tideman Geismar	£6 16*s*. groat

Today the debtor would simply give a check to the creditor who would endorse it and send it to his bank. The check would then be collected from the debtor's bank by way of the clearing house. The check, today, circulates in the opposite direction from the mediaeval book transfer.

It has been contended that the possibilities of a book-transfer system were rather limited without a centralized clearing system.[99] The Bruges account books do not substantiate this contention. They show that a book-transfer worked perfectly without centralized clearance if there was cooperation among the banks within the system and if they opened accounts to each other. In mediaeval Bruges specie payments within the local banking system were thus largely eliminated. This fact did not escape the attention of contemporaries who talked about 'the Exchange,' meaning the local banking and transfer system as a whole and not any exchange or bank in particular.[100]

Although mediaeval law and business practice in general favored the use of oral rather than of written orders of payment, some exceptions had to be made in dealing with public authorities or with non-resident customers. The oral order was inadequate in the one case and not feasible in the other.

It is obvious why it was not feasible to enforce the rule requiring the personal presence of the depositor in the case of customers who were out of town or even residing abroad. Non-resident depositors were frequently Hanseatic merchants who had returned to their homeland but who, for some reason or other, had left money on deposit with a money-changer or with a broker-innkeeper. The account book of Vicko van Geldersen, a merchant and cloth-dealer from Hamburg, who traded with Bruges contains a number of entries which show that assignments on money deposits in Flanders were currently bought and sold. Here is a typical entry from his account book, which is kept in a scarcely readable mixture of bad Latin and Low German:

> Heyne vamme Haghene tenetur 17 *lb.* gr. et 3 Vlamesche schilde, dat *lb.* gr. vor 5mk. et 1s., de ik em afcofte des ersten mydwekens in der vasten [March 7, 1375], unde dat is rede ghelt unde steyt by her Evert Ghudenrik.[101]

This entry tells us that, on the first Wednesday in Lent 1375, Vicko van Geldersen bought from one Heyne vamme Haghene Flemish exchange for an amount of seventeen pounds groat and three Flemish *écus* at the price of five marks and one shilling per pound groat. These pounds and these écus are said to be on deposit (*steyt*) in ready cash (*rede ghelt*) with the Bruges alderman, sire Evrard Goederic. In other words, the text clearly refers to a deposit payable on demand. The whole transaction, consequently, corresponds to the purchase of a sight draft on Bruges. The entry in the account book does not mention explicitly how Vicko van Geldersen disposed of the money assigned to him. Probably it was collected by his Bruges agent, at that time a relative named Vicko Elbeke Junior, and applied toward a purchase of Flemish cloth. Indeed, it appears from another entry on the same page of the account book that this agent sent several shipments to Hamburg about this same time.[102] Though the business of Vicko van Geldersen was by no means specialized, he was a regular importer of cloth which he sold in Hamburg both at wholesale and at retail.[103]

The fact that collections were often made by agents is further illustrated by another entry:

> Dominus Albertus de Gheldersen tenetur 20 *lb.* gr., dese rede stad by her Erverd Ghudenrik in Flanderen, de em Albert Hoyers afcofte achte daghe vor lichtmissen [January 26, 1375]. Desse 20 *lb.* gr. heft Make Screyge unfanghen.[104]

According to this entry, a certain Albert Hoyers bought from Dominus Albertus van Geldersen, a member of the Hamburg city council and a distant relative of Vicko, an amount of twenty pounds groat in Flemish money. As in the previous case, this money is said to be on deposit with Evrard Goederic, but the entry this time contains the additional statement that collection was made by Make Screyge. On the other hand, there is no mention of the price of the pound groat.

This Make Screyge, like Vicko Elbeke Junior, was van Geldersen's agent in Bruges. According to the account book, he bought cloth for the amount of £32 7*s.* 3*d.* groat and pepper for the amount of £7 14*s.* 2*d.* groat.[105] His purchases, consequently, totalled £40 1*s.* 5*d.* groat. They were paid partly with the above-mentioned twenty pounds groat and partly with another twenty pounds, payable at mid-Lent (March 29), 1375, which Vicko van Geldersen had bought from his uncle Albert Luneborch.[106] As for the remaining seventeen groats, the agènt Make Screyge paid them out of his own pocket and was later reimbursed by his principal. The only point which remains obscure in the whole transaction is the relationship in which Albert Hoyers stood toward Vicko van Geldersen. There are two possibilities: either Albert Hoyers bought the twenty pounds groat from Albert van Geldersen on his own account and resold them to Vicko, or else Hoyers simply acted as a broker between the other two. This second possibility is more likely.[107]

As these two examples clearly show, the draft on Bruges, whatever its diplomatic form, was collected in each case by someone who was the agent or the certain attorney of the assignee (the *certain commis* of French, and the *gecommitteerde* of Flemish, documents).[108] There was no need for an order clause,[109] but all the component requisites for a bill of exchange were present. At least four persons were involved: 1) the drawer, assignor, or seller of foreign exchange—Heyne vamme Haghene in one case and Dominus Albertus van Geldersen in the other; 2) the payor or drawee, the Bruges alderman Evrard Goederic; 3) the payee, Vicko van Geldersen's agent—Vicko Elbeke Jr. or Make Screyge; 4) the remittor or assignee Vicko van Geldersen, who, by remitting local currency, gave consideration for the draft or 'letter of assignment.' The transaction, it is important to note, merely involved the transfer of title to a sum of money available abroad.

Vicko van Geldersen's account book contains a number of similar entries relating to purchases of Flemish exchange, but they are more laconic and give less detailed information than the two texts which have been quoted. Only one more entry concerns Evrard Goederic.[110] Three others refer to money entrusted to one Juncvrouwe Tise in Bruges.[111] Only one of these entries presents any interest; it states that Vicko van Geldersen has twelve pounds groat on deposit with Juncvrouwe Tise, probably in his name, but the money is said to belong to one Vicko Sankenstede.[112] Juncvrouwe Tise, for all we know, might have been the landlady with whom the Hamburg merchants usually boarded when they were in Bruges. The fact that money was placed on deposit with Evrard Goederic is rather puzzling. The entries in the Hamburg account book date from 1375, but we know from other sources that Goederic withdrew from the money-changing business fourteen or fifteen years before. He is last mentioned as a money-changer in the municipal account for the fiscal year 1359-1360 (n.s.). His name is omitted two years later from another list and he has no clearing account in the Collard de Marke ledgers. The most plausible explanation is that Goederic did not retire entirely from business, but took up brokerage or trading. As we shall see, there was a tendency on the part of the Bruges innkeepers and brokers to act as cashiers for foreign merchants and thus to encroach upon the functions performed by the money-changers.

The examples just given may not be considered quite satisfactory, because we are so uncertain about the real nature of the business of Evrard Goederic and Juncvrouwe Tise at the time of the entries in Vicko van Geldersen's account book. Fortunately, there is plenty of evidence to show that money-changers outside Bruges often held deposits for non-residents.[113] This was the situation in Frankfort-on-the-Main whose fairs attracted merchants from far and wide.[114] South Germans trading with Venice not infrequently had money on deposit in the Rialto banks and paid their Venetian creditors by transfer from their bank accounts.[115] In 1485 the Antwerp money-changer Jacob van den Bloke testified before the court in Bergen-op-Zoom that he had received an amount of one hundred pounds Flemish from two merchants of Cologne in behalf of (*tot behouff van*) a John Brouck, grocer of London. The money-changer promised to pay out the said amount, either in Antwerp or in Bergen-op-Zoom, to the said John Brouck or—and this is significant—to his proxy (*gemachtigde*).[116] Not only merchants, but smaller towns sometimes had bank deposits in more important cities. In 1426 the towns of Kampen and Deventer in the dominions of the Bishop of

Utrecht had money standing to their credit at the exchange of Cologne, probably in joint account, because Kampen sent a messenger to Deventer with a proposal to transfer this money to Bruges.[117]

As Vicko van Geldersen's account book and these other examples prove, non-residents used to 'set over' or to sell their claims on money deposited abroad with a money-changer, a broker, or a host. Such assignments obviously could be implemented only by making out a draft or a written order of some kind. As far as North-Western Europe is concerned, apparently only two of such documents have come down to us. The extant specimens are not very good and have nothing to do with Bruges, but they are important because no others are known to exist. The more satisfactory of the two texts is a letter close given under seal by which a certain Henrik Knop confesses that he has received an amount of 165 marks in local currency from the money-changer Hoyger in Lübeck. In exchange the latter is to receive in Stockholm 330 marks Swedish which are said to be on deposit in ready cash with a Jacob Kron. The document dates from October 31, 1349, and is attested by two town-councillors as witnesses.[118] The second document is of 1378.[119] According to its contents a certain Hinrich Wulf of Stralsund declares to all concerned that he has sold sixty-five marks Prussian to a Johannes von der Este and requests Johannes Dyssowe of Danzig to pay this amount in cash on presentation of the letter.[120]

The two documents vary greatly in wording and from the point of view of diplomatic structure (one is a letter close, the other is a letter patent).[121] These dissimilarities prove that, in Northern Europe, commercial instruments had not yet assumed a crystallized form by the second half of the fourteenth century. In both cases there is, however, a noticeable tendency toward greater brevity. All redundant legal phraseology, so common in mediaeval charters and deeds, is left out. Another point of resemblance is that both documents take the form of a bill obligatory. Emphasis is laid, not on the request to pay, but on the maker's obligation and on the sale of exchange which motivates that request.[122]

The drawee who held the deposit was probably the drawer's partner, host, commission-agent, or correspondent. Most likely his obligation to honor the bill arose from the sale of consigned goods or from collections made in behalf of his partner, guest, principal, or fellow-merchant. It is certain that there were no banks in either Stockholm or Danzig, which in the fourteenth century were still backward business centers.

In Northern Europe business methods were still primitive as compared with those of Italy and the Mediterranean trading centers, where genuine bills of exchange and other forms of drafts were in general use by the end of the fourteenth century. Two good examples of drafts payable by money-changers rather than payable by merchant-bankers have been found: one in a Genoese, and another in a Spanish, document of the year 1392. The Genoese document is an order to pay directed by Niccolo Lomellini, temporarily residing in Savona, to the bookkeeper of the bank 'Benedetto Lomellini e Percevallo de' Vivaldi' in Genoa. The order, dated September 21, is made out in the name of one Gregorio Squarzafico and is payable on the following first of October.[123] The Spanish document is a bill of exchange drawn on October 26, 1392, for an amount of £17 10*s*. Barcelonese by Guillem de Muntbru, mintmaster of Majorca, on his colleague, a money-changer named Luques of Barcelona.[124] The bill was not payable on sight, but two months after date.

In Venice, by the beginning of the fifteenth century, some further progress had been made. The transfer banks (*banchi di scritta*) apparently encouraged their customers to make use of written assignments which were payable in bank, i.e., by book transfer (*contadi di banco*). These perhaps even circulated from hand to hand. A decree of the Senate dated September 25, 1421, put a stop to this practice. Because the banks did not keep adequate reserves behind demand deposits, the assignments were not readily convertible into cash. As a result they sold at a discount and had a depressing effect on the rates of exchange.[125]

An exception to the general use of oral contracts had also to be made in the case of dealings with public authorities. Even in the Middle Ages the principle was firmly established that public money could not be spent without a warrant signed by the city treasurer or some other responsible official. Moreover, a receipt was generally required, because public accounts were subject to audit and each item of expenditure had to be supported by an appropriate voucher. The municipal finances of the Flemish cities, for example, were placed under supervision from the end of the thirteenth century onward and accounts were rendered each year in the presence of commissioners appointed by the Count of Flanders.[126]

The Bruges money-changers were never fiscal agents of the city or of other administrative bodies, as was sometimes the practice elsewhere, chiefly where there was a municipal exchange or a publicly-owned bank.[127] A notable example is the Bank of Deposit established in Barcelona by a city ordinance of December 14, 1400.[128] This bank served as a fiscal agent for the city of Barcelona and the province of Catalonia, as well.[129] The bank was also the sole legal depositor of money which was subject to litigation or was being administered by trustees, executors, or guardians. Similar conditions prevailed in Strasbourg where the exchange was also a municipal agency.[130] In the Low Countries the *stadwissel* or 'municipal exchange' of Brussels was entrusted with the collection of the city's revenue and with the payment of most expenditures.[131] In Lille, also, the exchange was a depository of public funds.[132] The same seems to have been true in Marseilles.[133] In Italy, private bankers were sometimes entrusted with the management of public funds and an historian has recently been able to reconstruct the budget for the town of Piacenza for the fiscal year 1356-1357 from the records of a local money-changer.[134]

Although such practices were not followed in Bruges, one should not jump to the conclusion that the money-changers of this city never handled any public funds nor maintained any business relations with the local authorities. The latter sometimes needed foreign currency, when municipal officials had to go abroad on a diplomatic mission.[135] Naturally the necessary currency was supplied by the money-changers. They even occasionally made payments in behalf of the city.

In 1330 an amount of eighteen hundred pounds *parisis* or one hundred fifty pounds groat which Bruges owed to the powerful Peruzzi Company was paid by assignment on the exchange of Jan Cortscoef (*in cambio Johannis dicti Cortscoef*).[136] The transaction itself is less important than the manner in which it was carried out. The formality of the whole procedure contrasts sharply with the casualness which characterized dealings between private individuals. Jan Cortscoef evidently had to submit accounts to the city treasurers; hence the transaction had to be surrounded with all possible legal safeguards. Angelo de Montaquerelli, the local representative of the Peruzzi, was consequently requested not only to give quittance in due form, but also to prove that he had the necessary authority to act as the certain attorney of his principals. Both the receipt and the power of attorney are still preserved in the Bruges Municipal Archives. The receipt is made out directly to the two city treasurers—not to the money-changer—and is sealed with their seals and that of the Peruzzi Company—not with Montaquerelli's personal seal.[137] Apparently the presence of the two parties was still required despite the use of written documents.[138] The receipt is further attested by several witnesses and authenticated by a cleric named Jan Cramme, an apostolic and imperial notary.[139] The date is August 17, 1330. The power of attorney dates from the preceding twelfth of May. It was drafted in the city of Florence where the headquarters of the Peruzzi Company were located. The document is made out in the name of all the partners of the firm 'Tommaso dei Peruzzi & Co.' of Florence.[140] Both a general and a special power of attorney was bestowed upon Niccolo dei Peruzzi and Angelo di Montaquerelli who were given the necessary authority to represent the firm in Bruges and more especially to deal with the local municipal government. The instrument is signed by a notary public named Dino Manetti and his signature is acknowledged by the abbot of San Severino in the name of the bishop of Florence. The bishopric's seal is appended to the document by two silk cords. Public authorities, in the past as well as in the present, were not very businesslike. If a deed were required to validate each transaction in the ordinary course of business, it is clear that banking and trade would be well-nigh impossible.

The Bruges money-changers sometimes also held public funds as farmers of the excise taxes on wine, beer, and mead. These taxes were in the Middle Ages the most important single source of revenue of the Belgian municipalities.[141] In

1369 and 1370 the duties on those three commodities yielded nearly three quarters of the aggregate income of the city of Bruges.[142] The tax on wine alone represented more than fifty per cent of the total. This proportion may sound almost incredible, but it has been proved that the consumption of wine per capita was four times as great in the Middle Ages as it is today.[143]

Contrary to what one would expect, the farming of the excise taxes did not involve any advances to the city treasury. The farm did not have to be paid beforehand, but was apparently payable in installments, as the proceeds of the tax came in. This is at least the impression which one gathers from the records of Guillaume Ruyelle.

The tax on the consumption of wine—by far the most important of the excise taxes—was farmed out four times a year to the highest bidder, each time for a period of thirteen weeks. Tax-farmers were not infrequently money-changers, but other people of means also made bids. During the period from 1367 to 1372 Guillaume Ruyelle was awarded three contracts: one for the second quarter of 1367, another for the first quarter of 1368, and a third for the third quarter of 1369.[144] The money-changer Jacob Reubs had his bids accepted on four occasions during the same period. Some other successful bidders were rich brokers like Jacob Metteneye and Clais van der Beurse (or de la Bourse). A Jacob van de Walle who farmed the tax on wine for the last quarter of 1371 is mentioned in the Collard de Marke account books as a furrier.

According to the municipal accounts, Guillaume Ruyelle was the farmer of the excise duty on wine during the third quarter of the year 1369 or for thirteen weeks beginning the 3rd of July. This term is within the period covered by his ledger. Though it does not contain any explicit indication concerning this undertaking, a comparison of Ruyelle's accounts with those of the city yielded unexpected results and provided some clues which made it possible to trace the transaction.[145] It appears that Guillaume Ruyelle's cousin and assistant was in charge of the collection of the tax. He also paid the city-treasurer sire Jehan van Artrike. According to Ruyelle's ledger the total paid was £969 11*s.* groat. According to the municipal account, the city received only £929 11*s.* groat or £11,154 11*s.* 8*d.* *parisis*. The difference of forty pounds groat might very well have been a 'present' to sire Jehan van Artrike, the city treasurer. According to Ruyelle's ledger, total collections amounted to £1139 5*s.* groat. This figure less £969 11*s.* groat gives a gross profit of £169 14*s.* groat or nearly fifteen per cent. Net profit is more difficult to determine, since the ledger entries do not give any detailed information regarding the collection costs. The ledger accounts wind up with a credit balance of £23 15*s.* 9*d.* groat, which should represent net profit, if all entries were correctly made. However, as there are probably some omissions, the above figure is at best only an approximation and may even be entirely wrong. If the amount of £23 15*s.* 9*d.* groat were correct, it would show that the net profit was very low and barely exceeded two per cent of the aggregate proceeds.

In Bruges the local court frequently caused money in litigation to be deposited at the exchange and to be kept there pending the court's decision.[146] Such money evidently was impounded in a special account and could be released only by order of the court. Funds were sometimes also bailed to a money-changer in order to provide for the payment of the expenses of a lawsuit or of the charges for 'room and board' of an imprisoned debtor.[147] In case of the bankruptcy of the money-changer, it seems that the court or, in other words, the municipal government, was responsible and had to make good the loss suffered by whomever had a rightful claim to the deposit.[148]

Official business, however, remained a factor of minor importance. The Bruges money-changers, therefore, had to rely on a steady flow of private deposits. These deposits were attracted and retained because of the ease with which they were transferable and could be used as a means of payment. The effect, from the point of view of an economist, was that a circulation of bank deposits took the place of circulation of coin. This substitution probably went a considerable way, since many payments among business men were apparently made by assignment in bank.[149] The use of specie was thus reduced to a large extent. Such a condition did not pass unnoticed. In Italy, at least, the public authorities were aware of the fact that bank deposits were part of the circulating medium. As early as 1421 a Venetian document distinguishes between two kinds of money and uses the expression *contadi di banco* for bank money and *denari contadi* for coin.[150] Later one finds even the phrase *moneta di banco* which is a literal translation of 'bank money.'[151] The use of such expressions implies a clear recognition of the fact that bank deposits are money and perform the function of money.

[1]This appears from a study of Professor Robert L. Reynolds of the University of Wisconsin on a Genoese lawsuit in the year 1200 ('A Business Affair in Genoa in the Year 1200: Banking, Bookkeeping, a Broker, and a Lawsuit,' *Studi di storia e diritto in onore di Enrico Besta* [Milan, 1938], II, 167-181). This study proves the following points:

a) that it was customary for merchants to have a bank account.
b) that they could borrow from bankers on short-term by overdrawing their accounts.
c) that credit on the books of a bank was transferable.
d) that there existed some kind of inter-bank arrangement which allowed Mr. A, customer of bank X, to transfer money to the credit of Mr. B, customer of bank Y.

In my opinion the study of Professor Reynolds is of outstanding importance for the early history of banking. Margaret Winslow Hall's article ('Early Bankers in the Genoese Notarial Records,' *The Economic History Review,* VI [1935], 73-79) really does not contain conclusive evidence concerning the existence of banks in twelfth-century Genoa, although such existence may be presumed.

[2]Miss Hall admits that *bancherius* at first was synonymous with *cambitor,* money-changer, and that banks were referred to as money-changing tables, not as places for the transaction of general financial business (*op. cit.,* p. 73). Professor Usher remarks that 'In many parts of Italy, the term "banker" appears at an early date, but, unfortunately, without assured accuracy in usage' ('Origins of Banking: the Primitive Bank of Deposit, 1200-1600,' *The Economic History Review,* IV [1934], 400).

[3]See, for instance, the ordinance of December 20, 1389 (Gilliodts, *Inventaire,* III, 132). This ordinance enumerates: 'hosteliers, coulletiers, merciers, taverniers, changeurs, useriers, tafletticrs.' See also the ordinance of October 13, 1467 (*ibid.,* V, 540 f.).

[4]Margaret Hall rightly emphasizes this point (*op. cit.,* p. 73 and *passim*) and justly criticizes Monsieur Sayous for minimizing the role of the money-changer (*ibid.,* pp. 76, 78). According to Sayous, deposit banking also grew out of money-lending and the *banquiers de crédit,* rather than the money-changers, were instrumental in this development. See his article, 'Les opérations des banquiers italiens en Italie et aux foires de Champagne pendant le XIIIe siècle, *Revue historique,* CLXX (1932), 2, 6, 21. Conditions in Flanders do not bear out this theory.

[5]Regarding this custom, see, for instance, Edler, 'Accomanda,' *Glossary,* p. 20. On the knights-templars, the standard work is Léopold Delisle, *Les opérations financières des Templiers* (Paris, 1889).

[6]Sayous, 'Opérations des banquiers italiens,' *op. cit.,* p. 11.

[7]*Ibid.*

[8]The text is published in the appendix to Hénaux, 'Les banquiers liégeois au XIVe siècle,' *op. cit.,* p. 327.

[9]*Ibid.,* p. 328.

[10]*Ibid.,* p. 327.

[11]*Ibid.,* p. 328. The description given by Hénaux (*ibid.,* p. 322) concerning the procedure followed from then on, is not quite accurate.

[12]Sayous, 'Les opérations des banquiers italiens,' *op. cit.,* p. 10.

[13]Edler, *Glossary,* p. 20.

[14]Bigwood, (*Régime,* I, 430) writes: 'La situation sociale des changeurs, leur compétence particulière, la confiance qu'ils inspiraient ont amené des particuliers à leur confier des fonds. Ils estimaient avec raison qu'ils étaient plus en sûreté dans le coffre de ces spécialistes dont les locaux devaient être aménagés pour y recevoir et y conserver de la monnaie.' This was only true as long as the money-changers had not become deposit bankers. Bigwood, in general, underrates the importance of the money-changers and does not emphasize their banking activity.

[15]See Appendix No. I.

[16]Julius Landmann, 'Banking (History of Commercial),' *Encyclopaedia of the Social Sciences,* II, 427. Statements like the following by Endemann are consequently untrue: 'Depositen wurden um der Theilnahme am Gewinn willen am liebsten bei einem Wechslerbankier gemacht.' (*Studien in der romanisch-kanonistischen Wirthschafts und Rechtslehre,* I, 425).

[17]Elia Lattes, *La libertà delle banche a Venezia dal secolo* XIII al XVII (Milan, 1869), p. 120. The speech of Tommaso Contarini was pronounced on December 28, 1584, and is published *in extenso* by Lattes.

[18]*Ibid.;* cf. Sneller, 'Wisselaarsbedrijf in Nederland,' *op. cit.,* pp. 487-488. In July, 1608, the municipal authorities of Amsterdam issued an ordinance which forbade banking or *het kassiersbedrijf* altogether. The merchants immediately protested against this measure. They pointed out that they could not get along without *kassiers* or bankers for several reasons, one of them being the time wasted in counting money, if all payments were to be made in cash. See J. G. van Dillen (ed.), *Bronnen tot de geschiedenis der wisselbanken (Amsterdam, Middelburg, Delft, Rotterdam)* [The Hague: Nijhoff, 1925], Part I, p. 15, No. 18: Request dated between July 12 and July 29, 1608.

[19]E. Lattes, *op. cit.,* p. 120. Contarini uses this very expression: '. . . et siccome col mezzo del banco, in un momento nel qual si muove la penna sopra i libri, si satisfa al comprador et al venditor. . . .'

[20]*Ibid.*

[21]Cf. Letts, *op. cit.,* p. 22.

[22]This cadaster has been published in full by Gilliodts ('Les registres des "Zestendeelen",' *op. cit.*). According to his text, the number of houses is given separately for each district:

District of St. John	1,055 houses
District of St. Donatian	1,362
District of Notre Dame	1,672
District of St. James	1,824
District of St. Nicholas	1,397
Scarmers	818
Outside the walls	207
Total number of houses	8,335

The estimate of 8,400 allows for a certain amount of duplication due to the fact that some houses built in courtyards have the same number as those fronting on the street.

[23]Jos De Smet, 'L'effectif des milices brugeoises et la population de la ville en 1340,' *RBPH,* XII (1933), 636. The estimate of Häpke (*op. cit.,* p. 175) who sets the total population at 50,000 is probably too high.

[24]Appendix No. I. The first list actually contains twenty-seven names, but one of them, Jan Moens, is a money-changer. His name should therefore be dropped from the list for this purpose. The second list has eighteen, including three money-changers, which reduces the number of depositors to fifteen.

[25]See de Roover, 'Ruyelle,' *op. cit.,* pp. 92-95, doc. No. 7. The list of debit balances includes 28 items, but items 2, 20, 23, 24, 27 should be dropped because they certainly do not relate to customers' accounts.

[26]See Appendix No. III.

[27]See Collard de Marke Journal No. 2.

[28]*Ibid.*

[29]The author has made out a filing card for every account in this ledger and his collection contains about 1100 cards.

[30]Lane, 'Venetian Bankers,' *op. cit.,* pp. 189-190.

[31]The rector of St James, one of the Bruges parish churches (*Mesire Curet de Saint Jakes*), even had a bank account. See Collard de Marke Ledger No. 3, fol. 7.

[32]de Roover, 'Ruyelle,' *op. cit.,* pp. 93-94. The total given on p. 94 is £946 17*s.* groat, but item 61 amounting to £3 2*s.* 6*d.* should be subtracted.

[33]*Ibid.*, pp. 94-95. The figure of £69 2*s.* 2*d.* is obtained as follows:

	£	s	d	£	s	d
Total debit balances				661	14	10
Deduct:						
No. 27 Item folio	562	14	6			
No. 2 Williame Ruyelle	8	10	3			
No. 20 Medimysele	9	5	9			
No. 23 Hannekin Ruwel	6	0	0			
No. 24 Medimyselle	6	2	2	592	12	8
Total				69	2	2

[34]de Roover, 'Ruyelle,' *op. cit.*, p. 79, Table No. 10.
[35]Collard de Marke, Ledger No. 4, fol. 112:

Les Grands Cahorsins

Dr.	Cr.
Les grans Caoursins par Jakoppe Reups 7 en march....£29 1*s.* 4*d.*	doy par Conrart Boin Adone 5 en march...........£29 1*s.* 4*d.*

The corresponding entry in Jacob Reubs' account (Ledger No. 4, fol. 310, Cr.) reads as follows: 'Item par les grans lonbars 7 en march £29 1*s.* 4*d.*' These entries prove that *Grans Caoursins* and *Grans Lombars* had the same meaning. The fact that the lombards of Bruges had an account with the money-changer Jacob Reups is confirmed by a document published by Bigwood (*Régime,* II, 352). The estate of the lombard Jacques Maucegas, which escheated to count of Flanders in 1363, included an amount of £332 groat placed on deposit at the exchange of Jacob Reups ('lesquels lis dis lombards rechevoient et comptoient sur le change Jacop Reubz'). Bigwood (*ibid.*, I, 316) writes erroneously '. . . investis dans l'office du changeur Jacques Reubs.' This statement should be emended to read *déposés au change de Jacques Reubs*. It is unlikely that the lombards were partners of Jacob Reubs.
[36]Collard de Marke Ledger No. 4, fol. 98:

Jehan Diese de Castille, mestre de naves

Dr.	Cr.
Jehan Diese, mestre de naves me doit que je li fay conte ou fuellet 126........... 15 *lb.* 8*s.*11*d.*	fol. 98 doy par Lukin de Karle 21 en février........... 15 *lb.* 8*s.*11*d.*
Jehan Diese de Castille me doit par Jehan Senches de Liseguere à l'ostel Sire Jakoppe Matenaie 17 en march.............. 30 *lb.* gr. Et par lui contet à ce jour.. 5 *lb.* 8*s.*11*d.*	fol. 125v [126] doy par Abram Parvesin 16 en march.............. 20 *lb.* gr. Et par Lukin de Karle dou fuellet 98............ 15 *lb.* 8*s.*11*d.*

[37]To use the terminology of Professor Gras, the Hanseatic merchants were still in the traveling stage, while the Italians had already reached the sedentary stage of mercantile capitalism. See Gras, *Business and Capitalism,* chap. II, pp. 27-66, and chap. III, pp. 67-119. On this same topic, the reader should also consult the important study of Gunnar Mickwitz, 'L'economia medievale nei paesi baltici e nei paesi mediterranei,' *Rivista internazionale di scienze sociali,* XLVI (1938), 813-824.

[38]This is not necessarily true if one single money-changer is considered, but applies to the exchange as a whole (the local system of exchange-banks).

[39]These are a few of Collard de Marke's principal customers:
Native Merchants: Sire Jacques de Visch, Jan van den Vagheviere, Sire Jehan Bonin [burgo-

master of Bruges], Conrart Boin Adone, Jehan Bregelay (Briselaye), Sire Jehan Makaire, Bauduin van Assenede.

Brokers-Innkeepers: Sire Jakemes Matenaie (Metteneye?), Medimyselle de Rudevorde, Jakoppe van le Fine, Raoul Doucemin (de Coumines), Ernout Poultus, Jehan van der Leke, demiselle Isoie.

Drapier: Willem van de Neke.

Furrier: Jehan van de Walle.

Goldsmith: Jehan de Courtrai.

Italians: Nicolas Ammanati, Dimenche Cucul (Zondaghe de Florentijn), Sire Tiram Enperial Jakemon Fabe, Lucadine, Forteguerre, Lukin de Karle, Hanebaut Lommelin, Dine Malapris, Otebon de Marin, Barde Menchine, Marco Morosini [Venetian], Galigo da Piastre, Jehan de Priolle, Willaume Raiponde, Lois Robiert, Thumas Sarlande, Pierre Scandillon, Aubiert Spingle (Spinelli), Davin Tedaldin, Pierre Teste. This Dimenche Cucul's real name was probably Domenico Cocchi.

[40]Rudolf Häpke, *Der deutsche Kaufmann in den Niederlanden* ('Pfingstblätter des Hansischen Geschichtsvereins' [Leipzig, 1911]), p. 10: '. . . mit der Zeit wurde es freilich auch üblich, den Barvorrat "in den Wechsel" zu legen, d. h. bei einer der zahlreichen Banken arbeiten zu lassen.'

[41]This phrase 'by writings only' is found in Thomas Mun, *England's Treasure by Forraign Trade* (London, 1664), chap. IV, p. 42. (Also reprinted by the Economic History Society [Oxford: Basil Blackwell, 1933], pp. 16-17.) In Venice, to transfer credit on the books of the banks was called *scrivere e girare in banco.* See G. Luzzatto, 'Les banques publiques de Venise (siècles XVI-XVIII),' in *History of the Principal Public Banks,* ed. by J. G. van Dillen (The Hague, 1934), p. 41.

[42]I have emphasized this point from the very first, as far back as 1929, when I started working on the Collard de Marke account books. See de Roover, 'Les livres de comptes de Collard de Marke,' *op. cit.,* p. 30, and 'Guillaume Ruyelle,' *op. cit.,* p. 29; Carman, 'Flemish Accounting of the Fourteenth Century,' *op. cit.,* p. 117.

[43]Espinas, *La vie urbaine de Douai,* II, 157.

[44]*Ibid.,* III, 70, *pièce just.* No. 100, art. 1, 2.

[45]*Ibid.,* art. 3.

[46]Usher, 'The Origins of Banking,' *op. cit.,* pp. 410 ff. The oral contract has been mentioned casually by several historians, but none of them have seen its full importance as clearly as Professor Usher. See Goldschmidt, *Universalgeschichte des Handelsrechts,* p. 324; Sieveking, *Die Casa di San Giorgio,* p. 46 [330] (S. talks about an oral or a written order); André-E. Sayous, 'Les opérations des banquiers de Gênes á la fin du XIIe siècle,' *Annales de droit commercial français, étranger et international,* XLIII (1934), 291, 295; Luzzatto 'Les banques publiques de Venise,' *op. cit.,* p. 41; Lane, 'Venetian Bankers,' *op. cit.,* p. 190; Emmanuel Vogel, 'Der Giralverkehr in den oberitalienischen und den deutschen Handelszentren bis zum ausgehenden Mittelalter,' *VSWG,* XXXI (1938), 3.

[47]Reynolds, 'A Business Affair in Genoa,' *op. cit.,* pp. 170-171.

[48]That the money-changers at the fairs of Champagne were Italians is clearly established by a document published by Bigwood, *Régime,* II, 302. This document mentions the following money-changers: Rochin Bonnenseigne (Buoninsegna), Renier Compain (Compagni), Renier dou Pas (Pazzi)—all of Florence.

[49]Bourquelot, *Etudes sur les foires de Champagne,* pp. 300, 352-354.

[50]This expression is used by Gerard de Malynes, *Consuetudo vel lex mercatoria or the Ancient Law-Merchant* (London, 1622), p. 335.

[51]I owe this information to the kindness of Dr. Elizabeth Chapin Furber, author of *Les villes des foires de Champagne des origines au début du XIVe siècle* (Paris, 1937).

[52]Usher, 'The Origins of Banking,' *op. cit.,* p. 416.

[53]It is doubtful whether the written orders of assignment published by Bensa (*Francesco di Marco da Prato,* pp. 352-358) should be considered as real checks. Treasury orders, war-

rants, and similar documents issued by public authorities clearly cannot be considered as such. Real checks do not appear before the late sixteenth century. Goldschmidt (*op. cit.*, p. 326) gives the text of several early examples. Cf. Ernst Ludwig Jäger, *Die ältesten Banken und der Ursprung des Wechsels* (Stuttgart, 1879), p. 21.

[54]Elia Lattes, *op. cit.*, p. 91, n. 8.

[55]*Ibid.*, p. 107, Project of a statute for the first public bank in Venice, December 28, 1584.

[56]*Ibid.*, p. 113 (decree of April 11, 1587).

[57]Charles F. Dunbar, 'The Bank of Venice,' *QJE*, VI (1892), 389.

[58]van Dillen, *Bronnen*, Part I, p. 1, No. 2, Ordinance of June 2, 1604. The same prohibition was renewed on July 12, 1608 (*ibid.*, p. 12, No. 14) and on June 4, 1621 (*ibid.*, p. 47).

[59]This was already so in thirteenth-century Genoa. See Raffaele Di Tucci, *Studi sull'economia genovese del secolo decimosecondo: la banca privata* (Turin, 1933), p. 120: 'Ma già la polizza, o *charta*, almeno per le riscossioni dirette nel banco, non era necessaria, ed era sufficiente, per l'accertamento di un debito o di un credito, l'annotazione sul cartulario.'

[60]Paciolo, *op. cit.*, fol. 206: 'E pero è da notar che con lo bancho te poi communamente impaciare da te; ponendovi denari per piu tua sigureçça, overo, per modo de deposito a la giornata, poter con quelsi far tuoi pagamenti chiari a Piero, Giovanni, e Martino, *perchè la ditta del bancho è comme publico istrumento de notaro, perchè son per li dominii ascigurati* . . .' [italics mine]. Paciolo refers to Venice, but the same was true of Genoa (Sieveking, *Casa di San Giorgio*, p. 47 [331]), and of most Italian cities (Usher, 'Origins of Banking,' *op. cit.*, p. 410, n. 3).

[61]Thomas de Castellino, the bookkeeper of the Bank of St. George, called himself 'notary and bookkeeper of the bank, (*notarius et scriba*). The same was true of the bookkeepers of private banks. See Sieveking, *Casa di San Giorgio*, p. 47 [331], n. 1. By way of comparison, the projected statutes of the Banco di San Ambrosio in Milan (1593) also provided that the same credence should be given to the books of the bank as to notarial instruments (Jäger, *op. cit.*, p. 42). In Barcelona, too, the journals of the public bank, established in 1401, were kept by notaries (Usher, 'The Origins of Banking,' *op. cit.*, p. 411).

[62]Alberto Tofani, *Alcune ricerche storiche sull'ufficio e la professione di ragioniere a Firenze al tempo della repubblica* (Florence, 1910), p. 43.

[63]Usher, 'Origins of Banking,' *op. cit.*, p. 411.

[64]Gandi, *op. cit.*, p. 97. In Venice, as early as 1348, a money-changer who was guilty of tearing out leaves from his journal was debarred from the practice of his profession (Elia Lattes, *op. cit.*, pp. 29-30).

[65]Notaries had made their appearance in Flanders as early as the thirteenth century. Although this new institution spread rapidly—in Bruges there was a notary from 1304 onward—it did not assume an importance comparable to that which it enjoyed in Italy. Notaries in the Low Countries were clerics and derived whatever authority they had from imperial and apostolic commissions. The main function of these early notaries was to prepare diplomas and other official documents. H. Nélis, 'Les origines du notariat public en Belgique [1269-1320],' *RBPH*, II (1923), 267-277 and Jean Yernaux, 'Les notaires publics du XIIIe au XVIe siècle, spécialement au Franc de Bruges,' *Bulletin de la Commission Royale d'Histoire*, LXXXII (1913), 111-82. Yernaux points out that, according to the rules, only unmarried clerics in the minor orders were eligible to the office of notary: in fact, most Bruges notaries were priests.

[66]This is a general impression which one gets by going through the two volumes of Gilliodts-van Severen's *Cartulaire de l'Estaple*. On several occasions, foreign and native merchants were consulted on trade customs.

[67]M. M. Postan, 'Private Financial Instruments in Medieval England,' *VSWG*, XXIII (1930), p. 71.

[68]See Appendix No. I.

[69]Paciolo, *op. cit.*, distinctio 9, tractatus 11, fol. 206.

[70]Sieveking, *Casa di San Giorgio*, p. 46 [330]; Vogel, *op. cit.*, p. 3; Usher, 'The Origins of Banking,' *op. cit.*, p. 411.

[71]Sieveking has to admit this fact in a footnote, but it is not clear why he states in the text that the rule was effective (*Casa di San Giorgio*, p. 46, n. 5).

[72]Genoa, State Archives, *Registri Bancheriorum*, sala 24. This room contains several journals or *manualia*—not only one, as is stated erroneously by Alessandro Lattes—an almost complete series of cashbooks from 1390 to 1433, and one earlier volume for the year 1386.

[73]Alessandro Lattes, 'Gli antichi registri dei banchieri genovesi,' *Rivista del dirritto commerciale*, XVII[1] (1919), 616. Moreover, I had an opportunity to examine the Lomellini material during a visit to Genoa in 1938.

[74]See Sieveking, *Casa di San Giorgio*, p. 46, n. 5.

[75]This is a general impression based on the fact that I myself have been able to compare the Bruges with the Genoese material.

[76]Sieveking (*Casa di San Giorgio*, p. 46, n. 5) gives a good example of such an entry relating to a transfer of twenty lire from the account of Cristoforo Cataneo (assignor) to that of Juliano de Ventimilia (assignee). The journal entry reads as follows: 'Christoferus Cataneus pro Juliano de Ventimilia £20.' Examples from the Collard de Marke journals will be given in the next pages.

[77]Collard de Marke Journal No. 2, fol. 7.

[78]Collard de Marke Ledger No. 4, fol. 38. See Appendix No. II, Account 19.

[79]Collard de Marke Journal No. 2, fol. 109.

[80]Collard de Marke Ledger No. 4, fol. 124. See Appendix No. II, Account 18.

[81]*Ibid.*, fol. 79, account of Willaume Raiponde: 'Willaume Raiponde me doit—Et par sen compaignon contet 25 en février.' See Appendix No. II (17). Cf. Journal No. 2, fol. 7, December 27, 1368: 'Pierre Rougenelle me doit par Dimenche sen compaignon contet.' See Appendix No. III.

[82]Collard de Marke Ledger No. 5, fol. 385, account of Willem Ruyelle.

[83]Collard de Marke Journal No. 2, fol. 7. See Appendix No. III.

[84]Collard de Marke Ledger No. 4, fol. 26.

[85]de Roover, 'Ruyelle,' *op. cit.*, p. 78, Table No. 9.

[86]Collard de Marke Journal No. 2, March 28, 1369, fol. 82.

[87]Collard de Marke Ledger No. 4, fol. 79. See Appendix No. II, Account 17.

[88]*Ibid.*, fol. 124. See Appendix II, Account 18.

[89]de Roover, 'Ruyelle,' *op. cit.*, pp. 34-36. The assumption made in these pages that there must have existed some kind of written document circulating by indorsement is, of course, entirely wrong. While preparing my Ruyelle study, I was greatly puzzled by some of the entries, as I did not know about Professor Usher's work and the existence of oral, instead of written, commands to pay.

[90]For the supporting evidence, see *ibid.*, p. 75, Table No. 6, and p. 79, Table No. 10.

[91]The following money-changers all have accounts in Ledger No. 2: (1) Pietre d'Oudenarde, (2) Jehan de Courtray, (3) Jehan van Donc, (4) Jehan Eurle, (5) Jehan van Marc (6) Estievenes van dre Miers (Steven van der Meersch), (7) Jehan Mons (Moens), (8) Pietre le Potre, (9) Stasin Quatouc, (10) le demisielle Rapesart, (11) Jakoppe Reups, (12) Jakemes de Rouc, (13) Willaume Ruyelle, (14) le demisielle de Witte. Note that the list includes two women.

The following money-changers have accounts in Ledger No. 4: (1) Pietre d'Oudenarde, (2) Jehan van Donc, (3) Jehan Eurle, (4) Jehan van Marc, (5) Estievene van dre Miers, (6) Jehan Moriel, le cangeur, (7) Pietre le Potre, (8) le demiselle Rapesart, (9) Clais Rapesart, (10) Jehan Reups, (11) Jakoppe Reups, (12) Jakes de Rouc, (13) Willem Ruyelle, (14) le demiselle de Witte.

[92]This method was certainly *not always* used, as Emmanuel Hugo Vogel ('Der Giralverkehr im Mittelalter,' *op. cit.*, p. 4) seems to imply.

[93]Collard de Marke Ledger No. 4, fol. 320. See Appendix No. II, Account 12.

[94]Two corresponding accounts have been published twice: once by de Roover, 'Ruyelle,'

op. cit., p. 70; and the second time by Carman, 'Flemish Accounting of the Fourteenth Century,' *op. cit.*, p. 122.

[95]Wilhelm Koppe, *Lübeck-Stockholmer Handelsgeschichte im 14. Jahrhundert* ('Abhandlungen zur Handels-und Seegeschichte,' Vol. II, Neumünster in Holstein, 1933), pp. 132, 136, 194-195, 235, 250; Collard de Marke Ledger No. 4, fols. 26v and 84.

[96]de Roover, 'Ruyelle,' *op. cit.*, pp. 30-31 and 72, Table No. 3, for the accounts of France de Busschere and Tideman Geismar.

[97]*Ibid.*, p. 70, Table No. 1, and Carman, *op. cit.*, pp. 117, 122.

[98]de Roover, 'Ruyelle,' *op. cit.*, p. 69.

[99]J. G. van Dillen, 'De girobanken van Genua, Venetië en Hamburg,' *Tijdschrift voor Geschiedenis*, XLII (1927), 36.

[100]In Bruges it was common to talk about money placed on deposit 'at the exchange' *(in den wissele)*. See Bigwood, *Régime*, I, 432; Gilliodts, *Coutume*, I, 517; and Sneller, 'Het wisselaarsbedrijf in Nederland,' *op. cit.*, p. 496, No. 2. In Dutch the expression *leggen in cambio* was used, which is the same as the Flemish *leggen in den wissel* (*ibid.*, p. 497). The Liége statute of January 1315 (n.s.) talks about *la cange de la cité de Liege*, although there were certainly several exchange offices (Hénaux, *op. cit.*, p. 327). The officials of the brotherhood *(frairie)* were significantly called 'the masters of the exchange' *(li maistres delle cambge)* (*ibid.*, p. 328). In Italy *pagare in banco* was a commonly used expression.

[101]*Das Handlungsbuch Vickos von Geldersen*, p. 106, item 684.

[102]*Ibid.*, item 688.

[103]*Ibid.*, p. xxv. Vicko van Geldersen was called a *Wandschneider* or cloth-dealer.

[104]*Ibid.*, pp. 92-93, item 563.

[105]*Ibid.*, item 560. Make Screyge became later an important merchant. In 1386 he entered the Hamburg city-council. He was elected burgomaster in 1390 and died in 1419 (*ibid.*, p. 36, n. 10).

[106]The text of this entry is as follows: 'Luneborch tenetur 20*lb.* gr., de ik em cofte to twelften [Epiphany, January 6, 1375], tho mydvasten [March 29, 1375] to betalende. Dese 20*lb.* heft Make Screyge unfanghen.' (*Ibid.*, p. 92, item 562.) The editor gives erroneously the first of April as the date for Mid-Lent 1375 (*ibid.*, p. 92, n. 9).

[107]It is possible that Albert Hoyers was a brother-in-law of Albertus van Geldersen, who was the husband of a Tybbe Hoyeri (*ibid.*, p. xiii). Albert Hoyers himself became a member of the Hamburg city-council (*ibid.*, p. 45, n. 9). He was in close relations with Vicko van Geldersen and at least once acted as his agent in Flanders (*ibid.*, p. 110, items 714 and 715). Both were creditors of the dukes Wenceslas and Albert of Saxony and Lüneburg and of the duke Bernhard of Brunswick and Lüneburg (*ibid.*, pp. 185-186, Appendix item 1).

[108]Cf. André-E. Sayous, 'L'histoire universelle du droit commercial de Levin Goldschmidt et les méthodes commerciales des pays chrétiens de la Méditerranée aux XIIe et XIIIe siècles,' *Annales de droit commercial français, étranger et international*, 1931, p. 320; Brunner, 'Brügger Schöffensprüche zur Geschichte des Wechselrechts im fünfzehnten Jahrhundert,' *op. cit.*, p. 13. In Latin documents one often finds the expression *certus missus* or *nuncius*.

[109]If necessary, it could be replaced by a power of attorney.

[110]*Handlungsbuch Vickos von Geldersen*, p. 104, item 665.

[111]*Ibid.*, p. 92, item 561; p. 103, item 648; p. 104, item 667.

[112]*Ibid.*, p. 104, item 667.

[113]Collard de Marke had a great many foreign customers, but it is impossible to tell from his records whether or not they were residing in Bruges.

[114]Kriegk, *op. cit.*, p. 339.

[115]Heinrich Sieveking, 'Aus venetianischen Handlungsbüchern: ein Beitrag zur Geschichte des Grosshandels im 15. Jahrhundert,' (Schmoller's) *Jahrbuch für Gesetzgebung, Verwaltung und Volkswirtschaft im Deutschen Reich*, XXVI (1902), 200.

[116]Sneller, 'Het Wisselaarsbedrijf in Nederland,' *op. cit.*, p. 497, n. 3.

[117]*Ibid.*, p. 497.

[118]Max Neumann, 'Geschichte des Wechsels im Hansagebiet bis zum 17. Jahhundert,' supplement to *Zeitschrift für das gesammte Handelsrecht,* VII [Erlangen, 1863]), p. 119. Neumann publishes the following text: 'Ik, Hinrik Knop, bekenne des, dat ik hebbe upgheboret unde entfangen van Hoygere Wesselere hundert unde vive unde sestich mark an lubescheme pagimente, dar he wedder vore entfangen schal tho deme Stockholme drehundert mark unde dertech mark zwedesch in alsodaneme pagimente also dar ghenge unde gheve is. Dit vor benamede gelt schal eme bereden Jacob Kron van den seshundert unde sestich marken de ik, Hinrik Knop, unde Alvin van deme Stene van eme koften; tughe desser dink sint her Johan Plescowe unde her Seghebode Crispin, rathmanne; ghegheven an dem jare Godes 1349, in deme hilghen avende Alle Godes Hilghen. . . .'

[119]*Ibid.*, p. 122. As date Neumann gives 1328 in the document, but 1378 in the reference. The later date is probably correct.

[120]*Ibid.*, p. 122. 'Wythlich sy alle den ghuden luden de dessen bref sen adder horen lesen, dat ich, Hinrich Wulf, to Demezunde [Stralsund] hebe vorcroft eneme erbarn manne vorbenamet Johannes von der Este alse vele alse 65 mark prusch de schal eme antworden Johannes Dyssowe un bedde jo leve um dat jy dessen man to entrechten alse vort wanner he dar cumt; wente ic hebbe alse mit eme aufslosset dat hy det gheld rede vinden schal, to ever bewysinghe un tho ever betuchnisse so hebbe ic min ingheseghel vor dessen bref ghehanghen, schreve to Demesunde 1378.'

[121]This seems to suggest that the letter under seal tended to displace the more formal letter patent. Later the letter close itself was to give way before the informal letter missive.

[122]On the importance of this point, see Freundt, *op. cit.*, I, 64-77.

[123]Sieveking, *Casa di San Giorgio*, p. 235 [519], Appendix III, item 1.

[124]André-S. Sayous, 'Les méthodes commerciales de Barcelone au XIVe siécle, surtout d'après des protocoles inédits de ses archives notariales,' *Estudis universitaris catalans,* XVIII (1933), 234-235, Appendixes I and J. The text is also given in another article of Sayous, 'Les méthodes commerciales de Barcelone au XVe siècle,' *Revue historique de droit français et étranger*, 4th series, XV (1936), 277.

[125]The text of the decree which was published by Elia Lattes (*op. cit.*, pp. 47-50) is very obscure and confusing. Contrary to the editor's assertions (*ibid.*, pp. 50 f.), it is not clear from the text whether the *contadi di banco* were certificates of deposit issued by the *banchi di scritta* or assignments made out by the depositors. Cf. Alessandro Lattes, *Il diritto commerciale nella legislazione statutaria,* p. 206; Edler, 'Contado di Banco,' *Glossary,* pp. 85-86; Erwin Nasse, 'Das venetianische Bankwesen im 14., 15. und 16. Jahrhundert,' (Conrad's) *Jahrbücher für Nationalökonomie und Statistik,* XXXIV (1879), 337. The text of the decree of 1421 makes better sense if compared with the provisions of the decree of November 26, 1526, 'ordinationes circa bancos a scripta,' arts. 5, 12, 13, and 16 (E. Lattes, *op. cit.*, pp. 90-92). The purpose of both the decree of 1421 and the one of 1526 was to prevent the depreciation of bank money and the existence of a premium *(lazo)* on cash. See Edler, 'Lazo,' *Glossary,* p. 151.

[126]van Werveke, *De Gentsche Stadsfinanciën,* pp. 67 f.

[127]'Municipal exchange' *(stadwissel)* does not necessarily mean public ownership. In Brabant, it was simply a title given to the exchange which handled the municipal business and was exempt from certain taxes. In Strasbourg, on the contrary, the *Stadtwechsel* was a public agency.

[128]Usher, 'Banking in Barcelona,' *op. cit.*, p. 132, and *Early History,* I, 270.

[129]*Ibid.*, pp. 134-5.

[130]Cahn, 'Der Strassburger Stadtwechsel,' *op. cit.*, pp. 44-65.

[131]Bigwood, *Régime,* I, 404: 'Jusqu'en 1503 la ville confiait à un changeur qu'elle désignait à cet effet et qui devait être cautionné par des bourgeois, les revenus de Bruxelles. On payait également à son change les amendes judiciaires.'

[132]Benoit, 'Le "Beauregard" de Lille,' *op. cit.*, p. 17.

[133]André-E. Sayous, 'Les transferts de risques, les associations commerciales et la lettre de

change à Marseille pendant le XIVe siècle,' *Revue historique de droit français et étranger*, 4th series, XIV (1935), 491.

[134]Tommaso Zerbi *La banca nell'ordinamento finanziario visconteo, dai mastri del banco Giussano, gestore della tesoreria di Piacenza, 1356-1358* (Como, 1935), p. 118.

[135]Gilliodts, *Cartulaire de l'Estaple*, I, 183, No. 244.

[136]Gilliodts, *Inventaire*, I, 423.

[137]*Ibid.*, I, 423, No. 347.

[138]Usher, 'The Origins of Banking,' *op. cit.*, pp. 418 f.

[139]Jan Cramme is listed among the notaries doing business in Bruges during the fourteenth century. See Yernaux, *op. cit.*, p. 161.

[140]Gilliodts, *Inventaire*, I, 422, No. 347. This partnership was formed on November 1, 1324. The list of partners included in the power of attorney corresponds to the one given by Sapori, 'Storia interna della compagnia mercantile dei Peruzzi,' *op. cit.*, p. 22.

[141]de Roover, 'Ruyelle,' *op. cit.*, p. 42, n. 1. Cf. van Werveke, *Gentsche Stadsfinanciën*, p. 219.

[142]de Roover, 'Ruyelle,' p. 43, n. 2.

[143]Hans van Werveke, 'Le commerce des vins français au moyen-âge,' *RBPH*, XII (1933), 1100; de Roover, 'Ruyelle,' *op. cit.*, p. 44.

[144]*Ibid.*, pp. 89 f., doc. No. 4.

[145]Full evidence based on the figures of Ruyelle's ledger and of the municipal accounts will be found *ibid.*, pp. 46-52.

[146]Bigwood, *Régime*, I, 432; Gilliodts, *Coutume*, I, 517 and *Cart. de l'Estaple*, II, 448, No. 1422, March 29, 1514.

[147]*Ibid.*, II, 178 f., No. 1120, December 9, 1468.

[148]*Ibid.*, II, 448, No. 1422.

[149]This expression is used by Gerard de Malynes, *Consuetudo vel lex mercatoria or the Ancient Law-Merchant*, p. 335.

[150]Usher, 'The Origins of Banking,' *op. cit.*, p. 400.

[151]Luzzatto, 'Les banques publiques à Venise,' *op. cit.*, p. 41. Adam Smith also used the expression 'bank money' in the meaning of credit on the books of a public bank such as the banks of Amsterdam, Hamburg, Venice, and Genoa. He made a distinction between 'bank money' and 'the common currency of the country' or coin. See Adam Smith, *The Wealth of Nations* (New York: The Modern Library, 1937), Book IV, chap. iii, pp. 445 f.

Chapter 14

LOANS AND INVESTMENTS

BY organizing a system of payments which was, in most cases, more expedient than the slow telling of imperfect coins, the money-changers performed a service of outstanding usefulness to the business community. They apparently received no compensation for this service, although it entailed additional expenses which were far from negligible. These expenses had to be met in one way or another. Money-changers could only do so by finding an income-yielding use for some of the money entrusted to their care, but they had to keep enough cash on hand to avoid being short of funds in case of unforeseen and sudden withdrawals. This principle is called the fractional reserve principle and is still today the 'ABC' of commercial banking.

Bank management largely consists in putting into effect a policy which conforms to this guiding principle. Managerial problems, consequently, arise only in connection with the making of loans and investments. Accepting deposits and making transfers are not transactions which give rise to any managerial problems. The role of the banker remains purely passive and consists merely in the carrying out of instructions given by his customers, largely a routine procedure which can easily be delegated to an employee, as the job requires only a knowledge of bookkeeping and some proficiency in simple arithmetic. As we have seen, the mediaeval money-changers were sensible enough to leave to their staff all the clerical work. They themselves were thus free to turn their attention to the managerial problems arising from their loans and investments policy.

How to use the resources which the depositors placed at the money-changer's disposal was the most important problem. Such a problem exists whenever and wherever banks operate on a fractional reserve principle. This problem does not exist, of course, in the case of a public bank which operates with a one hundred per cent cash reserve—like the Bank of Amsterdam in its early years—or which is restrained from making any loans to private individuals, but has to invest all its excess reserves in the public debt. A good example of a bank of the latter type is the municipal bank of Barcelona, formally opened for business in January, 1401.[1]

As the money-changers of Bruges kept only part of their liabilities in cash and, consequently, operated on a fractional reserve principle, they had to manage their business in such a way that they neither became insolvent nor ran out of cash. Insolvency arises from bad loans and poor investments with the result that assets no longer cover liabilities. The bank is no longer able to pay its debts and goes bankrupt. Inasmuch as most liabilities are demand obligations, insufficiency of cash is often due to lack of liquidity, that is to say, in an emergency assets are tied up and cannot promptly be converted into cash. Insufficiency of cash may also be due to over-expansion of credit so that the reserve has been allowed to fall dangerously low. Whatever the cause of the trouble, insufficiency of cash, if acute, must lead either to bankruptcy or to a more or less prolonged suspension of specie payments.

The purpose of this chapter is to examine how our Bruges money-changers tried to cope with this crucial problem of finding a suitable use for the financial resources which were at their disposal. It should be realized that personal ability is not the only factor to be considered. Other factors beyond the individual's control also deserve consideration. The mediaeval credit structure had serious flaws. We should, therefore, be aware of the fact that several avenues open today were closed to the banker in the Middle Ages.

Credit can be extended and investments made according to different methods. These methods vary considerably between the United States and Europe, and differences are still greater between the practices of today and those of the Middle Ages. In order to avoid any confusion or misunderstanding, it appears necessary to clarify a number of concepts.[2]

The method of extending credit against interest-bearing promissory notes is distinctly an American practice which is unknown in Europe. As this practice was probably also unknown in the Middle Ages, it does not have to be considered here. In Europe, on the other hand, credit is often extended by discounting commercial paper and by writing the net proceeds to the credit of the borrower's account. Under certain conditions such paper can be rediscounted at the central bank. In the Middle Ages, however, there were no central banks and no facilities for rediscounting. Moreover, the lack of negotiable instruments, as we have seen, was a serious gap in the mediaeval credit structure. While the bill of exchange was not unknown, it was not endorsable and involved speculation on the exchange.[3] If the account books of Collard de Marke and Guillaume Ruyelle are reliable guides, the Bruges money-changers, as a matter of fact, did not speculate on the exchange and had no correspondents abroad.

The overdraft, which is regarded with some disfavor in the United States, is, on the contrary, quite popular on the other side of the Atlantic. European bankers are in the habit of granting a line of credit (*ouverture de crédit*) to their customers who are thus allowed to overdraw their accounts up to a stated limit. In Europe an overdraft (*avance en compte courant*) may be secured by collateral or even by a mortgage on the borrower's real property. A perusal of the Collard de Marke and Guillaume Ruyelle ledgers indicates that they contain a good many overdrawn accounts. Also in mediaeval Italy[4] and in Barcelona[5] the overdraft seems to have been the usual way in which bankers extended credit to their customers; only the Bank of St George in Genoa and, presumably, the private bankers of that city followed a different system, which, as far as we know, is without parallel elsewhere. In the ledgers of the Bank of St George there are two sets of accounts: the *rationes ad numeratum* or current accounts for all obligations subject to call and the *rationes temporum* to which were posted all entries relating to items not immediately due or collectible.[6] Credit was often created by debiting a *ratio temporum* and crediting a *ratio ad numeratum* with the same amount. Thus a claim maturing at some future date was the counterpart of a debt falling due immediately. Some of the loans granted in this way were secured by *loca* or shares in the Compere of St George, the association of state creditors.[7] If such a loan was not repaid at the appointed time, the *loca* would be forfeited. The transaction might be considered as a remote ancestor of the modern time loan. The Genoese system gave rise to other types of loans;[8] but a thorough discussion of this topic lies outside the scope of our inquiry. The case of Genoa shows, at any rate, that allowance should be made for regional differences.

The overdraft differs from other loans in that the obligation of the debtor is determined by the debit balance of his account in the bank's ledger. In the Middle Ages no other documents or supporting vouchers were necessary, as no entry in the books of the bank could be made without the customer being present or represented by his lawful attorney.[9] The only prerequisite was the banker's willingness to let the customer overdraw his account. Otherwise entries would be made in the usual form as described before.[10]

The most serious disadvantage of the overdraft is that it is not a self-liquidating loan, but may stay open on the books for an indefinite period of time. Thus the banker supplies the borrower permanently with part of his working capital or stock in trade. As a result, it is often impossible to force the liquidation of overdraft loans in times of stress. These are the conditions today. There is no reason to believe that they were different in the Middle Ages.

For Bruges the Collard de Marke and Guillaume Ruyelle account books are practically the only available source of information concerning the loan and investment policy of the local exchange banks. The ledgers of Collard de Marke, the more important of the two money-changers, reveal that the number of overdraft loans kept pace with the expanding volume of his business and grew from forty-nine on April 6, 1366, to one hundred seventeen on May 20, 1369 (Table 20). It also appears that most overdrafts were for small amounts according to figures based on the balances due from customers on five different dates between April 1366 and May 1369. From 38.5 to 49 per cent of these debit balances are below five pounds groat, from 47.8 to 73.5 per cent below ten pounds groat, and from 69.5 to 83.9 per cent below twenty pounds groat. Outstanding balances above fifty pounds groat represent only from 7.7 to 15.2 per cent of the aggregate; but the figure of 7.7 per cent recurs on two different dates. The figures given by Guillaume Ruyelle's financial statement are even more striking. This statement

TABLE 20

DEBIT BALANCES IN THE COLLARD DE MARKE LEDGERS

Frequency Distribution	Ledger No. 1 April 6, 1366			Ledger No. 2 April 19, 1367			Ledger No. 3 April 10, 1368			Ledger No. 4 December 24, 1368			Ledger No. 5 May 20, 1369		
	Number of Balances	Per Cent of Total	Cumulative Per Cent	Number of Balances	Per Cent of Total	Cumulative Per Cent	Number of Balances	Per Cent of Total	Cumulative Per Cent	Number of Balances	Per Cent of Total	Cumulative Per Cent	Number of Balances	Per Cent of Total	Cumulative Per Cent
Below £5 groat	24	49.0	49.0	26	44.0	44.0	35	38.5	38.5	41	35.6	35.6	48	41.0	41.0
£5 and under £10	12	24.5	73.5	7	11.9	55.9	20	22.0	60.5	14	12.2	47.8	21	18.0	59.0
£10 and under £15	4	8.3	81.8	5	8.5	64.4	11	12.2	72.7	17	14.8	62.6	12	10.2	69.2
£15 and under £20	1	2.1	83.9	3	5.1	69.5	10	11.0	83.7	11	9.6	72.2	7	6.0	75.2
£20 and under £25	1	2.1	86.0	3	5.1	74.6	...	.....	83.7	9	7.8	80.0	5	4.3	79.5
£25 and under £30	...	.....	86.0	2	3.4	78.0	2	2.2	85.9	5	4.3	84.3	3	2.6	82.1
£30 and under £35	2	4.2	90.2	2	3.4	81.4	1	1.0	86.9	1	.9	85.2	5	4.3	86.4
£35 and under £40	1	2.1	92.3	...	.....	81.4	2	2.2	89.1	3	2.6	87.8	1	.8	87.2
£40 and under £45	...	.....	92.3	1	1.7	83.1	2	2.2	91.3	...	.....	87.8	4	3.4	90.6
£45 and under £50	...	.....	92.3	1	1.7	84.8	1	1.0	92.3	1	.9	88.7	2	1.7	92.3
£50 and under £100	3	5.6	97.9	5	8.5	93.3	4	4.4	96.7	6	5.2	93.9	5	4.3	96.6
£100 and under £200	1	2.1	100.0	4	6.7	100.0	3	3.3	100.0	6	5.2	99.1	2	1.7	98.3
£200 groat and above	...	.....	.....	...	.....	.....	...	.....	.....	1	.9	100.0	2	1.7	100.0
Total	49	100.0	.....	59	100.0	.....	91	100.0	.....	115	100.0	.....	117	100.0	.....

Source: Bruges Municipal Archives, Account Books of Collard de Marke.

reveals that twenty-two customers were allowed to overdraw their accounts. Out of these twenty-two accounts, nineteen have balances below five pounds groat, two between five and ten pounds groat, and one only above fifteen but below twenty pounds groat.[11] The average is £3 2*s.* 10*d.* gr. Collard de Marke's average, as is to be expected, is considerably higher. It varies between a minimum of £13 9*s.* 7*d.* gr. on April 6, 1366, and a maximum of £23 16s. 6d. gr. on April 19, 1367. Except on April 10, 1368, the average is much closer to the maximum than to the minimum. With both money-changers the average overdraft is considerably less than the average deposit (Table 12). One should, however, not lose sight of the fact that averages are unduly influenced by a few large items. In Collard de Marke's case then, half the overdrafts are below ten pounds groat with only one exception when the ratio is 47.8 per cent or slightly less than half.

The prevalence of small debit balances leads to some interesting conclusions. It seems that the Bruges money-changers were eager to retain the good-will of their customers and, therefore, were rather lenient in letting them overdraw their accounts as long as trifling amounts were involved. Such favors were not usually abused, and overdrafts were in general promptly repaid. However, each of the Collard de Marke ledgers contains on the first and second pages a number of inactive accounts which probably represent distressed or frozen loans. There are not many such accounts and the total of overdue claims is small. Of course, such accounts should not have been left open on the books, but should have been written off as a loss. The existence of a few dubious or uncollectible items does not alter the fact that overdrafts of limited amount and of short duration cannot bring about a state of insolvency because the credit risk is rather well divided among many small items. There is only a remote possibility that a considerable number of debtors would fail to live up to their obligations at the same time.

Small overdrafts, consequently, are not objectionable from the standpoint of good management. The question is whether the same applies to overdrafts of sizable amount: let us say of fifty pounds groat or more. An audit of the Collard de Marke account books shows that these overdrafts are few in number but of considerable importance (Table 21). On April 19, 1367, and on May 20, 1369, nine overdrafts of fifty pounds groat or more represent respectively 64 and 53 per cent of the total loans outstanding among Collard de Marke's customers. At another date, December 24, 1368, thirteen overdrafts with debit balances exceeding fifty pounds groat account for 57.3 per cent of the aggregate loans while the remaining 42.7 per cent is spread over 102 different items (Table 22).

The four customers who, on April 6, 1366, owed balances exceeding fifty pounds groat are Jakes or Jakemart de Wallers, Medemiselle de Rudevorde, Jehan van Tinneskin le père, and Lambesin de Jaghere or Diagre.

Medemiselle de Rudevorde was one of Collard de Marke's regular and most important customers. The fact that her account was very active all through the

TABLE 21

List of Overdrafts above Fifty Pounds Groat on Five Different Dates According to Collard de Marke's Ledgers

On April 6, 1366

	£	s	d groat
1. Jackemart de Wallers	121	0	0
2. Lambesin de Jaghere	87	12	11
3. Jehan van Tinneskin	64	0	6
4. Medemiselle de Rudevorde	52	3	7
Total	324	17	0

On April 19, 1367

	£	s	d groat
1. Sire Ector Jucamiel	141	6	0
2. Lambesin de Jaghere	138	9	4
3. Jackemart de Wallers	121	0	0
4. Bette Dougardin	115	0	0
5. Pierre de Leurent	97	14	1
6. Medemiselle de Rudevorde	91	16	8
7. Jehan van de Walle	73	12	7
8. Simon Ongcriet	61	17	2
9. Jehan van Tinneskin, le pere	56	11	4
Total	897	7	2

On April 10, 1368

	£	s	d groat
1. Jackemart de Wallers	178	6	5
2. Lambesin le pere de Jaghere	121	19	9
3. Jehan van de Walle	100	1	6
4. Sire Jehan de Rudevorde	94	11	7
5. Georges Wandelaire	61	7	2
6. Gilles de Dec.	55	3	10
7. Pietre de Gérard	53	9	2
Total	664	19	5

On December 24, 1368

	£	s	d groat
1. Jehan vande Walle	220	13	2
2. Galigo da Piastre (Italian)	163	0	0
3. Jackemart de Wallers	158	6	5
4. Thumas Sarlande (Italian)	119	12	0
5. Carot de Galbert (Italian?)	111	2	9
6. Lambesin de Jaghere	107	9	7
7. Medemiselle de Rudevorde	107	9	6
8. Pietre van le Fine	95	9	7
9. Georges Wandelaire	89	14	2
10. Marke Mourisin (Venetian)	88	12	8
11. Jehan de Concorighe (Italian)	88	7	11
12. Gilles le Clerc dou Dam	74	16	6
13. Jehan de Quantin	71	17	11
Total	1,496	12	2

On May 20, 1369

	£	s	d groat
1. Lambesin de Jaghere	383	1	9
2. Jehan van de Walle	256	8	10
3. Williame Raiponde (Lucchese)	165	16	10
4. Jackemart de Wallers	164	5	5
5. Galigo da Piastre (Italian)	93	9	10
6. Thumas Sarlande (Italian)	86	15	3
7. Thumas de Gotier	80	0	11
8. Willem van de Nienoede	67	11	1
9. Pietre Sucrebout	50	12	2
Total	1,348	2	1

Source: Bruges, Municipal Archives, Account Books of Collard de Marke.

TABLE 22

RELATIVE IMPORTANCE OF OVERDRAFTS EXCEEDING FIFTY POUNDS GROAT ON FIVE DIFFERENT DATES ACCORDING TO COLLARD DE MARKE'S LEDGERS

Date	Number of Overdrafts Exceeding Fifty Pounds	Total Number of Overdrafts	Per Cent of Total	Total of Overdrafts Exceeding Fifty Pounds Groat			Aggregate Overdrafts (Pounds Groat)			Per Cent of Aggregate
				£	s	d	£	s	d	
April 6, 1366	4	49	8.2	324	17	0	660	10	2	49.2
April 19, 1367	9	59	15.2	897	7	2	1,405	12	10	63.8
April 10, 1368	7	91	7.7	664	19	5	1,478	10	0	45.0
December 24, 1368	13	115	11.3	1,496	12	2	2,611	18	2	57.3
May 20, 1369	9	117	7.7	1,348	2	1	2,553	11	9	52.8

Source: Bruges, Municipal Archives, Account Books of Collard de Marke.

period covered by the extant ledgers may serve as an indication that her business was of some importance. She owned an inn which was patronized by foreign merchants, chiefly Germans,[12] and probably combined this trade with that of broker and commission agent, as was customary in Bruges.[13] As one would expect, the balance of Medemiselle de Rudevorde's account fluctuated a great deal, but was consistently on the debit side up to sometime between Christmas 1368 and Pentecost 1369, when the scales tipped over in her favor. On May 20, 1369, Medemiselle de Rudevorde had an amount of £97 11s. 8d. gr. standing to her credit.[14] The ledger entries give no clue as to how she was able to pay off her indebtedness. It may be that the money came from the proceeds of a sale, but the best guess is that the money really belonged to some of her guests. In Bruges it was customary for foreign merchants staying at an inn to entrust their money to their host for purposes of safekeeping.[15]

That Medemiselle de Rudevorde's guests undoubtedly followed this practice appears from a charter of Louis de Male dated September 8, 1374. This charter describes 'Joncvrauwe Edele van Ruddervoorde' as being insolvent and greatly in debt to several Hanseatic merchants who had given her money 'in good faith' (*ter goeder trauwen*).[16] The conclusion is that Medemiselle de Rudevorde must have failed sometime between the summer of 1369 and September 8, 1374. Collard de Marke presumably went bankrupt during the same period. The two events may be interrelated, but the surviving records do not disclose whether the failure of the bank caused the failure of Medemiselle de Rudevorde or the other way around. Without more information it is impossible to decide whether or not Collard de Marke was wise in extending credit to Medemiselle de Rudevorde.

We are less well informed about the business of Lambesin de Jaghere, another of Collard de Marke's principal debtors. His account, like that of Medemiselle de Rudevorde's is very active but is constantly overdrawn. On April 6, 1366, Lambesin de Jaghere owed Collard de Marke an amount of £87 12*s.* 11*d.* groat.[17] A year later this amount had risen to £138 9*s.* 4*d.* groat.[18] On April 10, 1368, the outstanding balance was reduced to £121 19*s.* 9*d.* groat[19] and dropped further to £107 9*s.* 7*d.* groat by Christmas 1368,[20] but within the next five months Lambesin de Jaghere's debt grew to £383 1*s.* 9*d.* groat.[21] The ledger entries do not give any information which would enable us to explain this sudden jump.

A rapidly increasing debt to a bank may mean one of two things: either borrowing in order to finance expansion or else borrowing in order to cover up losses and to replenish a dwindling working capital. Which one of these two alternatives applies in the case of Lambesin de Jaghere can only be guessed. In 1379, he was made to contribute to the forced loan which was levied on all wealthy citizens.[22] In 1382, he was one of several officials who collected a war contribution from the Hanseatic merchants after the battle of Roosebeke.[23] On those two dates Lambesin de Jaghere was thus one of the leading citizens in the community. It is, therefore, unlikely that he would have failed or lost heavily a few years before, as few people recover quickly, if at all, from such a blow. The loan from Collard de Marke probably served to finance a commercial venture about which no inkling is given in the ledger records.

The account of Jakes de Wallers, unlike those of Medemiselle de Rudevorde and Lambesin de Jaghere, is not an active, but a dormant, account. The balance changes little over protracted periods of time. This immobility might lead to the mistaken inference that the loan to Jakes de Wallers was one of those dubious claims which have been referred to in a preceding paragraph. But a memorandum entry in the front of the earlier of the two extant journals hints at something quite different. This entry mentions 'li compagnie de Jakes de Wallers' and refers in this connection to letters of payment or bills of exchange from Brittany.[24] This word Brittany is the clue to the whole mystery. In all probability the 'compagnie de Jakes de Wallers' was some kind of a partnership formed for the trade in French wine from the Loire region or in salt from the island of Oléron, or perhaps even for the purpose of dealing in both of these commodities. An entry in one of the ledgers gives further support to this theory. Under the date of April 10, 1368, Collard de Marke records that Jakes de Wallers owes him a balance of £178 6*s.* 5*d.* gr. carried over from a preceding ledger and arising from a settlement which took place on November 10, 1367, 'before he [Jakes de Wallers] left for Brittany.'[25] Consequently, the balance of Jakes de Wallers' account is not an overdraft at all, but represents the money invested by Collard de Marke in this Brittany venture. Jakes de Wallers was presumably the active partner who traveled back and forth, while Collard de Marke was the investing partner who stayed at home but who, from a distance, probably kept an eye on the conduct of the venture. As this example shows, it may sometimes be difficult, in practice, to draw a line between a loan and an investment regardless of the fact that such a distinction may be clear from a legal point of view.

Sire Georges de Wandelaire (de Wandelaar) was another of Collard de Marke's customers who, at times, borrowed substantial amounts by overdrawing his account. On April 10, 1368, he had thus exceeded his credit to the extent of £61 7*s.* 2*d.* gr.[26] This debt rose to £89 14*s.* 2*d.* gr. on December 24, 1368.[27]

Sire Georges de Wandelaire—he is consistently given the title of *sire* or *heer* —was apparently someone of importance in fourteenth-century Bruges. He played a prominent role in the civil strife which troubled Flanders from 1379 to 1385.[28] In the early phase of the struggle, sire Georges de Wandelaire was a member of several diplomatic missions which represented the city of Bruges at peace conferences held in Tournai (November 1379) and Lille (January 1380).[29] In 1380 Georges de Wandelaire was chosen to fill the office of city treasurer.[30] Two years later the municipal government bought from him the horse on which rode Gérard de Saint-Omer, carrying the standard of Bruges, at the disastrous battle of Beverhoudsveld (May 4, 1382).[31] When in the summer of 1383, Bruges was threatened again by a sudden advance of the enemy,[32] sire Georges de Wandelaire and one Gilles Honin were commissioned to supervise the digging of a new moat and the building of additional defenses.[33] Georges de Wandelaire was still alive in the nineties; he is mentioned in the records as *échevin* or alderman in the years 1392, 1394, and 1397.[34]

These miscellaneous details about the life of sire Georges de Wandelaire are not particularly relevant to our purpose. They show only that he wielded considerable influence in the oligarchical government of Bruges. There is, however, no doubt that he could not have been successful in politics, had he not been successful in business, too. Oligarchies as a rule are not much impressed by demagogic oratory, and achievement is necessary to keep up prestige.

Jehan van de Walle, another customer who was granted a line of credit, is described as a furrier (*pelletier*) in the Collard de Marke ledgers.[35] As the laying in of a supply of furs involved considerable expense, it was necessary to possess some capital in order to practice this trade. In Bruges the furriers were among the wealthier crafts together with the gold- and silversmiths, the mercers, the fishmongers, and the butchers.[36] Most likely only a select group of tradesmen, in particular those whose trade involved an outlay of capital, could get credit accommodation from a bank. The rank and file of the craftsmen, if they needed financial assistance, had to borrow from the lombards by pawning their cloth, their supplies, or even their tools. Moreover, petty craftsmen, as they had little or no money invested in their trade, had no occasion to borrow except for consumption purposes. The money-changers, for reasons which will be given later, were not very much interested in this type of loans.

Jehan van de Walle's debt to the bank, instead of expanding and contracting, as one would expect in a seasonal trade like the fur trade, increased steadily from £30 0*s*. 4*d*. to £256 8*s*. 10*d*. groat over the period covered by the Collard de Marke ledgers (Table 21.) Such a steady increase arouses suspicions, and we would very much like to know what use was made of the proceeds of the loan. Jehan van de Walle's account is not a very active account.[37] One wonders, therefore, whether its balance does not represent an investment, this time in the fur trade, rather than a loan.

The Bruges sources give very little information about Pieter Sucrebout, a customer who, according to the financial statement of May 20, 1369, owed on that date an amount of £50 12*s*. 2*d*. groat to the bank.[38] On the preceding twenty-fourth of December there was only a balance of three pounds groat standing to his debit.[39] A certain Pieter Sucrebout, presumably the same person as Collard de Marke's customer, participated in 1380 in the campaign against Ghent as *hooftman* or captain in the Bruges militia.[40] This little detail, however, is not very helpful in settling the question whether Pieter Sucrebout deserved to be granted a line of credit.

Several of Collard de Marke's customers who were allowed to overdraw their accounts were Italian merchants or merchant-bankers. The members of the Lucchese colony in Bruges, in particular, seem to have favored Collard de Marke with their patronage: he handled the bank accounts of Forteguerra di Forteguerra, Jaquemard Faba, Guillaume Raponde or Rapondi, Galigo da Piastre,[41] and Davin Tedaldin or Tedaldini. Another regular customer was Thumas Sarlande who was in some way closely connected with the master of the mint Jehan Terminiel or Interminelli, another Lucchese, but the entries in the Collard de Marke ledgers do not disclose what this connection really was.[42] Important accounts are also those of the Italian merchants Mark Mourisin or Marco Morosini (from Venice), Nicolas Ammanati (from Pistoia), Dine Malapris, and Nicolas Boin Acourt or Bonaccorsi (from Florence or Lucca).

The accounts of these Italian merchants are usually very active ones. Unlike the Easterlings, the Italians were accustomed to make use of bank facilities in their homeland and as far as practicable made all their payments by transfer from their bank accounts. The example of the Italians most likely influenced the paying habits of other people and induced them also to open bank accounts.

From the point of view of sound banking, the loans to the Italian merchant-bankers were far from being as objectionable as some of the investment loans which have just been discussed. As these merchants were either heads or representatives of powerful international business houses, they did not rely on bank loans to supplement their working capital, but their balances with the local exchange-banks were likely to fluctuate in sympathy with the state of the money-market, the exchange-rates, and the movement of international trade. The Italian merchant-bankers dealt extensively in bills of exchange, engaged constantly in arbitrage, and maintained balances with correspondents in all important financial centers. If these balances, for example, were at a low ebb, such a situation would affect the exchange rates. Under such conditions, it might become profitable to ship bullion abroad rather than to purchase bills of exchange in order to build up the depleted foreign balances. Conversely, the Italian merchant-bankers might decide to bring bullion into the country if they needed money in Bruges, but had idle balances with correspondents abroad. The Italian merchant-bankers, because of their foreign connections, thus held a strategic position in the money market. How imports or exports of bullion affected the financial condition of the local exchange banks has been discussed in a preceding chapter, and there is no need to dwell upon this topic here.

The Collard de Marke ledgers yield little or no information concerning the mechanism of the money market. A cursory examination of the accounts of the Italian merchant-bankers does show, however, that they were constantly buying or selling gold. Between December 24, 1368, and May 20, 1369, a period of diminishing tension in the money market, the sales of gold coins to Collard de Marke seem to have been more numerous than the withdrawals of funds.[43] If this impression were correct, it would elicit the conclusion that bullion from outside was pouring into Bruges, thus relieving the existing strain on the money market.

This inquiry into Collard de Marke's loan policy is on the whole rather disappointing. No information at all is available about a number of the borrowers and, when some information is given, it is often irrelevant or inconclusive.[44] A few facts do, however, stand out. Almost all loans were unsecured overdrafts or fiduciary loans. The majority of them were for small amounts and did not constitute a potential threat to the solvency of the bank. It is a well-known fact that mediaeval people had little regard for maturity dates.[45] Judging by the Collard de Marke ledgers, depositors—with the connivance of the banker—were equally casual about drawing on their bank account without having sufficient funds. In most cases this carelessness seems to have been due to overtrading.[46] Mediaeval society suffered from a shortage of capital and borrowing was made difficult because of the usury prohibition and the lack of an adequate organization of credit.[47] People were, therefore, inclined to skimp on the most unprofitable form of wealth: money. Merchants and dealers often did not keep enough cash on hand, so they had trouble in meeting maturities. Either the creditor had to wait or the banker was asked to allow an overdraft.[48]

In so far as can be ascertained from our survey, only persons owning property and having a standing in the community were given open credit for substantial amounts. The proceeds of such advances were obviously used by the borrowers in order to expand their business. In other words, bank loans were made for production, and not for consumption, purposes. The borrowers—with one possible exception, Medemiselle de Rudevorde—appear to have been safe credit risks. In spite of all these good features, Collard de Marke's credit policy is not above criticism. Big overdrafts were few in number but absorbed a considerable proportion of the bank's resources. Such overdrafts were by no means temporary advances, but were in fact investment loans or even outright investments, as has been revealed by our investigation in one or two instances. For our purpose legal distinctions between what constitutes a loan and what constitutes an investment do not matter very much. Whatever the legal form adopted, the banker practically entered into partnership with the borrower and furnished him permanently with working capital. The danger of tying up funds is obvious, if one considers that the banker's main liability was made up of deposits payable on request.[49] However, it would be unfair to accuse Collard de Marke of mismanagement, at least as far as his loan policy was concerned. One should not forget that mediaeval banks were seriously handicapped by the absence of a discount market for commercial paper and of facilities for rediscounting. Lack of liquidity was a distinctive feature of the primitive bank of deposit in the Low Countries as well as in other parts of Europe.[50]

As already explained, no interest was paid by the money-changer on demand deposits. Strangely enough, it seems that no interest was charged on loans, either. Nowhere do the Collard de Marke and Guillaume Ruyelle account books contain any reference to interest paid on debit balances. If we may believe the Venetian senator Tommaso Contarini, the *banchi di scritta* of Venice did not charge anything either, if a merchant of good repute wanted to make assignments 'beyond the amount standing to his credit.'[51] The bankers are willing to render this service, Contarini explains, 'because it does not involve any disbursement of specie,'[52] and 'because they know that the merchants support the movement of trade whether in money or in goods.'[53] These utterances make it clear that temporary advances were often granted without charge in order to retain customers. As Contarini correctly points out, a transfer bank could extend credit without any immediate loss of specie simply by making an entry on the books, debiting the account of one customer and crediting the account of another. Contarini does not mention, however, that such a transaction would lower the reserve ratio of the bank, lead to an expansion of bank deposits, and result in the creation of additional purchasing power, or of additional money, which is practically one and the same thing.[54]

Mediaeval banks were not philanthropic institutions. If they charged no interest on their loans, they had to find some other way of covering their expenses and of making a profit.[55] The Collard de Marke account books disclose that the Bruges money-changers, instead of charging interest on outstanding balances, took their profit under the form of fees for the exchange of gold for silver and vice versa. The accounts of the Italian merchant-bankers contain a number of debit entries relating to such fees.[56] It is also quite possible that customers who had overdrawn accounts paid higher fees than others or received less favorable prices for bullion sold to the money-changers. But there is no evidence to support this supposition. As for investment loans and outright investments, there is little doubt that interest was charged under some concealed form.[57] Presumably the banker received a share in the profits of the venture. How this share was computed the available records do not reveal. The division of profits was probably determined according to a special agreement in each case. In the late Middle Ages the rate of return on productive investments varied from 8 to 15 per cent.

The adopted solution offered the additional advantage of evading the canonist prohibition of usury. The canonists objected to the lending of money for certain gain (Fr. *à gain certain,* Fl. *om seker gewin*), but did not disapprove of the investment of money in a business venture for a share in profit or loss (Fr. *à gain*

TABLE 23
ABRIDGED FINANCIAL STATEMENT OF GUILLAUME RUYELLE
MAY 24, 1370

RESOURCES	Amount (Pounds Groat)			Per Cent of Total
	£	*s*	*d*	
Cash: in till	15	10	5	1.6
in vault	262	11	10	27.7
Loans (overdrafts)	69	2	2	7.3
Investments (?)	562	14	6	59.5
Total of assets	909	18	11	96.1
Deficit	36	18	1	3.9
Total	946	17	0	100.0
LIABILITIES				
Due to Depositors	946	17	0	100.0

Source: R. de Roover, 'Ruyelle,' *op. cit.*, pp. 92–95.

et à perte, Fl. *op gewin oft verlies*). Thus putting money 'in adventure' was tantamount to a partnership and was not censored by the usury laws. The money-changers had to inspire confidence in their depositors and, therefore, had to confine themselves to legitimate business. Open or even secret violation of the usury laws would have undermined that confidence, because only the principal of a loan was recoverable at law. Furthermore, money lent on usury was subject to confiscation irrespective of other penalties. Several of the Bruges municipal accounts of the fourteenth and fifteenth centuries contain lists of fines collected from people who had been convicted of usury in the city court. In going through these lists I have found only one money-changer, a man named Jan Moreel or Jehan Moriel.[58] According to the Collard de Marke account books, his business was not very important. Jan Moreel, presumably, became a shady money-monger because he had not succeeded in earning a living by reputable and legal means.

Collard de Marke and Guillaume Ruyelle, the two money-changers whose business records have come down to us, did not follow the same loan policy. Guillaume Ruyelle placed even less emphasis on loans and more on investments than did his colleague. According to Ruyelle's financial statement of May 24, 1370, overdrafts amounted on the aggregate to only £69 2*s*. 2*d*. gr., whereas a total of £946 17*s*. groat was due to depositors.[59] The ratio of loans to deposits was thus less than 10 per cent (Table 23). The reserve ratio—cash to deposits—was 29.3 per cent.

These two totals are itemized on the original statement and may be considered accurate, since the figures of the statement and those of the ledgers have been collated and correspond. There is, however, one item of £562 14*s*. 6*d*. groat which, on the original, is added to the receivables but cannot be traced to the ledger and does not represent a ledger balance. The inclusion of this item is explained by the words 'Item folio' in the narrative column. The explanation can have only one meaning: the amount of £562 14*s.* 6*d.* groat is the aggregate of several items listed in detail on another complementary statement which is no longer extant. It is a reasonable surmise that the items in question were recorded separately because they referred not to loans but to investments, and because they were not taken from the extant ledgers, which concerns only Ruyelle's banking business but from some other account book. We know from frequent references in the ledgers of Collard de Marke that he did not use the same books for his banking business and his commercial undertakings. It is probable that Guillaume Ruyelle followed the same procedure.

If this explanation concerning the puzzling item of £562 14*s.* 6*d.* groat is accepted, the assets of Ruyelle's bank were made up as follows: cash reserve (including money in till and in vault), £278 2*s.* 3*d.* gr.;[60] loans (mainly overdrafts), £69 2*s.* 2*d.* gr.; and investments, £562 14*s.* 6*d.* gr. The major part of the bank's resources were thus invested directly in trade.

Incidentally, a glance at the summary statement (Table 23) will also show that assets do not cover liabilities and that there is a deficit of £36 18*s.* 1*d.* gr. In other words, Guillaume Ruyelle had made some bad investments and had lost not only the whole of his capital but money belonging to his depositors besides. If this analysis is correct, he was virtually bankrupt on May 24, 1370. Indeed, we know from other sources that Guillaume Ruyelle failed in the summer of 1370 and that some of his property was sold in pursuance of bankruptcy proceedings during the fall of the same year.[61]

According to the financial statement of May 24, 1370, the assets of Ruyelle's bank were distributed in the following proportion: 29.3 per cent of outside liabilities was kept in specie as a reserve, 59.5 per cent was directly invested in trade, only 7.3 per cent was applied to loans, and 3.9 per cent represented the excess of outside liabilities over assets. The assets were probably only the business assets and did not include any of the real estate which Ruyelle is known to have possessed.

We are not so well informed about Collard de Marke's financial condition, since no contemporary statement of assets and liabilities or any sort of balance sheet has come down to us. It is not possible to reconstruct such a statement from the available data. It has been possible, though, to compute the ratio of loans to demand liabilities at five different dates between April 6, 1366, and May 20, 1369, inclusive. As is apparent from Table 24, this ratio fluctuates between a minimum of 25.2 per cent and a maximum of 56.7 per cent. These percentages are both well above Ruyelle's 7.3 per cent, but are not quite high enough to warrant the conclusion that Collard de Marke stressed loans rather than investments. On the contrary, there is not the slightest doubt that, also in his case, a substantial part of the money belonging to depositors plus his own capital was directly invested in trade.

As has been explained before, Collard de Marke kept track of his commercial dealings in separate books. None of these have survived, but we know of their existence from occasional references in the extant ledgers. The account books thus referred to are a *papier des dras*[62] and a *petit papier des drapiers.*[63] There is consequently no doubt: Collard de Marke combined the trade in cloth with the management of a transfer bank.

As the *papier des dras* and the *petit papier des drapiers* are lost, it is not possible to go into great detail concerning Collard de Marke's cloth business. Fortunately, some information, although not very much, can be gathered from the extant records.

Collard de Marke was apparently engaged in the cloth trade, but not in the manufacture of cloth. From the records it is clear that he bought most of the the cloth in the province of Hainaut, especially in the manufacturing centers of Valenciennes and Maubeuge, from local *drapiers* or cloth manufacturers, who presumably concentrated on production, but were not in a position to market their product advantageously.[64] The cloth purchased in Hainaut was then transported to Bruges and sold there in the cloth hall, mostly to foreign merchants.[65]

Collard de Marke himself was probably not a native of Bruges but of the province of Hainaut. This circumstance would explain why he had connections in, and traded with, this region. Such an assumption rests on the following clues: de Marke or de Marque is a Walloon rather than a Flemish name; the name, moreover, is not found among the leading families of Bruges; frequent misspellings of Flemish names in the extant account books suggest that the atmosphere in Collard de Marke's office was French.[66]

That Collard de Marke had business interests in Hainaut is also shown by the fact that several non-resident customers were living in that region. As previously stated, the accounts of non-residents are grouped together in the rear of each ledger. Significantly, most of them have French-sounding names and those whom I have been able to identify were from Valenciennes or Mons, which were respectively the principal city and the capital of Hainaut.[67] Such is the case with Thierry Brochons who has a very active account in each of the extant ledgers. On February 12, 1369, this Thierry Brochons received credit for a shipment of 1,200 French francs in specie which he had sent to Bruges by one Collard le Brun, butcher of Valenciennes.[68] Furthermore, Brochons is the name of a well-known family of Valenciennes and some of its members had a stake in the woolen industry. In 1346, one Walter Brochons was among the *Treize Hommes de le Halle*, an official body with regulating power over the cloth trade.[69] Another citizen of Valenciennes who has an account in the Collard

TABLE 24
RATIO OF LOANS TO DEPOSITS ACCORDING TO THE COLLARD DE MARKE LEDGERS ON FIVE DIFFERENT DATES

Ledger	Date	Ratio of Loans to Deposits	Loans (Pounds Groat)			Deposits (Pounds Groat)		
		Per Cent	£	*s*	*d*	£	*s*	*d*
No. 1	April 6, 1366	28.6	660	10	2	2,310	9	2
No. 2	April 19, 1367	25.2	1,405	12	10	5,566	8	3
No. 3	April 10, 1368	29.2	1,478	10	0	5,071	4	4
No. 4	December 24, 1368	56.7	2,611	18	2	4,605	15	4
No. 5	May 20, 1369	45.8	2,553	11	9	5,575	6	1

Source: Bruges, Municipal Archives, Account Books of Collard de Marke.

de Marke ledgers is Jehan Moyses or Moyset. From 1358 to 1363 he was *prévôt de la ville,* a position equivalent to that of mayor.[70] This Jehan Moyses must have been very wealthy, because in 1361 Louis de Male sold him crown jewels with the option of repurchasing them a year later for 6,000 florins.[71] Another non-resident customer is described in one of the Collard de Marke ledgers as 'Lottier de Tournay demorant à Mons en Hainnaut.'[72] A cursory examination of the accounts of non-residents gives the impression that not all entries were based on banking or credit operations, but that some might have originated in commercial transactions connected with Collard de Marke's cloth business.[73]

As Collard de Marke could not very well assume the direction of a bank and look after other ventures at the same time, the management of the cloth business was entrusted to a partner named Pietre van le Fine.[74] It is a plausible assumption that this partner was in charge of the purchases and, for this purpose, traveled back and forth between Bruges and Hainaut. While he was on a trip the selling could conveniently be supervised by Collard de Marke himself with the help of an employee, because in Bruges the offices of the money-changers and the two cloth halls were all located on or near the Grand' Place.[75] It should perhaps be added that no cloth could be displayed and sold outside the cloth halls which had been especially built for the purpose.

As no partnership agreement has survived, nothing can be said about the relation between the two partners or about their respective shares in the common venture. The amount which Collard de Marke had invested in the partnership with Pietre van le Fine was rather considerable and certainly exceeded five hundred pounds groat.[76] Greater accuracy cannot be attained because of the many gaps in the available records. The two partners reckoned with each other from time to time, preferably in the presence of a third party who could be called on to witness in case of need.[77] Pietre van le Fine, it appears from a marginal note in the last of the extant ledgers, died in the summer of 1369.[78] No exact date is given. There is a possibility that Collard de Marke became entangled in serious difficulties, when he tried to wind up the affairs of his partnership with Pietre van le Fine. Mediaeval merchants, except the Italians, often relied too much on their memory and accounts were slovenly kept. Such conditions were likely to breed trouble in the event of sudden death.

The policy of making direct investments in trade was not peculiar to Collard de Marke and Guillaume Ruyelle. Other money-changers of Bruges followed the same course. In 1326, according to the toll records of Calais, the principal importers of English wool were three Bruges merchants. One of them was also a money-changer.[79] A few years later, in 1369, the burgomasters and aldermen of Bruges protested to the municipal authorities of Lübeck against the arbitrary seizure on the high seas of a cargo of meat and herring belonging *jointly* to two citizens of Bruges Jacob de Visch and the money-changer, Jacob Reubs, frequently mentioned in the Collard de Marke account books. This shipment was being accompanied by a servant of the two partners named Arnold Hont.[80]

The close association of banks and business, far from being prevalent in Flanders alone, was a widespread evil. 'In nearly all regions,' writes Professor Usher, 'bankers commonly had considerable sums invested in trade.'[81] It is not that the danger of such investments was entirely overlooked; but mediaeval bankers, it must be recognized, had little choice. The lack of discountable commercial paper, the canonist objection against the taking of interest, and the legal impediments resulting therefrom, left the bankers no other alternative but to seek a profitable use for surplus funds through the direct participation in commercial ventures.

The fate of the mediaeval transfer banks thus rested on the shaky foundation of long-term investments and short-term liabilities. No wonder that attempts were made at an early date to buttress the tottering walls of the mediaeval credit structure. The regulations on banking of the Venetian Republic give perhaps the best picture of the efforts which were made in this respect. In 1374, a statute was passed which forbade banks to trade in speculative commodities such as iron, copper, and tin.[82] In 1403 banks were enjoined by another statute not to devote to trade more than one and a half times the amount of their holdings of government obligations.[83] In other words the earning assets of a transfer bank were to be invested three-fifths in trade and two-fifths in the public debt.[84] This regulation was made necessary, it is stated in the preamble to the statute, 'because the *banchi di scritta* were in the habit of trading overseas for excessive sums, thus exposing their depositors to great risks.'[85] At the end of the sixteenth century practically the same argument was adduced by Contarini in his discourse in favor of the establishment of a public bank. Private bankers, his argument runs, cannot afford to be simply custodians of the money entrusted to them, but have to invest it in trade in order to make a profit.[86] Such investments are not only risky, but immobilize funds which will not be available, if there is a run on the bank.

In Flanders, regulations on banking were far less numerous than in Venice. Flemish ordinances have not touched upon the matter under discussion except for one important provision which is included in the privileges wrested from Mary of Burgundy after the death of Charles the Bold (1477). This provision restated the obligation of the money-changers to give bond and, further, forbade them 'to deal in commodities or to be partners to such dealings, either at home, or overseas, or beyond the mountains.'[87] In other words, henceforth, the money-changers were not supposed to make any direct investments whether in domestic or in foreign trade. How the money-changers were going to make profits is a point which is not elucidated. The restriction placed on the activity of the banks probably remained a dead letter as did many of the other concessions which Mary of Burgundy was forced to grant in order to gain time and to appease an aroused populace. The populace, for once, could be appeased with proclamations and did not give much thought to their enforcement. There existed in Flanders no administrative machinery by which banking control could be made effective. The already overburdened municipal authorities certainly were not in a position to take up additional duties. In Venice, at least, there was a special body of bank-examiners, the *provveditori sopra banchi* who saw to it that the decrees of the Senate were complied with by the Rialto banks.[88] In Genoa the supervision of the banks was a function delegated to the *Officium Mercantie* in the fourteenth, and to the *Officium Banchorum* in the fifteenth, centuries.[89]

The privileges granted by Mary of Burgundy were supposedly designed to redress the grievances of the public against the administration of Charles the Bold.[90] The demand for drastic regulation has, therefore, some significance. Apparently the public had been sorely hit by repeated bank failures and ascribed these failures to misguided investments on the part of the banks.

Because economic development in the Low Countries was considerably slower than in Italy, the analysis of the Bruges records sheds some light on the moot question of the early origins of banking.[91] As loans were less important than investments, the Bruges exchange banks—and the same applies to mediaeval transfer banks elsewhere— cannot be regarded primarily as specialized credit institutions.[92] To pretend that banking developed out of money-lending is a preconception which seems logical enough *a priori,* but which is not confirmed by any documentary evidence.[93] All banking apparently developed out of exchange transactions. At a later stage the decisive factor in the development of commercial banking seems rather to have been the change from regular to irregular deposits. Banking functions are unmistakably performed whenever cash reserves represent only a fraction of demand liabilities, and whenever bank deposits become transferable and are used extensively as a substitute for money.[94]

From the point of view of the economist it does not make any difference whether the resources of a bank, except the specie reserve, are utilized to finance trade in a direct way, by forming partnerships, or in an indirect way, by making loans.[95] Both methods have the same effect: the creation of additional purchasing power.

Legal writers naturally make a great deal of the distinction, which is essential for them, between partners and creditors, because these two classes of claimants have different rights in case of liquidation or of bankruptcy. But the economic historian does not care much about this question of equities and priority rights. A mediaeval bank interests him only as a going concern or as part of a banking system. What happens to defunct banks may be of great interest to the student of the history of law, but it is of minor interest from the point of view of the economic historian. For this reason he cannot accept the criterion of legal writers who contend that a banker is not a banker, if he is simultaneously engaged in trade and does not confine himself to lending.[96] Such a lack of specialization was the rule rather than the exception in mediaeval times.[97] Moreover, it is impossible to draw a clearly marked dividing line between loan contracts and partnership agreements. Many contracts cut across the boundary line[98] and the jurists have wrangled over them ever since the Middle Ages.[99]

Some Genoese partnership agreements of the twelfth century mention bankers appearing as parties to the contract. It is highly significant that the banker is always the investing, and never the traveling or active, partner.[100] Most of the contracts were concluded for overseas voyages, but the voyages were to nearby ports and hence did not involve great risks or a prolonged immobilization of funds.[101] Bankers appear also as lenders in a number of loan contracts, but these are less numerous than are the partnership agreements. In two contracts of the year 1200, an interest rate of five pennies per month or twenty per cent a year is stipulated.[102] No interest is mentioned in other contracts, but is certainly present under a disguise.[103] Most probably the borrower obligated himself for an amount greater than the one actually received. This assumption is based on the fact that, in at least one contract, the debtor explicitly relinquishes in advance the *exceptione non numeratae pecuniae*,[104] i.e., the debtor promises that he will not go to court and repudiate his debt, in whole or in part, by taking an oath that he has not received in full the amount for which he is bound by contract.[105]

The similarities between banking in Bruges during the fourteenth century and banking in Genoa at the end of the twelfth century are certainly striking, despite the difference in time and place. Interest, in fourteenth-century Bruges, continued to be carefully concealed and the bankers continued to divide their surplus funds between lending and direct investment in trade, but with emphasis on the latter.[106] As it was a practical impossibility to run a bank and to attend to other business at the same time, bankers in Bruges as well as in Genoa, confined themselves to the role of investing partners.[107] Management or travel was always left to the other party. Such was the relationship between Collard de Marke and his partners, Jakes de Wallers and Pietre van le Fine. 'Investing partner' does not mean 'sleeping or dormant partner.' In the Middle Ages, the investing partner, who supplied the major part of the capital, usually retained the right to interfere if something went seriously wrong. Nevertheless the choice of a reliable person as active partner was very important, because the investing partner was not always at hand to prevent mistakes. Frequently the success or failure of a venture depended upon the active partner's judgment and ability, chiefly in foreign parts.

The Bruges money-changers did not make loans secured by the pledge of personal property, they did not lend extensively to public authorities, and they did not discount bills of exchange. Why? An attempt will be made to answer this question in the following paragraphs.

The money-changers did not engage in pawnbroking, because they were not licensed to do so. Pawnbroking, as we have seen, was the monopoly of the lombards. Besides this fundamental reason, there were other factors which contributed to exclude the money-changers. Their offices, the reader will remember, were small and did not have any facilities for the storage of pawned articles. Pawnbroking, moreover, was socially in disrepute. As deposit banking rests on confidence, the money-changers could not disregard the feelings of the public and had to restrict the scope of their activity to legitimate business. The lombards also lent mostly to people of small means who wanted cash for consumption purposes and had no use for bank credit. This small-loan business did not appeal to the money-changers. They realized that their business depended upon an active movement of trade. They, therefore, tried to promote business activity by lending only to merchants or by participating directly in commercial undertakings.

In Italy, too, there was a clear demarcation between pawnbroking and deposit banking. In Florence, for example, the Jewish pawnbrokers who, after 1437, were given a monopoly to the exclusion of all Christians,[108] were allowed to lend only on pledges (*sul pegno*) but were not supposed to make any loans *ad scriptam* or under the form of overdrafts.[109] The Venetian transfer banks did sometimes grant credit with jewelry as security, but collateral other than gold or silver was probably not acceptable.[110] Another exception is Strasbourg where the municipal exchange banks lent money on pledges, apparently small sums on which interest was computed per week from one Monday to the next.[111]

The Bruges money-changers occasionally advanced money to the city of Bruges, but only in great emergencies. In 1304, the money-changer Janne van Ghent lent one hundred pounds for the campaign in Hainaut.[112] The following year the money-changers as a group made another contribution toward the prosecution of the war against France.[113] In 1359, they advanced an amount of £2,400 8*s*. *parisis* or £200 0*s*. 8*d*. gr. at the urgent request of the municipal authorities.[114] Three years later, the City of Bruges was again in financial straits and had to make another appeal for financial aid. This time she succeeded in raising 3,780 pounds *parisis* or 315 pounds groat of which the lombards contributed 480 pounds *parisis* or forty pounds groat and the money-changers 3,300 pounds *parisis* or 275 pounds groat. In 1366 the city of Ghent still owed 2,275 florins on an original amount of 3,020 florins to the heirs of the deceased Bruges money-changer Tideman Bloumeroot.[115]

On the whole the city of Bruges relied little on the money-changers. This source was only tapped in last resort. Bruges borrowed more often from the Italian merchant-bankers, but this method had the disadvantage of being expensive. Most long-term financing was done by selling life-annuities and rent-charges to private individuals.[116] Bruges like other Flemish cities favored this method all through the Middle Ages.

Life-annuities, it is obvious, were not a desirable investment for a money-changer. As for rent-charges, the return on them was so low that they were not desirable either. Besides, there was no organized market for them as there is today for government securities. To these remarks, it should perhaps be added that the money-changers were not financially strong enough to lend amounts as large as those which the Italian merchants, on several occasions, were able to supply. For all these reasons the money-changers did not play any conspicuous role in public finance. Their loans to the count of Flanders were even less numerous than those to the city of Bruges. The only known transactions of this kind are mentioned in the accounts of Philip the Good. Between 1422 and 1428 these accounts contain several references to the repayment of loans to two Bruges money-changers, Colin Lefèvre and Antonin de Vivalda.[117] The latter very probably belonged to the Genoese banker's family of that name.

With regard to public finance, conditions in Italy were very different from those prevailing in Flanders. The assets of the Italian transfer banks commonly included investments in the public debt. One should not overlook that public administration, including finance, was more developed in the Italian city-states than in Flanders.[118] In Genoa, for instance, the public debt was divided into shares (*loca*) which were secured by liens on specific sources of revenue.[119] Sales were registered in transfer books. In Flanders a similar organization simply did not exist. The Flemish cities enjoyed a somewhat better credit standing than the mediaeval rulers, but not as high a standing as the Italian republics.[120]

The main function of the Bruges exchange banks was to facilitate local payments by a system of book transfers. Collard de Marke and Guillaume Ruyelle, it is clear from their account books, did not deal in bills of exchange and did not have correspondents abroad. The local character of the business of the Bruges money-changers is not altered by the fact that they had a number of non-resident customers. Collard de Marke and Guillaume Ruyelle never undertook to remit money abroad. They did not go beyond the carrying out of instructions by making local payments for outside customers.[121] It often happened that bills of exchange, instead of being paid in cash, were paid by an assignment in bank.[122] Obligations between a buyer of foreign exchange and the seller of a draft payable abroad could be settled in the same way. In both cases the money-changer only came in as the recorder of the transaction. No discounting was involved. Nor was there any credit extended, except if bank credit was being used to buy or to honor a bill of exchange. A good example of the payment of a matured bill by means of a book transfer is given in the Collard de Marke account books.[123]

On March 6, 1369, one Jakemon Franche had to pay a bill of exchange (*un cange*) of five hundred Florentine florins to a certain Boin Accourt (Bonaccorsi) of Lucca whose agent in Bruges was apparently Jakes de Gérart (Gherardi.)[124] Jakemon Franche provided for the payment of this bill at maturity in the following way. A few days before, on February 28, an amount of four hundred French francs at the rate of 31½ groats apiece, or equivalent to £52 10*s*. gr. in money of account, was transferred to his credit from the account of Jakemon de Blaudain, another customer. On March 6, Jakemon Franche made a deposit of ten pounds groat in cash. This payment brought his total credit to an amount of £62 10*s*. gr. representing the equivalent of five hundred florins, the face value of the bill, at the rate of 30 groats apiece. This amount of £62 10*s*. gr. was then written to the credit of Jakemon de Gérart, representative or attorney of the payee,[125] and charged to the payor Jakemon Franche, whose account was cancelled in the process.

A transaction of this type obviously did not involve any extension of credit. But suppose that the payor or drawee did not have sufficient funds to pay the bill when it became due. In such a case the money-changer could allow him to overdraw his account. It is to be observed that a transaction of this sort would not differ in any important respect from an ordinary overdraft. As the entries in the Collard de Marke account books rarely give any particulars, I have not been able to discover a clear case involving a bill of exchange which was honored with the proceeds of a bank loan, although the practice must have been fairly common. The Collard de Marke account books contain at least one example of a loan being used, not to pay a draft, but to pay a letter obligatory, the mediaeval ancestor of our promissory note.

On several occasions Collard de Marke agreed to be surety or pledge for the debt of one of his customers. In the fourteenth century the letter obligatory, *chirographe* or *escrit obligatoire*, was still used to some extent as an instrument for witnessing debts. In Flanders the letter obligatory was a deed drawn up in the presence of two aldermen and not a letter under private seal like the English bond described by Professor M. M. Postan.[126] Surety contracts took the form either of co-debtorship or of an independent suretyship. In the first case, the surety was bound jointly with the principal debtor, but had the right of recourse against him either by virtue of a special proviso in the letter obligatory itself[127] or by virtue of a separate contract.[128] In the second case, the surety was liable only if the principal debtor failed to pay.[129] Of these two forms co-debtorship was by far the most common in Flanders.[130] It is this form which is found in the Collard de Marke account books.

According to a memorandum in the journal it appears that Collard de Marke was surety or pledge for one sire Jehan Baille and was jointly bound with him 'to refund and to pay' an amount of seventy-five pounds groat to an Italian named Boucasin Peluc.[131] This obligation was recorded in *une finanche* (a loan embodied in a letter obligatory) due April 20, 1369.[132] On the day of maturity the principal debtor sire Jehan Baille did not have enough money standing to his credit to pay his debt. The seventy-five pounds in question were nevertheless charged against his account[133] and credited to sire Jehan de Concorighe who was presumably the representative or attorney of the creditor Boucasin Peluc. On May 19, sire Jehan Baille's account had a debit balance of £31 4*s*. 11*d*. gr. which was carried forward to the next ledger.[134] On the same date Jehan de Concorighe had still £73 11*s*. 1*d*. groat out of the seventy-five pounds groat remaining to his credit at the bank.[135]

A few points should be stressed. The case shows how credit transactions could be cleared by book transfer without the bank losing any cash. There is manifestly no discounting involved, but the case presents an analogy with acceptance credit. Whether as surety or as acceptor, the banker is primarily liable for the obligation of his customer, but, theoretically, has the right to take recourse against him if he fails to provide the necessary funds at maturity. In practice, arrangements for credit accommodation are usually made in advance between the banker and his customer.

Two other cases of suretyship recorded in the Collard de Marke account books are less interesting than the transaction which has just been discussed. In one case, Collard de Marke was surety for an amount of two hundred pounds *parisis*, at twenty groats a pound, which Jakemon de Blaudain owed to one Gilles de Loo of Roulers as the result of a compromise (*une pais*) concluded on March 10, 1369. It had been agreed that Gilles de Loo had the right to ask for payment at any time after Palm Sunday or March 25, 1369.[136] Actually a settlement did not take place until April 7, 1369, when an amount of £16 13*s*. 4*d*. gr., equal to two hundred pounds *parisis*, was transferred from Jakemon de Blaudain's account to the credit of Gilles de Loo of Roulers.[137] The latter was not a regular customer of Collard de Marke's and withdrew immediately £8 6*s*. 8*d*. gr., or half the above amount, in cash. The balance was still standing to his credit when a new ledger was started on May 20, 1369.

The second case relates to an affair in which Collard de Marke was surety for six hundred francs which one of his customers, Jehan de Rudevorde, had to pay in Paris on March 22, 1369, to a Florentine named Bietremins de le Carde. The local representative of the creditor was apparently a Lucchese named Bielnar de Baudouce.[138] It is certain that Collard de Marke did not undertake to remit the above sum to Paris. On March 6, 1369, the equivalent of six hundred francs or £77 10*s*. gr. was transferred from Jehan de Rudevorde's account to the credit of Jehan de Quantin and, on the same day, from Jehan de Quantin's to the credit of the Italian Lois de Robiert.[139] The entries in the ledger do not give any clue as to the purpose of these two transfers. The whole transaction did not involve any extension of credit as the debtor Jehan de Rudevorde was able to supply the necessary funds on March 6, several days before maturity.

The account books of Collard de Marke and Guillaume Ruyelle contain many examples of overdrafts but not a single example of discounting. One must conclude that neither bills of exchange nor other instruments, such as letters or bills obligatory whatever their nature, were discountable. Conditions in Italy were similar to those existing in Bruges. As Alessandro Lattes, a prominent student of the history of commercial law, writes in one of his most important books: 'The Italian private banks [that is, the Italian exchange banks] were deposit and transfer banks, but never performed the more modern function of discount.'[140]

There is no evidence either that Collard de Marke or Guillaume Ruyelle extended credit to their customers by buying their bills of exchange. Not a single instance has been found among the thousands of entries recorded in the books of those two Bruges money-changers. Neither did they have any correspondents in foreign parts to whom bills could have been sent for collection. In this respect conditions in Italy were the same as in Flanders. In Italy, too, the local transfer banks did not as a rule practice the *cambium per litteras* or have a network of correspondents abroad. The only important exception to this rule is perhaps that of the Venetian *banchi di scritta* which extended credit to customers either by allowing them to overdraw or by buying their foreign bills. But this is one of those exceptions which confirm the rule.

The lack of negotiable instruments was perhaps a serious shortcoming of the mediaeval banking system but its great weakness was not there. A much more serious defect was that the rigidity of the credit structure was greatly increased by the lack of an elastic currency. Today central banks can expand or contract their circulations of notes. By rediscounting operations it is possible to substitute bank notes for bank deposits if there is a demand for more hand-to-hand currency. But, in the Middle Ages specie was the only form of currency. Any increase in the demand for more currency on the part of the public resulted, therefore, in an immediate and often drastic reduction of the cash reserves of the banks. Under those circumstances it is only natural that they tended to keep their cash reserves well above a level which is considered safe today. In other words, the reserve ratio of mediaeval deposit banks was in general higher than the reserve ratio of commercial banks today.

The reserve ratio of Guillaume Ruyelle was 29.3 per cent on May 24, 1370. Probably this figure is fairly representative. The reason is that banks have to keep in step. An individual bank can expand less, but not more, than the other banks in the same system. There is no reason to doubt that this economic law also operated in the Middle Ages. As we have seen, all the money-changers of Bruges were in account with each other. If one of them expanded more than the others, he would soon be warned against over-expansion by the rising adverse balances of his accounts with other banks. If this warning remained unheeded, his competitors were sure to ask for a settlement in cash of the balances due to them. Such an action was likely to result in the rapid exhaustion of the specie reserves of the un-cooperative money-changer and would thus compel him to contract or to stop expanding.

There is little accurate information available concerning the financial condition of mediaeval banks as very few bank statements have reached us. According to a summary statement published by Professor Usher, the Bank of Barcelona maintained on January 23, 1433, a cash reserve of £105,781 15*s*. 3*d*. *Barcelonese* against aggregate demand and short-term liabilities totalling £358,053 4*s*. 6*d*. *Barcelonese* These figures give a reserve ratio of 29.5 per cent.[141] The famous bank of St George in Genoa operated on a much lower ratio. According to the first statement prepared by the bank on January 1st, 1409, after nine months of operation, the cash reserves barely exceeded three thousand florins against liabilities to depositors of about forty or forty-five thousand florins.[142] The reserve ratio was consequently less than ten per cent. Such a ratio was below the safety limit. It is not surprising that the Bank of St George repeatedly ran out of cash and had to suspend specie payments.[143] The trouble was due both to over-expansion and to a mistaken monetary policy which the government expected the bank to carry out.[144]

The rigidity of the mediaeval banking system was still further aggravated by the fact that the assets of deposit banks were not convertible into cash without loss and without delay. Forced liquidation, chiefly of a stock of commodities, was likely to be disastrous in times of monetary stringency and of low prices. The consequence was that the banks placed all their hopes in their cash reserves rather than in their ability to cancel loans and to realize on their investments. As contraction of earning assets was difficult, if not impossible, the cash reserves were likely to suffer the brunt of the fluctuations in the money market. If the pressure on the banking system became too great, the money-changers were sure to clamor for debasement of the currency. And they were right: debasement was often the only way out.[145] History sometimes repeats itself. In 1935, the threatening collapse of the Belgian banks, too deeply engaged in industry, was among the chief causes of the devaluation of the franc. After all, 'devaluation' and 'debasement' are only different names for the same thing. Both devices involve a lowering of the standard by reducing the gold or silver content of the monetary unit.

Figures based on the Collard de Marke account books shed some light on the behavior of mediaeval banks in the face of changed conditions in the money market. These figures give us the aggregate loans, the aggregate deposits, and the ratio between the two on five different dates (Table 24). For three consecutive years this ratio varied little from one year to the next and stood at 28.6 per cent on April 6, 1366, at 25.2 per cent on April 19, 1367, and at 29.2 per cent on April 10, 1368. On December 24, 1369, however, there was a sudden jump from 29.2 to 56.7 per cent. As Table 24 shows, this increase was due to the fact that Collard de Marke continued to expand his loans while his deposits were falling off. Loans increased from £1,478 to £2,611 while deposits dropped from £5,071 to £4,605 groat. This demand for cash may have been due to a seasonal movement of funds. Money in Bruges was usually tight during December and the first half of January.[146] But the amplitude of the fluctuations seem to justify the conclusion that unusual stringency prevailed in the money market. In any case, there were two ways in which Collard de Marke could meet the emergency: either by curtailing drastically his investments or by sacrificing his cash reserves, as the above figures show plainly that he did not contract his loans. It is highly improbable that he was able or willing to liquidate his commercial undertakings. We must therefore come to the conclusion that the scarcity of money in the winter of 1368 resulted in a severe drain on Collard de Marke's cash reserves and presumably on those of the other money-changers in Bruges. The above figures even suggest that the situation must have been for a while extremely critical.

The succeeding months probably brought some relief to the money market. By May 20, 1369, Collard de Marke's financial condition had greatly improved. Our figures indicate that the ratio of loans to deposits had come down to 45.8 per cent. This improvement was due to the combined action of a contraction in the volume of loans and an expansion in the volume of deposits. All other things remaining equal, the net result must have been a substantial increase in Collard de Marke's cash reserves.

If this analysis is correct, it confirms that mediaeval bankers, in an emergency, relied on their cash reserves rather than on a contraction of their loans or a liquidation of their investments. One may question the wisdom of Collard de Marke's policy of expansion in the face of a tightening money market. Perhaps it was wise to lend freely. Curtailment of credit often precipitates a panic. Whatever the individual bank might or could do in order to weather the storms, the fact remains that the mediaeval banking system as a whole was not very flexible. As it did not bend under the strain, it had to break. Such breakdowns were not a rare occurrence.

If banks are considered as business institutions, the direct investment of their resources in mercantile ventures is evidently bad, since it involves an immobilization of funds and precludes an adequate division of risks. From the point of view of the economy as a whole, it does not make any difference how the banks use their resources as long as they operate on a fractional reserve principle. Transferable deposits not only are money substitutes, but *deposit banks create credit or purchasing power by their lending or investing activities.* It does not matter in the least whether the borrower gets currency or is given credit on the books, or whether the investments are made in foreign trade or in local ventures. The process is more devious or complicated in one case than in the other, but the ultimate result in each case is the same: additional money gets into circulation through the operation of the banking system.

That deposit banking had inflationary effects in the Middle Ages as well as today is a truth which does not rest on any documentary evidence but is arrived at by economic analysis. A satisfactory demonstration may be found in almost any American textbook on Money and Banking. However, the principle of credit expansion is not always understood in foreign countries or by persons with no training in economic theory. For the benefit of readers who are not professional economists, let us suppose that the Bruges money-changers operated on a 25 per cent reserve ratio (which is plausible) and that one of them received a new deposit of sixteen pounds groat. Of these sixteen pounds groat, the money-changer would, of course, add four pounds to his cash reserve and lend or invest the remaining twelve pounds. Let us suppose further that he allowed one of his customers to overdraw his account to the extent of twelve pounds in order to pay the customer of another money-changer. Twelve pounds would now be added to the latter's deposits. This second money-changer would now be in a position to expand by adding three of the twelve pounds to his cash reserves and by lending or investing the remaining nine pounds. Thus new deposits would be created in his own or other banks. In theory this process would repeat itself until the original sixteen pounds were used as backing for sixty-four pounds of transferable bank deposits. The economists call this phenomenon 'the principle of multiple expansion.'[147]

As bank deposits, in mediaeval Bruges, were extensively used as a means of payment, they replaced coin to a considerable extent and represented certainly a large fraction of the total monetary circulation. The displaced coin, there is no doubt, went abroad with the result that the supply of money in the mediaeval world as a whole was artificially increased.[148] Furthermore, since bank deposits were only partly backed by specie, the requirements of the Bruges trade *ceteris paribus* would have necessitated a much larger supply of coin if there had been no banks. To conclude, the exchange banks *created purchasing power, or money, as effectively as if they had been granted the privilege of issuing notes.*[149]

This is supported by the history of Venetian banking. Venice suffered repeatedly from the over-expansion of bank deposits with the result that bank money depreciated as would paper money if issued in excessive quantities.[150] On several occasions the banks were allowed to suspend specie payments but inconvertible bank money continued to circulate in the books of the Rialto banks. In the sixteenth and seventeenth centuries the Venetian Republic even used bank money extensively as a means of war finance. Bank deposits ceased to be convertible in specie, bank credits were then created against government loans, and war materials were simply paid by assignment in bank instead of specie. The result was a real inflation of the circulating medium.[151] Over-expansion of bank deposits has the same effect as the over-issue of paper money. Essentially there is little difference between bank deposits and bank notes. Both are fiduciary money resting on the confidence of the public in the solvency of the banks.

As we shall see in the next chapter, it is not impossible that the financial advisers to the dukes of Burgundy were aware of the fact, or at least suspected, that the money-changers of Bruges usurped monetary functions by their banking transactions. This truth strangely enough had to be rediscovered after five centuries by the Belgian Government which is the successor to the traditions of the House of Burgundy. It is only in the *Rapport au Roi* which precedes the Royal Decree of July 9, 1935, that the Belgian Government officially admitted that the banks of deposit *de facto,* if not *de jure,* performed the functions of a bank of issue, and that bank notes and transferable bank deposits were fundamentally identical. The relevant passage of the *Rapport au Roi* is very much to the point and is worth quoting as a conclusion to this chapter:

> Le rôle prépondérant que jouent, dans la plupart de nos institutions de crédit, les engagements à vue représentés par des dépôts ou par des promesses formelles d'avances en compte, leur confère en fait, sinon en droit, le caractère de banque de circulation. Les crédits sont accordés sous forme d'inscription en compte. D'autre part, par le jeu des virements et des compensations, la circulation des dépôts à vue a pris un caractère monétaire en tous points analogue à celui qu'avait à l'origine la circulation des billets au porteur.
>
> La science économique a, depuis longtemps déjà, fait ressortir l'unité foncière de la circulation de monnaie légale, telle qu'elle existe dans la plupart des Etats modernes sous forme de billets et d'engagements à vue de l'institut d'émission, et de la circulation scripturale des dépôts et d'autres engagements à vue des banques particulières.
>
> De grandes différences existent, sans doute, entre ces deux circulations, mais

> elles relèvent bien plus de l'aspect légal et juridique que de la réalité économique à laquelle l'Etat ne peut pas, le voulût-il, rester étranger.[152]

The *Rapport au Roi* contains one mistake. Bank notes did not precede transferable bank deposits, but bank money under the form of transferable bank deposits existed in Italy and Flanders long before there were any notes.

NOTES TO CHAPTER 14

[1]Usher, 'Banking in Barcelona,' *op. cit.*, pp. 135 f., and *Hist. of Deposit Banking*, I, 271.

[2]I refer here to the fact that an American scholar was unfairly criticized by a French reviewer who misunderstood the meaning of 'overdraft' and 'transfer of credit' and did not know about the American practice of loans secured by promissory notes. See AHES, V (1933), pp. 498 f.

[3]Of course, bills of exchange could be used in an indirect way as a credit instrument. For example, bills of exchange could be purchased with bank credit instead of with cash. On this topic, see Usher, 'The Origins of Banking,' *op. cit.*, p. 415.

[4]*Ibid.*, pp. 414-415, n. 2. The Venetian senator Tommaso Contarini in his speech of December 28, 1584, in favor of the creation of a public bank, clearly referred to the overdraft when he mentioned that bankers would accommodate their friends by simply granting them credit without any disbursement of cash or coin *(di denaro)*. See E. Lattes, *op. cit.*, p. 125, No. 42. His brother, Alessandro Lattes (*Il diritto commerciale*, p. 209) asserts that loans were frequently *(per lo più)* secured by pledges of personal property *(sopra pegno)* or by letters obligatory, but he adds immediately that one of the most common forms of lending was to open a line of credit without security *(credito allo scoperto*, Fr. *crédit à découvert)*. The two statements seem contradictory to me. I doubt very much whether loans secured by pledges or by letters obligatory were as common as A. Lattes assumes.

[5]Usher, 'Banking in Barcelona,' *op. cit.*, p. 129, and *Hist. of Deposit Banking*, I, 33 ff.

[6]Cf. Sieveking, *Casa di San Giorgio*, p. 49 [333].

[7]*Ibid.*, p. 56 [340].

[8]Chiefly in connection with the farming out of certain taxes.

[9]A good example is given by Sieveking (*Casa di San Giorgio*, p. 48 [332]). The archbishop of Genoa Jacoppo Fieschi had an account with his relative, the banker Antonio Fieschi. Money was deposited to the credit of this account or withdrawn from it, not by the archbishop himself, but by his 'factor' or servant. When the archbishop died in 1397, it was found that the account at the bank had been overdrawn to the extent of £100 17*s*. The archbishop's heirs tried to repudiate this debt by questioning the authenticity of the bank's records, but the *Officium Mercantie* or Commercial Court decided that the entries in the books were to be considered as satisfactory evidence and that the estate of the deceased was to be charged with the balance due to the Fieschi bank.

[10]Usher, 'The Origins of Banking,' *op. cit.*, pp. 414 f.; *idem*, 'Banking in Barcelona,' *op cit.*, p. 129.

[11]de Roover, 'Ruyelle,' *op. cit.*, pp. 94 f. The items above ten pounds and below fifteen pounds are: Williame Danoubel £14 15*s*. 1*d*. gr. and Jehan de Boghemakere £10 2*s*. 5*d*. The only item above fifteen pounds is a debit balance of exactly nineteen pounds groat due from a Segher Gherart.

[12]Gilliodts, *Cart de l'Estaple*, I, 274, No. 355.

[13]Ehrenberg, 'Makler, Hosteliers und Börse in Brügge,' *op. cit.*, p. 414.

[14]Collard de Marke Ledger No. 5, May 20, 1369, fol. 50.

[15]Ehrenberg, 'Makler, Hosteliers und Börse,' *op. cit.*, pp. 423-28.

[16]Gilliodts, *Cart. de l'Estaple*, I, 274, No. 355.

[17]Collard de Marke Ledger No. 1, fol. 14.

[18]Ledger No. 2, fol. 21.

[19]Ledger No. 3, fol. 23.

[20]Ledger No. 4, fol. 20.

[21]Ledger No. 5, fol. 34.

[22]Gilliodts, *Inventaire*, II, 349-53.

[23]*Hanserecesse*, II (Leipzig, 1872), 412, No. 342, sec. 5. Date: May 1, 1387.

[24]Collard de Marke Journal No. 1, April 19, 1367-April 10, 1368.

[25]Collard de Marke Ledger No. 3, fol. 1: 'Jakes de Wallers me doit par le reste de nos contes dou 2e fuellet de men autre papier devant cestuy, contet à lui 10 jours en novembre quant il en ala en Bretaingne.'

[26]Ledger No. 3, fol. 12.

[27]Ledger No. 4, fol. 14.

[28]Pirenne, *Hist. de Belgique,* II, 206-18.

[29]Gilliodts, *Inventaire,* II, 385 f.

[30]*Ibid.,* p. 387.

[31]*Ibid.,* pp. 412 f.: 'Item ghecocht jeghen den here Joris Wandelare, een banniere paerd ter stede boef, 't welke Gheraerd van Sint-Omaers reed metter stede banniere, ende coste 5 ℔. gr. Somme 60℔. par.'

[32]The troops of Ghent under the leadership of Frans Ackerman had taken Damme on July 1st, 1383 (Pirenne, *Hist. de Belgique,* II, 217).

[33]Gilliodts, *Inventaire,* III, 23.

[34]*Ibid.,* pp. 251, 278, 383 (No. 835), and 385 (No. 839).

[35]Collard de Marke Ledger No. 4, fol. 10 and Ledger No. 5, fol. 6.

[36]Pirenne, *Hist. de Belgique,* II, 212.

[37]His account on fol. 10 in Ledger No. 4 is charged with several transfers to the credit of Hanseatic merchants such as Cristofle Wetin, Gisselare Gier, and Thideman Rommelin Roede. It is a well-known fact that furs were one of the principal trading articles of the Hanseatic merchants. Thideman Rommelin Roede, or more exactly Remmelincrode, was in 1361 an elder or member of the local council of the Hanseatic League in Bruges. *Hanserecesse,* I (Leipzig, 1870), 129, No. 201.

[38]Collard de Marke Ledger No. 5, fol. 38v.

[39]Ledger No. 4, fol. 28.

[40]Gilliodts, *Inventaire,* II, 405.

[41]Ibid., III, 92. Galigo da Piastre is mentioned in 1384 as being the partner of Dino Rapondi. Cf. Bigwood, *Régime,* I, 108.

[42]Collard de Marke Ledger No. 4, fol. 3v has a ledger account with the following heading: Thumas Sarlande à le cause dou mestre de le monnoie.' The master of the mint was at that time Jehan Interminelli or Terminel. See Appendix II, Account 2.

[43]For example, important deposits of gold specie were made by Forteguerra (Ledger No. 4, fol. 124) and by Davin Tedaldini (Ledger No. 4, fol. 76).

[44]We have no information whatever concerning a number of borrowers whose balances at one time or another exceeded fifty pounds groat, as for example: Jehan van Tinneskin, sire Ector Jucamiel, Bette Dougardin, Simon Ongeriet, Pierre de Leurent, Pierre de Gérard, Gilles de Dec, Jehan de Concorighe, Carot de Galbert, Gilles le Clerc (dou Dam), etc.

[45]See, for example, Edler, *Glossary,* Appendix III, p. 398. This author made a very careful study of this issue on the basis of the Medici account books of the Selfridge Collection at Harvard University and came to the conclusion that credit terms were seldom observed. Discounts were sometimes granted in order to induce customers to pay before the stipulated credit term.

[46]An excellent paragraph on overtrading is found in Adam Smith, *The Wealth of Nations,* Book IV, chap. i, p. 406. Adam Smith points out that overtrading was the cause of the common complaints about the scarcity of money under mercantile capitalism. Cf. Viner, *Studies in the Theory of International Trade,* pp. 87-90. The author of a sixteenth-century Venetian document argues against the erection of a public bank on the ground that the merchants would be greatly inconvenienced because they would not be permitted any longer to overdraw, as they were used to doing with private bankers. A result of the creation of a public bank would thus be to force the merchants to increase their cash balances and to curtail their volume of business. See E. Lattes, *op. cit.,* p. 152, doc. 43.

[47]As Professor Viner points out, shortage of capital keeps interest rates high and makes it difficult to borrow on favorable terms (*Studies in the Theory of International Trade,* p. 88).

[48]Cutting down cash balances was not always a wise business policy. If the creditor refused to wait any longer and the bank refused to lend, such a practice was bound to lead to forced sales at inopportune moments.

[49]This danger was clearly seen in Italy, at least. In 1450 a Venetian statute forbade the *banchi di scritta* of the Rialto to make any transfers for speculators in silver, whether citizens or foreigners, unless they had sufficient funds. See E. Lattes, *op. cit.*, p. 70, doc. 22. On March 31, 1467, another statute was passed whereby bankers were not allowed to lend more than ten ducats to any one customer without good security (*ibid.*, p. 72).

[50]Usher ('The Origins of Banking,' *op. cit.*, p. 401) states rightly that 'the whole credit structure was jeopardized by the absence of a satisfactory type of short-time paper.'

[51]E. Lattes, *op. cit.*, doc. 43, p. 152.

[52]*Ibid.*, doc. 42, p. 125.

[53]*Ibid.*, doc. 43, p. 152.

[54]This statement may require some illustration for the benefit of readers who are not trained economists. Suppose that a money-changer who has no capital starts in business with only two customers, Mr. A. and Mr. B, each depositing an amount of fifty pounds groat. At this stage, the money-changer's balance is as follows: assets, cash £100 gr.; liabilities, due to depositors, £100 gr. Suppose now that the money-changer allows Mr. B to overdraw his account in order to transfer an amount of £75 gr. to the credit of Mr. C. As a result of this transaction, the money-changer's balance is changed as follows:

Assets		*Liabilities*	
		Due to depositors	
Cash	£100 0 0 gr.	to Mr. A	£50 0 0 gr.
Loans: Mr. B	25 0 0	to Mr. C	£75 0 0
	£125 0 0 gr.		£125 0 0 gr.

The cash reserve remains untouched, but the liability to depositors has risen from £100 gr. to £125 gr. The reserve ratio, which was formerly 100%, has now dropped to 80%. Furthermore, the expansion of bank deposits has created additional means of payment or additional money to the extent of £25 gr.

[55]Cf. Nasse, *op. cit.*, P. 339.

[56]For example, Guglielmo Rapondi's account (Ledger No. 4, fol. 188) contains the following debit entry: 'Et pour l'avantaige de l'or dessus dit, de tout l'or de nos contes, contet à lui à ce jour 1 ℔. 5*s*. gr.' A similar item is charged to Davin Tedaldini (Ledger No. 4, fol. 76).

[57]Nasse, *op. cit.*, p. 339.

[58] He was fined fifty pounds *parisis* for lending money at a rate exceeding 2*d*. per pound a week. Bruges Municipal Archives, Comptes Communaux, 1368-1369 (n. s.), fol. 18^{v}.

[59]The full text of this statement is found in de Roover, 'Ruyelle,' *op. cit.*, pp. 92-95, doc. No. 7. This statement, it is recalled, is written on a loose sheet of paper which was discovered by sheer accident inside the binding of Ruyelle's ledger. The statement was prepared by listing separately the debit and credit balances standing open in the ledger as of May 24, 1370.

[60]This amount is the sum of two items which, in the original, are labeled as follows: 'Item 262 *lb.* 11*s.* 10*d* en argent' and 'Item 15 *lb.* 11*s.* 5*d.* par mi conteit.' The smaller item, evidently, represents till money for which the bookkeeper-cashier—who also made out the statement—was accountable *(par mi conteit)*; the larger item refers probably to specie kept in a safe or strongbox. Mediaeval money-changers usually had two strongboxes in which their money was kept: a large one, containing the bulk of their specie reserve, which was kept in a vault or other secure place, and a small one, containing till money, which was kept in the office. For an example of this arrangement, see Sayous, 'La "Table des Changes" de Valence,' *op. cit.*, p. 137.

[61]Bruges, State Archives, Fonds des Métiers, No. 467 (Cartulary called Roobouck of the Fishmongers' Gild), fol. 1.

[62]Collard de Marke Ledger No. 2, fol. 101, and Ledger No. 5, fol. 23.

[63]Ledger No. 3, fol. 1.

[64]An entry in Ledger No. 3, fol. 10, mentions several bolts of cloth from Maubeuge and Valenciennes.

[65]Sales of cloth are mentioned in Ledger No. 2, fol. 101, and Ledger No. 5, fol. 23. Buyers of the cloth were Tideman Rommelin Roede (a Hanseatic merchant), Jehan van Marc (another money-changer), Pietre Vetinc, Olivier Kalve, Georges Boin Avoir (Bonaiuti), Martin Domingues (presumably a Spaniard), Dominges Janes (another Spaniard or Portuguese), Antonne van Zendre (a German), etc. Collard de Marke paid *hallegeld* or *hallage* on some of the cloth sold by him.

[66]Thus Lambesin de Jaghere is written Lambesin Diagre; Steven van der Meersch becomes Estievene van Dremiers; Jehan van den Acker, Jehan van de Nacre; Jakob Metten Eye, Jakes Mattenaie; Mattheus Janssens or Janssone, Mathins Jehan Senne; etc.

[67]Here are some of the names: Thierry Brochons, Hanin Quentin, Jehan and Pierre Moyses or Moyset, Jehan Hoket, Franche Louvet, Pierre Rasoir, etc.

[68]Collard de Marke Journal No. 2 (corresponding to Ledger No. 4), fol. 48. The entry in question reads as follows: 'doy Tiery Brochon ke il m'envoia par Colard le Brun, bouchier de Valenchiennes le 12e en février 1400 francs dou roy.'

[69]Espinas, *Documents relatifs à la Draperie de Valenciennes,* p. 262, No. 434.

[70]*Ibid.,* pp. 30, 38, 321, and *passim.*

[71]Bigwood, *Régime,* II, 344-48, No. XLIV, A and B. The contract is clearly a loan disguised under the form of a sales contract, because the option could be extended for another year on payment of 2,000 florins. Presumably, the interest rate was 50%, and not 33⅓% as Bigwood asserts (*ibid.,* I, 449). The loan was actually repaid on July 13, 1362, or before the end of the first year (*ibid.,* II, 348).

[72]Collard de Marke Ledger No. 5, fol. 410v.

[73]This possibility is suggested by an entry involving Thierry Brochons in Ledger No. 5, on fol. 23.

[74]In Ledger No. 5, fol. 23, there is a joint account in the name of 'Pietre van le Fine et Collard de Marke.'

[75]Some sales were also made by Pietre van le Fine. See Ledger No. 3, fol. 10. Collections, certainly, were often made by Collard de Marke, see Ledger No. 2, fol. 101.

[76]On April 6, 1366, the debit balance of the account of Pietre van le Fine in Ledger No. 1 (fol. 15) amounted to £548 14*s.* 11*d.* gr. On April 19, 1367, however, an amount of £358 13*s.* gr. was standing to his credit. It had increased to £1,090 10*s.* 10*d.* gr. by June of the same year. At that time the balance suddenly swung back to the debit side because of a transfer or nearly two thousand pounds groat from the *papier des dras.* At the end of June 1367, the debit balance of Pietre van Fine's account was £553 5*s.* 8*d.* gr. (Ledger No. 2, fol. 101). On April 10, 1367, there was again a credit balance of £700 14s. gr. representing, the ledger entry says, sales made by Pietre van le Fine (Ledger No. 3, fol. 10). On May 20, 1369, the aggregate debits exceeded the aggregate credits by £543 10*s.* 7*d.* gr. (£1,289 13s. 4*d.* gr.—£746 2*s.* 9*d.* gr.). It is impossible to know what these figures exactly mean. Possibly the debits represent money paid for purchases and the credits, sales made by Pietre van le Fine. But, I repeat, it is all more or less a guess.

[77]This assertion is based on the following entry (Ledger No. 3, fol. 10): 'Pietre van le Fine pour plusuers parties de dras de Valenchiennes et de Maubuege qu'il avoit vendus, dont nous en avons contet ensanble, présent Jehan Gronin 12 jours en avril [1368].'

[78]Ledger No. 5, fol. 23. The note reads as follows: 'sur les dras depuis que Pietre fu trespasés.

[79]Pirenne, *Hist. de Belgique,* II, 68-69, n. 2. Pirenne, unfortunately, does not give any names or precise references.

[80]*Codex diplomaticus lubecensis (Lübeckisches Urkundenbuch),* Part I, *Urkundenbuch der Stadt Lübeck,* Vol. III, (Lübeck, 1871), pp. 753-54, No. 693.

[81]Usher, 'The Origins of Banking,' *op. cit.*, p. 416; Gustav Lastig, 'Beiträge zur Geschichte des Handelsrechts,' *Zeitschrift für das gesamte Handelsrecht,* XXIII (1878), 161; Lane, 'Venetian Bankers,' *op. cit.*, p. 187. A case in point is that of the banker Giacomo da Giussano who had a bank in Piacenza during the years 1356-1358. His business was in many ways similar to that of Collard de Marke. Giussano, too, did not limit to banking the scope of his activity, but also traded in cloth, hosiery *(calzature)*, and other commodities. See Zerbi, *op. cit.*, p. 247. The same conditions prevailed even in Germany. See the contract concluded in 1403 between the city of Frankfort and the money-changer Johann Palmstorf. Speyer, *Die ältesten Credit- und Wechselbanken in Frankfurt am Main* pp. 28-29, sec. 10.

[82]E. Lattes, *op. cit.*, p. 13.

[83]*Ibid.*, p. 14.

[84]Roberto Cessi in 'Il problema bancario a Venezia nel secolo XIV,' *op. cit.*, p. 799, writes erroneously that the banker was not allowed to invest in trade more than one and one-half times his own capital. The original text says: 'nisi de tanto de quanto fecerit impraestita nostra communi, et de medietate plus.' See E. Lattes, *op. cit.*, p. 44, doc. XII.

[85]*Ibid.*, p. 42.

[86]*Ibid.*, pp. 125-26. Cf. the discourse against the establishment of a public bank, where an attempt is made to refute this argument (*ibid.*, p. 150).

[87]Bruges, Municipal Archives, Chartes politiques, 1e série, No. 1155, sec. 13, April 21, 1477: 'Item, dat de wisselaers ende banchouders in de onser voors. stede van Brugghe borchtucht stellen zullen van hueren banc ende wisselen, ter bewaernesse van elken, ende, dat zy gheene coopmanscepen doen, noch ghesellen in coopmanscepen wesen en zullen moghen binden lande, over zee, noch over sberchs.' Cf. Bigwood, *Régime,* I, 417 where he writes: 'l'ordonnance de Philippe le Hardi (1389) sur ses monnaies de Flandre défend aux changeurs de se livrer au trafic . . .' This latter ordinance has been published by Gilliodts (*Inventaire,* III, 130-35, No. 706). It regulates the trade in money and bullion, but, contrary to Bigwood's assertion, does not place any restriction upon the participation of money-changers in commercial transactions.

[88]A. Lattes, *Il diritto commerciale,* p. 201.

[89]Di Tucci, *op. cit.*, p. 131. In 1528 the *Officium Mercantie* and the *Officium Banchorum* were merged into one single office, the *Rota Civile.*

[90]Pirenne, *Hist. de Belgique,* III, 8-16.

[91]The whole discussion concerning this problem of origins centers around Genoese records of the twelfth century.

[92]This was true already in twelfth-century Genoa. See Hall, 'Genoese Bankers,' *op. cit.*, p. 75: 'In credit as in foreign exchange, merchants, not bankers, were the pioneers,' and p. 76: 'The earliest records, those from 1179 to 1186, contain almost no evidence of money-lending.'

[93]The chief exponent of this theory is the French economic historian André-E. Sayous, who has formulated it especially in his article 'Les opérations des banquiers italiens,' *op. cit.*, pp. 2, 6, and 21. Sayous further insists that banking did not develop until well into the thirteenth century. Recent publications by Raffaele Di Tucci, Margaret Hall, and Robert L. Reynolds have proven that banking in Genoa developed earlier than Sayous has been willing to admit. See the latter's article, 'Les opérations des banquiers de Gênes à la fin du XIIe siècle,' *op, cit.;* his review of Margaret Hall's study in AHES, VIII (1936), 109; and 'Les travaux des Américains sur le commerce de Gênes aux XIIe et XIIIe siècles,' *Giornale storico e letterario della Linguria,* XIII (1937), 88-89. Professor Reynolds, in his rejoinder ('Gli studi americani sulla storia genovese,' *ibid.*, XIV (1938), 15-19, 24, 25-26), has shown that the criticisms of Monsieur Sayous are not always fair nor well-founded in fact.

Sayous stresses the importance of short-term credit, as if there existed ninety-day paper in the Middle Ages, but he has to admit that borrowers had little regard for maturities. See 'Les opérations des banquiers italiens,' *op. cit.*, p. 29; 'Les opérations des banquiers de Gênes à la fin du XIIe siècle,' *op. cit.*, pp. 293, 295; 'Le capitalisme commercial et financier dans les pays chrétiens de la Méditerranée occidentale depuis la première croisade jusqu'à la fin du moyen âge,' *VSWG,* XXIX (1936), 280; and 'Méthodes commerciales de Barcelone au XIVe siècle,' *op. cit.,* p. 219.

[94]A clear case proving that bank deposits were transferable is found in a Genoese document of the year 1200. As such a practice did not spring up overnight, it must have existed prior to 1200. See Reynolds, 'A Business Affair in Genoa,' *op. cit.,* pp. 8 f., and Di Tucci, *op. cit.,* pp. 96 f. The evidence presented by Dr. Hall is not conclusive, because she does not establish beyond any doubt that bank deposits were easily transferable. This is the only criticism which I have to make of her study.

[95]Irving Fisher, *The Purchasing Power of Money* (New York, 1913), pp. 40 f.

[96]This is also the opinion of Monsieur Sayous who writes apropos of Di Tucci's book: 'D'une façon générale, les textes publiés par M. Di Tucci laissent l'impression que la spécialisation des banquiers était très médiocre; ils agissaient comme des commerçants ayant à tenir des échéances plutôt que comme des spécialistes du maniement de l'argent ayant des fonctions et préoccupations particulières,' and 'A la fin du XIIe siècle, les banquiers génois adaptaient à leur activité encore peu spécialisée le cadre ordinaire des opérations commerciales' ('Banquiers de Gênes au XIIe siècle,' *op. cit.,* pp. 293 f.).

[97]As a matter of fact, lack of specialization is a general characteristic of mercantile capitalism. See Gras, *Business and Capitalism,* pp. 74-81.

[98]The twelfth-century notarial records of Genoa contain a number of contracts in which bankers receive money on deposit and promise the depositors to pay them a share of the earnings rather than a fixed rate of interest (Di Tucci, *op. cit.,* p. 90, doc. XI; Hall, 'Genoese Banking,' *op. cit.,* p. 77, n. 2). More modern examples of such hybrid contracts are the French *commandite,* preferred stock, and income bonds on which interest is paid only if earned.

[99]Sayous, 'Banquiers de Gênes au XIIe siècle; *op. cit.,* pp. 289, 291.

[100]Di Tucci, *op. cit.,* pp. 106-109, docs. XXXIV-XLII.

[101]*Loc. cit.* Two partnerships were formed for voyages to Provence (docs. XXXIV and XXXIX), one for a voyage to Sardinia (doc. XXXVII), and two for voyages to Sicily (docs. XL and XLII). In two instances the text states that the partnership is formed for a voyage overseas, but does not give further details (docs. XXVI and XLI).

[102]*Ibid.,* p. 101, docs. XXVII and XXVIII. An interest of 10% was paid by the banker on time deposits (*ibid.,* p. 93, doc. XVIII and p. 95, doc. XXI).

[103]*Ibid.,* p. 100, docs. XXV and XXVI.

[104]*Ibid.,* doc. XXVI.

[105]J. Lameere, 'Un chapitre de l'histoire du prêt à intérêt,' *op. cit.,* p. 97.

[106]Usher, 'The Origins of Banking,' *op. cit.,* p. 412: 'We must assume that banking policy consisted chiefly in keeping some actual cash in hand, extending loans to promising customers, and making some investments in trade.'

[107]In the contracts published by Di Tucci, the banker is always the investing partner (*op. cit.,* pp. 106-109, docs. XXXIV-XLII).

[108]Ciardini, *op. cit.,* p. 29.

[109]*Ibid.,* pp. 4, 31, ii (doc. I), and xxiii (doc. VI).

[110]Lane, *op. cit.,* p. 196. The examples given by Professor Lane do not warrant, it seems to me, the conclusion that the Venetian bankers 'combined the now distinct businesses of pawnbroking and commercial banking.' This conclusion would only be justified if loans were made on collateral other than gold, silver, or government obligations.

[111]Cahn, 'Der Strassburger Stadtwechsel,' *op, cit.,* pp. 58-60.

[112]Gilliodts, *Coutume,* I, 518.

[113]*Loc. cit.*

[114]de Roover, 'Ruyelle,' *op. cit.,* pp. 37, 88-89.

[115]Bigwood, *Régime,* I, 100.

[116]Cf. van Werveke, *Gentsche Stadsfinanciën,* Book I, chap. ix, pp. 266-90.

[117]Bigwood, *Régime,* I, 45. The spelling 'Antonin de Vinalda,' given by Bigwood must be a misreading.

[118]Ehrenberg, *Das Zeitalter der Fugger,* I, 38.

[119]Sayous, 'Le capitalisme commercial et financier,' *op. cit.,* p. 281.

[120]On this topic, see Ehrenberg, *Das Zeitalter der Fugger,* I, 18-22.

[121]de Roover, 'Ruyelle,' *op. cit.,* pp. 58-61.

[122]For an example, see Gilliodts, *Cart. de l'Estaple,* II, 6, No. 913. The date of the document is March 9, 1452.

[123]Collard de Marke, Ledger No. 4, fol. 105.

Dr.

[124]*Loc. cit.:* 'Jakemon Franche me doit par Boin Acourt de Louc 6 en march d'un cange de 500 florins de Florenche à Jakemes de Gérart.......................... 62 *lb.* 10*s.*'

Cr.

'Doy par Jakemon de Blaudain 28 en février 400 francs françois à ½ gros [52*lb.* 10*s.*]
Et par lui contet 6 en march.. 10*lb.* gr.
Somme 62 *lb.* 10*s* gr.'

[125]Ledger No. 4, fol. 110.

[126]Postan, 'Private Financial Instruments in Medieval England,' *op. cit.,* pp. 27-42.

[127]Bigwood, *Régime,* II, 266, No. III. The letter obligatory dates from August 1261. The co-debtors are Evrars à le Take and Willaume Dorcies. But, if Evrars pays the letter, Willaume has to compensate him without delay ('Et Evrars en doit acuiter Willaume tout çuite'). Cf. *ibid.,* pp. 285-86, No. VIII.

[128]Georges Des Marez, *La lettre de foire à Ypres au XIIIe siècle* (Mémoires in-8⁰ de l'Académie Royale de Belgique,' LX [Brussels, 1900]), pp. 44-45.

[129]*Ibid.,* p. 160, No. 68.

[130]Bigwood, *Régime,* I, 472.

[131]Collard de Marke, Journal No. 2, fol. 1: 'Memore que je sui pleghes de sire Jehan Balle de rendre et payer à Boucasin Peluc au 20e d'avril 75 *lb.* gr. sik'il apert par men autre petit papier devant chesty ou fuellet 128. J'ay escrit sur leur comte.'

[132]Account of Jehan de Concorighe (Ledger No. 4, fol. 165): 'Item li doi-ge par Jehan Baille pour une finanche qu'il fist à Boucasin 75 *lb.* gr.'

[133]Ledger No. 4, fol. 173: 'Sire Jehan Baille me doit par sire Jehan de Concorighe pour une finance 75 *lb.* gr.'

[134]*Ibid.*: 'Item li doi-ge ke il me fait conte ou fuellet 32 de men papier apriès cesty 31 *lb.* 4*s.* 11*d.*'

[135]*Ibid.,* fol. 165: 'Item me doit-il ke je li fay conte ou fulliet 29 de men papier apriès cesty, 73 *lb.* 11*s.* 1*d.* gr.'

[136]Journal No. 2, fol. 2: 'Mémore que je sui pleges pour Jakemon de Blaudain à Gilles de Lo de Roulers de le somme de 200 *lb.* de parisis, 20 gros pour le *lb.* S'est à paijet à le volentet dou dit Gilles le jour de paskes flories passet. Ce fu fait 10 en march.'

Ledger No. 4, fol. 149, account of Gilles de Lo de Roulers: 'doy par Jakemon de Blaudain 7 en avril pour le cause d'une pais 200 lb. parisis, 20 gros pour le lb., somme 16 *lb.* 13*s.* 4*d.*'

[137]Ledger No. 4, fol. 131 and 149.

[138]Journal No. 2, fol. 2: 'Mémore que je sui pleghes de Jehan de Rudevorde pour 76 *lb.* 5*s.* gr. qui monte 600 francs lesquel il es doit faire donner à Paris à Bietremins de le Carde, Florentin, à 22 jours de march. Se les doit recevoir Bielnar de Baudouce de Lukes.'

[139]Ledger No. 4, fols. 96^{v}, 85, and 33.

[140]A. Lattes, *Il diritto commerciale,* p. 204: '. . . questi banchi privati furono soltanti banchi di deposito e di giro, e non esercitarono mai le funzione più moderne dello sconto.' Cf. Sieveking, *Casa di San Giorgio,* p. 49 [333]: 'Die Banken discontierten keine Wechsel, da die Form des Indossierens erst im 17. Jahrhundert mit dem Verfall der Wechselmessen üblich wurde.'; also Sayous, 'Les méthodes commerciales de Barcelone au XVe siècle,' *op. cit.,* pp. 275, 281. I do not agree with Endemann's statement: 'Und andererseits gab es für den Depositenverwahrer kein natürlichere Verwendung der bei ihm niedergelegten Werthe als im Wechselgeschäft, (*Studien,* I, 425).

[141]Usher, 'Deposit Banking in Barcelona,' *op. cit.*, p. 138; *idem, Early History of Deposit Banking*, I, 181.

[142]The summary statement published by Sieveking (*Aus Genueser Rechnungs- und Steuerbüchern*, pp. 36-37) gives only the totals of the balance, a detail which is not of any value. The figures given above are based on a photostatic copy of the original (Genoa, State Archives, Sala 24, Bancorum S. Georgii, Cartularium 1408, fols. 110v-113). Total liabilities amount to fl.54,295 14*s*. 1*d*. from which have to be subtracted more than ten thousand florins representing deposits made by various tax collectors and by the consuls of the Casa di San Giorgio. The money in cash was exactly fl.3,013 9*s*. 3*d*., according to the balance (*ibid.*, fol. 110v).

[143]Sieveking, *Casa di San Giorgio*, p. 72 [356], n. 2.

[144]*Ibid.*, pp. 62 [346], 67-75 [351-59].

[145]Because debasement would relieve the money market and stretch the cash reserves of the banks.

[146]Uzzano, *Pratica*, chap. xlviii, p. 156.

[147]Chester Arthur Phillips, *Bank Credit: a Study of the Principles and Factors Underlying Advances Made by Banks to Borrowers* (New York, 1920), pp. 32-64. The example is valid only in so far as it applies to the local system of exchange banks as a unit and not to any individual money-changer in particular. For a banking system as a whole, loans are offspring of deposits and deposits, offspring of loans (*ibid.*, p. 64).

[148]This process has been described by Adam Smith in his discussion on money (*op. cit.*, Book II, chap. ii, pp. 277-79 and *passim*).

[149]I do not agree with the following statement of Professor Z. W. Sneller, since it is in contradiction with my conclusions: 'Hij [de wisselaar] had in zijn bank of kantoor slechts te maken met het harde, reëele geld; de opkomst van een fiduciair betaalmiddel, schepping van den handel onder crediet, ging buiten hem om. Of, om het te zeggen in de taal der Wirtschaftsstufen: het bedrijf van den wisselaar wortelt geheel in de Geldwirtschaft; de ontluikende Kreditwirtschaft was product van den zich in breede vrijheid ontwikkelenden groothandel' ('Het wisselaarsbedrijf in Nederland,' *op. cit.*, p. 497).

[150]The same happened in Genoa. See Sieveking, *Casa di San Giorgio*, p. 66 [350] and n. 4.

[151]Lane, 'Venetian Bankers,' *op. cit.*, pp. 201 f., 205 f.

[152]Royal decree of July 9, 1935, called 'Arrêté royal sur le contrôle des banques et le régime des émissions de titres et de valeurs,' *Moniteur Belge*, CV (1935), No. 191, p. 4356. Cf. M. Allemandet, *Le contrôle des banques en Belgique* (Paris, 1937), p. 40.

Chapter 15

BANK FAILURES AND PUBLIC POLICY

IN the Middle Ages, commercial banking was not a conservative business but a risky game. The stability of mediaeval banks was jeopardized by a number of serious defects in the credit structure: there was no central banking institution which could help the other banks in a panic; there were no negotiable instruments, so that the overdraft was the most common form of extending credit; the usury prohibition and its legal implications were a serious hindrance to the development of credit; haphazard methods of bookkeeping were another source of difficulties because the mediaeval banker never knew exactly how large his commitments really were; banks, in general, were too small and hence vulnerable; and, last but not least, the direct participation in business ventures was not only risky but involved the immobilization of funds and prevented an adequate division of risks.

Under those circumstances, mediaeval bankers had to rely almost exclusively on strong cash reserves and they naturally tried to protect these by every means. In times of monetary stringency, the mediaeval bankers would not hesitate to resort to every possible subterfuge in order to gain time and to avoid paying out cash.[1] Customers asking for specie were sent from one bank to another until they were completely worn out or they could get payment only in undesirable black money so that they needed a cart to carry it home.[2] Sometimes the books were deliberately falsified, and the customer was told that there was an error in his account which had to be straightened out before any payment could be made.[3] Depositors were also promised special advantages if they would not ask for cash but would make all their payments by assignment in bank.[4] Another method was to shorten the office-hours. As the telling of specie required time, customers were thus induced to settle their debts by book transfer. Because of these practices, bank deposits ceased to be readily converted into cash. In Venice, about 1526, specie was at a twenty per cent premium over bank money.[5]

All these expedients tended to arouse suspicion as to the solvency of the banks. According to the Venetian Senator, Tommaso Contarini, a false rumor, the imminence of a war, the news that a commercial venture had gone wrong, the failure of a merchant in debt to a bank, and similar events were enough to shake completely the confidence of the public and to provoke a run.[6] As a banker could not repay all his depositors at once, he was often compelled to suspend payments after desperate efforts to raise money at excessive interest rates. Contarini points out that such panics were not a rare occurrence, and that numerous bank failures were the result. According to him, ninety-six out of one hundred and three banks which had existed at one time or another in Venice came to a bad end.[7] Only seven banks did not end in disaster. Professor Frederic C. Lane, who has made an extensive study of Venetian banking, believes that Contarini exaggerates and that the record of the Rialto banks is somewhat better.[8] Even so, it must be granted that bank failures were exceedingly frequent.

Conditions in Bruges were the same as in Venice. According to the available records, the following Bruges money-changers ended in a state of bankruptcy: Boidin Wegghebedde (1315), Diederic Urbaens' widow (1350), Guillaume Ruyelle (1370), Collard de Marke (1370?), Jan Baudeel (1409), Simon de Cokere (1453), Collard de May (1482), Willem Roelands (1482). This list is far from being complete.[9] A systematic investigation in the Bruges archives would undoubtedly bring more cases to light.

The usual expression for bankruptcy in the Bruges sources is *faute van den wissele* in Flemish and *faulte en le change* in French.[10] These expressions remained in use throughout the fourteenth century. The verb 'to fail' (Fl. *faelgieren,* Fr. *faillir*) does not occur before middle of the fifteenth century.[11] At a later date the expression *rompture desdictz bancquiers,* evidently an antecedent of the French *banqueroute* and the English 'bankruptcy,' is used in Maximilian's ordinance of 1489.[12]

Most of the information on bank failures in Bruges is based on court decisions and entries in the municipal accounts. Documents of this type naturally do not go into any detail regarding the causes of each bank failure. The available sources also give only sparse information regarding the legal procedure which was followed in case of bankruptcy. Of course, bankruptcy entailed a complete suspension of payments and the exchange office of a bankrupt money-changer was closed. He had to surrender all his property, which was placed in the hands of trustees appointed by the justices of the local court. The books of the closed bank were also seized and handed over to the authorities, a circumstance which probably explains the presence of the Collard de Marke and Guillaume Ruyelle account books in the municipal archives of Bruges. The property of the bankrupt was then sold for the benefit of the creditors.

This procedure is very well described in a deed concerning the sale of two houses belonging to Guillaume Ruyelle, who apparently went bankrupt in the spring or summer of 1370. According to the text of the deed, he had to turn over all his property to the municipal authorities, 'as was customary in such a case,' in order to satisfy the creditors of his bank. On November 16, 1370, the two houses standing on the Fish Market, then on the north side of the Grand' Place, were sold by Lambesin de Vos, burgomaster, *in the name of the City of Bruges,* to Peter Gaderpenninghe and Ghidolf Volkaerde, representatives of the Fishmonger's Gild. This document, of exceptional interest, has not come down to us in the original, but through a notarial copy made in the seventeenth century and inserted in a cartulary of the Fishmongers' Gild.[13]

Debts of the bankrupt were proved and allowed against his estate, if they were recorded in the 'papers' or books of the exchange. But if no record could be found, a creditor might have trouble in having his claim approved by the trustees or the sureties of the bankrupt.[14] In 1482 the city of Bruges appointed an examiner named Donas de Moor to audit the books of the insolvent money-changer Willem Roelandts.[15]

The distribution of the assets among the creditors was at first a thorny problem because of a conflict between the customary law of Germanic origin and the Roman law. The Roman law provided that the assets should be distributed rateably among the creditors. The customary law of Germanic origin, on the contrary, gave precedence to the creditor who was first to file a claim. Creditors who did not make haste were thus likely to be completely shut out from the distribution of the assets. In Flanders, *pays de droit coutumier,* there was probably a great deal of hesitation before definite rules of jurisprudence were worked out.

According to a document dated October 12, 1358, the authorities of Lille adopted a hybrid and rather unsatisfactory solution in a bankruptcy case involving a money-changer named Jehan le Nepveu. The claims of the city and of orphans were given priority rights and had to be paid before any others. Next came the depositors who received no interest on their deposits. The law adopted the view that the money-changer had trangressed his rights by using such deposits in his own business. If something was left after all these prior claims had been fully paid, the unsecured creditors could come in for their share in the order in which they had filed their claims, according to the principles of the old German law. If, after all these payments, there was still a small balance left, it was to be distributed rateably (*au sou la livre*) among the sureties and *fidéjusseurs*.[16]

It is by no means certain that the custom of Bruges and the custom of Lille were the same in the matter of bankruptcy, but there is, as far as I know, no Bruges document which gives the rules according to which the assets of a bankrupt were to be divided among the creditors. It seems, however, that some classes of creditors, such as orphans and privileged foreign merchants, had priority rights on the assets. After payment in full of the preferred creditors, the assets were to be distributed rateably among the depositors and the other unsecured creditors.[17] When the assets of the bankrupt plus those of his sureties did not cover the liabilities, the principal debtor and his guarantors might be imprisoned for debt, if the creditors could hope to gain something by blackmailing relatives.[18]

As has been explained, the money-changers were required by law to give surety. It is evident that the sureties were only secondarily liable: they could be called upon to pay the debts of the guarantee solely in case of bankruptcy. Usually the sureties obligated themselves only up to a given sum beyond which they ceased to be answerable. For instance, a certain Pieter le Cuers was surety up to the considerable amount of one thousand pounds groat for the money-changer Simon de Cokere who failed about 1460.[19] In 1410 the creditors of the bankrupt money-changer Jehan Baudel sued his surety, a certain Jean de Voghel, and obtained judgment against him for a bond of two hundred pounds groat.[20]

Often a money-changer had several sureties. After the failure of Diederic Urbaens' widow, between 1340 and 1350, one of the sureties named Jan van Bouchout sent a request to the aldermen and justices of the municipal court. He protested strongly, because another surety named Jan Hauwscild had cancelled his commitments without previous consent of the aldermen and without serving notice upon either the principal debtor or the other sureties. The petitioner contended that a surety should not be allowed to withdraw without providing an acceptable substitute, and that it was unfair to release one surety, thereby increasing the burden of the others.[21] Jan van Bouchout's request certainly raised some pertinent points. It is unfortunate that we do not know what action was taken by the court.

Although the Flemish used in the request is clumsy and uncouth, Jan van Bouchout must have been either very shrewd or well-advised. In the second part of his petition, he raised some further legal points and asked the aldermen whether the sureties were liable for all the debts of a bankrupt money-changer without distinction. According to him, the sureties were not responsible (1) for any deposits belonging to orphans on which interest was paid, (2) or for claims which were not recorded in the books, (3) or for any obligations arising from commercial transactions, (4) or for any balances due to other money-changers.[22] In other words, the responsibility of the sureties was limited to demand deposits which were duly recorded in the books and which did not bear interest. We do not know the final decision of the court, but it is questionable whether it was prepared to grant all the points raised by Jan van Bouchout. Point two has been fully discussed in a preceding chapter and there is, consequently, no need to dwell again on the same topic. As for point one, guardians often placed the money of orphans at interest in the exchange. Such transactions were not frowned upon by the canonists, and it was a general principle of mediaeval law to consider orphans, and sometimes widows, as preferred creditors. For these reasons Jan van Bouchout had little chance to convince the court with respect to the first point, but there is a possibility that he won out on points three and four. As precedents were so important in the Middle Ages, it is regrettable that we do not have the decision which was handed down by the court in this interesting case.

Another legal problem of great importance was raised in connection with the bankruptcy of the Bruges money-changer Simon de Cokere. One of his customers, a man named Jehan de Scrivere, had accepted a bill of exchange, amounting to forty pounds groat, for the English merchant Thomas Tikel. The presenter of the bill was the Italian Piero da Rabata. Before, or on, maturity date Jehan de Scrivere notified Piero da Rabata that the amount of forty pounds groat had been transferred to his name at the exchange of Simon de Cokere. After sending several messengers, Piero da Rabata himself tried to collect the money, but found that Simon de Cokere's office was closed. He then heard that the money-changer had failed.

As Jehan de Scrivere insisted that the bill had been paid by his assignment in bank, Piero da Rabata took the case to court, demanding payment for the sum of forty pounds groat. Jehan de Scrivere, as defender, contended that he owed nothing and that the debt had been duly discharged, since the forty pounds had actually been written to the credit of Piero da Rabata on the books of the exchange.

After consulting several merchants on commercial practice, the court found for the plaintiff and decided that Piero da Rabata had not been duly paid the said sum of forty pounds, but that Jehan de Scrivere had a claim in bankruptcy for the same amount against the money-changer Simon de Cokere.[23]

This decision, it should be stressed, was wholly in agreement with Italian merchant custom. In Venice, both the debtor and the creditor had to be present in order to make an assignment valid.[24] A Florentine municipal statute of 1355 was even more specific: if a debtor made a payment by transfer on the books of a bank or of a money-changer in the presence, and with the consent, of his creditor (*presente et volente creditore*), such a payment was valid whether or not the banker or the money-changer proved to be solvent.[25] The use of checks instead of oral orders of transfer has not greatly changed the legal principles on the matter. Today, either in the United States where the common law is the rule, or in Belgium where they have the Code Napoléon, a payment by check is not complete until the check is paid by the bank on which it is drawn. In Belgium the law requires the presentation of checks within a specified time. After that, the maker ceases to be responsible if the bank fails or if there are no longer sufficient funds to pay the delayed check.

The Bruges money-changers were often lax in observing the rule which required the presence of both the debtor and the creditor. After all, it was not quite so essential that the creditor or assignee should witness a transfer made in his favor. There is no doubt that the Bruges money-changers, for reasons of expediency, often made transfers simply on the strength of an order given by the assignor or debtor without securing the assent of the creditor or assignee. The prevalence of this practice would help to explain the strikingly great number of transitory or temporary accounts which are found in the Collard de Marke and Guillaume Ruyellle account books. Of course, the presence of the debtor was an absolute necessity, because nothing could be charged to the account of a customer without his being present or without his consent.

The fact that the money-changers were required to give surety did not always offer much protection to the creditors. It probably happened time and time again that the amounts for which the sureties were bound did not cover the losses resulting from bankruptcies. Some groups of foreign merchants, who were able to put pressure on the public authorities by threatening to leave Bruges and to carry their trade elsewhere, secured privileges by which all losses due to bank failures were to be assumed by the city.

Such a guarantee was given as early as 1309 to the Hanseatic merchants or to the merchants of the Holy Roman Empire, as they were officially called. Article twenty-four of the privileges which were granted to them in that year provided that 'in case any of the said merchants placed money on deposit at the exchange or received an assignment on a money-changer, the city of Bruges would be responsible for any losses suffered as a consequence of insolvency on the part of a money-changer.'[26] This provision was re-enacted with a few insignificant changes in the wording and the spelling, when the privileges of the Hanseatic merchants were renewed in 1359 after laborious negotiations which dragged on for several months.[27] These privileges were ratified by Louis de Male in 1360,[28] and confirmed again by Philip the Bold in 1392.[29] In 1480, the Hanseatic merchants obtained the same guarantee against losses due to bank failures from the city of Antwerp, but only up to the sum of six thousand crowns at 48 groats apiece.[30]

Besides the Hanseatic merchants, there were only a few other groups of foreign merchants trading in Bruges, who were able to obtain similar protection for the safety of the money which was entrusted to money-changers. In 1362, the merchants of Nuremberg were granted privileges which were almost identical with those of the Hanseatic League and contained the above-quoted provision concerning bank failures.[31] In 1411, the merchants of Portugal also secured the right to be compensated by the city for any losses caused by the bankruptcy of money-changers.[32] It seems that the same favor was also granted to the Spaniards.[33]

The privileges granted to the Italian colonies are significantly silent on this matter of bank-deposit guaranty. It is striking that guaranties were given exclusively to foreign merchants, who belonged to economically backward nations, who did not have banks in their home lands, who were not used to dealing with such institutions, and who stayed in Bruges only for short periods at a time instead of residing there permanently like the representatives of the Italian business houses. Among the Hanseatic merchants and some of these other national groups there was still a great deal of reliance on collective protection, which contrasts sharply with the individualistic spirit and the self-reliance of the more advanced Italians.

There is not the slightest doubt that the clauses regarding bank-deposit insurance in the charters to the foreign merchants were actually carried out. The municipal accounts of Bruges contain scores of entries relating to payments made in this connection to foreigners. As early as 1315, the city of Bruges paid the claims of several Hanseatic merchants against the insolvent money-changer Boidin Wegghebedde. On the other hand, the city recovered seventy pounds *parisis* from the bankrupt and his sureties.[34] In 1482, Jean Metteneye, as surety of the absconded and bankrupt money-changer Collard de May, reimbursed the city for an amount of £72 8*s*. 4*d*. groat which it had paid to several privileged creditors.[35] After the failure of the banker Willem Roelandts about the same time, the liabilities were so considerable that the city was unable to repay all the claimants at once and had to ask for respite. A scheme was devised by which they were to be repaid in installments. The claims of the Hanseatic merchants alone amounted to £1,244 14*s*. 11*d*. groat which were paid as follows: four hundred pounds groat immediately, on October 1, 1482, and the balance in two installments of £422 7*s*. 5½*d*. gr. each, on April 1 and on October 1, 1483.[36] The Spaniards presented claims totalling £69 17*s*. 4*d*. gr. and the Portuguese sued the city for £223 13*s*. 6*d*. gr. The lawsuit dragged on until 1487 when the city finally came to terms and agreed to compensate the Portuguese.[37]

There are some essential differences between bank-deposit guaranty in the Middle Ages and bank-deposit insurance today. In the Middle Ages only a few privileged foreign merchants were entitled to compensation and were given preference over all other creditors.[38] Today the purpose of the insurance scheme is to protect the small depositor, and all deposits up to a certain figure—in this country up to five thousand dollars—are guaranteed. The scheme is placed on an actuarial and statistical basis and all banks contribute toward an insurance fund out of which compensations are eventually paid. Of course, nothing simliar existed in the Middle Ages. Compensations were paid out of public, i.e., municipal, funds, but the city had the right of recourse against the bankrupt estate and the sureties of the bankrupt. Moreover, the case of Bruges was probably unique. Even on a limited basis, deposit insurance does not seem to have existed in mediaeval Europe outside the Low Countries.

Another question which interested the foreign merchants, especially the Germans, was that of the safety of the money entrusted to broker-innkeepers. All through the fourteenth century, this problem embittered the relations between the city of Bruges and the Hanseatic League.

In the first half of the fourteenth century, the Bruges innkeepers began to invade the banking business, as they had done successfully before with the brokers' trade, so that 'broker' and 'innkeeper' had come to mean the same thing. At first, the Bruges innkeepers accepted money only for purposes of safekeeping, but later they became bolder; they began to make transfers and payments for their guests and to invest surplus funds in their own business. By and by the innkeepers became competitors of the money-changers. This tendency was encouraged especially by the Germans who preferred to entrust their money to their hosts rather than to a bank!

The privileges granted in 1309 to the Hanseatic League provided that 'an innkeeper was responsible if his servant or employee went off with money or property belonging to guests.'[39] This innocuous provision became the source of all subsequent grievances. The trouble started in 1351 when the Bruges broker and innkeeper Laurent van der Beurse or de le Bourse died in straitened circumstances. He left many debts especially to his German guests who had entrusted their money to his care. In accordance with local custom, the municipal authorities stepped in and sold van der Beurse's property for the benefit of the native creditors, so that the aliens did not receive anything from the proceeds of the sale.[40] This action of the Bruges authorities aroused the ire of the Hanseatic merchants and was certainly one of the contributory factors which led to the break between Bruges and the Hanseatic League.[41]

When peace was restored in 1359, the League demanded that the above-quoted provision should be extended. The new privileges of June 1359, consequently contained the following addition: 'that the City was to be answerable, if a merchant suffered any loss because of an innkeeper.'[42] This was an exorbitant concession.[43] It became a further source of difficulties, because the city refused to live up to the agreement and tried by every subterfuge and legal quibble to evade responsibility.[44] Apparently the city of Bruges was willing to be liable for the money-changers who were few and who were required by law to give surety, but she was not prepared to vouchsafe the obligations of a crowd of innkeepers and brokers over whom she had no control. The Hanseatic League, on the other hand, kept to the terms of the agreement. The practical consequence was that its members could entrust their money or their goods to almost anyone and expect the city to be responsible in case of loss.[45]

The failure of Medemiselle de Rudevorde, Collard de Marke's customer, in or about 1370, revived the conflict.[46] In 1374 the case was finally taken to the count of Flanders for arbitration. Louis de Male, very wisely, refused to settle it as a legal issue (*ende niet over recht*), but decided that, in order to maintain friendly relations with the Hanseatic League, the city was to pay Medemiselle de Rudevorde's debts with the understanding, however, that such an action would not constitute a precedent.[47]

After 1387, the question of the city's liability for the debts of broker-innkeepers ceased to be an issue.[48] It is probable that, with the passage of time, the German merchants learned to make use of the existing banking facilities and discontinued the practice of entrusting money to their hosts.[49] The innkeepers were too numerous, also, to organize effectively a system of payments by book transfer. This is presumably the main reason why they did not succeed in supplanting the money-changers.

The promise made in a preceding chapter to explain the drop in the number of the Bruges money-changers and the decrease in their business during the fifteenth century has not yet been fulfilled. It was only pointed out at the time that this setback was not due to the decline of Bruges and to the rise of Antwerp.[50] The money-changers lost their importance all over the Low Countries and there is no evidence that their business was of any consequence in the Antwerp of Charles V. It is true that the frequency of bank failures had something to do with the decline of the money-changers' business, since they undermined the confidence of the public in the solvency of banks. But the convenience of settling debts by transfer was so great that this explanation is entirely inadequate. The unification of the coinage system under the dukes of Burgundy cannot have been the determining factor either, because the banking business of the money-changers was so much more important than their dealings in petty exchange. An explanation must consequently be sought elsewhere.

A careful study of the monetary ordinances of the fifteenth century reveals that the real cause of the decline of the money-changers' business can be traced to the monetary policy of the dukes of Burgundy. This policy was pursued with tenacity and, as time went on, became more and more hostile to banking.

As early as 1433, the monetary ordinances provided that 'it was unlawful, either in the City of Bruges or elsewhere, for any person whomsoever, whether a money-changer or not, to have a bank in order to receive the money of the merchants and to make their payments, under the penalty of banishment for three years.'[51] The same provision is repeated with little change in the ordinance of October 13, 1467.[52] The text of Maximilian's ordinance of December 14, 1489, is worded differently: 'After the promulgation of this ordinance,' the text reads, 'there will be no longer any *changeurs-banquiers,* that is, money-changers who accept the money of merchants, of burghers, and of other persons, and who use it daily to make payments for them.'[53]

Professor Z. W. Sneller, who has studied the question, believes that the purpose of these enactments was to break up the combination of the functions of money-changer and of banker.[54] This interpretation, however, does not fit in with the text of the earlier ordinances which says plainly that banking was forbidden 'to any person whomsoever (*aucune personne, changeur ne autre*).' Nor does this interpretation agree with Maximilian's ordinance. Its provisions—if one reads them all—make it absolutely clear that the purpose of the government was *the suppression of all banks.* After the passage quoted above, the ordinance states that 'if a money-changer, even in case he does not call himself a banker, accepts the money of merchants, of burghers, or of foreigners in order to make any payments, he will be fined two florins for every pound groat and the depositor, too, will be fined two florins for every pound.'[55] To this rule the ordinance admits only three exceptions: first, the cities retained the right to appoint treasurers or other officials in order to collect their revenue and to make their payments; secondly, the colonies of foreign merchants were allowed to appoint a clerk in order to make payments by transfer, but only among the members of the same group; thirdly, private individuals also could collect money for others, if those individuals were provided with a regular power of attorney or a similar document.[56]

Mediaeval ordinances and statutes were more often not enforced than carried out, but the repeated enactments on banking of the dukes of Burgundy and of Maximilian of Austria must have produced practical results. Chiefly the latter's ordinance of 1489 dealt a deadly blow to the banking business of the money-changers by frightening the depositors away with the threat of heavy fines. It is significant that history does not record the existence of any transfer banks in sixteenth-century Antwerp. In 1584 the Venetian senator Tommaso Contarini, who was well informed, compared advantageously the Venetian method of making payments by assignment with the clumsier methods in use in Antwerp and in Lyons. In Antwerp, according to his description, merchants were in the habit of transferring or 'of setting over' debts from one to another until someone was found who would pay cash.[57]

There were probably several reasons why the dukes of Burgundy tried to get rid of commercial banks and adopted a 'hard money' policy. Two reasons are stated explicitly in the ordinance of 1489. One of them is the great frequency of bank failures. 'These failures,' the ordinance declares, 'have wrought utter ruin among all classes of people, but especially among the merchants and the persons of note.'[58]

Next, the ordinance accuses the bankers of all kinds of offenses against the common weal and, more specifically, of picking and culling the currency, of sending bullion to foreign mints, and of bringing the underweight money of these mints into circulation.[59] These accusations were grave and should not be dismissed as humbug. The financial advisers to the dukes of Burgundy were not children in matters of finance. Picking and culling left only the lighter and abraded coins in circulation. The resulting deterioration of the currency had an unfavorable effect on the rates of exchange and encouraged the circulation of spurious coin. There is no doubt that the practice of picking and culling was greatly facilitated by the fact that the bankers accumulated in their coffers a considerable fraction of the total stock of specie. The hard money which was thus withdrawn from circulation was replaced by bank money under the form of transferable deposits, as has been shown before. The suppression of the banks and the institution of a purely metallic currency (through the elimination of bank money) would certainly reduce the opportunities for garbling the coinage by bringing back into circulation the specie reserves concentrated in the banks.

When, at the end of the sixteenth century, banking was revived in Amsterdam under the name of *kassiersbedrijf*, the banks were again accused of picking and culling the currency, undoubtedly not without reason.[60] Again attempts were made by the public authorities to suppress all banking activity, but these attempts were strongly opposed by the business community because of the convenience of making payments by transfer. The creation of the public bank of Amsterdam was the result of a compromise: it established a system of payments by transfer as demanded by the merchants and restricted the possibilities for picking and culling as desired by the public authorities.

Besides the two reasons given in the ordinance of 1489, the attitude of the public authorities toward banking was probably determined by other motives which were kept from the public. The financial advisers to the dukes of Burgundy were surely aware of certain facts, but it is difficult to tell to what extent all their implications were really understood. It is quite possible that some of these advisers saw dimly that the banks created money and usurped monetary functions.

There is no doubt that the dukes of Burgundy strove by all means to maintain the standard of their money.[61] The mints ceased to be farmed out and were entrusted to 'persons of substance' who were not seeking profits.[62] Such a policy was bound to clash with the interests of the money-changers who favored debasement whenever their cash reserves were running low because of a crisis in the money market. A policy of monetary stability thus tended to increase the number of bank failures, as neither contraction nor rediscounting but debasement was the safety valve of mediaeval banks.

In Flanders, the decline of deposit banking during the fifteenth century was caused as much by the direct action of hostile legislation as by the impact of economic forces set in motion by the monetary policy of the government. The defects of the credit structure were such that mediaeval banks of deposit throve best under conditions of a continuous inflation of the currency and of a rising price level. They were likely to wither away if these conditions ceased to exist. In case of debasement, the liabilities of the money-changers remained unchanged because they owed their depositors the same sum of pounds, shillings, and deniers groat as before. But the value of the money-changers' assets was likely to increase, if measured in terms of monetary units, that is, in terms of groats. The investments of the money-changers in business ventures were especially likely to gain in value in harmony with the rise of the price level. Even the bullion and the gold coins which the money-changers kept in their coffers would be worth more as a result of the depreciation of the currency. In contrast to debasement, a policy of monetary stability, if accompanied by falling prices, was likely to affect disastrously the financial condition of mediaeval banks, since their assets tended to decline in value, while their liabilities remained the same. For these reasons, the fourteenth century, a period of relentless debasement of the currency, was in Flanders the heyday of deposit banking.

[1]A. Lattes, *Il diritto commerciale*, p. 211. Cf. Dunbar, *op. cit.*, 317; Gerard de Malynes, *A Treatise of the Canker of England's Common Wealth* (London, 1601), pp. 25-26.

[2]van Dillen, 'De girobanken van Genua, Venetië en Hamburg,' *op. cit.*, p. 42.

[3]A. Lattes, *Il diritto commerciale*, p. 234.

[4]*Ibid.*, p. 211.

[5]van Dillen, 'Girobanken,' *op. cit.*, p. 42; Lane, 'Venetian Bankers,' *op. cit.*, pp. 200, 204.

[6]'Orazione del Senatore Tommaso Contarini (1584),' in Elia Lattes, *op. cit.*, p. 124.

[7]*Loc. cit.* Cf. Dunbar, *op. cit.*, p. 312.

[8]Lane, 'Venetian Banks,' *op. cit.*, p. 191.

[9]The dates given here are only approximate. In most cases the bankruptcy occurred some time before the date indicated, because it usually refers to litigation resulting from bankruptcy proceedings.

[10]Gilliodts, *Cart. de l'Estaple*, I, 137, No. 192, and 490, No. 589.

[11]*Idem, Coutume*, I, 460, 525; Bruges, Municipal Archives, Sentences civiles, 1453-1461, fol. 332.

[12]*Groot Placcaet-Boeck . . . der Vereenighde Nederlanden*, I, 2592-93.

[13]Bruges, State Archives, Fonds des Métiers, No. 467, a cartulary called *Roobouck* ['Red-book'] of the Fishmongers' Gild (Métier des Poissoniers), fol. 1. I am greatly indebted for this reference and the complete text of the deed to Mr. Albert Schouteet, Assistant Archivist of the City of Bruges, who found it while he was making an inventory of the material on the Bruges craft gilds.

[14]Bruges, Municipal Archives, Chartes politiques, 1e série, No. 445. See Appendix I.

[15]Gilliodts, *Coutume*, I, 525.

[16]Poignant, *op. cit.*, pp. 127-28 and 164-66, Appendix V.

[17]In a court decision of the fifteenth century it is stated that in case of failure, 'tous ses biens [of the bankrupt] et debtes devoient de droit appartenir à tous ses créditeurs, chacun pour rate de sa debte.' See Gilliodts, *Coutume*, I, 460.

[18]See the case of Boidin Weghebedde in 1315 (Gilliodts, *Cart. de l'Estaple*, I, 137, No. 192).

[19]Bruges, Municipal Archives, Sentences Civiles, 1453-1461, fol. 332.

[20]Gilliodts, *Cart. de l'Estaple*, I, 468, No. 565.

[21]Bruges, Municipal Archives, Chartes politiques, No. 445, fol. 1. See Appendix I.

[22]*Ibid.*, fol. 3.

[23]The text of the court decision, dated March 9, 1452 (n.s.), has been published in full by Heinrich Brunner, 'Beiträge zur Geschichte und Dogmatik der Werthpapiere: I), Brügger Schöffensprüche zur Geschichte des Wechselrechts, *op. cit.*, pp. 30-32. Cf. Gilliodts, *Cart. de l'Estaple*, II, 6, 913, and *Coutume*, I, 460.

[24]Elia Lattes, *op. cit.*, pp. 91, 107, 113; Nasse, *op. cit.*, p. 334.

[25]Lastig, 'Beiträge zur Geschichte des Handelsrechts,' *op. cit.*, p. 152: 'Si quis fecerit alicui persone vel loco scribi aliquam pecuniae quantitatem in libro tabulae alicuius campsoris tenentis publice tabulam sive mensam, presente et volente creditore, statim liberatus sit ab illo cui fecerit scribi usque ad quantitatem scriptam, sive talis campsor solverit sive non.' Cf. Lattes, *Diritto commerciale*, p. 227.

[26]Privilege of November 14, 1309, published in full in *Hansisches Urkundenbuch*, II, 68, No. 154, art. 24: 'Vord ware dat zake, dat enich van den vorseiden coeplieden gheld leiden in de wissel van Brucghe iof beheten ware van paiemente up enicghen wisselare, ende danof faute ware in den wisselare, danof zal de steide ghehouden wesen ende vor hem ghelden.'

[27]Privilege of June 5, 1359, art. 39. See *Hansisches Urkundenbuch*, III, 219, No. 452, and Gilliodts, *Inventaire*, II, 45, No. 532.

[28]Privilege of June 14, 1360, art. 32. See *Hansisches Urkundenbuch*, III, 261, No. 497.

[29]Privilege of May 12, 1392. See *ibid.*, V (1899), 21, No. 2.

[30]Privilege of December 7, 1480. See *ibid.*, X (1907), 539, No. 821. See also Bigwood, *Régime*, I, 422.

[31]Privilege of January 23, 1362, art. 32. See Gilliodts, *Cart. de l'Estaple*, I, 249, No. 319.

[32]Privilege of December 26, 1411, art. 48: 'Item que nostre ville de Bruges soit tenue de respondre pour les changeurs d'icelle de ce qui sera trouvé en vérité que les diz changeurs devront aux diz marchans de Portugal, se faulte est trouvé ès diz changeurs.' See Gilliodts, *Cart. de l'Estaple*, I, 490, No. 589.

[33]*Ibid.*, II, 262, No. 1243.

[34]*Ibid.*, I, 137, No. 192.

[35]Gilliodts, *Coutume*, I, 525, and *Cart. de l'Estaple*, II, 488, No. 1422. This Collard de May was a well-known money-changer who was in business for several years before he went bankrupt. In 1451 he had financial dealings with English merchants at the fairs of Bergen-op-Zoom (Power, 'The Wool Trade,' *op. cit.*, p. 67). Thirty years later, his name occurs in the Cely accounts. Apparently, the Cely partners paid some of their creditors by assignment on Collard de May (*ibid.*, p. 371, n. 136).

[36]*Hansisches Urkundenbuch*, X, 623, n. 1; £76 9*s*. 4*d*. gr., which Hanseatic merchants owed to Willem Roelandts were deducted from the first installment payment.

[37]Gilliodts, *Cart. de l'Estaple*, II, 262, No. 1243.

[38]The statement made by Häpke (*Brügges Entwicklung zum mittelalterlichen Weltmarkt*, p. 243) that the city of Bruges was liable for *all* the liabilities of the money-changers is not true.

[39]Ehrenberg, 'Makler, Hosteliers und Börse,' *op. cit.*, p. 423.

[40]*Ibid.*, pp. 423-24.

[41]The Hanseatic sessional records of this period are full of bitter complaints about the high-handed treatment which was meted out to the German merchants in Laurent van der Buerse's case. See *Hanserecesse*, Vol. I, p. 91, No. 158; p. 179, No. 251; Vol. III (Leipzig, 1875), p. 225, No. 238; pp. 231 ff., No. 239: sec. 3, §1 (p. 231), §8 (p. 232), sec. 6, §1 (p. 235), §2 (p. 236). In accordance with the treaty of 1359, the city of Bruges paid, in 1360, £1547 2*s*. par. in order to compensate the German merchants for losses in Laurent van der Buerse's case and for other damages (*ibid.*, p. 255, No. 266).

[42]See Ehrenberg, 'Makler, Hosteliers und Börse', *op. cit.*, p. 424; Gilliodts, *Inventaire*, II, 51, No. 532; *Hansisches Urkundenbuch*, III, 214-23, No. 452.

[43]Richard Ehrenberg ('Makler, Hosteliers, etc.,' *op. cit.*, p. 425) admits this point.

[44]In order to defend her position, the city of Bruges did not hesitate to twist entirely the meaning of the paragraph added in 1359 (*ibid.*, p. 426).

[45]Because the League pretended that the city was responsible not only for the debts of a broker-innkeeper with whom a member was boarding, but also for those of any broker-innkeeper with whom he entered into contract (*ibid.*, p. 426).

[46]This is probably the case mentioned in Ehrenberg, *op. cit.*, p. 425, and in *Hanserecesse*, I. 479, No. 518.

[47]Gilliodts, *Cart. de l'Estaple*, I, 274, No. 355.

[48]The question still gave rise to discussion in 1387 at a general session of the Hanseatic League. See *Hanserecesse*, Vol. II, p. 417, No. 343, §45; p. 431, No. 344, §36; p. 442, No. 345, §32.

[49]The practice of entrusting money to an innkeeper did not, however, disappear entirely, because a document of 1470 refers to a defendant who offers to place a disputed sum of money in the hands of *a money-changer or of his host (ès mains du change ou de son hoste)*. See Brunner, "Brügger Schöffensprüche,' *op. cit.*, p. 43.

[50]This convenient explanation is given by Bigwood, *Régime*, I, 395.

[51]Ghent, Municipal Archives, Chartres et Documents, No. 561, ordinance of October 12, 1433, art. 11: 'Item que aucune personne, changeur ne autre, ne puisse tenir en la ville de Bruges, ne ailleurs, table ne banc pour recevoir l'argent des marchans et faire leurs paiemens sur paine du ban de trois ans.'

[52]Gilliodts, *Inventaire*, V, 546.

[53]*Groot Placcaet-Boeck . . . der Vereenighde Nederlanden*, I, 2592: 'Item, est advisé, et conclud que, à l'éntrée de ceste ordonnance, n'y aura nulz changeurs-bancquiers: à sçavoir ceulx qui gardent l'argent des marchans, bourgeois et aultres personnes, dont ilz faisoyent payements journelement.'

[54]Sneller, 'Wisselaarsbedrijf,' *op. cit.*, p. 495; Bigwood (*Régime*, I, 437) gives the following interpretation: 'Les changeurs étaient ainsi amenés à pratiquer, à côté du change manuel, le change de place en place. Ce dernier genre d'opérations resta néanmoins, en ce qui les concerne, l'exception. Les marchands continuèrent à être chargés du soin de ce genre de règlement. En Flandre, le duc Philippe leur assura même une sorte de monopole, en interdisant, sous peine d'un bannissement de trois ans, à toute personne y compris les changeurs de tenir "table ne banc pour recevoir l'argent des marchans et faire leurs paiemens".' This interpretation, it seems to me, does not make sense.

[55]*Groot Placcaet-Boeck*, I, 2592-93.

[56]*Ibid.*, I, 2593.

[57]E. Lattes, *op. cit.*, p. 121. This practice migrated from Antwerp to Amsterdam where it developed so many bad features that it was forbidden by a municipal ordinance of March 9, 1619 (van Dillen, *Bronnen*, I, 45, No. 46). The prohibition was reenacted on June 4, 1621 (*ibid.*, p. 48, No. 50).

[58]*Groot Placcaet-Boeck*, I, 2592.

[59]*Loc. cit.*

[60]van Dillen, *Bronnen*, I, 1, No. 2 (Ordinance of June 2, 1604); p. 12, No. 14 (Ordinance of July 12, 1608); p. 47, No. 50 (Ordinance of June 4, 1621).

[61]Pirenne, *Histoire de Belgique*, II, 420. See also the preamble of the monetary ordinance of October 13, 1467 (Gilliodts, *Inventaire*, V, 538).

[62]Pirenne (*Hist. de Belgique*, II, 421) declares that the mints used to be farmed out *à la chandelle* or by auction.

Chapter 16

CONCLUSIONS

THIS study on banking in Bruges throws considerable light on several of the most controversial issues in economic history. These conclusions will restate and emphasize the principal contributions made in the preceding chapters toward a better understanding of the early development of credit institutions in the Low Countries and of mediaeval banking in general. Since banking in Bruges was only a beginning, it may be advisable to point out the importance of this early stage for the subsequent development of banking in the Low Countries, especially in Antwerp and in Amsterdam.

The main point which this study brings out is that there were in Bruges three different classes of money-dealers: the Italian merchant-bankers who combined foreign trade with dealings in bills of exchange, the lombards who were chiefly pawnbrokers, and the money-changers who assumed the important function of purveyors to the Mint and added deposit banking to this activity. From a legal point of view each group enjoyed a special status. The merchant-bankers were protected against any arbitrary acts of authority by their trade privileges which were in fact diplomatic treaties between the Count of Flanders and the Italian city-states. The lombards were merely tolerated as the lesser of two evils and were permitted to lend money at usury under the protection of a licence system. As for the money-changers, they were citizens who did not have any special rights or privileges and whose profession was strictly regulated. As dealers in bullion, the money-changers were expected to comply with monetary ordinances and were even entrusted with their enforcement.

This classification is not entirely new. It is found already in the great work of the Belgian jurist and historian, Georges Bigwood, on the legal and economic aspects of money-lending in mediaeval Belgium. Unfortunately Bigwood became badly confused in other parts of his book and failed to adhere to his own classification.[1] For example, he paid a great deal of attention to the licences which the rulers in the Low Countries granted to the lombards but he did not perceive that these licences did not determine the legal status of the merchant-bankers as well. On the other hand, the trade privileges of the Italian colonies are scarcely mentioned. This is not the only mistake in interpretation or in emphasis. The bill of exchange is dismissed in a couple of pages and its rôle as a credit instrument is entirely overlooked. Supposedly bills of exchange were used chiefly for the transfer of funds.[2] With regard to money-changers, Bigwood mentions that they received deposits and made payments for their customers, but these activities are regarded as relatively unimportant. According to Bigwood, petty exchange was the main function of the money-changers.[3] There is nowhere a reference to the fact that they created credit by allowing their customers to overdraw their accounts. On the whole, Bigwood's work contains valuable source material and is authoritative on the activities of the lombards but is unreliable with respect to the merchant-bankers or the money-changers.

Contrary to Bigwood's main thesis, banking in the Low Countries and elsewhere did not originate in money-lending but in exchange.[4] *Cambium minutum* or manual exchange gave rise to deposit banking on a local scale and *cambium per litteras* or exchange by bills to foreign banking or 'the business of exchange.'

One of the causes of the prevailing confusion on mediaeval banking is apparently the failure of modern scholars to see that the word 'lombard' in mediaeval sources has two different meanings.[5] Sometimes it designates a profession and is synonymous with Cahorsin or pawnbroker. In other texts it designates the nationality and is applied to any merchant from Lombardy and even from Tuscany or any other part of Italy. Consequently one should make a distinction between Lombards and lombards. In Bruges sources the pawnbrokers of St Gilles parish are commonly referred to as 'the lombards.' Although Giovanni Villani, the famous Florentine chronicler, was not a pawnbroker but a partner of the powerful Peruzzi Company, he is nevertheless called a 'Lombard' despite the fact that he came from Tuscany and not from Lombardy or Piedmont.[6] Forteguerra di Forteguerra, the Lucchese merchant-banker, is also described as 'den Lombaerd' in a Flemish document regarding the seizure of some goods belonging to Englishmen.[7] Another document refers to the Lombards who assembled on the place de la Bourse.[8] As we know, this public square was the favorite meeting place of the Italian merchants. It would not be difficult to give other quotations but those given will suffice to show that the word 'lombard' had a double meaning.

The sharp distinction which has been made between the activities of the Italian merchant-bankers and those of the lombards conflicts with the theory propounded some years ago by the prominent historian Josef Kulischer in a provocative essay on trade and money-lending in the Middle Ages.[9] His theory certainly needs revision. While Kulischer is undoubtedly right in stressing the association of banking and trade in the Middle Ages, he is in error when he denies the existence of lombards or Cahorsins who specialized in pawnbroking.[10] His examples for England and France all refer to the activities of the Italian merchant-bankers in those two countries. When he comes to the discussion of German conditions, he has to admit reluctantly that the Italians in Germany were mainly usurers from Asti, Chieri, and Milan who devoted themselves almost exclusively to money-lending, especially pawnbroking.[11] As has been pointed out in the course of this study, the Italian merchant-bankers did not establish branches in Germany. The Baltic trade was in the hands of the Hanseatic League and the merchants from Southern Germany traded chiefly with Venice. It is quite possible that Italian money-lenders in Germany occasionally dealt in spices and luxury articles. What Kulischer overlooks is that Germany was economically backward. What might be true of Germany did not necessarily apply to the Low Countries, to France, or to Italy.

Kulischer also denies, without justification, that there was much difference anywhere between a pawnshop and the office of a money-changer.[12] It is true that in some parts of Europe, for example, in Burgundy and Franche Comté, the lombards sometimes combined pawnbroking and money-changing.[13] One should not overlook local and regional differences and assume a degree of uniformity which in fact did not exist. In any case, pawnbroking was a specialized business in the Low Countries and in Italy.

The three classes of money-dealers which we have found in Bruges did not form hermetically sealed groups: it was sometimes possible to pass from one group to another. A striking example is furnished by the life of Simon de Mirabello who began his career as a lombard but ended it as a merchant-banker, although he still owned a share in the pawnshop of Ghent at the time of his death. Another case is that of Antonio di Vivaldi, from a family of Genoese bankers, who established himself as a money-changer in Bruges.[14] Such cases were, however, the exception rather than the rule.

In the matter of credit organization conditions in mediaeval Bruges resembled more closely those prevailing in Italy or Catalonia than those prevailing in Germany or even in France and England where banking had not yet taken root or was still something exotic. In Florence, for example, there were banks of different types which corresponded more or less to those found in Bruges: *banchi grossi,* which did an international business and traded in bills of exchange; *banchi in mercato,* which were the local transfer banks; *banchi a minuto,* which were small establishments doing some sort of goldsmith's business;[15] and *banchi di pegno*, which were pawnshops. After 1437 the latter were operated by Jews and licences were no longer granted to Christians.[16] All bankers—the pawnbrokers not included—were required to join the *Arte del Cambio* or the 'Exchange Gild.' The evidence does not support La Sorsa's theory that the great merchant-bankers were not members of the *Arte del Cambio* but of the Calimala, Wool, or Silk Gilds.[17] In Florence, it should not be forgotten, one could belong simultaneously to several gilds; thus the partners of the Peruzzi Company were members of both the *Arte del Cambio* and the *Arte di Calimala* and the historic Medici were registered with three gilds: the *Arte del Cambio,* the *Arte della Lana* or Wool Gild, and the *Arte di Por Santa Maria* or Silk Gild.[18]

Venice and Genoa were also blessed with a hierarchy of banks: from petty money-changers to international financiers. The situation in Barcelona was much the same. The petty money-changers who specialized in manual exchange were at the bottom of the ladder. Above them were the bonded money-changers or *banchieri in Loggia*—as the Italians in Barcelona called them—who were allowed to accept deposits and to have covers on their tables or banks.[19] The top of the credit structure was occupied by the representatives of the Italian banking houses who controlled the business of exchange and were in touch with Flanders and Italy. In 1401 the city of Barcelona started a new experiment and founded the first public bank, which became the fiscal agent of the municipality and of the provincial government of Catalonia as well.[20]

The lombards or Italian pawnbrokers had only a negligible influence, if any, upon the later development of banking.[21] Their direct descendants are the *monts-de-piété* on the Continent of Europe and the private pawnshops and small loan companies in Great Britain and the United States. It is not generally known that the mediaeval licence system has survived in Anglo-Saxon countries. In Great Britain licenced pawnshops may charge interest on small loans at a rate as high as 25 per cent a year.[22] The rate is even higher in the United States. Several states allow 3 per cent a month or 36 per cent on loans up to three hundred dollars. The maximum *legal* rate is even 42 per cent in five states: Arizona, Florida, Louisiana, Maryland, and Virginia.[23] This is not much below the 43⅓ per cent which was permissible in the Middle Ages. Modern laws regulating pawnbroking have many features in common with mediaeval grants and contain the usual provisions concerning the payment of an annual fee, the maximum rate of interest, the sale of unredeemed pledges, and the fixation of a minimum period during which pledges must be kept. Despite the high interest rates which, by law, pawnshops and small loan companies are allowed to charge, their profits are not higher than other enterprises because operating expenses, especially investigation costs, are also high. The same was true in the Middle Ages. This was an aspect of the usury question which the Churchmen were unable to understand.

Excommunicating usurers did not further the solution of the usury problem. Usury—manifest or secret—was bound to continue until something was found to take its place and to meet the demand for consumers' credit. The creation of the *monts-de-piété* was therefore a step in the right direction.[24]

The lombards should not be considered as bankers in the accepted meaning of the term. Their loans resulted in the transfer of purchasing power but not in the creation of new purchasing power or of additional money as in the case of the merchant-bankers and the money-changers. These two groups alone—and not the lombards—introduced practices which had considerable influence upon the later development of banking.

The merchant-bankers made a major contribution by developing the bill of exchange.[25] Its use in international trade considerably reduced the demand for specie, since shipments of gold and silver from one country to another were largely eliminated and replaced by a system of payments by compensation and transfer. In the Middle Ages, as has been pointed out, the bill of exchange was still what the term implies and generally involved an exchange, as well as a credit, transaction. Bills were not used for the purpose of discounting and still less of rediscounting.

When Bruges declined, the merchant-bankers moved to Antwerp, which inherited the position of Bruges as the financial metropolis of northwestern Europe. During the sixteenth century there was no major innovation in the machinery or the technical organization of the money market, but Germany and Castile were drawn into the orbit of international finance. Another important development was the emergence of the fairs of Castile, Frankfort-on-the-Main, and Besançon. Those of Lyons were already flourishing before 1500 but they became even more important as international clearing centers during the sixteenth century. The Italians lost their monopoly of foreign banking but held their ground despite the influx of Germans, such as the Fuggers, the Welsers, the Tuchers, the Hochstetters, and of Flemings, such as Erasmus Schetz and his sons, Gilles Hooftman, and Paul van Dale. The religious wars shook the credit structure in its foundations. Many of the great banking houses, too deeply engaged in government loans, disappeared in a succession of financial crises and state bankruptcies.

By 1600 Amsterdam instead of Antwerp was rapidly becoming the world's financial center. Although Antwerp had lost much of its former splendor, it remained the banking place of the Spanish and, later, Austrian Netherlands. In the eighteenth century Antwerp merchant-bankers maintained business connections with Paris, Amsterdam, Vienna, and Trieste; took an active part in the creation of colonial enterprises, such as the Ostend Company; had money invested in sugar refineries and other industrial ventures; were interested in underwriting; and founded the first insurance companies in Belgium.[26] There is, consequently, no breach in continuity: the business of the merchant-bankers at the time of Maria Theresa was no less diversified than that of the Italian financiers at the time of Louis de Male or Charles the Bold. The lack of specialization among merchant-bankers was not peculiar to the Low Countries but was a general phenomenon prior to the advent of Industrial Capitalism.

After the merchant-bankers had migrated from Bruges to Antwerp bills of exchange continued as before to be bought and sold through brokers at current or market rates. The famous Antwerp *bourse* was less a commodity exchange (*bourse commerciale*) than a bill market (*marché des changes*) where the exchange rates were determined daily by the forces of supply and demand.[27] According to the letters of Sir Thomas Gresham the mood of the market sometimes changed suddenly in the course of two 'burse times.' He erected in London a building that was a copy of the Antwerp *bourse*. It is significant that this building was at first called 'the burse' but that its name was changed by proclamation to that of 'Royal Exchange.' This terminology clearly indicates that the burse or *bourse* was originally a building erected to provide a meeting place for bill brokers and exchange-dealers rather than for merchants. It is evident that the *bourse* was soon used for both purposes since most exchange-dealers were also merchants.

The development of negotiability marks the beginning of a new chapter in the history of banking. Some of the earliest examples of endorsed bills are found in Antwerp around 1610. It is difficult to say where this practice started but it spread rapidly despite the opposition from conservative business men, lawyers, and legislators.[28] By 1650 endorsement had become a common practice almost everywhere in Europe. In spite of Gresham's efforts the business of exchange never took firm roots in England. Instead, the London goldsmiths around 1600 extended their activities to include deposit banking and developed the new practice of 'discounting' domestic or 'inland' bills.[29] This development in a secondary center such as London did not bear fruit until the eighteenth century. On the Continent foreign banking remained what it had been in the Middle Ages, that is to say, 'a traffic or commerce in money, which is remitted from place to place, from one city to another, by correspondents, and by means of bills of exchange.'[30] In England, foreign bankers of the old type were called 'remitters' in the seventeenth and eighteenth centuries. According to Malachy Postlethwayt, whose accuracy may be trusted in this matter, there were 'but very few' such remitters in London 'in comparison to the number there is in Italy, France, and Holland.'[31] It is amazing that Postlethwayt's description has escaped the attention of historians and economists.

The money-changers—those of Bruges as well as those in other places—did not handle bills of exchange, did not have correspondents in all places of Europe, and only exceptionally undertook to make payments outside the city.[32] The offices of the money-changers were essentially local transfer banks. Owing to the close co-operation among all the money-changers in the same city, the transfer system was so efficiently organized that a great many payments, chiefly among merchants, were made by transfer without resorting to the use of specie. As the money-changers operated on a fractional reserve principle, they brought additional means of payment into circulation reducing the quantity of currency that was required to meet the needs of trade.[33] The ratio of cash to deposits probably fluctuated around one-third but varied considerably with the state of the money market and the demand for coin.

During the fifteenth century deposit banking in the Low Countries suffered a serious setback because of increasing hostile legislation, beginning with the ordinance of October 2, 1399, which forbade the payment of bills of exchange by assignment in bank. By 1500 the money-changers had probably discontinued all banking activity. The absence of facilities for making payments by transfer was keenly felt in Antwerp, the great emporium of the sixteenth century. The merchants adopted the habit of assigning their claims or receivables to their own creditors. 'To set over debts' was, however, not as convenient as an organized transfer system. Sometimes a creditor was sent from one debtor to another, six or seven times, until someone was found who was willing to pay cash.[34] It was probably in Antwerp—because there were no transfer banks—that bills of exchange first began to circulate by endorsement, shortly after 1600. The absense of transfer banks perhaps also explains why the English merchants especially favored the circulation of bills of debt payable to the bearer and demanded that the Courts admit the validity of this clause and that no delays be granted to recalcitrant or dishonest debtors.[35] The evils about which the English merchants complained were partly due to the absence of adequate banking facilities.

It is no wonder that deposit banking was revived in Amsterdam under the name of *kassiersbedrijf* toward the close of the sixteenth century. The *kassiers,* like the mediaeval money-changers, combined manual exchange with deposit banking. It is not difficult to see why bankers came to be called *kassiers.* A commercial banker today still acts as cashier for his customers.

History often repeats itself. The *kassiers*—for the same reason as the Bruges money-changers—were threatened with suppression as early as 1604.[36] The public authorities accused the *kassiers* of garbling the money and of other malpractices which resulted in the deterioration of the currency and in the rise of the exchange rates.[37] But the merchants protested very strongly against the drastic action contemplated by the authorities and pointed out that they could not get along without *kassiers* and facilities for making payments by transfer.[38] In order to meet these objections, the authorities decided to create a public bank which would buy bullion from the merchants and give them credit in the books. The public bank of Amsterdam, founded on January 31, 1609, continued the traditions established by the mediaeval exchange banks and the later *kassiers.* It bought and sold bullion and made transfers upon receipt of written, instead of oral, assignments.[39] The public bank of Amsterdam did not trade in bills of exchange and was restrained by statute from extending credit to private individuals. Aside from this restriction, the public bank of Amsterdam performed the same functions as the Bruges money-changers and should be considered as their direct descendant.

Incidentally, the creation of the bank did not achieve the objective of the authorities: they were unable to prevent further depreciation of the currency, which was not due exclusively to picking and culling, and they did not get rid of the *kassiers,* who, far from disappearing, became competitors of the new institution.[40] Bank money was soon at a premium over the badly worn currency which was in circulation.

What has been said about the Wisselbank of Amsterdam also applies to the public banks of Hamburg, Genoa, and Venice. They were primarily local transfer banks, subject to public control. They did not deal in bills of exchange and did not issue notes; however, according to the famous description of Adam Smith, foreign bills were commonly payable, not in coin but in 'bank money,' that is, by means of a credit transfer in the books of the bank. Another feature of the public banks was that they bought or sold bullion by giving credit in bank money or by cancelling existing credits. The public banks, in short, continued to fulfill the same function as the mediaeval money-changers with the difference that clients were not allowed to overdraw their accounts, and that surplus reserves were not invested in business enterprises but in public loans. The banking system developed by the mediaeval money-changers and continued by the public banks of Amsterdam, Barcelona, Genoa, Hamburg, and Venice was based on the transferability of bank deposits rather than on the circulation of bank notes. This system lasted until the public banks themselves—with the lone exception of the bank of Hamburg—were swept away by the storm which the French Revolution loosened over Europe.

The view has been expressed that mediaeval capitalism was seriously hindered in its development by its failure to invent the bank note.[41] There is an element of truth in this statement but one must not forget that the mediaeval banking system created money substitutes under the form of bills of exchange and of transferable bank deposits. As a matter of fact there is no fundamental difference between bank notes and transferable bank deposits.[42] They are both fiduciary monies which rest upon the confidence of the public in the banks. For certain purposes, bank notes which circulate from hand to hand are a more satisfactory substitute than bank deposits. A major defect of the mediaeval banking system was that it lacked liquidity. In times of crisis it was impossible for the banks to shift the burden to other banks or to appeal for aid to a central credit institution. There was no way by which a contraction of bank deposits could be compensated by an expansion of bank notes.

The lack of liquidity of small local banking systems led to repeated breakdowns. Borrowing could not be discouraged by raising the rate of discount since this device was not available. In an emergency, the banks could, of course, refuse to lend and could call in their loans. But the ensuing contraction was more likely to increase the pressure than to bring relief. As already explained, debasement was the real safety valve of mediaeval banks against deflationary pressure. It is not surprising that the money-changers would clamor for debasement whenever their cash reserves were running out. Unfortunately for the banks, the authorities were not always prepared to debase the currency except as a last resort. They were not blind to the fact that continuous debasement impoverished the ruling classes and was destructive of the existing social order.

The support which the money-changers gave to debasement brought them into conflict with the dukes of Burgundy who tried to maintain the standard of their money. The outcome was that the authorities decided to abolish the banks in order to protect the currency.

I have pointed out that mediaeval bills of exchange were not discounted but purchased outright. Some may argue that this is a minor matter and that I have overstressed this point. It is true that, to some extent, it makes little difference whether a banker buys or discounts a bill. In both cases he extends credit since he gives a sum of money in exchange for a claim payable at a future date. But a mediaeval bill involved something more than a loan, namely an exchange transaction. The presence of exchange had two important consequences. One, it enabled the jurists and the theologians to contend that an exchange contract was not a straight loan or a *mutuum*. Consequently, exchange profits, so the learned doctors argued, were not usurious, since there could be no usury where there was no loan.[43] Two, as soon as exchange comes into the picture, the banker's profit ceases to be certain and becomes uncertain, since it depends entirely upon the unpredictable oscillations of the exchange rates.[44] I have given a complete analysis and its correctness is fully confirmed by the business records of the Italian merchant-bankers. Their profits, as the entries in their books plainly show, originated in exchange speculation and not in fixed interest charges. True, interest was included in the rates. This fact, however, does not alter the speculative character of foreign banking because the exchange rates responded to forces other than the rate of interest. Moreover, these forces were beyond the control of the bankers. They tried to forecast the course of the exchange but their guesses were not always right.

On all these points the demonstration given in this study is complete and decisive. One qualification needs to be made: my conclusions do not apply to the northern trade. There was no organized money market in the Hansa towns. There was such a market in England, but the English merchants had their own way of doing business and the Italian merchant-bankers were forced to adapt themselves to local conditions. Even in Bruges the facilities of the money market were used mainly by the members of the southern colonies: Italians and Catalans. The account books of the merchant-bankers rarely mention Flemish names in connection with exchange dealings.[45] This is not surprising since the carrying trade was almost entirely in the hands of foreigners. This situation did not change until the sixteenth century when a few Flemish merchants succeeded in gaining a foothold in foreign trade and international finance.

The conditions of equilibrium of the mediaeval money market have been fully described and determined. It has been possible to answer most of the questions with one important exception: Were there any business cycles in the Middle Ages? The available evidence shows that the money market was certainly subject to seasonal fluctuations and that they followed a pattern which was common knowledge among the bankers. If there are seasonal fluctuations, the existence of larger waves, that is, of cyclical fluctuations may be presumed and cannot be rejected *a priori*. Most theorists believe that business cycles do not antedate the Industrial Revolution or the Napoleonic Wars but there is not the slightest evidence to support this opinion. On the contrary, the few mediaeval business letters that have survived are full of references to business fluctuations and to alternating periods of good and bad trade. For the sixteenth century, the letters of the van der Molen, commission merchants of Antwerp, draw the same picture.[46]

Since mediaeval banks created credit against overdrafts, the contraction and expansion of bank money must have had disturbing effects on business activity and on the volume of production. Any contraction of credit tended to generate a crisis and any expansion to promote a boom. Among economists, Professor Schumpeter of Harvard University is a notable exception in that he admits that business cycles may be older than is commonly assumed.[47] Professor Schumpeter is also of the opinion that capitalism is as old as credit creation, which would carry us back to 1200 or thereabouts. Whatever the truth may be, the question should be raised even though it cannot be solved with the material which is available at present.

By way of a general conclusion it may be safe to state that the mediaeval banking system was based on the existence side by side of foreign banks and of local transfer banks, either public or private. This system apparently survived on the European continent until it was destroyed by the hurricane of the French Revolution. After the storm was over, William I, King of the Netherlands, founded the Société Générale de Belgique, which was a bank of discount, deposit, and circulation modeled after the English pattern. Thus the English banking system, so different from its mediaeval antecedent, was introduced into Belgium.

NOTES TO CHAPTER 16

CONCLUSIONS

[1]Bigwood (*Régime,* I, 181) classifies the Italians residing in the Low Countries into three categories: (a) the representatives of the great Italian banking and trading companies, (b) the Italians who became mintmasters or who were appointed to public offices, such as that of *receveur de Flandre,* and (c) the lombards or Italian pawnbrokers. As Bigwood deals separately with the money-changers, his classification is substantially correct. In other parts of his book, however, he fails to distinguish clearly between the Italian merchant-bankers and the lombards. For example (*ibid.*, p. 302), Pierre Cape and Pierre Scandillon—the latter a customer of Collard de Marke's—were merchants and not pawnbrokers. The same applies to Nicolas Chiavre, also mistakingly considered as a lombard. Mino Ricci (*ibid.*, p. 298) was a factor or employee of the Gallerani Company. Why is he mentioned as a lombard?

[2]*Ibid.*, pp. 650-55. Only 'dry exchange' resulted in the extension of credit (p. 653).

[3]*Ibid.*, pp. 420-37, esp. p. 426.

[4]The same theory is propounded by André-E. Sayous ('Les opérations des banquiers italiens,' *op. cit.*, p. 6) who writes: 'Le point de départ des opérations de banque a été des prêts, . . . il s'y est greffé des opérations de change.' In my opinion, just the opposite is true, and the text should be emended to read: 'Le point de départ des opérations de banque est dans le change. Il s'y est nécessairement greffé des opérations de crédit.' See my article 'Le contrat de change depuis la fin du treizième siècle jusqu'au début du dix-septième,' *op. cit.*, p. 114.

[5]Statements made by Simone Poignant in her book *La Foire de Lille* (for example, on p. 130) show how badly confused some historians are on this subject. On p. 132 this author even asserts that there was little difference between the business of the lombards and that of the money-changers! Cf. Piton, *Les Lombards en France,* I, 39. Benoît (*op. cit.*, p. 16), on the other hand, is right when he points out that a clear distinction should be made between *tables de change* ('exchanges') and *tables de prêt* ('pawnshops').

[6]Gilliodts, *Inventaire,* I, 265: 'Item Janne Vilaine, den Lombaert, van der compagnie van Perouze.' Cf. *Coutume,* I, 520.

[7]Bruges, Municipal Archives, Chartes politiques, 1e série, No. 616.

[8]Ehrenberg, 'Makler,' *op. cit.*, p. 451.

[9]Josef Kulischer, 'Warenhändler und Geldausleiher im Mittelalter,' *Zeitschrift für Volkswirtschaft, Sozialpolitik und Verwaltung,* XVII (1908), 29-71, 201-54. Cf. Franz Arens, 'Commerce d'argent et commerce de denrées au moyen âge à propos d'un travail récent,' *Revue de synthèse historique,* XVII (1908), 298-308; Raymond de Roover, 'Die rechtliche und wirtschaftliche Organisation des Münzhandels und Kreditgeschäftes in Brügge,' *Hansische Geschichtsblätter,* LX (1935), 369-70.

[10]Kulischer, 'Warenhändler,' *op. cit.*, p. 56: '*Will man jedoch den irreführenden Ausdruck* durchaus beihalten, so muss man jedenfalls sich stets gegenwärtig halten, dass unter den "Lombarden" und "Cauwerschen" keineswegs verhasste Wucherer zu begreifen sind sondern jene stolzen italienischen Handelsherren, welche die führende Rolle im Warenhandel als im Bankgeschäft übernahmen. . . .' Of course, this statement is in contradiction with the evidence presented in this study.

[11]*Ibid.*, pp. 52-56. Schulte (*op. cit.*, I, 325) is of a contrary opinion. Cf. Arens, 'Commerce de l'argent,' *op. cit.*, p. 301.

[12]Kulischer, 'Warenhändler,' *op. cit.*, p. 216.

[13]Gauthier, *Les Lombards,* pp. 261, 263, Nos. 125, 128. Document No. 125 is a grant of June 19, 1381, which allows usurers from Chieri to lend at usury and to establish a public exchange in the city of Dijon.

[14]Bigwood, *Régime,* I, 45.

[15]This expression *banco a minuto* occurs in a partnership agreement of 1483 between

Francesco di Giuliano de' Medici and Gabriello di Jacopo Davicano. The purpose of the partnership was the trade in bullion, jewels, precious stones, and jeweled belts. The partnership also made loans secured by jewels only (Selfridge Collection of Medici Mss, Harvard University, No. 495, p. 40).

[16]Doren, *Italienische Wirtschaftsgeschichte,* I, 447.

[17]La Sorsa, *op. cit.,* p. 15. On the other hand, La Sorsa is right when he points out that not all members of the *Arte del Cambio* were international bankers. Cf. Gustav Lastig, *Florentiner Handelsregister des Mittelalters* (Halle, 1883), pp. 22-26. The partners of the Peruzzi Company were all registered with the *Arte del Cambio* from 1299 until the time of the bankruptcy. Averardo de' Medici was one of the consuls of the same gild in 1419. (Sieveking, *Handlungsbücher der Medici,* p. 4). Doren (*op. cit.,* p. 457) follows La Sorsa, but the documentary evidence proves the contrary.

[18]Nicola Ottokar, *Il Comune di Firenze alla fine del dugento* (Florence, 1926), p. 26. With regard to the leading Medici, the unpublished matriculation lists in the State Archives of Florence give the following dates of admission to membership in the three gilds:

Arte del Cambio, Matricola No. 12

Cosimo, May 1, 1420 (fol. 86); his son Piero, December 15, 1425 (fol. 94); and Piero's two sons, Lorenzo and Giuliano, December 30, 1465 (fol. 112).

Arte della Seta, Matricole No. 8

Cosimo, July 18, 1433 (fol. 45); Piero, March 7, 1435 (fol. 179); Lorenzo, July 6, 1469 (fol. 137^{v}).

Arte della Lana, Matricole No. 21

Piero di Cosimo, March 21, 1434 (fol. 124^{v}).

[19]Usher, *History of Deposit Banking,* I, 239, 245.

[20]*Ibid.,* p. 271.

[21]Koch, *op. cit.,* p. 49: 'Auch für die Ausbildung des Bankwesens sind sie [the lombards] ohne Bedeutung gewesen, da ihre Schwerpunkt in dem lokalen Geldwucher beruhte.'

[22]The Pawnbrokers Act of 1872: 35 and 36 Victoria, c. 93.

[23]The laws vary from state to state. Some states have no laws which makes matters worse instead of better.

[24]A bill to establish such institutions in England was actually introduced in the House of Commons in 1571 but failed to become an act of Parliament (Tawney, Intro., Wilson, *Discourse,* p. 125). For another project of the same kind, see R. H. Tawney and Eileen Power (eds.), *Tudor Economic Documents* (New York, 1924), III, 370-77.

[25]The following authors are of the opinion that the bill of exchange was developed by merchants, not by money-changers: Bigwood, *Régime,* I, 437; Sneller, 'Wisselaarsbedrijf,' *op. cit.,* p. 487; A. Lattes *Diritto commerciale,* p. 204; Josef Kulischer, *Allgemeine Wirtschaftsgeschichte des Mittelalters und der Neuzeit* (Berlin, 1928), I, 331. Gras in his book *Business and Capitalism* (p. 143) states correctly that 'the peculiar creation of the sedentary merchant was the draft form of the bill of exchange.' Elsewhere in his book (p. 55) he points out that the traveling merchant was responsible for the development of the exchange contract in notarial form, a prototype of the draft.

The following authors are of a different opinion and erroneously attribute the invention of the bill of exchange to the money-changers: Vogel, 'Giralverkehr,' *op. cit.,* pp. 1-9, and Endemann, *Studien,* I, 107, 425.

[26]Hans van Werveke, *Brugge en Antwerpen: Acht eeuwen Vlaamsche handel* (Ghent, n. d.), pp. 185, 195-207, and the references given on pp. 212-13; Denucé, *Italiaansche Koopmansgeslachten,* pp. 157-74.

[27]Richard Ehrenberg, *Das Zeitalter der Fugger: Geldkapital und Creditverkehr im 16. Jahrhundert* (3rd ed.; Jena, 1922), I, 51: 'Dennoch hat es schon im Mittelalter Börsen gegeben; aber sie dienten noch nicht dem Waaren-, sondern in erster Linie dem Wechselhandel, genauer: dem Wechselbriefhandel.'

[28]Usher, *Hist. of Deposit Banking,* I, 94-109, esp. 102.

[29]R. D. Richards (*The Early History of Banking in England* [London, 1929], p. 46) mentions the appearance of the 'inland' bill but fails to point out that 'inland' bills in contrast to 'outland' bills were discountable.

[30]Malachy Postlethwayt, 'Banking,' *The Universal Dictionary of Trade and Commerce* (London, 1751), p. 193.

[31]*Ibid.,* p. 197.

[32]Bigwood, *Régime,* I, 437. Conditions in Italy were the same. Professor Lane ('Venetian Bankers,' *op. cit.,* p. 188) writes with reference to Venice: 'Venetian banks about 1500 were primarily local banks.' With regard to a money-changer in Piacenza, Zerbi (*op. cit.,* p. 248) observes: 'Ma non si ha motivo di credere che il banco Giussano negoziasse assiduamente in tratte su altre piazze.'

[33]In the seventeenth century Sir William Petty, commenting upon Dutch practices, pointed out that banks were capable of doubling the efficiency of the currency. See Eli F. Heckscher, *Mercantilism* (London, 1935), II, 232.

[34]van Dillen, *Bronnen,* I, 45. Cf. H. van Velden, 'Het kassiersbedrijf te Amsterdam in de 17[e] eeuw,' *De Economist,* LXXXII (1933), 59.

[35]Oscar de Smedt, 'De keizerlijke verordeningen van 1537 en 1539 op de obligaties en wisselbrieven,' *Nederlandsche Historiebladen,* III (1940), 15-35.

[36]van Dillen, *Bronnen,* I, 1, 12, 17.

[37]In Amsterdam exchange rates were generally quoted in local currency on the basis of a fixed quantity of foreign currency. A rise of the exchange rates, therefore, was equivalent to a depreciation of the local currency.

[38]van Dillen, *Bronnen,* I, 14-17, No. 18.

[39]For the text of such an assignment, see *ibid.,* p. 35, No. 39.

[40]The kassiers were again authorized to operate in 1621 (*ibid.,* p. 47).

[41]Marc Bloch, 'Economie-nature ou économie-argent: un pseudo-dilemme,' *Annales d'histoire sociale,* I (1939), 10: 'Pour n'avoir pas su et pu inventer le billet de banque, le capitalisme médiéval a été constamment handicapé.'

[42]It naturally makes no difference whether the bank deposits are transferable by written or by oral assignment.

[43]For instance, Panormitanus declares in his *concilia:* 'Usura non committitur nisi in contractu mutui.'—McLaughlin, 'Teachings,' *op. cit.,* I, 98. Cf. Sigismondo Scaccia, *Tractatus de commerciis et cambio* (Geneva, 1664), §1, Quaestio vii, Pars 1, Summaria, p. 131: 'Usura non versatur in alio contractu, quam in contractu mutui, sive sit mutuum explicitum seu implicitum.' According to Albertus Magnus usury was a gain resulting from a loan ('usura est lucrum ex mutuo').

[44]Tommaso Buoninsegni, *Dei cambi: Trattato risolutissimo et utilissimo* (Florence, 1573), fol. 5[v]: 'Ma variandosi la valuta delle monete per diversi accidenti, non si può in questo modo di cambiare, sperar guadagno certo.'

[45]The Medici account books mention a Polo Bociardo, who, I suspect, is a Fleming named Paul Bossaerts. The identification of Flemish names is complicated by the fact that they were Italianized.

[46]Edler, 'The van der Molen,' *op. cit.,* pp. 118 ff.

[47]Joseph A. Schumpeter, *Business Cycles: a Theoretical, Historical, and Statistical Analysis of the Capitalist Process* (New York, 1939), I, 225 ff.

APPENDICES

Appendix 1

Request to the Municipal Authorities of Bruges made by the Surety of a Bankrupt Money-Changer.

Bruges, Municipal Archives, Chartes politiques, No. 445.

Werde Heren Borghmeesters, Scepenen ende Raed van der stede van Brucghe, hu toghen Jan van Bouchout ende zine vriende over Joncfrouwe Lisebetten, 's vorseidz Jans wijf, dat hemlieden redene dinet, dat Jan Hauwescild sculdich es also verre ghehouden te wesene in de borghtucht van den wissele als 's vorseids Jans wijf van Bouchout, bi redenen dat de vorseide Jan Hauwescilt huter borghtucht niet ghedaen en was bi den ghemeenen hope van Scepenen, ende ooc so en gaf de vors. Jan Hauwescilt noch niemene van der wet weghe, Jans wive van Bouchout, noch Joncvrouwen Nannen Diederijc Urbaens wedewe, die principael stake was van den wissele, niet te kenne, dat hi quite wesen wilde van der borghtucht van den vorseiden wissele, dat men tandren tiden wisselaers ghegheven heift te kenne, als ghelike zaken ghevielen.

Voord so toght de vorseide Jan ende sine vriende over sijn wijf, dat men den vors. Jan Hauwescilde niet sculdich en hadde gheweist te doene huter borghtucht van den wissele, men hadder weder enen also soffisanten in sine steide ghestellet, ende hopt ooc de vorseide Jan ende sine vriende, dat men niemene sculdich en es te bescampene, noch den enen borghe hute te doene omme den anderen te verzwaerne sonder sijn weiten.

* * *

Dit sijn de persone die scult eesschen der wedewen Diederic Urbaens de welke men in den panpier vindt:

[1] Jan van den Eede	66 *lb.* 18*s.* gr. 2*est.*
[2] Jan de Wale Junior	5 *lb.* 6*d.* gr.
[3] Robeir de Wale	600 scilde payement
[4] Jan van der Waghe	51*s.* 8*d.* gr.
[5] Chrispiaen van den Voorde	11 *lb.* 1*d.* gr.
[6] Wouter van Viven	23 oude scilde
[7] Clais Oste	41 *lb.* 16*s.* gr.
[8] Daniel sinen cnape	15 *lb.* 14*s.* gr.
[9] Jan Pluems	10 *lb.* 14*s.* 8*d.* gr.
[10] France van Ypre	4 *lb.* 12*d.* gr.
[11] Heinrijc Rubijt	8 *lb.* 20*d.* gr.

[12] Jacob de Valkenare *dictus* Pollepel	9 *lb*. 3*s*. gr.
[13] Jan van Ardenbuergh	3 *lb*. gr.
[14] Clais van Lueghendorp	32*s*. gr. 21 scilde
[15] Clais de Kerseghieteren	100 scilde
[16] Jacob Tand	3 *lb*. 16s. 1*d*. gr.
[17] Lodewijc Bolleblomme	4 *lb*. 5*s*. gr.
[18] der Bernaerd Priem van Assisen	44*s*. 2*d*. gr.
[19] Gheraerd van den Meere	17*s*. gr.
[20] Jan van Rendscote	10 *lb*. 2*s*. gr.
[21] Clais ser Matheus cnape van der Burse	32 *lb*. 14*s*. 8*d*. gr..
[22] Jacob van Bouchout	8 *lb*. 2*s*. 6*d*. gr.
[23] Jan van den Ghavere	32*s*. 4*d*. gr.
[24] Pieter Enselkin	3 *lb*. 19*s*. 5*d*. gr.
[25] Brixsis Bakeman	52 graven scilden
[26] Lauwers, *filius* Langheghers	6 *lb*. 8*s*. 2*d*. gr.
[27] Jan Moens, de wisselare	20 graven scilden

Dit es d'antworde van Janne van Bouchout ende van sinen vrienden over Joncfrouwen Lisebetten 's vorseidz Jans wijf als van der scult die enighe persone eesschende sijn der wedewen Diederije Urbaens als van haren wissele dewelke scult men in't panpier van den wissele vonden heift, so welken tiden dat hu Heren Borghmeesters, Scepenen ende Raed van der stede van Brucghe ghelieven zal de vors. persone voor hulieden t'ombiedene; de vorseide Jan in baten van zinen vrienden over sijn vorseide wijf zal gherne elken zonderlinghe verandworden up sinen eesch in huwe presencie.

* * *

Dit sijn de persone die scult eesschen der wedewen Diederic Urbaens dewelke men in den panpiere niet en vindt

[1] Jan Hals	4 *lb*. gr. payement 5*d*. gr.
[2] Jan Vettinc	97 's graven scilden
[3] Jan Sac van Geneven	24*s*. 4*d*. gr.
[4] Jan van der Capelle, wisselare	41 scilden 10*d*. gr.
[5] Griele 's Brauwers	3 *lb*. 14*s*. gr.
[6] Riquaerd van Varsenare	148 's graven scilde
[7] Jan Hoinc	7 onsen goudz
[8] Jan Niewestad	3 *lb*. 16*s*. gr.
[9] Gheraerd van Hilts	11 's graven scilden
[10] Symoen Bisscop	4 *lb*. 9*s*. 4*d*. gr.
[11] Jan Moens de Wisselare	25 scilde
[12] Jan Adelaerd	24*s*. 6*d*. gr.

[13] Jan van den Hove	3 *lb.* 11*s.* 8*d.* gr.
[14] Liejaerd ten Baerse	19 *lb.* 8*s.* 4*d.* gr.
[15] Bouden de Vos	50 scilden
[16] Everaerd Goederic	9*s.* 9*d.* gr.
[17] Pieter Enselkin Tremanant boven 3 *lb.* 19*s.* 5*d.* gr. toten somme van	5 *lb.* 10*s.* gr.
[18] Jacob de Zwertslipere	250 scilden

Van weseghelde ende coopmanscepe

Jan Vettinc ende Clais Hauwescilt	22 *lb.* gr. ende de bate van 3 jaren
Clais ende Blote van den Casehuse	38 *lb.* 14*s.* gr.
Pieter de Scotelare ende Jan ende Godscalc Hauwescilt	31 *lb.* gr.

Dit es d'andworde van Janne van Bouchout ende van sinen vrienden over Joncfrouw Lisebetten 's vors. Jans wijf als van den schulden die enighe persone eesschende sijn der wedewen Diederijc Urbaens, als van haren wissele dewelke scult in 't panpier van den wissele niet vonden en es. Eerst so toghen de vorseide Jan ende sine vrienden over de vors. Joncvrauwe, dat zoe van der vorseide scult niet en es sculdich te antwordene bi der redene dat men 't in 't panpier van den wissele niet vonden en heift, noch so en es hie in den name van sine vorseide werdinne sculdich te andwordene van weseghelde daer men bate af gheift, noch van enighen gheleenden ghelde dat men gheleend mochte hebben deen wisselare den anderen, noch van gheene coopmanscepe die men buten wissele ghedreven mochte hebben.

Appendix 2

Sample Accounts from Collard de Marke's Ledgers.

For several reasons it has seemed inadvisable to follow the usual rules in publishing abstracts from the account books of the Bruges money-changer Collard de Marke. For one thing, business records should be copied accurately but there is no need to treat them with the same devout respect as diplomas, charters, chronicles, or literary manuscripts. A second reason is that there is no sense in adhering so closely to the original that the modern reader is completely confused unless he is familiar with the habits of mediaeval bookkeepers. In the matter of business records intelligibility is of greater importance than a servile reproduction of the original text. Finally, I believe that mediaeval business records should be presented, as far as possible, in a modern form by placing figures in columns, by clearly separating debits from credits, and by footing the columns even if the totals are not given in the original. On the other hand, additions, subtractions, and other operations should be carefully checked. Accuracy in this regard is in my opinion much more important than the publication of a meaningless array of Roman numerals. My purpose is not to show how mediaeval bankers kept their books but to produce the evidence for some of my assertions in this study. A page of Collard de Marke's ledger is reproduced: it will show how the original really looks.

The abstracts published here are only a small sample of the available records. The reader is reminded of the fact that there are in the Bruges archives five ledgers and two journals which once belonged to Collard de Marke, that each ledger is a large in-folio volume of more than six hundred pages or three hundred folios, that each contains nine hundred or more different accounts, and that the number of transfers and other transactions recorded in any one ledger runs into the thousands. The publication of all this material would fill several volumes, but I doubt whether its integral publication would serve any useful purpose except that of supplying the delighted antiquarian with a list of several thousand names without contributing much, if anything, to the history of banking.

Collard de Marke, following the prevailing custom, used Roman numerals for all figures. Since such numerals only create confusion, I have substituted Arabic notation for all sums of money and for all dates. In the original, the ledger accounts are divided vertically into two columns, one for the debit and one for the credit. I have added separate columns for the explanation and for the amount of the entries on both the debit and the credit side. Collard de Marke kept his accounts in pounds, shillings, and deniers groat. The groat was subdivided into three sterlings or 24 mites. In the original, the abbreviations used are the customary ones: *lb.* for the pounds, *s.* for the shillings, *d.* for the deniers, and *est.* for the sterlings. In order to save space, I have eliminated all unnecessary repetition by placing the symbols for the different monetary units at the head of the appropriate columns. Zeros have been added where there are none in the original. Thus 'xx lb. gr.' has been transcribed £20.0.0. The 'gr.' for groat has been dropped since the caption of each table indicates clearly that the accounts are kept in pounds groat.

Sometimes Collard de Marke does not give the equivalent of French francs or other gold coins in money of account. When necessary such amounts in francs or other gold coins have been extended in groats. Such extensions are given in italics in the extension column. The totals footing the extension columns are not in the original. Most of the time the debit and credit totals are equal which shows that Collard de Marke kept his accounts with a reasonable degree of accuracy. In a few cases there is a difference of one or two sterlings or even of one or two groats. The largest discrepancy occurs in the account of Mademoiselle de Rudevorde where there is a difference of seven groats and one sterling between the totals of debit and credit.

The old spelling has been preserved in the explanation columns. Abbreviations have been extended as usual. Thus 'Jeh.' has been transcribed as Jehan. With regard to 'Jak.' it is sometimes difficult to tell whether this abbreviation stands for Jakes, Jakop, Jakemon, Jakemes, or Jakemart. All these forms of the name 'Jacques' occur in the Collard de Marke ledgers, but the form 'Jakemon' is the most frequent. I have used Jakemon when there was no reason for preferring one of the other forms. Words omitted have been added between brackets. Brackets have also been used for any additions to the original text.

(1) Account of Pierre van le Fine, Collard de Marke's Partner
Ledger No. 2, fol. 101

Dr. Cr.

Explanation	Amount (Pounds groat)			Explanation	Amount (Pounds groat)		
	£	s	d		£	s	d
Pietre van le Fine me doit: par Jehan Hoket par le conte que je li fait en me petit papier. .	47	9	4	doy par pluisuers parties somme faites, si qu'il appert par le fuellet 9 de ce papier	1,090	10	10
Item me doit-il si qu'il appert par me papier des dras pour pluisuers parties, somme faites . . .	1,933	10	6	Item li doi-ge par lui contet 10 en juing [1367]	20	0	0
Somme 1,980 *lb.* 19*s.* 10*d.*				Item li doi-ge par Pierre de Vidac a ce jour	15	0	0
				Item li doi-ge par Pietre d'Audenarde de 14 en juing	22	16	0
				Item li doi-ge par Pietre le Potre 15 en juing	11	8	0
				Item li doi-ge par Jehan van der Windre a ce jour	20	0	0
				Item li doi-ge par Stasin Quatouc a ce jour	6	0	0
				Item li doi-ge par Dominges Janes de Baudri Ovre de Velt. . .	10	0	0
				Et par lui contet a ce jour	4	7	0
				Item li doi-ge par Antonne van Zendre de Radekin Vrane en Dourpt	25	0	0
				Item li doi-ge par lui contet 17 en juing	10	0	0
				Item li doi-ge par lui contet a ce jour	12	0	0
				Item li doi-ge par Pietre d'Audenarde	10	0	0
				Item li doi-ge par lui contet a ce jour	14	0	0
				Item li doi-ge par le demisielle de Witte 19 en juing	7	0	0
				Item li doi-ge par Pietre le Potre a ce jour	8	2	0
				Item li doi-ge par lui contet 20 en juing	14	0	0
				Et par Jakoppe van le Fine a ce jour	5	0	0
				Item li doi-ge par Pierre de Vidac 21 en juing	15	0	0
				Item li doi-ge par lui contet 24 en juing	25	0	0
				Item li doi-ge par Stasin Quatouc 24 en juing	6	14	0
				Item li doi-ge par Pietre d'Audenarde a ce jour	8	13	10
				Item li doi-ge par Jakoppe Reups a ce jour	4	12	6
				Item li doi-ge par Pierre Janes a ce jour	11	10	0
				Et par Nicollas de Gijen a ce jour	15	0	0
				Item li doi-ge par lui contet a ce jour	6	0	0
				Et	26	0	0
				Item li doi-ge par Stasin a ce jour	4	0	0
				Somme de tout 1,427 *lb.* 14*s.* 2*d.*			
				Item li doi-ge qu'il me fait conte ou fuellet 117	553	5	8
	1,980	19	10		1,980	19	10

(2) Account of Thomas Sarlande Concerning the Mint
Ledger No. 4, fol. 4

Dr. Explanation	Amount (Pounds groat) £	s	d	Cr. Explanation	Amount (Pounds groat) £	s	d
Thumas Sarlande a le cause dou mestre de le monnoie me doit:				Doy pour le reste d'un conte de men autre papier dou fuellet 87	400	0	0
Item me doit-il par lui que je luy fay conte ou fuellet 67 pour le cause de Jehan Terminel	50	0	0	Item li doi-ge pour le pourfit de lui, contet a lui au Noël l'an 68 [1368]	50	0	0
Item me doit-il ke je li fay conte ou fuellet 3 de men papier apries chiesty	400	0	0				
	450	0	0		450	0	0

(3) Account of Thomas Sarlande Concerning the Mint (Continued)
Ledger No. 5, fol. 4

Dr.	£	s	d	Cr.	£	s	d
Thumas Sarlande me doit: a le cause de Jehan Terminniel pour une reste que on me devoit a le monoie dou 17e jour d'avril [1369], et dou 28e jour d'avril, et dou 7e jour de may, contet l'an 1369, a ces journées a Jehan Jourdain, si qu'il appert par me papier de le monnoie	501	19	7	doy si qu'il [appert] par le fuelliet 4 de men autre papier . .	400	0	0
				a le cause dou mestre de le monnoie			
				Item li doi-ge que Jehan Jourdain m'envoia environ le premier jour jour [sic] d'aoust [1369]	51	19	7
				Balance	50	0	0
	501	19	7		501	19	7
Reste ke li dis Tumas me doit, contet a Jehan Jourdain a ce jour desu dit a le monnaye de Gand . . .	50	0	0				

(4) Account of Jehan Terminiel (Interminelli), Mintmaster
Ledger No. 4, fol. 103

Dr.	£	s	d	Cr.	£	s	d
Jehan Terminiel me doit: par Roulot Rabonne de Louvain pour une lettre qu'il m'envoia 24 en février	415	4	2	doy que je rechus a le monnoie 2 en march	415	4	3
	415	4	2		415	4	3

(5) Account of Roulof Rabonne of Louvain
Ledger No. 4, fol. 103

Dr. Cr.

Explanation	Amount (Pounds groat) £	s	d	Explanation	Amount (Pounds groat) £	s	d
Roulof Rabonne me doit: par Pietre d'Audenarde 26 en février [1369]	200	0	0	doy Jehan Terminiel 24 en février	415	4	3
Item me doit-il par lui contet a ce jour en 510 moutons g[rans] et 13 gros, 800 francs françoys et pour l'avantaige 3 *lb.* 9*s.* 2*d.*	215	4	3				
	415	4	3		415	4	3

(6) Account of Sire Jehan Baille
Ledger No. 4, fol. 173

Dr. Cr.

Explanation	£	s	d	Explanation	£	s	d
Sire Jehan Baille me doit: Par sire Jehan de Concorighe pour une finance	75	0	0	doy par le reste de nos contes dou fuellet 77 contet a lui 25 en avril	37	5	11
Par Gilles de Valenchiennes 25 en avril pour 100 francs a 32 gros	13	6	8	Et par lui contet a ce jour	20	17	6
Et par Olivier de Rosieres de l'ostel le dame van le Fine	24	17	6	Et par lui contet pour 100 francs	13	6	8
Somme 113 *lb.* 4*s.* 2*d.*				Et par Jakoppe Franchoys 5 en may	10	9	2
				Somme 81 *lb.* 19*s.* 3*d.*			
				Item li doi-ge ke il me fait conte ou fuellet 32 de men papier apries cesty	31	4	11
	113	4	2		113	4	2

(7) Account of the Money-Changer Guillaume Ruyelle
Ledger No. 4, fol. 315

Dr. Cr.

Explanation	£	s	d	Explanation	£	s	d
Willaume Ruyelle me doit: Et par Pietre Garighe 26 en march	5	0	0	doy par Jehan Bersvoc 6 en avril	16	9	9
Et par Jehan de Concorighe 27 en march	12	0	0	Et par Jehan de Hedines de Pierre de Pioce	4	15	0
Et par Nicolas de Gyen 21 en avril	8	0	0	Et par Hanekin contet	2	11	6
Et par Tideman Losebrec	2	11	6	Et par Jehan Sachet 9 en may	15	0	0
Et par le varlet Jehan Gardepeninc contet	11	4	9				
	38	16	3		38	16	3

(8) Account of Pietre Garighe, Probably an Italian

Dr. — Ledger No. 4, fol. 140 — Cr.

Explanation	Amount (Pounds groat) £	s	d	st	Remarks	Explanation	Amount (Pounds groat) £	s	d	st	Remarks
Pietre Garighe me doït: Item me doit-il que je li fay conte ou fuellet 141	55	5	8			doy par Barde Menchine 26 en march	50	0	0		or
						Et par Willaume Ruyelle a ce jour	5	0	0		
						Item li doi-ge par le reste de nos contes dou fuellet 32		5	8		
	55	5	8				55	5	8		

Dr. — Ledger No. 4, fol. 141 — Cr.

Explanation	£	s	d	st	Remarks	Explanation	£	s	d	st	Remarks
Pietre Garighe me doit: par Outre Scac 28 en march	50	0	0			doy par le reste de nos contes dou fuellet 140 contet a lui 27 en march	55	5	8		or
Et par Willem Tonnelaire 13 en avril	100	0	0			Et par Nicollas Outremarin 31 en march	30	0	0		
Et par Pietre van Collekierke 5 en may	18	13	3		or	Et par Jehan Aloet 9 en avril	10	0	0		
Et par Stasin Risse 5 en may a Jehan van Leke 37*s.* et par Pietre d'Audenarde 28 *lb.* 3*s.* gros	30	0	0			Et par Barde Menchine 12 en avril	50	0	0		p.
Et par Gilles van de Poulle 19 en may	20	0	0			Et par Gabryel Lery 13 en avril	50	0	0		p.
Somme 218 *lb.* 13*s.* 3*d.*						Et par Barde Menchine 19 en avril	15	0	0		p.
Item me doit-il que je pauay a Stasin Davit de Wervy 14 en avril	20	0	0		Contet	Et par Barde Menchine 20 en avril	6	9	10		
Item me doit-il que je li fay conte ou fuelliet 21 de men papier apries cesti	119	14	5			Et par Nicollas Amanat 21 en avril	9	0	0		
						Et par Jehan van de Buske 5 en may	9	0	0		
						Et par Jakemon de Gérart 19 en may	123	12	2		
						Somme 358 *lb.* 7*s.* 8*d.*					
	358	7	8				358	7	8		

(9) Account of Gilles de Loo from Roulers, a Small Town in Flanders

Dr. — Ledger No. 4, fol. 149 — Cr.

Explanation	£	s	d	st	Remarks	Explanation	£	s	d	st	Remarks
Gilles de Lo de Roulers me doit: par lui contet 7 en avril [1369]	8	6	8			doy par Jakemon de Blaudain 7 en avril pour le cause d'une pais 200 *lb.* parisis, 20 gros pour le *lb.*, somme	16	13	4		
Item me doit-il ke je li fay conte ou fulliet 22 de men papier apries cesty	8	6	8								
	16	13	4				16	13	4		

(10) Account of Jehan de Concorighe, Probably an Italian Merchant

Ledger No. 4, fol. 30

Dr.

Explanation	Amount (Pounds groat) £	s	d	st	Remarks
Jehan de Concorighe me doit: par le reste de nos contes dou fuelliet 287 de men autre papier	88	7	11		
Item me doit-il par Boucasin contet 12 en jenvier [1369] 24 nobles [crossed out]					
Et par Dine Malapris 15 en jenvier	10	16	9		or
Et par Polles de le Conte 18 en jenvier	100	0	0		or
Somme 199 *lb.* 4*s.* 8*d.*					
Item me doit-il que je li fay conte ou fuelliet 92, si a 40 *lb.* or*	163	0	3		
	362	4	11		

Cr.

Explanation	Amount (Pounds groat) £	s	d	st	Remarks
doy par Dine Malapris un en jenvier [1369]	72	18	9		or
Et par Stasse de Berghes 17 en jenvier	40	0	0		p.
Et par sen varlet contet 18 en jenvier	28	0	0		p.
Et par sen varlet contet 19 en jenvier 24 nobles [crossed out] 12 francs de Haynau [crossed out]					
Et par Jehan van Marc 29 en jenvier	129	15	5		10 parisis
Et par Thumas Sarlande 15 en fevrier	13	4	0		
Et par lui contet 19 en février pour 600 francs a ce jour#	78	6	8		
Somme 362 *lb.* 4*s.* 11*d.*					
	362	4	11		

Ledger No. 4, fol. 92

Dr.

Explanation	£	s	d	st	Remarks
Jehan de Concorighe me doit: par Lois de Robiert 21 en march	123	19	2		or
Et par Jakemon de Gerart 23 en march	123	19	2		or
Et par Gabrijel de Court 24 en march	100	0	0		or
Et par Gabrijel de Court 26 en march	100	0	0		or
Somme 447 *lb.* 18*s.* 4*d.*					
Item me doit-il que je li fay conte ou fuellet 143	261	19	9		
	709	18	1		

Cr.

Explanation	£	s	d	st	Remarks
doy par le reste de nos contes dou fuelliet 30 contet a lui 19 en février, si a 40 *lb.* gros or	163	0	3		
Et par Galigo da Piastre 20 en février	25	18	0	2	or
Et par Rafel Tripane 28 en février	32	0	0		p.
Et par Franchois Peninc 3 en march	60	0	0		or
Et par Flipre de Lorin 14 en march	64	16	10	2	or
Et par Gabrijel Lery 23 en march	40	0	0		
Et par Mathin Villain 24 en march	125	13	10		
Et par Jakemon Boubelle a ce jour	49	0	0		or
Et par Jehan Tignesin 27 en march	85	1	8		p.
Et par Flipre de Lorin a ce jour	52	7	2	2	or
Et par Willaume Ruyelle a ce jour	12	0	0		
Somme 709 *lb.* 18*s.* gros					
	709	18	0		

*The 40 pounds gold are obtained by deducting £110 16*s.* 9*d.* groat, the sum of the two items marked 'or' on the debit side, from £151 5*s.* 5*d.*, the sum of the item marked gold on the credit side plus £78 6*s.* 8*d.* equivalent to 600 francs.

#The 600 francs were reckoned at 31 groats and one sterling, or one third of a groat, each.

(10) Account of Jehan de Concorighe, Probably an Italian Merchant (Continued)
Ledger No. 4, fol. 165

Dr. | Dr.

Explanation	Amount (Pounds groat) £	s	d	Remarks	Explanation	Amount (Pounds groat) £	s	d	Remarks
Jehan de Concorighe me doit:					doy par le reste de nos contes dou fuellet 143 contet a lui 18 en avril	80	4	1	p.
par Jehan de Sclotelaire de Malines 28 en avril contet	5	14	2	or	Item li doi-ge par Jehan Baille pour une finanche qu'il fist a Boucasin	75	0	0	
Et par François Fidielle 14 en may a Jakoppe Reups	75	18	9	p.	Somme 155 *lb.* 4*s.* 1*d.*				
Somme 81 *lb.* 12*s.* 11*d.* gros									
Item me doit-il ke je li fay conte ou fulliet 29 de men papier apries cesty	73	11	1						
	155	4	0			155	4	1	

(11) Account of the Hanseatic Merchant Tideman Rebart
Ledger No. 4, fol. 16

Dr. | Cr.

Explanation	£	s	d	Remarks	Explanation	£	s	d	Remarks
Thideman Rebart me doit:					doy par le reste de nos contes dou fuelliet 245 de men autre papier	34	0	3	
par Jakoppe Reups 30 en décembre [1368]	34	0	0						
Et par lui contet			3						
	34	0	3			34	0	3	

(12) Account of the Bruges Money-Changer Pierre d'Audenarde
Ledger No. 4, fol. 310

Dr. | Cr.

Explanation	£	s	d	Remarks	Explanation	£	s	d	Remarks
Pietre d'Audenarde me doit:					doy par le reste de nos contes dou fuellet 305 contet	78	17	0	
par Gorge Wandelaire 15 en février [1369]	12	14	0		Item doi-ge par Henric de Semit 15 en février	7	0	0	
Et par Pietre van le Fine a ce jour	49	0	0		Et par Pietre de Vidac 16 en février	50	0	0	
Et par le varlet Pietre Semont a ce jour	15	0	0		Et par Ernout varlet Jehan Dop 15 en février	5	5	0	
Et par Jehan Prangiere 16 en février	18	0	0	contet	Somme 141 *lb.* 2*s.*				
Item me doit-il par Clais Diedric Zenne [Diedrickzone] a ce jour, contet	8	0	0						
Item me doit-il par Lambesin Diaghere [de Jaghere] 15 en février	6	0	0						
Somme 108 *lb.* 14*s.* gros									
Item me doit-il que je li fay conte ci-desous	32	8	0						
	141	2	0			141	2	0	

Item me doit-il que je li paiay pour avantaige d'or contet a ce jour, 8*s.*

(12) Account of the Bruges Money-Changer Pierre d'Audenarde (Continued)

Ledger No. 4, fol. 315

Dr.

Explanation	Amount (Pounds groat) £	s	d	Remarks
Pietre d'Audenarde me doit: par Lambesin Diaghere 26 en march	8	0	0	
Et par Clais Breton a ce jour, escrit au fuellet 380	20	0	0	
Item me doit-il qu'il rechut en un tonniel qui vient de le monnoie 26 en march*	158	3	10	
Item me doit-il que je li fay conte ci-desous	69	15	8	
	255	19	6	

Cr.

Explanation	Amount (Pounds groat) £	s	d	Remarks
doy par le reste de nos contes dou fuellet 314	222	6	7	
Et par Jehan Cras de Jakemon Franchois 27 en march	33	13	0	
si a l'avantaige de 128 *lb.* or				
	255	19	7	

Ledger No. 4, fol. 320

Dr.

Explanation	Amount (Pounds groat) £	s	d	Remarks
Pietre d'Audenarde me doit: par Jehan Vetinc 2 en may	23	0	0	
Et par Jehan sen varlet contet que je li envoiay par Copin Con 4 en may, 50 doubles mountons#	*10*	*8*	*4*	or
Et par Gorge Burlemay a ce jour	17	10	0	
Et par Lucadine a ce jour	8	7	7	
Et par Pietre Vetinc 5 en may	38	10	0	
Et par Dar de Revice 7 en may	31	0	6	
Et par Jehan van de Walle a ce jour contet	68	7	8	
Et par Clais Scepe a ce jour	11	0	0	
Et par Lambesin Diaghere	10	0	0	
Et par Pietre Sucrebout 8 en may	6	0	0	
Somme 224 *lb.* 4*s.* gros				
Et par Jacob van den Iede 9 en may	27	9	8	
Et par Lambesin d'Alos 12 en may	10	0	0	
Somme 261 *lb.* 13*s.* 8*d.*				
Item me doit-il par Denis de Wagenaire pour Henric Pininc 14 en may	23	13	4	
Item me doit-il que je li fay conte ou fuellet [323] contet 14 en may	82	19	7	
Item me doit-il que j'ay payet a Crestien pour l'aventaige de 120 *lb.* d'or que que [sic] je li pouie devoir, contet a lui a ce jour 29*s.* 6*d.*				
	368	6	8	

Cr.

Explanation	Amount (Pounds groat) £	s	d	Remarks
or 127 *lb.* gros				
doy pour le reste de nos contes dou fuellet [317 bis] contet a sen varlet 30 en avril	37	3	0	
Et par Jakemon de Gérart a ce jour	30	0	0	
Et par Marke Gras 5 en may	75	15	7	
Et par Gorge van Rondeville a ce jour de Hugelin Adelaise	15	10	0	
Et par Jehan de Bekout 5 en may de Raoul de Coumines	9	11	0	
Et par Stasin Risse 5 en may a Pietre Garighe	28	3	0	
Et par Jehan de Grave de Simon Ongeriet 5 en may	6	0	0	
Et par Jehan Martines 5 en may de Lambesin Diaghere	20	0	0	
Et par Jakemon Bibijen 8 en may	8	0	0	
Somme 230 *lb.* 2*s.* 7*d.*				
Et par Franche van Zinghe 11 en may de Comel de Soterive	20	0	0	
Et par Simon Serigem de Jehan Scadehourde	40	0	0	
Et par Lambesin Scepres 12 en may de Raoul Rogier	9	0	0	
Et par Jehan Martines a ce jour de Lambesin Diaghere	25	0	0	
Somme 324 *lb.* 2*s.* 7*d.*				
Et par Simon Serigem 12 en mai	12	0	0	
Et par Outre Nolande de Jakoppe Boubelle 9 en may	20	0	0	
Et par Jehan van de Buske 14 en may	12	4	0	
	368	6	7	

*This entry refers evidently to a keg of newly minted coin received from the mint.
#The *doubles moutons* apparently were reckoned at 50 groats apiece.

(13) Account of the Bruges Money-Changer Jacques Reubs or Reups

Ledger No. 4, fol. 320

Dr.

Explanation	Amount (Pounds groat) £	s	d	Remarks
Jakoppe [Jakes] Reups me doit: par le reste de nos contes dou fuelliet et 318	80	19	5	
Item me doit-il que je li envoyay par Hanekin Daniel 30 en avril, 120 heaumes	*27*	*0*	*0**	
Et par Jehan Minne a le cause de Hanotin a Thiery Brochons 30 en avril	20	0	0	
Item me doit-il par Jakemon de Rouc 2 en may	50	0	0	
Item me doit-il par Jehan de Vagheviere a ce jour	7	3	8	
Et par Jakemon de Blaudain a ce jour	9	0	0	
Et par Franche de Guir 4 en may	61	16	2	or
Et par Lambesin Diaghere a ce jour	7	6	0	
Et par Jakemon de Rouc 4 en may	50	0	0	
Et par Jehan Duc 5 en may	10	0	0	
Et par Clais Scepe 7 en may	9	0	0	
Et par Lambesin Diaghere	22	0	0	
Et par Willem van de Neke 8 en may	15	10	0	
Somme 369 *lb.* 15*s.* 3*d.*				
Et par Ernout Poultus de fil contet pour monnoie de Braibant pour un sien hoste	17	1	6#	
Et par Pietre Vetinc 9 en may	49	9	4	
Et par Lambesin d'Alos 12 en may	16	11	0	
Et par Lambesin Diaghere a ce jour	37	0	0	
Et par Jehan Duc a ce jour	9	0	0	
Et par Raoul de Coumines a ce jour	16	0	0	
Et par Jakemon de Rouc a ce jour	100	0	0	
Somme 614 *lb.* 17*s.* 1*d.*				
	614	17	1	

Cr.

Explanation	Amount (Pounds groat) £	s	d	Remarks
Doy par Gerart Lambins 30 en avril [1369]	23	0	0	
Et par Estievene Bieke 30 en avril	38	11	0	
Et par Flipot Jehan Zenne [Janssone] de Fortegerre 2 en may	54	3	4	
Et par Jehan van der Windre a ce jour	32	0	0	
Et par Boniface Leu 4 en may de Estievene Leu	60	18	9	
Et par Jehan Daro, Melonnois, 5 en may	30	15	0	
Et par Thideman Cousin 5 en may de Baudy Ovre Velt [Overveld]	17	0	0	
Et par Ricart Linc 5 en may de Jakemon de Gérart	80	0	0	p.
Et par Franche de Deman a ce jour de Gaudolf de Gerames	50	0	0	
Et par Henric de Brauere 8 en may de Rafel Tripane	10	0	0	
Somme 396 *lb.* 8*s.* 1*d.*				
Item li-doi-ge par Ricart Estefelt de Fortegerre	60	0	0	p.
Item par Jakoppe Fine 12 en may de Jehan Bauselin	13	19	7	
Somme 470 *lb.* 7*s.* 8*d.*				
Item li doi-ge qu'il me fait conte au fuelliet 322	144	9	5	
	614	17	1	

*The *heaumes* (*schilden*), gold coins, apparently were reckoned at the rate of 54 groats apiece. The amount of £27 in the extension column is based on this rate.

#Note this entry referring to an exchange transaction.

(14) Account of Jacques France Relating to a Bill of Exchange

Ledger No. 4, fol. 105

Dr. Explanation	Amount (Pounds groat) £	s	d	st	Remarks	Cr. Explanation	Amount (Pounds groat) £	s	d	st	Remarks
Jakemon Franche me doit: par Boin Acourt [Bonaccorsi] de Louc 6 en march [1369] d'un cange de 600 florins de Florenche a Jakemes de Gérart*	62	10	0			doy par Jakemon de Blaudain 28 en février 400 francs franchois a demi gros#	*52*	*10*	*0*		
						Et par lui contet 6 en march	10	0	0		
						Somme 62 *lb.* 10*s.* gros					
	62	10	0				62	10	0		

(15) Account of the Foreign Merchant Jacques de Gérard (Gherardi)

Ledger No. 4, fol. 110

Dr. Explanation	£	s	d	st	Remarks	Cr. Explanation	£	s	d	st	Remarks
Jakemon de Gérard me doit: par Jehan de Quantin 6 en march [1369]	67	0	7		or	doy par le reste de nos contes du fuellet 15 contet a lui environ le premier de march		4	5		or
Et par lui contet 7 en march	15	0	0		or	Et par Jakemon Franche 6 en march	62	10	0		or
Et par Tumas de Guir 12 en march	73	12	9			Et par Nicollas Boin Acourt a ce jour	38	0	5		
Et par Gabrijel Lery 13 en march	36	13	4		or	Et par Mikiel Genis 12 en march	125	6	11	1	or
Et par Jehan de Priolle 15 en march	61	7	5		or	Et par Henric Heu [should be Leu] 13 en march	12	6	6	2	
Et par Jakemon de Quantin 16 en march	35	16	8		or	Et par Lois de Robiert 14 en march	50	0	0		or
Et par Pietre Florent dou Dam a Jakes de Rouc 16 en march	5	0	0			Et par Jehan de Priolle 21 en march	63	8	9		or
Et par Jakemon de Galbert 12 en march	50	0	0		or	Et par Jehan de Concorighe 23 en march	123	19	2		or
Et par lui contet 21 en march 30 nobles a 65 gros [the words 'a 65 gros' are crossed out]						Et par Jehan Tignesin 24 en march	62	16	11	2	or
Et par Ricart de Reste 23 en march	50	0	0		or	Somme 538 *lb.* 13*s.* 2*d.* 2 esterlins					
Et par Davin Tedaldin 24 en march	45	4	2		or	Et par lui contet 25 en avril	131	0	7		p.
Et par Tumas de Gotier a ce jour	103	6	8		or	Somme 669 *lb.* 13*s.* 10*d.* gros					
Et par Galigo da Piastre 10 en avril	37	0	0		p.	Item li doi-ge qu'il me fait conte ou fuellet 184	46	3	2		
Somme 580 *lb.* 1*s.* 7*d.* et 30 nobles											
Et par Barde Menchine 25 en avril	53	6	8								
Et par Estievene Bieke a ce jour	38	11	0		p.						
Et par Willem van Eurne d'Audenarde contet 26 en avril	25	3	3								
Et par Jehan Doubesue a ce jour contet	18	14	6								
Somme 715 *lb.* 17*s.* gros											
	715	17	0				715	16	11	2	

*The florins apparently were rated at 25 groats each. The counterpart of this entry will be found on the credit side of the account of Jacques de Gérard or Gherardi. This bill of exchange, it will be noticed, was paid by transfer in bank.

#The 400 French francs were rated at 31 and one-half groats each.

Ledger No. 4, fol. 184

Dr. Explanation	Amount (Pounds groat) £	s	d	st	Remarks	Cr. Explanation	Amount (Pounds groat) £	s	d	st	Remarks
Jakemon de Gérart me doit: par le reste de nos contes dou fuellet 110	46	3	2			Doy par Lois de Robiert 30 en avril	117	0	0		p.
Et par Pietre d'Audenarde 30 en avril	30	0	0		p.	Et par Jehan de Paulle 2 en may	19	7	0		p.
Et par Ricart Linc 5 en may a Jakoppe Reups	80	0	0			Et par Barde Menchine 7 en may	70	0	0		p.
Et par Henric van de Comme de l'ostel dou Fauchon de Louvain a ce jour contet, a 32 gros plus 4 gros au cent, 400 francs	*53*	*8*	*0*			Somme 206 *lb.* 7*s.*					
Et par autre partie 37 francs ½	*5*	0	*1*			Et par Lois de Robiert 19 en may	101	3	7	1	
Somme 214 *lb.* 11*s.* 3*d.* gros						Et par Jehan Oursiel 1[illegible] en may	38	8	4		
Et par Pietre Garighe 19 en may	123	12	2			Somme 345 *lb.* 18*s.* 11 *d.* 1 esterlin					
Item me doit-il que je li fay conte ou fuellet 35 de men autre papier	7	15	6	1							
	345	18	11	1			345	18	11	1	

(16) Account of the Italian Merchant Thomas Sarlande

Ledger No. 4, fol. 87

Dr. Explanation	£	s	d	st	Remarks	Cr. Explanation	£	s	d	st	Remarks
Thumas Sarlande me doit: par le reste de nos contes de ci-deseure contet a Andrin 31 en jenvier [1369]	243	11	0			Doy par Copin contet qu'il rechut 7 en février	95	0	0		
Et par Estievene Bieke 31 en jenvier	60	0	0			Et par Ricart de Reste 15 en février	90	0	0		
Et par Tadi Moricon a Jakoppe Reups 10 en février	15	0	0			Et par lui contet 16 en février	25	13	3		
Et par Dine Sanoche 15 en février	40	0	0			Item li doi-ge par lui contet 17 en février 6*d.* gros moins	100	0	0		p.
Et par Jehan de Concorighe a ce jour	13	4	0		or	Et par Jakemon Fabe 17 en février	30	0	0		
Et par Mikiel Genis 17 en février	157	10	0			Et par Ernout Fin 26 en février	40	0	0		or
Et par Engijen Dapalaie 17 en février	20	0	0		p.	Et par Andrins contet 28 en février	100	0	0		p.
Et par Rafel Tripane 26 en février	35	0	9			Et par Françoys Peninc le premier de march	20	0	0		p.
Et par Catain Piniel 27 en février	25	0	0			Et par Jehan de Priolle 9 en march	38	6	8		or
Et par Barde Menchine le premier de march	21	16	1	1		Et par Tumas de Guir 14 en march	40	0	0		or
Et par Pierre Scandillon 10 march	20	0	0			Somme 578 *lb.* 19*s.* 11*d.*					
Et par Composte de l'ostel Ernout Poultus	66	7	0			Et par Fortegerre 16 en march	21	0	0		p.
Somme 717 *lb.* 8*s.* 10*d.* gros						Et par Gabrijel Lery 22 en march	51	13	4		
Et par Andrins contet a 8 mites 3 nobles*		*16*	*4*			Somme 651 *lb.* 13*s.* 3*d.*					
Et par Ernoul Poultus 23 en march	43	0	0		p.	Item li doi-ge pour le pourfit que Jehan Terminiel doit avoir contet a lui au Noël l'an 68 [1368]	50	0	0		
Somme 761 *lb.* 5*s.* 2*d.* 1 esterlin						Item doi-ge qu'il me fait conte ou fuellet 137	59	11	11		
	761	5	2	1			761	5	2		

*The nobles were apparently rated at 65 groats and one sterling, or 8 mites.

(17) Account of the Lucchese Merchant-Banker Guglielmo Rapondi

Ledger No. 4, fol. 79

Dr.

Explanation	Amount (Pounds groat) £	s	d	st	Remarks
Willaume Raiponde me doit:					
par le reste de nos contes dou fuelliet 16 contet a Ragoulin 5 en février [1369]	18	4	6		
Et par Ernout Fin 9 en février	89	3	9		or
Et par Karoc de Galbert 16 en février	91	12	9		
Et par Mahiu van de Brouke a ce jour contet	6	17	3		
Et par Marke Mourisin 17 en février	56	0	0		or
Et par Mikiel Genis 23 en février	38	0	0		or
Et par sen compaignon contet 25 en février	11	0	0		or
Et par Lois de Robiert 27 en février	67	10	0		or
Et par Franchoys Fidielle 8 en march a Jakoppe Reups	110	0	0		or
Et par Henric Touche 9 en march a Pietre d'Audenarde pour Jehan de Quantin	50	0	0		p.
Et par Gilles Visolle 10 en march a Jehan Jakelot de Wervy [Wervicq]	25	0	0		p.
Et par Antonne Raimonde 13 en march	35	0	0		or
Somme 598 *lb.* 8*s.* 3*d.*					
Et par Pierre Scandillon 16 en march	35	0	0		or
Et par Fortegerre 28 en march	40	0	0		or
Et par Gorge Enpereal 31 en march	78	12	0		or
Et par Jehan Levaie a Nicollas Halberine, Engles, a Willem Medilton a Pietre d'Audenarde a ce jour	100	0	0		or
Et par Mathiu Villain 5 en avril	45	16	7	2	or
Et par Lois de Robiert a ce jour	80	0	0		or
Somme 977 *lb.* 16*s.* 10*d.*	977	16	10	2	

Cr.

Explanation	Amount (Pounds groat) £	s	d	st	Remarks
doy par Karoc de Galbiert 9 en février	90	13	2	2	or
Et par Jakemon Fabre 16 en février	127	1	8		or
Et par Ernout Fin 16 en février	30	0	0		or
Et par Antonne Doupont 27 en février	76	17	6		or
Et par Mikiel Genis 8 en march	120	0	0		or
Et par Jehan de Priolle 13 en march	64	1	3		or
Somme 508 *lb.* 13*s.* 7*d.*					
Et par Jehan de Quantin 16 en march	35	0	0		or
Et par Dine Sanoche 21 en march	9	0	0		
Et par Gabrijel de Court 26 en march	129	3	4		or
Et par Gerart Burlemay 27 en march	3	2	0		
Et par Clais Barbesen 31 en march	87	0	0		p.
Somme 771 *lb.* 18*s.* 11*d.*					
Et par Thideman Relbe contet 9 en avril	40	3	0		
Et	12	17	0		
(Somme 53 *lb.*)					
Et par Pierre de Wille Nueve 28 en avril	12	0	0		p.
Et par Antonne Raimonde dou 9e jour de march	45	8	7		or
Somme 882 *lb.* 7*s.* 6*d.*					
Balance	95	9	4		
	977	16	10	2	

Reste 95 *lb.* 9*s.* 4*d.* or lesquels il me fait conte 188.

Ledger No. 4, fol. 188

Dr.

Explanation	£	s	d	st	Remarks
Willaume Raiponde me doit:					
par le reste de nos contes dou fuellet 79 contet a sen compaignon 2 en may	95	9	4		or
Et pour l'avantaige de l'or dessus dit, de tout l'or de nos contes, contet a lui a ce jour	1	5	0		
Et par Pierre Scandillon 4 en may	50	0	0		
Et par Lois de Robiert 19 en may	100	0	0		
Et par Fortegerre a ce jour	30	10	10		
Somme 277 *lb.* 5*s.* 2*d.*	277	5	2		

Ci.

Explanation	£	s	d	st	Remarks
doy par sen compaignon contet 2 en may	57	8	5		p.
Et par Piercevant de Griman 4 en may	3	9	5		
Et par sen compaignon contet 12 en may, pour 300 francs [a 32 gros]	40	0	0		
Et par Karot de Galbert 16 en may	10	10	6		
Somme 111 *lb.* 8*s.* 4*d.*					
Item li doi-ge ke je ly e fait conte ou fullet 37 de men papier apries cesty	165	16	10		
	277	5	2		

(18) Account of the Lucchese Merchant Forteguerra di Forteguerra
Ledger No. 4, fol. 124

Dr.

Explanation	Amount (Pounds groat) £	s	d	st	Remarks
Fortegerre me doit:					
par le reste de nos contes dou fuellet 94 contet a lui 14 en march [1369]	14	1	8		
Et l'avantaige de 150 *lb.* or, item 25 *lb.* item 60 *lb.*, item 31 *lb.*					
Et par Galigo da Piastre 16 en march	30	0	0		p.
Et par Bietremins Markadielle 16 en march	30	12	0		p.
Et par Lois de Robiert 16 en march.	31	8	8		p.
Et par Tumas Sarlande a ce jour....	21	0	0		p.
Et par Raoul Doucemin 17 en march	6	9	5		
Et par Dimenche Cucul 23 en march	33	0	5		
Et par Thumas contet 27 en march 700 frs. frs. [francs franchois]					
Et par Biernart Morille 28 en march	130	0	0		or
Et par Raoul Doucemin 6 en avril...	25	16	8		
Somme 322 *lb.* 8*s.* 10*d.*					
Et par Davin Tedaldin 16 en avril..	49	14	5	1	p.
Et par Barde Menchine 26 en avril..	65	12	6	2	p.
Et par Gabryel Lery 26 en avril....	52	10	0		p.
Et par Sauvaige Saijelet 27 en avril..	40	0	0		p.
Et par Jakemart Fabe 27 en avril...	20	0	0		p.
Et par Flipot Jehan Zenne [Janssone] de l'ostel Henric de Semit 2 en may, a Jakop Reups	54	3	4		
Et par Franchoys Bietremin 5 en may	20	0	0		p.
Et par Jehan Levaie a ce jour......	80	0	0		p.
Et par Robiert le Signeur 5 en may..	37	18	0		
Et par Davin Tedaldin 7 en may...	52	15	6		
Et par Galigo da Piastre 8 en may..	24	0	0		
Et par Ricart Estefelt 9 en may a Jakoppe Reups	60	0	0		p.
Et par Raoul Douchemin 11 en may	39	7	6		
Et par Gorge Boin Avoir 11 en may.	35	0	0		
Et par Jehan van Kouc 12 en may de l'ostel Pietre van Ake	125	11	0		
Et par Pierre Teste 16 en may......	40	0	0		p.
Et par le demiselle de Rudevorde 16 en may	80	0	0		
Et par Galigo da Piastre 19 en may..	20	0	0		
Et par Franchoys Bietremin 19 en may	40	0	0		
Et par Aubiert Spingle a ce jour....	11	12	6		
Et par le demiselle de Rudevorde...	14	13	5	2	
Somme 1,285 *lb.* 7*s.* 1*d.* 2 esterlins	1,285	7	1	2	

Cr.

Explanation	Amount (Pounds groat) £	s	d	st	Remarks
doy par Mikiel Genis 16 en march .	160	0	0		or
Et par Jakoppe de Blaudain a ce jour	10	11	1	1	p.
Et par Jakemon de Blaudain 27 en march 700 frs. frs. [francs franchoys]					
Et par Jakemon Fabe 28 en march	30	0	0		p.
Et par Tumas Sarlande 28 en march	85	0	0		or
Et par Willaume Raiponde 28 en march	40	0	0		or
Somme 325 *lb.* 11*s.* 1*d*					
Et par Tumas contet pour 400 frs. a 32 gros, somme	53	6	8		p.
Et par Antonne Raimonde 24 en avril	40	0	0		p.
Et par Thumas Sarlande 27 en avril	50	0	0		
Et par le dit Thumas a ce jour.....	50	0	0		p.
Et par Jakemon de Blaudain 27 en avril a 32 gros, 100 francs..........	*13*	*6*	*8*		
Et par Franchoys de Guir 4 en may	184	15	4		p.
Et par Flipre de Lorin 5 en may...	40	0	0		p.
Et pay Jehan Oursiel 5 en may....	53	2	0		
Et par Aubiert Spingle 5 en may...	106	5	0		
Et par Jehan Teste contet 11 en may	40	0	0		p.
Et par Gorges Boin Avoir [Buonaiuti] a ce jour	86	6	7		
Et par Gentil Gascon 12 en may..	35	0	0		
Et par Jakemon Franchoys 15 en may	100	0	0		p.
Et par Sauvaige Saijelet 17 en may	36	9	2		
Et par Dine Responde 19 en may..	30	10	5		
Somme 1,244 *lb.* 13*s.*					
Reste me doit 40 *lb.* 14*s.* 1*d.* 2 esterlins escrit ou fullet 18 de men papier apres cesty	40	14	1	2	
	1,285	7	1		

(19) Account of Mademoiselle de Rudevorde, Proprietress of an Inn, Failed Between 1370 and 1374
Ledger No. 4, fol. 38

Dr.

Explanation	£	s	d	st
Medemiselle de Rudevorde me doit: par le reste de nos contes dou fuelliet 339 de men autre papier	107	9	6	
contet par accort 24 en décembre				
Item me doit-ille par Lambiert d'Alos 30 en décembre [1368]	6	0	0	
Et par Pietre Ludinkouse 3 en jenvier [1369]	12	0	0	
Et par Lukin Karle 5 en jenvier	22	0	0	
Et par Jehan Gravestien a ce jour de l'ostel Sire Thideman de le Berghe contet	11	15	0	
Et par Gilles de Dec a ce jour	35	0	0	
Et par Laurent van Collekierke a ce jour	44	0	0	
Et par Bietremin Mercadielle 8 en jenvier	28	0	0	
Item me doit-il par Estievene Guillaume 9 en jenvier	12	18	4	
Et par Ernout Lauwerke 10 en jenvier	35	0	0	
Et par Nigle Ducdorp a l'ostel Lambesin van Saint-Omer a ce jour, a Jakoppe Reups	57	0	0	
Et par Albrec Zoussebrouc a ce jour	16	0	0	
Et par Jehan Alf Windre a ce jour	36	0	0	
Et par Jehan Scovedre 10 en jenvier	32	0	0	
Et par Lukin de Karle a ce jour	40	0	0	
Somme 495 *lb.* 2*s.* 10*d.* gros				
Et par Lambesin Diaghere 11 en jenvier	50	0	0	
Et par Hermant Hoft a Henric van Horiscem 13 en jenvier	30	0	0	
Et par Thideman Losebrec 16 en jenvier	24	0	0	
Et par Jehan Acar 17 en jenvier a Jehan Ferandes	14	0	0	
Et par Ernout Poultus a Jakoppe Reups a ce jour	15	0	0	
Et par Bietremin Mercadielle 18 en jenvier	31	0	0	
Et par Jehan van de Vagheviere 20 en jenvier	20	0	0	
Et par Vinçant van de Moure a ce jour	6	0	0	
Et par Herman Hoft a ce jour a sire Henry van Eirsce	10	0	0	
Et par Pietre Ludinkouse a ce jour	11	0	0	
Et par Catain Piniel a ce jour	7	0	0	
Et par Ghi de Brune a ce jour	11	0	0	
Et par Gilles de Dec a ce jour	6	0	0	
Et par Thideman Losebrec	15	0	0	
Et par Thideman Rommelin Roede 27 en jenvier	8	0	0	
Et par Jehan Scepe a ce jour	14	0	0	
Et par Jakemon Pietre de Leu a Jakoppe de Rouc	13	0	0	
Somme 780 *lb.* 2*s.* 10*d.*	780	2	10	

Cr.

Explanation	£	s	d	st
Doy par lui contet 29 en décembre [1368] pour 540 francs et 12 lion, somme	72	0	7	
Et par Olivier Kalve 2 en jenvier	37	17	10	
Et par Jehan de Rudevorde 4 en jenvier	25	11	8	
Et par Willaume Raiponde a ce jour	25	16	8	
Et par Robiert de le Crois a ce jour contet	26	4	4	
Et par Henric de Markengueville a ce jour contet	16	2	11	
Et par lui contet a ce jour pour 700 francs a 8 gros*	90	13	0	
Et par Dine Malapris 5 en jenvier	30	0	0	
Item li doi-ge par elle contet a 10 en jenvier pour 1,076 francs et 1 lion	139	14	4	
Somme 464 *lb.* 1*s.* 4*d.* gros				
Et par Gerart Bousenet 11 en jenvier	1	10	0	
Item li doi-ge par Collart Olle de Brinc 13 en jenvier contet	9	13	6	
Et par Leurent Aleval 15 en jenvier	13	18	0	2
Et par Aubert Ballet a ce jour contet	18	0	4	
Et par lui contet a ce jour	67	19	10	
Et par Rainmon Siriere	17	0	0	
Et par Thiery Brochons pour Jehan Baket 20 en jenvier	27	0	0	
Somme 619 *lb.* 3*s.* 0*d.* 2 esterlins				
Item li doi-ge qu'il me fait conte ou fuellet 66	160	19	2	
	780	2	2	2

*The expression '700 francs a 8 gros' means 700 francs at the rate of 31 groats each plus 8 additional groats for every hundred francs:

700 francs at 31 groats each	£90	8*s.*	4*d.*	groat
Seven times 8 groats or 56 groats		4	8	
Total	£90	13*s.*	0*d.*	groat

(20) Account of the Bruges Furrier Jehan van de Walle

Ledger No. 4, fol. 10

Dr. / Cr.

Explanation (Dr.)	£	s	d	Remarks	Explanation (Cr.)	£	s	d	Remarks
Jehan van de Walle, peletier, me doit par le reste de nos contes dou fuellet 203 de men autre papier	220	13	2		Doy par Jehan van Marc 24 en jenvier [1369]	6	18	0	
Et par Cristofle Wetin 31 en march	10	0	0		Et par Jakemon de Blaudain 23 en février	10	10	0	
Et par Gisselare Gier 21 en avril	20	0	0		Et par Pietre d'Audenarde 3 en march	19	14	4	
Et par Jakemon Bibijen 14 en may	25	0	0		Et par le demisielle de Rudevorde	2	2	0	
Et par Thideman Rommelin Roede	10	0	0		Item li doi-ge ke il me fait conte ou fuellet 6 de men papier apries cesty	256	8	10	
Et par Franche Begarot	10	0	0						
	295	13	2			295	13	2	

(21) Account of the Hanseatic Merchant Tideman Remmelincrode

Ledger No. 4, fol. 61

Dr. / Cr.

Explanation (Dr.)	£	s	d	Remarks	Explanation (Cr.)	£	s	d	Remarks
Thideman Rommelin Roede me doit: par Jehan Passe de Douse 24 en jenvier	6	0	0	contet	Doy par Lambesin Diaghere 20 en jenvier [1369]	20	0	0	
Et par Willaume Seladoc de Saint-Omer 26 en jenvier	14	0	0						
	20	0	0			20	0	0	

Ledger No. 4, fol. 73

Dr. / Cr.

Explanation (Dr.)	£	s	d	Remarks	Explanation (Cr.)	£	s	d	Remarks
Thideman Rommelin Roede me doit:					Doy par Thideman Losebrec 31 en jenvier	24	0	0	
par Willaume van Ainmere 15 en février	54	0	0		Et par le demiselle de Rudevorde	30	0	0	
	54	0	0			54	0	0	

Ledger No. 4, fol. 208

Dr. / Cr.

Explanation (Dr.)	£	s	d	Remarks	Explanation (Cr.)	£	s	d	Remarks
Thideman Rommelin Roede me doit:					Doy par Jehan van de Walle escrit ou fuellet 50 de men papier apries cesty	10	0	0	

(22) Account of the Hanseatic Merchant Tideman Geismar

Ledger No. 4, fol. 27

Dr. Explanation	Amount (Pounds groat) £	s	d	Remarks	Cr. Explanation	Amount (Pounds groat) £	s	d	Remarks
Thideman Ghissemare me doit:					doy par le reste de nos contes dou fuellet				
par Jehan Stochem 13 en jenvier........	13	10	0		281 de men autre papier................	18	0	0	
Et par Clais de le Bourse 26 en jenvier...	4	0	0						
Et par lui contet.....................		10	0						
	18	0	0			18	0	0	

Ledger No. 4, fol. 84

Dr. Explanation	£	s	d	Remarks	Cr. Explanation	£	s	d	Remarks
Thideman Gissemare me doit:					doy par sire Jehan de Bogemakre.......	5	12	11	
par Jakoppe de Soutre 16 en march	7	2	0		Et par Willem Ruyelle 16 en march.....	6	16	0	
Et par Martin Roulat 24 en march......	6	0	0	contet	Et par Jakoppe de Soutre		13	1	
	13	2	0			13	2	0	

Appendix 3

Sample of Collard de Marke's Journal beginning December 26, 1368

fol. 7

26 en décembre [1368]	
Doy Marke Mourisin par lui contet	46 *lb*. gr.
27 en décembre	
Raoul de Coumines me doit par sen varlet contet en monnoie de Braibant	8 *lb*. -*s*. 12*d*.
Pierre Rougenelle me doit par Dimenche sen compaignon contet 100 francs dou Roy	
Doy Jakop van de Walle le jouene par lui contet	56 *lb*. gr.
Jehan de Gant me doit par Gillis de Man et Ector Zecome Jehan	11 *lb*. gr.
Demiselle Soute van de Walle me doit par li contet	30 *lb*.
Doi France Maldre par lui contet	10 *lb*.
29 en décembre	
Doy Jehan Duc par lui contet	12*lb*. 8*s*. gr.
Raoul Doucemin me doit par Luc Poucier de l'Escluze contet	5 *lb*. gr.
Doy Jehan Acar contet	20 *lb*. gr.
Doy le demiselle de Rudevorde par lui contet pour 540 francs et 12 lion	72 *lb*. -*s*. 7*d*. gr.*
30 en décembre	
Nicolas Mondielle me doit par Jakemon de Galbert	40 *lb*. gr.
Sire Jehan de Vos me doit par Jakoppe Reups	4 *lb*. gr.
Henric Simon me doit pas Nisin de Bleweke à Jakoppe Reups	6*lb*.
Doy Jakemes Fabe par li contet	9 *lb*. 7*s*. 9*d*.
Jakoppe Reups me doit par Jehan le lonbart de Tournay	17 *lb*. gr.

*For the corresponding entry in the ledger, see Appendix II, No. 19, the account of Mademoiselle de Rudevorde.

Par mi contet qu'il reçut à Copin Velaine	10 *lb.* 18*s.* gr.
Jakemes de Blaudain me doit par Jehan le lonbart de Tournay	9 *lb.* gr. or
	fol. 7ᵛ
Nicolas de Pole me doit par Pieres Roudenelle	15 *lb.* 19*s.* 2*d.* or
Wilem van de Neke me doit par Grielle Seblekres contet	2 *lb.* 13*s.* 10*d.*
Et par Lisebete van Gent contet	2 *lb.* 13*s.* 7*d.*
Willem Medilton me doit par Jehan Edeghien	11 *lb.* gr.
Jehan van Single me doit par Tildeman Graveroit contet	5 *lb.* 16*s.*
Thideman Rebart me doit par Jakoppe Reups	34 *lb.*
Et par lui contet	3*d.* gr.*
Jakoppe Reups me doit par Gérar Burlemay	12 *lb.*
Et par Ellio Camens de la Rochielle	50 *lb.* gr.
Et par Outre van de Dike contet	7 *lb.* gr.
Doy Franche de le Porte par lui payet, à lui contet à che jour	65 *lb.* gr.
Henry Scoutekeleve me doit par Mertin van Tourout	4 *lb.* gr.
à le demiselle de Wite	
Jakemon de Blaudain me doit par Jehan Gontières de Prawes	21 *lb.* 16*s.* 3*d.*
payet à lui 1 *lb.* 16*s.* 3*d.*	
Ostage Frigo me doit par Pieres dre Deman à Jakoppe Reups	10 *lb.* gr.
Simon Ongeret me doit par Mikiel de Matenty à l'ostel le demiselle Trude, contet	6 *lb.*
Ellio Camens me doit par Lambiert d'Alost	20 *lb.* gr.
Jehan Duch me doit par Lotart Ghibieke de Mons	12 *lb.* contet
Et par Baudin Marchiel de Mons	8 *lb.* contet
Sire Jehan Bave me doit par Outre Vouty	3 *lb.* gr.
Jehan Scardebrouc me doit par li contet	2 *lb.* gr.
Jakop Wisolle me doit par Jehan van de Scure	10 *lb.* gr. contet
Bauduin van de Brouke me doit par lui contet	20*s.* gr.
	fol. 8ʳ
Jehan Edighien me doit par Estièvene Bieke contet à sen fil	5 *lb.* 18*s.* 9*d.*

*For the corresponding entry in the ledger, see Appendix II, No. 11, the account of Tideman Rebart, Hanseatic merchant.

Tumas Sarlande me doit par Tumas de Guir	75*lb*. gr.
Mikiel Tradinc me doit par Grigollo Fet	31 *lb*. gr.
Doy Dimenche [Domenico] Cukul par Copin sen varlet contet	22 *lb*. 16*s*. 11*d*.
Jakoppe de May me doit par Willem van Dierden contet	3*lb*. 12*s*. 10*d*.
Le demiselle Rapesart me doit par Lambesin Diaghere	14 *lb*. 16*s*.
Et	9 *lb*. gr.
Jakoppe Reups me doit par Lambesin Diaghere	3 *lb*. 6*s*.
Jakoppe de Soutre me doit par lui contet	9 *lb*. gr.
Lukin de Karle me doit par Willem Relin à Clais Rapesart 5 *lb*. 16*s*.	10 *lb*. gr.
Jakemon de Blaudain me doit par Pietre le Potre 2 en jenvier [1369]	24 *lb*. 19*s*.
Raoul Doucemin me doit par Luc de Poutier à le demiselle Rapesart	16 *lb*. 6*s*.
Et par Raoul contet	2 *lb*. 5*s*. gr.

etc. etc.

BIBLIOGRAPHY

Bibliography

Manuscript Sources

Belgian Archives

Bruges Municipal Archives

Account Books of Collard de Marke, Bruges Money-Changer:

Ledger No. 1, in-fol., April 6, 1366-April 19, 1367, 310 folios, Section I, fols. 1-244; II, 251-80; III, 287-301. Some folios are damaged and the ink has faded.

Ledger No. 2, in-fol., April 19, 1367-April 10, 1368, 400 folios, Section I, fols. 1-299, 370-88; II, 300-43; III, 352-66; Index.

Ledger No. 3, in-fol., April 10, 1368-December 24, 1368, 381 folios, Section I, fols. 1-291; II, 291-327; III, 332-61.

Ledger No. 4, in-fol., December 24, 1368-May 19, 1369, 443 folios, Section 1, folios 1-212; II, 300-23; III, 400-6; Index.

Ledger No. 5, in-fol., May 20, 1369-December 24, 1369, 470 folios, Section I, fols. 1-321; II, 350-87; III, 410-19.

Journal No. 1 (corresponds to Ledger No. 2), half-folio, April 19, 1367-April 10, 1368, no pagination.

Journal No. 2 (corresponds to Ledger No. 4) half-folio, December 24, 1368-May 19, 1369, 195 folios. The folios from 117 to 190 and 194-95 are blank.

Ledger of Guillaume Ruyelle (or Ruweel), Bruges Money-Changer, in-fol., 211 folios, January 1369-June 1370.

Municipal Accounts (Comptes Communaux), of the fourteenth and fifteenth centuries.

Chartes politiques, 1e série, Nos. 237, 445, 616, 1155, and 1307.

Sentences civiles, 1453-1461.

Bruges, State Archives

Gilden en Ambachten, No. 467, *Roobouck* van het Visch Ambacht (Fonds des Métiers, cartulaire du Métier des poissonniers).

Ghent, Municipal Archives

Chartres et Documents, No. 561.

Italian Archives

Florence, State Archives

Mediceo avanti il Principato, Filza No. 134, item No. 2. Ledger of the Medici branch in Bruges (1441).

Carte Strozziane, Series II, No. 20. Libro segreto di Francesco Sassetti, 1462-1472.

Florence, Biblioteca Nazionale

Codice Magliabechiano, XI, 97. Abaco Benedetto (after 1474).

Codice Palatino 601. Aritmetica (c. 1450).

Codice Panciatichiano 71. Modi e forme (1418).

Ms Palatino 573. Abaco Benedetto (1460).

Genoa, State Archives

Registri Bancheriorum, Sala 24: Capsiae Lomellini, 1386, 1390, 1392, 1394, 1396-

1433 (one for each year); Manuali Lomellini for 1397, 1398, 1399, 1400, 1402, 1406-1431 (for a few years within this period).

Registri Bancheriorum, Sala 24: Registri Bancorum S. Georgii, Cartulario, 1408. Sala (or Room) 24 contains an almost complete series of the journals and ledgers of The Bank of St. George from 1408 to 1445.

Lucca, State Archives

Corte dei Mercanti, Nos. 82-84. Libri dei Mercanti, 1371, 1372, 1381.

Prato (Tuscany), Datini Archives

No. 753. Carteggio da Bruggia, Fondaco di Genova.

No. 801 (old No. 169 in Nicastro's Inventory). Libro Verde C (1397-1399), Fondaco di Barcellona.

No. 802 (old No. 170). Libro Nero D (Feb. 1, 1399-Jan. 31, 1400), Fondaco di Barcellona.

Nos. 852-54. Carteggi da Bruggia, Fondaco di Barcellona.

No. 1146 (old No. 1078). Cambiali (Bills of Exchange).

Vatican City, Vatican Library

Vat. Lat., MS 4828.

American Archives

Boston, Harvard Graduate School of Business Administration.

Selfridge Collection, No. 495. Articles of Association of the Medici Family (15th-17th centuries).

Published Sources

Belgium. 'Arrêté royal sur le contrôle des banques et le régime des émissions de titres et de valeurs,' *Moniteur Belge*, CV (1935), No. 191.

Bigwood, Georges. 'Documents relatifs à une association de marchands italiens aux XIIIe et XIVe siècles,' *Bulletin de la Commission Royale d'Histoire*, LXXVIII (1909), 205-44.

Borlandi, Franco (ed.). See *El libro di mercatantie et usanze.*

Chastellain, Georges. *Chronique, 1419-1470.* Edited by Baron Kervyn de Lettenhove. Vol. III. Brussels, 1864.

'Clementynboeck, 1288-1414,' [editor unknown], *Bulletin des Archives d'Anvers (Antwerpsch Archievenblad)*, XXV (n. d.), 101-465.

Codex diplomaticus lubecensis (Lübeckisches Urkundenbuch), Part I, *Urkundenbuch der Stadt Lübeck*, Vol. III, Lübeck, 1871.

Davidsohn, Robert. *Forschungen zur Geschichte von Florenz.* 4 Vols. Berlin, 1896-1908.

Delepierre, Octave (ed.). *Précis analytique des documents que renferme le dépôt des archives de la Flandre Occidentale.* Vol. I. Bruges, 1840.

Deschamps de Pas, Louis. 'Essai sur l'histoire monétaire des comtes de Flandre de la maison de Bourgogne et description de leurs monnaies d'or et d'argent,' *Revue Numismatique*, 2d series, VI (1861), 106-39, 211-37, 458-78; VII (1862), 117-43, 351-65, 460-80. Also published in book form (Paris, 1863) with the addition of a calendar of documents entitled: 'Inventaire des pièces relatives aux monnaies pendant la période des comtes de Flandre de la maison de Bourgogne (1384-1481) existant aux Archives de la Chambre des Comptes à Lille.' Pp. lvi. A copy of the reprint is in the New York Public Library. A supplementary article appeared in the *Revue Numismatique*, XI (1866), 172-219.

Desimoni, Cornelio, and Belgrano, L. T. 'Documenti ed estratti inediti e poco noti, riguardanti la storia del commercio e della marina ligure: Brabante, Fiandra e Borgogna,' *Atti della società ligure di storia patria,* V, fasc. 3, 357-547.

Doehaerd, Renée. *Les relations commerciales entre Gênes, la Belgique et l'Outremont d'après les archives notariales génoises aux XIIIe et XIVe siècles.* Institut historique belge de Rome, Etudes d'histoire économique et sociale, Vols. II-IV. 3 Vols. Brussels-Rome: Institut historique belge de Rome, 1941.

Espinas, Georges (ed.). *Documents relatifs à la draperie de Valenciennes au moyen âge. Documents et travaux publiés par la Société d'histoire du droit des pays flamands, picards et wallons,* Vol. I. Paris: Domat-Montchrestien, 1931.

Espinas, Georges, and Pirenne, Henri (eds.). *Recueil de documents relatifs à l'histoire de l'industrie drapière en Flandre.* 4 vols. Brussels, 1906-1924.

Friedberg, E. (ed.). *Corpus Juris Canonici.* 2 vols. Leipzig, 1879.

Fumi, Luigi (ed.). *Registri del Archivio di Stato di Lucca.* Vol. II, *Carteggio degli Anziani (1333-1400),* Part I (1333-1368); Part II (1369-1400). Lucca, 1903.

Gaillard, Victor. *Recherches sur les monnaies des comtes de Flandre depuis les temps les plus reculés jusqu'à l'avènement de la maison de Bourgogne.* Vol. I: *jusqu'au règne de Robert de Béthune inclusivement.* Ghent, 1852. Vol II: *sous les règnes de Louis de Crécy et de Louis de Male.* Ghent, 1857.

Gessler, Jean (ed.). *Le livre des mestiers de Bruges et ses dérivés: quatre anciens manuels de conversation.* New York: Publications of the Institute of French Studies, 1931.

Gilliodts-van Severen, Louis. *Cartulaire de l'ancienne Estaple de Bruges.* 4 vols. Bruges, 1903-1906.

——————. *Cartulaire de l'ancien grand tonlieu de Bruges, faisant suite au cartulaire de l'ancienne Estaple.* 2 vols. Bruges, 1908-1909.

——————. 'Chartre de la Comtesse Marguerite de Flandre en faveur des marchands hanséatiques (13 avril 1253),' *La Flandre,* I (1867-1868), 243-46.

——————. *Coutume de la Ville de Bruges. Coutumes des Pays et Comté de Flandre. Quartier de Bruges.* 2 vols. Brussels, 1874-1875.

——————. *Inventaire des archives de la Ville de Bruges.* 6 vols., Introduction, Table analytique, Glossaire flamand. Bruges, 1871-1885.

——————. 'Les registres des "Zestendeelen" ou le cadastre de la Ville de Bruges de l'année 1580.' *Annales de la Société d'Emulation pour l'étude de l'histoire et des antiquités de la Flandre Occidentale,* XLIII (1894).

Groot Placcaet-Boeck inhoudende de Placcaten ende Ordonnantien van de Hoogh-Mogende Heeren Staten Generael der Vereenighde Nederlanden. Vol. I. The Hague, 1658. Copies are in the Library of Congress and in the John Crerar Library, Chicago.

Grunzweig, Armand (ed.). *Correspondance de la filiale de Bruges des Medici.* Vol I. Brussels: Commission Royale d'Histoire, 1931. Vol. II has not yet been published.

——————. 'Le fonds du Consulat de la Mer aux Archives de l'Etat à Florence,' *Bulletin de l'Institut historique belge de Rome,* X (1930), 1-121.

Das Handlungsbuch Vickos von Geldersen. Edited by Hans Nirrnheim. Hamburg, 1895.

Hanserecesse. 3 vols. Leipzig, 1870-1875.

Hansisches Urkundenbuch. 11 vols. Halle-Leipzig, 1876-1916.

La Marche, Olivier de. *Mémoires (1435-1488).* Edited by Henri Beaune and J. d'Arbaumont. Vol. III. Paris, 1885.

I libri di commercio dei Peruzzi. Edited by Armando Sapori. Milan: Fratelli Treves, 1934.

El libro di mercatantie et usanze de' paesi. Edited by Franco Borlandi. Documenti e studi per la storia del commercio e del diritto commerciale italiano, No. VII. Turin: S. Lattes & Co., 1936.

Limburg-Stirum, Count Thierry de (ed.). *Cartulaire des chartes de Louis de Male, comte de Flandre.* 2 vols. Bruges, 1898-1901.

Masi, Gino (ed.). *Statuti delle colonie fiorentine all'estero (secc. XV-XVI).* Milan: A. Giuffrè, 1941.

Oresme, Nicole. *Traictié de la première invention des monnoies.* Edited by M. L. Wolowski. Paris, 1864.

Paciolo, Fra Luca. *Summa de arithmetica, geometria, proportioni et proportionalita.* Venice, 1494; 2d ed. Toscolano, 1523.

Parmentier, Remi A. *Indices op de Brugsche Poorterboeken.* Bruges: Desclée, de Brouwer & Cie., 1938.

Pegolotti, Francesco Balducci. *La pratica della mercatura.* Edited by Allan Evans. Cambridge, Massachusetts: The Mediaeval Academy of America, 1936.

Recueil des ordonnances des Pays-Bas sous le régne de Charles-Quint (1506-1555). Edited by Ch. Laurent, J. Lameere, and H. Simont. Receuil des anciennes ordonnances de la Belgique, 2d series. Vols. I, IV, V. Brussels, 1893-1913.

'Het "Register van den Dachvaerden",' *Bulletin des Archives d'Anvers (Antwerpsch Archievenblad),* XIX (n. d.), 1-472.

Snellaert, Ferdinand Augustijn (ed.). *Nederlandsche Gedichten uit de veertiende eeuw van Jan Boendale, Hein van Aken en anderen, naar het Oxfordsch handschrift.* Brussels: Académie Royale de Belgique, 1869.

Uzzano, Giovanni di Antonio da. *La pratica della mercatura.* Published as Vol. IV of Gian-Francesco Pagnini, *Della Decima e delle altre gravezze, della moneta e della mercatura de' Fiorentini fino al secolo XVI.* Lisbon-Lucca, 1766.

Van Houtte, Hubert (ed.). *Documents pour servir à l'histoire des prix de 1381 à 1794.* Brussels: Commission Royale d'Histoire, 1902.

Secondary Material

Alfieri, Vittorio. *La partita doppia applicata alle scritture delle antiche aziende mercantili veneziane.* Turin, 1891.

Allemandet, M. *Le contrôle des banques en Belgique.* Thèse pour le doctorat, Université de Caen, Faculté de Droit. Paris: Librairie technique et économique, 1937.

Arens, Franz. "Commerce d'argent et commerce de denrées au moyen âge à propos d'un travail récent,' *Revue de synthèse historique,* XVII (1908), 298-308.

———. 'Grundsätzliches zur Problematik der "Kauwerschen" (Caorsini),' *Vierteljahrschrift für Sozial- und Wirtschaftsgeschichte,* XXV (1932), 251-60.

———. 'Wilhelm Servat von Cahors als Kaufmann zu London,' *ibid.,* XI (1913), 477-514.

Ashley, Sir William J. *An Introduction to English Economic History and Theory.* Vol. I, Part I, *The Middle Ages.* 10th impression. London: Longmans, Green & Co., 1919. Vol. I, Part II, *The End of the Middle Ages.* 4th ed., 9th impression. London: Longmans, Green & Co., 1920.

Babelon, Ernest. *La théorie féodale de la monnaie.* Mémoires de l'Académie des In-

scriptions et des Belles Lettres, in 4° series, Vol. XXXVIII, Part I. Paris, 1908.
Baudot, Jules. *Les princesses Yolande et les ducs de Bar de la famille des Valois.* Paris, 1900.
Bauer, Clemens. *Unternehmung und Unternehmungsformen im Spätmittelalter und in der beginnenden Neuzeit.* Jena: Gustav Fischer, 1936.
Beardwood, Alice. *Alien Merchants in England, 1350-1377: Their Legal and Economic Position.* Cambridge, Massachusetts: The Mediaeval Academy of America, 1931.
Benoît, A. 'Le "Beauregard" de Lille,' *Revue du Nord,* XXV (1939), 5-39.
Bensa, Enrico. *The Early History of Bills of Lading.* Genoa: Caimo & Co., 1925.
———. *Francesco di Marco da Prato: notizie e documenti sulla mercatura italiana del secolo XIV.* Milan: Fratelli Treves, 1928.
Bigwood, Georges. *Le régime juridique et économique du commerce de l'argent dans la Belgique du moyen âge.* Mémoires de l'Académie royale de Belgique, Classe des lettres et des sciences morales et politiques, Collection in-8°, 2d series, Vol. XIV, 2 parts. Brussels, 1921-1922.
———. 'Les financiers d'Arras: contribution à l'étude des origines du capitalisme moderne,' *Revue belge de philologie et histoire,* III (1924), 465-508, 769-819; IV (1925), 109-19, 379-421.
Bini, Telesforo. 'Sui Lucchesi a Venezia, memorie dei secoli XIII e XIV,' *Atti della I. e R. Accademia lucchese di scienze, lettere ed arte,* XV (1854), 1-248; XVI (1857), 1-174.
Biscaro, Gerolamo. 'Il banco Filippo Borromei e compagni di Londra (1436-1439),' *Archivio storico lombardo,* 4th series, XIX (1913), 37-126, 283-386.
Blancard, L. 'Note sur la lettre de change à Marseille au XIIIe siècle,' *Bibliothèque de l'Ecole des Chartes,* XXXIX (1878), 110-28, 388.
Bloch, Marc. 'Economie-nature ou économie-argent: un pseudo-dilemme,' *Annales d'histoire sociale,* I (1939), 7-17.
———. 'Ecrits sur la monnaie,' *Annales d'histoire économique et sociale,* X (1938), 360-62.
———. 'Le problème de l'or au moyen âge,' *ibid.,* V (1933), 1-34.
Boissonnade, P. *Le travail dans l'Europe chrétienne au moyen âge (Ve-XVe siècles).* Paris: Libraire Félix Alcan, 1921.
Bolsée, J. 'Une enquête sur les usuriers dans l'Ammanie de Bruxelles en 1393,' *Bulletin de la Commission Royale d'Histoire,* CII (1937), 141-210.
Bourquelot, Félix. *Etudes sur les foires de Champagne: sur la nature, l'étendue et les règles du commerce qui s'y faisait aux XIIe, XIIIe et XIVe siècles.* Mémoires présentés par divers savants à l'Académie des Inscriptions et des Belles Lettres, 2d series, Vol. V, 2 parts. Paris, 1865.
Boutillier, Jean. *Le grand coustumier général de practique, aultrement appellé Somme Rural.* Paris, 1537.
Brants, Victor. *Esquisse des théories économiques professées par les écrivains des XIIIe et XIVe siècles: l'économie politique au moyen âge.* Louvain, 1895.
———. *La lutte contre l'usure dans les lois modernes.* Louvain, 1907.
Bridey, Emile. *La théorie de la monnaie au XIVe siècle: Nicole Oresme. Etude d'histoire des doctrines et des faits économiques.* Paris, 1906.
Brun, Robert. 'A Fourteenth-Century Merchant of Italy: Francesco Datini of Prato,' *Journal of Economic and Business History,* II (1930), 451-66.
Brunner, Heinrich. 'Beiträge zur Geschichte und Dogmatik der Werthpapiere: I.

Brügger Schöffensprüche zur Geschichte des Wechselrechts im fünfzehnten Jahrhundert,' *Zeitschrift für das gesamte Handelsrecht,* XXII (1877), 1-58.

————. 'Beiträge zur Geschichte und Dogmatik der Werthpapiere: III. Zur Geschichte des Inhaberpapiers in Deutschland,' *ibid.*, XXIII (1878), 225-62.

————. 'Les titres au porteur français du moyen âge,' *Nouvelle revue historique de droit français et étranger,* X (1886), 11-51, 139-81.

Buoninsegni, Tommaso. *Dei cambi: Trattato risolutissimo et utilissimo.* Florence, 1573.

Cahn, Julius. 'Der Strassburger Stadtwechsel: ein Beitrag zur Geschichte der ältesten Banken in Deutschland,' *Zeitschrift für die Geschichte des Oberrheins,* LIII (1899), 44-65.

Calmette, Joseph. *La société féodale.* Paris: Armand Colin, 1923.

Carman, Lewis A. 'Researches of Raymond de Roover in Flemish Accounting of the Fourteenth Century,' *The Journal of Accountancy,* LX (1935), 111-22.

Cessi, Roberto. 'Il problema bancario a Venezia nel secolo XIV,' *Atti della R. Accademia delle Scienze di Torino,* LII (1916-1917), 781-99.

————. 'Le relazioni commerciali tra Venezia e le Fiandre nel secolo XIV,' *Nuovo Archivio Veneto,* N. S. XXVII (1914), 5-116.

Chiaudano, Mario. 'I Rothschild del Duecento: la Gran Tavola di Orlando Bonsignori,' *Bullettino senese di storia patria,* N. S. Vol. VI (1935), fasc. 2, pp. 40.

Ciardini, Marino. *I banchieri ebrei in Firenze nel secolo XV e il monte di pietà fondato da Girolamo Savonarola.* Borgo S. Lorenzo, 1907.

Coulton, G. G. *Medieval Panorama: the English Scene from Conquest to Reformation.* Cambridge: Cambridge University Press, 1939.

Cumont, Georges. 'Etude sur le cours des monnaies en Brabant pendant le règne de la duchesse Jeanne, veuve, depuis 1383 jusqu'à 1406,' *Annales de la Société royale d'archéologie de Bruxelles,* XVI (1902), 93-159.

Darings, J. H. 'Over de Lombaerden en Bergen van Bermhertigheid in België,' *Belgisch Museum voor de Nederduitsche Tael- en Letterkunde,* VI (1842), 333-72.

Davanzati, Bernardo. 'Lezione delle monete,' *Scrittori classici italiani di economia politica, Parte Antica,* Vol. II. Milan, 1804. Pp. 19-50.

————. 'Notizia de' cambi a M. Giulio del Caccia, dottor di Legge,' *ibid.* Pp. 51-69.

Davidsohn, Robert. *Geschichte von Florenz.* Vol. IV². Berlin: E. S. Mittler & Sohn, 1925.

De Bo, L. L. *Westvlaamsch Idioticon.* Bruges, 1873.

de Decker, Pierre Jacques François. *Etudes historiques et critiques sur les monts-de-piété en Belgique.* Brussels, 1844.

Delisle, Léopold. *Les opérations financières des Templiers.* Paris, 1889.

de Meulenaere, O. 'Jehan Boutillier: Esquisse biographique,' *Nouvelle revue historique de droit français et étranger,* XV (1891), 18-35.

De Mont, Pol. *La peinture ancienne au Musée royal des Beaux-Arts d'Anvers.* Brussels, 1914.

Denucé, Jean. *Italiaansche koopmansgeslachten te Antwerpen in de XVIe-XVIIIe eeuwen.* Malines: N. V. Het Kompas, 1934.

de Pauw, Napoléon. 'Les Mirabello,' *Biographie Nationale,* XIV (Brussels, 1897), 872-73.

de Roover, Florence Edler. See Edler, Florence.

de Roover, Raymond. 'The Account books of Collard de Marke,' *Bulletin of the Business Historical Society,* XII (1938), 44-47.

———. 'Le contrat de change depuis la fin du treizième siècle jusqu'au début du dix-septième,' *Revue belge de philologie et d'histoire,* XXV (1946-47), 111-28.

———. 'Discussion of N.S.B. Gras' paper "Capitalism—Concepts and History",' *Bulletin of the Business Historical Society,* XVI (1942), 34-39.

———. 'Early Accounting Problems of Foreign Exchange,' *The Accounting Review, XIX* (1944), 381-407.

———. 'A Florentine Firm of Cloth Manufacturers: Management and Organization of a Sixteenth-Century Business,' *Speculum,* XVI (1941), 3-33.

———. *Il libro dei conti di Guglielmo Ruyelle cambiavalute di Bruges (1369).* Translated by Mario Cittadini. Rome: Casa Editrice Castellani, 1941.

———. 'Le livre de comptes de Guillaume Ruyelle, changeur à Bruges (1369),' *Annales de la Société d'Emulation de Bruges,* LXXVII (1934), 15-95.

———. 'The Medici Bank,' *The Journal of Economic History,* VI (1946), 24-52, 153-72; VII (1947), 69-82.

———. *The Medici Bank.* New York University Graduate School of Business Administration Studies in Business History, Vol. II. New York: New York University Press, 1948.

———. 'Aux origines d'une technique intellectuelle: la formation et l'expansion de la comptabilité à partie double,' *Annales d'histoire économique et sociale,* IX (1937), 171-93, 270-98.

———. 'Quelques considérations sur les livres de comptes de Collard de Marke (1366-1369), précédées d'un aperçu sur les archives commerciales en Belgique,' *Bulletin d'Etudes et d'Informations de l'Ecole Supérieure de Commerce St. Ignace* (Antwerp, 1930). Pp. 33.

———. 'Die rechtliche und wirtschaftliche Organisation des Münzhandels und Kreditgeschäftes in Brügge,' *Hansische Geschichtsblätter,* LX (1935), 369-70.

———. 'What is Dry Exchange? A Contribution to the Study of English Mercantilism,' *The Journal of Political Economy,* LII (1944), 250-66.

Des Marez, G. *La lettre de foire à Ypres au XIIIe siècle: contribution à l'étude des papiers de crédit.* Mémoires de l'Académie royale de Belgique, Classe des lettres et des sciences morales et politiques, Collection in-8°, Vol. LX. Brussels, 1900.

de Smedt, Oskar. 'De keizerlijke verordeningen van 1537 en 1539 op de obligaties en wisselbrieven: eenige kantteekeningen,' *Nederlandsche Historiebladen,* III (1940), 15-35.

De Smet, A. 'L'origine des ports du Zwin: Damme, Mude, Monikrede, Hoeke et Sluis,' *Etudes d'histoire dédiées à la mémoire de Henri Pirenne.* Brussels: Nouvelle Société d'Editions, 1937.

De Smet, Jos. 'L'effectif des milices brugeoises et la population de la ville en 1340,' *Revue belge de philologie et d'histoire,* XII (1933), 631-36.

Despause, Albert. *Les dévaluations monétaires dans l'histoire.* Paris: Marcel Rivière, 1936.

de Stoop, P. 'Particularités sur les corporations et métiers de Bruges,' *Annales de la Société d'Emulation pour l'étude de l'histoire et des antiquités de la Flandre Occidentale,* 2d series, I (1843), 133-66.

Dieudonné, Adolphe. 'L'actualité d'hier: changes et monnaies au moyen âge,' *Revue des Deux Mondes,* 7e période, XXXVII (1927), 927-37.

Di Tucci, Raffaele. *Studi sull'economia genovese del secolo decimosecondo: la banca privata.* Turin: Fratelli Bocca, 1933.

Doehaerd, Renée. 'Les galères génoises dans la Manche et la Mer du Nord à la fin du XIIIe et au début du XIVe siècle,' *Bulletin de l'Institut historique belge de Rome,* Fascicule XIX (1938), 1-76.

Donnet, Fernand. *Coup d'oeil sur l'histoire financière d'Anvers au cours des siècles.* Antwerp: J. E. Buschmann, 1927.

Doren, Alfred. *Italienische Wirtschaftsgeschichte.* Vol. I. Jena, Gustav Fischer, 1934. Only one volume published.

Dunbar, Charles F. 'The Bank of Venice,' *Quarterly Journal of Economics,* VI (1892), 308-35, appendix, 371-97.

Edler (de Roover), Florence. 'Eclaircissements à propos des considérations de R. Davidsohn sur la productivité de l'argent au moyen âge,' *Vierteljahrschrift für Sozial- und Wirtschaftsgeschichte,* XXX (1937), 375-80.

———. 'The Effects of the Financial Measures of Charles V on the Commerce of Antwerp, 1539-1542,' *Revue belge de philologie et d'histoire,* XVI (1937), 665-73.

———. 'Francesco Sassetti and the Downfall of the Medici Banking House,' *Bulletin of the Business Historical Society,* XVII (1943), 65-80.

———. *Glossary of Mediaeval Terms of Business, Italian Series, 1200-1600.* Cambridge, Massachusetts: The Mediaeval Academy of America, 1934.

———. 'A Prize of War: A Painting of Fifteenth Century Merchants,' *Bulletin of the Business Historical Society,* XIX (1945), 3-12.

———. 'The Silk Trade of Lucca during the Thirteenth and Fourteenth Centuries,' Unpublished Ph.D. dissertation, Department of History, The University of Chicago, 1930.

———. The van der Molen, Commission-Merchants of Antwerp: Trade with Italy, 1538-44,' *Medieval and Historiographical Essays in Honor of James Westfall Thompson.* Edited by James L. Cate and Eugene N. Anderson. Chicago: University of Chicago Press, 1938. Pp. 78-145.

Ehrenberg, Richard. 'Makler, Hosteliers und Börse in Brügge vom 13. bis zum 16. Jahrhundert,' *Zeitschrift für das gesamte Handelsrecht,* XXX (1885), 403-68.

———. *Das Zeitalter der Fugger: Geldkapital und Creditverkehr im 16. Jahrhundert.* 2 vols. 3d ed. Jena: Gustav Fischer, 1922.

Einaudi, Luigi. 'The Medieval Practice of Managed Currency,' *The Lessons of Monetary Experience: Essays in Honor of Irving Fisher.* New York: Farrar & Rinehart, 1937. Pp. 259-68

———. 'Teoria della moneta immaginaria nel tempo da Carlomagno alla rivoluzione francese,' *Rivista di storia economica,* I (1936), 1-35.

Einstein, Lewis. *The Italian Renaissance in England: Studies.* New York: Columbia University Press, 1902.

Emiliani-Giudici, Paolo. *Storia politica dei municipi italiani.* 2 vols. Florence, 1851.

Endemann, Wilhelm. 'Die nationalökonomischen Grundsätze der canonistischen Lehre,' *Hildebrand's Jahrbücher für Nationalökonomie,* I (1863), 26-47, 154-81, 310-67, 537-76, 679-730.

———. *Studien in der romanisch-kanonistischen Wirtschafts- und Rechtslehre bis gegen Ende des 17. Jahrhunderts.* 2 vols. Berlin, 1874-1883.

Espinas, Georges. *La vie urbaine de Douai au moyen âge.* 4 vols. Paris, 1913.

Evans, Allan. 'Some Coinage Systems of the Fourteenth Century,' *Journal of Economic and Business History,* III (1931), 481-96.

———. (ed.). See Pegolotti, Francesco Balducci (under Published Sources).

Feys, E. and Van de Casteele, D. *Histoire d'Oudenbourg.* Vol. II. Bruges, 1873.

Finot, Jules. *Etude historique sur les relations commerciales entre la Flandre et la République de Gênes au moyen âge.* Paris, 1906.

Fisher, Irving. *The Purchasing Power of Money.* New York, 1913.

Freundt, C. *Das Wechselrecht der Postglossatoren.* 2 vols. Leipzig, 1899-1909.

Fris, V. 'L'historien Jean Villani en Flandre,' *Compte rendu des séances de la Commission Royale d'Histoire, LXIX* (1900), 1-7.

———. 'Note sur Thomas Fin, receveur de Flandre,' *ibid.*, LXIX (1900), 8-14.

Funk, Arthur Layton. 'The Movement of Reform and Revolt in Mid-Fourteenth Century France,' Unpublished Ph.D. dissertation, Department of History, The University of Chicago, 1940.

Gandi, Giulio. *Le corporazioni dell'antica Firenze.* Florence: Giannini & Giovannelli, 1928.

Gauthier, Léon. *Les Lombards dans les Deux-Bourgognes.* Paris, 1907.

Gilliodts-van Severen, Louis. 'La lettre de change, son emploi à Bruges au moyen âge et dans les siècles suivants,' *La Flandre,* XI (1880), 327-37.

———. 'La levée du dixième et du vingtième denier à Bruges, 1571-1583,' *Annales de la Société d'Emulation de Bruges,* LX (1910), 289-336.

Goldschmidt, Levin. *Universalgeschichte des Handelsrechts.* Stuttgart, 1891.

Gonnard, René. *Histoire des doctrines monétaires dans ses rapports avec l'histoire des monnaies.* 2 vols. Paris: Librarie Recueil Sirey, 1935.

Goris, Jan A. *Les colonies marchandes méridionales à Anvers de 1488 à 1567.* Louvain: Librairie Universitaire, 1925.

Gras, N. S. B. 'Bill of Exchange,' *Encyclopaedia of the Social Sciences,* II (1932), 539-40.

———. *Business and Capitalism: an Introduction to Business History.* New York: F. S. Crofts & Co., 1939.

———. 'Capitalism—Concepts and History,' *Bulletin of the Business Historical Society,* XVI (1942), 21-34.

———. 'Economic Rationalism in the Late Middle Ages,' *Speculum,* VIII (1933), 304-12.

———. 'The Growth of Rigidity in Business during the Middle Ages,' *American Economic Review,* XXX (1940), suppl., 281-89.

Grunzweig, Armand. 'La correspondance de la filiale brugeoise des Medici,' *Revue belge de philologie et d'histoire,* VI (1927), 725-40.

Gutkind, Curt S. *Cosimo de' Medici, Pater Patriae, 1389-1464.* Oxford: Oxford University Press, 1938.

Häpke, Rudolf. *Brügges Entwicklung zum mittelalterlichen Weltmarkt.* Abhandlungen zur Verkehrs- und Seegeschichte, Vol. I. Berlin, 1908.

———. *Der deutsche Kaufmann in den Niederlanden.* Pfingstblätter des Hansischen Geschichtsvereins, No. VII. Leipzig, 1911.

Hall, Margaret Winslow. 'Early Bankers in the Genoese Notarial Records,' *The Economic History Review, VI* (1935), 73-79.

Hecht, Felix. *Ein Beitrag zur Geschichte der Inhaberpapiere in den Niederlanden.* Doctoral dissertation. Heidelberg, 1869.
Heckshe r, Eli F. *Mercantilism.* 2 vols. London: George Allen & Unwin Ltd., 1935.
Hénaux, Ferdinand. 'Les banquiers liégeois au XIVe siècle,' *Bulletin de l'Institut d'Archéologie liégeois,* III (1857), 313-30.
Hosten, E., and Strubbe, Eg. I. *Geillustreerde Catalogus, Stedelijk Museum van Schoone Kunsten.* Bruges, n. d.
Huizinga, J. *The Waning of the Middle Ages.* London: Arnold & Co., 1924.
Huvelin, P. 'Compte-rendu de G. Des Marez; "La lettre de foire à Ypres au XIIIe siècle: contribution à l'étude des papiers de crédit",' *Revue historique,* LXXVII (1901), 152-72.
Jäger, Ernest Ludwig. *Die ältesten Banken und der Ursprung des Wechsels.* Stuttgart, 1879.
Jevons, W. Stanley. *Money and the Mechanism of Exchange.* New York, 1897.
Johnson, E. A. J. *Predecessors of Adam Smith.* New York: Prentice-Hall, 1937.
Keynes, John Maynard. *The General Theory of Employment, Interest, and Money.* New York: Harcourt Brace & Co., 1936.
——————. *Monetary Reform.* New York: Harcourt, Brace & Co., 1929.
Knight, Frank H. "Historical and Theoretical Issues in the Problem of Modern Capitalism,' *Journal of Economic and Business History,* I (1928), 119-36.
——————. 'Interest,' *Encyclopaedia of the Social Sciences,* VIII (1932), 131-44.
Knight, Melvin M. *Economic History of Europe to the End of the Middle Ages.* New York: Houghton Mifflin Co., 1926.
Koch, Sylvain. *Italienische Pfandleiher im nördlichen und östlichen Frankreich.* University of Breslau, doctoral dissertation. Breslau, 1904.
Koppe, Wilhelm. *Lübeck-Stockholmer Handelsgeschichte im 14. Jahrhundert.* Abhandlungen zur Handels- und Seegeschichte, Vol. II. Neumünster in Holstein: Karl Wachholtz Verlag, 1933.
Kriegk, Georg Ludwig. 'Frankfurter Geldgeschäfte und Handelsbanken im Mittelalter,' *Frankfurter Burgerzwiste und Zustände im Mittelalter.* Frankfurt am Main, 1862. Pp. 330-43.
Kulischer, Josef. *Allgemeine Wirtschaftsgeschichte des Mittelalters und der Neuzeit.* 2 vols. Munich and Berlin: R. Oldenbourg, 1928-1929.
——————. 'Zur Entwickelungsgeschichte des Kapitalzinses,' *Jahrbücher für Nationalökonomie und Statistik,* LXXIII (1899), 305-71.
——————. 'Warenhändler und Geldausleiher im Mittelalter,' *Zeitschrift für Volkswirtschaft, Sozialpolitik und Verwaltung,* XVII (1908), 29-71, 201-54.
Kuske, Bruno. 'Die Handelsbeziehungen zwischen Köln und Italien im späteren Mittelalter,' *Westdeutsche Zeitschrift für Geschichte und Kunst,* XXVII (1908), 393-441.
Kuznets, Solomon. 'Pawnbroking,' *Encyclopaedia of the Social Sciences,* XII (1934), 32-40.
Laenen, J. 'Les Lombards à Malines, 1295-1457,' *Bulletin du Cercle archéologique, littéraire, et artistique de Malines,* XV (1905), 23-40.
——————. 'Usuriers et Lombards dans le Brabant au XVe siècle,' *Bulletin de l'Académie royale d'archéologie de Belgique,* 1904, pp. 123-44.
Lameere, J. 'Un chapitre de l'histoire du prêt à intérêt dans l'ancien droit belgique,' *Bulletin de l'Académie royale de Belgique, Classe des lettres,* 1920, pp. 77-104.

Landmann, Julius. 'Banking (History of Commercial),' *Encyclopaedia of the Social Sciences,* II (1937), 423-31.

Landry, Adolphe. *Essai économique sur les mutations des monnaies dans l'ancienne France de Philippe le Bel à Charles VII.* Bibliothèque de l'Ecole des Hautes Etudes: Sciences historiques et philologiques, Vol. CLXXXV. Paris, 1910.

Lane, Frederic C. *Andrea Barbarigo, Merchant of Venice, 1418-1449.* Johns Hopkins University Studies in Historical and Political Science, Series LXII, No. 1. Baltimore: The Johns Hopkins Press, 1944.

———. 'Venetian Bankers, 1496-1533: a Study in the Early Stages of Deposit Banking,' *The Journal of Political Economy,* XLV (1937), 187-206.

La Sorsa, Saverio. *L'organizzazione dei cambiatori fiorentini nel medio evo.* Cerignola, 1904.

Lastig, Gustav. 'Beiträge zur Geschichte des Handelsrechts,' *Zeitschrift für das gesamte Handelsrecht,* XXIII (1878).

———. *Florentiner Handelsregister des Mittelalters.* Doctoral dissertation. Halle, 1883.

Lattes, Alessandro. 'Gli antichi registri dei banchieri genovesi: note per la storia del diritto commerciale,' *Rivista del diritto commerciale,* XVII[1] (1919), 616-18.

———. *Il diritto commerciale nella legislazione statutaria delle città italiane.* Milan, 1884.

———. 'Francesco di Marco da Prato,' *Rivista del diritto commerciale,* XXVII[1] (1929), 99-103.

———. 'Genova nella storia del diritto cambiario italiano,' *Rivista del diritto commerciale,* XIII[1] (1915), 185-99.

———. 'Note per la storia del diritto commerciale,' *Rivista del diritto commerciale,* XXXI[1] (1933), 535-40.

Lattes, Elia. *La libertà delle banche a Venezia dal secolo XIII al XVII.* Milan, 1869.

Laurent, Henri. 'Crise monétaire et difficultés économiques: en Flandre aux XIVe et XVe siècles,' *Annales d'histoire économique et sociale,* V (1933), 156-60.

———. *Un grand commerce d'exportation au moyen âge: la draperie des Pays-Bas en France et dans les pays méditerranéens (XIIe-XVe siècle).* Paris: Librairie E. Droz, 1935.

———. *La loi de Gresham au moyen âge: essai sur la circulation monétaire entre la Flandre et le Brabant à la fin du XIVe siècle.* Brussels: Université de Bruxelles, 1933.

Lazzareschi, Eugenio. 'Gli statuti dei Lucchesi a Bruges e ad Anversa,' *Ad Alessandro Luzio gli Archivi di Stato italiani: miscellanea di studi storici.* Florence: Felice Le Monnier, 1933. Pp. 75-88.

Lefèvre, Placide, O. Praem. 'A propos du trafic de l'argent exercé par les juifs de Bruxelles au XIVe siècle,' *Revue belge de philologie et d'histoire,* IX (1930), 902-12.

Lemoine, Robert J. 'Les étrangers et la formation du capitalisme en Belgique,' *Revue d'histoire économique et sociale,* XX (1932), 252-336.

Letts, Malcolm. *Bruges and its Past.* 2d ed. Bruges: Desclée, de Brouwer & Co., 1926.

Liebe, Georg. 'Die Anfänge der lombardischen Wechsler im deutschen Mittelalter,' *Zeitschrift für Kulturgeschichte,* 4th series, I (1894), 273-80.

Lopez, Roberto. 'Sensali nel medio evo,' *Nuova rivista storica,* XXII (1938), 108-12.

Lucas, Henry Stephen. *The Low Countries and the Hundred Years War, 1326-1347.* Ann Arbor: University of Michigan Press, 1929.

Luchaire, Achille. *Social France at the time of Philip Augustus.* Translated by Edward Benjamin Krehbiel. New York: Henry Holt & Co., 1912; reprinted by Peter Smith & Co., 1929.

Luschin von Ebengreuth, Arnold. *Allgemeine Münzkunde und Geldgeschichte des Mittelalters und der neueren Zeit.* 2d ed. revised. Munich-Berlin: R. Oldenbourg, 1926.

Luzzatto, Gino. 'Les banques publiques de Venise (siècles XVI-XVIII),' *History of the Principal Public Banks.* Edited by J. G. van Dillen. The Hague, 1934. Pp. 39-78.

———————. 'L'oro e l'argento nella politica monetaria veneziana dei secoli XIII e XIV,' *Rivista storica italiana,* 5th series, Vol. II, fasc. 3 (1937), 17-29.

———————. *Storia del commercio.* Vol. I: *Dall'antichità al Rinascimento.* Florence: G. Barbera, 1914.

———————. 'Sull'attendibilità di alcune statistiche economiche medievali,' *Giornale degli economisti e rivista di statistica,* 4th series, LXIX (1929), 122-34.

Machiavelli Niccolò. *Istorie fiorentine.* Edited by Plinio Carli. Vol. II. Florence, G. C. Sansoni, 1927.

McLaughlin, T. P. 'The Teachings of the Canonists on Usury (XII, XIII, and XIV centuries),' *Mediaeval Studies,* I (1939), 81-147; II (1940), 1-22.

Malynes, Gerard de. *Consuetudo vel lex mercatoria or the Ancient Law-Merchant.* London, 1622.

———————. *A Treatise of the Canker of England's Common Wealth.* London, 1601.

Marin, Carlo Antonio. *Storia civile e politica del commercio dei Veneziani.* Vol. V. Venice, 1800.

Meltzing, Otto. *Das Bankhaus der Medici und seine Vorläufer.* Jena, 1906.

———————. 'Tommaso Portinari und sein Konflikt mit der Hanse,' *Hansische Geschichtsblätter,* XII (1906), 101-24.

Mély, Fernand de. 'Les primitifs et leurs signatures: Quinten Matsys et Marinus,' *Gazette des beaux-arts,* XL (1908), 215-27.

Mickwitz, Gunnar. 'L'economia medievale nei paesi baltici e nei paesi mediterranei,' *Rivista internazionale di scienze sociali,* XLVI (1938), 813-24.

Mirot, Léon. 'La colonie lucquoise à Paris,' *Bibliothèque de l'Ecole des Chartes,* LXXXVIII (1927), 50-86.

———————. 'Les Isbarre, monnayeurs royaux,' *ibid.,* pp. 275-314.

———————. 'La société des Raponde, Dine Raponde,' *ibid.,* LXXXIX (1928), 299-389.

———————. 'Les Cename,' *ibid.,* XCI (1930), 100-68.

———————. 'Forteguerra Forteguerra et sa succession,' *ibid.,* XCVI (1935), 301-37.

———————. 'L'origine des Spifame; Barthélemi Spifame,' *ibid.,* XCIX (1938), 67-81.

[The first four of these articles were reprinted privately in book form under the title *Etudes lucquoises.* Paris, 1930.]

Mondaini, Gennaro. *Moneta credito banche attraverso i tempi.* 2d ed. Rome: S. A. Editrice 'Studium Urbis,' 1942.

Monroe, Arthur Eli (ed.). *Early Economic Thought: Selections from Economic Literature prior to Adam Smith.* 3d printing. Cambridge, Mass.: Harvard University Press, 1930.

———. *Monetary Theory before Adam Smith.* Cambridge, Mass.: Harvard University Press, 1923.
Morel, Paul. *Les Lombards dans la Flandre française et le Hainaut.* Lille, 1908.
Mun, Thomas. *England's Treasure by Forraign Trade.* London, 1664. Also reprinted by the Economic History Society, Oxford: Basil Blackwell, 1933.
Nasse, Erwin. 'Das venetianische Bankwesen im 14., 15. und 16. Jahrhundert,' *Jahrbücher für Nationalökonomie und Statistik,* XXXIV (1879), 329-58.
Nef, John Ulric. 'Industrial Europe at the Time of the Reformation (*ca.* 1515-*ca.* 1540),' *The Journal of Political Economy,* XLIX (1941), 1-40, 183-224.
———. 'Silver Production in Central Europe, 1450-1680,' *ibid.,* XLIX (1941), 575-91.
Nélis, H. 'Les origines du notariat public en Belgique (1269-1320),' *Revue belge de philologie et d'histoire,* II (1923), 267-77.
Nelson, Benjamin N. 'The Usurer and the Merchant Prince: Italian Businessmen and the Ecclesiastical Law of Restitution, 1100-1550,' *The Tasks of Economic History, The Journal of Economic History,* Supplement VII (1947), pp. 104-22.
Neumann, Max. 'Geschichte des Wechsels im Hansagebiet, bis zum 17. Jahrhundert,' Supplement to Vol. VII, *Zeitschrift für das gesamte Handelsrecht.* Erlangen, 1863.
———. *Geschichte des Wuchers in Deutschland bis zur Begründung der heutigen Zinsengesetze (1654).* Halle, 1865.
O'Brien, George. *An Essay on Mediaeval Economic Teaching.* London: Longmans, Green & Co., 1920.
Oman, Charles. *The Coinage of England.* Oxford: Oxford University Press, 1931.
Oosthoek's Geillustreerde Encyclopaedie, VIII (1936), 612: 'Lombard.'
Orchard, Dorothy Johnson, and May, Geoffrey. *Money Lending in Great Britain.* New York: Russell Sage Foundation, 1933.
Ottokar, Nicola. *Il comune di Firenze alla fine del dugento.* Florence: Vallecchi, 1926.
Pagnini, Gian-Francesco. *Della Decima e di varie altre gravezze imposte dal comune di Firenze. Della moneta e della mercatura de' Fiorentini fino al secolo XVI.* 4 vols. Lisbon and Lucca, 1765-1766.
Peruzzi, Luigi Simone. *Storia del commercio e dei banchieri di Firenze in tutto il mondo conosciuto dal 1200 al 1345.* Florence, 1868.
Phillips, Chester Arthur. *Bank Credit: a Study of the Principles and Factors Underlying Advances Made by Banks to Borrowers.* New York: Macmillan, 1920.
Pirenne, Henri. *Economic and Social History of Medieval Europe.* New York: Harcourt, Brace & Co., 1937.
———. *Histoire de Belgique.* Vol. I, 5th ed., Brussels, 1929; Vol. II, 3d ed., Brussels: Maurice Lamertin, 1922.
———. 'L'instruction des marchands au moyen âge,' *Annales d'histoire économique et sociale,* I (1929), 13-28.
Piton, C. *Les Lombards en France et à Paris.* 2 vols. Paris, 1892-1893.
Poignant, Simone. *La foire de Lille: contribution à l'étude des foires flamandes au moyen âge.* Bibliothèque de la Société d'Histoire du Droit des Pays flamands, picards et wallons, Vol. VI. Lille: Emile Raoust, 1932.
Postan, M. M. 'Private Financial Instruments in Medieval England,' *Vierteljahrschrift für Sozial- und Wirtschaftsgeschichte,* XXIII (1930), 26-75.
Postlethwayt, Malachy. *The Universal Dictionary of Trade and Commerce.* London, 1751.

Power, Eileen. 'The Wool Trade in the Fifteenth Century,' *Studies in English Trade in the Fifteenth Century.* Edited by Eileen Power and M. M. Postan. New York: The Macmillan Co., 1933. Pp. 39-90 and 365-72.

Prims, Floris. 'Heer Anselmus Fabri, onze tiende deken (1415-1449),' *Antwerpiensia, losse bijdragen tot de Antwerpsche geschiedenis,* XI (1937), chap. iii, 19-26. Antwerp: 'De Vlijt,' 1938.

Pusch, Gottfried. *Staatliche Münz- und Geldpolitik in den Niederlanden unter den Burgundischen und Habsburgischen Herrschern, besonders unter Kaiser Karl V.* Doctoral dissertation, University of Munich. Munich: Val. Höfling, 1932.

Raby, R. Cornelius. *The Regulation of Pawnbroking.* New York: Russell Sage Foundation, 1924.

Renouard, Yves. *Les relations des Papes d'Avignon et des compagnies commerciales et bancaires de 1316 à 1378.* Bibliothèque des Ecoles françaises d'Athènes et de Rome, fascicule 151. Paris: E. de Boccard, 1941.

Reynolds, Robert L. 'A Business Affair in Genoa in the Year 1200: Banking, Bookkeeping, a Broker, and a Lawsuit,' *Studi di storia e diritto in onore di Enrico Besta,* Vol. II. Milan: A. Giuffrè, 1938. Pp. 167-81.

——————. 'Merchants of Arras and the Overland Trade with Genoa, Twelfth Century,' *Revue belge de philologie et d'histoire,* IX (1930), 495-533.

——————. 'Gli studi americani sulla storia genovese (risposta a A. E. Sayous),' *Giornale storico e letterario della Liguria,* XIV (1938), 1-27.

Richards, Gertrude Randolph Bramlette. *Florentine Merchants in the Age of the Medici.* Cambridge, Mass.: Harvard University Press, 1932.

Richards, Richard David. *The Early History of Banking in England.* London: P. S. King & Son, 1929.

——————. 'The Pioneers of Banking in England,' *Economic History,* I (1929), 485-502.

Robinson, Louis N., and Nugent, Rolf. *Regulation of the Small Loan Business.* New York: Russell Sage Foundation, 1935.

Sabbe, Etienne. 'De Lombarden te Kortrijk in de XIIIe, XIVe en XVe eeuwen,' *Annales de la Société d'Emulation de Bruges,* LXVII (1924), 173-80.

Salzman, L. F. *English Trade in the Middle Ages.* Oxford: Oxford University Press, 1931.

Sanderus, Antonius. *Flandria illustrata sive descriptio comitatus istius.* 3 vols. 2d ed. The Hague, 1732-1735.

Sapori, Armando. 'Il commercio internazionale nel medioevo,' reprint from the *Archivio di studi corporativi* (1938, fasc. 3), 40 pp. Republished with some change in the *Rivista storica italiana,* 5th series, Vol. III (1938), fasc. 3, pp. 73-99.

——————. *Una compagnia di Calimala ai primi del Trecento.* Florence: Leo S. Olschki, 1932.

——————. *La crisi delle compagnie mercantili dei Bardi e dei Peruzzi.* Florence: Leo S. Olschki, 1926.

——————. 'La cultura del mercante medievale italiano,' *Rivista di storia economica,* II (1937), 89-125.

——————. 'L'interesse del danaro a Firenze nel Trecento: dal testamento di un usuraio,' *Archivio storico italiano,* 7th series, X (1928), 161-86.

——————. 'Il personale delle compagnie mercantili del medioevo,' *ibid.,* 7th series, XXXII (1939), 121-51.

————. 'Storia interna della compagnia mercantile dei Peruzzi,' *ibid.*, 7th series, XXII (1934), 3-65.
————. *Studi di storia economica medievale.* 2d ed. Florence: G. C. Sansoni, 1947. All of the above-mentioned articles and many others have been republished in this volume.
————, (ed.). See *Libri dei Peruzzi* (under Published Sources).
Sayous, André-E. 'Une caisse de dépôts: la "Table des Changes" de Valence (1407 et 1418),' *Annales d'histoire économique et sociale,* VI (1934), 135-37.
————. 'Le capitalisme commercial et financier dans les pays chrétiens de la Méditerranée occidentale, depuis la première croisade jusqu'à la fin du moyen âge,' *Vierteljahrschrift für Sozial- und Wirtschaftsgeschichte,* XXIX (1936), 270-95.
————. 'Dans l'Italie, à l'intérieur des terres: Sienne de 1221 à 1229,' *Annales d'histoire économique et sociale,* III (1931), 189-206.
————. 'L'histoire universelle du droit commercial de Levin Goldschmidt et les méthodes commerciales des pays chrétiens de la Méditerranée aux XIIe et XIIIe siècles,' *Annales de droit commercial français, étranger et international,* XL (1931), 199-217, 309-22.
————. 'Les méthodes commerciales de Barcelone au XIVe siècle, surtout d'après des protocoles inédits de ses archives notariales,' *Estudis universitaris catalans,* XVIII (1933), 209-35.
————. 'Les méthodes commerciales de Barcelone au XVe siècle, d'après des documents inédits de ses archives; la bourse, le prêt et l'assurance maritime, les sociétés commerciales, la lettre de change, une banque d'Etat,' *Revue historique de droit français et étranger,* 4th series, XV (1936), 255-301.
————. 'Note sur l'origine de la lettre de change et les débuts de son emploi à Barcelone (XIVe siècle),' *ibid.*, 4th series, XIII (1934), 315-22.
————. 'Les opérations des banquiers de Gênes à la fin du XIIe siècle,' *Annales de droit commercial français, étranger et international,* XLIII (1934), 285-96.
————. 'Les opérations des banquiers italiens en Italie et aux foires de Champagne pendant le XIIIe siècle,' *Revue historique,* CLXX (1932), 1-31.
————. 'L'origine de la lettre de change: les procédés de crédit et de paiement dans les pays chrétiens de la Méditerranée occidentale entre le milieu du XIIe siècle et celui du XIIIe,' *Revue historique de droit français et étranger,* 4th series, XII (1933), 66-112.
————. 'Les transferts de risques, les associations commerciales et la lettre de change à Marseille pendant le XIVe siècle,' *ibid.*, 4th series, XIV (1935), 469-94.
————. 'Les transformations des méthodes commerciales dans l'Italie médiévale,' *Annales d'histoire économique et sociale,* I (1929), 161-76.
————. 'Les travaux des Américains sur le commerce de Gênes aux XIIe et XIIIe siècles,' *Giornale storico e letterario della Liguria,* XIII (1937), 81-89.
———— (ed. and translator). See Sombart, Werner.
Scaccia, Sigismondo. *Tractatus de commerciis et cambio.* Geneva, 1664.
Schaps, Georg. *Zur Geschichte des Wechselindossaments.* Stuttgart, 1892.
Schaube, Adolf. 'Die Anfänge der Tratte,' *Zeitschrift für das gesamte Handelsrecht,* XLIII (1895), 1-51.
————. 'Die Anfänge der venezianischen Galeerenfahrt nach der Nordsee,' *Historische Zeitschrift,* CI (1908), 28-89.
————. 'Einige Beobachtungen zur Entstehungsgeschichte der Tratte,' *Zeit-*

schrift der Savigny-Stiftung für Rechtsgeschichte, Germanische Abteilung, XIV (1893), 111-51.

——————. 'Rechtsgeschäfte und Rechtsstellung der "Lombarden" in der älteren Zeit ihres Auftretens in Frankreich,' *Zeitschrift für das gesamte Handels- und Konkursrecht,* LXI (1908), 289-322.

——————. *Storia del commercio dei popoli latini del Mediterraneo sino alla fine delle Crociate.* Translated from the German by Pietro Bonfante. Biblioteca dell' economista, 5th series, Vol. XI. Turin, 1915.

——————. 'Studien zur Geschichte und Natur des ältesten Cambium,' *Zeitschrift für Nationalökonomie und Statistik,* LXV (1895), 153-91, 511-34.

Schmoller, Gustav. 'Die öffentlichen Leihhäuser sowie das Pfandleih- und das Rückkaufsgeschäft,' *Jahrbuch für Gesetzgebung, Verwaltung und Volkswirtschaft im Deutschen Reich,* IV (1880), 87-123.

Schouteet, A. *Marcus Gerards, de zestiende-eeuwsche schilder en graveur.* Bruges: Gidsenbond, n. d. [*ca.* 1941].

Schulte, Aloys. *Geschichte des mittelalterlichen Handels und Verkehrs zwischen Westdeutschland und Italien mit Ausschluss von Venedig.* 2 vols. Leipzig, 1900.

Schumpeter, Joseph A. *Business Cycles: a Theoretical, Historical and Statistical Analysis of the Capitalist Process.* 2 vols. New York: McGraw-Hill Book Co., 1939.

Sée, Henri. *Histoire économique de la France.* Vol. I, *Le moyen âge et l'ancien régime.* Paris: Librairie Armand Colin, 1939.

Sieveking, Heinrich. *Genueser Finanzwesen mit besonderer Berücksichtigung der Casa di San Giorgio.* Vol. II, *Die Casa di San Giorgio.* Volkswirtschaftliche Abhandlungen der Badischen Hochschulen, Vol. III, No. 3. Freiburg in Breisgau, 1899.

——————. *Aus Genueser Rechnungs- und Steuerbüchern: ein Beitrag zur mittelalterlichen Handels- und Vermögensstatistik.* Sitzungsberichte der Kaiserlichen Akademie der Wissenschaften in Wien, Philosophisch-Historische Klasse, Vol. CLXII, No. 2. Vienna, 1909.

——————. *Die Handlungsbücher der Medici. Ibid.,* Vol. CLI, No. 5. Vienna, 1905.

——————. 'Aus venetianischen Handlungsbüchern: ein Beitrag zur Geschichte des Grosshandels im 15. Jahrhundert,' *Jahrbuch für Gesetzgebung, Verwaltung und Volkswirtschaft im Deutschen Reich,* XXV (1901), 1489-1521; XXVI (1902), 189-225.

Smith, Adam. *The Wealth of Nations.* New York: The Modern Library, 1937.

Sneller, Z. W. *Deventer, die Stadt der Jahrmärkte.* Pfingstblätter des Hansischen Geschichtsvereins, No. 25. Weimar: Verlag Hermann Böhlaus Nachfolger, 1936.

——————. 'Het wisselaarsbedrijf in Nederland vóór de oprichting der stedelijke wisselbanken,' *Tijdschrift voor Geschiedenis,* XLIX (1934), 486-502.

Sombart, Werner. *Der moderne Kapitalismus.* Vol. I, 3d ed. Munich-Leipzig: Duncker & Humblot, 1919.

——————. *L'apogée du capitalisme.* Translated from the German with a preface by André-E. Sayous, entitled: 'Werner Sombart et ses récents exposés de l'économie d'après-guerre.' Paris: Payot, 1932.

Speyer, Otto. *Die ältesten Credit- und Wechselbanken in Frankfurt am Main (1402-1403).* Frankfurt am Main, 1883.

Strieder, Jakob. *Aus Antwerpener Notariatsarchiven: Quellen zur deutschen Wirtschaftsgeschichte des 16. Jahrhunderts.* Stuttgart: Deutsche Verlagsanstalt, 1930.

Täuber, Walter. *Geld und Kredit im Mittelalter.* Berlin: Carl Hegmanns Verlag, 1933.
Tawney, Richard H. (ed.). See Wilson, Thomas. *A Discourse upon Usury.*
———. *Religion and the Rise of Capitalism.* Harmondsworth, England: Penguin Books Ltd., 1938.
——— and Power, Eileen (eds.). *Tudor Economic Documents.* 3 vols. New York: Longmans, Green & Co., 1924, 1935, 1937.
Tofani, Alberto. *Alcune ricerche storiche sull'ufficio e la professione di ragioniere a Firenze al tempo della repubblica.* Florence, 1910.
Tourneur, Victor. 'De la méthode à suivre pour évaluer en monnaies modernes les valeurs anciennes énoncées dans les textes historiques belges du XIe siècle au XVIIIe,' *Revue belge de philologie et d'histoire,* I (1922), 101-12.
Unwin, George. 'London Tradesmen and their creditors,' *Finance and Trade under Edward III.* Edited by G. Unwin. University of Manchester Historical Series, No. 32. Manchester, 1918.
Usher, Abbott Payson. 'Deposit Banking in Barcelona, 1300-1700,' *Journal of Economic and Business History,* IV (1931), 121-55.
———. *The Early History of Deposit Banking in Mediterranean Europe.* Vol. I. Harvard Economic Studies, Vol. LXXV. Cambridge, Mass.: Harvard University Press, 1943.
———. 'The Origins of Banking: the Primitive Bank of Deposit, 1200-1600,' *The Economic History Review,* IV (1934), 399-428.
Van den Bussche, Emile. 'De Groote Cauwersine,' *La Flandre,* IV (1872-1873), 79-82.
———. 'Mémoire sur les relations qui existèrent autrefois entre les Flamands —particulièrement ceux de Bruges—et les Portugais,' *ibid.,* IV (1872-1873), 32-56, 117-48, 247-85; V (1873-1874), 103-18, 167-86, 303-18.
van Dillen, J. G. *Bronnen tot de geschiedenis der wisselbanken (Amsterdam, Middelburg, Delft, Rotterdam).* Rijksgeschiedkundige Publicatiën, Vol. LIX. The Hague: Martinus Nijhoff, 1925.
———. 'De girobanken van Genua, Venetië en Hamburg,' *Tijdschrift voor Geschiedenis,* XLII (1927), 33-58.
———. 'Valuta-moeilijkheden en giro-verkeer tijdens de Republiek,' *Tijdschrift voor Geschiedenis,* XXXIX (1924), 321-47; XLI (1926), 8-39.
——— (ed.). *History of the Principal Public Banks.* The Hague: Martinus Nijhoff, 1934.
van Houtte, Jean A. 'Les courtiers au moyen âge,' *Revue historique de droit français et étranger,* 4th series, XV (1936), 105-41.
van Velden, H. 'Het kassiersbedrijf te Amsterdam in de 17e eeuw,' *De Economist,* LXXXII (1933), 48-68.
van Werveke, Hans. *Brugge en Antwerpen: Acht eeuwen Vlaamsche handel.* Ghent: Boekhandel Rombaut-Fecheyr, n. d. [*ca.* 1942].
———. 'Le commerce des vins français au moyen âge,' *Revue belge de philologie et d'histoire,* XII (1933) 1096-1101.
———. 'De ekonomische en sociale gevolgen van de muntpolitiek der graven van Vlaanderen (1337-1433),' *Annales de la Société d'Emulation de Bruges,* LXXIV (1931), 1-15.
———. 'Der flandrische Eigenhandel im Mittelalter,' *Hansische Geschichtsblätter,* LXI (1936), 7-24.
———. *De Gentsche stadsfinanciën in de middeleeuwen.* Mémoires de

l'Académie royale de Belgique, Classe des lettres et des sciences morales et politiques, Collection in-8°, 2d series, Vol. XXXIV. Brussels, 1934.

——————. 'Monnaie de compte et monnaie réelle,' *Revue belge de philologie et d'histoire,* XIII (1934), 123-52.

——————. 'Monnaie, lingots ou marchandises? Les instruments d'échange aux XIe et XIIe siècles,' *Annales d'histoire économique et sociale,* IV (1932), 452-68.

——————. 'Le mort-gage et son rôle économique en Flandre et en Lotharingie,' *Revue belge de philologie et d'histoire,* VIII (1929), 53-91.

——————. 'Les origines des bourses commerciales,' *ibid.,* XV (1936), 133-41.

——————. 'De Vlaamsche munthervorming van 1389-1390,' *Nederlandsche Historiebladen,* I (1938), 336-47.

Verwijs, Elco, and Verdam, J. *Middelnederlandsch Woordenboek.* 9 vols. The Hague, 1885-1928.

Viner, Jacob. 'Review of Eli F. Heckscher, *Mercantilism,*' *The Economic History Review,* VI (1935), 99-101.

——————. *Studies in the Theory of International Trade.* New York: Harper & Brothers, 1937.

Vogel, Emmanuel. 'Der Giralverkehr in den oberitalienischen und den deutschen Handelszentren bis zum ausgehenden Mittelalter,' *Vierteljahrschrift für Sozial- und Wirtschaftsgeschichte,* XXXI (1938), 1-9.

Warburg, A. 'Flandrische Kunst und florentinische Frührenaissance,' *Gesammelte Schriften.* Vol. I. Leipzig and Berlin: B. G. Teubner (1932). Pp. 185-206, 370-80.

——————. 'Francesco Sassettis letztwillige Verfügung,' *ibid.,* pp. 127-58, 353-65.

Weber, Max. *Zur Geschichte der Handelsgesellschaften im Mittelalter.* Stuttgart, 1889.

Wilson, Thomas. *A Discourse upon Usury* [1572]: with an Historical Introduction by R. H. Tawney. London: Bell, 1925.

Yernaux, Jean. 'Les notaires publics du XIIIe au XVIe siècle, spécialement au Franc de Bruges,' *Bulletin de la Commission Royale d'Histoire,* LXXXII (1913), 111-82.

Zdekauer, Lodovico. 'L'interno d'un banco di pegno nel 1417,' *Archivio storico italiano,* 5th series, XVII (1896), 63-105.

Zerbi, Tommaso. *La banca nell'ordinamento finanziario visconteo, dai mastri del banco Giussano, gestore della tesoreria di Piacenza, 1356-1358.* Como: E. Cavalleri, 1935.

INDEX

Index

Names of persons mentioned only in the appendices are omitted. In the bibliography all Belgian names beginning with 'de' or 'van' are listed under 'D' and 'V.' A different practice has been followed in preparing the index. All prepositions, such as 'de, dei, degli,' and 'van,' and the Flemish article 'de' preceding family names have been disregarded because of the inconsistency in spelling and usage during the mediaeval period. In the records of Collard de Marke and in other sources, Italian names are often gallicized. When identification has been possible, the Italian form is added. Cross references have been used only exceptionally when there is considerable difference between two variants of the same name.

For Product Safety Concerns and Information please contact our
EU representative GPSR@taylorandfrancis.com Taylor & Francis
Verlag GmbH, Kaufingerstraße 24, 80331 München, Germany